# The Last European War

*September 1939 /*
*December 1941*

Books by John Lukacs

The Great Powers and Eastern Europe
Tocqueville: The European Revolution/Correspondence with
    Gobineau (editor)
A History of the Cold War
Decline and Rise of Europe
Historical Consciousness
The Passing of the Modern Age

John Lukacs

# The
# Last
# European
# War

*September 1939/*
*December 1941*

*Anchor Press/Doubleday*
*GARDEN CITY, NEW YORK*

1976

Library of Congress Cataloging in Publication Data

Lukacs, John A
The last European war.

Bibliography: p. 528
   1. World War, 1939–1945.   I. Title.
D755.L84 1976      940.53
ISBN 0-385-07254-6
Library of Congress Catalog Card Number 74-33649

*To the memory of my mother,*
*a woman of great beauty in whose life*
*those were years of suffering and anguish*
*and hope and faith*

# Contents

Contents

# Author's note

The scope of this book is the history of an entire continent during two years of an enormous convulsion. The size of the canvas is very large, perhaps unduly so. There is another difficulty. Europe is of one piece only when people look at her from the outside. There were few Europeans in 1939. The national differences were profound. From Albanians and Andorrans to Serbs and Turks: there were more European nations than there are letters of the alphabet. Still, many of their experiences—and, more important, their reactions to these experiences—were similar. What was common, or similar—similar, never analogous—in their lives and in their thoughts? In the first part of this book I have attempted to describe the war, the movements of entire states and armies, with few references to the lives of the peoples. My interpretation of many of these events, resting sometimes on the evidence of relatively new materials, may be unorthodox. Since Hitler's cause was an evil cause, there has been little "revisionism" about this war. This condition obscures many things. *All* history is revisionism of a kind. The revision of history is not—or, rather, ought not be—the monopoly of opportunists whose description of the past serves but their ephemeral interests of the present—*their* present; who are ever ready to twist or turn the record of the past in order to exemplify ideas that are intellectually fashionable. All history—indeed, all thinking—consists of the rethinking of the past. That this constant revising of the past must rest on evidence is a truism. It is true: only it is not true enough. Historical evidence is one thing; legal evidence is another. The ultimate purpose of the latter is justice; of the former, truth. Truth is not only a deeper, it is a greater matter than justice. The reservoir of historical evidence is potentially boundless. The material available about the Second World War is both immense and ungovernable. I attempted to describe some of its difficulties and opportunities in the Bibliographical Remarks at the end of the book.

In the second, larger portion of this book, I have attempted to write about the lives of the peoples, the sentiments of nations, the convergences of thoughts and beliefs, in a certain order of sequence, exemplifying certain principles of historical reconstruction that I set forth in some of my earlier works, mainly in *Historical Consciousness*. This book is, consequently, divided into I. The Main Events; II. The Main Movements. The first part attempts to describe how events happened, the second why they happened—even though how and why are not always and altogether separable, since the why is often implicit in the how. There is no further need to explain the structure of this book, which should clearly appear from the Contents—and, hopefully, unfold before the reader.

John Lukacs

# The Last European War

September 1939/
December 1941

# I. The Main Events

# 1 . Introduction: Germany and Europe

THE LAST EUROPEAN WAR began in September 1939. It became the Second World War in December 1941. The years 1939–41 were more than the opening phase, they were the decisive phase of the Second World War. Had Hitler defeated Britain in 1940 or had he conquered the Russians in 1941, he would have won the war. Before December 1941 he came close to winning it, closer than we are accustomed to think. After December 1941 he could no longer win it. Such clear-cut turning points in the histories of great wars are rare. Nothing like this happened in the First World War.

1939–41 was the Last European War. The peoples of Europe may yet experience revolutions and civil wars; they may be conquered from the outside; they may be set against each other. But a war in which one nation sets out to dominate Europe, with the result of an all-European war—that is very unlikely to happen. Unlikely not because of the prospects—dim, even now—of a united Europe, but because of the results of the Last European War.

The year 1941 was a turning point not only in the history of the Second World War but in the relationship of an entire continent to the world. After 1941 the destiny of Europe depended on two extra-European powers, the United States and the Soviet Union—a condition that has prevailed ever since that time. 1941 was also a turning point in the relationship of Europe with its central power, Germany—the last of the great states of Europe that had set out to dominate the continent.

The main event in the history of mankind one hundred years ago was the rising power and influence of the German people in Europe. In 1871 the greatest statesman of the nineteenth century, Bismarck, succeeded in uniting most of the Germans into an empire. They had never been united before. They were not completely united then, nor would they ever be.

[3]

Still, what the Scotch philosopher and historian Hume had written about them was coming true. "Germany is undoubtedly a fine country," he wrote in 1748, "full of industrious honest people; and were it united, it would be the greatest power that ever was in the world."

It was certainly the greatest power on the continent of Europe. It had a large population, ever growing, and youthful. In 1870 nearly 45 per cent of the Prussian population was under twenty years of age—a figure worth pondering by those who prattle on about Youth Revolutions and Generation Gaps a century later. Soon there would be two Germans to every Frenchman—a fact that alone suggests how the unification of Germany was in itself sufficient to upset the balance of power in Europe. True, for every inhabitant of the German Empire there were two inhabitants of the Russian Empire. Yet only one portion of the Russian Empire lay in Europe; also, compared to Germany, Russia was primitive and backward. By 1900 Germany was the greatest industrial power on the continent of Europe, surpassing not only Russia and France but also Great Britain. Neither the numbers of the German people, nor the German people, nor the material resources of the German land sufficed to explain this. Even—or, perhaps, especially—in this age of materialism, mind counted ever more than matter. Exceptional and, at times, alarmingly impressive were the industriousness and the discipline of the German people—the results of their mental habits and of their governing ideas. That was the substance of their history as, indeed, it is the substance of the history of every nation, especially in modern times.

Still there is no isolated nation, as there is no isolated virtue. Perhaps the very introspective qualities of the Germans obscured their better understanding of other peoples. At any rate, they had few great statesmen between Bismarck and Hitler. Through a kind of offensive shortsightedness, together with an eventually disastrous alliance, they threw themselves into the First World War. They had to face almost all the Great Powers of the world. It took the latter more than four years to beat the Germans down. The traditional order of Europe was mortally wounded during that struggle. The wounds of the German people were terrible, but far from mortal. The Germans were humiliated and impoverished, they were down and out for a while. They were sick at being treated, no doubt with a great deal of injustice, as pariahs among the nations of Europe, at any rate for a while. Soon they would rise again and treat in turn, with far more injustice, the other nations of Europe as *their* pariahs. Such are the dangerous oscillations of the German soul and mind.

Even after the First World War there remained a united German state. It would soon recover from its humiliations and mutilations, including its self-inflicted ones. During the world economic depression of 1929–33, in the miseries of which the Germans wallowed with especial enthusiasm, the strength of Germany among the powers of Europe was rising, not falling. The year before Hitler became their Chancellor, both in absolute and in relative numbers there were more jobless Germans than there were jobless Frenchmen or Englishmen. Yet by 1932 it was the latter two who were trying to reduce their armed forces, not the former. Neither the German Army, nor the German Navy, were cutting back. The prospect, as well as the present retrospect, was obvious. Germany was rising again; and soon she would be the strongest power in Europe. This German ascent was accelerated by Hitler, but it was not caused by him. What he did was to give the Germans an extraordinary injection of confidence and of aggressiveness; and the aggressively confident German can be a very ugly variant of the human species. He gave the impression of a frightening German garrison state; yet both the volume and the speed of German armament were less during the thirties than what the world, including the intelligence services of the other powers, thought at the time.

No matter: The impression, especially when resting on discipline and will, was reality enough. During the thirties, Hitler achieved an economic and political revolution in the middle of Europe. Within Germany he put an end to unemployment and created a new kind of mass prosperity—all through the new climate of national confidence. Without Germany he restored the traditional German primacy in the markets of neighboring countries to the east and to the south. Much of this was achieved through the unorthodox, and yet common-sense, method of nationalizing the German people instead of nationalizing the industries, and through emphasizing that German wealth depended on German production instead of German possession of gold. German mass production soon became superior to that of any great European power, including Britain—in turnout, distribution, often even in quality. A few figures will illustrate this point. Two states that traditionally traded with Germany (principally because the direction of their economic relations followed that of their political sympathies) were Hungary and Bulgaria. In 1933, when Hitler came to power, 11.1 per cent of Hungarian and 38 per cent of Bulgarian exports went to Germany; 19.6 per cent of Hungarian and 38 per cent of Bulgarian imports came therefrom. By 1938 these figures rose to 51 per cent and 64 per cent, and to 48 per cent and 58 per cent, respectively. They doubled, trebled, quadrupled. By the middle of the thirties this German primacy was becoming evident among France's allies, states that had been dependent on French finance. In 1933, 13 per cent of Yugoslav and 18 per cent of Romanian imports had come from Germany; by 1938 this percentage had risen to 50 per cent and 49 per cent, respectively. Soon this primacy of Germany began to extend even to states that previously had traded little with the Germans, such as Greece or Norway or Spain. By 1938 the volume of trade and business of the traditionally Anglophile Greeks that they carried on with Germany was nearly five times larger than their trade with Great Britain, and fourteen times larger than their trade with France.

Such were the advantages of trading with the Third Reich. The advantages of befriending the Third Reich were no less evident. The diplomatic revolution achieved by Hitler in the thirties was very impressive. In 1933 France had five allies on the Continent, while Germany had none. Reacting to the rise of Germany in 1935, the French made an additional alliance with the Soviet Union. As late as 1938 Germany did not have a single ally, while France still had five on paper. In reality, most of France's allies had already deserted her, even though their alliances were technically still in existence. The leaders of formerly anti-German states, such as Poland, Yugoslavia, Lithuania, and Greece, not to speak of Mussolini's Italy and Franco's Spain, now preferred the friendship of Germany to that of France. Men within the British, and perhaps the Soviet, governments had similar inclinations. Much of Europe was coming closer and closer to the German orbit, notwithstanding the bad reputation of the Third Reich for mistreating Communists, liberals, Jews, and other opponents of Hitler.

These achievements of Hitler during the thirties were comparable only to Bismarck's during the 1860s, seventy years before. In one sense Hitler did even better than Bismarck: He achieved all of this without war. What Bismarck had achieved through blood and iron, Hitler achieved through the mere threat of discipline and steel. Yet in more than one way Bismarck was the greater statesman of the two. Without Bismarck the domination of the Prussians over the Germans might never have come about. There are many reasons to believe that Germany would have risen to a pre-eminent position in Europe even without Hitler. Her rise would have been slower, more difficult, less dynamic. She would have risen nonetheless.

Much of this German primacy had to do with cultural rather than with "economic" factors. The French philosopher Renan wrote one hundred years ago that the victory of the Prussians over the French at Sedan was the victory of the German schoolmaster. There was much to that. For two or three generations after 1870 the German universities were perhaps the best in the world. Most of the Eastern European peoples after the First World War depended on German methods of teaching. Beyond the universities new generations of intellectuals appeared who were more impressed by German than by French modes of thinking. This was true of such distant countries as Spain, Greece, Italy, Russia, of Marxists as well as of conservatives. An analysis of the German educational system alone would be insufficient to explain this. German thinking, at its best and also at its worst, represented a reaction against the bourgeois materialism of the nineteenth century; and, since the great Romantic movement had originated mostly in Germany, also a reaction against the cold and increasingly lifeless rationalism of the eighteenth. Neo-idealism was the great German contribution in the intellectual history of Europe, ranging from philosophy to physics. Entire generations of Europeans were sympathetically attuned to this, even when, politically speaking, they were not Germanophiles. Other millions of people, often not more than half educated, admired the aggressive efficiency of the German as a kind of cultural prototype. In the second part of this book I must devote an entire chapter to these, often insufficiently noted, international inclinations and relationships. It may be enough to sum matters up here by saying that the period 1871–1945 represented not only the political and economic but also the cultural predominance of Germany in Europe It was a long chapter in the history of Europe, and not only a political one.

There was, however, a fatal flaw in this development, so full of promise for Germany in retrospect. The Germans could be tactless and inconsiderate; they would cultivate some of their virtues to such systematic extremes that these became vices. "The Prussians," wrote that great Victorian English wit Labouchère more than one hundred years ago, "are saints compared with the French. They have every sort of excellence: They are honest, hard-working, well-instructed, brave, good sons, husbands, and fathers; and yet all this is spoilt by one single fault—they are insupportable. . . . A Prussian lieutenant is the most offensive specimen of humanity that nature and pipeclay have ever produced. Apart from all political considerations, the supremacy of this nation in Europe will be a social calamity. . . ."* Eventually the Germans would destroy their best prospects, and their extraordinary leader Hitler was no exception to that.

There is still another consideration, of principal importance for this book. The Germans had the potential to rejuvenate old Europe, to extend the European age, and the primacy of Europe, in the world for centuries to come. They destroyed this prospect because of their obsession with their own primacy in Europe, finally and perhaps irrevocably, during the Last European War. In this respect, too, Hitler was but an extreme prototype of their talents and of their vices. Often stronger, and on occasion more thoughtful than others, Germans, from Nietzsche to Spengler to Hitler, would speak of the dangers to Western civilization, to the white race, to Europe. In practice, instead of consolidating, they would mightily contribute to the perils of the West, of Europe and, in the end, of their own Germany. The principal instrument in this was Hitler's Third Reich. And so we arrive at the year 1938, which was the peak of Hitler's career.

---

* Pearson, 105–6. Full titles of the works cited in this book are to be found in Abbreviations of cited references, pp. 539–51.

# 2 . Hitler's year[1]

THE YEAR 1938 WAS HITLER'S YEAR in the history of Europe and of the world. In that year this once forlorn Austrian orphan became the most powerful man in the world. The year 1938 was both the pinnacle and the turning point of his life. Within six months he made, by mere threats, a German Reich that was bigger and more united and more dominant than any Reich in the past. Thereafter the remaining European powers, including England and France, acquiesced in his domination of most of Eastern Europe. By the end of 1938 there was not one state in Europe that dared to declare its open opposition to Germany.

In 1938 Hitler had Germandom behind him more than ever before or after. He had reason to believe that he had achieved the kind of mysterious bond with his people that is the mark of a great national leader in the hour of destiny. He thought that destiny had wedded him to the German people; and that he was destined to unify them better than ever. In March 1938 he made his native Austrian people unite with the German Reich. He returned to his birthplace in a strange mood of somber triumph. He was born in Braunau on the Inn, a village on the Austro-German border, on a gray spring afternoon on Saturday, 20 April 1889. He came back to Braunau on 12 March 1938, on another gray spring afternoon on a Saturday. In the very first sentence of *Mein Kampf* he had written:

> Today I consider it my good fortune that Fate designated Braunau on the Inn as the place of my birth. For this small town is situated on the border between those two German States, the reunion of which seems, at least to us of the younger generation [he wrote these words in 1924] a task to be furthered with every means our lives long.

---

[1] 1938.

[8]

Hitler's ancestors were upper Austrian peasants on both sides. His genealogy could be traced back for centuries without much difficulty (in part because on occasion the families were close and almost inbred). For three or four generations the families moved gradually westward, from the valley of the Thaya close to the Austrian-Czech border, changing their homesteads until Hitler's father came to Braunau in the valley of the Inn on the German frontier. In the movements of the Hiedler-Hittler-Schicklgruber-Pölzl families, Braunau was the westernmost place. It was the culminating point of their family history. There they brought to life this child who was to become the most extraordinary man in the history of their people.

Save for the symbol of its location, Braunau had little importance in Hitler's life. His family moved away from Braunau before he was four years old; it seems that he had not come back to Braunau until his triumphant day in 1938. He crossed the border there. He stayed but for an hour or so, while jubilation reigned. Presently through the darkening afternoon he drove onto Leonding, to visit his parents' graves. (He remembered much more of Leonding than of Braunau; often he would talk among his circle about his childhood in this small suburb of Linz.) In the evening he drove from Leonding into Linz. There he was received by a crying and cheering mass such as the history of Linz or, indeed, of Austria, had never seen. According to some accounts 100,000 people had massed together, including thousands of peasants who had come in their carts or by foot (the population of Linz was less than 120,000 at the time). This enormous crowd pressed thick before the Hotel Weinzinger in the city that he had remembered with especial affection, and for which he would have even more affection thereafter (he made special provisions for it in his Testament, and a few days before his death he would still seek mental solace in talking about architectural plans for Linz). He responded to the crowd with a sudden impulse. Going beyond the plans for a political union, he would receive Austria in the bosom of his Reich. To the delight and surprise of the Linzers (Linz was one of Austria's more Nazified towns), Hitler stayed for nearly two days. Only on Monday afternoon, 14 March, did his motor cortege start eastward again, for Vienna, where another kind of jubilant reception awaited him.

There is reason to believe that no journey Hitler made as Fuehrer made a deeper impression on him than this return to Austria. An hour or so in Braunau, then Leonding, then a prolonged and sentimental forty hours in Linz, then on to Vienna . . . One wonders whether Hitler knew that in March 1938 he traced, almost exactly, the path of his early life, from his birth in 1889 to 1906, the year of his mother's traumatically tragic death. It was the peak moment of his life. There is, as we shall see, evidence that he felt and knew this himself.

[9]

In any event, few men and few nations in the entire history of Europe had risen so dramatically as had Hitler and his Germany from 1933 to 1938. Three of the other powers of Europe could have restrained the ascent of Hitler's Third Reich during this time: France, England, and Italy. France was the only one of these three that bordered on Germany. In 1933 France still had the largest army on the Continent. Four days after Hitler had been made Chancellor of Germany, he said to the commanders of the German Army: "Now we shall see whether France has statesmen or not: If so, she won't let us have time but attack us" (before the buildup of the German Army).[2] The French had no such statesmen nor did they have generals worthy of the Germans' respect. When Hitler remilitarized the Rhineland in March 1936—in many ways his greatest European gamble until the outbreak of the war—the French did little or nothing. They might have acted had the English backed them; but the English did not. The governments of England during the thirties were dedicated to the pursuit of domestic business and to pacific relationships with most of the world, including Germany. This kind of economic dedication was usually the result of a determined Anglo-Saxon unwillingness to recognize certain unpleasant realities. The English, Wilde once wrote, "are always degrading truths into facts. When a truth becomes a fact it loses all its intellectual value." "The central fact," said Philip Kerr, Lord Lothian, a Christian Scientist, and at that time a prototypical figure of the English political establishment, in January 1935, "is that Germany does not want war and is prepared to renounce it absolutely as a method of settling her disputes with her neighbours provided she is given real equality."[3] The mirage of this kind of "central fact" was to be pursued with a rigid and narrow determination by the rigid and narrow minds of the Chamberlain type, at least for a while.

Oddly enough, Italy was the key element in the European constellation of Powers in the mid-thirties—an amazing constatation in retrospect. She was a Great Power, mostly because of her prestige. Because of Mussolini the world forgot the Italians' mixed performance during the First World War and before. Bismarck was reputed to have said that Italy had a good appetite but poor teeth. Mussolini had put a lot of effort into national dentistry. By repeating and repeating that Italy now had teeth like a tiger, the world came to believe this. Few people noticed that the Fascist Italian teeth, no matter how gleaming white, were decayed on the

---

[2] *VFZ* (Oct. 1954), 435 (General Liebmann's notations). Goebbels often repeated the same argument within his circle.
[3] Butler, 336.

inside. Still we have to go beyond mouth and digestion to notice another element in favor of Italy's Great Power status. Italy, besides Germany, was the only power of any size east of the Rhine—one of the senseless consequences of the treaties arrived at by the Congress of Paris after World War I. In early 1936 the French Senate ratified an alliance of France with Soviet Russia. Unlike the French alliance with Tsarist Russia before World War I, the effect of this alliance on the European balance of power, including Germany's prospects, was about nil. It bothered Hitler not a whit (even as it furnished him with the pretext of marching into the Rhineland). Had the French succeeded in getting Italy into an alliance with them, Hitler would have had to face some serious problems.

Thus Italy was more important than the Soviet Union, in part because this was what people thought. An even sillier consequence of the Paris peace treaties was the condition that the traditional relationship of Austria and Italy was entirely reversed by the thirties: The independence of Austria now largely depended on Italy. Had France and Italy been closely allied, they could have blocked Hitler's progress, at least to the south and to the southeast, at least until 1936. There is no use to spin out this iffy hypothesis further. Mussolini, like Hitler, had no stomach for the French. He was convinced that, especially compared to Germany, France was weak and flabby. He attributed this—not altogether unreasonably— to the parliamentary democracy of France. He also convinced himself— again, not entirely unreasonably—that democracy had been eating into England's strength, like cancer. By glancing and glowering at the decaying teeth of the English he failed to consider the remnant strength of their jaw. But that was to come later. During the mid-thirties the very set of that jaw was slack. In 1935, during the Abyssinian crisis, the Sea Lords advised the Prime Minister that their fleet was in no shape to stand up to the Italians in the Mediterranean. It is useless to argue what would have happened if the Western European democracies had succeeded in pleasing Italy. Had they handsomely acquiesced in Italy's colonial conquest of Abyssinia, Mussolini would not have been impressed. He was set to draw close to Hitler—and not because of ideological affinities alone. As late as in February 1936 his Triestine Minister, Suvich, would still minute to Mussolini: "to sacrifice Austria would be a colossal mistake, in my view."[4] Exactly one month later, Hitler marched into the Rhineland, and the Western democracies did nothing. Mussolini felt confirmed in the rightness of his views. He would move toward an alliance with Hitler, at the expense of Austria, if need be. He also ditched Suvich by the way.

The independence of Austria was doomed. In July 1936 her government signed a treaty with Germany that satisfied Hitler for a while, and

---

[4] Suvich on 7 February 1936, cited by De Felice, *EF*, 211.

Mussolini considerably. In his view Austria ceased to be the chasm, it was becoming the bridge between Italy and Germany. He would speak accordingly of a "Rome-Berlin Axis" (in November 1936) around which the destinies of Europe would henceforth revolve. Exactly one year later Hitler summoned the German generals and commanders. He told them that the German armed forces must be prepared for war, if need be, within the next few years, and that the first principal item on his agenda was the solution of Germandom's relations to Austria and to Czechoslovakia. We shall have to come back later in this chapter to the sometimes debated and debatable record of that conference, the so-called Hossbach Protocol, in order to inquire—or, rather, in order to inquire whether it is worth inquiring—if Hitler really wanted war or not. He certainly wanted to take advantage of opportune situations on the borders of the Third Reich, sooner rather than later.

These opportunities now presented themselves. Late in January 1938 two secret police files containing scandalous evidence—one obviously true, the other complicated and obscure even now—gave Hitler the opportunity (which he did not take until after painful doubts and hesitations) to replace his War Minister, the Army Commander-in-Chief and, in the bargain, the Foreign Minister, with men who were his convinced followers and absolutely dependent on him. Not that this was a conflict between the remaining German conservatives and the radical Nazis: The dismissed "conservatives," Field Marshal Blomberg and General Fritsch and the Foreign Minister, Neurath, bent and bowed before the Fuehrer. It was another political Catholic and conservative, Franz von Papen (a man who fancied himself as the Talleyrand of the Third Reich, whereas he was not much more than its Sieyès), the German minister to Austria, who told Hitler, in the midst of this personnel crisis, that just now something could be done with Austria whose Chancellor Schuschnigg would be willing to pay a visit to Hitler. This opportunity Hitler grasped with energy. On the afternoon of 12 February 1938 Schuschnigg arrived at Hitler's mountain compound. Schuschnigg expressed his admiration over the view and the weather. "We did not come together to talk about the weather," Hitler said. This was characteristic of the rest of their conversation. Hitler was brutal, demanding, strong. Schuschnigg was shaken, unsure, and weak. Hitler demanded changes within the Austrian government, together with other reforms that would prepare the way for Austria to become, increasingly, a satellite of the Third Reich. In order to save the remnants of Austrian independence, Schuschnigg gave way. He could not count on Italy any longer, nor would France or Britain do much, if anything, for Austria. In early March he had a brainstorm. Perhaps he could count on world public opinion. He suddenly called for an instant plebiscite that would affirm Austria's independence to the world. Both the wording and the conditions of the referendum are instructive in retrospect. "Are you in favor of a free and German, an independent and social, a Christian and united Austria?" It was not only that Schuschnigg was afraid of Hitler's wrath, he was also afraid of the strong pro-German and pro-Nazi feelings current among his own people. He announced a plebiscite that was to take place a mere four days later, on a Sunday. Only people over twenty-four years of age were allowed to vote (he knew how much of Austria's youth were imbued with German and Nazi sentiments).

Hitler was stung to the quick. A day or so later he ordered the military occupation of Austria. A few telephone calls from Berlin were enough to make Schuschnigg resign. A new Austrian Nazi government took over. When Hitler crossed into Austria, immense throngs cheered and howled him on. In Linz, on his way to Vienna, on the spur of the moment, he announced the *Anschluss*—not merely a Nazified government for Austria, but a complete union of Austria with Germany. The German —and most of the Austrian—people found themselves at a high point of happy frenzy. There were some ugly scenes involving elderly Jews in Vienna, but few Germans cared. The Third Reich was greater than ever, it was a colossus over Central Europe. No one who has not lived in Central Europe in 1938 could understand the impact of Hitler's march into Vienna. Compared to it the Russian invasions of Hungary or of Czechoslovakia decades later were primitive police actions, running against the current of sentiment and the tides of time. The Third Reich seemed to be the oceanic wave of present and future combined— representing a new kind of order in Europe, perhaps in the world.

Mussolini accepted the conquest of Austria in silence. Hitler was overwhelmed: He kept repeating, in a strangely emotional message, that he would never forget this, never. The French hardly stirred. Russia was far away. During Hitler's year Stalin was preoccupied with police reports about his subordinates in the day, and he would make Ukrainian party secretaries dance the *gopak* on occasions when they would be, all, disagreeably drunk at night. Many men in the British government, including Chamberlain, had a whit of sympathy for Hitler. Germany seemed to represent at least some of the virtues that the Birmingham brand of Toryism (in reality, a kind of late John Bright Radicalism) respected: industry, order, thrift, noncommunism, national self-determination. Hitler merely wanted to practice something that the heirs of Gladstone, including Woodrow Wilson, had been preaching. The Austrians were Germans, after all. So were the three million so-called Sudeten Germans living within the rim of Czechoslovakia. Immediately after the *Anschluss* of Austria they were becoming restive—in a predictable and disciplined way. They were among the most respected, and best-protected, people within Czechoslovakia. No matter: They were convinced by their leaders that their situation was intolerable. Intolerable is what people don't want to tolerate. They no longer wanted to tolerate a situation in which they were deprived of the joys of being the military subjects of the Fuehrer's Reich.

This boded trouble. Unlike Austria, Czechoslovakia had allies, on paper at least. No matter how weak and soft and demoralized, the French would have declared war on Germany *if* the British had done so too.[5] There was method behind this mush. Ever since 1919 the French knew that they could not fight Germany alone. Their security depended upon Britain, even though the British had no binding alliance with them. In 1938 they did not know that even such an alliance would not deter Hitler, who knew that he could defeat the French without the British doing much about it. Consequently the French tried to commit the British government to the defense of Czechoslovakia. In retrospect, this was a hopeless task, for three reasons of ascending importance. The British Army and Navy and Air Force were not ready for war, even as their armament in the air was proceeding fast. The Dominions, for long an important reservoir of manpower, were in no mood for a European war in 1938 and told Chamberlain so, which no doubt was what he wanted to hear. Most important, Chamberlain and his government and the large inchoate majority that he seemed to represent were inclined, and, at times, determined to find something good in Hitler's Germany and, conversely, to find things that were bad (they were not hard to find) in the French and in the Czechs. In the end, these inclinations were decisive. They also sum up the so-called policy of the appeasement. The sorry thing about it is that in the summer of 1938 Britain, perhaps for the last time in her history, was the principal factor in world politics—not because of her strength but because this was what most people, including Hitler, believed.

He knew that the British were, in a way, playing for time; he was also furious when, in May 1938, a false press campaign gave the impression to the world that Hitler had been ready to attack but that he was backing down because of some measures of Czech mobilization. He was, however, not displeased by the British willingness to "meditate." In August 1938 Chamberlain sent an aged Gladstonian Liberal to "investigate" the Sudeten situation. Soon it became apparent that the British government, like the Germans, was contemplating not merely the granting of complete autonomy to the Germans within Czechoslovakia but also the German annexation of most of these territories—another *Anschluss*. Hitler proclaimed that he would not tolerate Czech resistance to his demands much longer. He fixed 1 October as the target date. Neville

---

[5] Whether the French would have done much more than declare war—that is, whether they would have attacked Germany in the West—is another question. The available records as well as their performance in 1939 suggest that they would have done nothing of the sort.

Chamberlain, looking more and more like an old bird, flew twice over to the Continent to talk with Hitler. The entire world was impressed, mistaking the old bird as an angel of peace. Such were the twilight conditions of the European climate in 1938.

The few people who saw things clearer were frightened into submission—the Czechs and a few German generals who had been whispering conspiracy. When Chamberlain first flew to Hitler, Mussolini said to Ciano: "There will be no war. But this is the liquidation of English prestige." Hitler, who often failed to comprehend the English, took Chamberlain's measure at a glance. All over the Western world people were making bitter jokes about Hitler, and in fabulous sun-drenched Hollywood, Chaplin was beginning to crank up a silly movie about the Great Dictator. Yet the funny toothbrush mustache belonged to Chamberlain, not to Hitler. After this second meeting with Hitler in Godesberg, when Hitler had thrown Chamberlain's proposals into the wastebasket, Chamberlain returned to England with the firm determination to surrender. There are few records of British Cabinets comparable to that of the afternoon of 24 September 1938, after Chamberlain had flown back from Godesberg. "P.M. made his report to us. I was completely horrified—he was quite calmly for total surrender. More horrified still to find that Hitler has evidently hypnotised him to a point. Still more horrified to find that P.M. has hypnotised [Halifax, the Foreign Secretary] who capitulates totally. . . ."[6] This was the record by Alexander Cadogan, then a supporter of appeasement and a loyal follower of Chamberlain. Cadogan was now deeply disturbed, and said so to Halifax. After a largely sleepless night, the Foreign Secretary decided that Cadogan was right and that Chamberlain was wrong. It did not make much difference. On the surface things were moving toward war, an all-European war, for the first time after twenty years. At the same time many people, including Mussolini, knew that Hitler could get all, or nearly all, that he wanted, at the cost of a single gesture in favor of a peaceful settlement.

This is how the Munich "Conference" came about. It matured quickly, in a few days. On 29 and 30 September the Prime Ministers of Britain and of France met with Hitler and Mussolini in Munich. Both Hitler and Chamberlain got what they wanted. Hitler got the rich rim of Czechoslovakia for nothing. Chamberlain got peace and a reputation inflated into the image of an honest British statesman of Victorian proportions. What he had not realized was that he had earned Hitler's contempt for him and for the French. In the Western world a temporary wave of euphoria reigned because war had been averted. Opponents of Munich

---

[6] *Cadogan*, 103, 105.

such as Winston Churchill were nearly censured for having dared to criticize Chamberlain.

Soon the opponents were proven right—indeed, strongly and painfully so. Yet in two ways they seem to have been wrong, in retrospect. First, they were convinced (indeed, many of them remain so convinced until this day) that Hitler was bluffing. This, from the evidence, seems quite unlikely. Hitler was ready to go to war with Czechoslovakia, and he believed that the latter's allies would do nothing. Even if France had declared war, in a few days he could have smashed Czechoslovakia in a rapid campaign and stopped, whereafter the British would have striven for a kind of peace. Later he would often rue the fact that he went to war in 1939 and not in 1938. He may have been quite right. A quick war with Czechoslovakia in 1938 might have given him the mastery of Europe for a long time, with the consequent assent of the British, which is what he had always wanted. The second consideration is closely connected with the first. In 1938 Czechoslovakia had another ally besides France. This was the Soviet Union. Most people, including those who ought to have known better,[7] believe even now that, while in 1938 the French and the British betrayed the Czechs, the Soviet Union was ready to enter a European war in order to stand by its democratic Central European ally; that therefore Munich was the main event that turned Stalin away from the West and eventually toward Hitler. Most of this is nonsense. Few people, even in France, knew that, unlike in 1914, Russia did not border on Germany. In September 1938 a few Soviet diplomatists, when hard pressed, dropped remarks to the effect that the Soviet Union would stand by the Czechs, provided that the French observed *their* alliance commitments; and, again, provided that Poland and Romania would let the Red Army pass through their countries to Czechoslovakia, something that was wholly out of the question. In 1938 Stalin was no more prepared for war with Germany than were Chamberlain or Daladier. Hitler, who in 1938 and before, preened himself as the world leader of anticommunism, hardly gave the Soviet Union a thought. If the accepted opinion, according to which the main thread running through Hitler's political thinking was the aim of an eventual German conquest of Soviet Russia, is true, we are permitted to wonder why in Hitler's war and political planning in 1938 the Soviet Union did not figure at all. In all probability he knew that the Russians would not do much, if anything, for Czechoslovakia (except perhaps for putting some Russian pressure on Poland).

In a furious passage in a vituperative speech before Munich, Hitler

---

[7] This includes Churchill, *The Second World War* (GS, 304–5). Still on many matters this often superb personal history has stood the test of time much better than what many academic historians are now willing to consider.

said that this was his last territorial demand in Europe. In view of this it is difficult to defend Chamberlain's attitudes—not so much at Munich but during the rest of Hitler's Year, and for some time afterward. Chamberlain had justified his going to Munich to himself and to his people as an inevitable "compromise," a sacrifice for the sake of maintaining the peace of Europe, a kind of painful amputation that, in the circumstances, simply had to be done. The amputation was, however, followed by the near-total neglect of the patient. Not only had the rest of Czechoslovakia become now a sorry ward of Germany, entirely within Hitler's sphere of influence, but also the British and, consequently, the French acted as if they were letting most of Eastern Europe go that way. The Munich Four-Power agreement provided, among others, the prospect that Polish and Hungarian demands upon Czechoslovakia (the latter were, in their way, even more justified than were those of the Germans) would be considered in due course. When the question of Hungarians under Czechoslovakian rule came up, soon after Munich, the British and the French governments expressed their disinterest. They let Germany and Italy arbitrate a border revision, the so-called Vienna Award, whereby on 2 November 1938 a portion of Czechoslovakia was translated to Hungary. In one way this was a minor event, the result of a bitter dispute between neighbors, a fatal consequence of the ways in which their frontiers had been unjustly drawn twenty years before. In another way this British and French abstention was significant; it suggested that, at least for the present, the Western European powers had written Eastern Europe off. It certainly marked the end of an era; it was the final dismantling of the edifice of a Europe that the Western democracies had tacked together, after World War I, which they had won at the cost of an enormous and unprecedented bloodletting of their own.

Thus at the end of 1938 Hitler was more powerful than the two Germanic monarchs combined in 1914. He may have been the most powerful man on this earth. Yet he believed that time was working against him—in more than one way.

It is possible now, thanks mostly to the preservation of many German records and to the assiduity of certain research historians, to reconstruct in detail much of this lonely dictator's life. These details will not, of course, explain the enigmas in the character of this so voluble, and yet essentially so secretive, a man. The mind of Adolf Hitler was a very powerful instrument. To deduce from his awesome defects of the heart that he was wanting insight or intelligence is the commonest mistake most people make about him. Nor was he mad. This is the simplistic interpretation to which Americans are especially prone: It corresponds to the modern American inclination to believe that the presence of evil in men is an abnormal condition. To ascribe the evil acts of men to "abnormality" does not only obscure our necessary understanding of Hitler, it also obscures and damages our necessary understanding of human nature itself. Besides, there is all of the historical evidence to the contrary. All the stories of the dictator foaming at the mouth, throwing himself at the carpet and chewing it in a mad rage, are false. The contrary was, rather, true. What was frightening in his character was his cold and almost inhuman detachment. Men and women close to him would remember the porcelain blueness of his eyes, and his fixed gaze. In contemplating his photographs in retrospect I am struck less by that pathetic quality that George Orwell observed[8] than by a certain cruel nakedness of that face; a sad and cold and cruel face (the nose and the chin and the mouth seem especially cruel in profile; it is only that famous little mustache that tends to divert one's attention).

Sad, cold, cruel: but not mad. There remains a question that is difficult to avoid at this point. Was Hitler an ideologue, or was he an opportunist? There is the thesis, accepted by most people, that Hitler's plans for world conquest were the result of his fanatical devotion to an ideology that he had set out in *Mein Kampf* for anyone who knew how to read. Yet Hitler himself did not always like to be reminded of *Mein Kampf*[9]; in 1940, for instance, he forbade the public display of the manuscript. Others have said that Hitler was the supreme opportunist. Harold Laski wrote in 1942 that Hitler was nothing else, a man without principles and theories, who simply wanted power for its own sake (whatever that means). Ten years later, Hitler's then principal biographer, Alan Bullock, said much the same thing: "an unprincipled opportunist." (There is some evidence that Bullock has since changed his mind.) Another ten years later, A. J. P. Taylor, in *The Origins of the Second World War*, described Hitler as yet another German politician in the fell clutch of circumstances who stumbled into war, having had no particular plan of his own. Behind these, sometimes thoughtful, and often thoughtless, dismissals of Hitler's vision one may detect a certain uneasy unwillingness to recognize the power of his mind, or even to con-

---

[8] In his controversial review of *Mein Kampf* in early 1940; *Orwell*, II, 12–14.

[9] In February 1936 he said to the French publicist Bertrand de Jouvenel: "You want me to revise my book [Jouvenel was concerned with some of the extreme Francophobic passages], as if I were a writer revising for a new edition. But I am not a writer. I am a politician. I make my revisions in my foreign policy directed at an understanding with France. [Hitler said this shortly before his march into the Rhineland.] My success in this would amount to a revision worthy of its name. I enter my revisions into the great book of history!" Maser, *MK*, 47–48.

sider certain essential features of the vision (as Professor Eberhard Jaeckel put it, if Hitler had not a *Weltanschauung*, he surely had a *Weltbild*)[10] that lay behind much of the dreadful rhetoric of *Mein Kampf* and of Hitler's many later pronouncements.

Hitler was not much of an opportunist. This is no argument in his favor. Scoundrels are less dangerous than fanatics. It is as simple as that. But, then, Hitler's fanaticism was a curious compound of a crude kind of idealism with a cruel kind of realism. The result of this was, on many occasions, an astonishing accuracy of insight into the motives of political men, of political groups, of the political leadership of entire foreign nations about which otherwise he knew little. Hitler's insight into the weakness of his potential opponents was the greatest source of his actual strength. He was an opportunist in this sense: He knew when to risk sudden, and even unexpected, moves in situations which, to him, seemed opportune when he knew that his opponents would do little or nothing. Thus he, and not his generals, was proven right when he said that the French would not fight as he sent the German Army into the Rhineland, that the French and the British would do nothing for Austria, that they would not fight for Czechoslovakia, that even if they declared war on him they would not attack while the German armies crushed their neighbor states in the East.

This brings us to the question of whether Hitler wanted war or not. In a way it is a pointless question. Like most other conquerors, Hitler preferred to gain his ends without war, if possible. This was true during his year, 1938; it was equally true in 1939. At this point we must return, for a moment, to the earlier-mentioned conference in the Reich Chancellery on 5 November 1937, the record of which bears the name of the Hossbach Protocol. Colonel Hossbach, a General Staff officer, made a record of this conference a few days afterward. This record was eventually brought to the attention of the world during Hossbach's testimony at the postwar Nuremberg war crimes trials, where it was registered as IMT Document No. PS-386. Like the record of another important Hitler statement, his speech to his generals on 22 August 1939,[11] there is some basis to question the accuracy of the Hossbach record, especially since it is not an exact verbatim transcript.[11] According to A. J. P. Taylor, the 5 November 1937 conference meant little or nothing. "The conference was a manoeuvre in domestic affairs." This is true but only in the sense in which some of this Professor's works are maneuvers in domestic histori-

---

[10] Jaeckel, passim, esp. 14–15, 24–25.

[11] See, for example, H. W. Koch, "Hitler and the Origins of the Second War: Second Thoughts on the Status of Some of the Documents" (*THJ*, 1968), 125–43.

anship. What Hitler said on 5 November 1937 was not a blueprint for war; it was not intended in that way; it was an admonition to the chiefs of the German Army and Navy that a resort to force might be necessary in the near future. Hitler described certain eventualities in case of which Germany would move against Czechoslovakia and Austria. Such eventualities included a conflict between France and Italy, or civil war in France, for example. Because this did not happen, Professor Taylor wrote that "Hitler's exposition was in large part daydreaming, unrelated to what followed in real life." This is not very convincing. The important matter in the Conference was not Hitler's speculation about eventualities, but his calculation that when his opportunity arose, France would be paralyzed by weakness. "Britain, almost certainly, and probably France as well, had written off the Czechs and were reconciled to the fact that this question for Germany would be cleared up in due course." This was a remarkably accurate assessment of matters in November 1937; this was exactly what happened a little less than a year later.

There is another element in this November 1937 conference that has not received the attention it deserves. Most historians will agree that Hitler had two principal beliefs that marked his political life to the very end. One was his obsession with the problem of the Jews, which he considered of fundamental importance; the other was his belief that Germany must reverse her course of 1914 and seek expansion at the expense of Russia. Yet he made almost no reference at all to Russia on 5 November 1937 (as he would make few references to Russia during the Czech crisis). He said something to the effect that in the event of war over Czechoslovakia, Russia would be preoccupied with Japan (which was true), and then there is this cryptic sentence: "Poland—with Russia in her rear—will have little inclination to engage in war against a victorious Germany." In other words: If Poland were to move against Germany, Russia might move against Poland. Here was something like the pattern of the German-Russian collusion against Poland nearly two years before it came about. Was Hitler contemplating this as early as 1937? Did this self-avowed champion of European anticommunism have a secret line to Stalin by that time? We have no evidence of it. Yet Hitler's lack of concern with Russia at that time is enigmatic, and it remains perhaps the principal enigma in the international history of the origins of the Second World War.

At this significant conference Hitler said that he had to proceed from the assumption that Germany's "problems" must be solved before 1943–45, after which time the European constellation would no longer be favorable to her. This tallies with the now available evidence of German armaments, since, as we shall see, Hitler prepared for short, decisive wars within Europe, not for a world war. It also tallies with what Hitler had told his friend Mussolini. It is, on the face of it, not a very extraordinary statement. Bismarck, who once said that the farthest ahead a statesman could see and plan was about five years, might have approved. Yet it is significant in retrospect because of a profound change in Hitler's mind during 1938.

Hitler's concern with his health reached a critical stage this year. Unlike Bismarck, Hitler was often in a hurry. Often he feared that Fate, or Providence, would not allow him to fulfill his great tasks for German-dom. All through his life he had suffered from minor ailments. While not a hypochondriac, he was frequently worried about his health. Soon after his triumphant progress to Vienna, he dictated a detailed and private will (on 2 May 1938). Throughout the rest of his year, 1938, there was a marked change in his manner and in his habits. He now shunned the least physical exercise; he withdrew from the convivialities of his cohorts. We also know many important details of his medical history, mostly due to Professor Maser's painstaking and detailed researches.[12] "His belief that he was ill and that there was little time left, henceforth rules all of Hitler's thoughts, plans, and acts."[13] Hitler's subsequent concentration on foreign policy was most probably a consequence of this.[14] There was not much time left.

During his year, 1938, this change in Hitler's mind was complete. From that year onward he thought he was actually more ill than he was. Yet "actually," in this context, is an imprecise word. His increasingly frequent gastro-intestinal ailments were, to use a modern and not very sat-isfactory word, at least to some extent "psychosomatic." Their etiology, as indeed is the etiology of many such illnesses, was existential, not merely functional—and this was bound to be an exaggerated condition in the life of a man whose force of character had its source in his belief in the power of the mind and of the will.

Perhaps we may detect God's hand in the development of this

---

[12] See especially Maser, Chap. 8.

[13] Maser, 331. The other eminent modern German historian of Hitler and of his movement, Professor Deuerlein, wrote much of the same thing. Deuerlein, 131. So did Speer recall the change in Hitler, to whom he was close at the time: "The speed, with which Hitler urged forward the construction of the new Reich Chancellery, had its deep springs in his concern with his health. He feared seriously that he wouldn't live much longer." Speer, 116.

[14] At the same time we must keep in mind how Hitler considered his foreign policy as a direct and unbroken consequence of his conquest of the Reich. "Wherever our success may lead us," he wrote in 1928, "it is only to another starting point of another struggle." Goebbels would at times express a similar argument. According to him, the Nazi conquest of Europe repeated, on a larger scale, their political conquest of Germany.

paradox: This man, who so often spoke of the primacy of mind over matter, and of will over flesh, now started to move downhill, and eventually into catastrophe—because of the developing state of his mind, which affected his body, whose symptoms, in turn, impressed him with the deep inner sense that he had not long to live. His belief in mind over matter raised him to the highest power on earth; and this belief was to destroy him in the end.

The terrible simplicity—or, rather, single-mindedness—with which Hitler impressed the world was but part of his character. We know now that he often considered alternative policies that were quite in contrast with those public statements that he declared with repetitive imperiousness. Evidences of such considerations were few, though sometimes he let them drop to certain close subordinates. Even less known were, and are, Hitler's frequent hesitations.[15] These would sometimes occur just after his great, and in some ways surprising, triumphs. Then he would often feel a profound sense of uncertainty or, rather, the pull of two diverse possibilities of action that he would sometimes fail to resolve, to his own peril. Such were his uncertainties after his victory over Western Europe in June 1940; and also after Munich. His love-hate relationship to England has been noticed by many people.[16] We must now note that all through his year, 1938, there were many evidences of this kind of duality. He could not reconcile it satisfactorily. He thought of Chamberlain, of Nevile Henderson, of Lloyd George and of those English politicians who were inclined to come to terms with him, alternately with contempt and respect. At the November 1937 conference Hitler spoke of England as a "hate-filled antagonist," and soon after he appointed the truly simple-minded Anglophobe Ribbentrop as his Foreign Minister; yet

---

[15] As Professor Peterson wrote in his study of the German bureaucracy under Hitler, "The bits of evidence accumulated strongly suggest that Hitler was never as sure of himself and his position as both his enemies and friends thought . . . [there are evidences] of real fear of opposition and then real surprise that the opposition melted away. This was not unlike his later surprise when his foreign opposition melted away at Munich. Like most common men, he overestimated the ability of his 'superiors.' When he himself was the 'superior,' he avoided meetings with subordinates who might question a decision, or he flooded them with monologue to prevent their raising any objection. This is a sign of weakness, not strength." Peterson, 430–1. There is much truth in this thoughtful passage, even though it may be a little too strong.
[16] He also misunderstood England more than he misunderstood any other people. See, for example, his statements about England's future in Hitler, *MK*, 956.

for a long time Hitler considered all sorts of attempts at reaching some kind of large-scale deal with England. At times he thought that Munich was a great triumph; at other times he thought that he may have been wrong for not having forced a war in September 1938, when the stars stood in his favor. This duality became soon apparent. Ten days after Munich he spoke at Saarbrücken, sharply and bitterly attacking those English politicians who wanted to restrain Germany.[17] By that time what remained of Czechoslovakia was on the way to becoming a pliant and subservient satellite of the Third Reich; but he was not content with that. He was about to order military preparations for the eventual absorption and virtual annexation of the rest of that rump state, oblivious of the effect that this might have on British opinion and on the British government. He, who had the fearful talent of possessing a deep insight into even the most foreign of men when he met them face to face, often failed to consider what their reaction to some of his acts might be when they were outside of his sway.

On 8 November 1938 a Jewish youth from Poland entered the German Embassy in Paris and shot and killed a German diplomatist. Consequent to this senseless act, Goebbels and other minions immediately organized two days of terror to "retaliate" against the remaining Jews within Germany. For two days smoke from burning synagogues dirtied the November skies of the Third Reich, while the pavements of German towns glittered and crunched with broken glass from the Jewish shops and houses. There is some evidence that Hitler was not altogether in favor of this kind of brutal terror, presented as it was as a popular outburst against the Jews.[18] Yet he did nothing either to stop or to mitigate it before the world. Chamberlain and others of his ilk would not let even this kind of barbarism deter them from pursuing a policy of goodwill toward the Third Reich. Yet it was acts such as these that were beginning to turn English, and American, opinion almost irreversibly against Germany —powerful currents of opinion that could not be merely attributed to Jewish influences and to Jewish propaganda. When, by the end of the year, evidence began to accumulate to the effect that Hitler, not content with his *de facto* domination of Central Europe, was probably bent on further territorial acquisitions by force, there were important forces at work against him, particularly in the United States. It was in January 1939, more than two months before his sudden and shocking invasion of the remnant Czechoslovak state, that the crystallization of a world opposi-

---

[17] Re a significant phrase in that speech, see below, p. 390.
[18] In his very first anti-Semitic speeches, in 1920, Hitler argued that the problem of the Jews must be treated "scientifically," not emotionally, as in the past.

tion against him in earnest began, with President Roosevelt being its principal instrument.

No one who did not live in Central or Eastern Europe then can understand the force of the impressions of Hitler's year. The Germans were now the master race. From Podolian villages to the avenues of great cities such as Budapest or Trieste or Prague, Germans, whether tourist visitors or their white-stockinged youth, walked or marched with an arrogance and self-confidence that had never been theirs before. They seemed, moreover, as if they were the incarnations of a new world: strong and contemptuous of the old bourgeois civilization of Europe, or what remained of it. They were feared and admired for this. To new generations coming of age across Europe, from Romania to Spain, National Socialism had become an object of emulation. This wave of sentiment reverberated beyond the edges of Europe, to South America and Japan. The crisis of Munich eclipsed the interest in the Spanish Civil War; Franco had nothing to do with Munich; yet somehow no one was surprised that at the end of Hitler's year the Nationalist army in Spain, after nearly three years of civil war, was on its way to final victory. In the dark recesses of the Kremlin, Stalin took note of this new dynamic force in the world. The twenties' England of *Crewe Train* had faded away to smoke and fine dust, it was far away, a Victorian remnant, like Cannon Street Station. Still, even the vulgarest and most vicious village Nazi could not shake the notion of a perfidious Albion from his mind. In order to rule the world, Hitler still must square his accounts with England.

# 3 . The coming of the war in 1939[1]

WITH THE RESULTS OF HIS YEAR, 1938, Hitler was not content. He was no Bismarck. People throughout Europe, and across the globe, sensed this. The pulsating energy of the new Germany was too strong to be self-contained. There would be another crisis, sooner rather than later; and then there would be war. This is exactly what happened. The outbreak of the war in 1939 caused a great shock in the lives of hundreds of millions in Europe. The outbreak of no other great war in the modern history of Europe caused so little surprise. Still we must trace the conditions of its outbreak in some detail.

In order to do this, we must put aside the more or less traditional canvas of Europe and set up a canvas of larger dimensions. The year 1938 was the last year when the conditions of war and peace depended on the European powers alone. Neither the United States nor the Soviet Union had much to do with Europe then. In 1938 even the Spanish Civil War had become a kind of sideshow, it had something of a North African or South American tinge about it, all of the previous excitements of Western European and American intellectuals notwithstanding. Now all of this would change. The United States and Russia, for different reasons, had withdrawn from Europe twenty years before. Now their shadows—if that is the word—began to move across the edges of the Continent again.

There still remains some mystery about the purpose and the conditions of their involvement. What did Roosevelt want in Europe? What did Stalin? There is the Franklin Delano Roosevelt Library in Hyde Park, New York, housing Roosevelt's papers and masses of historical paraphernalia. Whether Stalin left behind more than a handful of papers God alone knows. *His* Infinite Wisdom is such that He need not rely on the files of the Recording Angels. *We* know little or nothing, but we must

---

[1] 1 October 1938–3 September 1939.

try.[2] But we must understand, too, that masses of papers, especially of the twentieth century, do not necessarily help; often the contrary. Roosevelt, like Stalin, was a secretive man, though no doubt in a different way. Roosevelt relied much on personal conversations and on the telephone. Like many Presidents, he knew how to make sure that many of his words and deeds remained unrecorded for posterity. Often it is even more difficult to trace the true history of a great democrat than of a great tyrant.

At any rate, sometime after Christmas in 1938 Roosevelt decided to do something about Hitler. Less than three months before, Roosevelt, too, had been caught up by the euphoria about Munich, and so congratulated Chamberlain. Unlike the latter, however, Roosevelt had no illusions about Hitler's potential goodwill. In November Roosevelt had to face an unusually strong surge of Republican—the isolationist party then—gains in the biennial elections to the Congress. After Christmas, as was his habit, he perked up. He convinced himself—or let himself be convinced—that Hitler must be stopped. He began to suggest eventual American support to politicians in Europe who were known to him to be more or less determined to resist Hitler. Aware that he could count on little or no popular or congressional support for a course set on intervention in Europe, he relied on certain people he knew. These included ambassadors whom he had personally chosen sometime before, Bullitt in Paris and Kennedy in London. The first was somewhat excitable and unstable; the second, a powerful domestic Democrat, had a view of the world that was miles apart from Roosevelt's. Both Bullitt and Kennedy turned out to be eventually the bitterest enemies of their erstwhile patron and President; but by that time it was too late for them, they could do little against the man who had set the course of the gigantic American ship of state.

In 1939 most of this lay ahead. About his change of course Roosevelt said little or nothing in public. Yet soon the first evidences of this American inclination were registered by sensitive ears in Europe. One of the first dispatches suggesting it was that by the Polish ambassador to the United States, Count Potocki, to his Foreign Minister, Beck, as early as 12

---

[2] Kierkegaard: "If God held all truth concealed in his right hand, and in his left hand the persistent striving for truth, and while warning me against eternal error, should say: Choose! I should humbly bow before his left hand, and say: 'Father, forgive! The pure truth is for Thee alone!'" Dostoevsky: "If anyone could prove to me that Christ is outside the truth, and if the truth really did exclude Christ, I should prefer to stay with Christ and not with the truth." *Voilà* the great and profound chasm between the Western Christian and the Eastern Christian mind. Like Tolstoy, Dostoevsky was a great nineteenth-century fabulist. Like Tolstoy, his understanding of history was thoroughly false.

January 1939.[3] Within a few weeks, evidences of American encouragement to the anti-German side began to multiply in certain capitals of Europe. A typical summary of this kind of information was registered by the Polish ambassador to Paris, Lukasiewicz, who reported that Bullitt told him in early February 1939: "Should war break out we [the United States] shall certainly not take part in it at the beginning, but we shall end it." Hitler was aware of this. In his speech on 30 January 1939 he referred, for the first time openly, to American hostility to the Third Reich. Like Potocki and, possibly, Chamberlain,[4] he connected this with the purposes of the Jews. He warned the international Jews "inside and outside Europe" that if they were to "succeed" in bringing about another world war, the result will be "the annihilation of the Jewish race throughout Europe."[5] In 1939 the world paid little or no heed to this kind of talk, which seemed to be (indeed, it was) typical Hitler at the time. It is in retrospect that the significance of Hitler's terrible threat emerges. Thereafter the purposes of Roosevelt and of world Jewry became inseparably connected in Hitler's mind.[6]

At this point I must leave the larger canvas in order to concentrate on a small wretched province of Eastern Europe. There was (and is) a dark side of Europe, as there is a dark side of the moon. The distance between the Carpatho-Ukraine and, say, Normandy was hardly less than that between Canterbury and the Gobi Desert. The ignorance of the leading statesmen of the Western democracies regarding Eastern Europe was and remains inexcusable. Their ignorance regarding the Carpathian Ukraine at least was understandable. Yet, in a way, this province was the key to a great change in the entire Eurasian constellation of the Great Powers during the winter of 1938–39. I must sketch its complex situation as briefly as possible.

Between the wars the Ukrainian people lived under three sovereignties.[7] The large majority continued to live within the Soviet Union. After World War I 3½ million Ukrainians found themselves within the confines of the new Polish state, for which they professed little or no loy-

---

[3] *PD*, 9. The Germans found a copy of this dispatch and published it in 1940. Potocki was inclined to ascribe Roosevelt's European policy as the result of important Jewish influences. Even before this January dispatch Potocki had a significant conversation with Bullitt, on 25 November 1938.

[4] After the war (in 1945), Kennedy said to James Forrestal that in 1939 Chamberlain had told him: "The Americans and the world Jews had forced him into the war." *Forrestal*, 121–22.

[5] See a more detailed discussion of these statements below, pp. 429–30.

[6] See a more detailed discussion of this below, pp. 446–49.

[7] Four, if one includes the small Ukrainian minority in Romania.

alty. Finally there were another 600,000 in the easternmost province of Czechoslovakia, separated from their brethren to the northeast by the Carpathian Mountains: hence the name Carpatho-Ukraine.[8] It was a dark, muddy, mountainous province, superstitious and backward, light-years away not only from Western Europe but also light-months behind the neon-lit shopfronts of Prague. Its inhabitants, unlike many of the Ukrainians within Poland, had never lived under the sovereignty of the Russian Empire. Before 1918 they belonged to the Kingdom of Hungary —indeed, there was a considerable sprinkling of Hungarians within the Carpathian Ukraine. Now, in 1938, they became excited during the dissolution of Czechoslovakia.

In the wake of Munich, as we have seen, the new and weakened government of Prague chose, not unnaturally, to seek the friendship of the powerful Third Reich. Czechoslovakia came close to becoming Germany's satellite. This did not protect Czechoslovakia from further dismemberment, including the kind of dissension that, under the name of decentralization, would eventually result in the end of the authority of the central government in Prague. In October 1938 that government was compelled to grant near-complete autonomy to the Slovak part of the republic. (The very name of Czechoslovakia was hyphenated into Czecho-Slovakia.) A similar kind of near-autonomy was given to the Carpatho-Ukraine. All of this merely postponed the dissolution of the republic. When the final crisis came, in March 1939, the chain of events began as Prague felt compelled to dismiss the "Prime Minister" of the Carpatho-Ukraine on 5 March, ten days before Hitler would arrive in Prague. The Carpatho-Ukrainians believed (and the world believed) that Hitler's Third Reich stood behind them (as indeed it stood behind the Slovaks). Yet at this crucial time Hitler was not interested in the Carpathian Ukraine, as indeed he showed his disinterest in all of the Ukraine —an attitude that had a profound effect on Joseph Stalin.

To the contemplation of him we must now turn. Two years, even one year, before the outbreak of the Last European War, the Soviet Union counted little in the affairs of Europe. This may be very surprising now; and yet it was so. What happened in Europe for at least a quarter of a century after 1917 was the opposite of what Lenin had thought would happen. He thought that the Communist Revolution, starting in Russia, would soon engulf most, if not all, of Europe—certainly Eastern and Central Europe. The very contrary happened. The vast majority of the peoples of Europe—and especially the neighbor peoples of Russia—were repelled by communism: by its idea, by its practice, and, most of all, by

---

[8] It was often called "Ruthenia" then, an imprecise term.

the kind of people who represented it.[9] Even within Russia, the Communist government survived the civil war only at the cost of letting portions of the old Russian Empire go by the board. Entire portions seceded into independence—contrary to what Lenin had hoped, into a kind of nationalist, and often sharply anticommunist, kind of independence. Lenin was a revolutionary; he was not a statesman. His successor, Stalin, turned out to be a statesman, not a revolutionary. His education in statesmanship took, however, a good long time. During the thirties he kept the Soviet Union in untold[10] misery through the brutal collectivization of land, and through the oriental cruelty of his senseless (senseless to the Western mind, that is) mass purges, whereby he would eliminate all potential opposition (which was actually nonexistent) to himself and to his cohorts from the ranks of the Red Army and from the leading cadres of the Communist party. He had also made the isolation of the Soviet Union from the rest of Europe near-complete. In 1938 the Soviet Union gave the impression of a hobbled barbaric giant state. The heavy industry of this giant state, and the massive armament of the Red Army, were not sufficient to counteract this impression.

Sometime in January 1939 Stalin, like Roosevelt, began to change his course—and, perhaps, his mind. For one thing, Stalin began to slow down the purges and eventually put an end to them. For another, he was obsessed with the age-old Russian, and specifically Bolshevik, idea that the Western European bourgeois states, and specifically England, were willing to buy peace from Hitler at the expense of Russia. Stalin would not let this happen, come what may. Soon there were straws in the wind that this was not what Hitler had in his mind, either. The best clue we have for tracing this development is through the Carpathian Ukraine. In the past (for the last time in 1936), Hitler had spoken about the German desire to get hold of the rich granary of the Ukraine. Much of this wish to expand Germany toward western Russia had been set down in *Mein Kampf*. Immediately before and after Munich, the Ukrainian nationalists in Central Europe were stirring into activity. Yet they received practically no support from Hitler. In the end he even allowed Hungary to occupy, and incorporate, the Carpatho-Ukraine into Hungary on 16 March 1939, when Czecho-Slovakia had fallen finally apart.

This was not lost on Stalin. He realized that the immediate key to his relationship with Germany was no longer the Ukraine, it was Poland.

---

[9] Had Germany, not Russia, gone communist in 1918, the attraction of communism to most people would have been much greater.

[10] Untold because of many intellectuals and journalists in the Western world who would not tell certain truths—not because they were ignorant but because they were unwilling to face them.

After Munich Potemkin, a high Russian official in the Foreign Commissariat, had said to the French ambassador in Moscow: "My poor friend, what did you do? This may lead to the fourth partition of Poland"—an unusually forthright statement from a Soviet diplomatist. Whether Stalin was thinking in these terms as early as October 1938 we do not know. What we do know is evidence to the effect that he sought a better relationship with Hitler, long before the first significant contacts between the Soviet Union and the Third Reich began in April 1939. This relationship had to develop at the expense of Poland. Just as Austria was the key to the relationship of Germany and Italy, Poland was the key to that of Germany and the Soviet Union. By the spring of 1936 at the latest, Mussolini, as we have seen, would consider his rapprochement with Germany at the cost of Austria. By the spring of 1939 at the latest, Stalin would consider his rapprochement with Germany at the cost of Poland. In the case of Austria it was a great relief for Mussolini to know that Hitler, his professed German folkishness notwithstanding, would forget the German-speaking people of the South Tyrol,[11] if need be. In the case of Poland it was a great relief for Stalin to find that Hitler, *Mein Kampf* notwithstanding, would forget the Ukrainians and the Ukraine, if need be.

At this point the parallel ends. The Poles were not Austrians. They would fight for their independence: and the result was the Second World War. They also considered themselves as a European power of some standing; and so, unlike the Austrians, who had put all of their eggs into the basket of their dependence on Mussolini's Italy, the Poles would pursue a policy of independence, which looks exaggerated and reckless in retrospect. Yet they could do little else. In 1918 the defeat, the revolution, and the weakness of their enormous German and Russian neighbor states had made their independence possible. After 1920—at the latest by 1924—Germany seemed to become the more dangerous neighbor of the two. The Poles had an alliance with France. After 1930, at the latest by 1933, their leader Pilsudski, one of the greatest statesmen in the modern history of Europe, saw the French alliance for what it was: an alliance on paper, not much more. When Hitler came to power he needed peace and security on the long borders of Germany. The Poles saw this. The result was a nonaggression treaty between Poland and the Third Reich, signed in January 1934, and good relations between them for the next five years. Meanwhile the Poles were not fooled by high German statements of friendship. The Poles fooled themselves, however, on one crucial point. They could not believe that Hitler would ever revert to the old Prussian policy of seeking an alliance with Russia. They put great stock in Hitler's

---

[11] The German people of the South Tyrol, or Alto Adige, a troublesome minority, came under Italian sovereignty in 1919. See below, pp. 184–85.

"Austrian" (that is, non-Prussian) background, in addition to his extremely anticommunist ideology. They believed that Hitler's contempt for Soviet Russia was of the same kind as their own.

Because the Second World War broke out between Germany and Poland, the relations between their governments during the crucial weeks and months before 1 September 1939 have been studied minutely. Yet much more instructive is the devolution of their relations during the winter of 1938–39, between Munich and Prague, that is, *before* the anti-German revolution in British policy set in. On six or seven occasions between October 1938 and March 1939 Ribbentrop or Hitler had talks with the Polish Foreign Minister, Beck, or with the Polish ambassador, Lipski. A careful perusal of the records of these conversations will reveal a subtle but significant change in the German attitude. Having "solved" their Austrian and Czechoslovakian "problem," the Germans suggested that they wished to "solve" their remaining problems with Poland. This is not surprising in retrospect. Only we must look beneath the surface. The world thought then, and many historians still think now, that the "problems" consisted of Danzig and of the Polish corridor and of the existence of a German minority in western Poland. Some historians even discovered that in regard to these "problems" Hitler's demands on Poland were not excessive (incorporation of Danzig into the Third Reich and an extraterritorial highway and rail line athwart the corridor to connect East Prussia with the rest of Germany). They miss the essential point.[12] Hitler wanted the Polish state to come within his sphere of influence. Concessions on Danzig were to be the first step along a path that would make Poland become Germany's ally, junior partner, eventually a satellite—the first step toward which would be Poland's joining the Anti-Comintern Pact. In sum, he wanted to put an end—gradually, if necessary—to a Polish state that was independent enough to have an independent foreign policy. For this was what Hitler wanted of his neighbor states, almost always. It was not the Austrian government's treatment of local Nazis, it was Schuschnigg's last desperate attempt to assert Austria's independence that made Hitler act swiftly in March 1938. The same pattern explains his actions against Yugoslavia or Vichy France or Hungary later during the war. It was not incidents involving Germans and Poles in Danzig or Poznan, it was attempts such as the slight—very slight—move by Beck to improve his relations with Russia in order to continue the Polish policy of balance after Munich that turned Hitler on Poland. Forster, the Nazi *Gauleiter* of Danzig, reported to Swiss High Commissioner Carl J. Burckhardt in November 1938: Hitler "told me: 'I shall guarantee the

---

[12] Taylor, 196: "Only Danzig prevented co-operation between Germany and Poland."

existence of these people [the Poles] at least for the duration of my life, if they are reasonable, if they conform completely to our foreign policy (*wenn sie ganz unserer Politik anschliessen*), if they behave as the Czechs do now, but God help them if they fail to understand this!'"[13]

Even before Hitler's march into Prague the relations between Poland and Germany deteriorated. At the end of February, anti-German demonstrations occurred in Warsaw, a reaction to the brutal treatment of certain Polish students by some Germans in Danzig. Yet the Polish government was not behind these demonstrations; as a matter of fact, it was embarrassed by them. The German press, too, did not make much of these events; its concerted campaign against Poland did not start until 28 March, a delay that has a certain significance in retrospect. The Poles acquiesced in the German annexation of Bohemia and Moravia, while Hitler, as we have seen, did not object to the Hungarian annexation of the Carpatho-Ukraine that brought about a common border of Hungary and Poland. As late as 21 March, Ribbentrop told the Polish ambassador that Poland must work for "a reasonable relationship with Germany," for otherwise Poland would become "Bolshevist"; Poland should adhere to the Anti-Comintern Pact. On 25 March General Brauchitsch, the Commander-in-Chief of the German Army, put down in his diary that Hitler did not yet want to solve the Danzig problem "by force. He would not like to drive Poland into the arms of Britain by doing so." But military plans for an invasion of Poland must be made ready. (Some of these plans were spelled out in the diary.) At the same time "the Fuehrer does not want to go into the Ukraine. . . ."[14] The Fuehrer knew something that Brauchitsch did not know then: If Britain were to embrace Poland, Hitler would put out his hand to Stalin.

We have seen how the British government, during Hitler's year, chose to acquiesce in Germany's primacy in Central and Eastern Europe. "This German preponderance," Halifax wrote the British ambassador in Paris on 1 November 1938, was "inevitable."[15] That day Chamberlain rebuked the Leader of the Opposition, Major Attlee, who had asked in the House of Commons a question about the German Economy Minister

---

[13] Burckhardt, 232. Count Szembek, the Polish Undersecretary of State, recognized this in a conversation with the Polish ambassador to Moscow on 10 December: Poland's position was difficult, since what the Third Reich meant by good relations with Poland was that the latter would be Germany's ally against Russia. Szembek, 386–87.

[14] *IMT*, xxxviii, 275–76.

[15] *BD*, III (3), 252.

Funk's round trip through the Balkans. Chamberlain "regretted" that Attlee "found it necessary to insinuate that there were necessarily political motives behind" the Funk journey; Chamberlain took Attlee to task for "this kind of profound distrust," which was bound to lead to all kinds of problems, especially with Germany. Still Chamberlain's policy, while certainly uninspiring, was not necessarily shortsighted. His government knew that by 1939 Britain's military situation would improve—especially because of the increasing armament of the Royal Air Force.[16] The French, too, thought that time would work in their favor, which was not an unreasonable assumption. Their Foreign Minister, Bonnet, was bent on getting from the Germans a paper similar to the Anglo-German Friendship Declaration that Chamberlain waved to the crowd as he came home from Munich. After some negotiations, Bonnet got what he wanted. Ribbentrop arrived in Paris on 6 December to sign a Franco-German Declaration of Friendship. The French, who had trouble with the Italians at the time,[17] wanted to be sure that in the near future the Germans would not move against the West. For this they were willing to affirm their acquiescence in Hitler's domination of Central Europe—at any rate, for a while.

This, too, was not altogether a shortsighted policy. At the same time it was not as farsighted as the enemies of Chamberlain and Bonnet claimed, and still claim. Their claim, which soon became a favorite one of leftist and Soviet-inspired historians, was that stealthily Chamberlain and Bonnet wanted to encourage Hitler eastward, toward an eventual war with the Soviet Union, the result of which might be the destruction of communism and a Germany bled white in the bargain. The very opposite was true. No matter how they disliked and distrusted the Soviets, neither Chamberlain nor Bonnet wanted to see Russia destroyed by Hitler. The French kept up their frayed, but nonetheless existing, alliance with the Soviet Union. And here we must return to the wretched Ukrainian question—precisely because by December 1938 it began to intrude in Bonnet's and Chamberlain's minds. Both—assisted by faulty intelligence estimates

---

[16] Supporters as well as critics of Chamberlain's policy kept this in mind. See, for example, Vansittart's letter to Baldwin of Christmas 1936: "The year 1939 is the first in which we shall be able to breathe even with comparative relief, although much will yet remain to be taken in hand. We shall not even then have reached safety. . . . But on any showing Germany will be ready for big mischief at least a year—and probably more—before we are ready to look after ourselves. To the F.O. therefore falls the task of holding the situation at least till 1939. . . ." Cited in Colvin, *NB*, 118.

[17] A few days earlier (on 30 November) Mussolini's son-in-law Ciano made a sharp allusion in the Fascist Chamber to Italy's "natural aspirations." The Fascist parliamentarians jumped up and down, shouting, "Corsica, Tunis, Nice!"

—thought that Hitler's next step might be the encouragement of insurrectionists within the Soviet Ukraine. Both wanted to make sure that an insurrection in the Ukraine would not automatically engage France in a war on the side of the Soviet Union. Both considered such a prospect with anxiety, not with anticipation. When Chamberlain visited Mussolini in Rome in January 1939 he asked whether Hitler had ambitions regarding the Ukraine. Mussolini denied this, to Chamberlain's relief.[18]

Hitler was interested in Czechoslovakia and in Poland, not in the Ukraine. It took some time until the British and French governments realized what this meant. All through the winter of 1938–39 the rulers of the Third Reich wanted from the British and the French a formal recognition of the situation that, in many ways, existed *de facto* as a consequence of Munich: the *de jure* recognition of Germany's free hand in Central, and in perhaps much of Eastern, Europe. That far neither the British nor the French were willing to go. In November 1938 they had agreed among themselves that the formula in the Munich agreement, according to which all four signatories guaranteed the remnant Czechoslovak state, had no longer any practical importance. Perhaps because they were at last becoming aware of troubles brewing in Czecho-Slovakia rather than in the Ukraine, perhaps because they felt a whit stronger than a few months before, on 8 February 1939 the French and the British governments politely and modestly inquired of the German government's views on the status of the four-power guarantee to the Czechs. This mild Franco-British note brought about a commotion in Berlin. After two weeks of deliberations, Hitler himself—a rare occasion, this—took the trouble of drafting the German response. It was categorical. The question of Czecho-Slovakia's guarantee was for Germany to decide. This portion of Europe belonged to Germany's sphere of interest.[19]

The French and the British governments took this in silence. The results of Munich were coming home to roost. Within a fortnight Hitler took what remained of Czecho-Slovakia. By early March the Carpatho-

---

[18] Chamberlain's question to Mussolini soon transpired to Moscow, where Stalin may have misinterpreted it because of his age-old Russian suspicion of a Western conspiracy aimed at his empire. There are reasons to believe that Stalin thought that Chamberlain wanted to encourage a German move against the Soviet Union, and there are reasons to believe that this episode spurred him on in seeking a rapprochement with Hitler, one of the first steps to which was Stalin's speech on 10 March, about which see below, p. 41.

[19] The French ambassador to Berlin noted that this German text "indicates that the Western powers no longer possess any rights in Central Europe." *LJ*, 58, cited also in the thoughtful article by André Scherer, "Le problème des 'Mains Libres à l'Est,' " *RH2M* (Oct. 1958).

Ukrainians and the Slovaks (the latter were encouraged by certain German authorities) were on the verge of insurrection against the Czechs. Hitler's solution was a Slovak state that would be a reliable German satellite, and the German occupation of "Czechia"—that is, Bohemia and Moravia—in the form of a German proctectorate, within the German-Roman Empire, where they once had belonged. He was relieved when Hácha, the aged and trembling President of Czecho-Slovakia, signed the necessary documents in the early hours of the morning, after having been cajoled and threatened in the best brutal German fashion.[20] The next day, 15 March 1939, Hitler drove into Prague in a snowstorm.

This time there were no large popular demonstrations to greet him. This was not, however, why March 1939 was a turning point in his career. For there occurred now a revolution in British policy—or, rather, sentiment. Within two days—between the fifteenth and the seventeenth of March—Chamberlain changed his mind or, rather, his course. At first he responded to the news of the German invasion of remnant Czecho-Slovakia with the calm—so calm as to be infuriating—tones of moderation, indeed of appeasement. Then the English common sense of Moderation In Everything, Including Moderation, somehow asserted itself. In Birmingham on 17 March 1939 Chamberlain surprised his hearers and the world. He excused himself for his slow reaction in the House of Commons to the recent events in Prague. Then he said: "Is this the last attack upon a small state, or is it to be followed by others? Is this, in fact, a step in the direction of an attempt to dominate the world by force? . . . Any attempt to dominate the world by force was one which the Democracies must resist."

Much has been written, and speculated, about the causes of this moral revolution of Chamberlain's. In reality, its causes were hugely simple—except for one titillating detail, on another level of "cause." The main cause was the reaction of British public opinion to Hitler's march into Prague. "Public opinion" is an inchoate and messy thing for the historian to handle. Its image may be false or falsified. Those historians who attempt to reconstruct it from the press are often unduly naïve. Yet there are occasions when its surface manifestations are more or less authentic reflections of the deeper currents of popular sentiment. So it seems to have been among the English people after the Ides of March in 1939. They were genuinely shocked that Hitler had broken his word, given but six months before. They felt that appeasing the Germans may have been worth a try, but no longer. At last Chamberlain felt that this elemental surge of British

---

[20] According to one source Hitler was more than relieved, he was ecstatic to the extent that he asked his favorite secretaries to give him a kiss. Zoller, 84. Usually he would restrict his kissing to their hands.

impatience was authentic. He was, in any event, not the kind of politician who was capable of disregarding public opinion. He was, in all probability, also influenced by his Foreign Secretary, Halifax.[21] The latter may have been, in addition, taken in by a carefully planted rumor—the titillating detail referred to above. M. Virgil Tilea was the Romanian minister to London. He was an intelligent and ambitious man, and a thorough Anglophile.[22] He hoped that the British government would take a strong stand against Germany. The day after Hitler's entry into Prague, Tilea arrived at the Foreign Office with an alarming piece of news. The Germans had presented a kind of ultimatum to Bucharest, demanding a monopoly on Romanian exports. He was taken to Halifax the next evening. The latter was deeply, and sorrowfully, impressed. What Tilea told him may have, therefore, contributed to his impressing Chamberlain, in turn, before Birmingham. It may have contributed, too, to the sudden activity on which Halifax now embarked: trying to construct, as rapidly as possible, an Eastern European alliance system against Germany. Yet the information that Tilea had conveyed proved soon to have been incorrect.[23] Within two days it was disavowed by the Romanian Foreign Minister as well as by the British minister to Romania. That day Tilea himself had a *mauvais quart d'heure* with Alexander Cadogan.[24] No matter; the new course of British foreign policy was set.

---

[21] Cadogan on 16 March: "We ought perhaps to take a stand (whatever that may mean) but after P.M.'s speech [of 15th] can we? He speaking again at Birmingham tomorrow night. Think he's been binged up to be a bit firmer."

[22] Before the Prague crisis he was busy in trying to secure a British loan to Romania, and also the elevation of each other's legations to the level of embassy.

[23] Until the end of his life (he died in 1972), Tilea claimed that he had received a confidential telephone call via Paris on the morning of the sixteenth from a confidant of the pro-Allied Romanian Prime Minister Calinescu. (Private conversation.) There is some evidence that Tilea may have been spurred on perhaps less by this kind of telephonic information than by a lunch that he had with an unnamed high official of the Foreign Office that day, and that the latter wanted to use Tilea for the purpose of "binging up" Chamberlain through Halifax. If this is so—and some evidence points thereto—the discretion observed by Tilea during the more than thirty-three years that followed deserves respect. We must also add that there was a certain substance to the rumors of German pressure on Romania (see King Carol's message mentioned by Thorne, 116).

[24] The Cadogan-Tilea conversation on 18 March is instructive. FO 371/23060, C 3538/3356/18. Last sentence on the Cadogan minute: "On the whole I do not think that my interview with M. Tilea increased my confidence in him."

There is, moreover, all the reason in the world to believe that Halifax was setting out on a new course, Tilea or not. Of all the reasons, the principal one was Hitler himself. Not only did he fail to understand the British mind. He now would fall prey to the kind of monumental tactlessness to which the German race has often been prone.[25] If the news of a German ultimatum to Romania was false, a German ultimatum to Lithuania was all too true. Like Danzig, the port of Memel (Klaipeda in Lithuanian) had been taken from the Germans by the Versailles Treaty. Now Ribbentrop demanded that Lithuania return it within twenty-four hours. The Lithuanian Foreign Minister was summoned to Berlin much like Hácha, to sign under extreme duress. Only a week had passed since the Germans marched into Prague. Now a German warship was racing eastward for a triumphant reception in Memel, with no less a personage than Hitler on board. He was miserably seasick on the way. He came out of his cabins to look dyspeptically at the narrow stretch of the Polish coast moving by. Already the first guns of a German political offensive aimed at Poland had been fired. For once Halifax and Chamberlain reacted with un-British haste. During the last fortnight of March they started off on their construction of an alliance system in Eastern Europe. They offered a guarantee to Poland that its Foreign Minister, Beck, accepted on 31 March "between two flicks of the ash off his cigarette," as he himself later said. The revolution in British foreign policy was now complete. British acquiescence in Germany's domination of most of Europe was over. For the first time in her history Great Britain gave a guarantee to an Eastern European state.

Again, much has been written on the details of British and German and Polish diplomacy during these last days of March. Again, we cannot, and perhaps need not, describe their often unseemly misunderstandings and tergiversations, including certain false rumors that were leading thereto.[26] The British guarantee to Poland may indeed have been the

---

[25] True, the Germans tried to play down the portents of their imperialism. See, for example, Goebbels' instructions to the German press on 16 March: "Employment of the term Great German World Empire [Grossdeutsches Weltreich] undesirable. The latter to be reserved for later opportunities." Cited by Hillgruber, HS, 15, note 5.

[26] See especially the excellent articles by an Irish historian, T. Desmond Williams, "Negotiations Leading to the Anglo-Polish Agreement of 31 March 1939," IH (1956), 59–93 and 156–192. One of the elements that contributed to Chamberlain's unseemly haste at that time was the intelligence contributed by Ian Colvin, a British journalist, on 28–29 March to the effect that a German attack on Poland may have been imminent. In this respect Williams, above, 172, is instructive: ". . . the news department of the foreign office seems to have been waging subterranean warfare against the prime minister's policy over a

result of hasty and incomplete calculations of its consequences. Yet these calculations were but the results of a deeper emotion. The British people wanted to know that something was done.[27] Their calculations may have been insubstantial. Their emotions were real.

In most of Europe the spring in 1939 was rainy, and the summer was long and pleasant, as in 1914. Millions of people traveled to the beaches and to the lakefronts. There was a strange equilibrium in the minds of many of them. Time seemed to have been suspended between peace and war; and yet time moved on. This mood of the summer of 1939, unlike that of 1914, is difficult to reconstruct. It left few traces in the published material of the period, including novels. It was a strange compound of existentialist and fatalist attitudes; and yet it was preferable to that swift darkening of the European horizon that had marked the summer and fall of the previous year. There would be war, if war must come. This was the predominant attitude, nearly circular in its logic, but nonetheless honest for that.

This mood was reflected in the chancelleries of the great capitals, where there was little of the acute agitation that had broken forth in July 1914, or in September of the year before. A kind of anxious quiet reigned in the summer of 1939. Only during the last ten days of peace did the Angel of Desperation arrive to preside over each and every deliberation, trailing the twin gnomes of Confusion and Hurry in her train.

One of the reasons—perhaps the principal one—for this psychic equilibrium was the illusion that an equilibrium of power had been restored. Britain and France had now stood up to Hitler. The prestige of Britain shimmered out with a new kind of gleam. France, too, gave an impression of revitalization and of recovery, evident not only in statistics of her industrial production and in the slight rise of her birthrate but also in the very atmosphere of Paris. The King and Queen of England visited Paris, as they visited the United States for the first time, that summer; and the royal journeys were a great success. Paris glittered in July. On the second, there was the most elegant Longchamps in years; two days later a

---

number of years. It had the important advantage that it was in close connection with some of the newspapers, such as the *Daily Telegraph*, the *News Chronicle*, and the Manchester *Guardian*, whose correspondents shared skeptical opinions about appeasement. . . ."

[27] On 29 March the government announced the doubling of the size of the Territorial Army; on 26 April it introduced legislation for military conscription, for the first time in British history before a war.

great ball given in the gardens of the Polish Embassy, "féerique," with *tout Paris*, and the smart men and women of the Western world, with "Luka," the now so popular ambassador, dancing barefoot in the dewy grass after dawn. On 14 July the Republic arranged a military display that impressed the foreign military attachés, including the Germans: The sun was dazzling, the equipment was new, there was a contingent of the Grenadier Guards marching down the Champs-Élysées, and French and British planes flying overhead. The greatest crowd in the history of 14 July, reported the police prefect of Paris. "An unforgettable day" even in retrospect, "every kind of dream was permissible, illusions strong as ever, fears vanished."[28]

In the summer of 1939 the belief that Hitler was far from invincible had risen, mostly because of the British. This impression was misleading. Neither the resolution of the British government nor the strength of the British people were equal to what most people (including many of Britain's enemies) thought. We know now that the British government had not altogether abandoned its attempts to appease Hitler, and that throughout the summer of 1939 Chamberlain did not have his heart in fighting Germany, that he hesitated, literally till the very last minute.[29] The resolution of the British government did not harden until Churchill took it over, in May 1940. In the summer of 1939 people did not know that the British government was still irresolute. We may, in retrospect, using all kinds of evidence, reconstruct in great detail the flounderings and the maneuverings of the British government of that time. They did not count much in the long run. The vast majority of the British people were resolved to resist Hitler; in the end, this was what their government thought it had to do.

There was yet another factor in the resolution of the government. This was the memory of 1914. Then the British had had no binding alli-

---

[28] Destrem, 95; 14 July 1939 was filmed on television cameras of the BBC, even as only a handful of people in England had television receivers.

[29] Consider not only his hesitation in declaring war between 1 and 3 September (he was faced with something like a parliamentary revolt on the second) but also the fact that as late as thirteen minutes after 11 A.M. on 3 September (thirteen minutes after the British ultimatum to Germany had expired), Chamberlain, having received news that Goering was ready to fly to England, may have been thinking of postponing his broadcast, set for eleven-fifteen, the broadcast in which he was to announce the war to the people of Britain. "At eleven-fourteen the Prime Minister changed his mind again. With a sigh he rose to his feet. The broadcast was on again." Alvar Liddell of the BBC, in the London *Daily Express* of 3 September 1967, further elaborated in Mosley, 460.

ances; had the Germans known that the British would go to war on the side of France they might have—perhaps—acted otherwise than they did. If there was any way to deter Hitler from war, Chamberlain thought after March 1939, it was to convince him that a German attack on Poland would bring war with Britain and France. Hitler was not convinced; at any rate, he did not believe that Britain and France would fight him till the bitter end. Yet what else could Chamberlain have done? People who berate him for the hasty and ill-considered British guarantee to Poland fail to ask what would have happened if after March 1939 the British had not declared that they would stand by Poland. Others say that Britain should have concluded an alliance with Russia first, and with Poland only subsequently; and that the Chamberlain government's distrust of Russia, together with the Chamberlain government's preference for a Polish over a Russian alliance, was the sheerest kind of folly. This argument sounds convincing in retrospect; yet there is less substance in it than appears at first sight. It was Poland, not Russia, that was threatened by Hitler; and it was Poland, not Russia, that was willing to conclude an immediate alliance with Britain. True, the Chamberlain government was fumbling and ineffectual in its negotiations with Stalin; but was Stalin ready to conclude an alliance with Britain at all? This historian thinks not. Like Mussolini three years before, Stalin in 1939 preferred a deal with Hitler over a deal with the Western democracies. There was evidence of this even before the British-French negotiations with Moscow began.

The record of the talks between the Third Reich and the Soviet Union is perhaps the most interesting, and the most instructive, in the history of modern diplomacy. They reveal (far more than the inaccessible, and perhaps nonexistent, Soviet records might show) how the power and the interests of the Russian state govern everything, and the ideological categories of communism nearly nothing, in the acts of the rulers of the Soviet Union. It was not Hitler, it was Stalin, who indicated long before their eventual pact, that ideological elements need not stand in the way of their relations. There is some indirect evidence, as we have seen, that the necessity of collusion with Stalin at the expense of Poland may have entered Hitler's mind earlier than historians have been accustomed to see it.[30] On the other hand Hitler hesitated to reach a definite agreement

---

[30] There is some evidence that of the many German-Polish negotiations during the winter of 1938–39, Ribbentrop's visit to Warsaw on 25–26 January 1939 (the atmosphere was friendly but there was little of substance in the talks) may have been decisive in the latter's mind. His widow wrote later: "On our way home [Ribbentrop] remarked to his staff for the first time: 'Now only one way is left open to us. We must come to an agreement with Russia, unless we want to see ourselves completely encircled.'" *Ribbentrop*, 101, note 1.

with Stalin until August.[31] Before that, it was almost always Moscow, not Berlin, that made suggestions for the further development of their relations. Already on 10 March—before Hitler's march into Prague, and well before the British decision to seek an alliance with the Soviet Union—Stalin made a speech in which, on the one hand, he berated the French and British for not having pursued the principle of collective security (whatever that meant), while on the other hand he suggested the wish of the Soviet Union to maintain "peaceful, close, and friendly" relations with all European powers, including Germany. He asserted that Russia would not "pull the chestnuts out of the fire" for France and Britain[32]; he would not let them embroil Russia in a war with Germany. For a while Hitler, who was busy with other matters, either did not realize the meaning of Stalin's suggestion, or he willfully ignored it. Yet by April Hitler began to consider the Russian card,[33] at the latest by the seventeenth, when the Soviet ambassador to Berlin proceeded to the German Foreign Ministry with the first definite offer: "Ideological differences," said Merekalov, need not be "a stumbling block" to better and better Russian-German relations, "Soviet Russia had not exploited the present friction between Germany and the Western democracies . . . nor did she desire to do

---

[31] Goering to Hitler's minion Rosenberg as late as 20 August (after news of the imminent deal with Stalin was made known to Hitler's circle): "I must ask the Fuehrer between ourselves what he *really* wants" (*was er zuinnerst will*). *Rosenberg TB*, 91.

[32] These chestnuts soon became a frequent item on the menu of diplomatic rhetoric. It is interesting to note that this phrase of "pulling the chestnuts out of the fire" was often used by Russian critics of Britain and France during World War I. It is even more interesting to note that Hitler used the same phrase three weeks later in his speech at Wilhelmshaven on 1 April 1939: "Anyone who declares himself to be ready to pull the chestnuts out of the fire for the Great Powers must be aware that he might burn his fingers in the process." Did someone bring this phrase to Stalin's attention? We shall probably never know. On 17 May Ribbentrop told Orsenigo, the papal nuncio in Berlin: "Russia is not disposed to pull the chestnuts out of the fire for Britain." *VD*, I, 152.

[33] Maser, *MK*, 64, noted that the deluxe edition of *Mein Kampf*, published in April 1939, on Hitler's fiftieth birthday, was an exact reproduction of earlier editions, and yet "as consequence of the first contacts between Berlin and Moscow the reproduction (in the pictorial appendix) of a poster, of 4 August 1921, entitled 'Soviet Russia in Its Death Throes,' was missing." We must consider, however, that such a printing must have been made ready before 20 April 1939; also, none of the extreme anti-Soviet passages of the text were deleted from it.

so."[34] Two weeks later Stalin and his Foreign Commissar, Litvinov, stood on the high platform on Red Square, reviewing the Red Army parade on the first of May; but when the latter, proponent of the alliance with the Western powers, tried to catch Stalin's eye, the Chief ostentatiously turned away. Within twenty-four hours this prominent Jew was dismissed, and Molotov took his place as Foreign Commissar.

The significance of this was not lost on Hitler.[35] Yet he was still hesitant—or, in his way, calculating. For the next four months the fate of Europe depended on a triangular relationship whose main points were Berlin, London, and Moscow. Again, we cannot, and perhaps need not, trace their tortuous negotiations in detail. In essence the record amounts to a contest in international blackmail, in which Moscow was the most, and London the least successful, with Hitler in the middle. The British were trying to get Russia within their alliance system, letting the world publicly know this, hoping by the way that this would make Hitler more amenable. Chamberlain was also not above trying to suggest confidentially to Hitler that if the latter were only more reasonable over Poland, a propitious relationship between Germany and Great Britain might be in the offing. The Western-Russian negotiations were protracted and known to the world; the British-German contacts were sporadic and secret.[36] Neither amounted to much in the end. In turn, Hitler was not above letting hints drop to the British and the French about Germany's new contacts with the Soviet Union.[37] The British especially did not take these hints seriously, until it was too late. Secretive and cunning by nature, Stalin dropped no hints to the British about the Germans and few hints to the Germans about the British. (The Russian hints to the Germans were

---

[34] *NSR*, 2.

[35] Hitler in 1920: "An alliance between Russia and Germany can come only after the Jews are dismissed" (*wenn das Judentum abgesetzt ist*). Jaeckel, 35.

[36] An able summary of these, including an evaluation of the so-called Hudson-Wohltat conversations in July 1939, in Thorne, 162–63.

[37] These hints were numerous. Their principal channel was the French air attaché in Berlin, Colonel Stehlin, on the express instructions of Goering; other hints were made to Americans, and in the Vatican. (See, for example, *Moffat*, 231; Stehlin, passim; *VD*, I, 151–52; and, perhaps especially, Hitler's statement to C. J. Burckhardt as late as 11 August: "Everything that I undertake is directed against Russia; if the West is too stupid and too blind to understand this, I shall be forced to seek an understanding with the Russians, defeat the West, and after its defeat turn with all of my forces against the Soviet Union. I need the Ukraine, so that they cannot starve us out, as during the last war." Burckhardt, 348. Hillgruber, *HS*, 28–29, calls this "farsighted" (*visionaer*). In reality it was a Hitler move (he knew that Burckhardt was trusted in London) in order to frighten the Western powers into concessions.

the very opposite of the German hints to the British: the Russians kept suggesting to the Germans that their negotiations with the British and the French were *not* going too well.) Stalin and Molotov tried their worst in Moscow to make the British and French negotiators uncomfortable. True, these negotiators as well as their alliance offers were not very satisfactory from the Russian viewpoint. Still, whether the British and French failure to push more assiduously for a Russian alliance would have made much difference is open to question. There is not the slightest evidence that Stalin was willing to enter into any alliance with Britain *if* he could make a deal with Germany instead.

In the summer of 1939 Stalin found himself not menaced but courted by the two rival constellations of the European powers.[38] He would make the best of the bargain. This bargain involved territory, not arms; the partition of Eastern (or at least of Northeastern) Europe, in essence. The time had now come to recover some of the territories that the Russian Empire had lost after World War I. In March 1939 the Russians slyly suggested to the Poles a possible partition of the Baltic states between them[39]; in April the Russians turned to Finland with the request that they cede three islands to the Soviet Union.[40] By June the London and Paris governments knew that what the Russians wanted was a free hand at the expense of their Baltic neighbors. The British and the French were not quite willing to grant this, especially not in their then present position as guarantors of the smaller states of Europe. They hadn't even gotten to the problem of Poland and the Russian alliance when the Russians proposed that the military talks should proceed before the political differences are resolved. Reluctantly, the British and the French agreed. They sent a delegation on a slow boat to Russia. It did not make much difference.[41] By

---

[38] They included Italy. In April 1939 Mussolini told Goering: "But why don't you come to an alliance with Russia?"

[39] Grzybowski to Beck on 18 March 1939; Budurowycz, 146, note 2.

[40] The Finnish government informed the United States of this, and asked whether Washington could intervene in Moscow in Finland's favor. Washington refused; still, this was the first instance in a long series of developments when the intervention of the United States in behalf of a small Eastern European state was requested.

[41] It did at least bequeath us one of the few fine passages of evocative reminiscence of that strange summer of 1939, in the recollections of French General Beaufre, a member of the delegation: "During this time the *City of Exeter* was approaching Russia. On the evening of 9 August, deep in the Gulf of Finland, the nordic sky, pale as mother of pearl and extraordinarily clear, was reflected in the sea, which was as calm as a lake. Kronstadt came into sight reminding us of the first hours of Franco-Russian alliance, where the Soviet fleet made its existence known by several fast small craft, which maneuvered round the ship.

that time in August the Germans were ready to offer the Russians the partition of Poland.

Because of his military timetable it was now Hitler who was in a hurry; he wanted the agreement with the Soviet Union as soon as possible. In the end, while the hapless British and French military missions were stranded in Moscow, Hitler had to address a personal message directly to Stalin, on 20 August 1939. This was a great event, "a milestone in world history; it marked the moment when Soviet Russia returned to Europe as a Great Power."[42] Within three days this great event became known to the world. The Nazi Foreign Minister, Ribbentrop, had flown to Moscow; Stalin and Hitler had reached a nonaggression pact. It was the biggest bombshell in the history of diplomacy in hundreds of years.

The nonaggression pact meant that Western hopes for a Russian alliance were dead. There was, too, a secret protocol, which meant the partition of Eastern Europe. Poland was to be divided along the rivers Narew, Vistula, and San; Lithuania was to belong into the German, the rest of the Baltic states, including Finland, into the Russian sphere of influence, to which Bessarabia, a part of Romania, was also allotted. Ribbentrop found the dry Eurasian climate of Moscow invigorating. Stalin toasted Hitler: "I know how the German people love their Fuehrer." Hundreds of German Communists were hauling stones in the muck and mire of German concentration camps.

---

"The calm returned as we entered a long canal open in the middle of the Gulf, a dredged passage similar to *la Goulette*, which led to the city of Leningrad. Although it was eleven o'clock at night, the sky was still bright and opaline. Leaning over the rail, all the personnel of the mission, in mess kit, as behoved us on an English vessel, enjoyed this magnificent evening and looked across at the unknown shore where the real game was to be played out. Shortly before midnight the *City of Exeter* entered the port, an immense forest of cranes and quays piled with timber, and tied up beside a wooden shed, the sordid maritime station typical of the treatment of visitors of this great country, so isolated from the rest of the world.

"On the quay a few Soviet soldiers in green caps and two or three badly dressed bystanders could see on the bridge of the *City of Exeter* twenty-six officers in mess jackets and the Indian crew busy warping the ship in. It would be difficult to find a neater picture to sum up the difference between the two worlds which were now to confront one another." Beaufre, 61–62.

[42] Taylor, 251. This crisp statement is compromised two pages later (Taylor, 253) by the following nonsense: The Russian-German Pact "was in the last resort anti-German: It limited the German advance eastward in case of war. . . . [The Russians assumed . . .] that Poland would be compelled to yield, and with the Polish obstacle out of the way, defensive alliance with the West might then be achieved on more equal terms." More equal is good.

Hitler was willing to pay a high price for this accord with Stalin.[43] Hitler thought that it would deter the British; he did not think (or care) whether it would deter the Poles. On the night of 23 August, Speer remembered,

> we stood with Hitler on the terrace of the Berghof, and looked with wonderment at a rare display of nature. Unusually strong northern lights washed the legend-ridden Untersberg with a red glare for a long hour while the skies flickered with the strangest colors of the rainbow. The last act of Götterdämmerung could not have been staged with more effect. Our faces and hands glistened with an unnatural red glow. This scene produced an oddly pensive mood. Hitler abruptly said to one of his military aides: "This looks like lots of blood. This time things won't go without force."[44]

---

[43] To Speer: "I put everything on this card" (Speer, 176). More important, most historians have overlooked the important memorandum that Ribbentrop wrote for Hitler on 24 June 1940 when the latter raised questions about Stalin's claim on Bessarabia (GD, D, X, 10–11). The memorandum refers to a secret directive that Hitler had given Ribbentrop before the latter's trip to Moscow in August 1939, a directive that disappeared from the German archives. The memorandum must be cited in detail. Ribbentrop began by citing the text of the secret protocol, about Bessarabia. Then he continued: "As far as I can remember, the following took place at that time: At the time of the delimitation of the mutual spheres of interest in Eastern Europe, the Soviets stressed their interest in Bessarabia when the Southeast of Europe was mentioned. On this occasion, I stated orally our disinterestedness in the Bessarabian question. However, in order not to put down explicitly in *written form* the recognition of the Russian claim to Bessarabia because of the possibility of indiscretions . . . I chose a formulation of a *general nature* for the Protocol. This was done in such a way that when the Southeastern European problems were discussed I declared very generally that Germany was *politically* disinterested in these areas, i.e., in the Southeast of Europe. The economic interest of Germany in these European territories was duly stressed by me. [Up to now the italics are Ribbentrop's; from now the italics are this author's.] *This was in accordance with the general instructions given by the Fuehrer for the Southeastern Europe and also, as I recall it, with a special directive* ["Not found," GD, D, X, 11, n. 2] *of the Fuehrer which I received before my departure for Moscow, in which the Fuehrer authorized me to declare German disinterestedness in the territories of Southeastern Europe, even, if necessary, as far as Constantinople and the Straits. However, the latter were not discussed."*

[44] Speer, 177; see also 539, note 1 (about meteorological report of northern lights on the night of 23 August), note 2 ( about authentic source of Hitler's remark).

Hitler's directive for "Fall Weiss," the invasion of Poland, was given as early as 3 April. Unlike the conference recorded by Colonel Hossbach, this directive consisted not of a potential but of an actual plan for war. Poland would be attacked on 1 September. On 23 May Hitler repeated this to his commanders. On 22 August (his day of triumph in Moscow), he spoke to them again, referring to the attack on Poland in brutal tones; the next day he advanced the date of the attack to 4:30 A.M. on 26 August, a Saturday. There is some reason to believe that the ferocious nature of his speech was meant not only to impress the generals but also that its contents were meant to leak to the British in order to impress them, which is exactly what happened.[45]

Possibly he postponed the day of the attack by six days for the same reason. Yet his hopes were not quite fulfilled. True, Chamberlain's letter to him, written on the morrow of the Stalin pact, was suffused with the old plainsong music of appeasement; Henderson, the British ambassador in Berlin, openly expressed his regret to anyone who would listen[46] that the Poles were intractable; he was sentimental to the point of foolishness. Still the British government, shaky as it was, did not let itself be affected by the German-Russian pact. The mood of the British people would not allow this; also, for once, Chamberlain's low esteem of Russia stood him in good stead. Around 4 P.M. on 25 August, news reached the Chancellery in Berlin that the British had ratified their alliance with Poland. A little after six, the Italian ambassador brought a letter from Mussolini: He was not ready to enter the war. The Chancellery was buzzing. Hitler ordered the postponement of the attack by a few days. To Goering he said that during this time he'd see "whether we can eliminate British intervention"; to Keitel: "I need time for negotiations."

We have to say a few words about Italy at this moment. For the last time in the twentieth century she was a decisive factor in the fate of Europe—for a few days, not more. Mussolini wanted this; he did not want to be overshadowed by Hitler. Hitler's occupation of Prague had shaken Italian opinion, including Mussolini and Ciano. They decided to compensate their people by annexing Albania, a small country that for years had been *their* virtual protectorate. During Easter week they invaded Albania and annexed it to the Italian Empire. The British and the

---

[45] As with the Hossbach memorandum, there is some controversy about the exact text of Hitler's 22 August speech to the generals; see *VFZ* (April 1968, July 1971).

[46] He hoped, for instance, to work on the Poles through third parties; thus, for example, he searched out the Hungarian minister to Germany, a pro-German, to tell him that he, Henderson, "does not understand" Poland's "provocations." Ádám, *MMV*, 240–41.

French swallowed this without much protest. They did, in consequence, offer a guarantee to Greece, similar to the one given to Poland.[47] (They also offered a guarantee to Romania.) Despite certain inclinations of Ciano, Mussolini would not be budged from Hitler's side. On 23 May 1939, the Rome-Berlin Axis became a "Steel Pact." Grandiloquent as this was, Mussolini wanted to make it clear to Ciano as well as to Hitler that Italy (and, in his opinion, Germany too) needed "a period of peace of not less than three years. It is only from 1943 that a warlike effort can have the greatest chance of success."[48] Here was a great difference in the timing of the two dictators. Hitler felt that he had to go to war in 1939; indeed, as we saw earlier, he believed that after 1943 the European balance of power may develop against Germany. Mussolini, with a largely unprepared Italy behind him, believed not only that Italy would be better prepared by 1943 but also that the dynamic influences of Fascism would continue to undermine the prestige and the power of the Western democracies across Europe. It must be said for Mussolini that he saw the world situation clearly in the summer of 1939. Germany would not succeed with the Poles as she succeeded with the Czechs, "Poland will be crushed and the result will be a European war," he said to a number of people in May.[49] Contrary to the standard views, held especially by English historians, Mussolini was not altogether a poltroon or a puppet or a sawdust Caesar; nor is it true that he simply took fright and abandoned Hitler a few days before the outbreak of the war. In the above-mentioned memorandum to Ciano, then passed on to Hitler, Mussolini said: "Fascist Italy does not desire a premature war of European character, although convinced that it is inevitable. It may be also possible that within three years Japan will have brought the war in China to an end." Somewhat like the United States, Japan was a marginal factor in the coming of the war in

---

[47] Their guarantee to Greece was preceded by something like the Tilea rumor. The Greek military attaché in Rome advised the Greek Prime Minister that the Italians were about to invade and occupy the isle of Corfu. Metaxas informed London that (unlike the Romanians) he intended to fight back in such an event. He asked for the prospect of British help. The British guarantee to Greece followed immediately.

[48] Directive to Ciano, 4 May 1939. Mussolini repeated this to Ciano near the end on 8 February 1943: "If they had given us three years' time we might have been able to wage war under different conditions or perhaps it would not have been at all necessary to wage it." Ciano, 580. He was right.

[49] To P. Tacchi-Venturi, a Jesuit middleman between himself, and the Vatican, on 1 May 1939, *VD*, I, 13–14; to the Hungarian military attaché Szabó, Ádám, *MMV*, 238–39.

1939, though by no means negligible.[50] Like Italy, she was closely aligned with Germany, though not ready to enter the war against Britain in 1939. All of this did not bother Hitler very much.[51] He was not altogether surprised by Mussolini's choosing to stay out for a while. He would go at the Poles alone, in any event. He did not want war with England, though he did not fear it. He knew the profound distaste (if that is the word) of Chamberlain for a war with Germany. During this last week of peace Hitler tried to dissolve the British-Polish alliance. There was now no lack of communications between Berlin and London. All kinds of messages and envoys, official and unofficial, were passing back and forth. Chamberlain and his ambassador in Berlin were now more concerned with putting pressure on the Poles "to be reasonable" than on Hitler. Hitler now started his last double maneuver. He demanded that Poland send someone to Berlin to negotiate with full powers, at once (this sounded ominously like Munich or Prague); and he ordered Ribbentrop to present to Henderson a list of German demands on Poland, consisting of sixteen points, that looked surprisingly reasonable (unlike his demands before Munich or Prague). What he meant to achieve by this appears from the memorandum that his commander-in-chief received the day before Ribbentrop read the plan to Henderson. "Attack starts, September 1. Fuehrer will let us know at once if we are not to strike. [There followed a summary of the German demands.] England will perhaps accept Poland, probably not. *Wedge between them!*"[52] On the last day of peace, Warsaw consented to let Berlin know that it would "favorably consider" the British suggestion for direct negotiations. In a confidential second portion of

---

[50] During the mid-thirties among all the world powers Japan spent the largest portion of her national income on armaments (46 per cent). Hitler's pact with Stalin shocked the governing circles in Tokyo, and there was a change in the government. Yet the commonly held assumption, according to which the Japanese were alienated by this to an extent that they turned away, at least temporarily, from their pro-German course in foreign policy, is exaggerated. The Japanese military, as well as their ambassadors in Berlin and in Rome, continued to sympathize with Hitler (see, for example, Shiratori [Rome] to Plessen, 2 September 1939, *GD*, D, VIII, 11). In turn, Stalin's expansion in Europe was made possible by the effects of the pact which, among other things, nullified the prospects of a German-Japanese collaboration against him. Stalin's European moves were also made easier by the defeat that the Red Army inflicted on the Japanese during their intermittent border warfare along the frontiers of Outer Mongolia in late August 1939.

[51] He did justify his pact with Stalin to Mussolini with the argument, among others, that the Japanese were unwilling to enter into a full military alliance against Britain.

[52] *GD*, D, VII, Appendix 1.

this dispatch, Beck instructed his ambassador, Lipski, to be careful and not engage in "concrete negotiations." The Germans, having broken the Polish diplomatic code, were aware of this. Hitler ordered the attack to begin the next morning. Before that, the SS mounted a fake attack on a German radio station near the frontier, executed by criminals who had been taken from concentration camps for this purpose. They dressed up in Polish uniforms. Having fulfilled their task, they were executed in turn.

At a quarter before five on the morning of 1 September, Friday, German troops, trucks, and tanks broke through the borders of the Republic of Poland on three sides. The old battle cruiser *Schleswig-Holstein* roared shells at the Polish garrisons outside Danzig. Swarms of German airplanes dropped clusters of bombs on Polish airfields and on the edges of many cities. There was no declaration of war. At ten in the morning, Hitler drove through a silent Berlin to the Reichstag. He announced: "Since four forty-five this morning we are firing back." Wearing a field-gray uniform, he vowed that he would not relinquish it till the end of the war. He exalted the example of Frederick the Great, to which he would return, over and over again, during the dark end of the war, in 1945. "One word I have never known: Capitulation. If, however, there should be anyone thinking that we are at the brink of hard times, I urge him to consider the fact that at one time a Prussian King, ruling a ridiculously small state, confronted one of the greatest coalitions, yet ultimately defeated it in three campaigns, simply because he was possessed of that certain undaunted spirit and faithful heart that is required of us in these times."[53]

So the war began in the East of Europe; and yet in the West nothing happened. The French government, which knew more than the British what it meant to face the Germans in Europe without another strong continental ally, wavered in private (though not in public). Its Foreign Minister was quite willing to accept another offer by Mussolini for mediation—in short, another Munich—if only Hitler would stop his armies at certain points, it hardly mattered where. The Polish ambassador was desperate: "Must I conclude that France's word amounts to nothing?" While the French dragged their feet, Chamberlain dragged his mind. By the end of 2 September he was faced by a potential revolt in the House of Commons, perhaps even including some members of his government. Messages and certain persons were still flitting back and forth between Berlin and

---

[53] He also referred to Molotov, who had made an ugly speech the previous day. "I approve of every word in the speech made by Herr Molotov, the Russian Commissar of Foreign Affairs." At the end of the war, when Hitler was dead, Molotov was still the Russian Commissar for Foreign Affairs.

London. Goering himself was ready to fly to London for the $n$th time (his first such offer had been made on 21 August). Since Hitler would not halt the German Army, Chamberlain found no way out. A British ultimatum was presented in Berlin; it expired at 11 A.M., British Summer Time, 3 September. An immensely weary Chamberlain spoke to the British Empire fifteen minutes later. The French, after much British prodding, advanced the hour of the ultimatum to 5 P.M.[54] It was a calm and sunny Sunday.

For the last time we must glance at the Reich Chancellery, that quite magnificent (and unjustly maligned) monument of marble splendor built by Speer and made ready for Hitler by the first of the year in 1939, where Hitler now waited, surrounded by his confidants. It was a rare occasion. He had risen at seven, not at the customary ten o'clock, that morning. Ribbentrop and Goering were there. The former wanted war with England, the latter did not want it. The former refused to accept the ultimatum from the British ambassador, letting his chief interpreter take it from Henderson. Dr. Schmidt hurried to the Chancellery. Hitler and Ribbentrop read the document together. Schmidt recalled that Hitler looked fiercely at Ribbentrop, saying: "What now?" In the next hall stood Goering, surrounded by his minions. "If we lose this war, God have mercy on us," he said. On that day of 3 September 1939, a milestone in the history of Western civilization, Hitler stood between Ribbentrop and Goering; and, for a moment, he was closer to the latter than to the former.[55] Hitler, too, did not want war with England; and, perhaps for a moment, he rued that he had allowed Ribbentrop too much leeway. However, this mood

---

[54] Daladier tried to avoid a debate on the war declaration, since he feared a division in which perhaps more than 100 deputies would vote against the government. Herriot arranged then for a vote on a proposal of "war credits of 75 million francs in order to fulfill the obligations resulting from our alliances." This was voted by a show of hands.

[55] It is not only that on 1 September Hitler designated Goering as his second in command of the Third Reich, to be ready to step in Hitler's place if Hitler were to die. At that time Goering reflected something of the "Western" orientation that was close to Hitler's heart: the seeking of a German understanding with the "Nordic" powers of the world, at the expense of Russia, if need be. Unlike Ribbentrop, Goering was unhappy not only with the English war but also with the Stalin pact. He was sincere in sending his friend Dahlerus, a Swedish businessman, back and forth between Berlin and London, in order to obtain peace. Goering was one of the last representatives of a world view that had first appeared in the 1890s, with Neville Chamberlain's father Joseph having been one of its early proponents, proposing an alliance among the Nordic peoples of the world, principally Britain, Germany, and the United States, and including Scandinavia, for the sake of Western civilization, as he saw it.

passed quickly. Hitler not only sensed, he knew that the British and French declarations of war were formalities; he knew that they would not attack Germany from the west.[56]

A strange kind of silence had spread over the great thoroughfares of the capital cities of Europe that Sunday. This atmosphere was very different from 1914.

Already the predictions about the first hours of the Second World War were proving false. During the 1930s a spate of books had appeared describing in frightful detail the bombs from giant air armadas that would pour destruction on the great cities in the first hours of a war.[57] Now, instead of cracking fire and deafening noise, there was an eerie kind of calm. The children's noises had vanished from the streets of London and Paris. Nearly two million children had been evacuated from London (eventually this kind of evacuation caused many problems). A smaller number had been moved out of Paris. The instinctive intelligence of the Parisians, which would be sadly wanting later, now served them well. All through the summer of 1939 the people behaved better than some of the shaky figures in their government. *Il faut en finir* (there has to be an end to this) was the French popular slogan during the spring and summer of 1939, after Hitler invaded and threatened one cowered nation after another. For once the slogan corresponded with the sentiments of the people. Now, on this September Sunday, they sensed that this would be a curious war. By early afternoon the boulevards and the Champs-Élysées were filled. In the crowded cafes people sat, rather quietly. They were looking at their watches. Five more minutes; one more minute; and we are at war.

The news of the British declaration of war and of the British and French ultimatums reached Warsaw in the early afternoon, because of the

---

[56] On 15 May Henderson had said to the German Secretary of State, Weizsaecker that if war came it "would be conducted defensively by the Western Powers." *GD*, D, VI, 385. Hitler may have known this when on 29 August he told Weizsaecker: "In two months Poland will be finished; then we shall have a great peace conference with the Western Powers." Weizsaecker, 208. At this point it may be instructive to note that in August 1914, too, the then German Chancellor Bethmann-Hollweg, deducing all kinds of hopes from the slowness of British naval and military moves (mistaking British ineptitude for British subtlety), believed that the British would not fight a "hard war." See Zechlin, E., "Cabinet vs. Economic Warfare in Germany: Policy and Strategy During the Early Months of the First World War," *OFW*, 145–256.

[57] A British government study the year before expected one million casualties in the first days of the war.

time difference. Popular rejoicing took place. Thousands of people left their homes, they hurried into the squares, before the stately fronts of the French and the British embassies. Women brought flowers, many had tears in their eyes. Crowds sang the "Marseillaise," in correct and slightly Slav-accented French; "God Save the King" in Polish and broken English. All of this went on through the warm afternoon, even as people knew how the Germans had bombed their city the previous night, that they were to bomb it soon again, and that their armies were being scorched and slashed by the Germans.

The people of Warsaw rejoiced out of relief. For more than two days they, and the world, were not quite certain whether the great Western Allies would keep their word and declare war on Germany. Now Britain and France had done so. It was no longer an isolated Eastern European war between Germany and Poland. It was to be the Second World War.

Twenty-five years before, the peoples of Europe had swept into the First World War with virile enthusiasm. Now they went to war in a serious, disciplined way. The English went to war with silent determination. The Germans, who were supposed to have been whipped into a fanatic frenzy by Hitler's propaganda, took up arms with a fatalism that may have been toneless rather than serene: but it was no less serious for that, and it stood in grave contrast with their oceanic outburst of enthusiasm and relief—yes, relief—when their Emperor had called them to war in 1914.

In 1939 those Europeans who sought relief in the coming of the war were a small minority, the exception. In 1914 it was the majority that had found relief in it, almost everywhere. Entire libraries have been written on the admittedly complex origins of the War of 1914. They all deal with the decisions and the fumblings of the governing classes: of monarchs and prime ministers and chiefs of staffs and admirals and, on a few occasions, with the lords of the press, who at times were the most powerful of all. Few of them deal with the sentiments of the majorities. In 1914 many peoples of Europe (most of them the first generations of newspaper readers) wanted war—or, perhaps, relief from and through war—as much, and perhaps even more, than had many of their masters. Few historians have had the ambition to deal with this mass phenomenon in depth. There survives a small passage, superficial but by no means shallow, from the odd little book by an English writer, written after the First World War that he had opposed with every fiber of his character. "We must never forget," D. H. Lawrence wrote in *Movements in European History,* "that mankind lives by a twofold motive: the motive of peace and increase, and the motive of contest and martial triumph. As soon as the appetite for martial adventure and triumph in conflict is satisfied, the appetite for peace and increase manifests itself, and vice versa. It seems a law of life."[58]

Between the two World Wars in Europe there had been little peace and little increase. There was some; but very little. The vast majority of peoples remembered the First World War and the suffering that followed it, for a long time. Unlike in 1914, there stood no forty, fifty, sixty years of dull daily life behind them, from which they wanted, no matter how unconsciously, to escape forward into the blaze and fire of war. Unlike in 1914, they knew that wars were no longer brief and dangerous and glorious adventures. The memory of the First World War hung over their minds. There was hardly a general officer in 1939 who had not been in and out of the trenches twenty-odd years before. Unlike in 1914, there were many people—in Western and Central Europe the majority—who were no longer first-generation newspaper readers; they had a sometimes dumb, sometimes latent sense of disbelief in much of what they would read in their newspapers. Hence their somber discipline, and the great inward quiet with which they behaved in September 1939.

Unlike in 1914, they could not see far ahead. The future was obscure. In 1914 most people expected a grand and short European war. In 1939 no one expected a short war, perhaps with the solitary exception of Adolf Hitler. Without demur, and without the enthusiasm surging out of relief, people did what they had to do; but about the consequences of their actions they were almost wholly in the dark.

In 1914 the peoples of Europe knew that the war was to be a European war, another European war, the name of which only changed later to "World War" in the popular terminology (this usage started first among Germans and Americans). In 1939 everyone knew, and so spoke, that this was the start of the Second World War. No one knew that it was also to be the Last European War.

---

[58] Lawrence, 306.

# 4 . Reluctant war[1]

DURING THAT FATEFUL DAY of 3 September 1939 the German armies were marching and driving far into Poland.[2] There a new pattern of war appeared. Instead of large masses of soldiers milling and swarming across fields and forests, inching forward to battle the enemy along the horizon, compact swarms of them were moving fast into the heart of the enemy country along highways, roads, and lanes, behind steel carriages that were literally blazing the trail. For centuries the most formidable engines of war, the heavy guns, had been placed behind the masses of men in the trenches and in the fields. Now the engines of war moved ahead of the rest—on the ground as well as in the air. There may have been a symbolic significance to this. The nation that produced the modern storm trooper at home was the first to put the mechanized storm troops, of the armored divisions, in the field. Not for nothing had Hitler read the famous Clausewitz. War was the continuation of politics—a new and brutal kind of war, of a new and brutal kind of politics.

Ahead of the fast-moving front the cities of Poland crumbled during the day, while their edges were blazing in the night. The German bombing planes were a new kind of flying artillery. They had started at dawn on the first day of war to bomb the airfields where the small Polish Air Force ranged its planes. After two days the German fliers destroyed most of them. Now they turned on the factories and the barracks and the columns of their enemy. They were unchallenged in their unbroken straight

---

[1] 3 September 1939–10 May 1940.
[2] Hitler wanted them to move fast, for more than one reason. He wanted to make sure that if the Western Powers were to succumb to Mussolini's proposals of "mediation," the German armies would be in possession of large chunks of Polish territory.

paths in the sky; they could see their motorized comrades drive ahead, often unchallenged, on the ground.

The leaders of the Polish Republic were unready for this new kind of war. Their preparations were incomplete and faulty. The Polish Army was brave. It even slowed down the rate of their enemy's advance after about nine or ten days. By that time it was too late. They received no help from abroad. Soon they were to be stabbed in the back. Meanwhile fifty-six to sixty German divisions were cutting into the heart of Poland from three sides.[3] They included the twelve armored divisions of the Third Reich. The legendary stories of Polish horse cavalry charges with lances against the German tanks are false. Still on the river Bzura a Polish army counterattacked to the south and held the Germans for a while. The German Tenth Army reached the outer edges of Warsaw after eight days of advancing; then they found the Polish opposition to be stiff. They halted, encircled Warsaw, and wore down her defenders by massive gunnery and bombing, in the end, by an overwhelming superiority of force. Led by their inspiring mayor, the soldiers and the people of Warsaw held out for another three weeks: "magnificent and forlorn," in Churchill's words,[4] the first act in their heroic saga during the Second World War, it was not to be the last. Outside Danzig the small Polish garrison on the Westerplatte, surrounded from all sides, including the sea, resisted fiercely. Years had to pass until such bravery was shown in the face of Germans by European soldiers during this war.

Along the Rhine there was silence. The French armies did not move. The British bombers did not come through.[5] Had they moved in time, Hitler would have been shaken. Along the western frontiers of the Third Reich, between and behind the sporadic and incomplete "Siegfried Line," lay less than 43 German divisions, mostly reserve units, only eight first-line ones among them. Altogether 98 German divisions and 128 Polish and French and British divisions were in existence in September 1939. These figures were largely devoid of meaning.[6] The German General Staff may

---

[3] The southern attack came from their satellite state, Slovakia. The leaders (and many of the people) of this Slav and Catholic nation joined the Third Reich's war on Poland with enthusiasm.

[4] Churchill, GS, 447. It must be recorded that looting broke out in Warsaw in the last two days before its surrender.

[5] They made one, unsuccessful, raid on the German port of Wilhelmshaven on 4 September.

[6] There was no precise military convention co-ordinating the Polish and the Allied armies. True, in May the French commander-in-chief, General Gamelin, told Polish General Kasprzycki that the French would attack in the west sixteen days after the Poles were attacked in the east. But these were little more than words: There was no exact agreement to that effect. The question

have been worried; Hitler was not. He knew that the Allies would not attack. Chamberlain may not have read Clausewitz: but for Chamberlain, too, war was the continuation of his politics. He had been reluctant to engage Germany with the full power of Britain while peace still reigned; he was reluctant to so engage Germany now. Britain, said Hitler to his chief of staff, General Halder, even before the war broke out, would fight a "sham war," a "phony war."[7] He was largely right—though not quite. The war policy of the British government was not sham: its reluctance was not the product of dissimulation: it was authentic. It was to be a reluctant war.[8]

Hitler tried his best to foster a kind of pacific warfare with the British and the French. His first directives for the conduct of the war in the west were so aimed. On 4 September he forbade all German attacks on French and British passenger steamers, even when these were sailing in convoy.[9] Five days later his Directive No. 3 decreed that "even after the irresolute opening of hostilities by Great Britain at sea and in the air and by France on land[10] and in the air my express consent must be obtained" before any further attack on the British and the French. Hitler hoped, and perhaps even counted, on a British inclination to make peace after Poland was struck down. He also hoped that an early invasion of eastern Poland by the Soviet Union would make the British inclined to talk peace with him. Thus he urged the Polish campaign to a quick conclusion. Unlike in later campaigns, he drove up front in his large staff car, addressing his troops in the sun and dust. Apart from these excursions, he directed much of the campaign from a special command train stationed outside the Polish railway station of Gogolin.

The evidence suggests that, like Hitler, Stalin may have misread the British; that he and Molotov expected another Munich as late as 2 September, possibly through the Italian mediation. Thereafter their policy

---

also arises whether the Allies could have attacked in the west even if they had wanted to do so. By 10 September the Germans were able to move a number of divisions from Poland to the west. By the sixteenth the Poles were beaten.

[7] *GD*, D, VII, 279–81. According to H. L. Mencken, *phony* war was a British Americanism. Mencken, *AL*, Supplement One, 511.

[8] The French, with their quick intelligence, were the first to give this strange opening period of the war a name: *drôle de guerre*, the translation of which colloquial phrase, however, is not so much "phony war" as it is "some war!"

[9] Possibly with American public opinion in mind. The sinking of the British passenger vessel *Athenia* on 3 September, an unauthorized act by a German submarine, revived memories of the *Lusitania*.

[10] In the no-man's-land of the German frontier, between the outposts of the Maginot and Siegfried forts, the French had moved cautiously ahead by a few miles.

was an oriental compound of caution and opportunism. Ribbentrop kept urging them to go ahead at Poland. For a while they were reluctant to do so. Then the speed of the German advance impressed Stalin. On the night of 8–9 September he ordered Molotov to congratulate the Germans on their "entry into Warsaw." This congratulation was premature. The Poles, as we have seen, set down to defend their capital city. Two days later Molotov spoke to the German ambassador, coming "to the political side of the matter and stated that the Soviet Government had intended to take the occasion of the further advance of German troops to declare that Poland was falling apart and that it was necessary for the Soviet Union, in consequence, to come to the aid of the Ukrainians and White Russians 'threatened' by Germany. This argument was to make the intervention of the Soviet Union plausible to the masses and at the same time avoid giving the Soviet Union the appearance of an aggressor."[11] The Germans were not happy with this kind of argument. Four days later Warsaw was still the key to Stalin's opportunism. "The Russian Army had reached a state of preparedness sooner than anticipated . . . [but] it was of the greatest importance not to take action until the governmental center of Poland, the city of Warsaw, had fallen. Molotov therefore asked that he be informed as nearly as possible as to when the capture of Warsaw could be counted on."[12] One more day, however, and Stalin overruled this. (His resolve was probably strengthened by the armistice that Soviet commanders signed with the Japanese after their skirmishes in the vastnesses of Mongolia.) On 17 September, Sunday, Soviet Armies moved in a mass across the long, undefended eastern marchlands of Poland. At Brest-Litovsk, where twenty-one years before, Lenin and Trotsky surrendered a large portion of the old Russian Empire to the military masters of the Second German Reich, grinning tank officers of the Red Army shook hands with their counterparts from the Third Reich.

The government of Poland, or what remained of it, had gathered in a miserable village on the Romanian frontier. On the evening of the Russian invasion it passed, among a mass of exiles, into Romania. The government of the latter, even though a paper ally of Poland and a recipient of a 1939 British guarantee, feared the Germans sufficiently to limit the freedom and the movements of the government of its stricken friend and neighbor. Yet the spirit of most Poles in exile was unbroken and inspiring. Of the nearly one hundred thousand who left Poland, the majority made their way to France, where they immediately formed the government in exile. Because of the large number of Poles continuing to serve first under French, then under British command, the prestige and the authority of

[11] GD, D, VIII, 44.
[12] GD, D, VIII, 60–61.

this government rose from shadow to acquire a certain amount of substance. But the exiles were a small portion of the Polish people, the vast majority of which was now subjected to brutalities and humiliations by their two ancient enemies. When these had conquered the ancient Polish Kingdom in the past, the life of the vast majority of peasants and serfs had been largely unaffected by the political tragedies of the Polish state, at least in the short run. Now, in 1939, the condition of their subjugation was impressed upon the people at once by the administrations of their cruel and crude conquerors. Tens of thousands of Polish officers and officials were eventually transported to camps hidden in the frozen forests and plains of the Russian Empire; thousands of them were killed by mass executions in the spring of 1940 for no reason whatsoever. The majority of people in eastern Poland were forced down into the Soviet mold of largely senseless misery at home. In November 1939 these provinces were annexed to the "Ukrainian" and "Byelorussian" Soviet Socialist Republics. They were incorporated into the Soviet Union. The brutalities of German rule over Poland were more systematic. The Germans closed churches and schools, and subjected thousands of Poles to deportation and subjugation of an especially loathsome character. The large numbers of Polish Jews felt the flail of their terrible enemy Hitler at once. These few words are not sufficient to convey to the reader the desperate realities and the often not less desperate adjustments of daily life under this new kind of inimical tyranny. All kinds of extensive records of their existence, however, exist.

Almost until the very end of the Second World War the German regime chose to treat the Poles worse than they treated almost any other conquered nation. Far more than the ancient Prussian dislike of the Poles, Hitler himself was largely responsible for this. Unlike Napoleon, he was largely devoid of magnanimity. The bravery of the Polish Army affected him not at all: rather, the contrary. To Dahlerus, the Swedish amateur mediator, he said on 26 September: "It was insolence for such a debased country as Poland to dare to turn against a country like Germany."[13] He

---

[13] *GD*, D, VIII, 142. Hitler's savage references to Poland are numerous; but perhaps his statements in the summer of 1940 stand out. To Mussolini on 18 June 1940: "Poland is steppe. My administrators prefer to govern Negroes instead of Poles." In his 19 July 1940 speech: "One of the unreal creations of the Versailles *Diktat*, a fake scarecrow (ein aufgeblasener Popanz). . . . Germany's patience was exemplary, even as one move of Germany's arm was all that was needed to destroy this bladder inflated by stupidity and pretentiousness." Again there is a noticeable similarity of Hitler's phrases to those of

was furious at the Poles because their resistance led to his war with England.

Now, a month after the outbreak of the war, after the disappearance of the Polish state,[14] he once more hoped that England would retreat toward peace. There was a short-lived German peace offensive, pursued through all kinds of neutral intermediaries, including Dahlerus, culminating in Hitler's great speech of 6 October.[15] Yet Chamberlain, no matter how reluctant a warrior, did not respond. Contemptuous of England (he told Sven Hedin later in October: "she wasn't even decent enough to help the Poles"), Hitler did not wait for long. On 9 October he issued his Directive No. 6 ("Case Yellow"):

1. Should it become evident in the near future that England and, under her influence, France also, are not disposed to bring the war to an end, I have decided, without further loss of time, to go over to the offensive.
2. Any further delay . . . will also strengthen the military power of the enemy, reduce the confidence of neutral nations in Germany's final victory, and make it more difficult to bring Italy into the war on our side as a full ally.

The German armies would roll forward to attack France on 12 November, conquering Belgium and Holland on the way; after France was crushed, the British might make peace. There occurred now an unusual combination in the history of the Third Reich. For once, Hitler's military commanders were strong enough to oppose him with some effect. They included Reichenau, perhaps the most Nazified of all of his generals. On 5 November Hitler reluctantly agreed to postpone the attack in the

---

Molotov's speech about Poland (31 October 1939): "the ugly offspring of the Versailles Treaty."

[14] One fifth of the former Polish state, including about 5 million Poles, was annexed to the Third Reich. Another two fifths were made into a novel kind of German satrapy, under the name of "Generalgouvernement" (it included about twelve million Poles and Jews). Two fifths of former Poland had fallen to the Soviet Union, with a population of another twelve million people, of whom six million were Poles. These German dispositions were not made public until 8–12 October. There is some reason to believe that Hitler considered the creation of a small, subservient, but nominally self-governing Polish state, had the British responded to his peace offer. Between Germany and Russia, too, the possibility of a Polish buffer state was left open until 25 September, when both Stalin and Hitler decided to cancel it; three days later they redrew the lines of their partition of northeastern Europe.

[15] Dahlerus approached the British again in November, with Goering's approval. Woodward II, 187.

west until the spring. The poor weather was a factor, too. Again, he felt that time was working against him. He would rue this postponement later, as he rued the postponement of war because of Munich. Yet he need not have fretted himself. The inactivity in the west affected the French adversely. Their morale in the fall of 1939 was better than it would be in the spring of 1940. Mussolini, too, was far from ready. Also, some of the German generals were restive—at least potentially so—in November 1939; they would no longer oppose him in 1940. In any event, Hitler soon felt that Providence was on his side. On 8 November a brave solitary German, Georg Elser, a worker, placed a bomb in the Munich beer hall where Hitler was about to speak. Because of a change in schedule, Hitler left the hall an hour before the bomb burst.

The initial discipline that held the French together in September was now loosening. A small example: on meatless days duck and game were allowed, on spiritless days champagne was legal. Noël Coward was a propaganda officer of the British in Paris, his offices next to the Ritz. Yet all of this matters only in retrospect. Had the Allies been successful in battle, much of what now seems corrupt and slack would have been ascribed to a kind of insouciant nonchalance. The trouble was not only that the Allies were not successful at war, the trouble was their reluctance to engage in it. On 10 September, when Poland was scorched and burning and torn apart by the Germans, Chamberlain wrote his sister: ". . . what I hope for is not a military victory—I very much doubt the feasibility of that—but a collapse of the German home front. For that it is necessary to convince the Germans that they cannot win. . . . I hope myself we shall not start to bomb their munition centers and objectives in towns unless they begin it. . . ."[16] The trouble with this kind of reluctance is that, albeit resting on principle, it is subject to every kind of temptation promising an easy way out. During the winter of 1939–40 the British and the French governments were inclined to base their conduct of the war on

---

[16] Feiling, 418. Chamberlain to Roosevelt on 30 September: "I retain full confidence that we shall come out successfully in the end. My own belief is that we shall win not by a complete and spectacular military victory . . . but by convincing the Germans that they cannot win. . . ." The British chiefs of staff issued "most stringent instructions" to the RAF, "only purely military objectives in the narrowest sense of the word were to be bombarded." COS Paper 961 (39). From September 1939 there survives, too, the famous statement of the British Air Minister, Sir Kingsley Wood. When Leopold Amery suggested that the RAF bomb the timber areas of southwestern Germany: "Oh, you can't do that. That's private property. You'll be asking me to bomb the Ruhr next."

dimwitted calculations and, on occasion, on harebrained schemes. Dominant among the former were the calculations of economists, amounting to an article of faith: a little more of a blockade, and the German economy would collapse. Nothing could have been farther from the truth.[17] The more or less harebrained schemes included clandestine attempts at collusion with what were believed to have been anti-Nazi circles of conspirators within Germany; they also included plans for opening up fronts within the Arctic Circle or in the Caucasus—it hardly mattered where, as long as the front was far away from France (or, for that matter, from Germany).

One exception to this uninspiring kind of reluctance was the war at sea. As the war began, Chamberlain took Churchill into his Cabinet. The British Navy and the people welcomed this event. Immediately the signal went out to the Navy: "Winston is back." He arrived in the Admiralty to find the same room and the same map case he had left twenty-four years before. He threw himself at the task of waging war at sea with his expectable enthusiasm. Unlike in 1914, the German fleet was small. Also, in 1939 there was a modern and powerful French fleet, twice the size of the German one, except for submarines. Even there the Germans started the war with relatively few (fifty-six). Daring commanders of some of them would torpedo a few British warships early in the war, on one occasion even penetrating into the wet fastness of Scapa Flow. Still the British and, with them, the French ruled the Atlantic. Twenty-five years after Sturdee's smashing victory at the Falklands over Spee, a German compact battleship named after the latter was chased into Montevideo by three small British cruisers. Rather than be sunk by a converging British force, the commander of the *Graf Spee* blew up his ship on 16 December and blew out his brains the next day. It was one of the few inspiring moments for British morale during that winter. The other one came two months later, when a British destroyer captured the German raider *Altmark* in a Norwegian fjord, freeing British sailors who had been kept prisoners in her hold.

Yet with all of this naval superiority at hand, Churchill could not affect the balance of power in Britain's favor. Had the British Navy been able to penetrate the Baltic, some of this could have been achieved. Churchill was keenly aware of this. He had to abandon his Baltic

---

[17] See a discussion of this below, "The 'laws' of economics," pp. 227–38. The blockade was ineffective because the Germans received vast supplies from the Soviet Union; because they produced vast amounts and varieties of synthetic materials; and, most of all, because of the discipline and the excellence of their organization, whereby they had nearly everything they needed, even though their economy was not placed on a full war footing until February 1942.

plan (*Catherine*), partly because of the cautious bent of the Sea Lords (whose behavior was the very opposite of the fighting spirit their predecessors had shown in the early years of the last world war), partly because of the justifiable anxiety at what could happen to warships moving in narrow seas but a few dozen miles from Germany's airfields. Naval power was no longer dominant, as in the past. The old Lloyd George may have known this when in January 1940 he told the British newspaper magnate Cudlipp that he thought Britain would lose the war.

"I do not yet believe in this war," wrote the French Catholic writer Georges Bernanos in self-imposed exile from Europe on the edge of the Brazilian jungle, during the twilight winter,

> I don't believe in it any more than before, I haven't yet given it my faith. This war does not resemble the one I expect, the one which is going to come, it will come in its good time. That it has disappointed the manufacturers of catastrophes, that it has cost till now fewer dead in six months than had the other war in six days—this is not what counts. We know well that in a few hours the dead could pile up in hecatombs. But as long as this war is puffed up with the scent of blood in its nostrils, as long as she sits in silence on the banks of the Meuse, with her black skirt tight between her thighs, with her hands crossed on her foul stomach, this war will be merely hideous and not terrible, she is a farce out of Hell.[18]

During the winter London and Paris flickered, twilit and cold. (For the first time in decades the Thames froze hard for miles.) In the vast northeastern portion of Europe the winter of 1939 was not twilit, it was dark. A monster empire had risen in the East. Entire states were about to disapper under its shadow. Within a few weeks after the beginning of the war the political map of Eastern Europe changed beyond recognition. There was nothing *drôle* in this, not at all. In the West the frontiers of states and nations had been established centuries before. The rising importance of the eastern, as compared to the western, half of the continent is one of the major themes of the history of Europe during the twentieth century. Compared to this long development, the Bolshevik Revolution was an episode. Indeed, it was an exception in the history of Europe, since no Communist revolution succeeded anywhere except in Russia. In 1918 the Germans had won in the East, yet they were to be defeated in the West: that, too, was exceptional, a pattern that would not appear again.

---

[18] Unpublished pages, written in early 1940, printed for the first time under the title of "Journal 1940 (1)" in Bernanos, *Le lendemain, c'est vous!* (Paris, 1969). (See also *Les enfants humiliés* (Journal 1939–40), Bernanos, *EC*, I.

What would appear again was their unscrupulousness, especially when one recalls their self-conscious claims to being the champions of Western civilization. In 1917 the Kaiser and his Prussians chose to make it possible for Lenin to re-enter Russia. In 1939 the anti-Bolshevik Hitler and his Nazis chose to make it possible for Stalin to re-enter Europe. They were very successful in the short run. They destroyed themselves in the long run. Whether in 1917 the Bolsheviks would have been able to make their revolution if Lenin had stayed closeted in Zurich, or whether Stalin would have been able to get to Warsaw, not to speak of Berlin, if Hitler had not started the Second World War, is not for the historian to decide. When Hitler finally attacked Stalin, Churchill told his secretary that if Hitler invaded Hell, he, Churchill, "would make at least a favorable reference to the Devil in the House of Commons." Whether Stalin was the same as the Devil is, again, not for the historian to state. He can say, however, that there is a difference between making a favorable reference to the Devil and telling him to help himself to the house of your neighbor.

During the first two weeks of the Polish war, Ribbentrop urged Molotov to go ahead. For a while there was the prospect of two small satellite Polish protectorates, one under German, the other under Soviet tutelage. Then both sides changed their minds; they would simply incorporate their respective portions into their empires. Stalin, forever suspicious, was both relieved and impressed when Hitler ordered that the German units roaming far ahead in eastern Poland be withdrawn to the boundary lines agreed upon in the secret protocol. (Something of the same pattern would be executed on the tortured body of Germany by Americans and Russians less than six years later, but that Hitler would not live to see.) Toward the end of the campaign Hitler and Stalin decided to redraw the boundaries of their newly acquired domains. Again this took no more than two days in Moscow for Ribbentrop. The boundaries of German-ruled Poland were advanced to the rivers Bug and San. In exchange for this Lithuania was to pass to the Russian side of the line. There were few loose ends left.[19] By that time (28 September) the first of the unfortunate Baltic delegations were being summoned to the Kremlin. In no uncertain tones Stalin told the Foreign Ministers of Latvia, of Estonia, and of Lithuania, in turn, that what a weakened Russian Empire had

---

[19] The long-disputed city of Vilna (Vilnius) was awarded by the Soviets to Lithuania, to become its capital. A small corner around the village of Suwalki, including a few square miles, was coveted by Stalin to the extent that he would pay, after protracted and irritating negotiations, more than seven million gold dollars ( the purchase price of Alaska) to the Germans for it in January 1941. Less than six months later the Germans took it within the first few hours of the Russian campaign.

lost twenty years before, a strong Russia was now to recover. Russian military and naval units were henceforth to be stationed within the three Baltic states. On the other hand, Stalin promised not to interfere with the domestic order of these small republics. He kept observing this policy for a while, until June 1940, when the dramatic events in the West moved him to extinguish the remnants of their independence by one fell swoop.

In the fall of 1939 Stalin's policy was aligned with Hitler's in another main respect. Stalin, too, hoped for a conclusion of the war. In retrospect many people, among them Bonnet, and of course all anti-Communist ideologues, have argued that the Soviets enjoyed the prospect of a European war of which they would eventually reap their revolutionary fortunes. Let me repeat once again: Stalin, unlike Lenin, was far more of a statesman than a revolutionary.[20] He wanted territory, not revolution, in Europe. Almost everything indicates that he wanted to secure, and digest, his new accretions. Had Chamberlain made some kind of peace with Hitler after the fall of Poland, the Western Powers' acquiescence in the new order of northeastern Europe would have been a matter of course. The advance of his state borders westward also gave Stalin more security in front of Germany, even as he was careful not to stress this point.[21]

He was not prudent enough to avoid a conflict with Finland. That large country, populated by a small and valiant people, had also been consigned to his "sphere" by the secret protocol. Yet Finland was an unusual case. First, she was a hard nut to crack. Second, there is some reason to believe, though we have no written evidence to that effect, that Hitler did not understand the secret protocol to mean that Finland would be as-

---

[20] He was *Time*'s "Man of the Year" of 1939—in retrospect, a little exaggerated, but not much.

[21] He instructed the Communist parties in Europe to propagandize *against*, not *for*, the continuation of the war. Immediately after the fall of Poland, Churchill said in a speech (with which Chamberlain agreed: Churchill, *GS*, 449, also Feiling, 425) that "Russia has pursued a cold policy of self-interest" (which was true), and "that the Russian armies should stand on this line was clearly necessary for the safety of Russia against the Nazi menace" (an exaggerated attribution of Stalin's purposes). For the appetite for land, unlike that for money, does not always issue from a deeper need for security. (Montesquieu: "The object of war is victory; that of victory, conquest; that of conquest, retention. A conquest is an acquisition; the spirit of acquisition carries with it the spirit of conservation and use, not that of destruction.") Instead of Clausewitz, Stalin would have been better off to ponder Montesquieu. By 1941 it became evident that Stalin had done little to fortify the new advanced western frontiers of the Soviet Union, while the fortified points on the old border were in disrepair.

signed to Russia completely, lock, stock, and barrel, and that Stalin knew this. In any event, Stalin wanted from Finland not complete control over the state but, rather, certain territories for the sake of Soviet security. The southeastern frontier of Finland ran very close to Leningrad. Stalin also wanted certain islands in the Finnish Gulf, to further ease the exit of the Russian Navy into the Baltic. He suggested such a cession to the Finns as early as in the spring of 1939. Now, in October 1939, Russian pressure on Finland began in earnest. Like their unfortunate Baltic neighbors to the south, the Finns, too, had to dispatch a somber delegation to Moscow. Not all of the Russian demands were altogether unreasonable, especially in retrospect; they even included a transfer of Russian land to Finland along the long, unpopulated central portion of their forest frontiers. What were unreasonable were the unimaginative and brutal negotiating tactics of Stalin and especially of Molotov. The Finns felt that they had no alternative but to resist. For once it was Stalin, not Hitler, who was in a hurry. Using the pretext of a fabricated frontier incident the Soviets, having taken a leaf out of Hitler's book, attacked Finland on 30 November without a declaration of war.

Here was a supreme example of the unpredictability of war. The European war had begun between Germany and Poland, Britain, and France. Less than three months had passed, and the two states who were engaged in actual combat were Russia and Finland. For once Stalin the Russian statesman gave a bit of undue consideration to the propaganda of communism. Moscow announced that there was no war between the Soviet Union and Finland at all but that a "People's Government" of Finland, presided over by one Finnish Communist by the name of Kuusinen, had come into existence in a frontier village and that the Soviet Union was merely assisting this government in its struggle to liberate Finland. Few people were misled by this idiotic piece of propaganda, least of all the Finnish working class, whose single-minded patriotism was a sight to behold. Within a few days it was becoming evident that their massive ground assaults, and their cruel bombing of Helsinki notwithstanding, the Russian armies were making precious little headway against the Finns. Once the prospect of a long winter war began in earnest, Stalin no longer let his consideration of international communism interfere with his contempt for it.[22]

---

[22] The Kuusinen "government" simply disappeared during the winter war, at the end of which a peace treaty was concluded by a state that had claimed that it was not at war. One of the first instances of Stalin's change of mind came a mere two weeks after the outbreak of the war. In a conversation with the visiting Estonian General Laidoner, Stalin gave the impression that he "was not actually striving to incorporate Finland into the territory of the Soviet Union."

The winter war was indeed in earnest. The Red Army was fighting badly; around the frozen sparse central front the Finns were skiing rings around them; in two places the Finns crossed the Soviet frontier, encircling Soviet units, who surrendered in droves. There were international repercussions. The fact that the moribund League of Nations in December expelled the Soviet Union from its membership mattered little to Stalin; what mattered was the bad performance of the Soviet Army. The latter had an important, though transitory, effect on the calculations of the Italian and of the French and British governments; it also had a far from negligible effect on Hitler's mind. Still, the German government watched the struggle of the Finns, Imperial Germany's old friends and allies, in icy silence, publicly stating that the Finns were to blame for their troubles. Hitler needed Stalin's friendship against the Anglo-Saxons. The Japanese were beginning to understand this, if indeed they had ever failed to do so.[23] Italy, however, was another question. Mussolini (unlike Hitler, an ex-Socialist) had a profound distaste for Russia's reappearance as a Great Power in Europe. Near the end of the year, Germany and Italy were drifting apart a bit. On 16 December Ciano spoke in the Italian Senate, sharply attacking Russia, while letting hints drop that the speech meant a criticism of Germany as well.[24] On 3 January 1940 Mussolini wrote an extraordinarily frank letter to Hitler. He urged his dictator friend to revise his policies in Poland, and also his regard for Stalin. The Western democracies would welcome an occasion to make peace, after which their morale would further decline from within.[25] It was a clever

---

At one of the interminable Kremlin banquets, Stalin told Laidoner that "he would not drink a toast that would astonish some of the guests and might not meet the approval of all." He raised his glass "to the independence and the *national* [my italics] People's Government of Finland." *GD*, D, VIII, 686–87.

[23] In February 1940 the Japanese ambassador told Ribbentrop in Berlin what the Japanese statesman Count Goto had said a decade or so earlier: Germany, Russia, Japan, were a three-horse team; the Russian horse must be in the middle so that it cannot break loose. "This combination is the best imaginable." *GD*, D, VIII, 730. Ribbentrop was much impressed.

[24] The few people who took the hints were already convinced. On the other hand, Ciano was reasonably honest. On 21 December he told Msgr. Tardini before an audience with the Pope: "I had gone to Salzburg [in August] to say: Peace, peace. But they [the Germans] answered: War, war! So I could secure peace for Italy but not for Europe." *VD*, I, 347.

[25] Poland, wrote Mussolini, which "fought courageously, deserves a treatment which does not give occasion for hostile speculations. It is my conviction that the creation of a modest, disarmed Poland which is exclusively Polish, liberated from the Jews—for whom I fully approve your project of gathering them all in a large ghetto in Lublin—can no longer constitute any threat to the

letter, possibly the cleverest Mussolini ever wrote Hitler. Mussolini wanted to wait; but Hitler was in a hurry. Within three months Hitler, and the force of events, convinced Mussolini to go along with him.

Meanwhile the attention of the world was being consumed by the winter war, which had all the attributes of David vs. Goliath, heroism vs. ignominy. Volunteers were coming to Finland from many corners of the world, most of them from her Scandinavian neighbors. They gave the Finns a lift of spirit, but not much more. The Scandinavian monarchs and presidents and prime ministers met often through that darkening autumn of 1939. All of their ministerial or royal conferences notwithstanding, no Scandinavian government wished to risk war for the sake of brotherhood. Arms and volunteers were trickling into Finland from the democracies as well as from some of Germany's allies, Italy, Hungary, against which the Russians protested. On the German side all help, including fellow-Aryan sympathies, were forbidden on the orders of the sphinx Ribbentrop, determinedly stony and dumb. On the Western side, the Finnish war became *la grande cause des bien-pensants*, for all right-thinking men (and women) the inspiring thing to think. Such outbursts of public thinking are often less inspiring than they seem at first sight. In this case they were pregnant with trouble: like a reformed *demi-monde*, considering the prospects of a respectable marriage with sudden enthusiasm, Inspiration was inseparable from Calculation. To help the Finns would be an inspiring thing. By the way the Allies would get Scandinavia in the bag, the American people on their side,[26] Hitler and Mussolini would be driven

---

Greater Reich. . . . I believe that the creation of a Polish state under the German aegis would be an element that would resolve the war and constitute a condition sufficient for the peace. . . . I am profoundly convinced that Great Britain and France will never succeed in making your Germany, assisted by Italy, capitulate, but it is not certain that it will be possible to bring the French and British to their knees or even divide them. To believe that is to delude oneself. The United States would not permit a total defeat of the democracies. . . . It is my definite duty to add that a further step in your relations with Moscow would have catastrophic repercussions in Italy. . . . Permit me to believe that this will not happen. The solution of your *Lebensraum* problem is in Russia and nowhere else. . . . The day when we shall have demolished Bolshevism we shall have kept faith with our two revolutions. It will be then the turn of the big democracies, which cannot survive the cancer which is gnawing them. . . ."

[26] How important American opinion was in Allied calculations as early as October 1939 appears in a memo of the British chiefs of staff re Finland in that month: "The invasion of Finland by itself would be no military threat to the Allies, nor could the Allies give any assistance to Finland. . . . *The one strong argument* for action was that it should win us the sympathy of neutrals all

apart, and the German war economy would grind to a halt. It was not a case of trying to kill two birds with one stone; it was a case of trying to kill a flock of birds with a pebble.

It was one of the great abortive follies of the war. By sending troops —at first disguised as volunteers—into northern Finland, the Allies would pass through northern Norway and Sweden, getting hold of the port of Narvik and the Swedish iron ore fields. The French were especially enthusiastic about this plan—any plan—that would keep the fighting as far from France as was possible. They, and the British, let themselves be persuaded by economic experts (who depended, in turn, on intelligence proffered by Thyssen, a recent refugee German industrialist) to the effect that without the imports of Swedish ore the steel hearths of the Third Reich would cool down and die out. The British and the French also believed that their coming down on the side of Finland against Communist Russia would melt American hearts, and finally produce the unwonted smile on the American Gothic faces of the isolationist Republican masses in the Midwest with whom President Roosevelt had to contend. Besides—a more difficult task, this—it might mollify the ugly reluctance of French Rightists for this democratic world war. The French and the British governments, in one word, would risk war with the Soviet Union if this would convert the editorialists of the Chicago *Tribune* and of the *Action Française* to their side. From December to March the governments deliberated over all kinds of plans. Folly and bluff reigned supreme in these deliberations.[27] Eventually their particular kind of slowness that

---

over the world. *The open support of the U.S.A. would outweigh the enmity of Russia. . . .*" [my italics]. Cited in Butler, II, 95.

[27] No full account of this chapter of Allied folly exists, even as it is worthy of a master historian's researches and pen. There is an honest account of some of it in Derry, 12, "The Allies, for their part, while sincere in protesting their desire to save Finland, certainly had other objects in view to which they gave less publicity." There was, for example, an early French plan to land in Petsamo, on the Arctic coast, a project "which seemed to combine the maximum provocation to the Russians with the minimum of strategic advantage to ourselves." Derry, 13. Examples of public idiocy abounded, as that in the respectable and respected *Le Temps* of 9 January 1940, calling for a blockade of Murmansk in which the writer saw "nothing but gain . . . [it] would help to swing the decision in Finland to the side of justice and right, while naval operations in the Black Sea, with Odessa under Allied guns, would encourage Romania to stand firm in face of any attack in Bessarabia." "Odessa under Allied guns" was good. It was on 5 February 1940 that the Supreme War Council finally accepted a British plan to send two Allied brigades through northern Norway to Finland, plus five Territorial battalions to southern Norway. By 1 March time was running out, and the British War Cabinet realized that the French attitude

was compounded by halfheartedness came to their rescue, though no one saw it that way at the time. While the first French and British advance units were being embarked in a blustery port of Scotland, the winter war came to a quick end. By late February masses of Russian troops hammered their way through the Karelian isthmus, the so-called Mannerheim Line. Impressed by the fact that Allied help would be too little and too late, and by the condition that after taking a slice of Finland, Stalin would let the rest of it exist alone, the Finns sadly signed the Treaty of Moscow on 12 March 1940.[28]

Before we consider the consequences of this event, we must shift our view from the northeastern to the southeastern portion of Europe. Here was another difference between the two world wars. The Balkans, which used to be called the powder keg of Europe (and, indeed, so it was in 1914), simmered down in peace and quiet during the first year of the Last European War, in 1939–40. Greece, Bulgaria, Romania, and Yugoslavia put a damper on their differences. Even Serbs and Croats had settled into a kind of uneasy coexistence.[29] These small states had learned a lesson—at least for a while. There was a Balkan Pact, including Turkey, a neutral bloc that eventually amounted to nothing once the Germans started moving to the southeast. Still, the Balkans presented a picture of neutrality and good sense, providing the Great Powers would let them alone. The Russo-German partition line across Eastern Europe stopped at the northern edge of the Balkans. The Germans were anxious to divert Stalin's eyes therefrom.[30] They wanted the Russians to put some pressure on the British in Afghanistan, India, and the Middle East.[31] "Stalin,"

---

was "most disquieting. Their promises seemed to be bluff and to have been made in the knowledge that they could blame us for the failure to redeem them." Woodward, I, 92.

[28] Finland lost most of the Karelian straits, the city of Viipuri, Petsamo and its outlet to the Arctic, a small peninsula for a Russian naval base, and other portions along the forest frontier. President Kallio, signing the treaty, said: "May the hand wither that is forced to sign such a paper as this." A stroke paralyzed his right arm five months afterward.

[29] Their politicians signed an agreement, the so-called "Sporazum," on 26 August 1939. It would eventually vanish before the opportunities that the German invasion of Yugoslavia offered for the Croats.

[30] Stalin, in the grand Tsarist tradition, was interested in Bulgaria: He proposed a mutual-assistance pact to the Bulgarian monarchist regime already in September 1939.

[31] On 30 December Keitel told Ribbentrop that "it is highly desirable to direct the Russian forces in this direction [Turkey, Iraq, the Middle East] and thus probably away from the Balkans." Jodl recorded this in a memorandum a week later. GD, D, VIII, 632–33.

said Hitler to his admirer Sven Hedin in early March, "was no longer the international Bolshevist, but showed himself as an absolute Russian nationalist and was in the last analysis following exactly the same natural policy of Russian nationalism as the Tsars"[32]—the very condition that would incense Hitler a few months later.

Mussolini, who was not impressed with such arguments about the new Russia, was sufficiently impressed with the slowness and the incapacity of the Western Allies to finally cast his lot with Hitler. The temporary cloud over the relations between Rome and Berlin blew away with the winds of spring. Mussolini still felt compelled to tell the Germans that Italy "was in no position financially to sustain a long war."[33] He was, however, impressed by Hitler's determination and ability to wage a short and decisive war in the West. Less than a week after the end of the winter war, Hitler and Mussolini met on a blustery, shiny day on the Brenner. "The campaign in France will be decisive," Hitler told Mussolini. "Once France is finished, Italy will be the master of the Mediterranean and England will have to conclude peace."

Because of the end of the Finnish war the French government fell. This was one of the strangest of political events. On 21 March Daladier, facing all kinds of hostile combinations in the Chamber, had to resign, because he had been too slow in committing France to the fatal folly of getting into a war with the Russian empire somewhere in Finland. Largely impervious to criticism from the Left, Daladier could not withstand massive criticism from the Right. Such was the political climate of France. The government was reformed, with Reynaud, a little man of considerable talents and of not inconsiderable courage, presiding over it. Reynaud was an Anglophile and a reliable ally.[34] This did not please the opponents of the war, who were beginning to come out of the woodwork, here and there—the significant thing in this political crisis. Their case was one of selective indignation. They wanted more action against Russia, less action against Germany, and none at all against Italy. The Allied military staffs went on to encourage such follies for a while.[35]

---

[32] *GD*, D, VIII, 863.

[33] *GD*, D, VIII, 902.

[34] On 28 March he contracted a formal alliance with Britain, providing for no separate peace.

[35] For a while these planners were toying with the idea of putting an Allied force into Salonika. Their plans depended on the "Weygand Army"—a largely motley and phantom force of underequipped French and colonial soldiery wasted in Syria, under the command of General Weygand who, contrary to the usual phrase, did not deserve a better fate, as soon events would

Within three weeks all of this was to be washed away by the Scandinavian storm.

Throughout the war (indeed, as late as in 1945), Hitler feared a British descent on Norway. The dread of a northern front close to Germany's vitals, not the dearth of Swedish iron ore, was principal in his mind.[36] Throughout his career in politics and war, Hitler would justify his offensives by the preventive argument: He would declare that he was forced to forestall an imminent attack by an enemy. There was often little or no truth in this kind of propaganda justification. Yet it was largely true in the case of Norway. At the beginning of the war Hitler wanted absolute neutrality on his Scandinavian flank. It was his commander of the Navy, Admiral Raeder, an unattractive representative of the Old School, who tried to draw Hitler's attention to the advantages of German control over Norway. As late as in October 1939 Hitler allowed Danish food shipments to go to Britain as long as Denmark shipped enough food to Germany. In November 1939 the Norwegian shippers' association chartered the largest and best vessels of their merchant fleet to the British. German submarines were begining to interfere with and sink Scandinavian ships on occasion, but Hitler was still planning his campaign in the West, not in the North. Once the Finnish war was on, this would change. Hitler was immediately aware of the Allied plans to establish themselves in Scandinavia. From now on it was a race between the hare Hitler and the Anglo-French tortoise. Contrary to the proverbial tale, the hare beat the tortoise in the finish. Again, contrary to the tale, it was the hare who was reluctant in the beginning. It was not until 1 March that Hitler gave the definite order: The attack in the North ("Weseruebung") will precede

---

show. The greatest of these imbecilities, worthy of record if only in a footnote, were contained in those Anglo-French staff plans in March 1940 that considered the death blow to the Russian and German empires to be administered by ancient French and British warplanes alighting from Syria and dropping bombs on the Baku oilfields. In a report of the British chiefs of staff of 8 March 1940, entitled "Military Implications of War with Russia in 1940," these experts concluded that "even with a considerable amount of German help in reorganising their transport system, the Russians were unlikely to be able to increase their supplies to Germany in 1940" (wrong again). "We could bomb the Caucasian oilfields, and thus ultimately bring about a Russian economic and military collapse. . . ." WP (40) 91, cited by Woodward, I, 108. Melting the polar icecap and putting Russia under water would have been a comparable idea.

[36] At any rate it was Finnish nickel rather than Swedish ore that was irreplaceable for the industry of the Third Reich. Hitler's conference with General Falkenhorst, on 20 February 1940, cited in detail by Churchill, *GS*, 564–65, shows that Swedish iron ore was a minor consideration for Hitler.

the campaign in the West ("Yellow"). True, he had plans drafted as early as 14 December. But the first British and French plans went back even earlier than that.[37] However, once the decision was made in Berlin, preparations jumped ahead with precision and speed. The decisions made in London and Paris were hedged around with a carapace of compromises that slowed down the progress of the Anglo-French tortoise to an economic crawl.

It was Hitler's great opponent Churchill, at the Admiralty, who put his heart and brain into the Scandinavian scheme. For a long time he would not have his way: He was slowed by Chamberlain, by the French, not least by the cautious Sea Lords of his own Navy. Still he was spoiling for a fight. He had his way in the minor and inspiring incident of the *Altmark* in mid-February. There is some evidence that this *Altmark* episode was instrumental in crystalizing Hitler's mind. He saw that in certain circumstances the British were ready to disregard Norwegian neutrality. By the end of March Churchill was about to have his way on the larger issue. He was plugging for a dual move against the Germans. One operation ("Royal Marine") would consist of floating masses of mines down the Rhine in order to cause havoc in the German portion of that important waterway.[38] The other ("Wilfred") would consist in the Navy entering Norwegian waters to mine them and thus interrupt the flow of German ore ships coming down from the ore port of Narvik. By April 1940 it should have been evident that the Germans depended on the down shipping from Narvik far less than the Allies claimed, or than the Allies' economic experts had calculated earlier; moreover, within a few weeks the ice in the northern Baltic would break up, whereafter the Germans could ship their ore direct from Sweden, with little concern for Allied interference. What is seldom recognized, even now, is the fact that behind the economic considerations stood the desire to establish a British presence in Norway.

On 30 March Admiral Darlan in Paris correctly forecast a German descent on Denmark and Norway as their reply to the British mining of the Norwegian Leads. In a few days the British were embarking troops

---

[37] On 8 January the Secretary General of the Swedish Foreign Ministry said to the British *chargé* in Stockholm that a British move into Scandinavia would lead to a German occupation of Denmark, and more besides. Boheman added: "I should have thought that the British Government had the fate of a sufficient number of smaller states on their consciences as is." Quoted by Woodward, *BP*, 23.

[38] Woodward, I, 101, "it was due mainly to Mr. Churchill's desire (in contrast with the passivity of his colleagues) to do something, even if it were only of a harassing kind, which would give the impression of an Allied initiative."

for three Norwegian ports, in anticipation of a German countermove.[39] There was a last-minute flurry of trouble between the Allies. The French, true to their form of trying to keep war as far from France's borders as was possible, on 3 April rejected the plan for mining the Rhine, while they were in favor of mining Norway. Next day Chamberlain, in a public speech, referred to Hitler as someone who "had missed the bus." Another day, and the British chief of the Imperial General Staff, General Ironside, declared that "we are ready for anything that may start." Nothing could have been farther from the truth. It was the Germans who were ready for anything, it was the British who missed the bus, and much else besides.

In retrospect, Hitler's invasion of Denmark and Norway was a masterpiece of daring and of execution.[40] It also gives the lie to the usual argument that this continental warmaker and tyrant was ignorant of the realities of war at sea. He was certainly not ignorant of amphibious warfare, of what the British call Combined Operations, in which they had been the masters ever since the opening of the modern age. The Germans beat the British in the obscure race for four ports in Norway, including Narvik. The British, including Churchill, did not believe that the Germans might venture that far. The British Navy, though not lacking in bravery on occasion (as in the squally battle in the fjord leading to Narvik), was lumbering in the North Sea while the Germans raced stealthily northward in the black night. Worse was to come on land. The Danes did not put up a fight.[41] The armament of Norway was antiquated, the country having been left unprepared for war by years of democratic and socialist administrations. Treachery was not enough to explain this democratic catastrophe. In Denmark there were occasions when, as a matter of course, Danish sailors helped to warp in the German ships that landed in the morning hours. The Norwegian Major Quisling, whose name was soon to be anathema in the democratic world, contributed little or noth-

---

[39] The first embarkation of these troops took place on 6 April, more than two days before the German invasion of Norway. On one occasion the Germans captured the operational instructions of "Stratforce," issued to the 8th Battalion of Sherwood Foresters. "The intention of *Stratforce* is to effect a landing at 512, 547, and 548, and to occupy these ports with a view of closing them to Germany. It is anticipated that our assistance will be welcomed by the inhabitants, but the decision as to whether or not to land will rest with the Royal Navy." Reproduced in Appendix 2 in *GWB* (2).

[40] The self-confidence and the succinctness of the directive for "Weseruebung" (1 March) are impressive. "The forces employed in 'Fall Weseruebung' will be as small as possible, having regard to our military and political strength, in relation to the northern nations. Weakness in numbers will be made good by skillful action and purpose in execution." It certainly was.

[41] In 1914 the Danish Army mustered 55,000 men; in 1939, 15,000.

ing to the Germans' success.[42] After a moment of hesitation the Norwegian king and the Army chose to fight. More than a week passed before the British put troops ashore, not in Trondheim or Bergen but in two small ports that they would abandon soon again. Around these ports they moved in "a muddy waddle." Inland, where black ice still lay on the dark Norwegian lakes, they were outfought and outflanked on every occasion. They were no match for the Germans. Churchill himself felt compelled to record, after the war: "We were each time just too late. . . . We, who had the command of the sea and could pounce anywhere on an undefended coast, were outpaced by the enemy moving by land across very large distances in the face of every obstacle. In this Norwegian encounter, our finest troops, the Scots and Irish guards, were baffled by the vigour, enterprise, and training of Hitler's young men."[43] There remained a glimmer of hope in northern Norway: scouting among piles of rock, French, Polish, and British troops finally cleared the Germans out of Narvik by the end of May—the only small Allied victory on land during the first fifteen months of the Second World War, it did not last. A few days after the Allies had withdrawn from Dunkirk, the King and government of Norway withdrew from Tromso to England, not without reluctance.

This was the first round of the duel between the two great opponents, Hitler and Churchill. In this first round Hitler bested Churchill. For a moment on the morning of 9 April Hitler was exultant: The Scandinavian sally was more than a sideswipe against the English, it was a decisive day. "As the year 1866 was the source of Bismarck's Reich, from this day will rise the Grossgermanisches Reich."[44] Yet in three ways the Scandinavian victory cost Hitler much, in the long run. His middle-sized navy came out of it battered, with losses so heavy as to eliminate it as a principal threat to Britain later in the summer.[45] There is another matter

---

[42] He did request Rosenberg as early as June 1939 for a sum of 6.5 million marks, saying that he could "change decisively in a short time the political situation in Norway, provided he had the necessary money." *GD*, D, VIII, 133, note 3. When Hitler met Quisling on 14 December 1939 the theme was still Norwegian neutrality. On the confusing day of 9 April Quisling took over the radio in Oslo, unbeknownst to the Germans: This event contributed to their failure to lay their hands on the King and government, for the latter had been inclined to parley with the Germans until Quisling's broadcast changed their minds and they left the capital for the North.

[43] Churchill, *GS*, 649; "a muddy waddle," 664.

[44] *Rosenberg TB*, 126.

[45] Too much should not be made out of this. The Germans lost three cruisers and ten destroyers; but the bases they got in Norway were worth that. Also, two of the five British aircraft carriers were lost west of Norway. Nor had Hitler planned to invade Britain with cruisers and battleships.

worth considering. Hitler's invasion of Denmark and Norway melted away a large chunk of the American isolationist mass on which he had placed some hopes. The main strength of the isolationist (and, consequently, Anglophobe—that is, anti-anti-German) Republicans was in the Midwest, with its large numbers of Americans of Scandinavian extraction from whose ranks most of the isolationist congressmen and senators had come, during the First World War and after. Their support of absolute American neutralism was now beginning to weaken. Had Hitler lost the initial race for Norway—that is, had he let the British precede him by a few days—the anti-British cause in America might have gained, not lost, strength. As things turned out, the national convention of the Republican Party was to nominate the internationalist and anti-German Willkie on the very day that France capitulated to Hitler.

All of this pales, in retrospect, before the most important matters. Hitler's triumph in Norway brought Churchill to power in England. Churchill was greatly responsible for the British debacle in the North. The British people may not have known this; but they had had enough of the dispirited and bumbling reluctant warriorship of Chamberlain. Twenty-five years before, Churchill fell from power because of the failure of the Dardanelles campaign, advocating which he had been more right than wrong. Now the fact that he was more wrong than right in Norway counted little or nothing against him. On 6 May a debate opened in the House of Commons about the Chamberlain government's conduct of the war. Dozens of Conservative members were deserting Chamberlain. In a loyal manner Churchill took much of the blame for the Norway defeat upon himself. This did not matter. The representatives of the British people wanted a national government. The Labor leaders would not enter such a government under Chamberlain. They would enter such a government under Churchill. Gradually this became evident by the evening of 9 May. Next morning the Reluctant War turned into the past with a crash. Hitler's armies invaded Western Europe. At 9 P.M. that night the world heard from Chamberlain himself that Winston Churchill was now leader of England.

It was a dramatic night. It capped the fiery impressions of the day. The real struggle had begun. Many people throughout the world instinctively understood what the change in the leadership of England was to mean. They may have been wrong in thinking that Churchill came to power as a response to Hitler's invasion of the Low Countries; but, again, this did not matter. What mattered was that, finally, Hitler had a real antagonist.[46] Hitler had never met Churchill. Once, before Hitler had be-

---

[46] Throughout this book I have spoken critically of the shortsighted and antiquated politics of parliamentary government. Yet it must be said that in the

come the master of Germany, they had a chance to meet, but Hitler had avoided him.[47] Hitler, who did not really understand the English, still possessed a great and cruel talent of insight into the characters and weaknesses of people confronting him. He was not altogether wrong in sizing up Chamberlain. About Churchill's character he understood little, a shortcoming that eventually contributed to his undoing. This did not mean that he, Hitler, could not prevent or parry what Churchill would, or could, do against him. His armies were surging ahead triumphantly at the end of the first day of the great campaign. All went according to plan, or even better. But his rising old antagonist was confident to the very depths of his soul. "I cannot conceal from the reader," Churchill wrote many years later, after the war, "that as I went to bed at about 3 A.M., I was conscious of a profound sense of relief. At last I had the authority to give directions over the whole scene. I felt as if I were walking with Destiny, and that all my past life had been but a preparation for this hour and for this trial."[48] This sentence, so moving in retrospect, compares favorably with whatever Hitler had said in his fervent phrases when he assumed his leadership for the war.[49] "I was sure," Churchill thought then, and remembered later, "I should not fail. Therefore, although impatient for the morning, I slept soundly and had no need for cheering dreams." He knew Hitler better than Hitler knew him. Three days later Churchill made the first of his famous speeches in the House of Commons. "I have nothing to offer but blood, toil, tears, and sweat."[50] To know his foe was plenty. But was it to be enough?

---

often sorry history of the British Parliament in the twentieth century, the crisis of May 1940 stands out as an hour of high honor. The very kind of political government that Hitler despised proved, for once, capable of lifting an extraordinary personage into the saddle.

[47] About this missed encounter, see below, p. 441.

[48] Churchill, *GS*, 667. (See also De Gaulle's hour below, p. 78, n. 4.)

[49] See above, p. 49.

[50] Taylor, *EH*, 475: "In a speech which combined echoes of Garibaldi and Clemenceau." No. It echoed—if that is the word—the then largely unknown George Orwell, who in an obscure little magazine (*New English Weekly*) in an incisive (and later much maligned) article on *Mein Kampf*, published on 21 March 1940 (*Orwell*, II, 14), offering certain profound truths about Hitler, wrote among other things: "Whereas Socialism, and even capitalism in a more grudging way, have said to people 'I offer you a good time,' Hitler has said to them 'I offer you struggle, danger and death,' and as a result a whole nation flings himself at his feet." Had Churchill read this article? It is difficult to tell.

# 5 . *Germany triumphant*[1]

THE EVENT OF THE GERMAN INVASION of Western Europe
at dawn on 10 May, a Friday, did not find the Allies altogether unprepared. Certain opponents of Hitler, within the Abwehr, whispered
it secretly to the Dutch military attaché for days. By Thursday night the
Belgian government knew that the Germans were about to erupt. At half
past three in the morning the bombs burst. Within a few hours the long-
prepared Allied countermove started. A Franco-British army was rolling
into Belgium in the morning. Within days and perhaps within hours, it
would meet the advancing German Army along the middle rivers of Belgium. Thus would begin the great martial confrontation, deciding the fate
of Europe and the war.

It did not happen this way. Hitler knew what the Allies were planning to do. In one long perfect stroke, he sliced them off. "Sichelschnitt,"
the cut of the sickle, his plan was called; and so it was. Drafted by Rundstedt and by Hitler himself, it called for the principal German armor to
move west of the westernmost forts of the Maginot Line,[2] driving across
the Ardennes, where the Allies least expected it to strike, debouch at the
Meuse, and once across it, race fast to the Channel coast. The Franco-
British armies that moved into Belgium would be trapped. It was a plan of
genius.

---

[1] 10 May–31 July 1940.

[2] Much maligned in retrospect. Churchill: "Properly used in the French
scheme of war, the Maginot Line would have been of immense service to
France." *GS*, 474. True. Except for one point, the Germans were unwilling to
attack the Maginot forts even when the rest of the French armies had
crumbled to near nothing. The fact that the Maginot Line had not been extended all the way to the Channel was, again, due to considerations weightier
than French parsimony or lack of foresight. Unfortunately this is not the place
to discuss these military contingencies in detail.

Gamelin, the French commander-in-chief, ran true to form. Narrow, careful, and bland, his cautious defensive spirit gave way whenever there was a chance to confront the Germans as far from the French homeland as it was possible. Already on the day of Hitler's Norway invasion he had asked his government to allow the French-British army to enter Belgium as a response of sorts. Now, a month later, he had his way. Reynaud, who had become aware of Gamelin's astonishing incapacity, had been planning to get rid of him on the very day of the German invasion of the West. Now Reynaud was stuck with Gamelin, and with much else besides.

The German armies had jumped off on a Friday. In two days they drove through the Ardennes. By Monday night they were across the Meuse, near Sedan.[3] The Dutch Army capitulated in the north. The third-rate French units around Sedan broke and ran. On Tuesday night Reynaud called Churchill: The news was ominous. Early Wednesday morning Reynaud woke up Churchill on the telephone. "We have been defeated," he said, in English. "We are beaten; we have lost the battle."

Churchill may have known Hitler. He did not know the state of the French Army. He flew over to Paris on Thursday. It was a beautiful day, calm on the surface; but in the governmental quarters and in the hearts of its officials, panic reigned. Clerks were burning the archives of the Foreign Ministry of France in the courtyard of the Quai d'Orsay; the black bits of paper fluttered across the Seine. The British party was told that there was nothing, or almost nothing, to stop the German spearheads from swooping down to Paris in a day or so. "Where is the strategic reserve?" Churchill asked Gamelin. There was none, the latter answered, with a shrug. Churchill did not give in to despair.[4] "Remarkable for his energy and vehemence," Churchill sat, "crowned like a volcano by some of his cigars"[5]; he kept telling and telling his foreign colleagues that

---

[3] Three days before the German invasion, General Huntziger, the commander of the French Second Army, told the mayor of Sedan that the Germans "will never think of attacking in the sector of Sedan. . . ." Vidalenc, 55.

[4] Nor did De Gaulle. That day was the psychic turning point of his career as the savior of France, that he felt constrained to proclaim more than a month later. It was on that sixteenth of May, somewhere in the field near Laon, that, confronted with the craven surrender of French soldiers to the triumphant Germans ("We haven't time," they had been told, "to take you prisoner."), "I felt myself borne up by a limitless fury. Ah! It's too stupid! The war is beginning as badly as it could. Therefore it must go on. For this, the world is wide. If I live, I will fight, wherever I must, as long as I must, until the enemy is defeated and the national stain washed clean. All I have managed to do since was resolved upon that day." *De Gaulle*, I, 44.

[5] *Baudouin*, 33, no friend of Churchill's.

England would go on fighting, no matter what happened. Reynaud was grateful. Churchill offered ten more fighter squadrons of the RAF for the battle of France. That was the limit: The commander of Fighter Command told Churchill that the remaining twenty-five squadrons were the absolute minimum for the defense of Britain.[6]

Most people believed at the time that in the battle of France, German air superiority was the crux. Not really: The German planes, especially their dive bombers, created panic rather than destruction. The crux was the automobilized progress of the Germans along the highroads of northern France and of the Lowlands, a progress that was so unbroken as to seem sinister. Beyond Sedan the Germans, on motorcycles, trucks, and tanks, were driving to the west. They would appear fifty, sixty miles behind what used to be called a "front." The French units would melt away; some of their soldiers would throw their rifles away. There was a bulge on the map, a German bulge, stretching and inflating westward. To the south and to the west of the bulge the movements of the French and British troops were slowed down by a new and awful obstacle: the fleeing populations.

Masses of the people of Belgium and of northern France were going to the south. Nothing like this had happened in the wars of Western Europe for centuries. From early and ominous trickles of refugees, the exodus swelled to an ocean within a month. On the fresh morning of 10 May the first British troops moving into Belgium near Courtrai saw automobiles with Jews from Amsterdam driving in the opposite direction to the south. A month later entire villages in Picardy and Normandy would be deserted by their inhabitants.[7] For a few days the exodus was relatively

---

[6] The crucial paragraph in Air Chief Marshal Dowding's letter of 16 May 1940 read: "10. I believe that, if an adequate fighter force is kept in this country, if the fleet remains in being, and if Home Forces are suitably organized for resist invasion, we should be able to carry on the war single handed for some time, if not indefinitely. But, if the Home Defence Force is drained away in desperate attempts to remedy the situation in France, defeat in France will involve the final, complete, and *irremediable* defeat of this country." The crucial word "irremediable" was slightly misspelled in the letter and corrected by Dowding in his own hand.

[7] Why did they flee? The historian, at this point, would do well to consider the important distinction between two "whys," one referring to the motives, and other to the purposes of people. (Lukacs, *HC*, Chap. IV [5], "Motives and Purposes.") It is difficult, and probably senseless, to attempt to ascertain with any degree of certainty *why* these people would leave their homes in this war, which was to pass through their villages with a speed unheard of and often with a minimum of material damage. It is much less difficult to ascertain *wherefore* they were going. The historian can trace their progress with more

orderly. Most of the Belgians left for the South in trains. After the breakthrough at Sedan the panic grew fast. All observers agree on the physiognomy of this great population movement, which flooded the highways in successive waves. First came large luxury autos, often driven by chauffeurs; then more modest cars; then incredibly old jalopies out of garages and sheds, where they had been left for years; then municipal vehicles, trucks, and fire engines, as the Germans were reputed to be drawing near. Then there was a temporary pause. For a day or so the highways would empty again. Now appeared the first swarms of cyclists, most of them boys under the military age. After them came the saddest portion of this democratic exodus, the people on foot, often pushing a cart or a baby carriage. Yet behind them plodded the heavy carts of Belgian and French peasants, piled high with mattresses, cages, bureaus, and even cupboards, pulled slowly by their heavy horses, sometimes surrounded by colts, calves, even cows. Between, behind, and around them, the troops found it difficult to move. Soon they became part and parcel of this exodus, distinguishable from the civilian masses only by their uniforms, less and less by their bearing.

Much of this was made possible by the extraordinarily fine weather. It was blue, sunny, beautiful. In May 1940 it seemed that even God favored the Germans. Reynaud recalled in his memoirs: The very beauty of the sky "seemed implacable in those tragic days." In brilliant weather the Germans drove into Brussels, the sun shone when they gave a band concert on the deserted Grand-Place on 19 May. That afternoon an extraordinary ceremony took place in Paris. The dignitaries of the agnostic Third Republic came to pray in the cool vault of Notre-Dame under a dazzling sky.

There was, at that time, a temporary sense of relief in Paris, though not in London. The German threat to Paris seemed to have passed by. They were going west, toward the Channel, unlike in 1914. Reynaud dismissed Gamelin. The new commander-in-chief was Weygand. The time was now to counterattack, to cut the long German crocodile snout burrowing westward. Here and there British and French armor were able to score the skin of the crocodile; but the counterattack, unco-ordinated as a matter of course, failed. On the evening of the twentieth, German generals stood on the cliffs of the coast. The northern Allied army was cut off. Small British and French units were driven into Boulogne and Calais, while the Germans turned to the north. The British were pulling back into Dunkirk. The Germans were less than twenty miles from Dunkirk before noon on 24 May when Hitler surprisingly ordered them

---

or less exactitude. See a few indications below, "The uprooting of peoples," especially, pp. 188–91.

to stop, a decision to which we shall return. The British had something like two extra days in which to pull back toward the sea. Their withdrawal was also helped by the brave defense of Lille by the First French Army against now increasingly superior German forces.

Like their new leader, the English people were now possessed with a sense of occasion. Their sea blood had stirred. A week before the battle at Dunkirk began, moved by their ancient instincts, they began to collect every kind of ship and boat into the harbors and ports and coves of southern England. A week later they launched them across a calm, gray Channel, on the continental side of which the German guns were bearing down. The boats and ships came first in droplets, then in spots, until their scatteration enlivened an entire stretch of the sea. In the end this national reach across the Channel proved a great and inspiring success. Instead of the one out of five hoped for, nearly four out of every five British and French soldiers around Dunkirk were rescued by a motley English armada of warships and yachts and excursion steamers and paddleboats and motorboats, as symbolic of the Britain of 1940 as had been Drake's fleet of the rising England of 1588. There were, contrary to its legend, some ugly scenes in the contracting bridgehead of Dunkirk. All of the expensive equipment of the British Army was lost. Churchill himself said that "wars are not won by evacuations." Still, Dunkirk was for the British in 1940 what the Marne had been for the French in 1914. More important than the military statistics was the lift it gave the British people in that deadly and beautiful spring. Buttercups and daffodils were in full bloom in Kent and in the parks of London that stood shining and calm. A serious people went on with their business, including cricket. The returning soldiers, dirty and weary, were impressed with the superbly English scene.[8] Few

---

[8] Some of the foreign soldiers were both impressed and amazed. I am compelled to cite a fine passage of prose now, from the wartime reminiscences of the French medieval historian Marc Bloch, who had been rescued from Dunkirk with the others: "It is not the dangers and horrors of that day (1 June) which have stuck most firmly in my memory. What comes back with especial clearness is our slow movement away from the jetty. A marvellous summer night shed its magic on the waters. The sky was pure gold, the sea a mirror; and the black, rank smoke, pouring from the burning refinery, made so lovely a pattern above the low shore-line that one was cheated into forgetting its tragic origin. Even the name painted on the stern of our vessel (*Royal Daffodil*) was like something out of an Indian fairy-tale. . . . We landed at Dover. Then came a whole day spent in travelling by train across southern England. That journey had left in my mind the memory of a sort of drugged exhaustion broken by chaotic sensations and images . . . the pleasure of devouring ham and cheese sandwiches handed through the windows by girls in multi-coloured dresses, and clergymen who looked as solemn as though they

knew that the representatives of this people had just given absolute powers to their government such as perhaps no other government had at that time, certainly not by law.[9]

Dunkirk did not inspire the French.[10] They were falling into one of their least attractive habits, their national tendency to blame others for their failures. Led by their King, the Belgians had capitulated to the Germans on the first day of the Dunkirk battle; that was bad enough. The British success at Dunkirk then filled the French with a sense of desertion and, for the first time, with a bitter kind of envy.[11] There were exceptions to this national tendency; unfortunately few among the leaders of the French Army or the Navy. Already on 25 May (and again on the twenty-ninth), Weygand presented a defeatist memorandum to Reynaud, suggesting that the British be told that the French Army might have to give up the fight. Pétain, standing in the wings, congratulated Weygand. The British leaders were beginning to feel in their bones that the French might surrender. The French people did not know this until a week later, after the Germans had crossed the Seine and the war communiqués began to include localities such as Forges-les-Eaux, which had not seen the shadow of the Germans in the 1914 war. The exodus grew into monstrous

---

were administering the Sacrament; the faint, sweet smell of cigarettes showered on us with the same generous profusion; the acid taste of lemonade and the flat taste of tea with too much milk in it; the cosy green of lawns; a landscape made up by parks, cathedral spired, hedges, and Devonshire cliffs; groups of cheering children at level-crossings. But what struck us more than anything else was the warmth of our reception. 'How genuinely kind they are!' said my companions. Towards evening we re-embarked at Plymouth, and dropped anchor at dawn off Cherbourg. We had to wait a long time in the harbour. 'You see,' said the ships' officers (French this time), 'the dock officials don't get to their offices until nine.' We were back, alas, in the rear zones of a France at war. No more cheering crowds, no more sandwiches or cigarettes. We were given, on landing, a formal, dry, rather suspicious welcome. The rest camp was an inhospitable and squalid place brightened by the presence of a few ladies belonging to the Red Cross." Bloch, 20–21.

[9] On the evening of 14 May Eden called for Local Defence Volunteers (soon they were renamed Home Guard). Within a day, 250,000 men presented themselves.

[10] One poem survives: *"Les parfums du printemps le sable les ignore: Voici mourir le mai dans les dunes du Nord."*

[11] True, in 1940 the British had sent but 10 divisions to France (they had eighty divisions there in 1918). Yet they were not willing to abandon the French. After Dunkirk more than 120,000 British troops were sent to Normandy *again* from England.

and unmanageable proportions. Weygand, at any rate, was better in constructing defeatist memoranda than the defense of France.[12] Here and
there French soldiers fought well. But leadership and organization, not to
speak of inspiration, was sadly wanting.[13] The army in the Maginot was
stationary and determined. The rest of the army fell back to the south, in
a retreat that, in retrospect, was perhaps a little more orderly and less dis-
honorable than the panic scenes in the North a month earlier. Five days
after the Germans broke south across the Somme, Mussolini declared war
on the Allies. The government left Paris. One million Parisians followed
in its wake. Shining and sad, Paris lay open to the Germans, not like the
proverbial victim of rape in tatters, rather like a beautiful middle-aged
woman in her summer clothes, deserted.[14] She was, at any rate, the sym-

---

[12] Much has been written about the Byzantine maneuverings of the French
military and political leadership before the armistice was to be decided. Less
known, but more instructive, are statements by Weygand and Pétain at the end
of the first week of June, that is, *before* the German breakthrough northwest
of Paris occurred. "Are you going on with the war?" Weygand asked
Reynaud on the sixth. "And with what, if the Paris area, which contains 70 per
cent of the war industry, is captured?" Reynaud said he would fight in Brittany or in North Africa, if necessary. He had just elevated General de Gaulle
for his undersecretary of war. On the morning of the seventh, Pétain had ap-
parently nothing more important to do than to go to Baudouin's office in order
to complain against De Gaulle. "He asked me to use my influence with the
Prime Minister to prevent him being present at our morning meetings. The
Marshal was annoyed with General de Gaulle for having put his name alone
to a book which was written on the Marshal's orders, and very largely corrected by the Marshal's own hand." *Baudouin*, 84–85 (an untruth). "The
Marshal declared that General de Gaulle has few friends in the army." This
was the same Pétain who the next day told the other ministers: "Nothing had
been done for months, or rather for years." (He certainly had done nothing.)
"Everything in this country must be started afresh." On 9 June: "England has
got us into this position. It is our duty not to put up with it, but to get out of
it." (The Germans were advised as early as November 1939 by a confidential
estimate from Spain: "If the question of peace should become more acute in
France, Pétain will play a role." *GD*, D, VIII, 414.)
[13] The "Marseillaise" was the signal on the national radio, "*Aux armes, citoyens,*
sung by an acid and nasal voice, it depresses the bravest among us." Benouville,
14.
[14] On the twelfth the shining skies over Paris were soiled in part by the smoke
of an oil refinery burning in the suburbs. Late that day an errant herd of cows,
trooping from somewhere near Auteuil, was seen crossing the elegant and now
empty Place de l'Alma. Re other scenes of Paris in these last days, see also
below, pp. 206–7, 209.

bol of Western civilization.[15] The Germans entered on the brilliant morning of 14 June, somewhat self-consciously, impressing themselves and their new captives with marches and music down the deserted avenues. In the working-class districts many people greeted them with curiosity and relief.[16]

Hitler was well aware of the extent of the French collapse. On the morrow of the fall of Paris he ordered Lieutenant Colonel Boehme on his staff to prepare a text for an armistice. Two days later Hitler himself revised this draft, which called originally for the total occupation of France. A portion of France would remain unoccupied. One must divide France from Britain, Hitler said, and give her a "golden bridge" for a way out. What Hitler would call a golden bridge was, in reality, a cul-de-sac, a sordid little passage behind a wall. The French had no desire to be pressed against the wall; and in the cul-de-sac many of them, including politicians, could gather. By that time—17 June—their government had cracked. It had gone from Paris to Tours, then to Bordeaux on the fifteenth. There the cabinet accepted a sly proposal by the politician Chautemps to merely ascertain the German terms for an armistice and then see whether they were unacceptable or not. The following night Reynaud, having lost the confidence of the majority of his colleagues, resigned from power. Pétain was the new head of the government. Next morning he said on the national radio, in an unfortunate phrase, "Fighting must come to an end." (*Il faut cesser le combat.*) This signified how all was over, even though the armistice would not be signed for another five days.

Four times during the battle of France Churchill had flown over to encourage the government of his ally. He and Reynaud agreed to carry on the fight in Brittany or in North Africa, it mattered little where. But Reynaud, unlike Churchill, had to face not only the mounting hostility of his colleagues; he also knew that the departure of the French government to Algeria would be held by many French people as a kind of desertion. A last-moment appeal to President Roosevelt failed; the latter could not yet commit the United States to war. There occurred the last dramatic move. Shortly after noon on 16 June London broadcast to France, and to the world, an extraordinary proposal. It was a Declaration of Union between Great Britain and France. "The two Governments declare that France and Great Britain shall no longer be two nations, but one Franco-British Union. . . . Every citizen of France will enjoy immediate citizenship of Great Britain; every British subject will become a citizen of France." It

---

[15] To certain people, across the Continent, the fall of Paris meant the end of a life worth living. They, including a distant relative of this author, now took the supreme act of despair. Few Parisians acted thus. Among them was the great surgeon Thierry de Martel.

[16] See below, pp. 218, 395.

was a breathtaking move, even though it was undertaken as a last-minute measure.[17] One is entitled to speculate what the existence of such a Franco-British Union would have meant for the sake of a united Western Europe after the war.[18] It is interesting to note that one of its prime promoters was none other than General de Gaulle. His figure had attracted Churchill's eye[19] days before others noticed the importance of his presence. De Gaulle personally telephoned the draft to Reynaud. But the Pétain party—indeed, the majority of the French Cabinet—reacted to it with contempt and ridicule. They saw in it a desperate and selfish British act, nothing else.

To the emotions as well as to the purposes of the pro-armistice party, Anglophobia was now the key. They would have accepted almost anything Hitler was about to propose. The latter, for once, showed a remarkable diplomatic talent. His terms were hard, triumphant, but not impossible.[20] He would leave two fifths of France, containing more than one third of her population, unoccupied. The powerful and untouched French fleet would not have to be surrendered to the victors as long as it remained immobilized in French harbors, under their watchful eyes. Churchill would not get away with the French fleet. Hitler knew that this was the main concern of the British.[21] In the second round of their great duel, Hitler had bested Churchill again.

Here and there the French were still fighting. The cadets of Saumur made a fine stand at one of the bridges across the Loire. Some units in the Maginot refused to surrender until more than a week after the armistice. De Gaulle, surrounded by suspicion in Bordeaux, flew off to London in a small plane; as Churchill put it, "he carried with himself the honor of

---

[17] In the British Cabinet, Churchill said "that his first instinct had been against the idea, but in this grave crisis we must not let ourselves be accused of a lack of imagination. Some dramatic announcement was clearly necessary to keep the French going. . . ." Woodward, I, 279.

[18] See below, pp. 490–91.

[19] "Here is the Constable of France." Churchill, *FH*, 215. A perfect phrase, however, ten days earlier, Pétain had complained to Spears about De Gaulle: "Vain, ungrateful, he has few friends in the Army." "They called him 'Le Connétable,' at St. Cyr." Spears, II, 85.

[20] The British ambassador, Sir Ronald Campbell, on 22 June called them "diabolically clever." FO 371 (C 7375/7362/17).

[21] At 1:30 P.M. on that momentous day of 16 June Halifax instructed the British ambassador to tell the French that they may be released from their obligation not to inquire for separate terms "on the sole understanding that the French fleet is at once brought to English ports pending the negotiations." This instruction was overtaken by events later that day. On 18 June Hitler said to Mussolini that prudence made him let the French have some hopes about their fleet. "Once we will have defeated England, we'll see."

France." On the afternoon of 18 June—the day of Churchill's "finest hour" speech[22] De Gaulle, completely alone, sat down before a microphone in Studio B-2 of the British Broadcasting Corporation. "The flame of French resistance cannot go out," he said. "It will not go out." "France has lost a battle. She has not lost the war." He, too, felt as if he were walking with Destiny, and that all of his past life had been but a preparation for this hour and for this trial. It was a milestone in the history of two great nations. On this day of 18 June in 1940, did Churchill and De Gaulle recall that it was also the 125th anniversary of the Battle of Waterloo? of Waterloo, which was the end rather than the beginning of that great central chapter of the history of the Modern Age when France and Britain had been the two greatest powers in the world. Already at Waterloo Blucher's German Army tipped the balance—a fact often forgotten not only by the British but also by the French, who preferred to think that they were defeated by the British, not by the Germans. Ever since Waterloo, Germany had grown and France declined. In June 1940 came the terrible summation of this.

On 22 June a sad and dispirited French delegation signed Hitler's armistice in the clearing of the forest of Compiègne, in the same restaurant car in which the Germans had signed their defeat at the end of the First World War. Hitler ordered that the monument to 1918 be destroyed (and that the monument to Marshal Foch be kept standing). The famous carriage WL 2519 was taken to Berlin. Hitler had triumphed as never before.[23]

---

[22] See below, pp. 97–98

[23] Here is a mystery. The newsreel film of the French armistice shows Hitler dancing a kind of silly little jig as he walks through that clearing. Like Nero's fiddle, or the Emperor's itch, that jig has since entered the history books, and the iconographic memory of the world. Literally out of step with Hitler's character, this writer wondered about it for some time. Years later came the sorry confirmation of his doubts. The film was (and is) faked. A Canadian propaganda official and film technician, John Grierson, "looped" the frames of the film: and one high step was thus jerked into a veritable little jig. The "story" of this falsification was recounted with evident satisfaction by Laurence Stallings, an American film propagandist, in the October 1958 number of *Esquire*. So much for the newsreel as an invaluable "documentary" source of history.

The mystery is compounded, however, by the published records of witnesses. William Shirer was such an eyewitness. In *Berlin Diary*, an American best seller in 1941, he described how he saw Hitler dance at Compiègne. (Did he see the movie?) But then there is that supremely honest and tragic figure, Friedrich Reck-Malleczewen, a bitter aristocratic enemy of the Nazis, who re-

It is at points such as this that the historian, feeling responsible for the truthfulness rather than for the effectiveness of his narrative, faces great difficulties in reconstructing a picture of the past. How did the rest of Europe react to these astonishing events? One hundred and twenty-five years before, only a small minority among the peoples of Europe heard of Waterloo. Millions of them had not known the name of Napoleon, let alone that of Wellington. Now, in 1940, the vast majority read some kind of newspaper, while increasing numbers of them could listen to the radio. All of them knew the name of Hitler, probably even that of Churchill. But what did they think? And who were they, this majority of Europe? In more than one way there was no such thing as Europe. What did a Bulgarian peasant and a Swedish accountant have in common? Still we can establish certain generalizations. The peoples of Europe were stunned by these enormous events. It was their governments that reacted quickly, in order to adjust themselves to the new continental order that was suddenly taking shape.

One example was that of Italy. All evidence shows that most Italians did not want war, whereas Mussolini wanted it. As early as on 13 May he saw how the campaign in France was going. He told Ciano: "Some months ago I said that the Allies had lost the victory. Today I tell you that they have lost the war. We Italians are already sufficiently dishonored. Any delay is inconceivable. We have no time to lose. Within a month I shall declare war." He was as good as his word. Unfortunately for him, his word was not enough. He brought Italy into the war unprepared in almost every sense. What he did not realize was that his entry into the war was to reduce Italy's importance in Europe, even before her military incapacities would reduce her prestige and power

---

corded in his diary: "October 1940 . . . in a Berlin movie theater recently, I saw the newsreel in which Hitler, standing in front of the historic railway car in the Forest of Compiègne, receives the news of the capitulation of France; and then begins to dance on one foot, like an Indian . . ." (Reck-Malleczewen, 79). Were the Germans so stupid as to show the American version of the newsreel? (There were American newsmen at Compiègne.) Are there two versions of the film? Has Reck-Malleczewen's diary been tampered with? Did Hitler dance a little jig, after all?

In any event, a film *was* taken. My desultory inquiries on this topic, greatly assisted by the researches of John Toland, suggest that the film, by the German cameraman Walter Frentz, was made at Bruly-le-Pêche, Hitler's headquarters, early on the seventeenth, when the news of the French request for an armistice first reached him. (Another, similar, frame may have been taken on the morning of the eighteenth when Hitler's special train stopped somewhere in the Black Forest on the way from Bruly to Munich.)

further.[24] Mussolini, this senior Fascist and revolutionary, had become a junior partner of the Third Reich, nothing else.

The governments of most other European states reacted more cautiously but in a similar fashion. Franco was pleased that his ambassador to France had been asked by Pétain to be the intermediary between the new French government and the Germans. Now German infantry was parading at the frontier station where the western Pyrenees touched the sea. On the day of the French armistice, Franco and his incompetent and glib brother-in-law, Serrano Suner (he was to be elevated to Foreign Minister in October), saw both the British and the American ambassadors to Madrid. To the latter Franco gave the impression of being pleased with the prospects of a German victory; to the former, he said that he could not understand why the British would fight on. Within a month Franco raised the cry of ¡*Gibraltar!* for Spain. The Romanians, with their customary opportunism, were the quickest to adjust. Each one hundred miles of the Germans' triumphant progress in France meant the change of yet another member of the Bucharest cabinet. By the end of June Stalin yanked Bessarabia from Romania. Within a few days the King and the government hastened to assure Hitler of their utmost goodwill. They felt it necessary to demonstrate this publicly by kicking the few remaining British representatives around. The traditional Francophilia of Bucharest society disappeared with hardly a trace. Among the remaining neutrals, Sweden felt compelled to depart from her traditional neutrality and grant the German Army limited rights of passage in Swedish trains through Swedish territory. The President of Switzerland on 25 June said that his people ought to "adjust themselves" to the new realities of Europe. Of the traditionally neutral states, only Portugal and Eire, on the edges of Europe, continued their course largely unchanged.[25]

Deeper than these diplomatic movements ran the German tide. Many people in Europe began to see in the German triumphs the shape of a new Europe, national and socialist, to which they were adjusting their ideas.

---

[24] The Italian military sensed this. They treated the French armistice delegation with exceptional courtesy. (At any rate, the occupation zone allotted to Italy was small, hardly over 800 square kilometers, including less than thirty thousand inhabitants in the town of Menton.) One example of craven cruelty on the part of the otherwise more or less humane Italians must be recorded, however. During the last week of the campaign in France, their pilots took their pleasure in bombing undefended towns and bridges that were laden with refugees, in the valley of the Loire.

[25] As early as July 1940, Salazar of Portugal kept warning Franco against betting too much on Hitler. This was a serious and effective contribution to the British cause.

We shall deal with these ideological movements in the second part of this book in greater detail. Here we must only say that, had they been more tactful and provident, the Germans in the summer of 1940 could have grasped an obvious opportunity. For not only revolutionaries and radicals and opportunists but also all kinds of conservatives and even some democrats and socialists were ready to come to terms with the new order in Europe. The states of Western Europe were on the verge of profound political transformations. The Danish and the Norwegian parliaments were ready to collaborate. In early July a number of Dutch refugee political figures returned to Holland, where they formed a conservative movement of national union. The Belgian exile government that had at first disavowed the capitulation by their King now was in complete disarray, some of its members being ready to return to Belgium and form a chastened government of collaboration. Pétain and the French political crowd, setting up their quarters in Vichy, proclaimed their authoritarian course for a new and "national" France. Slowly, gradually, the peoples followed their governments. All of those who attempted to record, and later to reconstruct, the state of public opinion and of popular sentiment in the summer of 1940, agree: The majority of the peoples of Western Europe were willing to adjust their thoughts to the new order of things, and to embark on some kind of political collaboration with the Third Reich—with what it was, and with what it seemed to represent. So they had to adjust their clocks and watches. German time had been introduced in Western Europe. *L'heure allemande* had come to stay.

Europe now lay before the Germans' feet. Their management of the war had been supreme.[26] Hitler's realism was impressive.[27] He did not want to fight the English. He had an ambiguous love-hate—or, rather, respect-contempt—feeling toward them (very German, that). In the summer of 1940 his respect was greater than his contempt. Also, he did

---

[26] In May 1940 German military production amounted to less than 15 per cent of the industrial production of the Third Reich. They produced less than forty tanks each month (in 1944 they would produce more than two thousand monthly). Their six-week campaign and conquest of all of Western Europe cost them twenty-seven thousand dead, less than many a day's loss during the 1914–18 war.

[27] Gide, on 7 July 1940, ". . . perfidious, cynical if you wish, but here again he acted with a sort of genius." "His great cynical strength consisted in not deigning to take account of any token values, but only of realities. . . . He has never taken any but others in with fine words. One may well hate him, but he most decidedly has to be taken into account." Gide, II, 256, 257.

not want to rule the world. Unlike the Kaiser,[28] Hitler did not want a world war. He wanted to make the English quit the war either through persuasion or through force. He wanted to make them see the light which, in his eyes, amounted to the recognition that he had no wish to reduce, or even diminish, the British Empire. He did not understand why the English, and especially Churchill, all of their insularity notwithstanding, would not accept the German domination of Europe. They would have to listen to his terms which, in essence, meant the acceptance of his will. He sincerely thought that his terms were, or that they would be, generous, for England, and that the English ought to respond. In this he was quite wrong. He thought that the English did not understand him. In reality, he did not understand them.

They had not been ready to consider his terms after he conquered Poland; they ought to be ready to consider his terms now, after he had conquered France. He suggested this to them even before France fell, during the campaign. He did not attack England from the air. He let the British Army withdraw from the Continent to England. Here is a crucial episode in the history of the Second World War. Why did Hitler order the German armor to stop before crossing the canal line south of Dunkirk in the morning of 24 May? Military and political historians have tried to discuss, and sometimes to dismiss, the purposes of this decision. The accepted view, according to which he and General Rundstedt (who was close to Hitler at that time) grew suddenly anxious about the wear and tear of the German armored divisions near Dunkirk, may be right. Yet Hitler, so often voluble, was also a very secretive man, and there are at least some reasons to believe that he had another purpose in mind: a signal to the English that they could withdraw from the Continent and then make peace with him on that basis.[29] At a crucial moment it seemed to him that the English *were* withdrawing from the Continent and, perhaps, from the war. During the night (at 3 A.M.) of 23–24 May, the War Office ordered the evacuation of Calais "in principle." A few hours before, the last British troops had sailed from Boulogne, leaving the French garrison behind. In the morning hours of the twenty-fourth the

---

[28] The aged Kaiser, Wilhelm II, exiled in Holland since 1918, lived to see German soldiers arrive in May 1940. Churchill had offered him a refuge in England. Wilhelm refused to move. He showed no trace of sympathy for the tribulations of his hosts the Dutch, now under German rule. He died a year later.

[29] Halder, *KTB*, I, 308, entry of 25 May 1940: "Hitler: We seek contact with England on the basis of dividing the world. Jodl: The English could have peace (they must return some colonies.)" Did some of this filter through to Churchill and Halifax by 27–28 May? See below, pp. 95–97.

large vessel *City of Canterbury*, full of soldiers and equipment, was moving off the shell-spattered dock of Calais for England, before the eyes of the dismayed French. The Germans could see much of this, and they could read some of the War Office signals. That morning Hitler issued his order to halt before Dunkirk. Is it not possible that, for a moment, the general pattern was crystallizing before his eyes? The British were leaving the Continent. Let them have a chance to leave. Military and other historians dealing with the Dunkirk story have not considered the impression that the British evacuation not only of Boulogne but also of Calais (which was countermanded by Churchill a day or so later) may have made on Hitler's mind at that precise time. "Churchill," Hitler said on 26 February 1945 to his closest confidants, "was quite unable to appreciate the sporting spirit of which I had given proof by refraining from creating an irreparable breach between the British and ourselves. We did, indeed, refrain from annihilating them at Dunkirk."[30] There follows a sentence that suggests that at the edge of his abyss in 1945, in retrospect, Hitler regretted not that he had been more forceful but that he had not been more generous, that he had not made even more definite offers to the English in 1940: "We ought to have been able to make them realize that the acceptance by them of the German hegemony in Europe, a state of affairs to the implementation of which they had always been opposed, but which I had implemented without any trouble, would bring them inestimable advantages."

While the last phase of the campaign in France brought triumph after triumph, Hitler made statement after statement, privately and publicly,[31] about his wish to terminate the war with England. When France surrendered, the German people were stunned nearly as much as their victims. Many people, including foreign observers, noted the impassivity of the people in Berlin, in contrast with their jubilations during the 1914 war. Pleased as he was with his military and diplomatic success—for he was not at all eager to pursue the French to North

---

[30] *Hitler-Bormann*, 96. Here is the sequence of events: 24 May, 3 A.M.: The War Office orders evacuation of Calais "in principle." 8–9 A.M.: The largest vessel, *City of Canterbury*, leaves Calais. (Another ship, the *Kohistan*, sails before noon. British destroy some of their tanks on the quays.) 11:42 A.M.: Hitler's order to halt before Dunkirk. 11:23 P.M.: Uninspiring War Office order to British commander in Calais to fight on. (Churchill irritated with text.) 25 May, 2 P.M. and 9 P.M.: Eden and Churchill order the Calais garrison to fight till the end.

[31] His most significant public statements may be found in his interview given to the American isolationist journalist Karl von Wiegand on 13 June, printed in the New York *Journal-American* (a Hearst paper) the next day.

Africa[32]—Hitler waited for a signal from London. On the night of 24–25 June he spoke again to his closest circle: "The war in the West is over. France has been defeated, with England I shall reach an understanding very shortly (*in kuerzester Frist*). There will remain our settling of our accounts with the East. But that is a task that opens global problems, such as the relationship with Japan and the balance of power in the Pacific, problems that we may not be able to tackle perhaps before ten years, perhaps I'll have to leave that to my successor. Now we'll have our hands full for years, to digest and consolidate what we have achieved in Europe."[33] This was exactly what Hitler wanted to tell the English, too; and there is some reason to think that he wanted to have such a statement "leak" through to London.[34] London did not respond, though, as we shall soon see, Churchill was not above letting Hitler hope—a little.

Hitler now waited—a little. This was not altogether in harmony with his character. He sought this harmony. He went off to visit some of the battlefields where he had served during the First World War. He made a strange, furtive, and restless visit to a Paris washed by the rising sunlight of a summer dawn, surrounded by those who were closest to him, including Speer and the sculptor Arno Breker.[35] He canceled the plan for a mass attack, by 220 German bombers, on Southampton. He disappointed his Italian allies by his reiterated wish to make peace with the English.[36]

---

[32] Hitler to Mussolini on 18 June: (We) must proceed "in such a way as to secure if possible a French government functioning on French territory. . . . This would be far preferable to a situation in which the French Government might reject the German proposals, and then flee . . . to continue the war. . . ." On 30 June Halder noted in his diary the general relief in the German headquarters because the French colonies were acquiescing in the surrender. So much for the argument that Pétain saved what had remained of France, and her colonies, from the conqueror. The conqueror got what he wanted.

[33] Boehme, 79.

[34] There is, in this respect, an interesting discrepancy between two of his statements in June. On 2 June he said that he hoped that Britain would be ready for "a reasonable peace settlement," after which his hands would be free for his "great and principal task: the settling of accounts with Bolshevism." It is possible that by 24 June Hitler may have realized that the prospect of a German attack on Russia would encourage Churchill to keep on fighting Germany. He, Hitler, now wanted to rob Churchill of the hope of a German war with Russia.

[35] Hitler astonished them with his detailed knowledge of the architectual details of the Paris Opera, surprising the dignified French functionary who had been corraled to guide them through the building.

[36] "What does Germany want now, peace or war?" Ciano asked Ribbentrop on 18 June. Ribbentrop, who had said to him "War" ten months earlier, now answered, without a moment of hesitation: "Peace." Ciano, *EVC*, 562–63.

Now that Italy had come into the war Mussolini felt that peace could come only at the cost of Italian prestige. (As Churchill remarked in his memoirs, the Duce need not have fretted himself. Soon he was to get all the war he wanted.) Hitler did not return to Berlin until 6 July, three weeks after the French had asked for an armistice. He planned to make a great political speech on the eighth. Not having heard from London, he postponed this to the nineteenth. He thought, at first, that Churchill would follow Reynaud—the warmonger stepping down. On 13 July he repeated his usual argument to his chief of staff: He, Hitler, was "greatly puzzled by Britain's persistent unwillingness to make peace. He sees the answer (as we do) in Britain's hope in Russia,[37] and therefore counts on having to compel her by main force to agree to peace. Actually that is much against his grain."[38] Six days later, Hitler made his speech in Berlin. Publicly and loudly and tactlessly he "offered" a last chance of peace to the British Empire. "Tonight," said Goebbels excitedly to his collaborators, "the fate of England will be decided."[39] Goebbels even speculated that Churchill would now resign. But this kind of speculation was almost devoid of substance.[40]

Meanwhile, Hitler had ordered a plan for the invasion of England. His directive (No. 16) was made ready three days before his grandiose speech. This does not mean that his offer of peace was not genuine—genuine, that is, according to his ways. He had to have an alternative: if his diplomacy would not persuade the English to quit the war, he would have to persuade them by the force of arms. Yet he was reluctant. The wording of Directive No. 16—"Operation Sea Lion"[41]—reflects this. "Since England, in spite of her hopeless military situation, shows no signs of being ready to come to an understanding, I have decided to prepare a landing operation against England *and, if necessary, to carry it out.*" This was a succinct and accurate reflection of Hitler's mind. The italics are mine. "If necessary": he hoped that it would not have to come to this.

---

[37] The British official historian Sir J. R. M. Butler, *GS*, II, 536, calls this an "absurd theory." Why?

[38] "The reason is that a military defeat of Britain will bring about the disintegration of the British Empire. This would not be of any benefit to Germany. German blood would be shed to accomplish something that would benefit only Japan, the United States, and others."

[39] Boelcke, 430.

[40] Almost, though not quite. The British ambassador to Washington (Lord Lothian) seems to have been impressed by the German peace proposals, while Churchill and Halifax were not.

[41] *Seeloewe*, in German, is a large seal, not a particularly fierce beast.

He was already thinking of something else: of invading and defeating Russia, after which England would be deprived of her last hopes of finding somebody who would count against him on the Continent. Two days after his speech, on 21 July, when it had become evident that the English would not respond, he told his staff that England would come to terms when Russia was no longer a threat to Germany. He now ordered them to prepare the initial plans for a war against Russia, a decision to which we shall return.

I thought it necessary, a few pages before, to give the reader a glimpse, from contemporary reminiscences, of the splendid indifference with which the British people regarded (or, perhaps, did not wish to regard) their mortal dangers during the days of Dunkirk. In the second part of this book I shall return, once more, to a brief view of their national mentality at that time. On 28 May, when the situation at Dunkirk still looked very dark, Churchill made a brief statement in the House of Commons, after which he met his ministerial colleagues—the so-called Outer Cabinet—in his room. Among other things, he said to them, "quite casually, and not treating it as a point of special significance: 'Of course, whatever happens at Dunkirk, we shall fight on.'" "There occurred a demonstration which, considering the character of the gathering—twenty-five experienced politicians and Parliament men, who represented all the different points of view, whether right or wrong, before the war—surprised me. Quite a number seemed to jump up from the table and come running to my chair, shouting and patting me on the back. . . . I was sure that every Minister was ready to be killed quite soon, and have all his family and possessions destroyed, rather than give in. In this they represented the House of Commons and almost all the people. . . . There was a white glow, overpowering, sublime, which ran through our island from end to end."[42]

We must nonetheless qualify this picture, no matter how correct it was (or, rather, turned out to be) in its great general lines. Churchill's position was not as strong at that time as it was soon to be (and, consequently, as it soon was to seem in retrospect). He had, after all, become Prime Minister as a kind of last resort. Many politicians in Britain, including the American ambassador, Kennedy, still distrusted him, even though the former, true to the British national tradition of self-discipline, kept their thoughts within themselves.[43] We must not forget that for a

---

[42] Churchill, *FH*, 100.

[43] Throughout May and June, for example, when Churchill entered the House he was cheered mostly by members from the Labor side, while many of the former Chamberlainites were sitting on their hands. The restrained nature of

long time Churchill's reputation included elements such as impetuosity, recklessness, and grandiloquence. What if these very elements would bring Britain swiftly to disaster? Then people could say that the champion for extreme war had his chance and failed. This was what Hitler hoped for. It was not beyond the bounds of possibility.

On 26 and 27 May (that is, before the Outer Cabinet meeting so well recorded by Churchill), this profound issue came into the open—into the closed open of the discussions of the five-member inner War Cabinet. There appeared a chink in the armor of British resolution—a superficially small, but significant, divergence between Halifax and Churchill. Sunday, 26 May, was a busy day. Reynaud had come to London in distress and despair. He wanted to convince the British of the necessity to bribe the Italians—to offer territories to them—to keep them out of the war. The Cabinet was rightly against this. But behind it there lurked a more important issue. Not only Reynaud but Halifax and Chamberlain (he was still an important member of the War Cabinet) thought that Mussolini might be willing to mediate between Hitler and the Allies at this point. The previous evening Halifax had talked with the Italian ambassador, Bastianini, telling him that the British government was not averse to considering a settlement of peace and security for Europe, and "we should naturally be prepared to consider any proposals which might lead to this, provided our liberty and independence was assured."[44] Churchill thought that there was little or nothing to be gained by approaches to Mussolini. He told this to Reynaud. At 3 P.M., Reynaud left. There now ensued a discussion within the closed War Cabinet, of momentous significance in retrospect.[45] Churchill would fight. "We were in a different position from France . . . we still had powers of resistance and attack, which they had not. . . . If France could not defend herself, it was better that she should get out of the war rather than that she drag us into a settlement which involved intolerable terms." Halifax "was not quite convinced that the Prime Minister's diagnosis was correct and that it was in Herr Hitler's interest to insist on outrageous terms." There was an underlying strain in the debate between Churchill and Halifax. The latter "thought that if we

---

kind of support by the governmental party was noticed by foreign diplomats in the galleries until, in early July, this was brought to Chamberlain's attention; Chamberlain then instructed his friend the Whip to put an end to these attitudes.

[44] Woodward, I, 198.

[45] The minutes are full of hidden intimations of conflict. Their deep and secret and decisive nature are suggested by the remark of the recording secretary on the original sheets: "This record does not cover the first quarter of an hour of the discussion, during which the Secretary was not present." Cab. 65-13 WM (40), 140th Conclusions.

got to the point of discussing the terms of a general settlement and found that we could obtain terms which did not postulate the destruction of our independence, we should be foolish if we did not accept them."[46] In the end the Cabinet ministers agreed to discuss a draft of a message to Mussolini the next day; they went back to see Reynaud again.

This was perhaps the most dangerous juncture in the political life of the new Prime Minister. Alexander Cadogan, an accurate weathervane, recorded later that day in his diary (he had been in the discussion with Reynaud): "Settled nothing much. W.S.C. too rambling and romantic and sentimental and temperamental. Old Neville still the best of the lot." During the night Churchill's resolve strengthened. The crunch—if that is the word—came the next day. There were two Cabinets. The one in the afternoon was decisive. Churchill was strong against the approach to Italy.

> At the moment our prestige in Europe was very low. The only way we could get it back was by showing the world that Germany had not beaten us. If, after two or three months, we could show that we were still unbeaten, our prestige would return. Even if we were beaten, we should be no worse off than we should be if we were now to abandon the struggle. Let us therefore avoid being dragged down the slippery slope with France. The whole of this manoeuvre was intended to get us so deeply involved in negotiations that we should be unable to turn back. . . . The approach proposed was not only futile, but involved us in a deadly danger.[47]

But Halifax demurred. He tried to remind Churchill that the day before "if he was satisfied that matters vital to the independence of this country were unaffected, he would be prepared to discuss terms. . . . On the present occasion, however, the Prime Minister seemed to suggest that under no conditions would we contemplate any course except fighting to a finish." Churchill brushed this aside.[48] The Cabinet was over. Halifax told Cadogan: "I can't work with Winston any longer."[49] Cadogan told him to keep cool. Halifax and Churchill took a stroll in the garden. What Churchill told Halifax during their walk we don't know. It appears that he charmed Halifax though he did not convince him, a condition of

[46] Ibid.
[47] Cab. 65-13 WM (40), 142nd Conclusions. Confidential Annex.
[48] The issue "was quite unreal and was most unlikely to arise. If Herr Hitler was prepared to make peace on the terms of the restoration of German colonies and the overlordship of Central Europe, that was one thing. But it was quite unlikely that he would make any such offer." Ibid.
[49] *Cadogan,* 291.

which the entry in Halifax's diary for this momentous day is the evidence.[50]

Of course Churchill was absolutely right. In a few days the success at Dunkirk made his position stronger. In the end he had his way. Yet it must not be thought that he was without opposition, even though little of this filters through in retrospect. Decades later Lord Normanbrook felt compelled to record some of it.[51] Lloyd George kept telling people that Churchill was wrong in assessing Hitler as a guttersnipe when, to the contrary, Hitler was one of the greatest figures in European history, greater even than Napoleon. When France fell there was an underground tremor of shock going through Britain, even as the surface discipline of the people continued unbroken. Again there emerged a significant difference between Churchill and Halifax, which was noted by the Swedish minister to London, on that darkest of days, 17 June.[52] Next day Churchill made his "finest hour" speech, so famous ever since.[53] Contemporaries recorded

---

[50] "At Cabinet we had a long and rather confused discussion about, *nominally* [my italics], the approach to Italy, but also largely about general policy in the event of things going really badly in France. I thought Winston talked the most frightful rot, also Greenwood, and after bearing it for some time I said exactly what I thought of them, adding that, if that was really their view, and if it came to the point, our ways must separate. . . . I despair when [Churchill] works himself up into a passion of emotion when he ought to make his brain think and reason." Birkenhead, *Halifax*, 458.

[51] "Within Britain there was confusion and perplexity, and in some quarters morale was brittle." *Action This Day*, 18.

[52] That day R. A. Butler of the Foreign Office told the Swedish minister that "No opportunity would be neglected for concluding a compromise peace if the chance offered on reasonable conditions . . . the so-called diehards would not be allowed to stand in the way of negotiations." Halifax, through Butler, let the Swedish minister know that "common sense and not bravado would dictate the British Government's policy." Woodward, I, 204, note. Did Churchill know of this? The Swedish government believed that sooner or later Churchill would fall and Halifax might form a new government. On 18 June the Italian minister to Stockholm reported to Rome that the British minister had asked for an audience from the Foreign Minister of Sweden and declared that the London government was ready (*é disposto*) "to discuss peace." *DDI*, IX, V, 37. Fransoni, having first ascertained that this was no mere rumor, three days later clarified his dispatch: The statement referred to was made in London, not in Stockholm. Ibid., 61.

[53] He had spoken the previous day, too. King, 55 (18 June): "Last night the papers all sent representatives to the F.O. to hear the official reaction to the French collapse. They were given a more or less colourless handout, and so they asked when the P.M. would speak. They were told not till this afternoon. So they pressed very strongly that it was imperative that Churchill should say

that these phrases had fallen flat that day.[54] Yet this crisis of 17–18 June, like that of 26–27 May, passed, too; and in a few days Churchill felt as confident as ever.

He came through because of the trust of his friends, the people of Britain, and, in a way, because of the hopes of his enemy Hitler. Many exemplary evidences of the former survive, but perhaps it is interesting to record how different people would think about the same things in the same words. An admirable Englishwoman, Miss Vere Hodgson, wrote in her diary during the critical days of the French collapse that Londoners at this time were "rather like a quarrelsome family faced by a death in the house; and reunited by it."[55] George Orwell, surely unaware of Miss Hodgson's private little copybook, wrote down the very same thing a month or so later: The English were like a family, with many skeletons in the closet, but united in trouble[56]: Churchill felt this in his bones. It led not only to his unexampled mastery of national leadership but also that of his statesmanship at the time. This is especially remarkable because Churchill was seldom a great diplomatist. Yet during the crucial month after the fall of France he outfoxed Hitler. He knew that Hitler was hesitant to attack the island immediately. He knew that, in order to ready the island's defenses, the British desperately needed time. Consequently there are some indications that Churchill was not above suggesting that, under certain conditions, the British might negotiate, though not from weakness. Perhaps this explains his offer to Lloyd George to enter the Cabinet in early June, which Lloyd George refused. Churchill renewed the offer on 19 June.[57] He knew that Hitler knew that Lloyd George had a high opinion of Hitler. Also, Churchill did not altogether forbid the British envoys in Sweden and Switzerland (especially the excellent Sir David

---

something to the nation last night. The result—broadcast all over the world—including North America—was a few stumbling sentences to the effect that the situation was disastrous, but all right. Whether he was drunk or all-in from sheer fatigue, I don't know, but it was the poorest possible effort. . . ."

[54] The speech was rebroadcast that night. Nicolson, 19 June: "How I wish Winston would not talk on the wireless unless he is feeling in good form. He hates the microphone, and when we bullied him into speaking last night, he just sulked and read his House of Commons speech over again. Now, as delivered in the H. of C., that speech was magnificent, especially the concluding sentences. But it sounded ghastly on the wireless. All the great vigour he put into it seemed to evaporate."

[55] Cited by Mosley, *Back*, 55.

[56] In *The Lion and the Unicorn*, first published in February 1941. *Orwell*, II, 68.

[57] The offer was suggested to Lloyd George's wife through Churchill's close junior friend Brendan Bracken. Lloyd George, F., 264.

Kelly in the latter country) to listen to selected German emissaries who were offering contacts. To listen; nothing else. When, after a month of lull, Hitler broadcast his grand peace offer to the British Empire on 19 July, Churchill did not deign to answer. It fell to Halifax to refuse Hitler's offer unconditionally. From then on all important divergences between Halifax and Churchill were gone.[58]

Churchill did not succeed in everything, of course. He failed, after the collapse of France, to convince and suborn and bribe French officials in North Africa with sufficient success so that they would gather into a kernel of a combatant French government in that part of the world.[59] He failed to establish a propitious contact with Stalin. Yet above all of these matters rose the impression of his resolution. On 3 July 1940, in one of the most tragic episodes of the Last European War, British warships attacked and sank a group of French battleships in Oran (Mers-el-Kebir) after the latter had refused to sail to Britain or to the United States. The Anglophobes of Pétain's circle frothed with impotent anger, but they counted little.[60] What counted was the impression across Europe, including on men such as Ciano and Mussolini. "For the moment," Ciano wrote in his diary on 4 July, this event proves "that the fighting spirit of His British Majesty's fleet is quite alive, and still had the aggressive ruthlessness of the captains and pirates of the seventeenth century." This was already a long way from what Mussolini had thought and said but a few months earlier, that the British were of a last line of tired old men. Hitler was impressed. So was Roosevelt. British resolution was more

---

[58] There was a flurry in Washington where the British ambassador (Lord Lothian) was willing to listen to intermediaries, see above, p. 93, n. 40. Another flurry involved the Duke of Windsor in Lisbon. He was about to go to the Bahamas. German agents as well as Franco tried to dissuade him, at first with some success. To one intermediary Windsor "paid tribute to the Fuehrer's desire for peace . . . he was convinced that if he had been King it would not have come to war." *GD*, D, X, 398; *DDI*, IX, V, 311. At this point Churchill's former friendship with Windsor was instrumental. Churchill sent a common friend (Sir Walter Monckton) to Lisbon. The duke shut his mouth and departed for the tropics.

[59] Those French politicians who were inclined to continue the struggle against Hitler from North Africa were brought back to France and imprisoned by the Pétain government.

[60] Contrary to the general impression, Churchill agreed to the attack on the French with a heavy heart. Taylor, *Beaverbrook*, 438. The French attempted to show their revenge for this attack by their recent ally by dropping a few bombs on Gibraltar. Five days after Oran their battleship *Richelieu* was again attacked by British torpedoes, but without success.

impressive than British strength: In mid-July there were still only four fully equipped divisions, and less than 350 workable tanks on the entire island. Behind Britain, however, rose the United States, against which Hitler could do little.

Hitler's carefully prepared public statements and interviews in favor of the Monroe Doctrine ("America for the Americans; Europe for the Europeans") found no echoes in the United States. The agencies of the Third Reich supported isolationist politicans in America, with limited effect. The convention of the Republican party met in Philadelphia during the very days of the French capitulation; its isolationist elements failed to carry the day. The convention nominated Wendell Willkie, whose inclinations in foreign policy were not unsimilar to Roosevelt's. This was a great relief to the English, even though, unlike in 1914–18, their propaganda tried to keep aloof from American domestic politics.

Still the United States was not an ally of Great Britain during the hour of her greatest danger—at any rate, not yet. The sentiments of the vast majority of the American people were inchoate to the point of being often contradictory: They disliked Hitler and they didn't want war. They were presided over by a President who despised Hitler and who supported Churchill and yet who was deeply aware of the restraints imposed on his office by the neutral and isolationist mass of political sentiment, the powers of which he may have exaggerated. Roosevelt, who had a natural tendency to procrastination, was also unduly confident about the situation in the Atlantic. There was a painful crux in his relationship with the British, a potential misunderstanding involving the future of the British fleet. Roosevelt wanted to make sure that, if worse came to worst, the British fleet would come to America. Churchill wanted to make sure that the worst would not come to pass. There was a dangerous discrepancy between these respective priorities. It must be said for Churchill—who, as I said earlier, was more of a warrior than a diplomatist and who, as the history of the war was later to show, often fell prey to his own tendency to procrastinate when it came to serious differences between himself and Roosevelt—that he tackled this problem at once, and rightly so. As early as 15 May he told Roosevelt that if American help came too late "the weight may be more than we can bear." (He also asked that an American naval squadron be sent to call at Irish ports.) He restated his argument even more clearly on 20 May: "If members of the present Administration were finished, and others came in to parley amid the ruins, you must not be blind to the fact that the sole remaining bargaining counter with Germany would be the fleet, and, if this country was left by the United States to its fate, no one would have the right to blame those then responsible if they made the best terms they could for the surviving inhabitants." On 15 June he let Roosevelt know that "a point may be reached in the struggle where the present Ministers no longer have control of affairs and when very easy terms could be obtained for the British island by their becoming a vassal state of the Hitler Empire."[61] This was exactly what Hitler had in mind. As in the case of France, his plan called but for a partial occupation of the British island, with a Germanophile British government established in the north.

Several months later Churchill told Cecil King that for six weeks after the collapse of France the "Americans treated us in that rather distant and sympathetic manner one adopts toward a friend we know is suffering from cancer."[62] Perhaps this is a slight exaggeration. But the Americans, including Roosevelt, were still undecided. The six weeks following the fall of France were crucial. Gradually they convinced themselves that the British were worth supporting, because they would hold out. At a decisive Cabinet session on 2 August Roosevelt said that he decided to sell "directly or indirectly" fifty or sixty old destroyers to Britain. Churchill had asked him for such a deal already in May. The destroyers were not, by themselves, vitally important. What was important, and Churchill understood this, was the gesture, the meaning of the act itself, to the world. It meant a decisive departure from American neutrality.[63]

The end of July in 1940 was a turning point in the history of the world. Roosevelt took the first decisive step on the part of the United States against Germany at the very same moment (2 August) when Hitler took his first decisive move in ordering the German Army to plan for the invasion of Russia, on 31 July. It was also the first step toward the liquida-

---

[61] On 22 June he repeated this argument through the Prime Minister of Canada: "I have good confidence in our ability to defend this Island and I see no reason to make preparations for or give any countenance to the transfer of the British fleet [to the United States]. I shall myself never enter into any peace negotiations with Hitler, but obviously I cannot bind a future Government which, if we were deserted by the United States and beaten down here, might very easily be a kind of Quisling affair, ready to accept German overlordship and domination." *Moffat,* 313: Roosevelt "worries as to some of Mr. Churchill's phraseology."

[62] King, 109.

[63] That the destroyer deal was primarily political in its purposes is suggested by the fact that as early as 16 May Reynaud had first asked for a quick sale or loan of American destroyers to France.

tion of the British Empire; but this is a consideration to which we cannot, and ought not, now turn.[64]

How did the decision to plan for the invasion of Russia mature in Hitler's mind? The matter is not simple. The accepted version, according to which throughout his life Hitler's emotions drove him toward the East, that his overriding purpose was to conquer European Russia for the sake of the German people, is perhaps a bit too simple to be true. "I would rather walk to Flanders than bicycle to the East," he said on a later occasion. "It is only the force of reason which dictates our moving to the East."[65]

In July 1940 his reason, rather than his emotions, began to dictate that way. He was trying to find a way to win the war without having to invade England. But there was more to this. He was also growing dissatisfied with Stalin's interpretation of the partition of Eastern Europe and with the singlemindedness with which the latter was Sovietizing his new acquisitions. Hitler knew what the Soviet incorporation of entire nations would mean for the peoples living there.[66] For a while, as we have seen, Stalin refrained from the Sovietization of the Baltic republics even as he had moved his rooks forward, to station Russian troops within the Baltic

---

[64] At any rate, not until much later in this book. See below, pp. 496–501; also 510. By mid-August, Churchill felt free to promise Roosevelt what the latter wanted to hear. When on 18 August the Canadian Prime Minister and the President met in Ogdensburg, New York, the latter "told Mr. King that Mr. Churchill had at last given a sufficient pledge that he would under no circumstances surrender the British fleet to the Germans. Mr. King told the President that he thought Mr. Churchill, in hesitating during the month of June to give a satisfactory pledge, had been motivated by a desire to observe all the Constitutional niceties and not bind the hand of a possible successor. (Mr. King reminded me that he had cautioned Mr. Churchill not to try to use the British fleet to bargain with the United States)." *Moffat*, 329.

[65] Schramm, 22.

[66] There was another great event that has not received the attention it deserves. Consequent to his partition of Eastern Europe with Stalin, Hitler decided to bring the German populations of the Baltic states back within the confines of the Reich. First in the winter of 1939, then in the summer of 1940, hundreds of thousands of Germans left their ancient dwellings for the West. See below, pp. 184–87. This was the beginning of a great population movement that came to an end only after his death and the lost war when, for the first time in eight hundred years, the once-flourishing and potent German colonies in Eastern Europe were extinguished, perhaps forever—one of the most important long-range consequences of the Second World War.

states in October 1939. The rapid collapse of France then surprised Stalin. On the day Paris fell he moved, brutally, first in Lithuania, then in Estonia and Latvia. Within a matter of days these unfortunate countries were invaded by masses of Soviet troops. Within a matter of weeks they were forcefully incorporated within the Soviet empire proper, as "member republics." On the morrow of the French armistice, too, the Russians delivered an ultimatum to Romania, demanding the immediate cession of the province of Bessarabia, which Romania had taken from a weakened Russia after the Bolshevik Revolution. The Romanians gave in. This brutal and tactless Soviet grab made a bad impression on Hitler, even though Stalin was grabbing nothing that had not been allotted to him in the partition agreement.[67] Stalin also demanded a portion of Romanian Bukovina, which had not been expressly listed in the 1939 secret protocol. The Russians began putting pressure again on Finland, using the issue of the Petsamo nickel mines as a pretext.

In sum, Hitler was disappointed with Stalin.[68] Yet he ought to have

---

[67] See above, p. 45, about Ribbentrop's important contemporary memorandum to Hitler. On 21 January 1941 Hitler told Mussolini: "The treaties with the Russians all suffered from a one-sided interpretation of the provisions by the Soviet Union. . . . Russia's interpretation of the guarantee agreements with the Baltic States as implying the complete absorption of these states represented something unique." Like the American government after Yalta, Hitler was (or pretended to be) shocked by Stalin's "realism." Yet there is no doubt that Stalin's acts rebounded against him, as they would again in 1945–48. On 3 December 1940 Hitler told the Bulgarian minister to Berlin, warning Bulgaria against accepting any Russian offer for a pact: "The consequences of a Russian guarantee . . . could be observed abundantly in the Baltic states . . . in a very short time everything was Bolshevized . . . just nothing left. Not even a pencil could be had there any longer: Everything had been carried away. All who had risen above the masses, the intelligentsia and the middle class, had been exterminated and replaced by incompetent commissars. . . . [The Fuehrer] described in strong words the conditions of terrorism, the shootings, the deportations. . . ." GD, D, XI, 768.
[68] To the Bulgarian Prime Minister, Filov, on 4 January 1941: "Germany . . . had again made the observation in the Baltic countries that the Bolshevists *had not learned anything new* [my italics] in the way of constructive effort. Whenever they came . . . they brought with them nothing but hunger and distress. Culturally, too, they had laid waste to everything. . . . First, the Bolshevists installed Jewish commissars, who tortured their former opponents to death. Next came the Russian commissars who, in turn, displaced the Jews. . . ." GD, D, IX, 1,023. These phrases of selective indignation suggest, contrary to the general belief accepted by historians, first, that Hitler was both well informed and interested in what happened under Russian occupation; second, that in his mind Jews and Soviets were *not* inseparable.

been satisfied with Stalin's attitude to Germany. Stalin and Molotov congratulated Hitler on the occasion of his triumph over France. The press communiqués by Moscow insisted on the unshaken strength of Russian-German friendship. On 25 June Churchill addressed a letter to Stalin. The gist of the letter was that a new situation had arisen in Europe. Was the prospect of German hegemony in Europe in the interests of the Soviet Union?[69] On 1 July Stalin and Molotov received the British ambassador, Sir Stafford Cripps. Their conversation lasted nearly three hours. Stalin denied that Germany would, or could, dominate the whole of Europe. Within two weeks Molotov gave the Germans a memorandum of the Stalin-Cripps conversation,[70] in which Cripps had been quoted as saying, among other things, "that it was rightly the task of the Soviet Union to maintain the unification and leadership of the Balkan countries," whereupon Stalin was supposed to have answered that he "did not see any danger of the hegemony of any one country in Europe," and that "no power had the right to an exclusive role in the consolidation and leadership of the Balkan countries."[71] For the next month Molotov refused to see Cripps at all. The latter despaired of his mission to the point that he asked to be recalled from Moscow.

---

[69] The historical importance of this letter, the first that Churchill addressed to Stalin, is great, but we must note two reservations. First, the idea of sending such a message had come from Halifax, not from Churchill. Woodward, I, 465. Second, the British envoy "was warned not to let Stalin think that we were running after him in order that he should pull our chestnuts out of the fire." Ibid., 466. (Chestnuts again.) This first Churchill approach to Stalin showed, thus, little or nothing of Churchill's later willingness to sacrifice much for a friendly relationship.

[70] The Russian version of the conversation given to the German ambassador by Molotov, *GD*, D, X, 207–8, does not substantially differ from the British record summed up by Woodward, I, 468–69. Molotov told the same to the Italian ambassador, for at that time Mussolini had decided to improve his relations with Russia, with the possibility of a sphere-of-interest deal in the Balkans. On 7 July Hitler criticized such an approach to Ciano. Upon the latter's suggestion that Italy might be ready to settle accounts with Yugoslavia, Hitler said that this must not happen because, if so, Hungary would attack Romania, and Russia would move farther into Romania and the Balkans.

[71] Even though all evidence points to the conclusion that, in making this suggestion, Cripps was speaking for himself, without such instructions from the British government, here was the gist of British policy during the rest of the war, and even afterward. Of the two alternatives—Germany ruling all of Europe, Russia ruling Eastern Europe—the second was preferable to the first; half of Europe was better than none.

Stalin was obviously not willing to intrigue with Churchill. The time might come, however, when the English would profit increasingly from any move, or even from the mere existence, of the Russian colossus to the east of Germany. So Hitler reasoned. He must deprive Churchill of such hopes. Here was the triangle of the previous summer again—with larger stakes, with less opportunity for mutual blackmail, yet even more dramatic in retrospect. Hitler wanted an agreement with England. Churchill wanted an agreement with Stalin. Stalin wanted friendship with Hitler. In 1940, unlike in 1939, none of them got what they wanted, not even Stalin.

In November 1939 Hitler had said to Brauchitsch and to his commanders: "We can oppose Russia only when we are free in the West. . . ." (A few months earlier it had been the reverse.) On 21 July 1940 he told Brauchitsch: "England would come to terms when Russia was no longer a threat to Germany." Yet now, in July 1940, he was not quite "free in the West"; nor was Russia "a threat." What, then, Hitler said to his commanders on 31 July about Russia tells much, too, about his thinking about England. Air warfare against England was now beginning, Hitler said; but "if results of the air war are not satisfactory, [invasion] preparations will be halted." Then came the political crux of the matter: "ENGLAND'S HOPE IS RUSSIA AND AMERICA. IF HOPE ON RUSSIA IS ELIMINATED, AMERICA IS ALSO ELIMINATED, because enormous increase in the importance of Japan in the Far East will result from the elimination of Russia." "RUSSIA THE FACTOR ON WHICH ENGLAND IS MAINLY BETTING. . . . SHOULD RUSSIA, HOWEVER, BE SMASHED, THEN ENGLAND'S LAST HOPE IS EXTINGUISHED. Germany is the master of Europe and the Balkans." "DECISION: IN THE COURSE OF THIS CONTEST RUSSIA MUST BE DISPOSED OF. SPRING '41. THE QUICKER WE SMASH RUSSIA THE BETTER. OPERATION ONLY MAKES SENSE IF WE SMASH THE STATE HEAVILY IN ONE BLOW. Winning a certain amount of territory only does not suffice. A standstill during the winter hazardous. *Therefore better to wait*, but decision definite to dispose of Russia. . . ." "Aim: Annihilation of Russia's vital energy. . . ."[72]

The capitals are in the original German typescript. The italics are mine. *Better to wait.* He would not smash into Russia until next summer. Now, for six weeks after the fall of France, Hitler had waited—indeed, he may have dawdled—before striking at England. Had he flung troops across the Channel by air in June, even in early July, he might have won the war. This was not then beyond the realm of possibility. But the time

---

[72] Halder, *KTB*, reproduced in *GD*, D, X, 370–74.

for this was passing, even before what was to be called the Battle of Britain began in the air.

At the end of July the peoples of Europe knew nothing of Hitler's decision to invade Russia. What they were beginning to see was that Hitler had not yet won his war. Slowly the wave of belief in the virtue, and perhaps even in the necessity, of co-operating with a new German Europe was beginning to ebb, especially among the peoples in the western half of the Continent, for two reasons. One was the German lack of response to the immediate physical and political needs and wishes of these peoples; the other was the increasing evidence that the British were holding their own, that they would fight on.

Perhaps the clearest evidence of this reassertion of sentiment for national independence existed in Switzerland. On 12 July General Guisan, the chief of the Swiss Army, commanded all officers of this small army to assemble on the plateau of the Rütli, the historic field of Swiss independence, on 25 July. (The day came exactly one month after the President of the Swiss Confederation, in an awkward speech, suggested that his people "adjust" themselves to a new order in Europe.) The general of a democratic citizen-army spoke without notes, without a microphone, in quiet tones of determination. He instructed his officers to hold themselves in utmost readiness to defend the independence and the liberties of their country. There survives a photograph of this event: the officers in a circle, leaning forward, listening earnestly in their long greatcoats, on that grassy cliff above a silent lake on a cool and gray day. The sky over the Rütli was typical of that July. For, on the morrow of the capitulation of France, the unbroken, dazzling skies in Western Europe floated away. German time had been introduced west of the Jura, rain began to fall, and clouds covered the lands of Western Europe during much of the rest of the summer.

# 6 . Germany governant[1]

L ATE IN AUGUST and early in September 1940 a rumor bloomed
on the Continent: The Germans had tried to invade England, and they
had disastrously failed. The English had poured oil on the surface of the
sea and set it afire. Thousands of burned bodies of their soldiers were
being collected by the Germans. There is no evidence that the rumor
had been started, or even fed, by the English. Its simultaneous appearance
belongs to the unwritten history of mass psychology. Its origins were, and
are, obscure. Almost surely its substance was the outgrowth of anticipa-
tions. People expected the dramatic pace of the war that had begun in
April to continue. The Germans had not conquered England; the Germans had suffered a disaster; their collapse was imminent. (Indeed, the
Germans had not conquered England; but they did not suffer a disaster,
and their collapse was far from imminent.)

In many ways the Last European War was an ideological war—less
ideological than people thought in 1940, still ideological to a considerable
extent. The German triumphs revitalized the cause of Fascism and of National Socialism across Europe, including the conquered nations. Most
movements of the "radical Right," pro-Fascist and pro-National Socialist,
had risen in the early thirties—a fresh and new and dangerous wind blow-
ing across the Continent. Most evidence, including electoral statistics,
suggests that by 1939–40 the zenith of their attraction had passed.[2] Now,

---

[1] 31 July 1940–1 March 1941.
[2] In Belgium the Fascist Rex movement of Degrelle received 12 per cent of the
popular vote in 1936, but only 4 per cent in 1939. In Sweden, Norway, England,
France, Switzerland, Ireland, Greece, Finland, Bulgaria, and the Baltic states, the
various parties and movements of the radical Right reached their respective
peaks some time between 1932 and 1936; thereafter their strength declined. In
Spain and Hungary the "peak" of the radical nationalist sentiment among the

in the summer of 1940, the radical Right was revitalized by the opportunity that a triumphant Germany presented. This did not mean that they were an important fifth column. With few exceptions, the military victories of the Germans owed little or nothing to their ideological allies. What the German victory meant to the different Fascists and Nazis was proof that they had been right, proof often at a terrible cost to their own people. Full of bitterness and self-righteousness and ambition, they saw a new prospect: to collaborate with the Germans in the construction of a new Europe."[3]

At this juncture the radical Right received a gaggle of new adherents. There were many intellectuals on the Continent who saw a symbol in the fall of France: It was the fall of bourgeois Europe, the beginning of a new era. Many of them were sincere in their newly found Germanophilia, in their wish to collaborate in the making of a new Europe. All of them were overwhelmed by their sense of occasion. Intellectual opportunism is a complicated phenomenon; I cannot here discuss its manifestations in detail. In any event, these tendencies, in 1940, were not altogether insignificant, nor were they insincere. Yet they did not rise to important heights. The principal reason for this was the tactless and increasingly harsh manner in which the Germans ruled in the occupied countries. Hitler was interested in the opportunity for German overlordship in the Continent, not in the opportunities for its union.

There was, however, a cumulative effect of the efforts of the collaborationist intellectuals. They were now in charge of the press and of the radio. Their propaganda filled many people with revulsion. Many other people remained indifferent or skeptical. Yet there were many people—young ones, first generations of newspaper readers, especially in Eastern Europe—who had known or read little else, so that they were not sufficiently immune to the cumulative effects of this kind of propaganda. The result was a new time-lag, a double phenomenon. On the one hand the Germans' chance of attracting the people of Europe, and especially of Western Europe to their side, diminished after August 1940. On the other

---

masses came in 1938–39. Romania may be the only exception to this trans-European phenomenon, where the Iron Guard emerged triumphant in 1940; but it had risen in the wake of a national catastrophe, the result, not the cause, of a great political transformation.

[3] Thus, while in some instances it was probably true what Sir Oswald Mosley and other Fascist leaders stated, that the police measures against them had been unjust and unwarranted because most Fascists, at least in England, were ready to fight the German invaders just as any other loyal and patriotic citizen, the question still remains: How would they have acted *after* the Germans occupied their country?

hand, the number of people who were committing themselves to the Germans' cause rose steadily, until 1943 at least.

Over and above the effects of propaganda on both sides there was the slow movement of the events of the war. The Germans had not won the war in 1940; but they were not yet losing it. Between the minority of dedicated anti-Nazis and the smaller minority of dedicated pro-Germans lived the mass of populations, for whom daily life was becoming more and more difficult and who looked ahead to the coming winter with gloom. The Germans held back the sun by two hours in the morning. Children had to get up in icy darkness and throw cold water on their faces and hands. "It was as if Paris had been moved beyond the Arctic Circle."[4] "The acid cold green of springtime" (Colette) was to bring little relief. People now knew in their bones that the war would be long. None of them knew that they would have to suffer through four or five more winters until they were to be liberated from the Germans.

We must now establish an unpalatable truth. The Battle of Britain was a halfhearted effort on Hitler's part. The British people stood up to the Blitz. "London could take it." All of this is true. Yet the Battle of Britain was not the turning point of the war. Hitler was skeptical of the ability of Goering's airmen to bomb the British into surrender; rightly so. After 1940 the history of the twentieth century is full of examples in which bombing by air has failed to force a nation to surrender. It is no way of imposing one nation's will on another, which is what victory consists of. People are not slabs of meat; pounding will make them tougher, not softer. The British people deserve our admiration, to say the least. Still, their finest hour may have come in June, perhaps as early as during the week of Dunkirk, when they did not flinch before the prospect of immediate defeat, or when they were indifferent and perhaps even relieved after the fall of France.

Across the Channel the Germans were assembling barges and all kinds of landing craft. They were beginning to pound Dover with their guns. Yet deep in the heart of the Continent, in his Supreme War Leader's lair, Hitler on 22 July told his then favorite field marshal, Rundstedt, that German preparations for a landing in Britain were principally psychological rather than military, a "maneuver" (*ein Scheinmanöver*).[5] German attacks on British ships increased, but their effects were not decisive. On 1 August Hitler issued his Directive No. 17. The intensification of air war could begin on 5 August. He still forbade "terror bombing in retalia-

---

[4] Audiat, 88.
[5] Hillgruber, *HS*, 170.

tion."⁶ Hitler now allowed Goering to unleash Goering's cherished Luftwaffe. The first mass attacks on southern England began. By 13 August they reached a high intensity. On 15 August, a glorious day (the sun was blazing in the sky), the Royal Air Force shot down 75 German planes (it claimed 182).

On the twenty-fourth Hitler still forbade attacks "against the London area and terror attacks." That day began an odd concatenation of events, pregnant with the eventual death of hundreds of thousands of English and Germans and other Europeans. That night a few German planes dropped bombs on London by mistake. Churchill chose to strike back. For the next few days British planes went over Berlin. Their bombing was quite ineffectual. Its purposes were, of course, far more psychological than military. A handful of German civilians were killed. Hitler grew frustrated and angry. On 30 August he lifted the ban on the bombing of London. The long summer days of August, with "the scent of crushed grass in the canteen tent, a honky-tonk piano battering out "Deep Purple" and "Somewhere Over the Rainbow,"⁷ were over. The sense of suffering and death now came to this great city. Yet Hitler's decision contributed to Britain's salvation. The fighter strength of the RAF was wearing away by the end of August. Had the Luftwaffe tried systematically to destroy the RAF the danger to Britain would have been so enormous as to be perhaps insurmountable. Now the brunt of the German bombing fell instead on London, and the British fighters were left free. On 7 September the massive bombing began. At first there was great destruction, and the beginnings of panic in the East End along the Thames. Soon it became evident that London could take it. It also became evident that the Germans could not take her. A few more days, and Hitler canceled Sea Lion.⁸

---

⁶ The first bombs on a peaceful German town had fallen in May 1940. They were dropped by a German plane by mistake. Yet in his 19 July 1940 speech Hitler used this bombing of Freiburg-im-Breisgau to threaten the British who "under the pretext of so-called military objectives . . . [bomb] open towns, market places, villages, houses, hospitals, schools, kindergartens. . . . Until now I have ordered hardly any reprisals, but that does not mean that this is, or will be, my only reply. . . ."

⁷ Thompson, *1940*, 145.

⁸ Around 8 September there was another clandestine flurry of German peace tentatives. Hitler's deputy Hess was consulting with Professor Karl Haushofer, probably not without Hitler's knowledge. They were about to approach certain Englishmen through Portugal (including the Duke of Hamilton, to whom Hess was to fly across the dark North Sea eight months later). As Haushofer put it: "From the whole conversation I had the strong impression that it was

Having said all this, the historian ought not mistake Hitler's necessity for some hidden kind of virtue. He may not have had his heart in attacking England. But this man had a very hard heart. Had he known that he could invade or destroy England, he would have done so. It is a mistake to pay too much attention to his repeated statements of admiration for the English race. They may have been rationalizations of his failures to come to grips with them. Nor was he ready yet to attack Stalin's empire. Ever since Hitler's 31 July order to prepare for such a campaign, the number of German units in Poland was gradually increasing; but there is not the slightest evidence that he canceled Sea Lion because of his concern with the Soviet colossus in the East.

The Battle of Britain was over, even as the Blitz had only begun. With the exception of only one, London was raided on seventy-six consecutive nights. They were nights of fire and ruin. The people became accustomed to the new landscape of jagged blackness, to the awful smell of pulverized brick, to the swift onrush of death, to their nightly dangers which, though by no means exhilarating, were things they could live with. The fires of London gleamed across the Atlantic as no other fires of the war. It was during the fall of 1940 that the sentiments of increasing numbers of Americans, especially of those of English and Scotch origins, were crystallizing into a new kind of resolution: The cause of helping Britain was slowly rising into a national ground swell, an American cause.

---

not conducted without the prior knowledge of the Fuehrer. . . ." *GD*, D, XI, 81; also 60, 79. The gambit failed. (As Dr. Albrecht Haushofer warned Hess in his memorandum, ibid., 79: "If worse came to the worst, the English would rather transfer their whole Empire bit by bit to the Americans than sign a peace that left to National Socialist Germany the mastery of Europe.")

As late as 13 September Hitler told Goering's second, General Jeschonnek, that "attacks on strategic targets must have first priority. . . . Bombing calculated to create mass panic must be left to the last. . . . [It] must be our last trump." On the seventeenth Jeschonnek reported that there was, as yet, no mass panic in London. He requested permission to bomb the residential quarters with greater intensity. "Raeder supported him strongly. But Hitler sheered off." Ansel, 297. On 25 September Hitler repeated his usual cantata to the air ace Galland: "He had the highest appreciation for the Anglo-Saxon race . . . the annihilation of Britain would produce a vacuum that could not be filled." Galland, 81–82. On 4 October Hitler lied to Mussolini, blaming the weather for the failure to invade Britain. On 6 February 1941 Hitler's Directive No. 23 summed up "The efficacy of our warfare against England up to now": (a) air attacks against shipping were the most useful; (b) air attacks against the armament industry were difficult to assess; (c) the most doubtful were the effects of bombing on the morale of the English people.

The common assumption, prevalent among many historians, even now, is that Hitler was willfully ignorant of the United States, an inclination that eventually led to his downfall. Not so. Hitler knew how much Churchill depended on Roosevelt. Hitler also did his opportunistic best to avoid giving Roosevelt a pretext for going to war. He would ignore Roosevelt's anti-German moves and provocations. When the news of Roosevelt's decision about the destroyer deal reached Hitler, Hitler's mind sprang forward. He would offer an alliance to Japan. This would divide American attention, keep most of the American fleet in the Pacific, and reduce American help to Britain. On 10 August he sent a special envoy, racing across Siberia, to Tokyo. The Japanese had begun to itch with excitement as the collapse of the European powers opened before them the prospect of a grand Far Eastern empire.[9] It took them very little time to accept Hitler's offer. The so-called Tripartite Pact, among Germany, Italy, and Japan, was signed on 27 September 1940. It included a special provision that its terms were not directed at the Soviet Union. They were clearly directed at the United States. This news had little effect on Europe, or on England. Since it had come on the morrow of a failed British expedition against Dakar in French West Africa, Joseph Kennedy cabled Roosevelt from London that it was "another nail in England's coffin."[10] To the contrary, it was another plank in the rising scaffold of the *de facto* Anglo-American alliance.

Hitler soon realized this. Reluctantly[11] his attention turned to the

---

[9] They were even ready to make peace with Chiang Kai-shek for this purpose, though preferably on their own terms. The latter, much maligned later by Americans during his long life, was wise. He knew that by saying figs to the Japanese he'd get all the apples from the Americans that he wanted.

[10] The crunch had now come in the latent conflict between Kennedy and Roosevelt. In the same telegram Kennedy, who disliked Churchill, said: "I cannot impress upon you strongly enough my complete lack of confidence in the entire conduct of this war." (The German chargé in Washington promptly received a copy of this telegram as well as of other cables. On 2 October 1940, for example, Ribbentrop told the Italian ambassador in Berlin about Kennedy's cables: England was bound to be crushed [*liquidata*]. Alfieri's dispatch, hitherto overlooked by American diplomatic historians, in *DDI*, IX, V, 641.) Roosevelt was not impressed. In October Kennedy retired from the London Embassy. He took the train to Hyde Park, New York, where, closeted with the President, they had a violent altercation. Some people think that they were trying to blackmail each other. (There was at least one lively skeleton in the private closet of each.) Kennedy, in any event, did not have his way.

[11] He told Quisling on 16 August: "He found himself forced, against his will,

western Mediterranean. There the British were beginning to assert their presence. The Italians had moved forward into the western desert of Egypt and British East African possessions, even as they had lost other opportunities.[12] Together with the Spanish, Hitler thought, the Germans could capture Gibraltar, closing the Mediterranean to the British, besides getting important bases on the northwestern bulge of Africa. In this Hitler did not have his way. The Spaniards were cautious, calculating, and patriotic. They were also glib, voracious, and incompetent. At first Franco was greedy with the prospect of cashing in on the collapse of the French empire. He wanted Gibraltar, all of Morocco, part of Algeria, and even a small slice of France northeast of the Pyrenees. He sent his brother-in-law, the singularly voluble Serrano Suner, to Berlin. The latter made a poor impression on Hitler, even as Serrano mouthed Fascist rhetoric.[13] Then, having replaced his conservative minister Beigbeder with Serrano in October, Franco met Hitler at Hendaye, on the Franco-Spanish frontier, on the twenty-third. Hitler was aghast at meeting a statesman who outtalked even him.[14] He felt that he had gotten nothing from this swarthy little Spaniard. Roaming through southern Spain by now were groups of German intelligence officers, clad in civilian suits cut of stiff German tweed, taking notes on roads and railways and on the trajectories of artillery sites on the Spanish coast across from Gibraltar. Franco was admonished by the Portuguese, cajoled by the Vatican, and blackmailed by the United States[15] to keep out of the war. On 7–8

---

to wage war against the English. . . . He was interested only in northern Europe, in the south of Europe not at all. The Mediterranean countries had always been the racial death of the Germanic peoples." *GD*, D, X, 494.

[12] On the day Italy declared war there were but three British airplanes on the field of Malta, which island the Italians could have captured without much difficulty.

[13] During their meeting Suner said many loathsome things, among them that "Portugal had no right to exist." (This was the neighbor and friend to whom Nationalist Spain may have owed its life.) He tried to avoid Hitler's suggestion that the Cape Verde Islands should receive a German base, saying that these islands could be defended against Anglo-American attacks by coastal artillery from Spanish Morocco. Hitler reminded him that they were 160 miles from the coast.

[14] Franco had also kept Hitler waiting. This event, later attributed to Franco's subtle diplomatic talents, was in reality a result of the incompetence of Spanish railway officials. (Hitler later said that he'd rather spend hours at the dentist than spend time with Franco again.)

[15] Roosevelt was putting pressure on Franco. He used the American Red Cross for this purpose. In December 1940 he authorized the Red Cross to send flour and grain to Spain.

December Admiral Canaris, the head of German military intelligence, a Hispanophile and an old anti-Communist friend, visited Franco in Hitler's behalf. Canaris, who disliked Hitler, dropped a hint to Franco that Hitler might not win the war.[16] Franco took the hint, and asked Hitler to excuse him, at least for a while.

This event, exactly one year before the great turning point of Pearl Harbor, was one of the minor turning points of the war. Hitler was now compelled to drop Operation Felix, including the capture of Gibraltar. With all the respect due to Franco's successful procrastination, however, it was not so much patriotic conservatism but geography and hunger that had forced him to lie low. He was very much aware of the presence of the United States across the ocean, who with the British could descend on Spain's islands in the Atlantic. Moreover, Spain had been suffering from the terrible aftereffects of three years of civil war. There were conditions of near famine in southern Spain that winter. On 21 January 1941 Hitler sent a sharp message to Franco, reminding him that "without the help of the Fuehrer and the Duce there would not today be any Nationalist Spain or a Caudillo . . . the Fuehrer and the Reich government are deeply disturbed by the equivocal and vacillating attitude of Spain." By that time Franco was no longer shaking in his boots (there is some evidence that he had been very much worried on his way to Hendaye.)[17] Hitler's main attention had shifted from the western to the eastern Mediterranean, from southwestern to southeastern Europe.

The cancellation of the Spanish project—Felix infelix—may have been a diplomatic defeat for Hitler. It did not mean, as Goering alleged later, that thereby Germany lost the chance to win the war. Had the British lost the Mediterranean they would have gone on fighting nonetheless. Indeed, much of Hitler's Mediterranean strategy had a preventive purpose. He was worried lest French North Africa revolt against the Axis, with the aid of the British and the Americans, who would then establish their bridgeheads against the soft underbelly of Europe—Churchill's later phrase, with the essence of which Hitler would fully agree. Hitler was worried in 1940 about what took place two years later, in 1942. Some of his people, especially the Navy, begged him to consider the prospects of a

---

[16] Canaris's account to Hitler read: "General Franco made it clear that Spain could enter the war only when England was about ready to collapse. Upon receipt of Admiral Canaris's telegram, the Fuehrer decides that Operation *Felix* is not to be carried out, since the necessary political prerequisites no longer exist." *OKW/KTB*, in *GD*, D, XI, 816–17.

[17] Once more Hitler tried: He asked Mussolini to try to prevail upon France. The two Latin dictators met in Bordighera in February. Nothing came out of that either.

Western European alliance against the British, an alliance led by National Socialist Germany and Fascist Italy, including the near-Fascist Franco and Pétain's "new" France. Hitler was skeptical of both of the latter. To him Vichy France, all of its authoritarian rhetoric notwithstanding, was nothing but the remnant of an old and corrupt republic. The photos of Pétain's Cabinet showed dwarfish gnarled little men with rundown mouths and mugs. If Hitler was pleased with De Gaulle's and Churchill's failure to conquer Dakar (on 25 September a Gaullist force, supported by British warships, was repulsed by the French there), he also saw the increasing number of French colonies across the world that were rallying to De Gaulle and to Churchill.[18] Returning from Hendaye, Hitler had met Pétain at Montoire, on 24 October. He sized up the latter: an old soldier, verging on senility, who may deserve a little respect but practically no consideration. He was also aware of Pétain's reluctance to commit his remnant France on Germany's side, *tout court*. Immediately after the cancellation of Felix, Hitler issued his Directive No. 19, Operation Attila, which called for the swift military occupation of Vichy France, and of the French fleet, if necessary, "in case those parts of the French colonial empire . . . should show signs of revolt"—another 1940 plan that would be put in effect in 1942.[19]

Still it was not Franco or Pétain but Mussolini who forced Hitler to divert his attention to the Mediterranean. We have seen that the governments and the peoples of the Balkans wished to remain neutral and be left in peace. We have also seen that after the fall of France, Mussolini was considering the opportunity of dividing the Balkans into spheres of interests, possibly including a deal with Russia.[20] He wanted some gain and glory for Italy now that Hitler was packing most of Europe within his domain. Hitler, on the other hand, wanted peace and quiet in the

---

[18] Between August and November the Cameroons, French Equatorial Africa, New Caledonia, the New Hebrides, Gabon, and the French colonies in India declared for De Gaulle. Togo (the former German colony) kept on Pétain's side.

[19] Ignorant of these brutal and contemptuous German plans, Pétain, urged by some of his conservative advisers, on 13 December dismissed Laval from his government and put him under private internment. This was the lowest point of Vichy-German relations during the war. The German response was immediate. Laval was released after three days. Eventually he entered the Pétain government again.

[20] The Russian response was encouraging. Molotov to the Italian ambassador on 25 June 1940: "In the Mediterranean, the Soviet Government would recognize Italy's hegemony, provided that Italy would recognize the Soviet Government's hegemony in the Black Sea." Toscano, 42.

Balkans, at least for a while.[21] Abandoning his idea of attacking Yugoslavia, Mussolini turned to the plan of invading Greece. On 15 August he let his navy arrange a brutal provocation: An Italian submarine torpedoed the Greek cruiser *Helle*, in harbor, bedecked on the occasion of a religious holiday. Hitler, for his own good, should have dissuaded Mussolini with the same kind of energy with which he had dissuaded him from taking on Yugoslavia. He did not do so. His main Balkan concern at that time was Romania. That country, inflated in size after World War I, had just been pared down by Russia; she was threatened by her neighbors Hungary and Bulgaria, each of which had justified territorial demands against her; she was ready to put herself under German tutelage. Just as he warned Mussolini against attacking Yugoslavia, Hitler warned the Hungarians not to attack Romania. At the end of August the Romanians submitted to an arbitration by Germany and Italy. The Second Vienna Award gave Hungary the northern half of the province of Transylvania. Bulgaria on her own received another piece of the province of Dobrudja. In Romania there occurred an earthquake, something between a revolution and a *coup d'état*. The King had to flee, and under the nominal kingship of his son, a radical nationalist dictatorship was set up, including fanatics of the Iron Guard but led by a general, Antonescu, whom Hitler grew to like and appreciate. Antonescu promptly asked Hitler for German "training troops" to be sent to Romania. Stalin was not amused. Nor was Mussolini. He told Ciano: "Hitler always faces me with accomplished facts. Now I'll pay him back by his same currency. He'll learn from the papers that I have occupied Greece. So the balance will be re-established."[22] On 15 October Mussolini and the Italian High Command decided on the invasion of Greece. He was not as good as his word. After all was said, he thought it better to let Hitler know. He wrote Hitler: "As regards Greece, I am resolved to end the delays, and very soon. Greece is one on the main points of English maritime strategy in the Mediterranean."[23] By the time the letter was sent, Hitler was on his way to meet Franco and Pétain. It wandered after Hitler, eventually catching up with him on the twenty-fifth.[24] He had hardly arrived back in Munich from

---

[21] Rejecting Italian plans for an attack on Yugoslavia, the *OKW/KTB*, as cited in note 4, *GC*, D, X, 483, read: "[The Fuehrer] wishes peace at the southern frontier of Germany and warns against giving the English an opportunity to establish their Air Force in Yugoslavia."

[22] Ciano, 353.

[23] It must be said that the principal subject of this letter was France, not Greece. Mussolini tried to warn Hitler not to offer the French much in the way of collaboration.

[24] See Martin van Creveler, "25 October 1940: A Historical Puzzle" in *JCH*, vol. 6, no. 3 (1971), 96.

his tour through France when he had to set out again for the South, to meet Mussolini. He heard of the Italian attack on Greece in the station of Bologna on the morning of the twenty-eighth. A little later he told his circle that the Greeks were not bad soldiers and that Italy might not win.[25] Yet he thought it best not to remonstrate with Mussolini when they, the two super-condottieri, met in the Palazzo Vecchio in Florence on the twenty-eighth.

Early that morning—or, rather, late in the previous night, at 2:30 A.M.—the Italian minister to Greece had presented himself at the house of the Greek Prime Minister and dictator, General Metaxas. The old man came to meet him, blinking, with a coat over his old-fashioned night-gown, wearing carpet slippers. The Italian note was not even an ultimatum; it left the Greeks no way out: It demanded the surrender of Greece to Italy, nothing less. "*Alors, c'est la guerre*" the old man said to the Italian. It was a brilliant night, with a myriad stars gleaming over Athens. Soon the sirens would howl, announcing Italian air raids. On the northern Greek frontier with Albania, however, the wind howled and the cold rain came down in sheets. "We are walking in mud," said one of the first Italian field reports.

At that time Hitler's thoughts were not unlike Bismarck's: All of the mud of the Balkans was not worth the bones of a Prussian grenadier. Like Bismarck, he wanted some kind of a compromise with the British Empire.[26] Unlike Bismarck, he got himself into a war with the British, and he could not get out of it. Unlike Bismarck, he was thinking of conquering Russia. He was not altogether happy with that prospect either. He had to consider one more alternative. Perhaps Stalin would conform to his wishes, which meant not one Russian step beyond the partition line, not one move beyond the status quo on Eastern Europe. He had ordered the planning for a campaign against Russia; but he had not yet issued his definite directive for that purpose.

A year before, the Third Reich and the Soviet Union had drawn a line of partition across northeastern Europe. Now surveying parties from both sides were completing the exact measurements of their imperial frontiers along the sodden fields of Poland, meter by meter, mile by mile. It is a common mistake to believe that the essence of diplomacy is deliberate imprecision. The contrary theory is true: Precision and exactitude are the

---

[25] Hillgruber, *HS,* 286.

[26] He mentioned this to Mussolini on 28 October for the first time, speaking of France: In the event of a compromise with the British Empire, the French would have to pay the costs.

best guarantees for written agreements between states. Yet there are exceptions even to the best of theories. No matter how precise the agreement, Hitler was disturbed by Stalin's interpretation of it. What was his, was his, the latter thought; and he proceeded to incorporate his new holdings within his imperial domain. In doing this Stalin may have been a supreme realist, but he was not supremely clever. He could be even more tactless than Hitler. "It is often better to have on the frontiers states which are weak and disunited," wrote the great French diplomatic historian Albert Sorel, "than to conquer them and share them with a powerful neighbour, who may through a temporary combination have become an ally, but who always remains a rival."[27]

In June 1940 Stalin not only subjugated and incorporated the Baltic republics in one brutal stroke, he was also putting new pressures on Finland. Finland was on his side of the partition line, the only land that was not yet fully conquered by the Russians. The Finns were frightened out of their wits. Like the Romanians, they were willing to put themselves under the protection of Germany. In early August Hitler began to respond. He ordered the sending of armaments to the Finns more and more openly. The Russians made protests but little more. In essence Finland was passing from their sphere of interest; but they had only themselves to thank for this.[28]

Hitler thought that Stalin's profits due to their treaty were large and sufficient. Stalin thought that Hitler's profits due to his benevolent neutrality were also large, which they undoubtedly were. (The German economy and industry were receiving very large benefits from continuous imports from the Soviet Union.) Stalin was not averse to extending their partition agreement to cover all of Eastern Europe, including the Balkans. While the Italians were interested in such a bargain, Hitler would have none of it.[29] Romania, even more than Finland, was passing into the Ger-

---

[27] Sorel, 59.

[28] Stalin learned his lesson in regard to Finland. In 1948 he would act according to Sorel's principle. He let Finland remain relatively free because of his appreciation of American public opinion, and also because of a tacit deal with Sweden: He would not Sovietize Finland if Sweden remained outside of NATO, a condition that has prevailed up to this day. In this respect he acted like Frederick the Great, who wrote in his political testament regarding a small duchy: "I have left it alone because the game is not worth the candle. It is a meager morsel, and it would not compensate for the outcry it would raise."

[29] He was worried that the Russians, after their fast grab of Bessarabia and Bukovina, might move farther into Romania. He was irritated at the Hungarians, who were threatening to go to war with Romania. The Romanian problem came to a head at the end of August when Hitler ordered the strengthening of

man sphere. Stalin wanted a little more balance in the Balkans. Already in September 1939 he had proposed to Bulgaria—ancient ally and suppliant of Tsarist Russia—a nonaggression pact. The Bulgarians declined then. Now the Russians renewed their entreaties. They also tried to blackmail and frighten the Romanians by snatching islands in the Danube Delta, along their new frontier.

These were troublesome issues between the two great continental powers in the autumn of 1940. But beside these issues were larger vistas in which especially Ribbentrop was interested. He urged Hitler to let him invite Molotov to Berlin. Ribbentrop wanted to align the Soviet Union with the Third Reich, Italy, Japan. The result would be a vast quadripartite alliance ruling Eurasia and possibly Africa, against the power of which the Anglo-Saxon democracies would be largely ineffectual. Ribbentrop wanted to convince Stalin not only of the advantages but also of the opportunity thereof. On 12 October he wrote him, "For one thing is sure: The war as such has been won by us anyway. It is only a question of how long it will be before England, under the impact of our operations, admits to complete collapse." Stalin was not convinced of this one sure thing. He and Molotov refused a proposal that Cripps, again on his own, advanced a few days later, which would have recognized the *de facto* Eastern European conquests of the Soviet Union in exchange for a more balanced neutrality on its part in the British-German war.[30] At the same time Stalin refused the proposal that the Japanese, in the wake of Ribbentrop, made for a nonaggression pact; and he set out cautiously to improve his relations with the United States, especially in regard to China. He also set Molotov's visit to Berlin and the announcement thereof to occur not before but after the American presidential election.

Molotov arrived in Berlin on 12 November, for three days. We have very detailed accounts of his talks with Ribbentrop and Hitler. Unlike Ribbentrop's visit to Moscow in 1939, Molotov's visit to Berlin in 1940

---

German divisions in southeastern Poland, ready for "a quick intervention to protect the Romanian oil districts" in case of necessity. Contrary to his original intention, he let Ribbentrop arbitrate between Hungary and Romania in the Second Vienna Award. For the first time since their treaty, Stalin sent a diplomatic protest to Berlin, saying that the Soviet Union should have been consulted about the partition. The Germans refused to listen.

[30] In Finland the British made it increasingly clear that, in face of the loss of their (and Canadian) control over the Petsamo nickel mines, they would rather see the Russians prevail in these complex negotiations, even as the Russian demands, as compared to the German ones, were brutal and extreme. On 20 November 1940 Hitler told the visiting Hungarian Prime Minister, Count Teleki: If they thought it necessary, the British would hand over the Balkans to the Soviet Union.

was a failure: But the fault was not all on the German side. The legend, enthusiastically propagated by people such as the Dulles brothers, according to which Molotov was a modern-day Mazarin or Talleyrand, a master diplomatist of the twentieth century, is nonsense. All that this unimaginative bureaucrat, with his cold slab of a face, could achieve was to irritate Hitler no end. Ribbentrop and Hitler talked about the division of Eurasia and of the world. Molotov came back, again and again, to the Russian wish to obtain naval bases in Finland and in Bulgaria. Yet during their conversations Hitler, not Molotov, was the realist.[31] The latter did not know how his wooden repetitions incensed Hitler. Molotov knew, of course, that all of Ribbentrop's declarations notwithstanding, the Germans had not yet won the war against England; but to see this in November 1940 one did not have to possess the insights of a Mazarin or of a Talleyrand.[32] When Molotov left, Hitler told his military circle: "Nothing came out of this, as he had thought. Molotov let the cat out of the bag."[33]

Instead of letting his cats out of his traveling bag, Molotov should have tried to bell the German cat, tiger that it was. He did not see it that way. He returned to Moscow with his tale. Stalin's big Caucasian nose sniffed the danger. He felt that there was trouble in Berlin. There now occurred a temporary reversal of Russian policy. Stalin removed the bland Soviet ambassador, Skvartsev, from Berlin, replacing him with Dekanosov, one of Stalin's own minions. On the twenty-fifth a special Soviet envoy flew to Bulgaria, where he made an extraordinary declaration: "If Bulgaria accepts the mutual assistance pact with the Soviets, Bulgaria may join the Tripartite Pact which Russia herself would probably, almost certainly, join."[34] That day a Russian draft for a grand treaty was given to the German ambassador in Moscow, on Stalin's instructions. He

---

[31] One example. Hitler: If "the United States could get a foothold in [Scandinavia] in case of participation by Sweden in a possible [Soviet-Finnish war], would Russia declare war on the United States, in case the latter would intervene?" *GD*, D, xi, 557. Molotov tried to weasel out of this.

[32] In 1942 Stalin told Churchill a story that subsequently became famous. During Molotov's visit to Berlin, Churchill sent a few bombers over Berlin in order to impress the party. Going down to the sumptuous cellars, Ribbentrop was supposed to have told Molotov: "England is finished," whereupon Molotov was supposed to have answered: "If England is finished, why are we going down the cellar, and whose are the bombs that fall?" Molotov may have thought this. That he said it to Ribbentrop is most unlikely.

[33] "This would not even be a marriage of convenience. To let the Russians into Europe means the end of Central Europe. The Balkans and Finland, too, are dangerous flanks." General Engel's diary, cited by Hillgruber, *HS*, 358.

[34] *GD*, D, XI, 713.

wanted to get along with Hitler. The Soviet Union was ready to discuss the Four-power Pact, subject to four, somewhat reduced, Russian provisions that were negotiable.[35]

Hitler did not bother to answer. Beginning in early December he would talk more and more about the Germans' ability to smash the Russian Army, if necessary. The American commercial attaché in Berlin heard about all this; so did Bulgarians, Turks, and others. Hitler talked for effect: but he meant it seriously. His Directive No. 21, Operation Barbarossa, was finally issued on the eighteenth. The German Army "must be prepared to crush Soviet Russia in a quick campaign. . . ." The final objective "is to erect a barrier against Asiatic Russia on the general line Volga-Archangel. The last surviving industrial area of Russia in the Urals can then, *if necessary*, be eliminated by the Air Force." *If necessary:* Hitler respected Stalin, who, he thought, might yet give in to him.[36] "Stalin was a wise man," he told Field Marshal Bock in early December. But Russia must be smashed. "Either the English give then in or Germany could pursue the fight against England under most favorable conditions. . . ."[37] Behind Russia, England; and behind England, America. The same story, again; and the need to hurry.[38] "In 1941 we must solve all

---

[35] German troops withdrawn from Finland, in exchange for which Russia guarantees peace with Finland and protection of German nickel interests there; a Soviet-Bulgarian mutual assistance pact; the area south of the Caucasus, in the general direction of the Persian Gulf, recognized as lying within Russia's future interests; Turkey to grant a small base to Russia in the Bosphorus or along the Dardanelles; Turkey forced to fall within the four-power sphere; Japan renouncing her concessions in the northern half of the island of Sakhalin. Stalin proposed no less than five secret protocols about these matters. *NSR*, 258 59.

[36] Dekanosov presented himself to Ribbentrop on 12 December, bringing among other things a signed picture of Stalin. Dekanosov's first audience with Hitler took place on the nineteenth, the day after Directive No. 21 had been issued. No German record of their conversation exists.

[37] Bock diary, cited by Hillgruber, *HS*, 364.

[38] Throughout this book I have argued, and shall further argue, that there was method and not just madness in Hitler's decision to attack Russia. He hoped that the eventual elimination of the Soviet Union would make the British and the Americans think twice about continuing the fight against him. There was reason within these calculations. Yet this does not mean that his calculations were correct, and that he had no other alternative. The most detailed study of Hitler's strategies in 1940–41 is Hillgruber, *HS*. This work is indispensable for scholars of that period. Yet it must be used with caution, since at times Hillgruber slips enough to reveal a certain sly suggestiveness through which later generations might find substance to rehabilitate Hitler. According to Hillgruber, Hitler had *no* alternative but to attack Russia, if he did not want

remaining problems on the Continent, since from 1942 on the United States may be ready to intervene."[39]

Barbarossa was set to start on 15 May 1941. Before that, Hitler got himself involved in the Balkans. He would later blame Mussolini for this condition, which kept Hitler preoccupied in southeastern Europe and the eastern Mediterranean for the first five months of the new year, and which may have postponed his attack on Russia for five weeks, with perhaps fatal consequences. Yet this argument is exaggerated. Exercised by Stalin's ursine diplomacy, Hitler was determined to exclude the Bear from anywhere in the Balkans, even before Mussolini's war on Greece upset matters further. Hungary and Romania were now allies of the Third Reich. The Bulgarians did not want to enter into a pact with Russia; eventually they would enter into a pact with Germany. Yugoslavia was pressed by Hitler to act accordingly. These pressures would have developed—indeed, they were beginning to develop—before Mussolini's helmet was knocked askew by the Greeks. That event, however, unquestionably strengthened the hearts and minds of those who did not want the victory of the Axis. In early November their welcome surprise came. The Italians could make no headway in the mountains of Epirus. Indeed, the Greeks were driving them back into Albania. In early December Mussolini had a momentary collapse of nerve. He was on the verge of asking the Germans to help negotiate an armistice. The crisis passed in a few days, but other disasters descended. The spirited small British army in western Egypt surged forward and beat the Italian army, chasing it into Libya, eventually capturing 130,000 prisoners, nearly 500 tanks, and more than 1,000 guns. The reputation of the Italian navy had been crushed, too, earlier, through the daring British attack on Taranto, where a few ancient

---

to capitulate altogether. This argument is concealed, for example, in a very long German sentence, consisting of hundreds of words and no less than six clauses, including this parenthetical remark: ". . . the military Eastern solution (which within the framework of the all-out war in the situation of 1940 was factually inevitable if Hitler did not want to 'capitulate')" Hillgruber, *HS*, 393. Yet Hitler was not sure that England would give in even after Russia was defeated. If he had to compromise with England, why not before his attack on the Soviet Union? To be sure, he tried: but without offering to the English any conditions that they would, or could, accept. He also kept telling his commanders (on 9 January 1941, for example) that "The smashing of Russia will also enable Japan to turn against the United States with all her forces. This will prevent the latter from entering the war"—in which he was wrong.
[39] To Jodl, *OKW/KTB*, I, 996.

British warplanes succeeded in sinking and damaging a number of Italian capital ships. The notion of the invincibility of the Axis now lay smashed on the ground. Hitler was furious. He let Canaris try to mediate between Greek and Italian diplomats in Madrid. The attempt failed, even as the Greek government kept assuring the Germans that they would not allow the British to occupy more than a few airfields in Crete. Hitler had some sympathy for the Greeks[40]; but he felt he had no way out. He had to settle the Balkan situation for good. His purpose was political necessity, not ideology. In January he let German tanks help Antonescu crush the radical rebellion of the Iron Guard, the very Nazis of Romania. President Roosevelt sent Colonel Donovan, a trusted confidant, later the head of the first American international intelligence service, into the Balkans, in order to stir up resistance against Germany, especially in Yugoslavia and Bulgaria. On 31 January Hitler issued a directive for Operation Marita: German armies would join the Italians in attacking Greece, through Bulgaria, in the beginning of April.

By the end of February German military engineers, reaching out from the Romanian shore of the broad Danube, began to build the pontoon bridge across which German troops would pour southward into Bulgaria. That small country, over which reigned a sad-faced and intelligent monarch, was in more than one way the touchstone of the greater circle of events. Studiously neutral at first, the Bulgarians avoided the Russian offer for a pact; they were reluctant to accept the German alliance; they listened to Russian protests and to the American legate but, in the end, they felt that they had no other choice but to go along with the Germans. On 1 March 1941 the Bulgar adherence to the Tripartite Pact was announced. The Germans began to cross the Danube. That day the conservative and Germanophile (in that order) Bulgarian Prime Minister, Filov, wrote in his diary: "If we don't let the Germans through we'll be treated as an occupied country. From an English victory we can expect nothing, for if German power should disappear, we would become Bolshevized."[41]

Hitler had his way. There remained Yugoslavia and Greece. He was to fix them within his orbit soon. Then he would meet Russia head on.

---

[40] At the end of January Hitler would point at Albania on the map: "All of this because of that piece of dirt! (*Und alles wegen dieses Drecks da!*) If I attack [Greece], the world will say that I'm jumping on the back of a small and brave people who defended their freedom just as had the Finns." Colonel Clemm's record, cited in Schramm-Thadden, 220. We must add, however, that Clemm was the German military attaché in Athens; no doubt Hitler's words were to some measure intended for Greek ears.

[41] Schramm-Thadden, 158.

Did he know that he had been moving around Europe in a circle, counterclockwise? In September 1939 he had met with the Russians in eastern Poland; then his attention moved to Scandinavia; then to Western Europe; then to Spain and the Southwest; then to the Balkans and the Southeast, before it would move up again, to the gray and green marchlands of eastern Poland, full force set straight to the East.

# 7 . Germany conquerant[1]

SPRING IN 1941 came early in the Balkans. The ice in the mountains melted into mud, and the sun shone on the metal of the German Army moving through Bulgaria. To the south, the Greeks knew that their turn was coming. They had taken comfort for some months from the condition that Mussolini's ally Hitler had not declared against them. They had asked their British allies to restrain their presence in and around Greece. But now the Greeks' supreme danger had come. Therefore Churchill faced a profound dilemma. The British forces in the western desert were doing well, they were pursuing the Italians beyond Libya into Tripolitania. Were they now to halt their prospects for further triumphant progress, in order to transfer a goodly portion of their troops and airplanes to Greece? At the end of February[2] Churchill decided—and not only for military reasons—that he could not abandon Greece to her own efforts. Yet his dilemma, profound as it was, did not compare with the stakes that the Greeks had to ponder. Many Greek generals respected and liked the Germans. On the day of the German crossing into Bulgaria the commanders of the Army in Epirus asked the royal government to try to make a deal with Hitler. They would not be able to withstand a German invasion from the north. The King and the Prime Minister[3] turned this Germanophile suggestion down. The die was cast. British troops were now coming to Greece. In another week the Italians started their offensive on the Albanian border, where there now stood twenty-six

[1] 1 March–22 June 1941.
[2] A German general, Rommel, whose name was hardly known then, was unloading in Tripoli. As late as October 1940 Mussolini did not want German armor in North Africa. Now the tables had turned, in more than one way.
[3] M. Korizis, the brave old Metaxas having died suddenly on 31 January.

Italian divisions against fifteen Greek ones. The Italians made little progress. No matter: Hitler's date for Operation Marita was set for 1 April. For once everyone knew what he was about to do, and soon.

North of Greece, Yugoslavia was the last remaining country in the Balkans that had not yet aligned herself with the Third Reich. For years its government tried to navigate with great caution between Hitler and Mussolini, pulling close first to one, then to another, while maintaining its traditional good relationships with the Western powers. Trying to put more into the balance, the Yugoslavs even established diplomatic relations with the Soviet Union, after the fall of France.[4] The world knew much about the traditional fighting qualities of the Serbs. It knew little about the fatal weakness of this multinational state, a weakness due to the deep river of hatred that ran between Croats and Serbs, a division that had been papered over by a judicious agreement reached between their moderate politicians shortly before the outbreak of the European war in 1939. Hitler wanted to eliminate the nonconformity of Yugoslavia on his Balkan flanks. He pressed the Regent, Paul, to join the Tripartite Pact. He offered the Yugoslavs unusual conditions. They would not have to sign a military alliance with Germany; he would not even demand rights for the passage of German troops through Yugoslavia. He also told Prince Paul that he might attack Russia in the summer—a statement with ulterior purposes, no doubt.

The Yugoslavs' dilemma was as cruel as that of the Greeks. With utmost reluctance, the Regent and his government felt that they could not refuse Hitler's demand. But there now occurred a powerful British—or, rather, Anglo-American—counterpull. Missives from Churchill, from President Roosevelt, from King George VI, poured on Belgrade. Churchill told the British minister that this was no time for polite recriminations. "Continue to nag, pester, and bite." Before Churchill's eyes revived the prospect of a Balkan front, reminiscent of World War I and Salonika days: Greece and Yugoslavia, perhaps Turkey. Beneath this diplomatic counteroffensive moved the powerful direct currents of agents. For the first time during the war the British secret service (with the help of substantial American money and persuasion) was about to pull off a great coup: to snatch an entire country from the Germans' trap. In a few dramatic days all of this came to a head. Three Serbian ministers resigned. Still the Yugoslav Premier and his Foreign Minister took the

---

[4] Until 1940 Yugoslavia was one of the few European states (in addition to Switzerland, Ireland, Portugal, and Spain) that refused to recognize the Soviet Union, in her case because of the distaste of the Yugoslav royal house for the regime of Tsar-killers. Now they were ready for the friendship of a new Tsar.

train to Vienna, where they signed their country's adhesion to the Tripartite Pact on 25 March. Hitler's terms were not only unusually modest, he also treated these Balkan statesmen with a certain degree of understanding: He "understood the feelings" of the Serbian people against the pact, he said. He had his own forebodings: He told Ciano that he sensed trouble coming in Belgrade. So it came. There was a revolution in Belgrade—or, rather, a *coup d'état*—overnight. The ministers had not yet returned when a group of Air Force and Army officers took over the government, deposed the Regent, Prince Paul,[5] and proclaimed the young Peter II King. The *coup* was, at least partly, engineered by the British; but there were wild scenes of patriotic enthusiasm. "Better war than pact!" people shouted. British, American, even French flags appeared. The spirit of the Entente, of the First World War, flew again. "Yugoslavia found her soul," Churchill announced to the House in London. Even the Russians seemed to have been moved—a little.[6] The British Navy sank three Italian cruisers off Cape Matapan in Greece. A lengthening row of British successes seemed to appear across the moving landscape of the war.

Reality was otherwise. The luck of Hitler's opponents was running out. He swung around to order an instant plan—Directive No. 25—for the invasion of Yugoslavia, "to be carried out with unmerciful harshness." On 2 April Rommel drove against the British encampments near Benghazi, forcing the latter to retreat. Hitler had ordered the setting up of the German Afrika Korps on the day when he ordered the construction of the bridge across the Danube to Bulgaria. Soon he would score another triumph in his duel with Churchill. The Germans could wage war with success simultaneously in Africa and in the Balkans. The British, as events would soon prove, could not.

---

[5] The British took it upon themselves to transport the prince into exile, as they had spirited the wily pro-German statesman Stoyadinovic out of the country a few days earlier.

[6] In March the Russians seemed to welcome cautiously the prospects of an anti-German front in the Balkans. They encouraged Turkey to resist German pressures. They did not go so far as to agree to Cripps' importunings, or even to listen to them (as when on 21 March Cripps asked that Moscow, too, exert pressure on the then still vacillating government in Belgrade). By that time support of the Soviets hardened into definite British policy in the Balkans. For example, on 26 February 1941 the British, in Istanbul, signed over all the remaining British and Dutch ships in the Danube waterway to the Soviet Union. The Romanians confiscated these vessels, and the Russians thought it better not to press their claim to them—an episode typical of the British-Russian relationship in the Balkans at the time. After the Yugoslav *coup*, Hitler said that the British had engineered it, even though people would think that the Russians stood behind it—a perceptive remark.

Hitler decided to smash Yugoslavia "with unmerciful harshness" not only because time was pressing. He also wanted to make a precedent. No state in Europe should think that, consequent to some change in the fortunes of the war, it could turn away from the Third Reich with impunity. The new Yugoslav regime tried to convince the Germans that it was not inimical, it would even remain with the Tripartite Pact, if wanted. The Yugoslavs knew what was threatening. The German menace grew by the hour. In a grimly demonstrative manner, German motorized divisions were passing through Hungary, in full view of the population, roaring and clattering southward along the river quays of Buda and Pest, in agreement with the pro-German chiefs of the Hungarian Army. Yet Hungary had signed a nonaggression pact with her Yugoslav neighbor only a few months before. Deeply aware of this condition, and of what Hungary's entry into the war on the side of Germany against Yugoslavia would signify to Britain and America, the conservative Premier, Count Teleki, blew out his brains on the night of 3 April. Through this dramatic act of suicide he wanted to let the world know that Hungary had been forced into dishonor. It did not change the course of events. Nor did another act, involving another pact, in the far north, where Stalin finally stirred. At midnight on 5 April the Yugoslav minister was summoned to the Kremlin. Stalin and Molotov announced that they were ready to sign a nonaggression pact with Yugoslavia.[7] There was, of course, no occasion for aggression between these two states, separated as they were by hundreds of miles, by entire states, and by German armies. The pact was meant to be a gesture of Slav solidarity, against German displeasure, if need be. As in 1914, an anti-German front in the Balkans was coming into existence.

Within a few days, perhaps within a few hours, it was shattered into pieces. In the very dawn hour when the Yugoslav minister returned to his legation in Moscow, hundreds of German airplanes rose from airfields still in the dark. Ahead of them lay the roofs of Belgrade, lit by the morning sun. The Germans cast down their chains of bombs without discrimination, to drive terror into the hearts of the people. In a few hours the town lay dazed in rubble and smoke. Meanwhile the Germans broke across the Yugoslav frontiers in a dozen places. In front of their motorized roar the Yugoslav Army dissolved. Within two days almost all of the Croat soldiers deserted. South of Yugoslavia the Germans reached Salonika in three days. Another two days, and Hitler's and Mussolini's Croatian allies and suppliants proclaimed a Croatian state. The remnants

---

[7] They had informed the German ambassador the day before.

of the Yugoslav government, the King, the diplomats, retreated pell-mell through the Serbian mountains to the south. On 17 April a general of the Serbian Army signed an armistice of surrender. By that time the German Twelfth Army, commanded by Field Marshal List, was halfway through Greece. Hitler and Goebbels had thought that the Balkan campaign would take two months.[8] Their troops wiped the Yugoslav Army and state off the map in ten days. They would take the Greek mainland in another ten, the British presence there notwithstanding.

For once Stalin was quick to react. On 13 April, a mere eight days after his Slavic pact with the Yugoslavs, he made a sharp turn in the course of his enormous Soviet ship of state, to the right. The day before his henchman Vishinski had been instructed to deliver a strong rebuke to the Hungarian minister in Moscow on the occasion of Hungary's participation in the Axis attack on Yugoslavia. The Japanese Foreign Minister, Matsuoka, was in Moscow. Stalin now took up an earlier Japanese proposal for a nonaggression pact, an event with momentous consequences to which we shall return. That night, 13 April, Stalin chose to follow this up with a gesture to Hitler. Stalin arrived, unexpected, at the Moscow railway station to see off the departing Japanese party himself. After wishing a cordial farewell to the Japanese, excited as these were by this high honor, Stalin publicly asked for the German ambassador. With some difficulty (Count von der Schulenburg was tall and Stalin small in stature), Stalin threw his arm around this Prussian shoulder at hand: "We must remain friends; you must now do everything to that end!" he said. A few minutes later he embraced the German military attaché: "We will remain friends with you—in any event!" The gesture had all the subtlety of a bear trying to tango. The Germans present were deeply impressed. Hitler was not.

The rapid collapse of Yugoslavia showed the world that the Germans were still masters in the art of war. It also showed the fatal weakness of multinational states. The Yugoslav state fell apart, almost at the first German blow. The hatred of Croats for Serbs gushed forth, breaking the weak dikes of their politic unity in a matter of days. It was a repetition, on a much larger and more tragic scale, of the Belgian experience, where Flemish soldiers had, on occasion, deserted their Walloon comrades. From these tribal outbursts of patriotism Hitler profited in the short run. Yet they were not altogether to his advantage in the long run. Yugoslavia was about to be partitioned. There was a Croatian state, a new Axis satellite, many of whose leaders were afire with murderous ambitions. Italy, Hun-

---

[8] Boelcke, 658.

gary, and Bulgaria took slices of the Yugoslav state. Out of this controversies, quarrels, and clandestine warfare were to rise, not at all to the Germans' liking. Soon they found that, unlike in the more civilized states of Western Europe, their mastery in conquered Yugoslavia or Greece was far from complete. They ruled the cities, but they had not enough troops in order to assert themselves in the countryside. Very soon various patriotic—and, a few months later, Communist[9]—groups of bandits were beginning to gather and roam in the mountains, descending on villages here and there. This was later to be proclaimed as partisan warfare, a new kind of war. In reality it meant the reappearance of the ancient practice of patriotic banditry in the Balkans, an art of rapacious guerrilla warfare that lay close beneath the surface of the memories of these Balkan peoples, who had practiced it against the Turks but two or three generations before.

To the south the Germans were rumbling into Greece. Having broken through the brave Greek defenders at Rupel Pass, they drove into Salonika fast. The British and New Zealand and Australian units could not hold them. They tried to make a stand at some of the passes, including Thermophylae, to no avail. Before them German armor proved superior in quality and especially in numbers. Behind them the Luftwaffe destroyed the port of Piraeus on the first day of the campaign. On 23 April the northern Greek armies surrendered to the Germans. Athens fell a few days later. The British imperial troops and some Greek units slipped away from the mainland to Crete. The behavior of the Greek populace was impressive: Unlike the Belgians and the French, they were not inclined to blame the British for their disasters; they cheered the weary British soldiers driving off to the south. Some of their generals, and a few politicians, were ready to politick with the Germans, whom they preferred to the Italians. Much of this was in vain. The Germans were hard masters; the Italians were more human and self-conscious. Within a few weeks there were few villages in Greece whose inhabitants would not prefer an Italian garrison to a German one.

There came now a novel campaign in the history of warfare. Hitler did not want a large island south of Greece to function as a British base. He ordered an assault on Crete. The Germans had no ships for this purpose, but they had parachute troops. Their commander convinced Hitler, who had been doubtful at first, that he could take Crete from the air. On 19 May German gliders and parachute troops descended on three airfields on Crete. The British and imperial troops failed to drive them off the main one, mostly because of failures in communications. For a day or two the battle hung in the balance. On the third day the Germans had a

---

[9] See below, pp. 263–66, 486.

bridgehead at Maleme airfield in hand. From there they took the other airfields on the north shore. Four more days, and the disorderly retreat of British, Australian, New Zealand, and Greek troops through the wild mountains of Crete to the southern shore began. A portion of the British and Greek forces, together with the Greek King and government,[10] were evacuated across the Mediterranean to Alexandria, which city, for the first time in perhaps two thousand years, became the temporary seat of a Greek government again. On 30 May the Battle of Crete was over. It happened exactly one year after Dunkirk. Unlike Dunkirk, there was little glory in it for the British. Their navy fought well but, for the first time, its superiority at sea could not balance the German domination of the air.[11] The British lost one out of every two of their soldiers in Crete. Three of their cruisers and six of their destroyers were sunk.

We know now what people did not know then with certainty. All of these sun- and blood-soaked scenes of war in the South of Europe would soon pale before the enormous event of Germany smashing into Russia in the East. That would decide the war, not the acrobatic bravery of the German troops leaping down onto Crete. Yet nearly 2 months after the fall of Athens, 2½ months after the fall of Belgrade, Hitler had not yet attacked the Soviet Union. His armies were not quite ready. Had the Balkan campaign upset his timetable? Had the Germans jumped off on 15 May, as they had originally planned, they might have been in Moscow before the winter came. In defying Hitler, the Serbs lost; but they made Hitler lose the greater war. Many people have argued this since that time. Hitler himself kept repeating it till the very end, blaming the Italians for his Balkan involvement and delay. Yet there is little substance in these speculations. The chiefs of the German Army established even before the military revolution in Belgrade that they could not start the eastern campaign before 15 June.[12] Oddly enough, Hitler's eventual defeat in the East

---

[10] Korizis committed suicide before Athens fell. The King, and the new government, had few doubts about the ultimate victory of their British patron and ally.

[11] On the other hand, the Germans used up their only parachute division. Their interpretation of British prisoners also showed that the spirit of these British troops was unbroken: "In spite of the many setbacks to the conduct of the war there remains, generally, absolute confidence in Churchill." Many years after the event, Churchill (*GA*, 303) recorded this with gratitude.

[12] As early as 16 March General Halder noted that Marita might interfere with Barbarossa. The next day Hitler ordered plans for the occupation of all of Greece (the original plan for Marita called only for the occupation of the northern part of that country). Already at that time the German High Com-

may have been due not to Yugoslav resistance but to the very opposite, to the amazingly swift collapse of the Yugoslav and Greek field armies. This did not only give Hitler overconfidence but, had Hitler had his hands full with them for two months, he might have had to postpone the war against Russia for another month, perhaps even to 1942.

In May he had yet another alternative. He could have gone through the Near into the Middle East, with relative ease. The German victories made a deep impression on some of the peoples of the eastern Mediterranean.[13] Already in March a pro-German nationalist, Rashid Ali, had intrigued himself into becoming Prime Minister of Iraq. Admiral Darlan agreed to let German and Italian planes land in the French protectorate of Syria. Without undue difficulty the Germans, before or after Crete, could have leapfrogged across the eastern Mediterranean to Syria, Iraq, Cyprus at least. Beyond these places Iran, Egypt, Afghanistan were potential German allies. Yet Hitler felt that he could not afford this. Unlike Napoleon, he had little interest in the career of Alexander the Great. His directive of 23 May (the day of the decisive German success in Crete) made this clear: The Germans would support the Iraqis, but the final attack on the British in the Near and Middle East could occur only after Barbarossa. Perhaps he had, again, not only military but also political calculations in mind.[14] Almost certainly he missed a chance. With a little more effort he might have been able to destroy the entire British presence in the Near and Middle East, an event with hardly calculable consequences. As it happened, the latter, after a few critical days, re-established the balance in their favor. British and Indian troops landed at Basra at the mouth of the Persian Gulf. In early May Rashid Ali attacked British airfields in Iraq, with the help of a few German and Italian planes from Syria (and a few German troops wearing Iraqi markings on their German uniforms). The small British garrisons held out. As the prospects of the battle for Crete were darkening, those of the battle for Iraq were brightening for the British. The beleaguered airfields were freed by the advancing British column, and a week later Baghdad fell to the British on the day when the last badly battered British and imperial troops sailed away from Crete.[15]

---

mand began to consider a postponement of Barbarossa for six weeks. There were also extraordinary floods of the Polish rivers along the German-Soviet frontier, especially of the Bug.

[13] On 14 April, for example, King Farouk of Egypt sent a secret message to Hitler through Farouk's father-in-law, the Egyptian minister to Persia: He hoped that Germany would liberate Egypt soon "from the British yoke."

[14] On his thoughts about the British before his invasion of Russia, see below, pp. 133, 135–36.

[15] Meanwhile, the British had also conquered Abyssinia, the capital of which had fallen to the British on the day Belgrade was smashed by the Germans. On

Rashid Ali fled across the desert frontier to Persia. Eight days later a combined force of British, Gaullist French, and Polish brigades coming from Palestine, attacked the Vichy forces in Syria. The Vichy French struggled bitterly until they felt forced to capitulate, perhaps not altogether inappropriately, on Bastille Day. A few weeks later British and Russian troops invaded Persia, forcing the national leader, Reza Shah Pahlevi, to abdicate, and installing a pro-Allied government. But at that time the war between Germany and Russia was already at full fury.

Wherever British and German soldiers met face to face, the latter still carried the day. Encouraged by the Germans' inability to descend on the Middle East, Churchill pressed General Wavell to attack General Rommel in the western desert, after the latter had pushed the British back into Egypt. In a courageous naval operation (Tiger), Admiral Cunningham had succeeded in bringing a substantial number of British ships, carrying nearly three hundred tanks, across the Mediterranean in May. Supplied with these, Wavell attacked Rommel on 15 June. Within two days Operation Battleaxe failed. As Wavell himself felt constrained to explain: The German tanks and armored cars were better than the British, the training of the British troops was inferior to that of the Germans. It was a small battle, but "to me a most bitter blow."[16] Churchill was badly shaken. He dismissed Wavell.

I have been running ahead of the story of what was still the central theater of the war. Through the autumn and winter and spring the Germans went on bombing England relentlessly, with incendiary bombs. On 14 November 1940 they succeeded in setting Coventry afire in a raid that lasted for ten hours. On Sunday evening, 29 December, occurred the Second Great Fire of London, 274 years after the first. The spring was worse. The Clydeside towns were pounded for days in a row. So was Plymouth, where during the first night of the bombing something like a collective hallucination happened: "People had sworn that they had heard Drake's Drum beating, for this as for other momentous occasions."[17] By May morale sank to a dangerous low. Liverpool, bombed night after night, was swept by ominous rumors: People whispered that food riots had taken

---

17 May the Duke of Aosta, Italian commander-in-chief in East Africa, surrendered to the British. This dignified man died a few months later in captivity. Two Italian garrisons held out in the fastnesses of Ethiopia for a few more months. That was the end of Mussolini's African empire.

16 Churchill, *GA*, 343. "I went down to Chartwell, which was all shut up, wishing to be alone. . . . I wandered about the valley disconsolately for some hours."

17 T. H. O'Brien, cited in Calder, 211.

place and that desperate groups were marching around the streets with white flags. On 10 May, one year to the day since Churchill had come to power, London had her worst night, with nearly fifteen hundred people killed. American reporters saw unshaven men going to work; some of them felt that the morale of the people was breaking.[18]

That night—it was a Saturday—a German plane, solitary in the evening sky, crossed the east coast of Scotland. Picked out by observers, it flew inland, undisturbed, as night was falling fast. The pilot let the plane crash; he bailed out. He was no less of a personage than Rudolf Hess, Hitler's deputy. He came on his own, to tell the British about Hitler's goodwill, to make peace. We met him once before, in these pages,[19] in a footnote when he had been talking with his friends the Haushofers about peace with England, and of his contact with the Duke of Hamilton, at the height of the Battle of Britain. Now he had flown to Britain at the height of the Blitz. He was an idealist Nazi, a brave man, and a naïve German. He was naïve and ignorant about the British, thinking, among other things, that the Duke of Hamilton, who bore the title of Lord Steward of the Household, had the ear of the King. (As Churchill put it to a friend: "I suppose he thinks that the Duke carves the chicken and consults the King as to whether he likes breast or leg.")[20] Hess was not naïve about Hitler, and there is reason to believe that he levanted to England with Hitler's tacit knowledge. Of course Hitler and Goebbels instantly disavowed Hess, announcing that the latter suffered from delusion. Probably Hitler knew of Hess's plan, though not of his timing. Certainly Hitler and Hess were of the same mind. To make peace with Britain before the German invasion of Russia was Hitler's main wish. It was worth a try. Hess was astute enough not to tell the British anything about the coming war with Russia. He was far from astute in his estimate of British psychology. He kept repeating how kindly Hitler felt toward the English people, and how

---

[18] On 7 May Lloyd George said in the House of Commons: The idea that Britain could invade Europe was "fatuous." Churchill answered that this was "the sort of speech with which, I imagine, the illustrious and venerable Marshal Pétain might have enlivened the closing days of M. Reynaud's Cabinet." Nicolson in his diary on 8 May: "It is true that nobody actually speaks of the possibility of defeat or surrender but this silence is a bad sign of repression. I feel that people will jump at any escape which will make cowardice appear respectable. . . . Morale is good—but it is rather like the Emperor's clothes." On the other hand, according to Calder, the attitude of the people was "superficially depressed, but in fact courageous," 219. He cites a working-class woman in Portsmouth: ". . . sometimes I feels I can't stand it any more. But it don't do to say so." Very English, very true.

[19] See above, pp. 110–11.

[20] Pawle, 96.

it pained the Fuehrer to wage war against English women and children. He certainly did not impress Churchill. On the other hand, Churchill did little to exploit the propaganda value of Hess's flight, perhaps because of the then trials of the British people: They should not be thinking much about peace emissaries from Germany.

A few days later the air attacks were dying down. The German air fleets were moving east, to Poland. Slowly, gradually, the people of Britain breathed with relief, a relief that continued throughout the year, and that may have had much to do with their emotional—so emotional as to be un-British—outburst of Russophilia later.[21] They felt little relief, however, about their war with the Germans. There was the depressing defeat in Crete, where their Navy could do little. That week there was high drama, too, in the Atlantic. Two German warships, one of them Hitler's newest and largest, the *Bismarck*, sank the *Hood*, the largest battleship of the British, off Greenland, in a matter of minutes. An entire fleet of ships drove out for the *Bismarck*. Hunted down after four days, she was finally sunk. It was a thrilling naval episode—for onlookers. A fantastically successful German bull's-eye shot; the British inability to hit back in time; their maddeningly slow comeback; Churchill insisting and insisting that the German be tracked down, hell or high water; the undisclosed American participation in the search; "Various Parties Converging on the Sea"[22]; the assembly of overwhelming force; surrounded and pounded from every side, the burning and rudderless German still floats and floats; she sinks in the end. Few people knew that the course of the episode was to be a microcosm of the course of the entire Second World War.

A year had now passed since their finest hour. Britain would not be invaded; and, gradually at least, America was coming in. Yet for the peoples of Europe, the prospect of a British victory had become more remote. From the edges of Europe the British had been rolled back again. It was to be a long war, after all. Their enemies, including the new Germanophiles on the Continent, convinced themselves more and more that in the duel of a young Germany and an old England, the former was invincible. The friends of old England, at the same time, did not lose heart. A propaganda campaign, mounted by Goebbels across the Continent, to raise the letter "V" into a symbol of Victory for the Third Reich, misfired. "V" became a Churchillian symbol instead. The Morse code equivalent of "V," three short strokes and a long one, became the signal of the European broadcasts of the British Broadcasting Corporation, to

---

[21] See below, pp. 165, 411–13.
[22] Chapter heading in John Buchan's *The Thirty-nine Steps*.

which millions listened on the Continent. It was also the rhythmic sound of the first bar of Beethoven's Fifth Symphony. A bar of German music as the official symbol of British defiance: During the war of 1914–18 this would have been inconceivable. Now it was a matter of course. England, after all, was fighting for the traditional humanist civilization of Europe, to the heritage of which Beethoven belonged. London was not only a harbor, a refuge, a last bastion. She was the capital of traditional Europe, of a free Europe, she was the focus of hope, perhaps unduly so, a memory that later quickly faded but that, in retrospect, commands respect. She was the seat of the President of Poland, of the King of Norway, of the Queen of Holland, of the Constable of Free France, of the legal Belgian, Yugoslav, Greek, and other governments, and of many respected dignitaries and diplomatists who had chosen to resign from the service of their German-dominated governments, to form a focus of future freedom in the midst of this proud and blackened city. The streets of London were full of unusual color: Besides the smart outfits of Canadians and Australians there was the international touch of Polish soldiers, French sailors, Dutch marines. It must be recorded that the morale of these people remained high, practically without exception.

"It looks as if Hitler is massing against Russia," Churchill wrote General Smuts on 16 May.[23] Hitler certainly made few efforts to hide this. He cared not whether people, including Stalin, knew it—a condition that vastly reduces the import of the information conveyed to Stalin by secret agents whose achievements have been inflated later to legendary proportions. Hitler told of his intention to attack to the Yugoslav Prince Regent, to Finns, Romanians, and others weeks, sometimes months, before the day. Did he want to impress Stalin to the point where the latter would surrender to all kinds of German demands? This is unlikely. Hitler had not formulated such demands. In this war there would be no Brest-Litovsk. It seems, on the contrary, that he wanted to impress the British and the Americans. Here was their last chance to stop fighting Germany.[24] Hess obviously failed. Around mid-June the tireless Dahlerus appeared again in

---

[23] Churchill, *GA*, 283.

[24] Hitler to his circle on 4 February 1945: "Later, when I attacked eastward and lanced the Communist abscess I hoped thereby to rekindle a spark of common sense in the minds of the Western Powers. I gave them a chance, without lifting a finger. . . . But the hatred felt by these hypocrites for a man of good faith is stronger than their sense of self-preservation. I had underestimated the power of Jewish domination over Churchill's England. . . ." *Hitler-Bormann*, 30–31.

the wings of the world scene, if only for a moment. He tried to transmit a message to the British in Stockholm. Goering had told him that Germany would soon attack the Soviet Union.

For the last time we must contemplate Hitler's decision. It was the loneliest he had ever taken. Perhaps with the only exception of the light-weight Nazi ideologue Rosenberg, whom Hitler did not take seriously, none of the hierarchy of the Reich were plumping for war against Russia. Hitler would not be dissuaded by his advisers or underlings, Ribbentrop, Raeder, Weizsaecker, Schulenburg, either by Nazis or by conservatives.[25] More than on other occasions, he had to justify his decision, in order to convince himself, first of all. His arguments were economical, tactical, strategic, and political, in ascending importance. Germany had profited from the economic deals with the Soviet Union; but he did not want to depend on Stalin. This was not much of an argument. He was getting from Russia much of the stuff he wanted.[26] The tactical argument Hitler summed up but once, to the visiting Romanian Marshal Antonescu ten days before the invasion: Russia might not attack Germany directly but press against Finland and Romania, binding down ever greater German forces on the flanks of the Reich.[27] The strategic argument made more

---

[25] He told Ribbentrop of his definite decision only on 6 April. It must be noted, however, that some of his generals were, for once, full of confidence.

[26] On 15 February 1945 he justified his decision to his circle: "Another reason was that the raw materials which the Russians were withholding were essential to us. In spite of their obligations their rate of delivery decreased steadily, and there was a real danger that they might suddenly cease altogether." *Hitler-Bormann*, 63–65. (Some of this argument is restated by Hillgruber, *HS*, 257: Hitler's economic and political dependence on Stalin was bound to increase.) This was quite untrue. Cf. Ritter circular, 11 January 1941, in *GD*, D, XI, 1071–72: "The Soviet Union has delivered everything that she promised. In many fields she has delivered even more than had originally been agreed upon. In the organization of the high shipments, the Soviet Union has performed in a really admirable manner . . . the biggest economic treaty complex that has ever been concluded between two states." The extent and punctuality of Russian deliveries was even more impressive in June than in January.

[27] Another, less ingenuous, version Hitler would offer later, as for example to his admirer Sven Hedin in October 1942, ". . . people who thought to do evil have done good. If Poland had been prepared to accept the agreement I offered, then it would never have come to war. But in that case Russia would have been able to complete her armaments to a scale that we only know now and are in a position to estimate. Another five years of peace, and Europe would simply have been crushed flat under the weight of the Bolshevik war machine. For it is obvious that, once the German-Polish dispute had been settled, the Reich and above all the National Socialist movement would have turned their attention in the first place to culture and above all to the social

sense. Instead of creating a two-front war, he would put an end to it. When Russia was eliminated, Britain's last hope on the Continent would be shattered. Time was of the essence, for Britain was still not strong enough to cause serious trouble in Germany's rear. "Now we have the possibility to smash Russia while our backs are free. This opportunity will not recur.[28] There was a political consideration behind this argument. The defeat of Communist Russia might rekindle American sentiments of self-interest. Americans may be impressed not only with Germany's invincibility in Europe, but they might also take some comfort from the final defeat of communism. The opponents of Roosevelt, who were far more anti-Communist than anti-German, would rise in strength.[29] In any event, Hitler issued a stringent directive on 21 June, the eve of his invasion of Russia: German submarines, ships, and airplanes must *"avoid under all circumstances* [italics in the original] clashes with American naval forces."[30]

These calculations were not altogether insubstantial. Hitler's decision to attack Stalin's Russia was not the result of madness; there was method in Hitler's mind. At any rate, he pondered it deeply. Four years later, on the verge of defeat, he said to his circle: "No decision which I have had to make during the course of this war was graver than that to attack Russia. I had always maintained that we ought at all costs to avoid waging war on two fronts, and you may rest assured that I pondered long and anxiously over Napoleon and his experiences in Russia."[31] All of this reduces the simplistic argument of those historians who, resting their case on the evidence of *Mein Kampf* alone, argue that war against Russia was Hitler's singleminded obsession, the ultimate opportunity of which he looked forward all through his life.[32] True, on 22 June he wrote Mussolini that his partnership with the Soviet Union had been often "very irksome to me" and that he was "happy to be relieved of these mental agonies." On the

---

questions. . . . Bolshevism would have succeeded in sending a synthesis of millions of fanatical and brutal fighting men with an inconceivable weight of armament to pound its way across harmless old Europe." *Hedin,* 251. "Harmless old Europe" is good. Did Hitler believe this argument himself?

[28] "I should be a criminal, neglecting the future of the German people, if I do not act." Bock diary, 30 March 1941. The same argument on 15 February 1945, in retrospect, in *Hitler-Bormann,* 64–65.

[29] Churchill was aware of this danger. He alluded to it in his message to Roosevelt on 15 June 1941, in Churchill, *GA,* 369.

[30] This strict order was repeated on 10 July, twice in September, and for the last time on 21 November 1941.

[31] *Hitler-Bormann,* 63.

[32] His singleminded obsession was the Jews, not Russia. See below, pp. 446 *et seq.*

other hand, his astonishing sense of premonition asserted itself again. By the middle of June, when his military advisers were declaiming that Russia would be beaten in no time and when someone spoke of Russia as a "big bubble," Hitler suddenly became thoughtful and said that Russia was rather like the ship in Wagner's *Flying Dutchman*. "The beginning of every war is like opening a door into a dark room. One never knows what is hidden in the darkness."[33]

He was wrong when he tried to convince himself that Stalin was about to move against him. Nothing was farther from the truth. No bourgeois statesman ever cowered before Hitler in the way Stalin and Molotov behaved for at least two months before the dreaded day came. They paid fulsome attention to Germany, they fulfilled and overfulfilled their deliveries, they ignored and insulted the British, they refused to acknowledge British and American information about the assembling German armies along their border, they kicked out of Moscow the representatives of Britain's allies, they gave recognition to every ally and satellite of Germany and to every enemy of Britain, they allowed German planes to fly deeper and deeper over their western frontiers without protest, in the end they even drafted an abject communiqué that was broadcast to the Soviet Union and to the world on 13 June, denying that there was, or could be, any trouble between Germany and Russia, pleading afterward for a single German reassurance of goodwill. Consequently the Russian people were wholly unprepared for the war. The alert of the Soviet armed forces was either incomplete or nonexistent. There were but two moves by Stalin that attest to his statesmanship during this agonizing time: One was his nonaggression pact with Japan, signed on 13 April, which eliminated the danger of a two-front war for the Soviet Union, at least for a time. The other was his self-elevation to the head of the government. On 6 May 1941 Stalin ceased to be merely the secretary of the party, he became Chairman of the Council of People's Commissars, an event that was not widely appreciated at the time.

Gradually, mechanically, systematically the German armies were put into a state of readiness. The code name Dortmund for the attack went out after noon on 21 June. The coming night was that of the summer solstice, the shortest night of the year. Hundreds of thousands of German soldiers would remember that pale summer night along the river of Poland, the loud croaking of thousands of frogs on the low banks of the Bug. Shortly before midnight the Moscow–Berlin express passed over the frontier bridge near Brest. It was followed by a long Russian goods train for Germany. The German motors began to roar. At 3:15 A.M. the flash of thousands of German guns lit up the sky. Above them swarms of Ger-

---

[33] Zoller, 142–43.

man planes were on their way to destroy the Soviet Air Force on the ground before the full day shone forth.

It was a hot June Sunday, with the sun shining over most of Europe. In Italy Mussolini as well as the Soviet ambassador had gone bathing in the sea. It was a day of historical memories and of new prospects for the French, whose hearts and minds were filled with new hopes.[34] So it was for many people, including Churchill, who prepared his broadcast during the day in the garden of Chequers. It was a speech full of purple rhetoric as well as cool and carefully calculated common sense. He did not care for communism. "But all this fades away before the spectacle which is now unfolding. . . . I have to declare the decision of His Majesty's Government . . . at once, without a day's delay. I have to make the declaration, but can you doubt what our policy will be? We have but one aim and one single, irrevocable purpose. We are resolved to destroy Hitler and every vestige of the Nazi regime. From this nothing will turn us— nothing. We will never parley, we will never negotiate with Hitler or any of his gang. . . . Any man or state who fights on against Nazidom will have our aid. Any man or state who marches with Hitler is our foe. . . ." This was a leonine roar, even more impressive than that of the German gunnery.

In the Kremlin there was a stunned silence that day. When the declaration of war was handed to him, Iron Man Molotov came close to apologizing. "Do you believe we deserved this?" he asked the German ambassador. At the same hour in Berlin the Soviet ambassador, Stalin's Georgian minion, asked Ribbentrop whether there wasn't a mistake, after all. Dekanosov took some comfort from the fact that Ribbentrop did not seem very happy. Stalin, too, hoping against hope, at first ordered the Soviet artillerists not to fire back at the Germans. The Moscow radio opened its daily service with a program of calisthenics. Later in the day Molotov went on the radio with a dull speech. By that time almost one half of the Soviet Air Force lay wrecked on the ground, and the returning German planes could see the dust clouds raised by the German tanks and trucks cascading forward many miles to the east of the borders of the Soviet Union.

---

[34] One of their writers recorded this in his diary with a kind of noble simplicity. "*Dimanche matin, les Français ont connu un grand bonheur. Le Reich dans la nuit avait déclaré la guerre aux Soviets.*" Guéhenno, 124.

# 8 . Germany rampant[1]

ON 22 JUNE the news in the morning was a bombshell event. Still for millions of Europeans it was but another German invasion, the start of yet another German campaign on a Sunday morning. It certainly began according to what had become the pattern. The Germans were driving forward fast. Hitler told Goebbels that the campaign might take four months. Goebbels reported this to his collaborators, adding that in his opinion it would be shorter, eight weeks: National Socialism was far superior to Communism, in organization as well as in spirit; this condition would manifest itself on the battlefield.[2] And so it appeared. Three weeks after the invasion, Hitler told the Japanese ambassador, Oshima, that he did not think that the Russian war would last more than six weeks. The projections of British and of American Army intelligence were similar: four weeks, six weeks, three months at the most.[3] Laurence Steinhardt, the American ambassador in Moscow, a principled and intelligent man, cabled before 22 June that he doubted whether Stalin's regime could survive a German invasion. His predecessor Joseph Davies, a silly millionaire who had swallowed most of the lies of Stalinite propaganda during the 1936–39 purge trials, told Roosevelt the very opposite: that Stalin would undoubtedly beat Hitler, which was what Roosevelt wanted to hear. Eventually Davies was proven right for the wrong reasons. Steinhardt was wrong, though for the right reasons. Such is the irony of history—if that is the right phrase, which this writer somehow thinks it is not.

At this point a philosophical question arises. Is the process of history the same as its results from retrospect? Yes and no. It is not the business of the historian to speculate (not much, at any rate) about what may have

---

[1] 22 June–1 November 1941.
[2] Boelcke, 659.
[3] Woodward, 150, note 1, 153; Eden II, 269.

happened when it did not happen. Yet his business is the mental reconstruction of the past: He must remember and record what people thought and knew at a certain time, even if they were to be proven wrong. He must understand that actuality and potentiality cannot be always separated, no more in the present than in the past. We know that Hitler lost the war in Russia. By 1942 many people knew that he was about to lose the war in Russia. What we seldom consider is that he came very close to winning it in 1941. On 22 June he flung three fourths of his mighty Army forward into the Soviet wasteland.[4] Within two days the Germans took Vilna and Kaunas. In eight days they were in Lwow. Seven days later they were in Riga, having done in a week what had taken the Imperial German Army three years during World War I. The Finnish and Romanian armies[5] moved with them along the flanks. Italy, Hungary, Slovakia, Croatia declared war on the Soviet Union; Spain sent a volunteer division on its own. A small but increasing number of volunteers came from the Western and Northern European countries that had been conquered by Hitler. The latter decided to accept all foreign states who wanted to participate in his "crusade."[6] Half of the Soviet Air Force was destroyed, more than twenty-five hundred planes in the first two days of the war. The Red Navy lumbered uselessly in the Gulf of Finland. Everywhere the Soviet armies were reeling back. Their generalship was far inferior to that of the Germans.

Stalin did not gather sufficient resolution to address the people of the Soviet Union until 3 July, in a monotonous speech, though significantly replete with ancient patriotic allusions. He had ordered the Soviet armies to launch counterattacks against the Germans and stand firm without giving up ground. With one minor exception (Yelnya before Smolensk), all of the counterattacks failed, and the Germans began to encircle larger and larger masses of Russians. In the middle of August Smolensk fell, an event that Moscow would not admit to its people for four more weeks. The Germans reached the outskirts of Leningrad. On 18 August Hitler or-

---

[4] On 22 June there were 153 German divisions in the East, 8 in Norway, 38 in Western Europe, 2 in North Africa, 7 in the Balkans, and 1 in Germany.

[5] The latter produced 30 divisions, more than all of the other satellites counted together.

[6] On 24 June, the Soviets helped to provoke the Finnish declaration of war by sending bombers over Helsinki prematurely. The incident prompting Hungary's declaration of war (on 26 June) remains a mystery. Three planes, with strange markings, dropped a few bombs on a Hungarian town. Some people, including historians in retrospect, think that they were German, others that they were Russian, again others that they were Slovak, of all things. Still it makes little difference. The majority of the Finnish government and of the Hungarian government were resolved to go along with the Germans.

dered a halt of the forward movement of Army Group Center, which was advancing along the Smolensk highway to Moscow. German losses had begun to mount; the Russians' fire could be murderous; the size and the armor of some of the Russian tanks proved to be impressive. "We may have underestimated the Russian colossus," the German chief of staff noted in his war diary on 11 August. Still nowhere did the Russians succeed in defeating the Germans. Hitler was coming close to winning his Russian campaign and, with it, the Last European War.

"The political testament of the German nation," Hitler had written at the end of *Mein Kampf*,[7] "should and must always read substantially: Never tolerate the establishment of two continental powers in Europe. . . . See an attack on Germany in any such attempt to organize a military power on the frontiers of Germany. . . . See to it that the strength of our nation is founded, not on colonies, but on the European territory. . . . Never regard the Reich as secure while it is unable to give every national offshoot for centuries his own bit of soil and territory. . . ." Now, finally, Hitler acted in accordance with this. Only now he got himself into a two-front war, against a large empire whose chief had succeeded in avoiding this very condition. Stalin's pact of nonaggression with the Japanese, signed in April, had been of very great help to Russia. True, the same Matsuoka who had signed it—a representative example of Japanese chivalry, no doubt—was now agitating in Tokyo that Japan join the Germans and attack the Soviet Union. Yet on 2 July 1941 a long imperial conference in Tokyo decided against this. Japan would prepare for war against Britain and the United States, not against the Soviet Union. This was a decision of monumental importance. Had the Japanese attacked Stalin's empire from the rear during that burning July they, and the Germans, might have won the war. One of the reasons why they did not do so was that Hitler did not press them for it—rather the contrary.[8] Japan's task was to tie America down, away from Europe. He wanted to win the war against Russia singlehanded in 1941.

But what did he mean by winning the war against Russia? We must, at this point, raise a question that has perhaps not received the attention it deserves. The brutal measures of subjugation and terror that Hitler and his cohorts ordered for Russia—we shall return to them in a moment—

---

[7] Hitler, *MK*, 963–64. The entire passage is underlined in the book.
[8] Already on 5 March 1941, under the heading "Co-operation with Japan," his Directive No. 24 read, among other things: "The common aim of strategy must be represented as the swift conquest of England in order to keep America out of the war."

overwhelm the picture, especially in retrospect. Hitler waged total war against Russia, and total war meant total conquest. Yet these are powerful but vague terms. Hitler knew that he could not occupy the entire Soviet Union, just as he did not want to occupy all of France or all of Britain. The directive of Barbarossa said that the "final aim" of the operation would be the line of the Volga, on to Archangel in the North. But what would happen after that? Did Hitler think that Stalin's regime would collapse and some kind of Russian Pétain or Quisling would appear, an anti-Communist from somewhere in Siberia, asking for an armistice? Everything indicates the contrary. Hitler had a high opinion of Stalin, a sentiment that the latter reciprocated. In February Hitler had told Field Marshal Bock that after the conquest of the Ukraine and Moscow and Leningrad "the Soviets would surely consent to a compromise."[9] In July he told Papen that Stalin was a great man, and that after reaching the Volga-Archangel line he might be ready to deal with him.[10] He repeated this in his closer circle.[11] In sum, Hitler may have thought about letting Stalin have a way out—after he had thoroughly beaten him in the field.

This may explain much, though not all, about the two cardinal errors attributable to Hitler already during the rampant progress of his armies across the Soviet Union in 1941. One was the brutality and the neglect with which he ordered that the peoples of the Soviet Union be treated. The other was his order halting his Army Group Center in August along the road to Moscow. About the first, mountains of nonsensical speculation have been written and spoken. The accepted view in the Western world, even now, is this: Under Stalin's tyrannical communism the peoples of the Russias were living in abject misery. (True.) They were ready to welcome the Germans as their liberators. (Partly true.) Hitler made a terrible mistake in neglecting these sentiments; he could have made millions of people rally against the Soviet regime. (Untrue.)[12] Most of the people

---

[9] Hillgruber, *HS*, 373–74.

[10] Hassell, 229–30.

[11] The Army's propaganda instructions for Barbarossa also warned against "premature" propaganda suggesting that the German war aims included the breakup of the Soviet Union into national states. *OKW*, 144/41, signed Jodl, in "Sammelmappe Barbarossa," III W 59–1 (Bundesarchiv Koblenz).

[12] A good example not only of misjudgment but of possible unconscious falsification occurs in the book by the eminent British military historian General J. F. C. Fuller: "Everywhere the Germans were welcomed as liberators by the common people." Fuller, 262–63. Fuller goes on to cite Reitlinger, who wrote the best work on the Germans' rule in Russia. Fuller's citation reads: "'Had the Germans,' writes Reitlinger, 'brought with them to Russia something like President Wilson's Fourteen Points of 1918, Russia would have

who welcomed the Germans did so because they believed that the Germans were winning, that they were to be the new masters. The exception were the Baltic peoples, only recently subjugated by Stalin, who really welcomed the Germans as liberators and not merely as new masters, and some of the Ukrainians. But Hitler did not intend to exempt them from his kind of iron Machiavellianism. He believed that it would be folly to share the government of the conquered lands with the native peoples.[13] Only trouble would issue therefrom. The best way was to treat these peoples sternly, from the beginning. In the event of a rapid German victory, the initial disillusionment with the severity of their new masters would disappear. In the event of a lengthy campaign, the more discipline the better. Hitler may have been right about the reactions of the conquered Soviet peoples: The Germans' brutality and resolution impressed them, as it impressed Stalin, whose opinion of Hitler remained high throughout the war. Hitler's actions and Stalin's reactions proved again how much truer than Marx was Proudhon, who said that people respond less to social contracts or ideologies than to the realities of power.

The war in the East, Hitler told his commanders, shall be a different war from the war fought heretofore. It will be a war of annihilation, where utmost brutality and resolution must go hand in hand. He issued an unprecedented "Commissar Order," according to which captured political officers of the Red Army were to be shot on the spot. Whether a better German treatment of Soviet prisoners would have led to their whole-

---

disintegrated just as Germany had done then' . . . 'Hitler never have diverted his armies from Moscow, in order to secure the Ukraine, since the Ukrainians would have offered to him.' " The reference reads: "Ibid., p. 22." But Reitlinger did not write this, on page 22 or anywhere else. He quoted a memorandum by Braeutigam, an able Nazi official, adding: "The notion that Russia could be easily split by psychological warfare . . . is bunkum."

[13] In March 1941 Hitler still considered the establishment of "weak socialist states" in the conquered lands of the Russian empire. By 16 July he changed his mind: no such states should exist. The memorandum of his conference held at Angerburg states that the political organization of the eastern states should be left in abeyance; this included the Ukraine, where on occasion the army and other German authorities, working at cross purposes with each other, for a while tolerated the existence of Ukrainian "governments." Still, as Reitlinger put it: "Hitler was nearer to perceiving the realities of the situation in the Ukraine than Rosenberg and the pro-Ukrainians, in spite of his astonishing limitations." Reitlinger, House, 160. It is noteworthy that the phrase "final solution" (Endloesung) first appeared in the minutes of the Angerburg meeting, kept by Bormann. It did not yet refer to Jews, nor to the physical extermination of peoples.

sale surrender is difficult to tell. At any rate, not one of his generals protested in the beginning. So far as tactics and movement went, they prepared to fight the same kind of war as heretofore: large motor-driven slashes into the enemy country, driving ahead so fast as to create panic and havoc among the enemy, encircling large numbers of them who would eventually surrender. After a while it dawned on both Hitler and his generals that this kind of *blitzkrieg* in Russia would not suffice. The country was too vast; the steel fingers of German armor were writing their paths in sand and mud. The enemy was too numerous; it reappeared again and again, ahead of the Germans, along their flanks, even behind them. The Germans would have to assert their presence. The vast lands between the few highways and gravel roads would have to be cleansed and occupied. For a while this was possible without much difficulty, but at an increasing cost in men. By the end of July, German losses were mounting. Relatively few of their officers and soldiers fell in set battles or sieges. They were often hit by Russian fire unexpectedly, after the main front was thought to have moved ahead. The peoples of the Russias were sullen, passive, unthinking. The very primitiveness in which the Soviet regime had kept them made them indifferent to material deprivations, and unaccustomed to questioning their indigenous rulers.[14]

We do not know exactly why Hitler ordered the halt of Army Group Center. We know that many months earlier, during the planning of Barbarossa, he kept repeating that too much importance must not be attributed to the capture of Moscow. It is unlikely (though not impossible) that by this halt on the road to Moscow Hitler wished to signal something to Stalin. Most probably Hitler thought that a certain amount of caution was in order. It may have been fatal, but it was not altogether foolish, no matter what the German generals would say in retrospect. Before the winter, Hitler ordered on 21 August, the aims to be achieved included the conquest of the Crimea, the Donets basin, and Leningrad. The latter was about to be encircled. Hitler did not want to spend an army on its siege. At the same time the German commanders before Leningrad did not extend to their opponents the customary offer to surrender. Hitler did not want to have to feed the people of Leningrad. He believed that because of starvation the defense of the city would eventually collapse. Unlike Stalingrad a year later, Leningrad was of secondary impor-

---

[14] Unlike the British in 1940, they did not have to suppress the temptation to think of alternatives. These simply did not occur to them. On the other hand, once the alternative entered into their minds, they would go over to the Germans almost instantly, on occasions that were otherwise unpredictable. About this momentum of minds, see below, pp. 425-26.

tance to him. Hitler said this before, not after, the siege. In any event, the order to halt and replenish on the road to Moscow did not mean a temporary lull on the other principal fronts—rather the contrary. Leningrad was nearly encircled, the Dnieper was crossed, the southern group of the German armies drove deep into the Ukraine. On 19 September Kiev fell. The Ukrainian population waved on the Germans; the Jews cowered in dark fear. Within a week Army Group South announced the capture of 655,000 prisoners in the battle movements around Kiev alone. The Germans had now taken more than 2.5 million Soviet prisoners. The Russian Air Force had no more than 1,200 planes. Winter was still more than a month away. The Soviet Union was on the verge of collapse.

*The Soviet Union was on the verge of collapse.* These are not merely the words of a single historian, writing comfortably in retrospect. "The Soviet Union," Stalin cabled Churchill on 3 September 1941, was "in a position of mortal peril."[15] On that day—two years to the day since she had gone to war with Germany—so was Britain. Had the Soviet Union surrendered to Hitler, Churchill and Roosevelt would have been faced with the gravest of problems. Hitler might have gotten what he wanted. In sum, the early autumn of 1941 was as critical as the early summer of 1940 had been.

Did Churchill and Roosevelt know this?[16] Yes and no. Having finally seen the Lend-lease and the Selective Service Acts through a recalcitrant and often tiresome Congress, in the summer of 1941 Roosevelt was in a kind of doldrum. The United States were becoming the Arsenal of Democracy: But what did this mean? With all the American help the British

---

[15] Stalin to Churchill, 3 September 1941, annexed to the Cabinet meeting record, Cab. 65/23 WM (41) of 5 September 1941. The text of his message is slightly altered in the Soviet publication of the Stalin-Churchill wartime correspondence. ("This has resulted in a lessening of our defence capacity and has confronted the Soviet Union with mortal danger.") Stalin-Churchill, 21.

[16] Did Hitler know it? Again, yes and no. There is something odd about his behavior during this victorious phase of his Russian campaign. Somehow or other his interest in the campaign would flag to a desultory level. In a different way from the time of Sea Lion, it seems as if his mind—mind, rather than heart—was often not wholly committed to the development of Barbarossa, a kind of unwillingness of concentration for which Hitler compensated by his orders for a brutal and aggressive waging of the war. In times of crisis, however, this relative vagueness of concentration would disappear—as, for example, in the winter crisis of December 1941–January 1942.

alone were not able to defeat Hitler. The latter, in turn, was clever enough to refrain from responding to Roosevelt's provocations in the Atlantic. In the summer of 1941 isolationist—that is, Anglophobe and Russophobe—sentiment among the American people was still strong.[17] In the event of a German triumph over Communist Russia it might have become overwhelming.

In the middle of August Churchill and Roosevelt met secretly off Newfoundland. This Atlantic conference was the first summit of the war. It resulted in the proclamation of an Atlantic Charter, an improvement over Wilson's Fourteen Points in one important respect: It contained only eight. Otherwise it was not a very successful conference. Churchill told Roosevelt that Russia might be beaten. With Russia out of the war and the United States not yet in the war, what would happen? It was urgent that the United States should somehow come in. Roosevelt agreed. He would try to "force an incident." Yet both he and Churchill knew that Hitler wasn't likely to play that game. At the end of August, after his return to London, Churchill admitted to Harry Hopkins that the War Cabinet found the situation depressing. If Russia were to be knocked out and Britain were to remain alone, "all kinds of dangers may arise."[18]

Stalin was suspicious of the British,[19] less suspicious of the Americans. Yet ever since 22 June the British had been his allies. He and Churchill began to exchange private messages in July; they signed a pact not to conclude a separate peace; they sent military missions to each other; they shelved the difficult Polish problem through Russia's formal recognition of the Polish government-in-exile; they dealt together with Persia. Throughout August, British intelligence estimated that the Soviet government would not do a Brest-Litovsk. But at the end of August there were ominous symptoms. For the second time Stalin was losing his nerve. On 26 August the Soviet ambassador suggested to Eden, and a week later to Churchill, that Russia might be forced to drop out of the war.[20] This was

---

[17] See, for example, Roosevelt's concern with American Catholics in his letter to the Pope on 3 September 1941, below, p. 507.

[18] Wilson, 259. Churchill to Hopkins, 29 August. To Hopkins, Churchill may have been harping on the Russian danger in order to force the pace of American intervention.

[19] He was also unsure with them, as was most of the Kremlin hierarchy. Thus Vishinski, on 22 June, in his first meeting with the British chargé after the German invasion, showed himself to be extremely nervous rather than relieved.

[20] Eden to Cripps, 26 August 1941: "The ambassador begged me to believe that something must be done quickly to remedy this state of affairs if we were to avoid the danger of growing mistrust between our two countries." FO 371, N 4840/78/G. Cripps to Churchill, 3 September, asked for a "superhuman

the gist, too, of Stalin's message of 3 September to Churchill. The British were doing very little in the West. They ought to send an expedition across the Channel or into the Balkans, to draw off thirty or forty German divisions from the Russian front, plus "a minimum monthly aid of 400 aeroplanes and 500 tanks. . . . Without these two kinds of aid the Soviet Union will be either defeated or weakened to the extent that it will lose for a long time the ability to help its Allies by active operations at the front against Hitlerism."[21] On 5 September Churchill and the Cabinet met to discuss these serious matters.[22] Churchill drafted an answer to Stalin. The British could not attempt a landing on the Continent: Their expeditionary force would be wiped out, with grievous consequences to the entire Allied cause. Stalin was now depressed enough[23] to suggest something extraordinary. On 13 September he asked Churchill to send twenty-five or thirty British divisions to the Soviet Union proper, either through Archangel or from Persia. Shades of Lenin and of the Russian Civil War! It is a pity that it did not come about. What a book Evelyn Waugh could have written, about the adventures of the Sherwood Foresters in the Ukraine.[24] Perhaps Churchill should have thought about it a little more. But he did not have the extra ships, or the extra men. All that he could promise Stalin was more arms, more bombs on Germany, and the pros-

---

effort," "take action to save collapse here." Churchill answered: "When you speak of a superhuman effort, you mean, I presume, an effort rising superior to space, time and geography. Unfortunately, such attributes are denied us." Gwyer, Butler, III, 194.

[21] Stalin-Churchill, 21.

[22] The Cabinet met with the chiefs of staff first at 10:30 A.M. Half an hour later they repeated their arguments to Maisky. Cab. 79/14, 479. The Cabinet met again at 4:15 P.M. to discuss Churchill's draft reply to Stalin. "Although there was nothing in the actual words that M. Maisky used to justify it, he (the Prime Minister) had the feeling that the possibility of a separate peace could not be altogether excluded." Cab. 65/23 (WM) 90. Two days later Churchill sent Beaverbrook to interview Hess in secret. Eventually Beaverbrook gave a translation of a memorandum by Hess to Stalin. Beaverbrook did not, however, give Stalin the transcript of his conversation with Hess. (Part of the transcript is given in Taylor, *Beaverbrook*.) Whether Churchill's main purpose was to impress Stalin or whether it was to sound Hess out is difficult to tell.

[23] On 7 September Cripps found him "very depressed and tired," "with some return of the old attitude of suspicion and distrust." Woodward II, 33. At the same time he told Cripps that he would not make a separate peace. Cripps to Eden, 7 September, FO 371, N 5113/78/38.

[24] Possible titles: *The Red Miss Chief; Comrades in Arms: Kommissarovka Revisited.*

pects of a British landing in northern Norway. Soon the chiefs of staff would tell Churchill that this, too, was impossible at the time.[25]

Hitler's great mistake in Russia may not have been his treatment of its peoples; it may have been his treatment of Stalin. Hitler ought to have let Stalin know in September 1941 what he let the French know in June 1940, that the end of resistance in the field did not mean the end of the Soviet state. But Hitler would not let Stalin retire from the field with an army that, no matter how badly beaten, was not yet thoroughly broken up. He surely was on his way to that, Hitler thought.

On 30 September Army Group Center lunged forward in the direction of Moscow. Operation Taifun was commanded by Field Marshal Fedor von Bock, a Prussian aristocrat, of the type whom people prefer to contrast with the vulgar Nazidom around Hitler: a "conservative" of the "old school." Yet this writer finds it difficult to command much sympathy for Bock who, no matter how conservative, went along with the most brutal and radical directives not only of Hitler but also of the Nazi party hierarchy. Despite (or, perhaps, partly because) of his Prussian traditions and of the many Russian connections of his family, Bock behaved in Russia like a caricature of a Prussian general: narrow, single-minded, unimaginative, and cruel. Thin, aged, skeletonlike, he was afire with the ambition of marching into Moscow before anyone else, and before winter came.

Nearly everything went well. German motorized infantry stormed into Orel so fast that people on the crowded trolley cars waved at them, unaware that they were Germans. After a week of fighting the panzer pincers closed around another enormous pocket, in the region of Vyazma and Bryansk, capturing another 660,000 Soviet soldiers. A single German division corralled 108,000 prisoners, more than what the entire German Army had captured in August 1914 in the decisive Battle of Tannenberg. During the second week of October Kaluga, Kalinin, Vyazma, and Bryansk fell, ninety-odd miles before Moscow. The German advance was slowing down, but before them the Russian armies were beginning to disintegrate. Already in mid-September Stalin had been forced to admit: "Unfortunately, firm and steady commanders and commissars are not

---

[25] Churchill knew how desperate the situation was. He demanded that the chiefs of staff prepare immediate plans for a British descent on Trondheim in Norway. The latter, powerfully assisted by the First Sea Lord, refused to go along. Bryant, 206. Churchill despaired of his generals: "I sometimes think that some of my generals don't want to fight the Germans"—a sentiment expressed by Stalin on occasion, to Churchill's dismay.

very numerous in our ranks."[26] On 12 October Zhukov was named commander of the Russian Western Front. The ranks were beginning to crack, infantrymen were disappearing from the field, though most of them would return. It was not like the French Army in 1940; it was, rather, like the Russian Army in 1917.

The most serious development was the panic in Moscow. This was a hidden event in the history of the last war. For four days—from 15 to 19 October—the vast majority of the people of Moscow expected the Germans to arrive at any moment, and they acted as if that even were not altogether unwelcome.[27] On 15 October the Soviet government left the capital, for Kuybishev on the Volga, six hundred miles to the east. The high party functionaries were leaving Moscow in great haste. On the road leading to the east there developed the first traffic jam in the history of the Soviet Union. Marauders attacked some of the cars, rifling and blackmailing the occupants, especially when these were recognizable as Jews. Within Moscow groups of deserters and workers began to plunder stores. Rumors circulated to the effect that the sacred body of Lenin had been removed from Red Square. Many of the workers ignored the orders of their evacuation to the east. The police had disappeared. People were buying up German-Russian dictionaries. The accepted view, according to which the Muscovites were bracing themselves for a heroic last-ditch resistance, building barricades day and night, is a myth. The mass of the Muscovites awaited the Germans with a mixture of expectation and apathy.[28] Moscow lay open for the taking. The Germans did not know this. Their famous, or infamous, intelligence failed them,[29] just as it had failed them in May 1917 when they did not realize how close to mutiny entire French divisions had been. A single German parachute regiment could have taken Moscow. Neither Hitler nor Bock realized their chance.

On the front winter had not yet begun. But the rains came. Rows and rows of German tanks and trucks and guns and motorcycles were mired in the mud, even on the main roads. The very motorization of the German Army stalled it in its tracks. There were muddy, desperate scenes everywhere within the German half circle before Moscow, a traffic jam far more consequential than was the ugly scene behind Moscow involving the fleeing Russian cars on the eastern highway. The German commanders and their soldiers cursed and prayed that frost would come, making

---

[26] Message to Shaposhnikov on 15 September, cited in Blackstock, 22, note 6.

[27] See about this below, p. 389.

[28] See below, p. 389, 397.

[29] The wise old former ambassador, Schulenburg, later too "attributed the German failure to capture Moscow to poor intelligence." Goure, Dinerstein, 218.

the roads and the fields passable again. Soon they would get all the frost they wanted.

Stalin, who watched the slowing down of the German advance, now did not lose his nerve. Time was working for him, he thought. On 19 October he reappeared in the Kremlin. He asked Shcherbakov, the cruel chairman of the Moscow Soviets: "Should we defend Moscow?" It was a rhetorical question. There and then a decree proclaimed a state of siege, and a curfew, in Moscow. The people were amazed, a little shameful, a little disappointed. Sixty miles away on the main road, Mozhaisk had fallen that day,[30] but the crisis was passing. On 23 October Molotov, who had complained about Britain to the Polish ambassador the day before, flew back to Moscow from Kuybishev. Stalin did not leave the capital again. On 29 October Army Group Center was ordered to halt. The next day the first snowstorm swept along its front; but the hard frost would not set in for another week.

We know now: In many ways, though not in all, mid-October 1941 may have been the turning point of the struggle for Moscow. But people, including the people of the Russias, did not know this then. Discipline in Moscow was restored; but behind the front, desertions continued; near the front, even peasants were beginning to abandon the collective farms. The thought that the war might be over, that the Germans had won, began to lodge within their skulls, here and there. We have few written evidences of this, partly because of the conditions of those times, partly because many who lived through them would not admit it later; but fragments of such evidence survive in the reminiscences of certain Russians, on occasion in the captured personal papers of Russian officers.[31]

Thus along the Moscow front the German armies were worn down,

---

[30] That day Beaverbrook presented a memorandum, entitled "Assistance to Russia," to the British Cabinet. "The chiefs of staff would have us wait until the last button has been sewn on the last gaiter before we launch an attack. . . . If we do not help them now the Russians may collapse." Cab. 69/3, DO (41) 22, 19 October 1941.

[31] For example, the diary of Lieutenant S., 31 October 1941: Last night "we crossed the Orel-Tula highway near Gorbatchevo-Plavsk and arrived in the village of Feodorovka. The number of desertions had risen to an incredible extent. [Some of our men] took the officers' horses, including mine. . . . Some officers! . . . In our battalion 80 per cent are deserters, including seemingly reliable persons. They go into the villages, throw away their uniforms and weapons. . . . In the villages the peasants are breaking up the collective farms, dividing the horses, the carts, and household implements. They drive away from the barns with sacks of stuff. Speeches are made that the war is lost and soon there will be no collective farms." Cited in Carell, I, 144–45.

while the spirits of the Russians were close to collapse. But neither side was aware of the possibly fatal weaknesses of the other; and during the first two weeks of November the fighting before Moscow narrowed down to a few bitter local attacks.

# 9 . *Germany halted*[1]

A DAY OR SO after the offensive toward Moscow was in full development, on 3 October Hitler addressed the Reichstag in Berlin. "This enemy is broken and will never rise again!" On 9 October, the day after Orel had fallen, Otto Dietrich, the Reich press chief, announced before German and foreign correspondents: "For all military purposes, Soviet Russia has been defeated." On 12 October the *Voelkischer Beobachter* ran a headline: "The Great Hour—The Eastern Campaign at Its End." For once the masses of the German people seemed inclined to take these proclamatory announcements at their face value. The year before their sentiments had lagged behind the rush of events. They could not quite believe that victory in the West was at hand. Now the contrary was true. Their wishes were fathers of their thoughts. They wanted to believe that the Eastern war, which was becoming more and more murderous every week, was over. Disillusionment came rapidly within two weeks. "A portion of the population had been gripped by an excessive optimism, based on the expressions of the Reich press chief," noted the anonymous summarizers of the secret SS reports on German public opinion on 27 October. "Dr. Dietrich's words and the attitude of the press had been taken literally by certain folk-comrades."[2]

The Germans were not alone in this. It was then, in the autumn of 1941, that the notion of a quick war, with all of its attendant hopes, disappeared from the minds of most peoples, of opponents as well as of friends of Germany. The peoples of Europe now saw that a long and enormous struggle was developing, that the Russians were holding out, at least through the winter, and that the entry of the United States against Germany would shortly occur. Six hundred thousand Soviet prisoners, again six hundred thousand Soviet prisoners, these numbers did not impress

---

[1] 1 November–7 December 1941.
[2] *Meldungen* (No. 252), 172.

them; what impressed them was that neither Moscow nor Leningrad had fallen. Among the opponents of the Third Reich the prevalent mood was not enthusiasm, it was a compound of confidence and resignation. The privations and the duress of the war were to continue, indeed, they were to last for a long time. In their darkened and rain-soaked cities (the autumn of 1941 was unusually wet in most of Europe), the chilly populace went about their daily chores, struggling with the difficulties of daily life.

Their hardships were not only material ones. In the fall of 1941 the Germans extended as well as tightened their control over the peoples of the Continent. The harshness of their police measures increased. Beyond their earlier demands for discipline and order, they were demanding a subservient conformity from their client governments. In Vichy France, for example, many of the vestigial remnants of freedom were now disappearing. In occupied France on 21 October for the first time a German firing squad shot fifty French hostages because of the killing of a German officer—a marked turn of the screw. In November the weakening Pétain met Goering without, however, fully committing himself to collaboration with the Third Reich.[3] Pétain's wavering policy did not work. Hitler knew what was in the back of Pétain's mind.[4] Pétain knew little of what was in the back of Hitler's mind. After the war against Russia is over, he would lay down the law for the Vichy crowd, Hitler told Mussolini in the autumn of 1941.

Far more drastic than their tightening of the screws in Western Europe were the changes in the Germans' treatment of the Jews in the East. After June 1941 occurred the first mass murders of them in eastern Poland, and Russia. Extermination, not merely concentration, camps were being built and given trial runs, here and there. To liquidate the mass of Jews of occupied Europe was no longer an ominous expression of Nazi rhetoric; it was on the way to becoming official German policy, an evolution corresponding to a change in Hitler's mind to which we shall have to return.[5] But here we meet again the problem of reality and retrospect. In retrospect the German decision to exterminate, and not merely imprison or subjugate, the Jews in Europe was an enormous turning point. Yet by 1941 the peoples of Europe had become accustomed to the brutalities of the Third Reich to an extent that nothing would surprise them, not even such a decision, had it been publicly announced (it wasn't).

---

[3] In November 1941 Darlan himself made a tentative approach to the English. Woodward II, 76, note 1.

[4] Pétain told Carl Burckhardt in November: "If only the English could see what's in my mind" (le fond de ma pensée). Nicolson, II, 192.

[5] See below, pp. 165–66; 434–35; 450–51.

This was true of the opponents as of the friends of the Third Reich. The German invasion of the Soviet Union revitalized temporarily the cause of a new—that is, German-led and National Socialist—Europe. In 1941, unlike in 1940, German propaganda went to considerable efforts to enroll new adherents en masse. Unlike in 1940, new adherents of intellectual quality were relatively rare. A few embittered and doctrinaire anti-Communists joined the cause of the "crusade," people whose fear and hatred of communism were greater than their love of liberty and decency. The Vatican and the Catholic churches in general refused to give public approval to the anti-Bolshevik crusade. The Germans succeeded in enrolling a motley variety of volunteer units, including a Spanish division and different Western and Northern European brigades. They proceeded to transform their Tripartite Pact into a renewed anti-Comintern Pact, signed in Berlin on 25 November 1941 which, in addition to states such as Romania, Hungary, Croatia, and Slovakia, included governments that had not declared war on the Soviet Union, such as Bulgaria and Denmark. On that cold day the German army was still grinding its way toward Moscow. Frozen villages were in flames, some of them less than forty, others less than thirty miles from the outskirts of the sprawling Russian capital.

The last German offensive in 1941 had begun to unroll in the icy mornings of 18 and 19 November, on the central front, which had rigidified in a half circle, about fifty miles before Moscow, during a relative lull in the fighting two weeks earlier. On the twelfth the chief of the General Staff had flown to the abandoned Russian town of Orsha. He conferred with the representatives of the Army group commanders. The question was: hold the armies where they were, or start another march forward? The chiefs of staff of Kluge and Leeb, of Army Groups North and South, would stay put. The representative of Fedor von Bock spoke otherwise. Bock had told him to tell Halder and Brauchitsch that he, Bock, would make the last push for Moscow. Moscow had to fall before the end of the year. Halder was reasonably satisfied. Bock could go ahead. In the last minute Bock, faced by Kluge's reluctance on his flank, asked for a postponement of the offensive for four days. Thus the frontal attack broke forth on the nineteenth. The temperature had dropped. The Russian country was covered with snow. The frost was harder and deeper than the Germans had expected. Still their offensive moved forward. Bitter fighting developed thirty miles ahead of Moscow. Hitler's and Bock's plan was to encircle Moscow rather than thrust directly at it. Against very large odds, German troops forged ahead in a northwestern direction, reaching the village of Khimki, a mere fifteen miles from Red Square. On

27 and 28 November Stalin and the Soviet Stavka[6] found the situation very critical. Yet now, unlike in mid-October, there was no panic in Moscow. The Soviets were beginning to realize that their enemies were no longer invincible. No matter how hardened and embittered, many of the German units were at the end of their resources, in more than one way. The larger numbers of the Russian troops, moving ahead and around them, were beginning to tell. On 28 November, when the front before Moscow was cracking and bending before the desperate thrusts of the Germans, the Russians reentered the city of Rostov in the far South. It was the first sizable town from which the Germans were forced back in Russia—indeed, except for Narvik, in more than two years of war in Europe. Two days later Zhukov proposed to Stalin and the Stavka that the time was ready for a Soviet counteroffensive before Moscow.

When the German chief of staff had been told at Orsha that Field Marshal Bock wanted to resume the attack on Moscow, General Halder was relieved. Halder had feared Hitler's reaction to the news that the leading generals were declining to press forward at this late stage, preferring the defensive. But Halder need not have fretted himself. By that time Hitler himself discounted the prospects of the last big push for Moscow. The accepted notion according to which Hitler was chasing his generals into the maws of frozen death is untrue. It was to become largely true a year later, in Stalingrad; it was not true before Moscow. It was Bock, not Hitler, who was ruled by the desire to reach Moscow by Christmas. Hitler should have told Bock to desist. But, as on other occasions, Hitler may not have had the courage of his premonitions.

For premonitions they were. Behind the legend of Hitler's madness in Russia there looms another, which it is our duty to disprove. It concerns not Moscow or even Russia but the entire war. This is the legend according to which Hitler would not, because he could not, admit to himself that he could not win the war; according to which his blind fanaticism and his megalomania made Hitler believe in a German victory until the very end, when his enemies were closing in on his lair in Berlin. Yet there is evidence that as early as 19 November 1941—that is, before Pearl Harbor, and on the very day when Bock's army was rolling forward, close to schedule, in the direction of Moscow—Hitler knew that he could no longer win the war. To a group of generals in his headquarters he dropped this remark: ". . . the recognition, by both of the opposing coalitions, that they cannot annihilate each other, leads to a negotiated peace."[7] This is especially significant when we consider that Hitler did

---

[6] Stavka: the high command, reverting to its old nomenclature from the time of the last war and the era of the Tsars.
[7] Halder, *KTB*, III, 295: ". . . *die Erkentniss, dass die beiden Feindgruppen sich nicht vernichten koennen, zu einem Verhandlungsfrieden fuehrt.*"

not always share his secret thoughts with his generals, nor did he always trust his chief of staff. Four days later, when Bock's troops were still advancing on both sides of the main road to Moscow, Halder noted another Hitler remark in his war diary: "We must face the possibility that neither of the principal opponents [Germany and Britain] succeed in annihilating, or decisively defeating, the other."[8]

From this moment, till the very last week of his life, Hitler had but one overriding design: to prolong the war, and to impress his opponents with the unbeatable toughness of Germany, so that their unnatural coalition would sooner or later fall apart, so that the Russians or, preferably, the Anglo-Americans, would feel compelled to negotiate peace with a great Germany still largely puissant and intact. He did not realize—at least not for two more years[9]—that his enemies would not negotiate with him. His will had started the Last European War. His will could no longer end it.

For the last time the outcome of the war balanced on the thin edge of the sword, around the thickening suburbs of Moscow.[10] The Germans still ground ahead, breaking into villages thirty, at times twenty miles away: Klin, Solnechnogorsk, Istra, Venev. But they were on their last legs, literally speaking. The terrible winged feet of the *blitzkrieg* Army were now frozen clumps. Their steadfastness in trying to move ahead is amazing in retrospect. When evenly matched, they almost always drove the Russians out of the burning villages, no matter how close these were to their holy capital. But they were seldom evenly matched. There were more and more Russians rising out of the ground, all around them. For weeks now the manpower crisis was German, not Russian. After a terrible drop in the Russian reserves, from the middle of November onward the situation changed: The number of available Russian units on the front was rising, that of the Germans was falling. By 5 December, twenty-three out of every hundred German soldiers who had been sent to the Russian Campaign were dead, wounded, or missing, a statistic compiled by their High Command. That night the last German units on the central front were told to halt their forward movements. Next morning the Russian

---

[8] Ibid., 306. *"Wir muessen der Moeglichkeit ins Auge sehen dass es keinem der beiden Hauptgegner gelingt, den anderen vernichtend zu schlagen, oder entscheidend niederzuringen."* As General Jodl told his colleagues after the collapse in 1945: Hitler knew by the winter of 1941 that "victory could no longer be achieved." Schramm, 26–7, also 161; also Maser, 416.

[9] See below, pp. 164–65.

[10] To speak of "suburbs" of Moscow is not quite correct. Unlike European cities, Moscow had no walls during the Middle Ages or after.

command went over to the offensive at a number of points along the fatal semicircle before Moscow.

There was, strictly speaking, no Battle of Moscow. Somewhat like the Battle of the Marne, there were desperate movements by both sides, with very bitter fighting here and there, seldom above the level of major skirmishes. Yet even more than the Battle of the Marne, it was the principal event of a great European war. Bock knew it days before the edge of the frozen sword had actually turned. On 30 November he spoke to Brauchitsch over the telephone. "I emphasize that the Army Group Center is at the end of its strength. . . . The entire attack has no depth. The men are physically exhausted. . . . Please inform the Fuehrer that Army Group Center is no longer in the position to achieve its objective. We do not have the strength any more. . . ."[11] The sick Brauchitsch (not brilliant even at his best) had called Bock to ask, in Hitler's name, when Moscow was expected to fall. Brauchitsch spoke as if Hitler were singleminded about this. Did Brauchitsch know that Hitler had not really expected Moscow to fall? It is difficult to tell, and perhaps irrelevant. Bock had understood for some time that Hitler was shying away from a direct push into Moscow, preferring an encirclement instead. The next day, therefore, Bock sent a message to the High Command: "The combat strength of the Army Group permits no classical movement of encirclement. The attack now in progress will gain some ground but at bloody costs. It will destroy some of the enemy, but it will not force a decision. . . ."[12] Two days later Bock tried to telephone Hitler. He got through to Jodl. The attraction of Prussian rhetoric still persisted. To break into Moscow was still possible, Bock said. "The last battalion will decide the issue." It didn't.

There were many more Russian battalions. They were better equipped for the war in the winter. But the German halt before Moscow cannot be attributed to the weather. The Russian winter was terrible. But in early December 1941 the temperature around Moscow was normal. Many German reminiscences, including those in English translation, speak of temperatures of fifty degrees below zero on 4–5 December.[13] They do not correspond to reality. The meteorological station in Moscow registered no unusual temperatures during the first week of December 1941.[14] It was cold enough, to be sure. It was snowy enough, to be sure. But there

[11] Bock, *KTB*, 30 November 1941, cited by Turney, 148–49.

[12] Bock, *KTB*, 1 December 1941, ibid.

[13] At that point the Fahrenheit and the Centigrade scales are very close: minus 50° F equals minus 46° C; minus 50° C equals minus 58° F.

[14] At 7 A.M. on 3 December the temperature was 19° F, at the same hour on 4 December 0° F, on 5 December minus 13°, on 6 December minus 15°, on 7 December minus 20°, and on 8 December rising to 5° above zero.

was little frost or snow at Rostov, where the Germans had been driven back the week before, by an increasing number of Russian battalions.

By the late afternoon of 7 December, a Sunday, Zhukov's counterattack had forced the Germans to retreat from most of their advanced positions. Amidst the agitation of Hitler's headquarters, where the sick Brauchitsch offered to resign, Hitler drafted his Directive No. 39, which was issued the next day: "The severe winter weather which has come surprisingly early in the East, and the consequent difficulties in bringing up supplies, compel us to abandon immediately all major offensive operations and to go over to the defensive."[15] In that very hour, half a world away from the snowy scene of war in Muscovy, on a tropical morning bombs were falling that, unlike the proverbial American shots 166 years before, were heard instantly around the world. The turning point of the entire war, perhaps of an entire century, had come within the same moment, half a world apart. The Last European War had become the Second World War.

Let us, for the last time, attempt to survey the larger human scene on that fateful afternoon. There are the peoples of Western Europe, and England, resigned to a long war, but sure of the Germans' defeat. There is Hitler, his feet set firmly amidst all of this drama, a man full of wrath and determination, a demagogue who nonetheless, in his innermost self, knows that he will not live long and that he can no longer win the kind of victory that would secure what he wanted for the German people. There are the German people who do not know this; yet they are beginning to know the premonitions of defeat. They are stunned by the news that America has, again, come into a world war on the side of their enemies. That their great army is halted in the middle of Soviet Russia, by that enemy of Western civilization, is hardest for them to comprehend. But God writes straight with crooked lines.

---

[15] The next day the official German war communiqué announced: "Due to the onset of the Russian winter the operations in the East are being curtailed. On most parts of the Eastern Front only local engagements are taking place."

# 10 . A second world war[1]

EXACTLY FIVE HUNDRED DAYS after the Ides of March in 1939, when the British had decided to fight Hitler if they must, they found themselves on the verge of the abyss. There came then a great change. Two decisions were reached, one in Berlin, the other in Washington. At the end of July 1940 Hitler, after some hesitation, decided to finish off Russia before invading Britain, at the very moment when Roosevelt, after some hesitation, made his decision to commit the United States on the side of the British. Another five hundred days later[2] came another great event. In the snowy wasteland before Moscow and in the sunny wastes of the Pacific the war was decided. In December 1941 the duel between Hitler and Churchill stood at a draw: 3–3. Hitler bested Churchill in Scandinavia and in Western Europe. Churchill scored in the battle over Britain: 2–1. Hitler scored again in the Balkans: 3–1. Now, at the onset of the winter in 1941, the Russian and American events evened the score for Churchill. Only it was no longer a duel predominantly between Churchill and Hitler. Russia and America were deciding the war, which had truly become a world war, at the end of which two great powers would remain, Russia and America, a development that would determine the fate of Europe ever since that time.

Few people in Europe sensed this in December 1941. In some curious way the news of Pearl Harbor was an anticlimax. The peoples of Europe, and of England, had taken the eventual entry of the United States into the war for granted for some time. Among those who hated and feared the Third Reich there was a sense of relief, rather than of enthusiasm. As so often in their history, the Americans had been telegraphing their punch for what to many people seemed a long and weary succession of months,

---

[1] 7 December 1941–
[2] 493 or 494, to be exact.

perhaps years. On 11 December 1941 Harold Nicolson noted in his diary: "Not an American flag flying in the whole of London. How odd we are!" Perhaps the people of London were not so odd, after all. Perhaps they knew in their bones that while Hitler was definitely losing the war, *they* were no longer the ones who were winning it.[3] As American slang would say, it was a new ball game. Something new had begun that at the same time was the end of something that had been glorious and ancient.

Hitler, too, knew what American entry in a world war meant. Only the suddenness of Pearl Harbor surprised him. For more than a year he had expected American intervention by 1942.[4] During the year 1941 Hitler and Goebbels were preparing the German people for war with the United States. They were discounting the influence of the isolationists within America.[5] Hitler did not underestimate the might of the United States. What he had wanted, ever since 1938–39, was to win his war in Europe before the United States could intervene.[6] In 1941 he hoped to defeat Russia before America would come in[7]—a not altogether unreasonable strategy. He wanted, as we have seen, to deny Roosevelt any pretext for an incident in the Atlantic; on the very eve of his invasion of Russia he ordered German submarines to avoid engagements with American ships, even in the event of extreme provocation by the latter.

Japan's war on the United States forced an end to these cautionary tactics. Immediately Hitler ordered the German Navy to attack American ships, three days before he declared war on the United States. Many peo-

---

[3] Shortly before Pearl Harbor, British prestige had gone down another half a peg. Their desert army had attacked Rommel, forced him back, but failed to deliver a decisive blow at him, in spite of a large British superiority in tanks. Still, the British were girding themselves for a long war. In December 1941 the National Service Act obliged men from eighteen to fifty, and women from twenty to thirty, to serve if needed.

[4] Hitler to the Hungarian Premier, Count Teleki, on 20 November 1940: Britain's only hopes were Russia and America. The latter would not be ready until the winter of 1941–42. *GD*, D, XI, 632.

[5] See, for example, Boelcke, 626, 759.

[6] See Hitler's unsigned memorandum of 9 October 1939: "The main danger to Germany of a long war lies in the fact that certain states may be drawn into the enemy camp. . . ." The United States may come in, sooner or later. "Here, again, time is working against Germany." *IMT*, ND, L-052. He repeated this argument to his generals on 23 November 1939. *GD*, D, VIII, 440.

[7] He predicted, once or twice, a future conflict between a German-led Europe against the United States but, he said in 1940, "possibly only after my lifetime." Hillgruber, *HS*, 147. He repeated this argument to Ciano on 25 October 1941. By early 1945 he would often say that "this war against America is a tragedy." *Hitler-Bormann*, 87, and passim.

ple have been speculating about his declaration of war on America, as if this had been some kind of rash decision. In reality Hitler had no other choice. Both in the timing of their entry and in the choice of their principal enemy in the Second World War, the Japanese were stupid.[8] Yet, had Hitler betrayed their alliance by not declaring war on the United States, he would have achieved nothing. The Japanese, feeling cheated, would have betrayed him at their future opportunity. Roosevelt would have gone on waging war against Germany *de facto,* even if not *de jure,* a practice of which the leaders of the American democracy proved capable neither for the first nor for the last time. Already in February 1941 the chiefs of the American Army and Navy had agreed on their general war plan, Rainbow 5, according to which Germany, not Japan, was the principal opponent, whence the defeat of the first had priority over the defeat of the second. There is no reason at all to believe that, had Hitler not declared war on the United States on 11 December 1941, these essentially reasonable[9] American dispositions would have substantially changed. In turn, the notion that Hitler was taken aback by the Japanese attack on the United States is an exaggeration. To the contrary, he feared the prospect of America coming into the war against Germany *before* Japan went to war with the United States. He wanted the latter to occur first. In this respect there was a discrepancy between him and Ribbentrop.[10] The latter attempted to push Japan into attacking Russia after June 1941. Hitler

---

[8] The timing of the Japanese defies reason. They could have attacked the British in the Far East in June 1940 with far-reaching effects. Instead they chose to sign an alliance with Germany in September 1940, a few days *after* Hitler had abandoned the idea of invading Britain. Again, the Japanese attacked the United States a few days *after* the Germans had been turned back before Moscow.

[9] Essentially unreasonable were the rhetorical statements by Roosevelt and Hull, attributing purposes to Hitler. On various occasions Roosevelt said that Hitler wanted nothing less than "the complete domination of the world." Hull said that Hitler was the most devastating conqueror "in the last thousand years and we believe there is no geographical limit whatsoever to his infamous plans"; that Hitler was ready for "a march of invasion across the earth with ten million soldiers and thirty thousand airplanes." These statements are cited by Compton, 255. On the preceding page Compton writes: "Down to December 1941 there was no German plan for a military attack on the United States." In the remaining pages of his work Professor Compton tries to square what he wrote on page 254 with what he cited on page 255, without success.

[10] On 9 November 1941 Ribbentrop instructed the German ambassador to Tokyo to tell the Japanese that they should attack anywhere but not touch American territories. Woodward, II, 152–53. As late as January 1942 Hitler did not ask the Japanese that they attack Russia. Hillgruber, 25–26.

was indifferent to that prospect until later in 1942. That was a great mistake, in retrospect. Hitler should have urged the Japanese to attack the Soviet Union in 1941. Whether they would have done so—and whether, in that event, Roosevelt would not have ordered the American Navy in the Pacific to engage in a *de facto* war against them—is another question.[11]

We have to follow Hitler a little farther. He did not let the turning point of the war overwhelm him. The German retreat before Moscow did not develop into a catastrophe. For this he, Hitler, was alone responsible. His generals, practically without exception, counseled a strategic retreat to winter quarters around Smolensk. He was convinced that such a retreat could become a catastrophe of Napoleonic proportions. He ordered the armies to stand fast, except for tactical retreats here and there, establishing strong points around which the Russian attacks would surge and eventually die down. He dismissed the ailing Brauchitsch and became the commander-in-chief of the German Army. All kinds of people, from generals put out to pasture to postwar historians, have ridiculed Hitler's pretensions of being a *Feldherr,* a war commander: wrongly so. In December 1941 Hitler was again right and his generals were wrong. The Russians pushed the Germans back, here and there, but they were unable to break them during that winter. In April 1942 Hitler remarked about the winter crisis before Moscow: "We have mastered a destiny which broke another man 130 years ago."

Hitler failed in his political, rather than in his military, strategy. While he knew that he could no longer win his war—that is, he could not wholly impose his will upon his opponents—he thought that he could still make Germany unbeatable, so that his enemies, particularly the Anglo-Americans, would be sooner or later compelled to deal with him. He did not realize that it is easier to start a war than to end it, especially when one's opponents are large democracies, whose public opinion, rightly or wrongly, is a principal factor. He hoped to split his opponents. He counted much on the British and American fear of Bolshevism.[12] He did not yet realize that his reputation had become so evil that this made it

---

[11] After all, Roosevelt, in justifying Lend-lease aid to Russia, said on 7 November 1941: "I have today found the defense of the Union of Soviet Socialist Republics vital to the defense of the United States."

[12] From January 1942 he had again tacitly permitted the exploration of certain tentatives toward the Western powers. An early example of such a tentative were the talks in Ankara of the German ambassador Papen with the—then very naïve—papal nuncio Roncalli, later to become Pope John XXIII. *VD,* 5, 575–76.

impossible for his opponents to negotiate with him, even if they wanted to; and they, with the possible exception of Stalin, did not want to.[13]

At any rate, he now had a world war on his hands.[14] Consequently two decisions of his, taken in the winter of 1941–42, stand out. He ordered a general mobilization of the industry and of the economy of the Reich. Until December 1941 his triumphant armies could wage rapid campaigns dependent on a national economy that was only partly mobilized for war. Now Hitler ordered a directive to prepare for a long war, and for full industrial mobilization.[15] His technicians proved to have been better than his generals. They prolonged the war for at least two years. They made up for almost all of the deficiencies in raw materials. Had Germany not been invaded from all sides by the end of 1944, the war could have gone on perhaps indefinitely, no matter what the world economists' calculations would say.

He also tacitly agreed with the implementation of something awful: the mass extermination of the Jews. A police conference to that effect was supposed to have met on 8 December 1941, the day after Pearl Harbor, in Berlin; it was then postponed to 20 January 1942, when the administrative decision was made at the so-called Wannsee Conference. No document, no written or even spoken evidence connects Hitler directly to the

---

[13] It took him two years to realize this. To Rommel he said in 1943: He, Hitler, too, "was aware that there was very little chance left of winning the war. But the West would conclude no peace with him—certainly not the people who were then at the helm. And the people who would have been prepared to negotiate with him had no power. He had never wanted war with the West. But now the West would have their war—have it to the end." *Rommel*, 427. Once Hitler came to realize this—that is, to admit it to himself—he again could be more realistic than some of his cohorts. At the news of Roosevelt's sudden death in 1945 it was Goebbels, not Hitler, who, in raptures, broke out a bottle of champagne. Jodl, before his condemnation in Nuremberg, in 1946, said in a memorandum: ". . . his military advisers—today one often hears it said—should certainly have made it clear to him earlier that the war was lost. What a naïve thought! Earlier than any other person in the world, Hitler sensed and knew that the war was lost." Schramm, Appendix II, 204.

[14] To the Japanese ambassador, Oshima, 3 January 1942: "He [Hitler] did not yet know how the United States was to be defeated."

[15] "Sometime between 3 December 1941 and 10 January 1942 Hitler decided that the present effort was insufficient and that the *blitzkrieg* [strategy] must be abandoned." Milward, 63. His Directive *Ruestung Ost* "marked the decisive break with the economic policy of the *blitzkrieg* period." Ibid., 64. In order to expedite this, the hierarchy of the Reich would depend on an increasing number of foreign workers, of whom nearly four million were already in Germany by the end of 1941.

Wannsee decision, but it is not difficult to reconstruct the main lines of his thinking in this regard. England opposed him because behind Churchill stood Roosevelt, and behind Roosevelt stood the Jews. Instead of taking the Jews out of Europe, they had gone to war with him. So the Jews of Europe would pay the price of this world war. He might not win the war, but at least he would put an end to the Jewish presence in Europe. At that time, in the winter of 1941–42, the drafting of the definite "final solution" was but a minor administrative decision. There is no reason to believe that it gave Hitler a sleepless night or even a difficult hour. Yet it turned out to be the most monstrous of all of his decisions, the consequences of which would destroy his reputation and that of his Reich for a very long time, perhaps forever.[16]

And now we may leave this extraordinary man, to whom La Rochefoucauld's maxim truly applies: "There are evil men who would be less dangerous if they had no good in them." What was good in him? He had a powerful mind. He was brave. He could be generous to those who worked closely with him. All of this adds up to a certain strength of character. Yet the fundamental source of Hitler's strength was hatred. Compared to the power of his hatreds, even his love for his people—the living purpose of a great national leader—amounted to little. In this he was quite unlike Napoleon.

We shall also say farewell to the people of England. They had borne the standard of Western civilization during the Last European War. Now they knew that they were no longer the principals in the battle. They were greatly relieved when the Russians took the brunt of Hitler's blows. An extraordinary wave of Russophilia swept across Britain after June 1941. Deep down the English may have been a little ashamed of this. To most Europeans they remained the standard-bearers. In reality this was less and less true. The English recognized this long before their friends and admirers in Europe became aware of it, in some instances not until many years later, after the war.

More than thirty years later, we can see how during that decisive time of December 1941 not only the outcome of the war but the fate of Europe for decades to come was crystallizing into recognizable forms. The British government was beginning to defer to Russia—at the expense of some of Europe, if need be. Two days before Pearl Harbor Britain, reluctantly yielding to Stalin's insistent demands, declared war on Romania, Bulgaria, Hungary, even Finland. The Polish government-in-exile, thankful for British support, had for months sufficient evidence to

---

[16] See a discussion of this below, pp. 451–52.

know that this kind of British support was far from unconditional. Only two days after the re-establishment of diplomatic relations between the Soviet and the Polish governments, brought about through British mediation, an editorial in the London *Times*[17] said: "Leadership in Eastern Europe can fall only to Germany or Russia. Neither Great Britain nor the United States can exercise, or will aspire to exercise, any predominant role in these regions." The Poles protested, but in vain. During the months that passed they had increasing reasons to worry. When in March 1942 Churchill conferred with their leader, General Sikorski, Churchill admitted "that his own assessment of Russia did not differ much" from that of the Polish general; "however, he underlined the reasons which made it necessary to conclude the agreement with Russia. She was the only country that had fought against the Germans with success. She had destroyed millions of German soldiers and at present the aim of the war seemed not so much victory, as the death or survival of our allied nations. Should Russia come to an agreement with the Reich, all would be lost. It must not happen. If Russia was victorious she would decide on her frontiers without consulting Great Britain; should she lose the war, the agreement would lose all its importance."[18]

The agreement about which Churchill and Sikorski were talking was the one proposed by Stalin to Eden a mere few days after the tide had turned before Moscow. In the dark days of December 1941 Eden arrived in Moscow with drafts of an Anglo-Russian declaration. Stalin said that he wanted an agreement, not a declaration. "A declaration I regard as algebra, but an agreement as practical arithmetic."[19] He produced a detailed Russian draft agreement about how Europe should look after the war, replete with secret protocols again.[20] They are very interesting in retrospect. They tell us volumes about Stalin the practical statesman as opposed to his mythical image as a world revolutionary. They sum up the Russian attitude toward Europe for most of the twentieth century. They are very similar to the propositions of Tsarist diplomacy during the First World War: an Eastern Europe dominated by Russia, a Western Europe presided over by Britain, and a weak and divided Germany in between. Aware of the Americans' objection to secret treaties, the British told Stalin that they could not make such a commitment in such terms. After some months of sullen haggling, the Russians dropped their draft. By the time the division of Europe came up, later in the war, Stalin found that he could profit even more from American algebra than from British arith-

---

[17] 1 August 1941.
[18] Conversation between Sikorski and Churchill, *DPSR*, I, 297–98.
[19] Woodward, 191.
[20] Their detailed description in Woodward, II, 222.

metic, from joint declarations with Roosevelt than from agreements with Churchill. In the end, after Yalta and Potsdam, the result was not very different: an Eastern Europe ruled by Russia, a Western Europe presided over by the United States, and a divided Germany in between.

However, it was not so much poor statesmanship on the part of Churchill and Roosevelt that eventually led to the division of the Continent. It was the slowness of the British and the American warfare against Germany. The English and the American peoples had the will, and the determination, to defeat Hitler. They did not have the determination, or the will, to invade Europe fast enough or wide enough—in other words, to liberate Europe while the Russians were still fighting in the East. In the end the United States was to react against the then ominous and overbearing Russian presence in Central and Eastern Europe even slower than had the British. No matter: By the end of the war the Americans, and the Russians, were the masters of their respective halves of the Continent. To a large extent this is still true today, more than thirty years after the Last European War had developed into the Second World War, and nearly thirty years after the termination of the latter. So much for those who prattle about the breathtaking speed with which things change in this so-called "revolutionary" age.

At any rate, 1941 marked the beginning of the final demise of the European state system that had lasted for at least three hundred years. Still, the end of the European state system did not mean the end of Europe or of its peoples. There was more to the Last European War than a phase of the Second World War; and it is therefore that I must now turn to the second, and principal, portion of this book, to the internal lives of the peoples.

# II . The Main Movements

# 1 . The lives of the peoples

LET ME NOW ATTEMPT to reconstruct certain matters about the lives of five hundred million people of a continent during the war: how they lived, and what they thought, during two or three years when the world around them and the powers ruling them changed often rapidly and violently, and when the order of the continent that they had known was transformed in ways that no one had foreseen. The difficulties of such a reconstruction are very great. First, there is the problem of "Europe," of a continent whose very limits are debatable. Is Russia of Europe? Is Turkey? Is Iceland? What does "Europe" consist of, what did it consist of? This problem of "Europe" is a recurrent problem of historical definition, which will not be solved until it is outgrown—that is, until Europe becomes more or less one, until most Europeans think of themselves principally as Europeans. This is not so now; and it was not so during the Last European War, when there were few Europeans who were thinking of themselves as Europeans. They were, instead, thinking of themselves as Englishmen, Frenchmen, Spaniards, and consequently they lived as Englishmen, Frenchmen, Spaniards. In 1939 "Europe," like "European," had a connotation only for certain people, certain aristocrats, certain bourgeois, certain intellectuals, certain cultivated men and women—and, of course, because of the perspective of distance, to Americans.[1] And nowhere does this relative absence of "European" people present greater problems for the historian than when he is trying to say something about the everyday life of nations; for the principal factors in the history of

---

[1] See below. When in 1936 Thomas Mann had come to Budapest for a lecture, the poet Attila József greeted him with a poem: ". . . üdvözöllek itt/ Fehérek között, egy európait." "A European, not merely a white man." By 1939 Mann, as many other "Europeans," was living in California, on his way to becoming an American citizen.

Europe in 1939 were nations, not classes; states, not societies; peoples, not economics. In 1939 there were (and thirty-five years later there still are) great and profound differences between Finland and Portugal, Holland and Albania, Greece and Switzerland—not only in their economic institutions, not only in their social structures, not only in their forms of government but in the ways in which their populations lived and spoke and thought—the matters with which every responsible historian ought to be concerned.

Another difficulty is that of the sources. The principal records from this period of Europe's history are concerned with the decisions and with the vagaries of statecraft, rather than with the lives of millions. The interested historian will have no great trouble in finding not only what a Hitler or a Churchill but also what a Ribbentrop or an Eden may have said at a certain time; but if he is trying to find how, say, the "average" Sicilian or Slovene lived, worked, and ate in the summer of 1940, he is running into all kinds of problems. In 1939 history was still principally the history of states, rather than the history of societies; the history of those who governed, rather than the history of those who were being governed. Scholarly contributions in social and economic history, statistical records of certain governments and municipalities had been in existence for a century at least; but their systematic organization and their availability was still sporadic and fragmentary, especially in the southern and eastern states of the Continent. The student of the diplomatic or military history of Europe during the Second World War does face—or, rather, he ought to face—certain complexities and difficulties that the student of earlier wars did not have to face; but whoever attempts to reconstruct honestly the sociography of Europe at that time faces not merely certain complications but often altogether different problems, not the least of which are the paucity, the unreliability, and the fragmentary character of his sources.

Nevertheless, we may establish certain generalizations. In 1939 the national populations of Europe were more homogeneous than ever before; for the democratic and industrial development of peoples nationalizes perhaps even more than it internationalizes them. In 1914 a German banker may have had more in common with a French banker than with his clerks; in 1939 this was no longer the case.

Continuity proved to be at least as strong as change. In 1941 there were still millions of people in Europe who lived as they have always lived, in some countries even after the violent waves of fire, bombardment, and foreign armies had surged over them. This was perhaps the other side of the coin: the phenomenon of a new kind of war where the previous distinctions between soldiers and civilians were being washed away. During the First World War, the life of a soldier was something entirely different from his life in peacetime; his warriorship meant an almost total break with his past. This was less so during the Second World

War—with many exceptions, of course, especially in the East of the Continent, where a new (or, in some ways, very ancient) kind of brutal warfare was begun by the Germans in June 1941.

On the other hand, the war, and the dramatic events on the Continent during 1939–41, *affected the thinking* of far more people than during the First World War. The mental earthquake was bigger than the physical one. This had something to do with the nature of the war, of course, but also with the widespread nature of universal literacy, of mass communications, and, probably, with the evolution of consciousness—meaning the increasing intrusion of mental processes in the structure of events —that, in the still unorthodox opinion of this writer, may be the only kind of meaningful evolution there is.[2]

By 1941, the reactions of large populations throughout Europe to the conditions imposed upon them suggested, in many ways, a surprising persistence—indeed, on occasion, a significant resurgence—of vitality. And this was most apparent as we contemplate the most fundamental phenomenon in the history of peoples: the transmission of life.

## THE TRANSMISSION OF LIFE

¶ For at least thirty years before 1939 the increase of Europe's peoples had been slowing down. Much of this was due to the First World War, though perhaps less so than it is commonly believed: Almost everywhere in Europe the size of families had begun to decrease before 1910. This decline in the size of families is not altogether attributable to the decline of religion (at the time of the most widespread erosion of religious practices among the lower classes, during the second half of the nineteenth century, the size of families in many countries hardly changed at all) or to contraception (during the entire nineteenth century the size of bourgeois families shrank, long before contraceptive devices for males became available; indeed, the use of such devices began to spread around 1900 not so much because they served contraception as because they were regarded as safeguards against venereal infections). The slowness of the growth of populations had much to do with industrial work and urban living, as a consequence of which large families were becoming burdensome. These consequences of social mobility were even more evident among the middle than among the lower classes, since they involved rising expectations from education, whereby the older bourgeois custom of sacrifices in

---

[2] Lukacs, *HC*, esp. Chap. IV; also 215–16.

order to insure their children's education led directly to limitations of family size. On the other hand, an important factor in the continued, even though slow, growth of national populations was the elongation of life expectancy, passing from a European average well below 50 years in 1910 (in France, Germany, and Italy, around 47–48; in European Russia, around 35) to over 60 by 1939 in many instances (in Scandinavia, Germany, and Britain, for example).

The population of the entire Continent (excluding Russia) increased by about 15 per cent between the wars, from about 328 million people in 1920 to about 380 million in 1940 (for the sake of comparison, the population of the United States increased by exactly 25 per cent during the same period). Most European peoples could register less than 1 per cent of average growth duing the thirty years before 1939, and no nation grew more than 2 per cent yearly; the largest growth was that of the Albanians (around 1.9 per cent), the smallest was that of the French (an annual average increase of 0.4 per cent between 1910 and 1940). In Western Europe only two peoples grew more than 1 per cent per annum during these thirty years: Holland (1.34 per cent) and Iceland (1.16 per cent); in three instances—Latvia, Estonia, and Ireland—the population actually decreased during the first forty years of the twentieth century. In the Balkans the least industrialized and least urban of people showed the greatest relative rise in their population.[3] On the other hand, there was not much of a relationship between religion and the size of families (in Ireland the birthrate dropped in Catholic South and Protestant North with hardly any difference). National cultures made more difference than similar social structures (in Western Europe the Dutch birthrate was exceptionally high, the Belgian and Luxembourgeois birthrate unusually low; in Eastern Europe the population of Latvia fell, while that of Lithuania increased).

At first sight the routine dogmas of economic determinism seem to be proven: There is a definite relationship between economic condition and the foundation of families; in many European nations the low point of births was reached during the economic crisis of the early thirties, whereafter the marriage rate and the birthrate were rising nearly everywhere. But at this point it is worth observing how this demographic recovery varied greatly from nation to nation. The steepest rise was that in the populations of Germany and of Italy, a 20 per cent or even 30 per cent increase in marriages and births in a few years. The number of mar-

---

[3] At the same time infant mortality in the Balkans was still higher than what it had been in Western Europe a generation before: in 1940 nearly 15 per cent in Romania, for example.

riages in Germany in 1932 was 511,793; in 1936, it was 611,114; even more significant is the rise in the number of births: 971,114 in 1932; 1,279,025 in 1936; meaning that for every two children born in Germany in 1932, three were born four years later. The yearly number of marriages among Italians, hovering steadily around 280,000 in the early thirties, and hardly influenced by the economic depression then, jumped to 317,000 in 1936 and to 377,000 in 1937. The Italian birthrate, dropping slowly but steadily since the beginning of the century from about 26 to 22 per thousand, rose to 22.9 per thousand in 1937 and to 23.8 per thousand in 1938. It is, I think, unreasonable to slur over these figures by simply referring to the so-called populationist policies of the German and Italian dictatorships of the period. Of course, Hitler and Mussolini encouraged large families, and offered certain financial and social benefits for them. But no dictator can force fathers to beget children; certain dictators with strict populationist policies would show no results (under Metaxas, for example, the number of marriages and of births in Greece actually dropped); and anyone who knows even a little about the supple intelligence of the Italian people (and about the far from unlimited extent of Fascist police rule over their everyday lives) must doubt that they could be influenced in the exercise of this most intimate and most personal act by a governmental exhortation.

This most intimate and most personal act . . . We know very little why people have children; we know a little more why they marry, the first act involving something that is rather impulsive, the second something that is rather deliberate. There remains, after all, a certain amount of mystery beyond human choice in the procreation of children: It involves an act of the consequences of which the participants are necessarily uncertain. And yet even as he knows very little about *why* people have children, the historian, with the aid of certain facts, may speculate a little about *when* they have children. I write facts, not a favorite word of mine, because certain statistics (provided that they are reliable) about the transmission of life are perhaps the *only* hard facts that exist in the world, since birth and death are indisputable, which is not true of most "facts" of a scientific or economic character.

It seems, for example, that in modern industrial societies births become more numerous during two, rather different, conditions: first, when large numbers of people have an increase of confidence in the future; second, when the lives of large numbers become, by necessity, compressed; and both of these conditions have surprisingly little to do with economic "factors." Confidence in the future had far more to do with national perspectives than with economics. The years 1936 and 1937 marked, for example, the highest points along the curve of the Italian birthrate during the entire Fascist period. Even Mussolini's harshest critics agree that the high point of his popularity occurred after the Abyssinian

War, in 1936 and in 1937—at a time when, economically speaking (or, rather, figuring), the Italian recovery from the agricultural and industrial trough of the early thirties was far from complete, and when the economic and financial sanctions decreed by the League of Nations against Italy had certain effects. And thus it may not be fanciful to point out how the absolute rise and fall in the number of Italian marriages mirrors *rather precisely* the relative rise and fall of Italian popular sentiment about the future of the nation: the enthusiasm and the confidence of the mid-thirties beginning to change, in 1938, with certain new concerns and new anxieties setting in; after 1940, then, the popularity of the war becoming widespread.

ITALIAN MARRIAGES IN THOUSANDS[4]

| 1935 | 1936 | 1937 | 1938 | 1939 | 1940 | 1941 |
|------|------|------|------|------|------|------|
| 288  | 317  | 377  | 325  | 322  | 314  | 274  |

German popular support for Hitler and his regime was at its highest after his conquest of Austria and of Czechoslovakia. It was then, in Hitler's year 1938 and in 1939, that the highest marriage rates in *all* of Europe were registered in Germany (9.7 and 11.8 per thousand), superseding even the prolific peoples of Eastern Europe.[5] In 1940, probably for the first and the last time in the history of modern Europe, the highest marriage rate on the Continent occurred in England. The historian, at this point, would do well to consider at least the possibility that in the psyche of peoples economic and sociological factors, including class consciousness, may be often superseded by what, no doubt inadequately, may be called the responses of the national psyche to a certain kind of confidence in one's nation:

---

[4] Consider that at least one half of the births in a given year (1937 and 1941 may be especially telling examples) are the results of their having been begotten during the previous year. The year 1938 as a turning point in the popular support to Fascism has been suggested, too, by the most knowledgeable Italian historians of the period, the excellent Renzo de Felice, for example.

[5] It is perhaps significant, too, that in 1939 among Germany's cities, Danzig and Gleiwitz, on the Polish border, registered phenomenally high birthrates, over 24 per thousand (the average of German cities of comparable size was 17.5 per thousand); even more phenomenal was the marriage rate in Linz, this then prototypically Nazi town, the cradle of Hitler as well as of Eichmann, with 25.8 marriages per 1,000 inhabitants, more than twice that of the national average.

MARRIAGES PER 1,000 INHABITANTS

|  | *1938* | *1939* | *1940* | *1941* |
|---|---|---|---|---|
| Germany | 9.7 | 11.8 | 9.1 | n.a. |
| England | 8.6 | 10.4 | 11.1 | 9.3 |
| France | 6.7 | 6.3 | 4.4 | 5.8 |
| Italy | 7.5 | 7.3 | 7.1 | 6.1 |

It is, I submit, not altogether unreasonable to detect in these figures the reflections of some things that are infinitely more profound than responses to material conditions.

We must insist at this point on a distinction that is all too often overlooked by people nowadays: Social conditions are not material conditions, just as social history is not economic history. All generalizations about different national societies leak,[6] because of the different tendencies of national societies even at similar stages of their material or institutional development, and also because of their different reactions to national triumphs or catastrophes: in one word, because of their different habits of consciousness. The phenomenal rise of the German birthrate in the thirties was even steeper than the rise of the marriage rate, while in England the jump of the marriage rate in 1939 and 1940 was much higher than the rise in the birthrate (fewer children were born in England in 1941 than in 1940). There are all kinds of surprising statistics hidden in these basic demographic figures. In Holland, for example, a sudden jump in the number of marriages in 1939 did not affect the birthrate until later years. In Albania the number of marriages in 1939 (Italy occupied the country that year) fell by nearly 25 per cent, yet the Albanian birthrate in 1940 jumped from 27.8 to 31.4 per thousand, the highest in Europe at the time.

Consider France. Her population in 1939 had shown very little

---

[6] I mentioned the existence of very great differences in neighboring nations with similar economic and social structures (before the war in Western Europe, Holland had the highest birthrate, and Belgium and Luxembourg one of the lowest); yet in 1939 the Dutch marriage rate jumped from 7.7 to 9.2 per thousand when the Belgian and Luxembourgeois rate dropped more than considerably (in 1940 the Belgian marriage rate, 4.3 per thousand, was the lowest in Europe, lower even than that of the French). There are all kinds of fascinating problems latent within these data, full of potential interest to the social historian. How about border areas, for example? Did towns and regions on both sides of the Dutch-Belgian border reflect the important divergences in the marriage and birth patterns of the two respective nations? Was there an appreciable influence of language? Were the Walloon portions of Belgium closer to the French pattern near the Franco-Belgian frontier?

increase over 1914 (from about 39.6 million to 41.6 million). If we adjust this figure by keeping in mind the recovery of Alsace-Lorraine (1.7 million people), France's liberal immigration policies (more than 2.5 million foreigners), together with the natural increase of longevity, the result is one of the few negative balances in Europe, certainly the only one among the great powers of the world. Also, where the continental average of the aged (over sixty years) was 9 per cent, in France it was 14 per cent of the entire population. (In 1939 there were 2.6 million Frenchmen between 20 and 30 years of age, among them nearly 600,000 foreigners—compared to 10 million Germans and Italians in the same age group). These were the basic facts and factors of French decline, even more than the slowness of her industrial production or the antiquated leadership of her Army. Throughout the thirties, there was little fluctuation in the overall birthrates and marriage rates, unaffected as these were by the ups and downs of the French economy: In 1937 and 1938, for example, the years of strikes and of two devaluations, the monthly average of births remained around 50,000 throughout. In the summer of 1939, for the first time in the decade, the number of births suddenly rose by 3,000 (6 per cent) in the single month of July—most of these were babies who had been conceived in October, shortly after the retreat into peace after the war scare of the Munich crisis. It is true that late in 1938 the government finally introduced severe legislation against abortions, and that in 1939, for the first time, serious social legislation, the "Code de la Famille," providing not inconsiderable family allocations, launched a populationist policy; but the effects of this, while appreciable, were far from decisive. Unlike in Germany, in France the declaration of the war and mobilization in 1939 led to an extraordinary drop, so that in June 1940 (that is, babies begotten in or about September 1939) merely 33,600 French babies were born (35 per cent less than the 1938–39 average). Even if we discount the possible stillbirths in that invasion month, this figure is remarkable; nothing like this decline had occurred either in Germany or in Great Britain at the time.

BIRTHRATES

| | *1939* | *1940* | ... | *1943* |
|---|---|---|---|---|
| Germany | 20.5 | 20.4 | | 16.0 |
| Great Britain | 15.3 | 14.6 | | 16.6 |
| France | 14.6 | 13.3 | | 15.9 |

But, then, look at the last figure. By 1943, for the first time in many decades, the French birthrate was close to the German one (if one considers the millions of young Germans under arms at the time, one should consider, too, the captivity of 1.3 million French prisoners of war). Already by May 1941 the number of French babies born reached the prewar average of 50,000 (a remarkable figure in view of the fact that these babies had been begotten immediately after the great debacle of the preceding summer); and by the spring 1942 their number begins to rise well beyond that of the thirties. And here we come upon a remarkable phenomenon: The war and its sufferings brought families together.

So had the deprivations of the economic depression a decade earlier; but then the birthrate had not risen, not at all. In almost every country of Europe more people married in 1940 and in 1941 than in the years before, and they begot more children than before. This happened even in countries that had been vanquished or subjugated by foreign armies.[7] In the German-occupied countries after the first shock, the number of births increased:

### BIRTHS IN THOUSANDS

|  | 1940 | 1941 | 1942 |
| --- | --- | --- | --- |
| Denmark | 68 | 72 | 79 |
| Norway | 48 | 46 | 53 |
| Holland | 185 | 182 | 190 |
| Belgium | 111 | 101 | 109 |
| Luxembourg | 4 | 4.1 | 4.6 |

The Russians began to install themselves in the three unfortunate Baltic republics in 1939, and brutally annexed them in 1940; yet in each of these countries the marriage rate increased (in Lithuania spectacularly, from 7.5 per thousand in 1939 to 9.3 in 1940). In Romania, a state mutilated by her giant neighbor Russia and by her smaller neighbors Hungary and Bulgaria in 1940, a country convulsed in addition by revolutions, by a serious earthquake, by German occupation, and by a new war against the Soviet Union within a twelvemonth, the marriage rate nevertheless rose, from 7.9 per thousand in 1939 to 9.1 in 1940 and 9.6 in 1941. In Finland, which suffered the threat of invasion, bombardment, mutilation, war (twice), and chilly poverty, the marriage rate remained the same in 1939 and in 1940, increasing by 20 per cent in 1941, when the number of births, too, jumped more than 25 per cent (though it was to drop in 1942). Figures in the Balkans remained relatively constant in 1939

---

[7] In certain countries the occupation by friendly foreign armies resulted, of course, in an increase of marriages and of births—in the case of Iceland, for example, a 20 per cent increase in marriages in 1941.

and 1940, with a slow rise (but, then, unlike in World War I, these states were not involved in the war in the beginning).[8]

The same phenomena of family consolidation and rise in the population were true of the threatened neutrals of Europe, whether in the middle or on the edges of the German-conquered continent:

| | MARRIAGES IN THOUSANDS | | | | BIRTHS IN THOUSANDS | |
| --- | --- | --- | --- | --- | --- | --- |
| | *1939* | *1940* | *1941* | | *1941* | *1942* |
| Switzerland | 32 | 32 | 36 | | 72 | 79 |
| Sweden | 61 | 59 | 58 | | 100 | 144 |
| Portugal | 49 | 47 | 55 | | 184 | 188 |
| Ireland | 15 | 15 | 15 | *but:* | 57 | 66 |

In the case of Spain, the significance of statistics is blurred by the end of the Civil War in 1939, with the consequent return of hundreds of thousands of soldiers to their families: This explains the large fluctuation of the annual marriage figures (144,000 in 1939; 216,000 in 1940; 190,000 in 1941); but if we keep in mind the very difficult agrarian conditions of the country, which resulted in near famine in Andalusia in the winter of 1940–41, the number of births was still remarkably high (511,000 in 1941; 531,000 in 1942). At this point the wisdom of Dr. Johnson seems, again, to have been more enduring than the ponderous hypotheses of certain sociologists. "It is not from reason and providence that people marry," he said, "but from inclination. A man is poor; he thinks, I cannot be worse, and so I'll e'en take Polly."

There is, of course, more to this. Ancient poverty is but one kind of misery, modern war and the police state are another; if misery likes company, so does loneliness; families come together through unplanned suffering but also through planned prosperity; as war tears up the routine fabric of society, the circle of men's acquaintances becomes wider while, at the same time, wartime restrictions, privations, curfews, and blackouts constrict the radius of their movements, keeping them indoors, together with their women, for unseasonably long hours. Moreover—and this is more significant—the shock of war and of defeat in 1940–41 in most European nations brought forth a rather spontaneous revulsion against much of the selfish individualism that seemed to have been characteristic of the liberal-democratic order (or disorder) of matters before the war. This reaction

---

[8] The extraordinary exception to the above is Greece, with its relatively low marriage rate and high birthrate, both of which dropped sharply in 1940 and 1941, facts that are not altogether explainable by the war that came to Greece only at the end of October in 1940.

was both deep and widespread enough not to be simply attributable to the effects of German propaganda. Some of the ideas of the "new Europe" were not without their effects, of course[9]; and at least the original meaning of the Pétainist motto of *Travail, Famille, Patrie*, replacing *Liberté, Egalité, Fraternité*, would accord with the then sentiments of many Europeans, including those who otherwise had no sympathy for Fascist political philosophies and no taste for collaboration with Hitler's Germans. Everywhere, including England, the privations of the first year of the war were unaccompanied by any nostalgia for the ways of life and for the uneasy security of the prewar years; rather, the contrary; that was very different from the First World War.

Divorces and suicides were, all, dropping, in some instances precipitously, during 1940 and 1941.[10] (Certain typical examples: in Britain, 8,700 divorces in 1939, and 6,800 in 1941; in France, 21,800 in 1939, and 14,600 in 1941[11]; in Luxembourg, 123 in 1939, and 57 in 1941; in Romania, 11,000 in 1939, and 7,860 in 1941. There was no significant change in the Scandinavian countries.) This was, of course, a general phenomenon happening in modern societies during wartime. On the other hand, contrary to the now classic sociological asseverations about suicide in peace and in war, in 1939–41 the decrease in the number of suicides was less than that in the number of divorces (though in certain countries the falling off of suicides, too, was remarkable).[12] With these figures of divorces and suicides we are, however, entering into statistical regions where figures are sometimes scarce and often far from reliable. The categories are no longer hard.

Let us not speculate about them further. What is certain is the amaz-

---

[9] As the excellent and unexceptionable F. Baudhuin wrote about the rise in the Belgian birthrate during the miseries of the early years of the German occupation (20 per cent higher in 1941–42 than in 1918): "One of the few positive consequences of the ideas of the New Order. . . ." (*On se trouve partiallement ici en présence d'une des rares conséquences positives des idées d'ordre nouveau, favorable à la famille. . . .*). Baudhuin, 198.

[10] During the thirties the divorce rate rose in every European state except for Norway, Portugal, and, perhaps surprisingly, France (529 per million in 1932; 524 in 1939). In 1939 Latvia was the country with the highest rate, 980 per 1 million inhabitants, the same nation with the most negative record of population growth in the thirties.

[11] A total of 11,300 in 1940, including a 50 per cent drop in the July–September period.

[12] The annual average of suicides in Britain was slightly over 5,000 in the thirties, dropping to 3,657 in 1941; in Germany the number of suicides committed by young people under 20 dropped *80 per cent* during the first six years of the Hitler regime, from 1,215 in 1932 to 250 in 1939.

ing fact that in December 1941—well into the third year of the Second World War—more people were alive in Europe than when the war began in September 1939. The principal cause of this surprising fact was, of course, the radically new character of war: Far fewer soldiers died in the first phase of the Second than in that of the First World War, mostly as a result of the new type of *blitzkrieg;* but we must consider, too, another factor, that of the continued vitality of Europe's peoples.

Against this fact we must stack up the increasing numbers of civilian dead, a consequence of the precipitous increase of technology and of the precipitous decline of traditional civilization; for the first time in many centuries women, children, and old people were killed by the hundreds of thousands, while the traditional distinction between soldiers and civilians was melting away. The numbers of people who lost their lives through air bombardment between 1939 and 1941 was still low, even in England and Germany; it was very much lower than what the estimates had been before the war began. The most horrible single fact of death that would eventually push the civilian hecatombs higher than the tall stacks of dead combatants, the fact of the millions of Jews killed, too, was not yet a deed, since the policy of their extermination, which had begun to crystallize in the second half of 1941 within the highest circles of Germany's administration, had become the official tenet of German policy only in January 1942. In the eastern marchlands of Europe the systematic killing of civilians, predominantly of Jews, had begun with the German invasion of Russia in June 1941; there occurred, too, a mass murder of Serbians by Croatians in the summer of 1941; but this kind of barbaric savagery was sporadic in character, that is, until the summer of 1942.[13] Still, this new policy of the planned extermination of national, political, and racial opponents[14] of certain Great Powers *was* developing, and it would grow into a new and horrid reality by 1942, soon after the entry of the United States in the Last European War would bring about the Second World War of this century. Together with another novel policy, that of the planned uprooting and transplantation of entire populations that was put into effect in a number of instances from 1939 onward, it marked the increas-

---

[13] It would be instructive to consider the numbers of marriages, births, suicides, and divorces among Jews in different countries after 1938 and before 1942, comparing these conditions from country to country: but such statistics, to the best of my knowledge, exist only in few instances, whereby the comparative basis for generalizations is missing.

[14] And not only of opponents. Between September 1939 and August 1941 nearly 50,000 brain-damaged German men, women, and children in the Third Reich were killed through the method of euthanasia. In August 1941, Hitler ordered a halt to this, after the protests of certain Catholic bishops had become audible. See below, p. 464.

ingly revolutionary character of this war and the steep decline of traditional European civilization.

## THE UPROOTING OF PEOPLES

¶ In the movements of our ancestors during the past two thousand years there were three great general epochs. Their migrations, generally westward, into the present countries of Europe took place before A.D. 1000. There followed at least eight hundred years of thickening and settlement, permanence of habitation having been characteristic of the feudal as well as of the bourgeois epochs of European civilization. During the past one hundred years large-scale migration began again, though of a different nature. It involved the movement of perhaps as many as seventy million people from Europe to new continents. Within Europe there was an even larger mass migration from the countryside to the cities, a movement that is still going on. But we must recognize the one large and important exception to this modern restlessness. While many people moved from one continent to another, and many more from one place to another within the same country, few people moved from one national state to another during the past two centuries. The only major exception to this were the Jews; and we must devote, later, a separate chapter to the extraordinary tragedy of this extraordinary minority.

During the nineteenth and the early twentieth centuries the history of Europe was becoming the history of nations even more than the history of states. It is instructive to note, for example, that before the end of the First World War, William II and his imperial government, no matter how ambitious their world-political designs may have been, showed very little interest in German populations abroad; they showed none in the Germans of Russia nor in those of Switzerland, not even in the Danube Germans (the Swabians) living in Romania, Hungary, and Serbia. The first attempts of a German government to cultivate some of these minorities in order to establish certain cultural and, implicitly, political ties between them and the German "homeland" were made during the Weimar Republic.[15] This fact illustrates the evolution in German political ambitions. It also illustrates the evolution of international affairs: that governments were beginning to appreciate that their relations must go beneath and beyond their relations with other governments, to include relations

---

[15] "The Germans of the Reich knew little about them, and cared less." Taylor, 26. Wrong.

with peoples and, on occasion, with peoples living in other states, under other governments.

After the First World War a new Eastern Europe had come into being. Oddly enough, no large-scale migration of populations from one country to another developed during this chaotic period, in spite of the drastic remaking of new frontiers and of new states (the only large enforced migration, that of the Anatolian Greeks from Turkey, occurred in Asia Minor, and the only large-scale emigration was that of three million Russians leaving their country in the wake of the Bolshevik Revolution). At the same time the idea of the transplantation of large numbers of people from one country to another, for the sake of stabilizing national homogeneity, was no longer new or shocking. The League of Nations had arranged and supervised the population exchange of hundreds of thousands of Greeks, Turks, and Bulgarians in the twenties, a new kind of mass transfer with varied and sometimes painful results but also with the indifferent consent of the rest of the world. In the twenties and in the thirties the majority of those who were troubled by the Jewish "problem," anti-Semites as well as Zionists, considered that its "solution," too, would be emigration, in order to enhance national homogeneity.

Then, in 1939, there began a series of large-scale transplantations of peoples, mostly in Central and Eastern Europe, an organized movement of certain populations on a scale that the civilized world had not seen perhaps in a thousand years. I can but sum them up in the briefest manner.

Hitler and Himmler brought about an immense resettlement of Germans who lived to the south and east of the borders of the Reich in 1939. This resettlement was achieved either through treaties or by the conquering Germans' fiat. Before the end of 1941 this involved the movement, to the Greater German Reich, of about 560,000 Germans who, added to the Austrians and to the Sudeten and Bohemian Germans incorporated into the Reich in 1938–39, raised the increment of new Germans in the Reich to nearly 11 million between 1938 and 1941.

The first of these treaties (and in many ways the most problematic one) included the majority of the inhabitants of the "South Tyrol," or "Upper Adige," which had been annexed by Italy from Austria in 1919; about 230,000 people, German in language. Very early in his public career Hitler had recognized that these former subjects of the Austrian Empire could be obstacles to the alliance that he wished to conclude with Mussolini's Italy. He understood, too, that the price for such an alliance, and for Mussolini's eventual consent to the German incorporation of Austria, would have to be a solemn German pledge to recognize the Alps for the Italian frontier, at the expense of this German-speaking enclave in one of Italy's northern provinces. It is interesting to note that the initiative of resettling some of these German-speaking people into Germany proper had come from Italian, not German, diplomacy, immediately after the German annexation of Austria in March 1938; in any event, Hitler took up the idea. In June 1939 German and Italian officials agreed on the principles of the resettlement. A definite treaty was signed on 21 October 1939, providing for a new kind of residential plebiscite, according to which the inhabitants of the said territory had to declare until the end of the year whether they wished to exercise their option of settling in the Reich or remain in Italy (their actual relocation would come later). Despite some subtle and some not too subtle Italian propaganda (and certain local Catholic warnings), about 75 per cent of the 230,000 South Tyroleans opted for the Third Reich. Their movement across the border was, however, rather slow: Less than 40 per cent (less than 75,000) of the German optants left their verdant fields and valleys before the end of 1941 (two thirds of them settling in the neighboring provinces of Austria). This resettlement was, thus, far from completed. It was not altogether a success, partly because of the often halfhearted and insincere attitudes of the two governments involved (the Italian government hoped to Italianize some of the Germans, while certain Nazis, especially Austrians, had not given up the hope of eventually reclaiming the South Tyrol for the Reich).

Far more complete and decisive was the transportation of the Baltic Germans to a Germany that some of their ancestors had left as long as eight hundred years before. Hitler knew what his 1939 treaty with Stalin meant: It meant, among other things, that millions of people in Eastern Europe would now disappear behind an iron curtain (this word, designating the Soviets' frontier with Europe, had been current in Germany since the early twenties). So Hitler would bring back the Baltic Germans, and perhaps the isolated German settlers from Volhynia, Galicia, and western Russia, later. A single powerful appeal from Germany would suffice to evoke an immediate and solid response from these people who had, in one way or another, always looked to Germany for the sustenance of their cultural and national consciousness. Treaties with Estonia and Latvia in October 1939 brought about this historical exodus of more than 61,000 Germans (80 per cent of the German population) from these once Hanseatic cities and lands of the Teutonic Knights. Then the German government turned to Moscow proper. Four times (3 November 1939, 5 September 1940, 22 October 1940, 10 January 1941) it signed treaties with the Soviet Union to arrange for the evacuation and the resettlement in Germany of those Germans who had come under Soviet rule through the Russian occupation of eastern Poland, of Bessarabia, and of northern Bukovina. The last of these treaties provided for the removal of the remaining Germans from Latvia, Estonia, and Lithuania, incorporated as these states were into the Soviet Union proper in the summer of 1940.

All of this involved the movement of about 350,000 people. What were Hitler's purposes in this? Much has been written on the racial and national policies of the Nazis in the East, mostly based on the heaps of surviving documents: policies marked by cruelty to a degree seldom surpassed in other fields of the Third Reich's administration, especially in Russia, after the German invasion, about which the title of Gerald Reitlinger's detailed study is both telling and appropriate; the great Eastern Nazi edifice turned out to be, in the end, *a house built on sand*. On the other hand, there are some reasons to believe that Hitler, at times, kept a minimum aim in mind: that of concentrating all of the German-speaking peoples of Eastern Europe into one Greater Germany. In his speech of 6 October 1939 he said: "The East and South of Europe is to a large extent filled with splinters of the German nationality. . . . In their very existence lies the reason and cause for continual international disturbances. In this age of the principle of nationalities and of racial ideals, it is utopian to believe that members of a highly developed people can be assimilated without trouble. It is, therefore, essential for a farsighted ordering of the life of Europe that a resettlement should be undertaken here so as to remove at least part of the material for a European conflict. Germany and the Soviet Union have come to an agreement to support each other in this matter. . . ." Even after his invasion of the Soviet Union there is some evidence that Hitler, in contrast to Himmler, gave but superficial consideration to the extensive peopling of the conquered Eastland with Germans. The Baltic Germans, for example, were expressly forbidden to return to their German-liberated territories; and in 1940 and in 1941 the Germans brought back people not only from behind the iron curtain but even from southern Bukovina and the northern Dobrudja, under Romanian administration. Of course, German policy was entirely different in Poland, especially in that part of western Poland that belonged to the German Reich before 1914 and that was annexed anew to Germany in 1939; that portion had to be Germanized as quickly as possible (for this purpose the eastern resettled Germans, though not the South Tyroleans, were considered as being especially useful).

Toward the end of the war Hitler tacitly permitted the reflux of millions of Germans toward the center of Germany as they fled before the advancing Russians, a movement that by 1945 became an enormous flood, inhibiting at times the movements and the priorities of his own armies. It seems that, after he had realized that he could no longer win the war, Hitler was to take some consolation from the condition that he was close to achieving two of his minimum historical goals: the elimination of Jews from Europe, and the concentration of all Germans in a united Germany. He failed to complete both, though he came a long way. In any event, one of the most important historical consequences of the Second World War was a drastic simplification of the national geography of

Eastern Europe. For this first time in eight hundred years, after 1945 virtually no significant German minorities remained in existence anywhere east of the Germanies. The first phase of their uprooting and transplantation, begun in the autumn of 1939, had been completed by the autumn of 1941. A new great migration of peoples, largely from east to west, had begun—until now, when this is written, the states of Europe, with few exceptions, are more homogeneous than ever before. Thus Wilson's (and Hitler's) ideals of national self-determination have come largely true; but at what cost! and under what conditions!

Other governments, too, resorted to these new policies of moving entire national populations after 1939. At the end of the winter war 400,000 Finns moved from their Karelian homesteads and towns back west into Finland, an increment of more than 10 per cent to the national population. A few thousand Lithuanians fled to East Prussia in the last moments of the twilight June days in 1940 before the occupying Soviets; and a few thousand Swedes were allowed to leave their Estonian homeland in October 1940. Sixty thousand Bulgarians migrated from the northern Dobrudja to southern Dobrudja after the annexation of the latter by the Bulgarian regime in the fall of 1940; nearly 100,000 Romanians moved in the reverse direction. About 80,000 left northern Transylvania as it was reannexed by Hungary in September 1940. In turn, the Hungarians repatriated 16,000 Hungarians of ancient stock (the Csángó-Magyars) who lived beyond the Carpathians, in isolated communities in Moldavia and Bukovina, in late 1941.

Most of these people were transported in accord with their will. This is not what happened in the event of deportations to the nearly 50,000 Germans from Polish Silesia, deported eastward in early September 1939 by the Warsaw government (most of them returned after the German victory); to the nearly 1,500,000 Poles who were removed to central Poland fom the newly Germanized Polish provinces in western and southern Poland; to the 1,200,000 Poles deported to the Soviet Union in 1940–41; to the more than 50,000 Ukrainians and White Russians who were transported to the Soviet Union from Germanized Poland and from the Memel region in 1940–41; to the 65,000 Lithuanians, 64,000 Latvians, and 63,000 Estonians who were deported to the Soviet Union in the early summer of 1941; to the 400,000 Volga Germans who were deported to Siberia and to Kazakhstan; to the more than 100,000 Serbians who were thrown across the new state "frontier" of Croatia, stripped of their belongings, in the summer of 1941. Add to these cruel and radical deportations of entire peoples entirely without their consent, the forced transportation of German and Eastern European Jews to the first Polish ghettos, and we are faced with the uprooting and removal of about 4 million people, organized by governments during the European phase of the last world war—an enormous precedent to the approximately 11 million "displaced" and expelled persons huddling in camps in the Germanies in 1945, at the end of the war.

Need we speculate about the psychic state of the unfortunate peoples who were compelled to leave their homes? Curiously enough, almost always there was a glimmer of hope amidst the despair that seemed to overwhelm them: This made their life bearable (there were, for example, Jews who actually believed that their concentration in the Polish town ghettos meant an improvement, not only of their social and legal status, but in the prospects of their future). Significant, too, were the reactions of the voluntary resettlers. Why did most of the people follow, more or less spontaneously and, more or less instantly, the call of the "fatherland" —or, rather, of representatives of a fatherland? Not many of the South Tyroleans who opted for Germany in 1939 were Nazis. Among the Baltic Germans the majority were not convinced National Socialists, and among the German peasant communities of Volhynia or Bessarabia tens of thousands thought of Hitler as a new monarch of sorts.[16] The principal reason for their option—and the same thing seems to be the case of Bulgarian peasants in the Dobrudja or of Hungarians in old Romania—seems to have been their sharpened consciousness of nationality. This general tendency toward national homogeneity was more than an idea of Hitler's. It was the principal factor in the historical movements of the peoples of Europe during the first half of the twentieth century, something far more widespread and also far more profound than class consciousness or ideology.

Clearest were the purpose of the populations who were moving toward German Europe from under Soviet rule or before the threatening Soviet shadow. Except for a handful of Polish Jews and Ukrainians, virtually no spontaneous migration occurred in the opposite direction. These people (and they came from all classes) had not the slightest doubts about the barbarian misery and the terror that would await them under Soviet Russian rule. The circumstances were poignant, at times worthy of the pen of a superb poet or novelist; consider, for instance, the dark Baltic early winter months of 1939, in Riga and Tallinn. During snowy nights

---

[16] The first time that the Danubian Swabians saw great numbers of Reich Germans was in 1918, when Mackensen's Army was retreating, well-equipped and well-disciplined, along the Danube; this made a deep impression on an entire generation. And there were thousands of pathetic Jews who in 1940–41 fled from the Sovietized territories to western, German Poland: These simple Jews were moved by the memories of World War I and by the atavistic memories of a Germany whose government, no matter how stern, would be less barbaric than that of Russia. Soon they were to be gassed to death.

thousands of German families were packing, leaving their houses where some of them had lived for two hundred years. They were a stolid and unimaginative people, these Baltic German Lutherans; and little that is noteworthy records their departure from their Hanseatic towns after so many centuries. Their old, semipatrician (and consequently only pseudo-Nazi) newspapers printed some of the sentimental speeches of their leaders before the newspapers, too, closed down:

> When the ship weights anchor today, we shall see our homeland for the last time. The last glance will be one of gratitude, not of reproach. For we must be grateful for what we are, not only to our people but also to the country that gave us and our fathers an opportunity to conduct a hard and beautiful fight for existence. . . .

A spokesman for the German aldermen of Tallinn:

> From the founding of this town until today . . . that is, for 720 years . . . the Germans have shared in the building of its government and defense. In good times and bad, through pestilence and famine and wars, the Germans and Estonians have lived together in this town, as children in the same house. . . . It is painful for us to go away from this town where our fathers lived, fought and died.[17]

The German schools closed; the last German Lutheran service was held in Riga on 10 December 1939; "Germanism in Latvia is dead forever," the Latvian Minister of the Interior declared.

Through a silent sea, under the black Baltic night, the white German ships steamed toward the west. Not thus traveled the first Jewish deportees eastward; or even the German peasants from Bessarabia and Bukovina, who trekked westward, in wagon trains of about two hundred carts each, moving along the snowy plains at a rate of about thirty miles each day. An intelligent and cosmopolitan Countess Waldeck saw this "spectacle which reminded me of engravings of the American frontier era: a long line of wagons, covered with white canvas, oxen-drawn, sometimes a colt or a horse running alongside."[18] It was also reminiscent of the Cossacks' treks two or three centuries before. Barbarism had reappeared in Eastern Europe, with a vengeance.

Still, the largest movement of peoples during the Last European War —a temporary one, to be sure—happened not in Eastern but in Western

---

[17] In the *Rigasche Rundschau*, 9 December 1939, cited by Schechtman, 101.
[18] Waldeck, 101.

Europe. It was the panic and exodus of May–June 1940, when perhaps as many as ten million Belgian and French people left their homes, fleeing southward. Nothing like this happened during the First World War.

The historian may trace their progress with more or less exactitude.[19] More than three million Belgians left their homes at a few hours' notice, nearly two thirds of the entire populations of certain provinces. Hounded by fear, by German bombers, starved and plagued by thirst under the relentless sun in May 1940, most of them eventually halted their weary progress north of the Somme and the Seine; still, 1.5 million wandered farther south, coming to a halt in the southwestern part of France, where the region around Toulouse became a veritable little Belgium at the time of the armistice. This was an extraordinary mass movement, propelled by panic.[20] It swelled within four days, beginning late on 11 May; on the afternoon of 15 May the last train for France left Brussels.[21] Among the French the exodus started a little later. It involved perhaps as many as 7 million French men, women, and children ( as many as 1 million Parisians fled their city between 10 and 13 June). On the southern side of the Seine and of the Somme in the department of the Eure, in lower Normandy, 90 to 99 per cent of the population packed up and left within three days: in the town of Evreux on the evening of 11 June, 172 inhabitants remained out of nearly 20,000; in Vernon, 150 out of 8,000.[22] We have seen their photographs, thousands of them, period pictures by now; the pushcarts among the sharp-nosed little Renaults and

---

[19] See Vidalenc, op. cit., the standard work on the subject, in the Foreword of which, however, the author points out the often insufficient character of statistical information.

[20] Disorder and panic were responsible for a sordid episode in Abbeville on 20 May, when a group of Belgian political prisoners, Rexists and pro-Germans, were shot by drunken soldiers in cold blood.

[21] The French had sent trains for the purpose of evacuating Belgians to the south. The French government proposed to receive 400,000 Belgians; ultimately four times that number came. On 16 May the Belgian government ordered all young people between 16 and 35 years of age who had not yet joined the ranks of the Army to assemble at Roulers, near the French frontier. It was a desperate and senseless bureaucratic order. These young people were put on trains for France. There was no opportunity to equip them with arms. The trains moved slowly; eventually their disconsolate progress came to a halt. Crammed full of unarmed youth, they made a deplorable impression on the French populace.

[22] Vidalenc, 138–39, cited the example of Marlemont, a small French village of the Ardennes: of 195 inhabitants, 171 left. Of these, 26 traveled but a short distance, a few miles from the village. Most of them moved toward the southwest, 79 of them reaching the department of the Vendée, on the Atlantic.

Citroëns, the mattresses and the proverbial cages holding the family canary, tied on the top. . . . By the end of May, 10,000 refugees had passed each day through the Seine bridges moving southward; by the end of June, nearly every village in southeastern France doubled its population. And then it was in the villages that there was not enough food.

The armistice came. Between 1 July and 1 October 1.5 million Belgians returned to their homes (400,000 of them by repatriation trains, 35,000 in automobiles, the rest through mixed means of transport). Ninety-eight per cent of the Belgians and 80 per cent of the French refugees came home by the end of the summer.[23] Many of them found that their houses had been pillaged by their neighbors.

## Food, drink, sleep

¶ Let us now look at the record of the availability and of the consumption of the essential materials of life: What and how did the peoples of Europe eat during the first two years of a world war, when most of the Continent fell under German domination? One would think, at first, that in our age of massive administrative records and economic statistics, this would be relatively easy to reconstruct from a humdrum mass of facts that must be eventually vitalized by the insights of the comparative historian. Not so. Not only does the availability of statistics vary from country to country (relatively much in Western, and little in most Eastern European countries), but also, in studying them, one runs up against a distressing condition: for, contrary to the general belief, economic "facts," including statistical ones, are not at all "hard"; indeed, often they are so soft as to be useless. That elusive thing, the "cost of living," for example, is subject to all kinds of exceptions and variations, even in the most orderly of societies in times of peace. Its computation and its categories vary from place to place; for what are "essentials" in "the cost of living" to certain people at a certain time are something quite different for another people at another time. When it comes to wartime, then, statistics of income and of expenditures must take into account an enormous variety of personal incomes and expenditures that, by the nature of things, go generally unreported. Even if someone could get hold of "primary" sources—say, the personal accounts of a number of family households—these would be incomplete and confusing, excluding as much as what they include. In any event, they would seldom include the irregular transactions of people, including

---

[23] A year later, in July 1941, there were still 800,000 refugees, including Jews, Czechs, Poles, Dutch, and Belgians in Vichy France.

those of the black market—failing, therefore, to register some of the most widespread and most important economic transactions of everyday life.

We can, however, essay certain generalizations. There was no famine in Europe during the Second World War, as there wasn't in the First[24]; but there was very widespread malnutrition (which, however, did not reach its peaks until 1944 and 1945, in many cases after the war was over). There emerged, early, the great vulnerability of industrialized nations. The governmental control of food was even more widespread than during the First World War. Its effects varied so widely that no generalization about rationing would do. They were rather successful in some countries, nearly completely ineffectual in others.

The amazing success story in this field is that of the Germans. During the entire war the German people did not suffer from malnutrition. None of the dreary and at times horrible war winter experiences of 1916 and 1917 repeated themselves; there was at least enough food for everyone. This is especially remarkable when we consider the following conditions: The Germany of 1939 was far less agricultural than the Germany of 1914; it was more dependent on imports; among its allies there was no large agricultural empire comparable to the Austria-Hungary of 1914; Germany in 1939, as we now know, had not prepared for a long war. In reality the food supply of the German people functioned with surprising reliability throughout the war, even at the time of the most destructive bombardments of their cities.

Rationing in Germany was decreed on 28 August 1939; it was further extended on 25 September. No more important extension was decreed until 6 April 1942,[25] when potatoes and other foodstuffs were added (Germany was the largest potato-growing country in Europe at the time). Thereafter rationing covered most foods. It was reasonably sufficient. The 2,400 grams of the weekly allotment of bread in 1940 and in 1941 was large enough so that many people did not take all of it; until 1942 the same thing was true of ersatz coffee (the quality of which was far superior to the ersatz coffee of World War I). The content of calories of rationed food in Essen, a typical German industrial city, was 1,552 in the spring of 1940, 1,515 a year later, 1,751 in the spring of 1942—com-

---

[24] Exceptions: Leningrad 1941–42, certain ghettos, concentration camps, and certain districts of Andalusia in late 1940–41.

[25] One significant extension was that of the rationing of tobacco, beginning on 7 November 1941 (foreigners were to get the full German tobacco ration; Polish and Russian prisoners one half of the German ration; Polish and Russian women and Jews none at all—this was typical). About the significance of the early 1942 turning point in German economic planning during the war see above, p. 165.

pared to the meager 1,176 in the summer of 1917.[26] The yearly total of rations for grown-ups in Essen was the following (in kilograms; eggs in numbers):

|  | Bread | Meat | Fats | Cheese | Eggs |
|---|---|---|---|---|---|
| 1940 | 124.2 | 26.2 | 14.0 | 3.1 | 89 |
| 1941 | 117.0 | 23.0 | 14.0 | 2.5 | 62 |
| 1942 | 111.8 | 18.5 | 11.6 | 2.3 | 42 |
| (Compared with 1917: | 107.3[27] | 18.6 | 3.2 | n.a. | 30) |

The rationing was also effective. With their usual discipline, compounded by the fearful respect accorded to the administrative organs of the police state, almost without exception all of the foodstuffs and other rationed materials were obtainable in Germany, at the official (and therefore low) prices. Except for certain luxury items (men's textiles), the black market hardly existed at all. Nor was the relative well-being of the German population altogether attributable to the looting of food from the conquered countries of Europe in 1939 and 1940. It is true that *within* these conquered countries the Germans arrogated to themselves most of the privileges of conquerors. Starting from an extremely favorable exchange rate set by themselves, the Germans ate and drank with plenty of ease in France or in Poland. But there is little material evidence to the effect that, with the exception of certain luxury items, the German population profited much from the conquest of, say, France or Belgium. The Germans ate well in 1940, but not better than in 1939; after their Western triumphs their rations were hardly increased at all. On the other hand, there was only a limited evidence of Spartan living, the virtues of which Hitler and Goebbels were to extol as the war proceeded. Food in Germany (as well as in Austria and Bohemia) was adequate, if not plentiful. Even imported luxuries such as coffee, tea, and chocolate were available; the natural rhythm of the year was not interrupted (the rationing regulations included, for example, special provisions for such occasions as weddings or baptisms or silver or gold wedding anniversaries). A few famous restaurants functioned with few restrictions on their rather impressive menus, not only the restaurants of certain grand hotels carefully maintained by the Nazis, but also places such as Horcher's in Berlin (where a first-class meal cost, however, twice as much as in Paris: about 50 RM per person), or the Three Hussars in Vienna (catering to some of the more cosmopolitan bigwigs of their hierarchy—to Goering, for example).

Let us now pass to the other extreme of France, where rationing and

---

[26] Schmitz, 10 and passim.
[27] Of much inferior quality.

food price controls were chaotic, inadequate, and inefficient from the very beginning of their imposition, and where malnutrition became a problem for millions as early as in 1941. The principal cause was the German occupation, of course[28]—but there were other contributory factors. France by 1939 was no longer the orchard, or the agricultural Canaan, of Western Europe. She had only recently passed the point of no return for a modern society, the point after which the majority of her people were no longer engaged principally in the production of food. For a Western European power this development had been very slow, coming rather late (the rural population declined very slowly, from 58 per cent to 48 per cent from 1900 to 1936). Her agriculture and her methods of food distribution were antiquated even in those regions where French industrial production was relatively modern. Indeed, by 1939 the French had become dependent on imports of foods. Perhaps as much as one third of their food was imported from abroad by the mid-thirties, whereas in Germany, in a country that no one could call the orchard or the breadbasket of Europe, dependence on food imports was constantly reduced in the interwar years, from about one third in 1927–28 to 17 per cent in 1938–39.[29] And while in nearly every state of Europe, including the majority of those that had been conquered by the Germans, the production of food, stimulated as it was by the exigencies of wartime, rose, in France it fell: French agricultural production in 1940 was 15 per cent less than in 1939; in 1941 it dropped another 6 per cent.

At the beginning of the war—indeed, nearly until the end of 1940—an unusual and unexpected situation arose: There was more food to be had in the cities than in the countryside. This included even Paris, under German occupation, one of the reasons why many of the well-to-do returned from Vichy France to Paris in the fall and winter of 1940.

---

[28] The discrepancy between the victor and the vanquished was especially sharp in their rationed food. In February 1941, for example (in grams):

|  | RATIONS FOR GENERAL CONSUMERS | | RATIONS FOR HEAVY WORKERS | |
|  | Germany | France (occupied zone) | Germany | France |
| --- | --- | --- | --- | --- |
| Daily bread | 340 | 300 | 700 | 400 |
| Weekly meat | 500 | 360 | 1,200 | 360 |
| Weekly fats | 270 | 100 | 740 | 100 |
| Weekly sugar | 1,200–1,500 | 500 | 1,200–1,500 | 500 |

[29] Petzina, 95, who points out that it was in the agrarian field, among others, that the Nazi Four-year Plan was not altogether a success.

This condition was a consequence of the accumulated reserves of the townspeople, and perhaps also of the extraordinary cold first war winter in 1939–40, which had depleted some of the reserves in the villages. If we consider the enormity of the catastrophe of 1940, it is remarkable how relatively stable prices remained that year: According to the French national institute of statistics, the wholesale price of foods (*Indices pondérés des prix de gros de 135 marchandises: produits alimentaires*), compared to a 100 base in 1939, climbed relatively slowly, to 105 in 1939 and to 139 in 1940[30]; thereafter the rise was more rapid (171 in 1941, 201 in 1942). On the other hand, we must keep in mind that France had experienced the morally as well as economically debilitating effects of enduring inflation in the otherwise depressed thirties: Despite two devaluations, French prices nearly doubled between 1934 and 1938. Thus the relatively slow rise of prices during the first two years of the war does not tell all of the story. There is reason to think that the average Frenchman spent not 1½ but at least 3 times as much money on his food by the end of 1941 than at the beginning of the war.[31]

Much of this had to do with the steadily waning public confidence in the paper money, but also with the fact that wages rose less rapidly than prices, both in occupied and in unoccupied France (in Paris the index of the prices of services in 1940 rose only 9 per cent, and in 1941 merely 13 per cent above that of 1938). By early 1941, thus, the usual wartime pattern appeared: Except for the poorest portions of the countryside, the peasants, and even most of the inhabitants of villages, were better off than the people in the towns. This condition involved more than staple foods. By the winter of 1940–41 the inhabitants of cities suffered more from cold than from low nutrition, especially in houses that were centrally heated and thus dependent on external sources of fuel supply, whereas wood, or at least scrap lumber or peat, was available with less difficulty outside the cities. At the end of 1941 the black-market prices of beef, eggs, milk, and

---

[30] The rise in 1940: January 126, July 138, November 148, December 152. In 1941: from January, 156 to December, 186. Sugar was the first item to be rationed in unoccupied France, beginning October 1940.

[31] In his perverse and incomparable *Journal de la France*, Alfred Fabre-Luce accused the French of gluttony and alcoholism: According to him, there were 100,000 more bistrots in 1939 than in 1919; the rate of alcoholism was higher than ever; "in 1939 the Parisian working-man spent three times as much on his food than what was necessary for him to subsist" (II, 397); also II, 399: "In May 1940 the French Army is surprised by war in a state of full digestion. One sees men throwing away their rifles while clutching a bottle." My cursory researches indicate that Fabre-Luce was wrong: The rate of alcoholism was dropping after 1938. In any event, it was lower than after 1870, or at the time of Zola's *L'Assommoir*.

potatoes in Paris were about three times those of the official prices, while the price of coal was more than ten times higher (later these food prices doubled again, while the price of coal more than trebled—by 1944 it was 30 times that of the official price). Until 1942, food, while expensive,[32] was always available in France. Unlike in Germany, every town had its share of black-market restaurants, openly tolerated by the German and the French police, where meat was usually served on the bottom of a plate, covered by vegetables or, on occasion, by eggs.[33] A new stratum of black-marketeers arose, immortalized by Jean Dutourd in his satire *Bon Beurre* after the war. Also, because of the cold, and because of the necessary (though temporary) energy that the consumption of a hot meal would provide, Frenchmen, especially in Paris, reverted to the customs of the early nineteenth century, when the main meal, the dinner, was eaten in the middle of the day (the midday meal had become the *déjeuner*, literally "breakfast," during that century).

Generally speaking, the more "backward" the social structure of a country, the better was her food situation: In the Balkans and in the Danubian countries, for example, there were few food shortages during the first two years of the war (in Hungary, rationing was not introduced until May 1941). Since the Germans paid relatively well for the food they imported and also because of the existing full employment, the living standards of the working classes of these populations actually rose in 1940 and in 1941. In Italy, too, the backward South suffered less than the industrial North.[34] There were, of course, exceptions: Greece, Poland, and the Baltic countries, where the new regimes brought with them an almost instant impoverishment for large numbers of people. Again, the political conditions determined the economic situation, rather than the reverse: In Denmark, where the Germans leaned over backward to demonstrate their moderation and nonintervention, the consumption and the availability of food was near normal throughout 1940 and 1941: Prices, too, rose relatively little (less than 50 per cent between 1939 and December 1941). By

---

[32] Representative black-market prices in France, September 1941: a chicken 200 to 300 F, eggs 6 to 10 F apiece; in the spring of 1941 a good bourgeois dinner in a black-market restaurant would cost 180 F upward. Early 1942: a kilogram of pork or beef or a liter of milk, 80 F apiece; butter, 180 F a kilogram; coffee, 500 F a kilogram.

[33] A German regulation in Paris in late 1941 allowed five de luxe restaurants to serve meat, in exchange for a 10 per cent surtax. They were: Tour d'Argent, Capironne, Maxim's, Drouant, and Carton-Lucas.

[34] Italian living costs in December 1939 were only 3 per cent higher than in December 1938; by December 1941 they rose nearly 40 per cent, according to a government computation.

and large, rationing worked well in occupied Norway, in Finland, in Britain[35] (where prices rose, however, nearly 50 per cent during the first two years of the war), and among the neutrals in Sweden and Switzerland (though in neutral countries, too, prices would double, on the average, between 1939 and 1942). Among the German-occupied countries rationing worked miserably in Holland and in Belgium, and hardly at all in Poland and in Greece. Statistics about the Soviet Union are not available; but even if they were, they would tell us little. There the population lived often amidst the primitive conditions of a barter economy, scrounging food through the most irregular and often unpredictable means, yet maintaining their vitality even in the darkest months of 1941, accustomed as they had been to a scarcity of food and to other Spartan conditions for long years, suffering from truly extreme conditions perhaps only in the encircled and famine-ridden city of Leningrad.[36]

In summing up the food situation, we can see two turning points during the first two years of the war: The German victory in Western Europe in the early summer of 1940 marked the first, and the late winter of 1940–41 the second. From August 1939 to April 1940 the general cost of living rose relatively slowly[37]: In 1941, then, food prices began to

---

[35] Rationing in Britain did not begin until January 1940 (ration books had been issued earlier). It involved ham, sugar, and bacon. Meat rationing followed in the spring; tea in the summer of 1940; canned foods and biscuits, etc. in 1941.

[36] This is a good example of the imbecility of the categories that are usually applied in order to designate different societies. In 1941 Churchill's England was a prototype of the conservative-capitalist and Stalin's Russia of the totalitarian-Communist state. Yet in England most of the food was strictly rationed, and some foods were altogether unobtainable outside of rationing, whereas in the Soviet Union most of the food was bought at primitive free markets, through haggling with peasants, including the infamous Sennaya in Leningrad, where in 1941 and 1942 fresh meat patties made of human flesh were openly sold and avidly bought by desperate people—the ultimate logical consequence of the principles of Adam Smith, I suppose.

[37] Rise in per cents from August 1939 to March 1940:

|  | Wholesale prices | Living costs |
|---|---|---|
| Belgium | 40 | 11 |
| Great Britain | 33 | 15 |
| Denmark | 51 | 8 (!) |
| Holland | 24 | 10 |
| Sweden | 25 | 10 |
| Switzerland | 25 | 6 |

Baudhuin, 100.

outrace all of the rest. About 35 per cent of the budget of a Dutch family went for food in 1935; this rose to 45 per cent by early 1941, while wages had risen only half as much. The cost-of-living index in Holland in 1940 stood 15 per cent higher than in 1938; it was 33 per cent higher in 1941 and 41 per cent higher in 1942, while food prices in 1940 were 18.3 per cent higher in 1940, 42 per cent higher in 1941, and 55 per cent higher in 1942. It was in early 1941 that a new element entered into the psyche of most Europeans: a mild obsession, a concentration on food, of which one result was to be the tremendous postwar interest in gastronomy in countries and among classes of people who had not been particularly interested in the varieties of good eating before the war. By 1941 dreams about meals were as frequent as were erotic dreams in the nocturnal fantasies of many Western Europeans. Also, their menu changed: They became dependent on simpler, ruder, and more fattening sources of food. Many fastidious Frenchmen and Belgians, for example, discovered the virtues of the lowly potato, some of them taking daily trips into the countryside for this now principal staple. The virtues of lard, too, were coming home to Belgium which, even more than France, had been hitherto the motherland of buttery cooking (a kilogram of lard, worth 20 Belgian francs in August 1940, cost 300 francs in early 1942 on the black market). There were periodic shortages of an extreme nature as early as at the end of January 1941, when no meat at all could be had in the poorer quarters of Brussels.[38] On the other hand, food was *always* available at a price. There were more stocks than what had been believed, even chocolate and tea were to be had, and while it is true that such luxuries were reserved, by the nature of things, to the rich (or, rather, to the newly rich), even factory workers could—indeed, they had to—buy certain staples at black-market prices.[39] Still, according to later estimates, the average Belgian and Dutchman by March 1941 had lost 10 to 15 pounds of his weight.

While wine and beer were becoming scarcer and weaker (in occupied France the rationing of wine was introduced in the summer of 1941), there was relatively little increase in alcoholism, even in countries

---

[38] In February 1941, 30 per cent of schoolchildren in Brussels arrived in their schools without having had breakfast. Gerard-Libois, Gotovitch, 337.

[39] Certain black-market prices in Brussels, May 1941: eggs 5.50 F apiece; a kilogram of potatoes, 15 F; of butter, 120 F; of beef, 100 F; of port, 130 F; of flour, 50 F; of sugar, 40 F; of coffee, 140 F; of tea, 500 F. Textiles (including "good English cloth" were always available: a good suit cost 6,000 to 10,000 francs (1,200 in 1939). Shoes were more difficult to get. In Normandy in April 1941 a kilogram of beans cost 50 F; of carrots (!), 16.50 F; a head of cabbage was worth 8 F; a head of lettuce, 5 F.

where the consumption of strong spirits would act as a potent defense against the insufficiency of heat. It is of some interest to note that the consumption of strong spirits among German soldiers was higher than during World War I, partly due to social, partly to geographical causes: Many of the younger soldiers were no longer abstemious, they wished to demonstrate their ability to drink strong stuff; also, the Eastern European taste for vodka, that potent and odorless generator of inner heat, largely unknown outside of Russia, Poland, and the Baltic countries before 1939, was brought back by the German and satellite troops from Poland and Russia. But the great success story was that of coffee. Millions who had been earlier unacquainted with it (in many countries of Central and Eastern Europe real coffee, as distinct from chicory,[40] had been a middle-class and upper-class staple) and other millions who knew it only in its mild breakfast or afternoon beverage forms, developed rapidly a taste for strong, compressed coffee of the Italian espresso type. Like the great Balzac a century before, they discovered strong black coffee as the principal stimulant; indeed, their daily existence became dependent on it.[41] In the vivid wartime account by Stefan Korbonski, *Fighting Warsaw*, he describes the places where "war millionaires celebrated their illegal transactions with glasses of vodka," together with the small restaurants in that tragic city, which were still "the rendezvous of gourmets," and "shady characters everywhere, wearing overcoats and suspiciously stout at the waist, whispering hoarsely, 'Vodka, vodka, vodka'"—blackmarketeers, offering their wares. "Crossing Jerusalem Avenue one entered the coffee-bar quarter . . . dozens of them, sometimes very tastefully decorated. . . ."

> Coffee bar . . . black coffee . . . how inseparably it was all linked up with conspiracy in Warsaw! One remembers so much that took place within their walls. Warsaw was still starving when the coffee bars began to appear, like mushrooms after a good shower of rain. Cozy and attractive, they became meeting places for all the world. I can still hear the orders: "Large black." "Small black." "Small black in a large glass" . . . the last being given in the hope that a small portion would be poured out

---

[40] Hence the disappointment of many Europeans during the war, and also after, with the coffee they received, on occasion, from the eldorado of the United States: American coffee, lightly roasted and preground, proved to be disappointingly weak for their palates and stomachs. (On the other hand, American nylons, seeping into Europe through Lisbon after 1940–41, were among the most coveted luxury goods, veritable status symbols.)

[41] Nicotine consumption increased too. In May 1941 the German manufacture of cigarettes was more than double the rate of two years before.

more generously into a large glass. The wits were ordering "A large small coffee." Coffee was expensive and every drop had a price. The coffee bars became regular conspiratorial places . . . letter-boxes. . . .[42]

We must note, finally, that in Western Europe at least there were no great fluctuations in life expectancy during the first two years of the war: In Belgium, for example, infant mortality in 1940 and in 1941 fell below prewar times; this is surprising. The new sulfa drugs reduced the extent and the duration of many infectious diseases. Partly due to the occupying armies, partly due to weakened physical resistance, venereal diseases rose even where prostitution had not (in Holland the annual incidence of gonorrhea in 1941 was three times that of 1939). The war brought about a sporadic increase in the professional employment of women, though only in a few countries (Finland, Russia, Britain, and Sweden) were there large numbers of women serving as auxiliary soldiers. Many women wore trousers for the first time (mostly in winter, as a defense against the cold); the fashion of long hair that had come back during the thirties and was to continue until the late fifties prevailed, perhaps unaccountably so.[43] The war of 1939–45 did not mark an important phase in the so-called progressive emancipation of women. The very exigencies of wartime life made the tasks of wives and mothers more time-consuming and more difficult. In 1939–41 there was only a slight rise in illegitimate births, and in many places a decrease of prostitution occurred together with a decrease in other kinds of criminality. The generally symptomatic growth of juvenile delinquency would arise only in the latter stages of the war, with guerrilla warfare, the *maquis*, the near collapse of traditional authorities, and the general disorder contributing thereto.[44]

A widespread psychosomatic symptom among millions of men in the Western European nations (and also in Poland) was polyuria, excessive urination; other widespread symptoms were excessive perspiration, cold feet and hands, and impotence among soldiers after their war experiences, lasting for months thereafter, since this involved a kind of fear that activates itself. A very widespread psychic symptom was hypnomania, the

---

[42] Korbonski, 149.

[43] In Spain no women wore trousers; women also had to wear skirted bathing suits, except on the portions of the beaches reserved for the diplomatic corps.

[44] It is interesting that in Germany, where a massive drop in juvenile criminality occurred, criminality among young girls (14–18 years old) in 1940 was almost as high as during the disorderly depression year of 1932 (144 convictions per 100,000 young people in 1932; 140 in 1940), whereas among boys of the same age group the rate fell by almost one half. In England juvenile delinquency rose sharply from 1939–41 and even more thereafter.

desire for excessive sleep. Sleep, indeed, was the great daily drug against the worry and the despair and the cold suffered by millions of Europeans. From Parisian patricians to Jews huddled under grimy comforters in the Warsaw ghetto, millions discovered an appetite for sleep such as they had not known before. And it was their deprivation of sleep rather than the other physical and psychic discomforts that millions of Londoners and other inhabitants of England found most difficult to bear during the first winter of the Blitz. For Germany and for most of the Continent the long-dreaded months of sleeplessness lay in the future.

## RÊVEUSE BOURGEOISIE

¶ *Rêveuse bourgeoisie*—sleepwalking bourgeoisie—was the title of a novel, written in the interwar years, by Pierre Drieu la Rochelle, the most intelligent, and perhaps the most tragic, figure among the French Fascist collaborationists with the New Europe in 1940. He was a *haut bourgeois malgré lui*, by which I mean that this aristocratic Fascist could never divest himself of a deeply rooted side of his character and mind: Still, throughout his writing ran the red thread of his hatred at what he saw as the deadly weakness, the death rattle of the bourgeoisie, everywhere in the West, but especially in France. And of course this view, and the political philosophy that sprang from it, were very typical not only of Fascism and National Socialism and of their many adherents but also of the spirit of what Europe seemed to have become in 1940, when the defeat of France was not only the defeat of France, and not only the collapse of the political order of the Europe erected at Versailles, it was also the defeat of bourgeois Europe, the collapse of the European bourgeoisie, the end of the Bourgeois Age in the history of the world.

There seemed to be, at the time, much truth in this; there is still truth in it; but it was not the entire truth. The bourgeoisie went on living, and it survived the war. What Drieu, what the fanatical "Rightists," what many intellectuals, including most Leftists, thought they saw in the thirties was, in one important respect, the same projection that Goebbels, even more than Hitler, saw and proclaimed toward the end of the war, before the Hitlerian *Götterdämmerung:* Whatever the outcome of the war, Goebbels cried, at least the bourgeois era is over and done with, the bourgeoisie will have been fatally weakened, eliminated by history, in Germany, and also elsewhere in Europe. There was some truth in this; but it was not the entire truth, especially not in Central and Western Europe. As a matter of fact, the principal social consequence of the war was the rise of new middle classes, both in Western Europe and ultimately even in communist Eastern Europe. If the result of the war was not altogether a restoration of bourgeois Europe, it did nonetheless lead to the Americanization of the social structure of the Continent. But this was a later development with which we are not concerned here, albeit we shall see its first evidences appearing as early as during the first phase of the war, when the institutions of the bourgeoisie seemed to have collapsed in ruins. What is remarkable, for our purposes, is that the European bourgeoisie—or, to be more exact, the bourgeois classes of Europe's nations—came through this period of their worst and most disheartening trials not better but perhaps not worse than any of the other classes in Europe.

The principal problem for the historian as he attempts to discuss their record is the great difficulty in defining, or even circumscribing, the term *bourgeoisie*, especially as it existed in Europe thirty years ago. We must recognize, first of all, that *bourgeois* and *middle class* are not the same things. The first is a historical, the second a sociological phenomenon. Middle classes exist everywhere in the world; in every kind of a society one may discern an upper, a lower, and a middle class. But bourgeois, like the European city, has been a specifically European phenomenon.[45] During the nineteenth century, when the Bourgeois Age was reaching its peak, when the ranks of the bourgeoisie were swelling sometimes beyond recognition, bourgeois had become a pejorative word, not only in the minds of supercilious aristocrats or in those of snobs, but also in those of artists, intellectuals, and radicals; of this new usage the Marxist anathema on the *bourgeois* is best known. Yet during the early twentieth century, at the very time when bourgeois ideals and bourgeois politics were attacked by both Left and Right, there were more bourgeois in Europe than ever before, all of the current ideologies notwithstanding; for the new swelling ranks of the middle classes could not divest themselves of bourgeois standards of bourgeois ways of life.

The social structure of most European nations by 1939 was neither predominantly aristocratic nor proletarian. It was predominantly middle-class, including those countries where the middle classes were not yet large. These countries were those in the South and in the East of the Con-

---

[45] The *bourgs* and cities of medieval Europe had particular characteristics of their own. The European city (and not only the castle or compound of the rulers, as in Asia or even in Russia) was surrounded by walls; there was a sharp separation of the city from the surrounding countryside; and, consequently, a sharp distinction between citizen (*citoyen, cittadino*) and country dweller. There was the celebrated German saying *"Stadtluft macht frei"* (the city air makes you free). *Bourgeois, burgher, Bürger, borghese* were not merely an economic stratum, they represented a mentality of their own. See Lukacs, *PMA*, Chap. 18.

tinent: Portugal, Spain, Poland, Hungary, Greece, the Balkan and the Baltic countries. Historians, especially American and British ones, often describe their social structures of the time as "feudal." This is largely nonsense. It is true that in places such as Hungary or Spain members of the former nobility still possessed, on occasion, very large estates; but even there the present belonged to industry, to new managerial groups, and to political meritocracies. And even in those European nations where commerce, industry, finance, and certain professions were overpopulated by Jews (in 1939 these were Romania, Hungary, Slovakia, Poland, Lithuania, Latvia), it was no longer reasonable to speak, as many foreign observers, Nazis as well as visiting English intellectuals, spoke, of a largely Jewish bourgeoisie. For the era of the national middle classes had by then arrived, the feudal, the pre-industrial era, the age of aristocracies having gone, and the era of the proletariat still a chimera, far away.

But at this point I must again insist on the distinction between *bourgeois* and *middle class*. A sociography of most European countries by 1939 would reveal that the middle classes have already risen, that they were multiplying rapidly, surprisingly fast, in spite of the only recent depression of the early thirties. But who constituted these classes? By 1939 the evolution of societies reached a stage where many previously unknown occupational categories would swell the middle ranks of societies to a point where, in one way or another, millions of former proletarians (and thousands of the former nobility) would feel and, on occasion, say that they belonged to the middle class. *In one way or another:* because, in many ways, a garage manager, an air force sergeant, a printing-shop foreman, an assistant superintendent, and a high-grade mechanic were no longer simply classifiable as belonging to the "working class" (in itself a more and more anachronistic term).[46] One may have finished his high school, previously the preserve of the middle and upper classes; the second may have possessed a motorcycle, a camera, and an apartment, all symbolic middle-class possessions; the third may have had an income higher than that of a university man, etc. On the other hand, they have not yet divested themselves of most of their lower-class memories and sentiments.

By 1939, therefore, in most European continental countries, possibly even in the Soviet Union, one of the most significant divergences was no longer among "lower," "middle," and "upper" classes but between a lower-middle and an upper-middle class. And this distinction cannot be

---

[46] Except in one important sense. At least until 1939, in most European countries the principal division persisted between two kinds of people: those who had domestic servants (even if only a single slatternly daymaid) and those who did not.

fixed by statistical constants, defining the two groups on the basis of income levels or occupational categories. Their differences involved, primarily, attitudes of mind rather than material possessions, perhaps even different forms of consciousness, certainly different kinds of aspirations. But, then, it was always certain kinds of aspirations, rather than possessions, that formed the substance of the bourgeois. And these bourgeois aspirations were still conditioned by the traditions of an older society. Patronizing the arts, pretending to be country gentry on occasion, cultivating the pride of family and clan, professing self-denying service to the state: These were patrician aspirations, a mixture of earlier bourgeois and aristocratic standards. I write "earlier" because during the nineteenth century in Europe as well as in England, the *grande bourgeoisie* became more aristocratic, while the aristocracy became more bourgeois. All of this has been described, sometimes very well, sometimes not so well, in a plethora of great novels of that period. My point is only that the European upper-middle classes, by 1939, had their share of certain aristocratic aspirations, which was not true of the newer and lower segments of the middle classes, as these became middle class without becoming bourgeois. And, in many ways, this was the key of the divisions of 1939–45; in many ways between upper-middle-class and lower-middle-class ideas and frames of mind.

For one thing, the European bourgeoisie was Anglophile. This was true of the entire Continent, Germany included. The origins of this attitude go back, of course, to the nineteenth century or, to be more exact, to the second half of it, when the type of the English "gentleman" became something of an idealized type for many of the remaining aristocrats and practically for all patricians and aspiring bourgeois, emulating the temperament, the manners, the imagined political preferences and, literally above everything, the clothes of "the gentleman." But this was not merely a superficial kind of imitation. This kind of Anglophilia was more than a social fashion, it meant a cultural preference; and, consequently, it was replete with political and ideological consequences. It was not shared by the lower-middle class; indeed, it was alien to it and to the masses of new arrivals in its ranks. Thus one of the most important divisions in Europe (and, to some extent, in other places of the world, too) during the Second World War was the one between Anglophiles (who were, consequently, Germanophobes) and Germanophiles (who were nearly always Anglophobes), and in nearly every country this corresponded amazingly with the divided attitudes of the upper middle classes and lower middle classes.[47] This was a phenomenon of such importance that I shall have to

---

[47] The only important exceptions seemed to have been that of the French, and of the French-speaking peoples of Belgium and Switzerland.

return to it when I write, later, about international relations, involving the sentiments of entire nations toward each other.[48] Its mention here was, however, an inevitable part of my introduction of my attempt to describe some things about the behavior of the European bourgeoisie during the first, crucial and traumatic, period of the Second World War.

*Rêveuse bourgeoisie?* Whatever one can say about them, they were not sleepwalking. Their behavior was sometimes cowardly, sometimes brave: I shall sort out some of the evidence, although I can illustrate it only through a few fragments. Before that, I must write briefly about the continuity of life, fascinating and intriguing, as it was: the amazing persistence of habits, institutions, constructs of life, patterns of thought—even on the morrow of cataclysms, on the edges of catastrophe, in the dead centers and in the deadly wakes of historical hurricanes.

There was, of course, continuity on low levels of life: Large portions of the lives of peasants in the vastnesses of Russia, for example, were not much different in 1939 from what they were in 1914, the communization of the Russian empire, their kolkhozes and tractor stations notwithstanding (it is seldom realized, for example, that in 1939 less than 10 per cent of Russia's villages had a Communist party cell). There was, too, the factor of momentum, on all levels of society and of life, the reflexlike continuation of everyday habits. But what I have in mind is a matter that is somewhat different: It is the resistance of traditional ways of life, together with the continuing stimulus of patrician aspirations. This is the kind of thing that seldom appears in the literature of the period, and it is not to be found in the memoirs at all. A brilliant exception to this vast literary lacuna is the novel, with the perhaps unfortunate title *Oedipus siegt bei Stalingrad,* by the Austrian writer Gregor von Rezzori, describing as it does the lives (and, more important, the thoughts and the aspirations) of German gentry, aristocrats and would-be aristocrats, snobs and habitués of "Charley's Bar" in metropolitan, cosmopolitan Berlin in 1938–39. There is

---

[48] See below, pp. 383–414. Here is an example from the dispatch of a German Embassy official in Rome in January 1940: "The broad mass of the Italian people, and this applies to all classes, never liked us. The German character with its frequently ponderous thoroughness is foreign to the superficial Italian. That has always been the case and is probably true today to an increased degree. There are few Italians who seek personal association with German circles. In general, the Italians prefer to be among themselves. Association with foreigners are fostered primarily by so-called society, and then mostly with the British and the French. . . ." Plessen, in *GD,* D, VIII, 612. Consequently Ribbentrop sent a gaggle of Bismarcks to Rome "in order to maintain contact with Roman society circles." *GD,* D, VIII, 744.

hardly a word about Nazis and Nazism in this book, whose pages are nonetheless suffused by its presence; and it is therefore that they are descriptive and telling. For this was one facet of Berlin, described later by no other foreigner as well as by George Kennan in his *Memoirs*. "What struck one about wartime Berlin," he wrote about 1939–40 from the retrospect of more than twenty-five years, "was the undemonstrative but unmistakable inner detachment of the people from the pretentious purposes of the regime, and the way in which ordinary life went on, as best it could, under the growing difficulties of wartime discipline." And later: "The news of the fall of Paris was received with the same inscrutable silence and reserve. I rode miles, that afternoon, on the enclosed upper deck of a bus, where practically everyone's conversation was audible. I heard no one as much as mention the event; the talk was all of food cards and the price of stocking."[49] The Nazi German hierarchy, too, all of their rantings and their professed radicalism notwithstanding, could not always divorce itself from a peculiarly German bourgeois past, sticking to it sometimes laughably indeed; for there was something deadeningly German-*bürgerlich* in those diplomatic receptions for Slovakian or Manchurian ministers in the Hotel Kaiserhof, the favorite place of Ribbentrop's Foreign Ministry for receptions, full of the solid reproduction furniture of the late twenties, "Stilmöbel," with lace doilies under the glass tops of the highly polished round coffee tables. (Few of those present would, to paraphrase Saki, try to forgive the furniture, which started out with an obvious intention of being Louis Quinze, but relapsed at frequent intervals into Wilhelm II.)

The continuity of life: coming back from the hell of Dunkirk, the trains, crowded with soldiers, ran past pastoral English scenes: "All along the line young men in flannels . . . playing cricket in the sunshine on beautifully tended fields shaded by stalwart oaks and poplar trees."[50] De Gaulle remembered London in early June 1940: ". . . a look of tranquillity, almost indifference. The streets and parks full of people, peacefully out for a walk, the long queues at the entrances of cinemas, the many cars, the impressive porters outside the clubs and hotels. . . ."[51] After the daze and the smoke of the terrible bombing of Rotterdam, a Dutch burger picks his way across the street, through the rubble, to his customary tobacconist, finding it open, dusty but unharmed, and buys his weekly box of cigars from the shelf. . . . The dirty pall of smoke over Paris, 10 June 1940, when the reserve oil tanks had been set afire on the edges of this, now frightened, great city: The evening falls, the govern-

---

[49] Kennan, *M*, 108.
[50] Henrey, 100, cited by Calder, 111.
[51] *De Gaulle*, I, 27.

ment has fled, one million Parisians are pushing their way southward, and yet there are spectators (true, not more than a handful) in the Odéon and the Oeuvre theaters; the mime goes on, and it is followed by the agreeableness of a walk in the soft liquid June evening beneath the dirtying clouds. . . . The first snow in Vienna in late November 1940, coming on a Sunday morning, a bright and tiring day when after Mass erect old ladies gather for a glass of coffee in high-ceilinged rooms, under pale chandeliers, and the soft gurgling of white tile stoves in their corners. . . . A rabbit hunt in Transdanubian Hungary, September 1941, with gentry and aspiring snobs from the city jostling each other for the Lucullan cold platters in the cool of a long porch, illuminated by the reflections of tremendous plane trees, drenched with gold. . . . The last afternoons before Christmas in the dimly lit streets and richly lit stores of Zurich and Madrid and Stockholm, with the slightly acrid smell of wet furs and snow. . . .

These are vignettes, nothing more. Far more meaningful are those tragic glimpses we can still get from life in the Warsaw ghetto, that horrible and depressing antechamber of death in 1940–41; depressing not only because we know what was going to happen, and not even because some of the things—fright, hunger, brutality, terror, occasional murder—that were already happening there, but because of the ominous presence of certain monuments from the past. I am thinking, for example, of the monstrous apartment houses, thick *Mietkasernen*, monumental tenements dark with grime and soot, keeping the narrow streets in their eternal shadow, blocking sunlight out even when the rest of the Polish plain was warmed by summer. There was something ominously Germanic in these Eastern European apartment houses where now thousands of Jews lived, herded together, as if the death and the horror of the Hitler era had been forecast —in this instance, literally foreshadowed—by the enormities latent in the shapes of Wilhelmian architecture. Their black shapes, surviving in the few photographs we have of the Warsaw ghetto, freeze at least this writer's heart even more than the pitiful photographs from Auschwitz, showing the hundreds of terrorized and weary new arrivals lining up along the railway siding on a gray morning.

And in the ghetto, too, as Reitlinger noted in passing, relying on some of its chroniclers, Immanuel Ringelblum and the strangely disingenuous Mary Berg, an American citizeness, "luxury was achievable"[52]: Restaurants, cafes, nightclubs (and, what is less surprising, brothels) existed, taking in fantastic sums. On Sundays the rich and the powerful of the Jewish families would sit there in gluttonous comfort; in the evening the atmosphere was glutinous with honey and soot, perfume and ashes, as

---

[52] *Berg*, 145.

beautiful shameless Jewish girls sat, eating rich food, sometimes with their temporary German SS lovers. Yet all this time, as Gerald Reitlinger records, corpses (including corpses of children) "were thrown out into the streets naked so that their roommates could keep their rags. . . ."[53] It would take a very great writer, someone infinitely more sensitive than Dostoevsky, to tell us something about these profundities of the alchemy of the human soul, about this, far from invisible and very close, coexistence of shamelessness and shamefulness, of luxury and degradation; alas, he will not be forthcoming.

Everywhere, in the darkened Europe of 1940–41, we encounter evidences of insistence on pleasure. Does this mean that people were consoling themselves with the pleasures of the flesh amidst their daily difficulties and the uncertainty of the future? Not necessarily; as we have seen earlier, there was no great general increase in prostitution or even in adultery. I am inclined to think that the desire or, rather, the consolation of traditional pleasures was the result of a mental attitude rather than that of physical appetites: The knowledge of ability of men and women to acquire, or to maintain, if only on occasion, certain traditional bourgeois comforts and pleasures, was more than ever a necessary ingredient of their mental equilibrium, involving their self-esteem. And it is quite surprising, in retrospect, how much of the prewar way of life persisted. People in occupied Holland, Belgium, and Denmark in 1941 still went on summer vacations. From Lyon and Vichy people went skiing to the Puy-de-Dôme in the winter of 1940; others spent a fortnight on the Riviera after the chilly winter. The self-composure of certain patrician families in Paris could be brave: This elite continued to wash in cold water and at their frugal parties refused to talk about food and heat. Less inspiring was the evidence of desperate gluttony among some people, their grim interest in eating in restaurants such as the Chapon Fin in Bordeaux, which for a transitory few days in the third week of June in 1940 had suddenly become the center of French politics and intrigue, attracting people in droves even after the government took off for Vichy. Even less inspiring was the behavior of those who, instead of disdainfully ignoring the occupants and the new regime, tried their social best (or, rather, worst) in conforming to it. On the cover of *L'Illustration*'s number of 28 December 1940 there is a large photo of the staircase of the Paris Opera at the occasion of a gala performance for the Sécours National: With the splendid uniforms of the Gardes Républicaines, the elegant silvery gowns and evening clothes, glistening under the seemingly undiminished light from the chandeliers, it is indistinguishable from any picture taken from a gala

---

[53] Reitlinger, *FS*, 60.

before the war (or after). In Belgium in 1941 the puritanical collaborationists of the Germans as well as the patriotic Cardinal van Roey condemned "the frivolous attitude of a portion of the *jeunesse bourgeoisie*
who seem to think of nothing beyond pleasures and dancing." Galas and
festivals would crop up on occasion, older musicals were much in
demand, especially those of Lehar. . . . As late as in the winter of
1941–42 Paul Struye wrote: It is a strange fact, "in spite of innumerable
material sufferings, the general image of the country does not give the impression of a grieving and badly wounded nation."[54]

It was amazing how quickly some of the bourgeois amenities of life
reappeared, sometimes at the very moment when the cyclone of the German conquest was passing over them. There is the picture of Bruges at the
end of May 1940, even before the announcement of the Belgian armistice,
a city spared artillery fire and bombardment by the Germans who drove
into it one night. The next day (the twenty-seventh) was full of sunshine,
the guns from Flanders were clearly audible as the battle of Dunkirk had
by then begun. It was a crowded city, crowded with the cars of people
who had fled from the east and by the newly parked masses of German
vehicles, crowded with refugees who were sitting in its large squares, and
thousands of them on the pavements of its streets, while other citizens
were sitting in the cafes, enjoying the open air and the sun, often but a
few tables away from German officers. In Paris it was not until 6 June
that for the first time the receipts of the Opera and of the state theaters
fell to below one half; on 10 June there were still a few people going into
the theaters. Then a parenthesis; but on 6 July the Palace Music Hall
opened again, on the twelfth the Concert Mayol, on the thirty-first the
Folies-Bergère, on 22 August the Opéra Comique, on the twenty-fourth
the Opéra (with a performance of *Faust*). By September Sacha Guitry was
performing at the Madeleine Theater, and Jouvet was playing Anouilh.
On 12 October racing at Auteuil started anew.

Still, war is a great social leveler: The fluid mobility of classes, this
principal characteristic of the twentieth century, accelerated with a spurt,
perhaps as never before. Men and women now rode in the Bois de
Boulogne, drove automobiles in Budapest, ate in the best restaurants of
Brussels, mingled with the Polish gentry and aristocracy in Warsaw cafes,
people who were never seen in those places before. The charming French
reserve officer, whom General Spears encountered in one of the Loire
châteaux in June 1940, amidst the cracking, creaking disruption of a rapidly sinking world, who could still, due to his connections, get him a car:
"He spoke perfect English and knew as much about hunting in the

---

[54] Struye, 98.

Midlands as I did," was already a figure of the past.[55] The present seemed to be marked by a newer class of people, and one of the principal status symbols of the latter was their possession of automobiles. By 1939 (in Western Europe at least) the mark of a new, mobile, class division (mobile in more than one sense of the word) was between those who had cars and those who did not. In any event, from these beginnings of an automobile civilization the Germans and their armies, because of their advanced motorization, profited, and the conquered peoples, because of their increased dependence on automobiles, suffered.[56] (Could the great Western European exodus in May–June 1940 have involved all of those millions of people, had it not been for the existence of cars?) Unlike in 1914, in 1940 the full extent of their dangers struck Parisians only on the day (10 June) when they saw the top personnel of the ministries leave for the south, now not from feverishly crowded railroad stations but driving in their cars. (The following day, 11 June, a handful of ugly incidents marred, on occasion, the frightened calm of the city: Men, at times with pistols in hand, would commandeer cars in municipal garages, and sometimes even from private ones.) A few days later the nascent automobile civilization that began to blossom (if that is the word) in the capitals of Western Europe around 1925, and that was to reappear again after 1947–48, came to a sudden end.[57] Thousands of cars, with their fenders staved in, out of gas and oil, lay on the sides of the roads; other thousands were carefully hidden in barns, rusting away for the next five years. On the streets there were now few: The Germans had the monopoly of their kind of imperious traffic. By November 1940 there were less than 7,000 French cars running in Paris: Most of these (with the exception of certain physicians) belonged to the new class who sought and, on occasion,

---

[55] In late 1939 Churchill would still minute angrily to the second and fourth Sea Lords about the fact that the commission of able and eager candidates was being withheld in the Royal Navy because of their lower-class provenance. Churchill, *FH*, 758. Spears recounts (I, 84–85) how in February 1940 the sons of petty officers and of naval ratings were turned down for officer's school because "their fathers came from the lower deck."

[56] The English understood this novel danger. In May and June 1940 "Precautions were introduced to prevent the enemy from augmenting his resources with British transports. . . . Special wheel-locking devices were fitted on buses to immobilize them while they were unattended. Armed guards protected the garages at night. Under a new order, motorists were compelled to immobilize their own cars when they parked them—the usual method was to remove the rotor arm of the distributor. If this was not done, the police would deflate the tires or pull out the ignition leads. Prosecutions were common, and fines of up to fifty pounds were imposed. . . ." Calder, 120–21.

[57] Gasoline for private cars was forbidden to be sold in Italy after 1 November 1941. In Sweden no foreigner was allowed to drive a car or a taxi.

received the favors of the Germans. On Sundays all motor circulation by Frenchmen was forbidden, and German motordom reigned absolute on the broadest of boulevards and the sleekest of avenues. In Belgium, where more than 150,000 private cars were registered in 1939, less than 7,000 were allowed to run by the end of 1941, meaning that 95 per cent of private cars (and 91 per cent of the prewar taxis) were out of commission. Some buses continued to move, relying on artificial propane and charcoal-gas systems.

This contributed to one aspect of the German era: to a widespread feeling that some things were reverting to the distant past in some ways. In the September 1940 number of *L'Illustration*[58] the fine writer Léon-Paul Fargue wrote a little sketch essay on Paris, with the title, "Resurrection of 1900," as he described the emptiness and the silence of the streets without cars, and the reappearance of bicycles and horse cabs.[59] One of the pleasant results was the greenness of the trees, lasting into October; now they were unaffected by the fumes of gas and oil. Bicycles became suddenly a very good thing to have (they also helped in keeping many bourgeois in surprisingly good physical shape through the war). By late 1940 a used bicycle in Paris would bring 2,500 francs. There were innumerable, and ingenious thefts of them, one of the consequences of which was the additional exercise imposed on the bourgeois under stress: Arriving at their destination, they would carry their bicycles upstairs.

The principal shortcoming, rife among the bourgeois, was not so much collaboration and adjustment but, rather, cowardice and opportunism. Of this we have innumerable vignettes from June–July 1940, at the time of the collapse of the French Republic which was, then, the prototype of a corroded bourgeois state, with some of its bourgeois the prototypes of a corroded bourgeoisie.[60] What struck observers in Bordeaux,

---

[58] *L'Illustration* reappeared in August: Very typical of the times, the first page of this urban and *haut-bourgeois* magazine carried the idealized photo of a woman with a scythe, "illustrating" the lead essay on the virtues of a back-to-the-earth philosophy by De la Varende.

[59] There were also velo taxis, pedicabs, that were allowed to circulate beyond the curfew: They were vilely expensive.

[60] Corroded: because of the hopelessly out-of-date impression, even of things: the inimitable picture, for example, of the château on the Loire requisitioned by the fleeing government where, on 12 June, Churchill had no option but to use the only telephone, a hopelessly antiquated one, hanging next to the lavatory; or the matutinal scene the next day in the graveled driveway, where General Spears watched the French Prime Minister's mistress "in a dressing-gown over red pajamas, directing the traffic from the slopes of the main entrance. . . . I had not seen red trousers on French legs since 1914." Spears, II, 178, 190.

for example, were the ugly evidences of fear: the trafficking, the jostling, the nervous clamor, the abandonment of friends; and before the Spanish frontier the briberies of the rich, stuck in their Delages and Delahayes in long lines under the blazing sun. . . . One of the sorriest impressions one gets from this 1940 debacle is the unconcealed relief with which many of these people were looking out for themselves on the morrow of the armistice. Many of them were on their way to Vichy; and there was little that was dignified in that diminished seat of a national government in mourning. "*Ce hammam planté d'arbres*" (this oriental bathhouse lined with trees): This is how someone described the new "capital," this seat of government, with its rattan chairs, and *grand-bourgeois* 1900 hotels, where the great campaign of national rejuvenation was presided over by an octogenarian, and where an entire republican national assembly chose to put an end to liberal democracy, decreeing the inauguration of a new era of patriotism and of austerity in a memorable session, sitting in the dusty plush chairs of the Casino. "This is the day of the National Assembly," wrote the new Foreign Minister, Baudouin, about 10 July 1940 in Vichy. "The dining room of the Hotel du Parc was as full as a restaurant in the Bois on the day of the Grand Prix. Ambassadors, politicians, and women (far too joyful and overdressed) are mixed up together. Jewelry is beginning to appear again. The general atmosphere is more painful than ever." The impressions of Du Moulin de Labarthète, possibly the best delineator of the atmosphere of the early Vichy period, were exactly the same: "too many people, certain Parisian faces. Dust and feverishness. Old friends greeting each other. Too many faces smiling which one would have preferred more sober." "A crowd of office-seekers, ruffians, crooks, women in all stages of age and beauty."[61] The hunt for all too scarce hotel rooms[62] and for all kinds of positions[63] began.

---

[61] Du Moulin, 15, 17, 20. Adrienne Hytier records the impressions of an ex-diplomat, Louis de Robien (who had lived though the Russian Revolution in 1917), in Vichy in late 1940: "a haven for . . . the duds in all walks of life, the impecunious ne'er do-wells who no longer hoped to find Jewish heiresses to marry . . . most of the people were simply intriguers: tycoons, wholesale grocers, esthetes, parliamentarians, journalists, aviators, actors, tennis or automobile racing champions, orchestra conductors, blackmailers, Red Cross nurses, better at exchange speculations than at the bedside, dolls in pursuit of their guys who had skipped off with the cash at the time of the exodus, nitwits dying to deliver the lectures they felt in them, not to speak of the Geneva 'précieuses,' now the faithful supporters of the Marshal, in order to go on playing a role." Hytier, 100.

[62] In the beginning Pétain worked at the Hotel Sévigné, taking only his meals at the Hotel du Parc, where only a screen separated him from the *grand monde;* later he moved to the third floor of the Parc (the second floor was

This sort of bourgeois opportunism and cowardice may have been most evident in France, but it existed elsewhere, too, including countries whose record was nearly unexceptionable during this year of trial, 1940. In Switzerland, for example, two hundred prominent citizens in July 1940 sent a letter to the government, requesting "a stricter control" of the free press, including the dismissal of certain democratic editors. The President of Switzerland at the time was Marcel Pilet-Golaz, a descendant of one of the great Genevan patrician houses, a typical representative of the cautious bourgeois stance who, addressing his people on the national radio on 25 June 1940, told them not only that they must take the realities of a new Europe into account, but he also welcomed, strangely in retrospect, "the great relief" that the end of the war in Western Europe (thus, implicitly, the defeat of France) had brought to Switzerland. A month later the descendant of another French-Swiss bourgeois family, General Guisan, took his brave stand, exhorting the Army and the people to the spirit of patriotic resistance.[64] Two patricians: two different spirits. There exists a photograph from early 1940 of both of them, side by side: General Guisan, with his severe but kindly blue eyes, with the seamed face of a patrician general-citizen, and Marcel Pilet-Golaz, the citizen-president, in his furred coat and top hat with his anxious face in his shiny patent-leather shoes, walking with mincing steps at the side of the spare soldier.

So much about the weakness, and about the sometime cowardice, of certain bourgeois. The word and the meaning of "bourgeois" was in disrepute in 1940: Long before the Nazi and Fascist triumphs, the meaning of the word had been made execrable by radicals, artists, intellectuals. But had artists and intellectuals behaved better than had the bourgeois of Europe in 1940? Not at all. "The republic of letters," wrote Jean Guéhenno, somewhat sadly, in his diary in June 1941, "certainly has few

---

occupied by Laval and by the Ministry of Information, the first by the Foreign Ministry: other ministries (Finance, Justice) were set up in the Hotel Carlton, Weygand and the Defence in the Hotel Thermal, the diplomatic corps in the Ambassadeurs. When the famous actress Elvira Popesco was put out from the Parc in July she made a grand scene.

[63] All kinds of positions, coveted by all kinds of people. For example, the archdemocratic champion of the League of Nations, Alexis Léger (later the author of elegant and incomprehensible verse) would offer his services from Washington to Pétain; Bertrand de Jouvenel, the self-professed spokesman for patrician conservatism and for Europeanism, visited Baudouin in September, confessing that his "hopes [!] when the Germans first arrived in Paris have been disappointed. . . . He wants a post abroad, either in the United States or in Ireland." Of course.

[64] See above, p. 106.

men of character." If only the Muses would keep silent during this war, as they once used to do! the excellent Wladimir Weidlé remarked. "Unfortunately, they keep talking, and we cannot listen to them without certain feelings of embarrassment and shame."[65] In England the cowardice and the intellectual dishonesty of intellectuals drove George Orwell to bitter sarcasm. On the Continent considerable numbers of artists and intellectuals scurried to accommodate themselves to the New Europe of the Germans. There was a floating population on the increase, a meritocracy of artists, entertainers, and professional intellectuals of all sorts.[66] Many examples of their opportunism existed in France. When in October 1941 the German government issued a generously paid invitation for a cultural visit to Germany to famous Parisian artists, it was accepted instantly not only by Fascists and pro-Nazis such as Drieu la Rochelle, Bonnard, and Brasillach, but also by Derain, Dunoyer de Segonzac, Vlaminck, and Van Dongen: a scintillating list of names. Upon their return from Germany, Vlaminck and Van Dongen, the latter a handsome little old bearded satyr, one of the most prototypical artist *illustres* of the freemasonry of the Third Republic, of what had been the society of *tout Paris,* wrote enthusiastic articles. The others at least remained silent. (To their honor, Braque and Matisse refused the invitations.) In Belgium, which (Baudelaire's nineteenth-century strictures on the dumb and dull bourgeois Belgians notwithstanding) was the home of some of the finest European avant-garde painting in the thirties, the surrealist Magritte was cosseted by the Germans, while Delvaux and Ensor rejected their bribes. Such bribes came often in the form of honoraria in new and profusely illustrated journals such as *Apollo,* in Belgium, where artistic freedom of expression served but to conceal the political purpose of subtly spreading a propaganda of Germanophilism. In Paris the news quickly spread in journalistic and artistic circles that Radio-Paris, under German control, was paying exceptionally well (and that its payments were made in cash, unreported and unreportable to the French tax authorities). Already in the late summer of 1940, therefore, hundreds of journalists, radio announcers, actors, actresses, singers, and musicians presented themselves in the waiting rooms of this powerful German-run radio station. Its German directors proved accommodating, with the result that Radio-Paris succeeded in giving the impression to millions of listeners "that nothing, or that almost nothing, has changed. They heard again the familiar voices of

---

[65] Weidlé, 291.

[66] Political opportunism seemed to be more tempting for journalists than for serious writers, for popular entertainers than for more serious musicians. (An interesting figure: As late as December 1939 only 8 of the 110 musicians of the Berlin Philharmonic were Nazi party members.)

certain actors and singers, and some of their favorite orchestras, too. . . ."[67] It took some time until the people of France knew by heart the repeated Gaullist jingle broadcast from London about Radio-Paris, the Lying German Radio: *"Radio-Paris ment. . . . Radio-Paris est allemand."*

Now to the other side of the coin—and it is a large side, thank God. If there was any class throughout Europe that even in 1940 disbelieved in the prospects of an ultimate German triumph, it was the bourgeoisie. From its ranks came the first resistants (the "Réseau Interallié," for example); and while it is true that many of the bourgeois did not go beyond repeating a few skeptical jokes aimed at Hitler, it must be recorded that Hitler's crusade against Bolshevism, against that deadly enemy of all that was bourgeois, elicited hardly a single assent or conversion from the bourgeois of Europe—rather the contrary. (There were, on the other hand, proletarian leaders in many countries who chose to be converted, or who finally completed their conversion, to Hitler's anti-Bolshevik philosophy in 1941.) And the internal history of Europe's nations in 1940 and 1941 is not devoid of high examples of patrician courage. There was, for example, François Joseph van de Meulebroeck, the burgomaster of Brussels, going far beyond his call of duty, and superseding perhaps even the patriotic courage of the great burgomaster Adolphe Max, of World War I fame (who, having died in November 1939, lived to see the beginning of another world war, though not another German invasion of his country). The Germans let Van de Meulebroeck occupy his office until June 1941, when he was confronted with the demands that he consent to the removal of four of his *echevins*, colleagues in the Brussels City Council. In that event, he was informed by the relatively moderate Germanophile Romsée, another city father, that Van de Meulebroeck could keep his post; but the burgomaster refused. On the twentieth Van de Meulebroeck's noble patrician manifesto appeared on the walls of Brussels. *"Mes chers concitoyens,"* it began, in the spirit of a trusted mayor of an older, close-knit communal past.[68] The German authorities tore down the posters.

---

[67] Audiat, 49. Also: "The choices of the Germans directing [Radio-Paris] were guided by principles that were not much different from those that had governed the selections of their French predecessors: appreciation of true talent, with occasional consideration of amorous services. This time, however, the latter services were no longer offered by the female votaries of art, music and the stage: The conquerors showed that their tastes were more eclectic."

[68] "The German authorities inform me that I must cease exercising my functions as burgomaster: I cannot but incline before this kind of order, even though it unlawfully violates the Hague convention: It is entirely unjustified. I have, in

Nevertheless, many of the Bruxellois came to the Hotel de Ville to acclaim their burgomaster, some bringing him large bouquets of flowers. Two days afterward Van de Meulebroeck was arrested. The printers of the poster and the citizenry were severely punished by the Germans.

Numerous examples of civic bravery took place in the small democracies of Western Europe during the first two years of the occupation. In December 1941, 95 per cent of the faculty of the University of Brussels refused the reforms and the new appointments imposed upon them by the Germans. In September 1940 Professors P. Scholfen of the University of Amsterdam and B. M. Teldens of Leyden drafted a petition against the dismissal of their Jewish colleagues, which was sent to the German governor of the Netherlands: A total of 60 to 80 per cent of the faculties were brave enough to sign this. When the greatly respected Jewish Professor E. M. Meijers was dismissed from Leyden in November 1940, a demonstration in his support was held in the same Maxima Aula where Grotius had sat three hundred years before; the dignified and brave speech by Professor R. P. Cleveringa was broadcast through loudspeakers to a large crowd of students outside. Cleveringa was arrested the next day, and the University of Leyden was closed. Similar manifestations of civic bravery occurred in Norway and Denmark. In Yugoslavia the small Serbian bourgeoisie was redoubtably Anglophile and Francophile. In Switzerland the refusals of the patrician owners and editors of great newspapers such as the *Neue Zürcher Zeitung* were actually inspiring, especially as they stood in contrast to the tendencies of some of their bourgeois countrymen, whose cautious advocacies of a dignified "adjustment," *Anpassung,* in the fall of 1940, were not very different from the less dignified behavior of the *paniquards* of the previous May (of rich Swiss who had fled to the southern mountain regions from the cities at the time). And even in Germany in 1940 there remained that core of patriciandom who believed that Hitler's cause was wrong *and* that he would not win the war. This is an important point, for many of the Germans

---

effect, loyally and sincerely tried to carry out the difficult and painful duties that are incumbent upon the mayors of cities and of villages occupied by the enemy. . . .

Contrary of what is being said by some, I have not quit my office, and I have not offered my resignation. . . .

*I am, I remain, and I shall remain the sole lawful burgomaster of Brussels.*

Taking my leave temporarily I ask of you to suffer your material and moral hardships with calmness, courage and confidence. . . . Those who are really of us fear but one thing in this world: their failing to do their duty, and the loss of their honor.

Keep together! Your unity makes your strength; it will assure you a better future. God will protect Belgium and her King."

who later gradually abandoned their faith in Hitler did so because of their increasing skepticism in one of these matters but not both. At any rate, hundreds of thousands of Germans in 1940 would still say "Hitler," not "Fuehrer," and they would read the relatively conservative *Frankfurter Zeitung* or *Deutsche Allgemeine Zeitung*. Admittedly this was not much of a "resistance," but it was more than nothing. And the condition that this resistance was felt in the name of patriotism under a triumphant nationalist regime, and in the midst of a people impressed with nearly incredible victories, should nonetheless elicit a certain quiet respect from us in retrospect.

I, for one, salute these people in retrospect, in Germany as well as in England. Especially in England, where many men and women of the middle class and the aristocracy exemplified the spirit of bravery during their finest hour, in 1940. There was (and still is) a widespread tendency, at times justifiable, to consider the British conservative middle-class responsible for the weakness of the thirties, as if the stupidity of the Colonel Blimps had been the main obstacle against recognizing the dangers of Nazism and Fascism: The now faded cartoons of David Low illustrate this idea. In reality, this was not so: For the failures of British vision, the Laborites, during the thirties, were nearly as responsible as were the Tories; and it was Churchill, with his many aristocratic attitudes, who proved to be the savior of England. Also, in 1940, few of the Blimps grumbled. Bravely, unthinkingly, they followed Churchill (whom, because of his flamboyance, many had earlier mistrusted) to the hilt, which in that event meant to the brink of death and, if necessary, beyond. One of the few surviving intelligence reports coming to Germany from England picked something of this up, reporting in the summer of 1940: "Here warmongering (*Kriegshetze*) only among Blimps. Workers fed up. Wives more so. Troops not keen. Anti-Semitism spreading. . . . Cost of living steeply mounting. . . ."[69] The only evidences of near panic during the bombing of London occurred in the East End, in the working-class district of Silvertown, on 7 September 1940; the West End, which should not have known how to take it, took it all right. We now know of the extraordinary secret plan for a guerrilla underground network with extensive points of radio contact, strung out across Britain, in the event of a successful German invasion, after which thousands of British men and women would resort to sabotage and isolated ambushes of Germans. Nothing like this had been prepared anywhere in Europe, certainly not in the Western European countries, in a way not even in Russia or Serbia. It was almost entirely an "Old Boy network," the thing against which British and other intellectuals have been screeching and railing before and ever

---

[69] Cited in Fleming, 127; also 118.

since the war: a network manned by Blimps, unmarred by a single instance of individual defection out of weakness. David Lampe described this nearly three decades later: "At every level of the . . . organization 'the old boy net' was brought into play, for the officers at the top had more confidence in this than in all the positive vetting in the world."[70] At the end of the year 1940, referring to an article by the New York intellectual Clement Greenberg, who had written in *Horizon* "that the working class is the only class in England that seriously means to defeat Hitler," George Orwell wrote in the *Partisan Review* that this "seems to me quite untrue. The bulk of the middle class are just as anti-Hitler as the working class, and their morale is probably more reliable. The fact which Socialists, especially when they are looking at the English scene from the outside, seldom seem to me to grasp, is that the patriotism of the middle classes is a thing to be made use of."[71] As early as 5 October 1940 Orwell wrote in his diary: "It *is* a fact, though one mustn't mention it—that working-class people are more frightened than middle-class."[72] But, then, in Paris, too, many people remarked that the German Army in June 1940 was received much better in the *banlieue rouge*, in the working-class suburbs than in the bourgeois *quartiers*, and in Czechoslovakia the icy murderer Heydrich himself remarked how the workers were not only docile but also more ready to collaborate than the Czech bourgeoisie.[73]

---

[70] Lampe, 71. They also knew how to keep quiet about it. "A well-known Master of Foxhounds in East Suffolk, one of the first in his country to be taken into the Resistance, told me, 'All I even did was go out at night to help train members of the Home Guard.' And that was the only thing he would say. Lampe, 70. Almost all of the British regional commissioners (heading the underground resistance networks) in 1940 were knights or peers. Their list in Lampe, 156. The American diplomat Lewis Einstein remembered about the Home Guard: "The men were mostly farmhands and labourers but also included Sir George Clark, who had lately retired as British ambassador in Paris. He who had been the best dressed of diplomats, who looked like an eighteenth-century worthy and spoke like a Victorian Cabinet minister, now became private clerk and responded to the military orders given by the family butler, who had been a former sergeant major in the Life Guards. . . ." Einstein, 228.

[71] *Orwell*, II, 50. See also the sorry episode of the stevedores from England at Calais, below, p. 419.

[72] *Orwell*, II, 378. Later he also defended dukes who let themselves be killed in Flanders. He could, of course, work himself up to a fine froth about the lady of the Rolls-Royce car during the Blitz, "more damaging to morale than a fleet of Goering's bombing-planes."

[73] "Heydrich instilled the Czech working classes with narrow materialism and obedience, thereby further strengthening their political impassivity." Mastny,

Of course, it was (and is) not as simple as all that. In Greece (especially in the South), the lower classes of the population resisted the Germans with greater fervor than the sometimes opportunist middle class. In England, too, country hotels, in the winter of 1939–40, were "filled with well-to-do refugees, who too often have fled from nothing. They sit and read and eat and drink . . ." wrote Constantine Fitzgibbon,[74] who remembered a constant stream of private cars and London taxis driving up to his mother's front door in the Thames Valley in September 1939, "a horde of satin-clad, pin-striped refugees." And, if the record of the British aristocracy and of the royal family was irreproachable (in the summer of 1940 King George VI was practicing pistol shooting in the gardens of Buckingham Palace), there is something unpleasant in the record of the Duke of Windsor, who on that most tragic and dramatic of days, 16 June 1940, called the British Embassy in Bordeaux by telephone from Nice, asking for a British warship to pick him up and carry him to safety (the ambassador suggested politely that he set off and drive to Portugal through Spain).[75]

That was the Lisbon Route, "one of the most typical symbols of this Year of Grace 1940," as Denis de Rougemont put it, who took that route himself in late August 1940: This narrow escape route from Geneva, wending its way between the German and Italian control stations through Vichy France and Franco Spain to Portugal. "How easy it would be to pinch this thin little artery where our old world is being emptied, in drops, of its elite and of its parasites! (An elite that is too gamey, and parasites grimly intent on their own survival. . . .)"[76] Perhaps, mused Rougemont, the new powers of Europe were not altogether unwilling to let this thin drainage tube run on. Once in Lisbon, the rich refugees fought and scurried for places on "the last ships of the last line connecting Europe to America, all of their vessels' names beginning with "Ex": *Exeter, Excalibur, Excambion*. And all they carry, in effect, are ex-people: ex-directors, ex-Austrians, ex-millionaires, ex-princes, toward their exile." One may add: ex-patricians as well as ex-crooks; for not all of the refugees from Nazi Europe were men and women of sterling virtue. But, then, within that imprisoned Europe, human realities weren't so simple, either. Men are neither beasts nor angels, the young Arthur Schlesinger,

---

354. Heydrich's material incentives were more than narrow: They included concerts, services, old-age insurance benefits, special provisions for minors, etc. The workers' impassivity at times evolved into collaboration: In 1940–41 many Czech workers volunteered to work in Germany, where jobs were plentiful.

[74] Fitzgibbon, 25.

[75] About the duke's temptations in Lisbon, see above, p. 99, n. 58.

[76] Rougemont, 123.

Jr., would write in America during the war,[77] a phrase accurately reflecting the American liberal consensus to the effect that mankind represents an evolutionary gray, between the two abnormal extremes of black
and white. To any European who lived through the Second World War
such a statement reflects an abyss separating American from European
thinking: What we learned, at the latest by 1940, was Pascal's greater
truth to the effect that man was *both* brute and angel—an infinitely more
profound thing—and that "the pity of it is that in trying to behave like an
angel man behaves like a brute."[78] There were a few men in the German
SS, the sons of butchers, who became humane and compassionate; and
there were Central European aristocrats, the descendants of three centuries of high breeding and Christian schooling, who turned into criminal
crooks, accomplices of Nazi brutes. One is impressed by the bravery, the
good humor, the spiritedness of the first resistance agents as their first networks were spun out in 1941; yet some of the best of them would break
under the first pressure, betray their friends, and seek passing solace in
sordid love affairs with their grinning captors. On the other hand,
members of the corrupt and cynical high society of a Levantine capital
such as Athens, described by Peyrefitte and its Alexandrian appendages
by Lawrence Durrell, would furnish hundreds of courageous, patriotic,
irreproachable officers during the war with the Italians and the Germans.
Often contradictory characteristics emerged on the surface of the same
person. It is easy to scoff at the grandiloquent patriotic rhetoric of Paul
Reynaud, that little dapper man, with his oriental cast of eyes, at first
sight a prototypical ministerial figure of the corrupt Third Republic, with
his pestering countess-mistress, to whom he was deeply devoted; yet he
resisted her political opportunings, he refused to surrender. There is
Reynaud, in the midst of collapse, in one of the Loire châteaux, crouching
late at night in pajamas with his secretaries, with a large map of France on
his knees, studying possible defense lines farther west and south. . . . One
has to have some respect for this little man, though to a past he did
belong.

The past: That was a very important point, a touchstone of many attitudes. The principal opponents of Nazism, of Hitler, of Germany in
1939–41 were conservatives, often reactionaries, in Germany as well as in
England—indeed, nearly everywhere. In Portugal and Spain, for example,
the most determined opponents of the New Order (which was not devoid
of medieval features) were archreactionaries, such as Cardinals Cerejeira
and Segura, absolutely unwilling to see anything good in Nazism, giving
no support even to its crusade against Bolshevism in 1941; and this was

---

[77] At the end of his *Age of Jackson* (1945), which established his reputation.
[78] *Pensée* 358.

true in every European country. Churchill, too, was more historically minded than was Chamberlain; so was De Gaulle; so were all those men and women who saw in Hitler the incarnation of something evil whose roots were dark medieval and supermodern at the same time. The opponents of the Nazis were looking backward as much as forward, toward the decencies of a bourgeois, conservative Europe.[79] The best minds among them were without illusions, since they were motivated not by nostalgia but by a powerful and at times inspiring sense of the past. In 1941 even a Tito and a Stalin found that there was something inspiring and liberating in the condition that they could draw on ancient patriotic resources of rhetoric, and they could portray (and, what is more important, perceive) themselves as patriotic chieftains, national leaders. It was Péguy, not Alain, who inspired patriotic Frenchmen, including many Communists, within the first resistance. Within Germany the Nazis were especially aware of the dangers of the "reactionary opposition."[80]

This consciousness of the past was largely absent in the minds of the new class that was arising everywhere in Europe during the war. These were people who were thinking in terms of a new world, rather than of a new Europe: mechanics, engineers, technocrats. In France, for example, some of them gained a temporary hold on statecraft during 1941, when they formed part of the new government presided over by Darlan: Bedaux, Pucheu, Barnaud, and Lehideux were "technocrats" (some of them called themselves "synarchists"), usually admirers of American techniques, of James Burnham's "managerial revolution"; soon they proved their ineptitude in politics. The time seemed right for the rule of "hard-headed" technicians. Their way of thinking intruded into the imagination of everyday people. The thoughtful Viktor Klemperer who, in his capacity of a persecutee philologist, kept one of the most telling diaries

---

[79] Extraordinary, in retrospect, was the nostalgia for monarchy in 1940, including Germany. Goebbels was worried about popular reactions to the death of Wilhelm II in Holland, in June 1941 (Boelcke, 615, 762–63). Hitler sent a wreath. In Spain there were popular demonstrations on the occasion of the death of Alfonso XIII, in exile, in February 1941. In Holland portraits of the Queen (who had not been extremely popular before 1940) were hung in many houses. The Belgian adulation for Leopold III in 1940 was extraordinary; it was similar to the first French sentimental wave of enthusiasm for Pétain. The peoples needed a father figure. The attitude of children and fathers was manifest in many ways: flowers and cheeses, prize tomatoes and cakes, were sent to Pétain, even after his meeting with Hitler. This intensity of monarchical desires was enormous, and it did not begin to abate until later in the war.

[80] See below, pp. 290–91; 307. Also the German Nazi was a different type: younger, darker, and thinner than the German militarists of the First World War, who had been massive, middle-aged, corpulent.

during the Third Reich, entitled *Lingua Tertii Imperii* (The Language of the Third Reich), noticed this early, when a young mechanic, having repaired something for him, asked, *"Habe ich das nich fein organisiert?"* ("Haven't I organized this real good?"). "The words 'organization' and *'organisieren'* (to organize) were in his ear, his mind was overladen with images to the effect that every kind of a job must first be 'organized' . . . instead of 'performed,' 'fixed,' or simply 'done.'" And later: "This simplistic mechanization of the human person was typical of [the new language]."[81] It affected not only everyday life but it also had a powerful attraction for many young people.

Much of the new totalitarian order depended on an increase of administration, all of its cult of youthful activity notwithstanding. In 1933 Hitler said that he wanted every young German to spend at least a month each year at manual labor—a clear break with the sedentary sickliness of the bourgeois era. And yet in Germany the portion of the population living on the land, and engaged in agriculture, was falling (it was 30.5 per cent in 1925, and 26.1 per cent in 1939); the percentage of those employed in industry was exactly the same in 1939 as it was in 1925 (42.1 per cent); what had increased was the section of the population employed in administration and services (*Oeffentliches Dienst und private Dienstleistungen*), from 6.6 per cent in 1925 to 10.4 per cent in 1939. A new amorphous class was coming into being, whose competences and professions were less and less clearly determinable, with an ephemeral style of life of their own. Informal and yet standardized, unreflecting and yet mentally formed by mass communications, they were no longer strict Middle German Heinzes but Bavarian and Swabian Beppos, whose German *Life* was the magazine *Signal*, and Zarah Leander their Ginger Rogers. After the war they would very easily fit into the new world of an Americanized West Germany, where the more enterprising among them started very profitable trucking firms. The origins of such enterprises went back to the war. It is interesting to observe how much of everyday life on the Continent depended on trucks as early as 1940 and 1941. We have seen that 90 per cent of private automobiles had disappeared at that time; but the number of trucks increased. There were more of them in Paris, for example, in 1943 than in 1940; in Belgium more than 24,000 trucks were run by private persons in January 1942. For not only did this war demonstrate, throughout Europe, the growing importance of unscheduled and irregular transportation of goods on the existing highways; it showed, too, that it was no longer merely the commercial middleman but also the transporter of goods (and, on occasion, of people)— of all kinds of goods and all kinds of people—who became a new kind of

---

[81] Klemperer, 126, 191.

indispensable and powerful entrepreneur. Indeed, in many profitable instances the middleman and the transporter of the goods was the same person. Most truck driver-owners were involved in the black market, often trafficking with the German occupants (there was an astonishing number of collaborationists among them, while in Germany the postwar trucking business had a goodly share of ex-Nazis).[82] These were the forerunners of the new middle class, rising quickly from its lower reaches (for the successful truck-operator during the war had to be not only a driver but also a mechanic). It was no longer "hard-faced men who made out well of the war." Their faces were often round, pasty, young. And the growing shadowy world of espionage and conspiracy was full of them too. For one thing, never were low-ranking agents as well paid as during the Second World War. As the wife of a low Soviet agent reminisced about the winter of 1940–41 in France and Belgium: "It was *la belle vie*. We went out every night, and danced all the time." Twenty-five years later she remembered winning dance competitions, and spending a marvelous New Year's Eve at the casino of Namur, "it was absolutely wonderful."[83]

At the time of this writing it has become fashionable to speak of a "generation gap": But that gap was there in 1939–41, wider than before. In 1940 the collapse of the corroded bourgeois world seemed to call for the rise of youth, and not only in Germany, in the fatherland of its cult. The octogenarian Pétain was enthusiastic about the establishments of the *Chantiers de Jeunesse*, that short-lived Spartan experiment of patriotic boy-scoutism, in France (one of the first Chantiers was set up not by a Fascist but by the later Gaullist hero, General de Lattre de Tassigny, in the deserted southern French village of Opme, in the summer of 1940). The ex-Communist and pro-Nazi Doriot wrote before and during the war about *la lutte de Jeunes;* Bertrand de Jouvenel remarked as early as 1935 that the social struggle was less "between workers and *patronat* as between the young and the old." A recent sociographic study of the SS Totenkopf Division in Germany shows that the majority of officers were around thirty years old in 1941; they had been born between 1903 and 1914.[84]

---

[82] A Dutch public-opinion survey after the war reported that, in retrospect, those questioned thought that 41 per cent of the Dutch people under occupation behaved "well," 49 per cent "fairly," and 10 per cent were "bad." Doctors, priests, teachers, and students received the best rating, truckers and contractors (among the latter 78 per cent were reported "bad") the lowest. Romein, "The Spirit of the Dutch People During the Occupation," *Annals* (May 1946).

[83] Perrault, 38.

[84] Hentig, "Beitrage zur einer Sozialgeschichte des Dritten Reiches," *VFZ* January 1968.

In 1940 and in 1941 the resistance was not yet marked by the presence of the young. There is perhaps a lesson inherent in this, applicable to our days: When the young are told that the world is theirs, youthful idealism is largely wanting. Juvenile delinquency, that previously hardly known phenomenon, began to appear in the occupied cities: Gangs such as the Amsterdam "Ace of Spades," roaming in 1941, could not be called resistants. What the young, including Nazis and non-Nazis, had in common was their contempt, sometimes outspoken, sometimes silent, for the bourgeois past. There is a vignette in Camus' *Notebooks* in 1939 about a family scene at the time of the mobilization. "The eldest son is leaving. He is sitting in front of his mother and says: 'It won't come to anything.' The mother says nothing. She has picked up a paper that was lying on the table. She folds it into two, then into four, then into eight." This was, of course, 1939, not 1914. But the youth of 1914 had been different.

So many institutions, so many habits crumbled. Contrary to modern belief, youth is not infinitely adaptable; on the other hand, young people, perhaps especially in our century, are existentialists without so knowing: They relish the breakdown of "systems." At any rate, they learned early during the war how to get along. Whether because of a natural desire for independence or because of sheer laziness, youth likes cutting corners, jumping sideways, and, sometimes, ahead.

*L'héroisme tombe au niveau du débrouillage* (instead of heroism, the knowledge of how to get around); for once, Fabre-Luce's scathing cynicism of France after her defeat contains much of the truth; indeed, *débrouillage*, especially for the young, may have been the first substitute for resistance. A substitute, but also a kind of step; for *débrouillage* was not merely a new attitude, it was a necessary way of thinking and way of living in a world where the black market was the everyday reality, sometimes the strongest one.


## BLACK MARKETS

¶ "Black markets" have a long, and seldom recorded, history. During the Second World War they reappeared, in full bloom. "Black" means selling and buying that is forbidden. In this sense every society has a black market, since the open marketing of certain goods (of certain drugs, for example) may be illegal. In times of national emergency and war, however, modern governments have found it necessary to restrict the availability and the distribution and the prices of all kinds of goods, especially foodstuffs. This kind of rationing and regulation was widespread during the First World War, though it was not particularly effective. Already at that time its effectiveness depended less on the availability of goods than on the authority and efficacy of the enforcing state. During the Second World War there was relatively little black-market activity under the draconian authority of the Third Reich within Germany. In states where the national cohesion and self-discipline of the peoples were strong—England or Finland, for example—there was relatively little black-market racketeering, at least during the early years of the war. After 1941 a certain war-weariness set in, and this kind of patriotic self-discipline began to unravel here and there. Among peoples who had a long tradition of looking at government as a natural evil, their dislike and contempt for alien or rapacious bureaucracies resulted in something like a universal black market from the beginning of the war: This was especially true of the Balkans, but also of Italy, all of the rhetorical severity of the Fascist regime notwithstanding. In other countries the collapse of political authority led to a surge of disrespect for government in general—in Vichy France, for example. Elsewhere the black market, perhaps for the first time in the modern history of Western Europe, became an instrument of resistance against the occupiers and against their local collaborators in government, against their stringent decrees, associated with insensitivity and misery. The diversity of economic conditions in Europe in 1939–41 in many instances reflected, rather than created, the diversity of political and social conditions; for economic conditions depended less on the existence of materials than on their distribution, and on the importance attributed to their availability—which were, properly speaking, political and cultural rather than economic factors.

The word "black market" has an unpleasant connotation for English and American ears. "Black," for anarchists, means *free:* and, for once, this connotation could be correct on many occasions. While on the one hand black-marketeering, springing up in the early phase of the Second World War, was often the breeding ground of some of the most repellent kind of operators, double agents, collaborationists, of a new floating class of people who were to rise to the scummy surface of a decaying social order during and after the war, on the other hand the very existence of the black market often signified a defiance of the stringent and stupid laws of occupiers and of authoritarian governments. The operation of the black market was, therefore, often a daily triumph—a small and costly triumph but, still, a triumph—of the resistance of life over imposed regimentation and official theory. That this was especially true in a subjugated nation, such as Poland, should not be surprising (there some of the habitués of Napoleon Square, of the vast black-market center, or some of the operators of some of the most celebrated black-market restaurants turned out to be among the most dauntless of patriots). More significant was the history of the black market in the orderly bourgeois democracies of Western Europe. In Belgium, where the successful black-marketeers (popularly called "soap barons") had been widely disliked during and after the First World War, they became respectable and even liked during the Second World War (after the liberation of Brussels, in 1944, a fresco was painted on the walls of one of the department stores, with the title: *A la gloire du Smokkelaar* [To the glory of the black-marketeer]). "The black market," wrote Professor Raoul Miry in 1946, "quite plainly saved the nation from slow starvation." It assumed "the character of a national institution, spontaneously created beyond the law by the tacit but effective consent of all citizens, great and small, rich and poor, regardless of class or profession." The dreaded frequency of tuberculosis and edema "diminished as the organization and the expansion of the black market became established. What was actually occurring was a vast movement of self-assistance, participated in by the entire nation under the noses of the administration as well as the Germans, whenever they obtruded in the situation."[85]

The collaborationists denounced black-marketeers vigorously and unceasingly. By 1941 a new element appeared: The bourgeoisie and some of its capitalist and industrial institutions began to collaborate with the black market, and not merely for the selfish reasons of their own personal sustenance. In Holland, Luxembourg, France (both occupied and unoccupied), and especially in Belgium banks, factories, and industrial companies after the first difficult war winter of 1940–41 turned to the unorthodox policy of giving supplementary salaries and, more important, foodstuffs, often secured by wholesale barter on the black market, as supplementary payments for their workers. These unorthodox benefits explain in part what is otherwise inexplicable: how workers' families could go on living, more or less normally, at a time when food prices had risen five to ten times while their wages had doubled at most. By 1941 this was so widespread a phenomenon that bureaucrats such as the Belgian De Winter, in charge of agriculture and alimentation, were ridiculed by the most conservative bourgeois in Belgium because of De Winter's continued insistence on a disciplined and egalitarian policy of rationing. It had become evident that the black market helped the peoples to live. Those better off simply had to spend much money on their food. The amazing thing was that, with the exception of a habitually indigent small minority, the large mass of populations proved capable of managing somehow; and, as we have seen, they did not greatly mind the sometimes enormous profits pocketed by the black-marketeer and smuggler-middleman.

On the other hand, the dissolution of authority had important long-range consequences. It contributed to the disrespect for the state by an

---

[85] Miry, 65.

entire generation: This produced cultural and social consequences that were to last long after the war. By 1941 in most European countries one could no longer point to the existence of a certain class of people who were law-abiding because of habit and of civic tradition. A Belgian social historian wrote after the war that the regime of the occupation transformed Belgians into a people of smugglers (*un peuple de fraudeurs*). This was true in more than one sense of the word "smuggler," and it was true of many of Europe's peoples.

Thus, while the defeat of the bourgeois democracies and the triumph of National Socialist Germany demonstrated the collapse of the remnant liberal assumptions about the ultimate reality of materialism, it soon became evident that the systems of planned econony were vulnerable, too, because of the obstinate survival of some of the most elementary manifestations of the acquisitive (acquisitive, rather than capitalist) spirit. These manifestations depended on particular national conditions (thus, for example, the German system of planning worked well only among Germans). In any event, the famous Horatian line of "nature coming back at you, even after you drove it out with a pitchfork" was applicable, for once, against the "vitalist" Germans. Yet, while the widespread existence of black—that is, free—markets was an existential reality, signifying a triumph over enforced socialistic systems, it did not quite mean a latter-day triumph of Adam Smith, or of Keynes, or of Economic Laws.

## THE "LAWS" OF ECONOMICS

¶ "No government action could overcome economic laws, and any interference with those laws must end in disaster"—this is what the president of the Board of Trade told the House of Commons in London at the beginning of World War I. It is one of my favorite quotes, for a number of reasons. It is a prototypical expression of that superficially broad-minded but, in reality, narrow-minded kind of Victorian Liberalism that had professed to believe that Economic Laws are Hard, Basic Facts, such as the Laws of Gravity or other Principal Laws of Nature. It is perhaps significant that the author of this principal admonition was none other than Walter Runciman, a prototypical English Liberal figure, who reappeared on the international political scene, if only for a short moment: In 1938 Chamberlain sent him to Czechoslovakia to find a compromise "solution" to the Sudeten crisis. In 1938 the Runciman mission seemed to represent the best in the English tradition of pragmatism and compromise and fairness. In reality, it represented the feeble and antiquated ideas of tired old men. Such a manifestation of weakness, too, was the belief of the

British government in 1939 that Germany would be defeated be economic warfare, by an economic blockade; that certain Economic Laws were insuperable, and that Hitler himself would be incapable of overcoming them.

The Chamberlain government was not alone in believing this. "There was," as A. J. P. Taylor put it, "an almost universal dogma among economists that Nazi autarchy was itself a symptom of impending breakdown, and the dogma was sustained by information from German refugees, who naturally gave Hitler no credit for anything."[86] This kind of economic determinism was a holy principle of the socialist Left as much as of the capitalist Right. Of course, orthodox economic liberalism, meaning the desirability of no government action in economics whatsoever, was a dead dogma by the thirties; but the Keynesian dogmatology that had succeeded it believed in economic determinism, too, though in a more sophisticated kind. Some of its pragmatic applications helped the United States out of the depths of the 1929–33 depression, and thereafter created comfortable chairs for a number of famous economists. For the conduct of the war against Germany its dogmas were of no use whatsoever. Few people recognized that the very phenomenon of Hitler's Germany—as, too, of Stalin's Russia, Mussolini's Italy, or even Roosevelt's America—were living illustrations of The End of Economic Man, the title of a book by the judicious refugee writer Peter Drucker in 1939. Few people recognize it even now.

One of the most, if not the most, successful economist of the twentieth century was Adolf Hitler. He did not believe in Economic Man; he knew nothing of Economic Laws. "Why should I nationalize the industries?" Hitler told Rauschning. "I will nationalize the people," which is what he did. Whether Krupp of Rheinmetall or I. G. Farben were "private" or "public" corporations made no difference at all. They were national. Hitler reduced unemployment in Germany about thrice as fast as Roosevelt or Mussolini, not to speak of Baldwin, Chamberlain, or Blum.[87] Nor did Hitler achieve this through coercion or through forced armament programs. The German public-works program was not very large in the mid-thirties, and the armament industry did not significantly

---

[86] Taylor, *EH*, 514, where he adds this delicious footnote: "The exception was C. Guillebeaud in *Germany's Economic System*, 1933–38. His reputation never recovered from this recognition of the truth." See also the now indispensable basic books by Klein, Milward, Petzina. I must add that the British official publications after the war, no matter how usually bland, are fairly honest in recognizing the shortcomings of these fundamental assumptions.

[87] In Britain there were still as many as 1.3 million unemployed in January 1940.

increase employment until after 1936. He achieved this because he under-stood, instinctively, that economics, in the broadest sense of its meaning, involves fiction rather than fact[88]; that economic conditions are often the consequences of confidence, rather than the reverse; and he was one of the most terrifying creators of national confidence. Because of this confidence the German currency, unlike the currencies of many other dictatorships, remained remarkably solid; for, even though Hitler in 1939 departed from Schacht's boldly conservative financial policies, Hitler probably understood that the 1929–33 depression was an aberration in the history of the twentieth century when the danger is almost always not that of deflation but that of inflation. Of course, Hitler was not successful in everything: In many instances his policy, including the Four-year Plan, was only a limited success; but, again, contrary to accepted opinion, not because the ideal of autarchy for a modern industrial power such as Ger-many was altogether ridiculous (we shall see how remarkable was the German production of synthetic materials), but because Hitler underes-timated the indispensable element of foreign trade, including Germany's own imports. (He did succeed in reducing Germany's imports somewhat. In foodstuffs Germany's dependence on imports by September 1939 was down to a fraction of what it had been in 1914.) National Socialist Ger-many, unlike most socialist states, demonstrated that it was possible to maintain a high standard of living under a rigid and centralized dicta-torship. (This writer remembers the anti-Nazi books and pamphlets that abounded in Europe in 1939 with statistics about the starving masses of the German people and about the inability of Hitler to wage modern war; he remembers, too, crossing Germany in the summer of that year that gave a rather different impression from the articles and books that he had been devouring; he was barely rising sixteen then, and not an expert on world affairs or economics; still, this experience laid the basis of his subsequent, and on occasion extreme, skepticism about the pretensions of economists.) In any event, to the people of Paris in June 1940 the previous jokes about German cardboard tanks and hungering soldiers rang singu-larly hollow. They should ring even more hollow in retrospect. For we now know that, contrary to prevalent opinion, German economy before the war, and well into the war, was quite able to produce both guns and butter.[89]

---

[88] *Fictio*, in Latin, means construction, including mental construction.
[89] A confidential police report on 30 January 1941 reported the rise of prices in Germany during the eight years since Hitler had come to power. Between January 1933 and December 1940 food prices had risen about 15 per cent, cloth-ing prices 41 per cent; and the general price index had risen 14 per cent—remarkably little, in retrospect.

Hitler's Germany produced fewer guns than had been supposed for a long time. Until January 1942, the German economy was not geared to "total war." The Germans did not reduce their production of consumer goods.[90] The greatest German victories were achieved during 1939–41 when German war production and war economy functioned on a limited scale—a kind of miracle, in retrospect.[91] Or perhaps it is not a miracle: It only shows how limited were, and are, the mental categories and processes of those people who think in terms of economic determinism. Until the summer of 1940 it was practically an article of universal belief among the Western democracies that Germany was soon bound to run out of essentials: of oil, of steel, of chromium, of vanadium, of food. This belief curiously coexisted with another belief to the effect that Germany had spent enormous amounts on armaments. (Hitler himself contributed to this fiction, perhaps by calculation: On 1 September 1939 he proclaimed that Germany was wholly ready for war, having spent 90 million RM for rearmament. All Western economists accepted that figure, including British economic intelligence. In reality they overcalculated by about 100 per cent: Germany's rearmament expenditures between 1933 and 1939 amounted to about 45 million RM.)

The Germans surely overcame the laws of economics very efficiently. It is instructive to look at the rough estimate of the Great Powers' armament production, in billions of dollars:

|               | 1939 | 1940 | 1941 | 1493      |
| ------------- | ---- | ---- | ---- | --------- |
| Germany       | 3.4  | 6.0  | 6.0  | 13.8(!)   |
| Great Britain | 1.0  | 3.5  | 6.5  | 11.1      |
| Soviet Union  | 3.3  | 5.0  | 8.5  | 13.9      |
| United States | 0.6  | 1.5  | 4.5  | 37.5[92]  |

I shall not comment on these remarkable figures. They again reveal that it is the efficient employment of arms, not their quantity, that counts. Here are more surprising data: In 1939 German aircraft production was

---

[90] The total value of consumer goods produced in the Third Reich amounted to 13.8 million RM in 1940; 14.3 million RM in 1941; and 13.1 million RM in 1942.

[91] "The main lesson that comes out of Germany's experience is simply that a nation's economic war potential may be a very poor measure of her actual military strength. It is hardly surprising that Germany eventually lost the war to a combination of powers whose economic potential vastly exceeded hers. What is much more surprising is how well she did, despite the economic odds against her." Klein, 238.

[92] Petzina (Table 21).

about the same as British production, and German tank production even a little lower than British. In 1940 and 1941 Britain alone produced about 30 per cent more aircraft than had Germany, and also more tanks. From 1939 to 1942 German munitions production less than doubled (it rose 93 per cent), while munitions production in the British Isles during the same period rose nearly eightfold (760 per cent). We have seen how during the first eight months of the war the entire strategy of the Western Allies was based on the false assumption that Germany's economy would have to collapse if she were to be deprived of her access to Scandinavian iron ore. Similar predictions were made concerning oil. Yet Germany, even with her much motorized army, was able to manage. Her annual consumption during the war was between 7 and 8 million tons; her stocks at the beginning of the war were low, and foreign imports, except during the 1939–41 years of German-Soviet pacts, were never higher than 2 million.[93] But more than one third of her needs were covered by synthetic gasoline, of which Germany produced 2.8 million tons as early as in 1939: This was four times larger than her synthetic production capacity in 1935. Even more successful was the Germans' production of synthetic rubber, rising from 22,000 tons in 1939 to 69,000 in 1942. This was more than what was needed for the entire military and civil consumption in Germany, so that the Germans could even export a little of the rubber surplus. During all of this time German manpower was mobilized at a lower rate than were English or Russian manpower.[94] The percentage of the German population drafted by the military services plus the entire civilian labor force remained the same in 1939, in 1940, and in 1941: It was 51.5 per cent of the entire population. (The contribution of slave labor by foreigners and prisoners of war become considerable only in 1942 and after.)[95]

---

[93] Germany's imports from the Soviet Union were nonetheless considerable. In the year 1940 the latter supplied 70 per cent of Germany's chrome, 40 per cent of her manganese, and 33 per cent of her oil needs.

[94] The Reich Labor Service made labor compulsory for men between 18 and 25 in September 1939; also for unmarried women (for a maximum period of 6 months; this was extended to 8 months in August 1941). Yet there was no drafting of women. The Minister of Economy, Funk, said that this was "unbearable to the party for psychological reasons during the years 1939 to 1942." Homze, 22.

[95] In May 1939 foreign workers amounted to 0.8 per cent of the entire German labor force. By the end of the year they were augmented by 110,000 Polish workers, plus 300,000 Polish prisoners of war. The foreign workers' participation thus rose to 3.2 per cent by the end of May 1940 (of these, 30 per cent were employed in agriculture). A shift to industry began in 1941. "From the summer of 1940 until the winter of 1941, the German attempt to utilize

Let us now turn to economic intelligence, of which much was available in Paris and London and Washington. Until 1939, and in many ways after that, Germany was a more or less open country, and much of her economy was an open book, as indeed her economic geography was an open map, with all kinds of details available to anyone who could read. The consensus of experts, including British economists, in 1939 was that Germany's stocks could last no more than six months to one year. We have seen how different Germany's position was in reality. On 3 September 1939 the British Ministry of Economic Warfare was set up (this title was preferred to the First World War name of Ministry of Blockade). Its main activities are recorded in a number of reasonably honest, though regrettably bland, official publications, such as W. N. Medlicott's *The Economic Blockade*, whose first sentence reads: "Too much, it is now agreed, was expected of the blockade in the Second World War."[96] Until 1940 "the story of economic warfare was one of great expectations." Indeed, Great Expectations reigned, at least on paper, in the Bleak House of the London School of Economics where, until March 1940, the new ministry had its home. In that bleak house certain peculiar traits of bland idiocy were flourishing. Thus, for example, the aging Keynes tried to impress (and nearly succeeded in impressing) on the Ministry of Economic Warfare the idea of a "policy of temptation," whereby the Germans, by artificially stimulated Allied competition, would be goaded to conspicuous consumption, into purchasing all kinds of stuff abroad that they didn't really need—an economic idea that might have sprung from the brow of Calvin Coolidge. For once the intellectuals' and the businessmen's mentalities were in accord. Chamberlain's war strategy rested on his trust in the efficacy of the blockade; he believed in Germany's serious economic difficulties, and he "did not believe that the enemy could face a second winter."[97] "Upon the economic factor depends our only hope of bringing about the downfall of Germany," wrote the British chiefs of staff in May 1940. Theirs was a modest assessment, compared to the more sanguine reports of the Ministry of Eco-

---

[foreign] labor was characterized by modesty and restraint." Homze, 45. "Until the latter half of 1941, the Army followed closely the Geneva Convention, which forbade the use of prisoners of war in war industries." Ibid., 49. By October 1941 there were 3.5 million foreign workers in Germany, 39 per cent of them prisoners. In certain industries, of course, the total was higher; in December 1941 more than 42 per cent of the work force in the Hermann Goering-Werke was not German.

[96] Vol. I (London, 1952). It is fair to add that the French were skeptical of the efficacy of the blockade throughout.

[97] Macmillan, 4.

nomic Warfare about imaginary sabotages in Germany, predicting a "general industrial breakdown throughout Europe"[98] in 1941 and fatal German shortages in war materials.[99] Even Churchill, admittedly no wizard in economics, could be wrong. In his letter to Roosevelt on 8 December 1940 he wrote that "saturation point is reached when the maximum industrial effort that can be spared from civilian needs has been applied to war production. Germany certainly reached this point by the end of 1939." He was off by five years at least. As Wagenfuehr, the principal German economic chronicler of the war years, put it, until the middle of 1944 "the German economy had no general difficulties in providing its raw materials."[100]

Without knowing these figures, some of Hitler's bitterest enemies understood this at the time. When in the dark early December days of 1941, the Polish General and Premier Sikorski visited Stalin, during their difficult discussions (probably too, with a view to impress Stalin with his anticapitalist convictions) Sikorski said: "Hitler had taught everybody how it is possible to achieve great things without gold and only with labour. Mr. Commissar," he turned to Molotov, "don't imitate the finance ministers in the West who, to begin with, haggle over each million." "STALIN (nodding) 'Good!' "[101]

That conversation in the Kremlin took place at the time of the turning point of the war. Hitler recognized that turning point. Sometime between 3 December 1941 and 10 January 1942 he decided "that the present war effort was insufficient and that the *blitzkrieg* (planning) should be abandoned."[102] His directive, *Ruestung Ost*, on 10 January 1942, marked the decisive break with the economic policy of the *blitzkriegs*.

Ignorant as he was of the laws of economics, Hitler almost won his war. Just as the outbreak of the First World War had been living proof

---

[98] Gwyer, Butler, III, 21.

[99] According to the estimate of the Ministry of Economic Warfare, German copper stocks from 1940 to 1942 should have fallen from 200,000 to 75,000 metric tons, whereas in reality they rose from 183,000 to 265,000 tons; the British Ministry experts also projected a 70 per cent decline in lead and 50 per cent in tin stocks, whereas German lead stocks remained on the same level, and tin stocks nearly doubled. Klein, 114.

[100] Cited by Petzina, 192.

[101] Kot, 141.

[102] Milward, 63. A few weeks later the able Speer took over the direction of the German war economy, his predecessor Todt having died in an accident. Todt, too, was an able man, and the eventual shortcomings of the German *blitzkrieg* economic planning cannot be ascribed to his shortsightedness.

of the fallacious belief in the primacy of class struggle, the Last European War proved the fallacy of economic determinism. (Social savants, Marxist theorists, and all kinds of economists persist in professing their ignorance of this development—to their profit, I must add.) There was another lesson implicit in the history of the last war. The capacities of modern destruction were matched by the capacities of modern reconstruction. The most startling evidences thereof appeared in Europe after the war. But already by 1940 it was becoming evident that modern warfare, including bombing from the air, disrupted the daily lives of people and the production of certain goods to a lesser extent than it had been supposed. In Holland, Belgium, Luxembourg, and occupied France more than 90 per cent of all railroad lines were back in service by the end of 1940; by May 1941 all of the destroyed rail and highway bridges and tunnels had been rebuilt. In Belgium, an "average" state under German occupation midway between the extreme harshness of the German regime in Poland and the Germans' "model" of an occupied Denmark, the reconstruction of industrial capacity was amazing:

BELGIUM, 1939–41

|  | Steel production (millions of tons) | Electricity (millions kw/h) | Gas (mill. m³) | Coal (Average monthly no. of employees, in thousands) |
|---|---|---|---|---|
| 1938 average | 184 | 440 | 57 | 126 |
| December 1940 | 147 | 405 | 53 | 129 |
| December 1941 | 121 | 434[103] | 61.5 | 124 |

Another important lesson was that of the amazing potentialities of agricultural autarchy. The neutral states furnish some good examples of this. They, all, fared much better than they had fared during the First World War, when they—with the partial exception of Switzerland—had given little thought to increasing their agrarian self-sufficiency in the beginning. The Swiss, financially well off, were able to import much of their food after 1939; but they knew that this was not enough. Immediately after the outbreak of the war the Swiss government started a determined program to increase arable land. It also promoted the breeding of

---

[103] In France (occupied and unoccupied zones), the production of electricity actually rose: millions of kw/h consumed in 1929: 1,196; in 1938: 1,548; in 1941: 1,588; in 1942: 1,576.

pigs, while it cut back the raising of beeves, steers, and calves. The Swiss idea was simple common sense[104]: The Swiss drastically reduced the production of fodder and increased the surface of arable land, no matter how poor. They concluded (this, for them, represented a rather radical break with traditional practices) that the kind of food produced by and through animals, no matter how desirable or healthy, requires a considerable wastage of terrain, while intelligent and modern practices of intensive cultivation may produce surprisingly large amounts of foodstuffs for large numbers of people.[105] Between 1939 and 1942 the cereal-growing terrains in Switzerland nearly doubled. In Britain they increased by 70 to 75 per cent. In Belgium the unfortunate De Winter refused to consider such a policy, putting his hopes instead in strict rationing and agricultural imports from other German-controlled lands, with the result that in 1941 and 1942 the surface of arable land in Belgium increased merely by something like 15 per cent still remaining less than what it had been in 1929. In plain English, all over Europe the people who grew their own potatoes and ate and sold them themselves made out best[106]—a kind of gross but healthy thing to do,[107] with results that no matter how widespread, seldom made their way into the statistical columns adding up the Gross National Product.

How often people forget that money, and its exchange, represent little more than a social contract, dependent on common presuppositions! Trade follows politics, and money follows power, rather than the other way around. In the operations of high finance, too, among black-marketeers of money, including the smartest experts of arbitrage in international finance, we may detect an illustration of the truism that what happens is what people think happens, surely in the short run, and often in the long run, too. Here are, for example, the sums in francs that a Frenchman on

---

[104] It was explained by the government official principally responsible for its administration, the excellent Dr. Wahlen, in 1943: Wahlen, passim; cited also by Baudhuin, 255.

[105] The Wahlen plan, further extended in November 1940, called for a vast increase in the production of bread, cereals, and beet sugar, together with compulsory cultivation of potatoes and vegetables, while livestock, except for pigs, was reduced.

[106] In Britain agricultural wages rose 61 per cent, while wages in manufacture rose 42 per cent between 1939 and 1942.

[107] "What a satisfactory job ploughing is," wrote an Englishman in his diary shortly after the war had broken out. ". . . I have not personally ploughed a furrow since 1928, but I find that I have not forgotten my old skill." Arthur Street, cited in Calder, 418.

the "free" (that is black) market had to pay for an American dollar
before the fall of France:

|  |  |
|---|---|
| 1 September 1939 | 43.80 |
| 18 September 1939 | 45.87 |
| 27 March 1940 | 50.70 |
| 28 May 1940 | 56.00 |

Thus on 28 May 1940, the day when Belgium surrendered, when
Dunkirk was besieged, when the supreme commander of the French
Army suggested the necessity of considering capitulation, the calculations
of the most sophisticated speculators of the world merely lagged behind
events: The value of the franc had dropped less than 30 per cent. Another
example: The reputation and, therefore, the value of the English pound—
not only in its relationship to the German mark but to the franc and to
the dollar—was highest in early 1942 throughout the Continent, which,
especially in retrospect, makes little sense. (The fluctuations of the German mark on the black market reflected the popular estimate of the prospects of German power more accurately: The official ratio was 20 francs
to 1 RM, but on the black market the rate was 8 francs in 1941, and 4 to 5
francs in 1943.)

The existing stock markets, too, usually lagged behind the general
inflationary development. In Amsterdam, where the stock exchange was
reopened on 15 July 1940, all through that year stock prices were not
only lower than in 1930 but they also registered only faintly the tremendous upheavals that had befallen Holland and the Continent (the share
index was 88.6 in August 1939; 83.9 in April 1940; and 87.7 in August
1940). Stock prices responded somewhat stronger to the general rise in
living costs and prices, as they moved from 87.7 in August 1940 to 149.9
in November 1941; but they continued to reflect the prevailing sentiments
of "financial circles" that were, more than often, produced by wishful
thinking as much as by existing realities. Before the entry of the United
States into the war, for example, having overestimated American, and underestimated Japanese power in the western Pacific, the index of Dutch
East Indian shares rose from 79.5 (August 1939) to 130.4 in November
1941 (dropping to 74.6 by August 1944). The general index of shares on
the eight principal stock markets of the world shows that Americans and
Swedes may have underestimated, Frenchmen and Belgians overestimated,
and Englishmen and Swiss more or less correctly estimated the general
world inflationary spiral:

GENERAL INDEX OF SHARES (1938:100)

|  | 1939 | 1940 | 1941 | 1942 |
|---|---|---|---|---|
| Amsterdam | 92 | 127 | 156 | 148 |
| New York | 108 | 96 | 82 | 88 |
| London | 93 | 87 | 98 | 116 |
| Paris | 116 | 191 | 353 | 594 |
| Brussels | 84 | 182 | 322 | 339 |
| Stockholm | 75 | 82 | 97 | 106 |
| Berlin | 103 | 135 | 144 | 152 |
| Zurich | 87 | 82 | 102 | 110 |

And, finally, we encounter the ancient and enduring mystery of gold. In many ways this seemed to have been the end of the age of gold: The greatest states of the world had abandoned the gold standard years before; the gold production of the world was diminishing: Here, again, Hitler's supreme contempt for the ancient bourgeois standards seemed to be proven by events. The Germans would explain this to their occupied peoples. When, in the summer of 1940, they told the Belgians and the Dutch that they had to pay the occupation costs, the administrators of these countries replied that they had no money. You must then print money, the Germans said. But there was no gold backing for such issuances of new currency, these people replied. You don't understand, the Germans said. This is passé, it is no longer necessary. Look at us, they said. The value of the money is work, the labor of the nation. Gold is nothing. And so it seemed. The French in 1939 began the war with twice as much gold as their treasury had in 1914: What good did that do?

And yet, at the very time when gold was dismissed from the minds of economists in Berlin and Rome and even in Washington and Paris, its value began to rise, and it rose precipitously, far beyond the calculations of financiers and economists, rapidly outrunning the general prices of stocks and bonds, and even the prices of the most valued currencies. Stocks, dollars, gold: They rose in ascending order. In Paris:

|  | Price of the napoleon d'or | Price of the average stock (stock index 100:1938) | Price of the U.S. dollar |
|---|---|---|---|
| End of May 1940 | 267.50 | 134 | 56 |
| End of Dec. 1941 | 1975.00 | 376 | 150 |
| End of Dec. 1942 | 4000.00 | 590 | 170 |

In other words, from the collapse of France to the American entry in the war, the value of the average industrial stock a little more than doubled, the value of the dollar nearly trebled, and the value of the napoleon d'or increased more than sevenfold. So gold amounted to something, after all. And the Germans knew it, too. There is a very good account of their, at times carefully hidden, attitude from a French officer who observed them closely during the Wiesbaden meetings of the Franco-German Armistice Commission in 1941:

> . . . without being economists or financiers, one can observe how, through the years, the partisans and the adversaries of gold confront each other yet events have not proven either of them right. But what one can observe definitely is *the attraction that the Germans have for gold* [his italics]. Officially they keep proclaiming that the relationship of European currencies is independent of the gold standard: but their actions tend to get as much gold for themselves as possible. . . .[108]

Thus during the Second World War the power of money proved far less solid than the value attributed to gold. The institutions of the last century crumbled, while older realities remained surprisingly valid. So did some of the assumptions of the Enlightenment crumble, though not everybody was ready to admit this. This continental world, stretching from elegant Parisian collaborationists to the crudest of blackguards in Ukrainian ghettos, was closer to the world of Hobbes and Rabelais and Ivan the Terrible than that of Rousseau or Adam Smith or Marx. It reflected the hollowness of theories about social contracts, noble savages, laws of economics, struggles of classes; but there remained within it a strong substance of selfish vitality, of national cohesion, and of the consciousness of the past.

---

[108] *Compte-rendu* by Lieutenant Colonel Vialet, 27 June 1941, *CDA*, IV, 590–91.

# 2 . The march of the armies

HISTORY CONSISTS PRINCIPALLY of change, of movement; and the Second World War was a war of movement. Its history was full of episodes of high drama, far more than the history of the First World War. The Second World War produced generals with a daring and resourcefulness that had not appeared during the First. During the First World War the civilian leaders of the warring empires were determined men, yet most of them knew little about war in particular. During the Second World War Hitler, Churchill, Stalin, each of them had a military side to their genius: They understood not only the enormous stakes but also the actuality of warfare better than had many of their generals. During the Second World War the sharp lines separating war and peace, and soldiers from civilians—distinctions that may have been one of the most important achievements of European civilization after the seventeenth century—were being washed away. Perhaps this was the most important —and ultimately the most barbaric—development of the war. It may also explain why there have been, as yet, no great military historians of that war. In the past, military history and the history of war were almost, if not quite, the same things. During the Second World War they no longer were. Military historians deal with the history of armies; and this is no longer enough. During the First World War entire peoples were enrolled in the cause of war, in the service of their armies; still only the armies moved, only the armies fought. During the Second World War the movements of armies were often inextricably involved with the movements of populations, and the physical movements were involved with the movements of minds. At the same time, during the Second World War the decisive movements occurred faster: A few thousand determined and well-equipped soldiers could conquer entire states in a few days, sometimes in hours. This is partly—but only partly—explainable by mechanization. The Second World War was not decided by the technical, and perhaps not even by the material, superiority of one side over

[239]

the other. It was decided by large numbers of men. The 180 million people of the Russian empire, together with the 150 million of the American empire, their willingness to fight even more than the quality of their equipment, decided the war.

All of this developed after 1941: It would carry us beyond the confines of this book, which ends with the turning point of the war. In other respects, too, 1941 was a turning point. This has been stressed especially by Germans. They say that until June 1941 the war was essentially a limited war, with certain ground rules accepted by the combatants, a more or less traditional contest of arms, with a more or less traditional treatment of prisoners. With the war in Russia all of this changed. There were Hitler's and Himmler's orders, best known among them the infamous *Kommissar-befehl*, providing for a war without quarter, in which entire categories of prisoners were to be eliminated. Certain German historians, such as Andreas Hillgruber, speak of a *Europaeisches Normalkrieg* (a normal European war) before June 1941, implying that the war in the West was one thing, but the war in Russia another, the kind of total war in which totalitarian savagery was only to be expected. I have often felt a mixture of admiration and envy for the proverbial old Irishwoman whose response to a query involving odds and bits of malicious information about a younger neighbor of hers was that "It is not true; but it is true enough." As a historian, I am compelled to work from the opposite assumption: Often I must say that "It is true; but it is not true enough." So with the claim that the Second World War changed in nature on 22 June 1941, implying that the German military were compelled to change their nature then and there. What is true is that, generally speaking, they treated their Soviet prisoners more brutally and inhumanly than they had treated prisoners of other nationalities. Otherwise they waged war in Russia as they waged war elsewhere: as much as they could, and as much as they thought would serve them. Total war is a myth, just as total victory or total peace or total love. For example, the Germans hardly bombed Moscow at all—certainly not as they bombed London or Coventry or Rotterdam or Belgrade. Their siege of Leningrad may have meant one million dead, but it was a siege closer to the practices of war in the seventeenth century than to the siege of Verdun: The Germans wanted to starve out the population. They did not use gas, except in the death factories on the sad plains of Poland. On the other hand, this *except* was a big thing. What the Germans did in Auschwitz after 1941 was implicit and, at times, explicit in some of the things they said, and did, before 1941. In Russia the Germans did not reap what they sowed; they reaped as they reaped before, only they tried to reap big. Their treatment—and, more important, their attitude—toward the "European" Poles in 1939 was not much different from their treatment of the "Asiatic" Russians in 1941; and their ultimate treatment of the Jews of Amsterdam was hardly different from their treatment of the Jews of Minsk. In sum, differences in their methods of warfare before June 1941 and after, wherever they existed, were differences of degree, they were not differences of kind.

The Second World War was a revolutionary war, different from the First World War not so much in the nature of war aims as in the method of their execution. War is one way in which to impose one's will on others. The Germans wanted to dominate Europe, including Russia. When governments and nations would resist this, they would conquer their cities and countries with their armies. The extent and the brutality of these conquests might differ, but the aim was largely the same: to break the will of those people who would resist them. In a large sense there was nothing new in this. The revolutionary novelty of the war lay in its methods. Hitler had an instinctive and often profound understanding of this. As early as in 1932 he told Rauschning: "The next war will be quite different from the last world war. Infantry attacks and mass formations are obsolete. Interlocked frontal struggles lasting for years on petrified fronts will not return. I guarantee that. They were a degenerate form of war."

Military men are often criticized for preparing for the war that happened before. In one important sense this criticism is unjust, for that is the only experience they can draw upon. (The question should be: *How* do they draw upon it?) In another sense this criticism is justified: This is how the French failed in the 1930s. Military planners, too, are prone to the intellectual habit of projecting the continuation of whatever seems to be going on, when they should be especially aware of this failing, since war is even less predictable than are most ambitious human endeavors. No doubt it is because of this kind of unpredictability that in war certain amateurs have been better than many professionals: No doubt this was one of the reasons behind Hitler's many successes. On the other hand, Hitler was not altogether an amateur at war: His memories of World War I, when he served at the front for four years, stood him in good stead.[1] At the same time, Hitler was one of those men who are able to perceive the potential meaning of new developments; for the independent mind is not the mind of a man who can liberate himself entirely from experiences of the past—that way lie illusion and folly—it is, rather, the mind of a man who, in recognizing certain new developments, detaches his mind not from experiences of the past but from the accepted intellectual categories of the present.

The predictions and the projections of most people, including ex-

---

[1] Before the Norway campaign he was supposed to have studied—at any rate, he looked at—von der Goltz's expeditionary campaign in Finland in 1918. The British professionals studied nothing of the kind.

perts, about the Second World War proved wrong. In 1939 they thought in terms of enormous material battles, entire cities burned up by mass bombardments from the air in the first few days of the war; blockades and air power would be decisive. The opposite happened. The economic blockade had surprisingly little effect: We have seen this in the foregoing chapter. Its main agent, sea power, declined in importance. After four or five hundred years, land power became dominant again, principally because of the automotive engine. After many decades, mobile warfare returned. Motorized armies would conquer at the speed of dozens of miles a day. Their movements were even swifter than were Napoleon's along the then sparse highroads of Europe.[2] Contrary to the projections of most experts, gas was not used in combat; and aerial bombing was not decisive.[3] Great campaigns were decided by relatively small armies. These were not quite the professional *armées de métier* projected by De Gaulle in the thirties. They consisted of a mix; some of the most reckless Storm Troops, like some of the Germans' SS units, were raised from the ranks of the people.

Rapid armies; rapid, small wars; this was much of the pattern of the Last European War, at least until the autumn of 1941. In the two months of the Norway campaign the casualties were 1,869 British, 5,296 German, 530 French and Polish, and about 1,500 Norwegian officers and men. During the Balkan campaign of 1941, in which the Germans conquered two states in three weeks, the entire German Second Army had less than 5,000 casualties. (It captured 90,000 Yugoslav, 270,000 Greek, and 13,000 British prisoners.) One of its divisions lost one officer and less than seventy men during the whole campaign. The Germans used small armies by choice, the British often by circumstance, as in Belgium and France in 1940. In Belgium, where bitter fighting raged for three weeks, the Belgian Army lost about 5,700 men, while the higher loss of civilians (about 12,000) foreshadowed the realities of a new kind of war. Still, after all was said, the *blitzkrieg* operations hurt the conquered less than had many wars of

---

[2] In Russia, however, Napoleon, whose armies moved on foot, reached Moscow six weeks faster than the spearheads of Hitler's motorized columns.

[3] The first air raid alarm of the war in London was symbolic of the erroneous projections, before and after. Fifteen minutes after the declaration of war had gone into effect, at 11:15 A.M. on 3 September 1939, the sirens went on all over southeastern England and London. This was a false alarm. It later transpired that an unarmed French courier plane had been crossing the Channel without having made the necessary signals to the British air warning system. It is less known that the first British air losses in the war occurred because of this false alarm. Two British fighters, which had risen into the air, were shot down by their nervous comrades.

the past. What hurt them were the deprivations and the tyranny of the occupation that followed.

Those military opponents of the Germans who failed to comprehend this in the beginning were wrong, I repeat, not altogether because they were hidebound theorists with their eyes fixed to the past; to a large extent their failure was due to their obsession with the accepted ideas of a supermodern present. Thus, for example, the British government in 1939 projected 1 million casualties in London alone during the first two weeks of the war—far more than what were to be the civilian casualties of the entire British people during the six years of the entire war. Thus, for example, the British and the French believed after the first German breakthrough at Sedan that the Germans had an enormous superiority in tanks and airplanes, whereas in reality this was not so. Having first underestimated the Germans' potential, after 1940 the opinions of the experts quickly changed, overestimating the quantity of the materials and armaments that the Germans were supposed to have had at their disposal. The German military production was much lower than had been thought[4]; the German expenditure of munitions, too, was surprisingly low.[5] In March 1940 the bland and uninspiring slogan of the French government, posted all over France, read: "We shall win because we are stronger." "Thanks to her colonial empire," wrote the editorialist in the March 1940 number of *L'Illustration*, "which numbers more than seventy million inhabitants, our country can raise all the soldiers that are deemed neces-

---

[4] See above, pp. 230–33.

AIRPLANE PRODUCTION IN 1941

| *Germany* | *Great Britain* |
|-----------|-----------------|
| 11,030 | 20,100 |

TANK PRODUCTION IN 1941

| | |
|-------|-------|
| 5,200 | 4,855 |

[5] In September 1939, for example, the munitions issued to the German armies in the Polish campaign were often incomplete in extent. Another surprising fact: German munitions production in 1941 was only 1 per cent higher than in 1940. Also, there was no great difference in the expenditure of munitions on the Eastern, from that of the Western, front: The rate was the same during the *blitzkrieg* campaigns and in the slugging battles with the Russians. G. Donat, "Der Munitionsverbrauch der deutschen Wehrmacht im Zweiten Weltkrieg," *WWR* (August 1966).

sary." These numbers mattered little. Strength lay not in them.[6] This was true of the Second World War at least during its first dramatic two years.

Even in Russia—and this is often overlooked—the German Army was not an enormous mass. The German line had no resemblance to the massed lines of men, dug in and out, that snaked across entire provinces and countries during the First World War. Gerald Reitlinger, not a military historian, was one of the few men to note this, with his discerning eye. The German-Russian War, too, was "an extraordinary war. On the German side a smaller number of soldiers held a line more than twice the length of the Russian front as it had been in the First World War. . . . Often the front was an imaginary line like the Equator."[7] Like the Equator, this imaginary line could have a powerful effect on the minds of men. During the First World War the advancing armies simply picked up the frontier posts and tried to move them forward, like armed land agents. During the Second World War they drove fast ahead, like armed tourists. During the First World War the spearheads were blunt little spikes closely welded to the massive body of the army. During the Second World War the job of the spearheads was to pretend that they *were* the conquering armies, en masse. "Spearheads" were really spearheads: They were thrown ahead. Often they succeeded, not only in impressing frightened and witless civilians, but also large masses of bewildered enemy soldiery. This explains the enormous bag of prisoners that relatively small armored and motorized units of infantry could pretend to encircle and collect. Thus the Germans captured 1.9 million Frenchmen in May–June 1940; 3.5 million prisoners in Russia in 1941.[8] Thus a few thousand British soldiers bagged nearly 40,000 Italians in the western desert in December 1940.

Compared to these novel forms of warfare, the organization of armies remained remarkably traditional. Nearly every state in Europe had some kind of universal military service in 1939 (the British passed their

---

[6] Nor was military intelligence particularly useful. In 1940 French intelligence about the German armies was better than that of the British, and in some instances even than German intelligence—with no worthwhile results. (The French military attaché in Berne, for example learned on 30 April that the Germans would attack between 8 and 10 May, and that their main thrust would come through the Ardennes, toward Sedan.) During the Second World War the influence of military attachés was high; yet their performances were often less than mediocre, including those of the respected and feared German military attachés.

[7] Reitlinger, *House*, 231.

[8] Only about one half (1.8 million) of these Soviet prisoners were collected in the so-called encirclement battles (*Kesselschlachten*) in 1941. These battles, too, were different from those of the First World War: Instead of frontal confrontation of armies, they were the result of great encircling movements.

conscription law only in 1939; for political reasons, Northern Ireland was excluded from the draft). Mobilization was made through the state postal services (except for a few Eastern European states, including Poland, which still depended on posters). Compared to 1914, in 1939 the speed of mobilization or even the duration of military training mattered little. The small democracies of Northern and Western Europe let their armies shrivel during the thirties, especially when Socialist governments were in power: Norway was a prime example of this. In 1940 the Norwegian Army fought poorly, the Danish Army and Navy did not fire a shot. The Netherlands Prime Minister, Colijn, said in 1936: "We no longer have an army; it will have to be created at the time of mobilization." Unlike the Norwegians, the Dutch passed a military service law in 1938, but the organization and the equipment of their army remained poor. The traditional ranks of the armies (their nomenclature deriving usually from the French pattern of centuries before) remained largely the same, including those of the Soviet Union. (One exception were the special ranks of the SS troops: a parallel army to the German Army, and eventually a parallel arm of the entire state apparatus.) The size of infantry divisions varied from about 12,000 to 20,000 men.[9] A few divisions formed an army corps; two to four army corps, an army. (The Russians called their army corps, armies; several of their armies formed a "front.") The ratio of general officers to soldiers varied little from country to country (it was very high in Spain). Different armies had different equipment, of course. In 1939 the armies of most European states, including Russia, were still largely horse-drawn. Nearly every army kept a few cavalry units as late as 1941.[10] The Germans were first in having special armored divisions. After the Western European campaign (when the French had two armored brigades), others followed them.

One great difference between the two world wars was in the propor-

---

[9] The precise count of divisions mattered little. There could be a discrepancy in the mere counting of divisons. Thus, for example, the French Army in May 1940 numbered 115 divisions according to Weygand's, 81 according to Reynaud's memoirs, and 94 according to the British War Office.

[10] The last cavalry attacks during the Second World War, and perhaps in the history of modern war, occurred in 1941. On 21 January 1941 at Keren, in Eritrea, 60 Italian cavalrymen, led by a Lieutenant Togni, attacked the British in a brave charge, in which 25 died and 16 were wounded (Barker, 84). In Russia two regiments of the 44th Mongolian Cavalry Division attacked Germans near Mushino on 17 November 1941 (Carell, I, 153.) Contrary to the general belief, mounted Soviet troops served on occasion throughout the war. The Germans also learned in Poland and in France that horse-drawn transport could be often more useful than motorized haul: The former could cross pontoon bridges of much lighter weight and construction.

tion of the troops who were in actual combat. During the Second World War, especially in the West, the majority of troops were not at the "front" (wherever that was). This was even true of the Russians. The "divisional slice," an Americanism, meaning the proportion of the non-combat troops needed to sustain the combatant units, was growing everywhere, because of the increasing mechanization (and also because of the bureaucratization) of war. In the foregoing chapter I suggested that one overall social division that cut across Europe in 1939 was the division separating those people who had automobiles from those who had not. This new kind of transitory elite was reflected by its employment in the war. In most of the armies the ability to drive was a decisive qualification: It determined the military employment of a recruit or of a draftee for the rest of the war.

In the end, equipment told: but never apart from the martial qualities. Of all the states, the Soviet Union under Stalin had spent most on military equipment: from 1.5 billion rubles in 1933, the Soviet budget increased military expenditures to 34 billion rubles by 1938. Whatever the propagandistic purpose in inflating these figures may have been, the events of the war showed that they were not altogether unreal. In 1941 the Soviet Union had a very large army, not altogether well equipped,[11] often poorly led (especially in 1941), frequently poorly trained, yet with hardly any other alternative than to fight on. The positive factors prevailed over the negative ones. Equipment and morale, leadership, and the willingness to fight contributed to each other, they were inseparable; but morale was the decisive element, as indeed almost always in the history of war—even as this had been obscured at times during the horrible slaughter of the First World War, when discipline seemed even more important than morale—indeed, when discipline absorbed morale.

The Germans fought well, the French fought badly, the Italians even worse, the English kept carrying on; Poles were brave, Serbians hot-headed, Romanians calculating, Greeks cunning and tough; the German Army was better than the British Army, the British Navy gave as good as it got, the Russian Navy was lumbering and largely useless,[12] the French fought much better outside their country than within it, Italians were better individually than collectively, Finns fought better in winter than in summer. These generalizations tell something about the Second World War. They were not—or, rather, they should not have been—a surprise

---

[11] In June 1941 only one of five Soviet planes was of a modern design. No anti-tank guns were available before October 1941. Gallagher in Keep, 228.

[12] In June 1941 the Germans had five submarines, ten minelayers, and a few motor torpedo boats in the Baltic; the Russians had two battleships, three cruisers, thirty-five destroyers, and ninety-three submarines. Yet the Russians were on the defensive: They could make no use of this naval superiority at all.

to anyone who knew something about these peoples and of their history of the past hundred years. (The few surprises were the Russians—how they kept fighting on—and, to some extent, the Romanians, who fought better than the Hungarians during the Second World War, this writer must admit.) The qualities of the armies reflected the qualities of nations, but only in certain ways. The trouble with these generalizations is not that they are too sweeping (generalizations, like brooms, are supposed to sweep, not stand in a corner). The problem, for the historian, is that they do not include the behavior of populations—and, as I said earlier, the history of war now included entire populations. Part—but only part—of this were the resistance movements. The Danes put up little fight in the beginning but considerable resistance later. The Slovaks put up no fight and little resistance. London and the English people would take it; the English commanders and their troops in Singapore would not. The people of Leningrad would put up with the prospect of mass starvation at the very time when the people of Kiev were not displeased with the sight of the Germans killing off their Jews. The history of peoples is not easy to write: The historian of the democratic epoch faces a monster task on his own.

Ever since Clausewitz the Germans have been criticized for proceeding by the maxim that war is but the continuation of politics by other means. It is often overlooked that the result of this may be timidity as well as aggressiveness. In the beginning of the war the Western democracies acted according to Clausewitz, though surely in a not very inspiring way. Already during the Munich crisis the British urged the French not to take the offensive even if war were to start over Czechoslovakia. In September 1939 the British and the French went as far as to declare war—and, as we have seen, no farther. They carried their politics of appeasement and of limited commitment into the war, leaving the thinly held German line in the West unharmed, dropping leaflets, not bombs, on Germany. Hitler, as we have seen, did much of the same thing: His Directives Nos. 2, 3, and 4 in early September ordered that "the opening of hostilities must be left to our opponents." He forbade the bombing of English and French cities and French passenger vessels. He was trying to impress his actual opponents, primarily the English, to reconsider the war against him; he was also trying to impress his potential opponents, the Americans. We have also seen that he refrained from bombing English cities until August 1940, and that he restrained the German Navy in the face of many kinds of American provocations until Pearl Harbor. Eventually in the heat of the war these politic restraints melted away on both sides. By September 1940 the Germans were considering fluorine gas shells against Gibraltar that would be sucked into the casemates by the air vents; General Guderian, later a favorite of British and American military historians, was a strong advocate of this. There is some reason to suspect, too, that had the Germans invaded England, the British may not have hesitated to use gas against them.[13]

Eventually the most radical change in the war involved not new weapons but the democratization of warfare. By 1941 the Germans found that no matter how quickly they could force an army to surrender, this was not enough: They might have to face the consequences—of the hostility of entire populations. During the First World War, the wars of states developed into wars of entire nations. During the Second World War, wars became wars among entire peoples. The appearance of partisan warfare in Eastern, and of armed resistance in Western Europe during the second half of 1941, while not decisive in itself, was a turning point in the history of civilization: It signaled the beginning of a new chapter in the history of warfare. Hitler, who knew how to turn Clausewitz upside down, understood this, but understanding was no longer enough. The prospect of the Germans' ultimate defeat in the face of an overwhelming coalition affected the minds of entire peoples, bringing forth among some of them a new kind of participation in war. "This war," said a young French officer to Marc Bloch already at Dunkirk, "taught me a lot, and one of its greatest lessons has been that there are a great many professional soldiers who will never be fighters, and a whole heap of civilians who have fighting in their blood."

## LAND WARFARE

¶ World wars are decided by the command of the seas: This seemed to be the rule during three hundred years. It seemed to be true of the Second World War. "Naval power in world affairs" still governs history, Roosevelt cabled Reynaud on 12 June 1940, in answer to the Frenchman's desperate plea. In 1940 Hitler, without a navy, could not invade England. Four years later the Allies, in command of the seas, invaded the Continent. Hitler did not understand the importance of sea power: He let the war begin with a very small German Navy: that was one of his egregious strategical blunders—this is the still accepted view. But we must look at this again. During the Second World War the most important front was in Eastern, not Western Europe. In 1918 the Western Allies were able to defeat Germany even after Russia had dropped out of the war. During the Second World War they could not have achieved this. On D-Day, in 1944, for each German division in the West there were four German divisions in the East. Had Hitler not had his hands full with the Russians,

---

[13] Lampe, 8.

he could have rushed masses of soldiers to the beaches and thrown the Anglo-American invaders back into the sea.

After many centuries, during the Second World War the primacy of land power returned, in part because of the employment of the internal-combustion engine. It took the British some time to understand this. For hundreds of years one of their principal instruments of victory, especially on the Continent of Europe, were combined operations. Having secured the command of the sea, they could transport and land small armies at points of their choice with impunity, and with the strong prospect of further success. During the Second World War this became a very risky endeavor. In December 1939 the chief of the Imperial General Staff still "pointed out that the Germans were inexperienced in combined operations, and that an invasion of southern Scandinavia would be a very large commitment for them."[14] Soon things turned out otherwise. The Germans' inexperience hurt them not at all; rather, the contrary: The British were defeated in Norway even as they kept their command over much of the North Sea.

The meaning of much of this has been obscured or, rather, misread since that time. The airplane made the battleship obsolete—yet it was (and is) not as simple as that. From the era of land power to that of sea power to that of air power—a kind of technological Darwinism especially dear to American minds—yet air power, while a very important element, was not the decisive one. The Germans could not break the British through air power alone in 1940,[15] and the Allies could not break the Germans through air bombardment in 1941 and after, no matter how massive. Had the Germans been able to throw masses of troops against them in 1943 and 1944, the Anglo-American invasion bridgeheads would have foundered, no matter how many of their planes might be in the sky.[16]

During the Last European War the importance of sea power declined. In 1939, unlike in 1914, the British and the French navies were many times larger than the German one. From this imbalance in their favor the British and the French profited little. Conversely, the Germans were not much hurt by this imbalance during the decisive phase of the war, before 1942. They had a Plan "Z," providing for the construction of a large fleet; but this plan, somewhat hurriedly decreed in 1939, was abandoned soon. No German warship larger than a destroyer was launched during the entire war. Their submarine program, too, advanced slower

---

[14] Woodward, I, 51.

[15] It must be noted, however, that in 1940 nine tenths of the British Isles were beyond the radius of German fighters.

[16] The Anzio operation in January 1944 was an example of this. The Allied control of the sea *and* of the air over their bridgehead availed them little.

than it was (and still is) generally thought: Their admirals Raeder and Doenitz wanted to see at least two dozen new submarines come from the shipyards each month; yet for ten months after the outbreak of the war the average monthly production was three U-boats, rising to six during the second half of 1940. In October 1940 there were less than sixty German U-boats at sea, while there were more than one hundred Italian submarines in the Mediterranean and in the Atlantic.[17] The German submarine danger to Britain was substantial, though far from decisive. Their peak successes occurred in 1942, that is, after America's entry into the war. Nor was the day of the battleship entirely over. The *Scharnhorst* and the *Gneisenau* sank twenty-seven British and Allied vessels in the Atlantic during February–March 1941—more than double the tonnage sunk by the entire German submarine fleet during the same time.[18]

The triumphs of the British Navy in the Atlantic and in the North Sea (the scuttling of the *Graf Spee*, the capture of the *Altmark*, the sinking of the *Bismarck*) were triumphs of prestige rather than decisive events in the sea war. (The same was true of the successful dash of the two German battleships through the English Channel in February 1942.) The prospect—rather than the activity—of British sea power was decisive in the defense of the island against German invasion and in the sea rescue from Dunkirk. The effect of sea power was not as unequivocal as it may seem at first sight. Hitler could have successfully invaded England with parachute troops in June 1940; we have also seen that, had not Hitler ordered them to halt, the German Army could have rolled up the Dunkirk bridgehead, in which event there would have been no one for British ships to rescue.[19] In the Mediterranean, the British Navy defeated the Italian Navy on several occasions; yet the British Navy could not prevent the German invasion and conquest of Crete, or of the Greek islands, or the transport of Rommel's troops and tanks to Africa. We have also seen that the British sea blockade of the Continent was not as effective as had been

---

[17] For more than two years the Italian submarine fleet was the largest in the world. Their performance in the Atlantic was poor, in the Mediterranean inconclusive. One exception to this generalization is the sometimes daring exploits of their midget submarines. Carrying frogmen, they caused havoc among British warships moored in Alexandria at least on one memorable occasion in December 1941.

[18] True, these were attacks on single ships; the German pocket battleships steered clear of most convoys.

[19] We must recall that the British lost almost all their equipment at Dunkirk: of 2,794 British guns that had been shipped to France, only 322 were brought back; 85,000 of their 90,000 vehicles were lost; so was 99.5 per cent of their oil and gasoline supplies in the bridgehead.

thought. This condition persisted even after the American Navy joined the British in the Atlantic. On the other hand, the prestige of American sea power was enormous: It was, in all probability, the primary consideration in Franco's mind in the autumn of 1940 when the latter chose not to commit himself on Hitler's side.

From the very beginning of the war, the Sea Lords were extremely cautious. They would not enter the Baltic, they would not penetrate the Skagerrak even when the Germans landed in Norway, they withdrew from attacking Trondheim. Their slowness could be exasperating on occasion. The mad genius of a Céline had a premonition of this. In 1937 he wrote: "Hah! The English allied with us! Their famous balancing act! Even slower and weaker than the last time! One year for mobilization . . . another year for preparation. . . . By that time we're stuck up for good . . . a 'wait and see' *formidable*. . . . They'll send over a few planes . . . a few generals to lunch *chez* Maurois . . . and discuss a bit with the Ministry about the tunnel under the Channel. . . ."[20] While Churchill's impulsive interventions contributed, at least on one occasion, to the failure of British naval operations (off the coast of Norway on 8–9 April 1940), on many more occasions his imaginative projects had to be abandoned because of the cautious conservatism of his naval chiefs. (Hitler seldom let himself be dissuaded by his generals and admirals; Churchill was compelled to listen to them.) In the fall of 1940 the British Navy did not penetrate the Adriatic, it did not interfere with Italian transports to Albania; in the spring of 1941 the Sea Lords decided against a plan to conquer the feebly garrisoned Italian islands of the Dodecanese in the Aegean; when in October 1941 Churchill, to help the Russians, ordered preparations for a British landing in Norway, he was dissuaded by his generals and admirals, to the great relief of the latter. The First Sea Lord, Sir Dudley Pound, dozed through these important meetings, waking up at the crucial moment of the debate with Churchill in order to put in his bit: a firm no.[21]

Perhaps he should have slept on. Perhaps sleeping sea dogs should be allowed to lie. For that was the time when Stalin said to Beaverbrook: The British must become a land power as well as a sea power. He was entirely right. Indeed, had the British chosen to become a land power, the map as well as the destiny of Europe after the war would have been very different. It is true that Stalin understood little about the difficulties of sea warfare, and that some of his demands for British landing and supply operations in 1941 were not only unreasonable but impossible. Yet Stalin was largely right as he contemplated what, to him, seemed absurd:

---

[20] Céline, *Bagatelles*, 87.
[21] Bryant, 215.

With all of their navy, the British were unable and unwilling to establish their presence anywhere along the long and undefended coasts of an entire continent at the time when the bulk of the German Army was fighting in Russia. Britain ought to have a large army as well as a navy, Stalin told Lord Ismay in September 1941. She could no longer rely on France, even in peacetime. "If Japan can have both an army and a navy, why not England?"

Hitler's underestimation of sea power may have stemmed in part, like Stalin's, from his landlocked (in his case Central European) background. Yet his vision of land power contained elements of his projection of the future. He had a great interest in automobiles. Already in 1924 he wrote in *Mein Kampf:* "The universal motorization of the world, which in the next war will be overwhelmingly decisive in the struggle . . . [Weimar] Germany remained shamefully behind in this most important field. . . ."[22] The passage continued with an expression of his contempt for the Russians, who could not produce a car that would run. Hitler had an interest in cars throughout his life. Immediately after he came to power, he started the building of the *Autobahnen,* expressways that in the 1930s were ahead of the rest of the world, including the United States. Hitler wanted to promote the building of automobiles in the Third Reich; he dropped the excise taxes on them as early as 1933. His engineers were at work on a German People's Car, of which a model was ready by 1938. One of the few photos that show Hitler smiling survives from that year: Hitler contemplating the Volkswagen.[23] The philologist Viktor Klemperer was impressed with the connection between Nazism and *Automobilismus* during the thirties. One of the typical outfits of the thirties in Germany was "the mummified racing driver, with his thick helmet and thick driving gloves . . . ,"[24] moving on to tanks in 1939. The German racing champion Bernd Rosemeyer, who died in a fiery crash in the thirties, was a popular hero whose cult reminded Klemperer of the cult of Horst Wessel. During the halcyon days of Danubian Nazidom, in the late thirties, young Germans of Austria, Hungary, Bohemia, and Slovakia rode

---

[22] Hitler, *MK,* 958. At that time Hitler professed considerable admiration for the United States and for Henry Ford, Sr., with whom his movement had some connections through a middleman.

[23] The 1939 model was very similar to that of the first postwar (1948) Volkswagen. The war cut short the projects for its mass production; the motor and the chassis were used for scout cars and amphibious cars instead. (In this respect, too, Hitler may have been motivated by certain Fascist achievements that he then would supersede: Fiat in Italy had produced cheap cars, with excellent lines and performance, during the 1930s—the Balilla and the Topolino.)

[24] Klemperer, 12.

their motorcycles on the dusty highways in the summer as if they owned the roads (this writer remembers them in their plus-fours and white stockings, standing stiff against their engines at the crossings.)[25] In Hitler's plans for a German-ruled Eastern Europe, automobiles and roads played an important role. The relationship of the ruling Germans to the Slavs would be the relationship of a motorized people to a pedestrian one: "Let them know just enough to understand our highway signs, so that they won't get themselves run over by our vehicles," he said to his circle in October 1941. The Germans shall change the character of the land in Russia: It will no longer remain an Asiatic steppe, "we'll Europeanize it. With this object, we undertake the construction of highways that will lead to the southeastern points of the Crimea and to the Caucasus."[26] Around the cities "in a depth of 30 or 40 kilometers, we shall have a belt of handsome villages, connected by the best of roads. . . ."[27] "The weapons of the future?" Hitler mused in September 1941. "First of all the land armies, then the air arm, and sea power only in the third place."[28]

Hitler's knowledge of tanks was "astounding," said Jodl after the war.[29] Yet Hitler underestimated both the extent and the efficacy of the Russian tank arm. Before November 1941 he believed that the Russians would not be able to do much in the winter.[30] It must be noted that the latter were slow in recognizing the early military lessons of the war in 1939 and 1940. They had masses of tanks, employing them with success against the Japanese in the Mongolian border fighting in 1938 and 1939. Still, as late as in May 1937 their famous Marshal Tukhachevsky attacked the idea of "independent tank formations," which had been proposed by

---

[25] In 1939 Germany had more motorcycles per capita than any other nation in the world: 23.8 per 1,000 inhabitants, a total of nearly 2 million. (The ratio of cars per capita was lower in Germany than in Britain, France, Belgium, Denmark, Luxembourg, Norway, and Sweden: 25 per 1,000 inhabitants. Comparable figures in 1939: Britain 51, France 54, United States 227, Romania 2, Poland 1, Bulgaria 0.7.)

[26] *Hitler TG*, 100.

[27] Ibid., 301 (8–11 Sept. 1941).

[28] Ibid., 34 (10 Sept. 1941).

[29] Schramm, 200–1.

[30] He told the Italian diplomat Magistrati on 2 February 1940: " 'The fact is that nothing can be done with a modern army in winter.' The Fuehrer went into a lengthy discourse regarding the effect of a hard winter on modern mechanized warfare, describing the influence of the cold upon motorized troops. . . . He pointed to parallels in history, remarking that Napoleon would not have been overthrown if the Russian winter had not destroyed his army. . . ." Hitler predicted that the Russians would not take the offensive in Finland before May or June. He was wrong. *DDI*, IX, III, 734.

Fuller, Liddell Hart, and De Gaulle around that time: He attributed to the idea of a highly trained technical army "the bourgeois fear of the masses."[31] In September 1939 the Russians were surprised by the rapid movements of German armored formations in Poland. In November 1939 Stalin ordered the dissolution of the independent Russian tank units. They were reorganized after the Western European campaign, in July 1940.[32] A year later the Russians had sufficient tanks to withstand the tremendous losses inflicted on them by the Germans. Their massive and strong KV and T-34 tanks were in production by 1941, just in the nick of time.[33]

"The internal-combustion engine," Colonel Charles de Gaulle wrote in 1934, "which is ready to carry whatever one wants, whenever it is needed . . . which, if it is armored, possesses such firepower and shock power that the rhythm of the battle corresponds to that of its movements."[34] The French command gave not a thought to De Gaulle's advocacies. The French Tactical Instructions of 1936 were an antiquated rehash of the tactics of the last war. The Germans, of course, recognized this.[35] The French put together two light mechanized divisions by November 1939; two small armored divisions were to be ready by the spring of 1940. Reynaud understood the potential of motorized armies better than had the French generals.[36] During the First World War the

---

[31] Fuller, *CW*, 277.

[32] Bialer, 145, 575–76. Even A. J. P. Taylor could not avoid the sentimental temptation of British intellectuals in attributing qualities to the Soviets that the latter did not possess: in 1939, ". . . as Communists, [the Russians] automatically favored a strategical doctrine more dynamic and revolutionary than that held in the decadent capitalist West. The Russians held that cavalry offensives, now in mechanized forms, were irresistible . . . the Russians asked to go through Poland [in 1939] because they believed, however mistakenly, that this was the only way to win a war. Political aims may have existed as well; but they were subordinate to genuine military needs." Taylor, 247–48.

[33] Relatively few British and American tanks reached Russia in 1941. On 25 November 1941 the Germans encountered a few British Mark III tanks near Solnechnogorsk, destroying most of them. They found Cyrillic instructions chalked on the instrument panels.

[34] *De Gaulle*, I, 16, citing his *Vers l'armée du métier*.

[35] See the German General Eimannsberger's article on the published French Tactical Instructions in *MWB* (28 May 1937): ". . . the tactics of armored units as laid down in this document represent a gigantic misunderstanding."

[36] One German general who was dubious about their effectiveness was Beck, chief of staff in 1938, and later a tragic and pathetic figure in the 1944 conspiracy against Hitler. His hatred of the latter may have overwhelmed his judgment. The French Army was the strongest in Europe, he said to a confidant in 1938. Hitler's offensive in Western Europe, he said to another in October 1939,

masses of troops tramped and crawled ahead in fields; now the armies would advance along the highways of Europe; road maps (such as the excellent Michelin maps in France) were on occasion even more useful to their officers than the standard detailed military maps. The Allies failed to read the lessons of the Polish campaign. In May 1940 the swift thrusts of German motorized infantry caught them by surprise.[37] Even more important than daring infantry attacks on strong points, including parachute descents (such as the successful German attack on the principal Belgian fortress of Eben-Emael), was the condition of the rapid and relatively easy movement of motorized troops around and through the main Belgian "K-W"[38] defense line, for example. The decisive German thrust was, of course, that through the Ardennes—a forest region where, save for the brave resistance of groups of the Belgian Chasseurs Ardennais, the Germans met with no obstacles until they arrived at the Meuse near Sedan. We have seen how the French command neglected this potential movement. In 1934 Pétain wrote that the Ardennes sector was "impenetrable . . . as this front has no depth, the enemy cannot commit himself there. If he does throw his strength at this point, we can pinch him off again, when he comes out of the forests. This sector, therefore, is not dangerous."[39] Impenetrable were not such regions such as the Ardennes, but regions of his mind. On one occasion he muttered at the table of defeat, on 26 May 1940: "We ought to use carrier pigeons. . . . It is regrettable that we have abandoned the use of carrier pigeons. . . ."

But the Fuddy-Duddies were not the only ones who were wrong. So were the New Fogies: the air enthusiasts. In 1921, an Italian general, Giulio Douhet, made a name for himself: He predicted that the next war would be decided in a matter of days, by terrible lightning strikes by bombers, from the air. To predict the future along a simplistic line, as the ever growing continuation of the present (or, rather, what seems to be the present), may be even more wrong than simplistic reliance on the past. The Douhet theory was even more wrong than Pétain's avian recall

---

"is bound to get stuck, I cannot tell where, but that it will get stuck is told me by my forty years of experience." Deutsch, 161–62.

[37] On one occasion, perhaps the last in the history of modern war, an armored train played an important role. The Germans drove it across an important bridge at Gennep in Belgium, at 4 A.M. on 10 May, capturing the bridge intact. The function of the train, however, was different from that of the armored trains of the First World War: This train carried an entire infantry brigade.

[38] Keerbergen to Wavre.

[39] Pétain praised the obtuse work by General Chauvineau, *Une invasion est-elle encore possible?* (Paris, 1938). Invasion: Is it still a possibility? The rhetorical answer of these French worthies was an unfortunately resounding NO.

of pigeons.[40] We have seen that the expected mass-bombing attacks on cities at the start of the war did not happen. We have also seen that air fleets were not decisive: German air power was unable to force Britain to surrender.[41] Later, with less excuse, those American and British strategists who believed that a bombing offensive would break the Germans were even more wrong. In late June 1941 the Germans wiped out nearly half of the Soviet air fleet; even this mattered little in the long run.[42] The airplane was a revolutionary weapon, but only in conjunction with land or sea power. Much of the relative ineffectiveness of sea power has been attributed to the ascendancy of the air: But this is a half truth. It was the Germans' control of land, of coastal bases and airfields along the inland seas and shores of the Continent wherefrom airplanes could rise and attack, that restricted the movements of the British Navy. In this respect, too, the airplane served as a novel kind of artillery rather than as an independent new arm. It was not the airplane but the aircraft carrier that superseded the era of the battleships, even in the Pacific, where the decisive Battle of Midway in June 1942 was fought by swarms of airplanes, for the first time in history. But these had risen from the decks of their carriers: To talk of the Battle of Midway in terms of airplanes alone is as if one talked of land battles solely in terms of bullets and shells, without referring to guns and rifles and the soldiers who manned and carried them. Air power in land warfare was decisive when it performed the function of flying artillery, destroying tanks, trucks, trains, disrupting the troops and supplies of the enemy as it moved along the road.

We have seen how, contrary to most predictions, the Second World War started without bombing attacks: Both sides were cautious, and with reason. Errors marked the first long-range bombing attempts, even in Poland, where the German bombing of towns produced relatively little damage or panic. On 4 September 1939 the RAF attacked a German seaplane base for the first time. The British lost 24 out of the 28 planes,

---

[40] A Luftwaffe commentator in 1944 wrote that Douhet's failure had been due to the character of the Italian people, that Douhet knew how Italians would react to massive bombing and that Douhet simply projected this knowledge to the level of a general rule. This is vastly unfair, for many reasons, one of them being that in 1921 Douhet's futurism was very much in line with much of avant-garde thinking—with Marinetti's futurism, for example.

[41] "Before 1940 there was little to choose between British and German air intelligence. Extraordinary blunders were made on both sides." Wood-Dempster, 48.

[42] True, the Luftwaffe lost nearly one thousand planes in Russia during the first six months of the war.

and managed to drop two bombs on the Danish town of Esbjerg. The Luftwaffe attacked the Shetlands for the first time on 13 September, without much effect. The reluctant war on land was reluctant war in the air, too (though not, as we have seen, at sea). Nocturnal bombing was even less accurate, even less decisive.[43] The Winter War was pockmarked by ugly Russian hit-and-run bombing of Finnish towns, again without much effect. The tenth of May in 1940, however, marked not only the beginning of the real war on land in Western Europe, but also in the air. On 10 May 1940 bombs fell on the German university town of Freiburg-im-Breisgau. The Germans immediately accused the Allies of "terror bombing" when, in reality, those bombs had been dropped by a Luftwaffe pilot by mistake: He had mistaken Freiburg for Dijon (over 150 miles apart). The Germans were now bombing French and Belgian airfields and factories and Dutch cities, including Rotterdam. Eighteen British bombers dropped bombs on the industrial city of München-Gladbach in the Ruhr. On 15 May a combative British Cabinet authorized the strategic bombing of military targets in Germany. On 3 June the Germans bombed the suburbs of Paris; on the night of 9–10 June French seaplanes made a brave lunge at Berlin, which was then bombed on the night of 25–26 August by the RAF for the first time. Consequently Hitler who, as we have seen, forbade the Luftwaffe to attack residential districts of British towns and cities until then, lifted this ban on the bombing of London on August 30[44]: Still, he ordered that "bombing with the object of causing mass panic must be left to the last."[45]

The tragic as well as the dramatic effects of aerial bombing were vastly exaggerated at the time. The Dutch Foreign Ministry, for example, claimed that during the German terror bombing of Rotterdam 30,000 people had lost their lives; in reality the dead numbered less than 1,000.

---

[43] In the beginning German radar functioned better than British radar; by 1940 this was no longer so. A Zeppelin had flown along the east coast of England in May 1939 trying to detect British coastal radar stations. German radar scored an impressive victory in December 1939; as its consequence German fighters were able to destroy two RAF squadrons making for the North German coast.
[44] See above, p. 110. In 1940–41 there was a tacit agreement between the Italians and their enemies. Rome and Athens were spared of bombing. On the other hand, the Italian Air Force would, at times, bomb with a kind of opportunistic cruelty, as for example, its bombing of the undefended Loire valley towns of Gien, Cosnes and Sens a few days before the armistice, or their bombing of the Greek town of Larissa in March 1941, a few days after an earthquake had destroyed 40 per cent of its houses.
[45] The British Cabinet decided to attack German cities without discrimination on 22 February 1942. The first mass bombing by the RAF hit Lübeck on the night of 28–29 March.

Air intelligence was equally at fault. Planes made enormous misses in navigation. The British frequently overflew Switzerland, not always on purpose.[46] In 1941 the Germans dropped bombs on Ireland, on one occasion on Dublin. The bombing of Berlin in 1941 had little more than psychological and demonstrative purposes (the first Soviet air raid on Berlin occurred on the night of 8–9 August 1941). Aerial intelligence made gross errors in the evaluation of air battles. On 8 August the high command of the Luftwaffe concluded that in the heavy operations of the preceding days the ratio of German to English losses in planes was one to three. In reality the Germans had lost 145 planes, the British 87. On 30 August the Luftwaffe evaluated the results of the month: It reported the loss of 791 British planes; the true figure was 261. By and large the Germans reported three British planes for every one that had been lost in reality; the British exaggerated the German losses two to one. On 8 August, for example, the RAF shot down 31 German planes, claiming 60; the Germans shot down 20 British planes, claiming 49. The Germans were the bigger liars.[47]

Early in the war the RAF learned the painful lesson of what could happen to low-flying attacks against bridges and other points defended by massive anti-aircraft artillery. During their brave attack against the bridges on the Meuse, on 14 May alone they lost 40 out of 71 bombers. Later their daylight attacks on German barges and ships assembled in the putative invasion ports were almost wholly ineffective[48]; so was the British bombing of Germany throughout 1940 and 1941, all of which took place at night; so were British attacks on German warships in their docks. The German nocturnal bombing of Britain was also ineffective. On the one hand, the Germans lost less than 1 per cent of their planes during these nocturnal operations; on the other hand, British production rose steadily, even in heavily bombed areas such as Coventry and Bristol.

---

[46] Until 9 November 1940 there was no blackout in Switzerland; its towns and villages remained illuminated, in order to make this neutral land visible from the sky. The blackout was introduced after the Germans had protested that this illumination assisted the navigation of British planes.

[47] Note, however, that the score—as distinct from the meaning—of the British victory in the Battle of Britain (slightly less than two to one in the RAF's favor) is one-sided in the sense that the British mostly lost fighters, while the Germans lost slower-flying planes, mostly bombers. Thus during the crucial week of 7–14 September the RAF lost 94 planes, the Luftwaffe 135—but the latter were mostly bombers or fighter-bomber escorts, flying near the outside limit of their operational radius.

[48] By mid-September 1940 the Germans collected about 3,000 vessels (155 transports, 1,748 barges and lighters, 1,161 motorboats) in the Channel and Lowlands, ports opposite England. By 21 September the RAF sank 9 ships and 52 barges of these. Hillgruber, *HS*, 109, note 119.

We have seen that Hitler was skeptical of the effects of long-range bombing. As early as 23 May 1939 he told his assembled military chiefs that a country could not "be brought to defeat by an air force," including Britain. On 18 November 1940 he told Ciano that "German experience in air warfare over German and English territory had shown that airfields were quickly restored . . . to [retaliatory raids] the English remained quite indifferent and the experience Germany had gained in the air war against England indicated that it did not pay to bomb purely civilian targets."[49] Reynaud, who was right in estimating the importance of tanks, overestimated the importance of air power. Having abandoned Paris, as late as 11–12 June 1940, he still professed to believe that large-scale British air attacks might stem the German tide. He was woefully wrong, while Dowding and Churchill were more than right in keeping the RAF in Britain for what they saw was coming. The record of Churchill's expectations of air power is mixed. He went ahead with the mass bombing of Germany, yet he did not quite trust those of his experts who claimed that 80 per cent of German production could eventually be destroyed from the air. The mass bombing of Germany was the result of his pugnacity, his will to hit and hurt the Germans; but it was also part and parcel of his "Erastian" strategy, hoping to win the war without a mass bloodletting on the Continent, without repeating the horrible land battles of the First World War.[50] By 1941 the British had dropped more than 30,000 tons of bombs on Germany (by 1944 this tonnage of bombs would rise more than twentyfold; still German production was rising). At the same time, the British were also beginning to learn that "the chances of a direct hit on a target . . . were so small as to be negligible."[51] Apart from the very small damage they inflicted on German war production,[52] the raids of 1940–41 cost the lives of more British fliers than of German civilians.[53]

---

[49] *GD*, D, XI, 607.

[50] On 25 July 1941 Churchill told Roosevelt of the British plan to bomb Germany and Italy ceaselessly. "These measures may themselves produce an internal convulsion or collapse." If not, the British would have to land in Europe, "coming to the aid of the conquered populations by landing armies of liberation when the opportunity is ripe." In other words, not a conquering mass army but a rescuing force.

[51] Gwyer, Butler, III, 36.

[52] There was one important difference, seldom noted in retrospect. In 1940 the Germans dropped far more explosive bombs than fire bombs on England. Until 1941 the ratio of the former to the latter was five to one. The British proportion of bombs cast on Germany was the very opposite: three fire bombs to each explosive bomb. After 1942 the British began to change this ratio, having found that fire bombs were less destructive than were explosives.

[53] Calder, 20; also Taylor, *EH*, 519.

Churchill was less sanguine than the American experts.[54] In February 1941 the State Department estimated that bombing would cause the "complete economic collapse" of Germany. General H. H. Arnold of the U. S. Army Air Corps in mid-1941 reported that his visit to England "left me with the impression that by air alone we might bring Germany so completely to her knees that it might be unnecessary for the ground forces to make a landing. . . . Air power and air power alone could carry the war home to central Germany, break down her morale, and take away from her the things essential to combat. . . . Modern war had completely changed the old concepts."[55] This kind of adolescent projection was hardly more valid than were the senile musings of a Pétain; it was certainly unreasonable after the experiences of 1940.[56]

Still, the airplane was a new instrument of warfare, especially when it was employed tactically, in support of land armies; its neglect could be dangerous and inexcusable. Here, too, the French had been especially hidebound and neglectful,[57] while the Germans were especially imaginative in profiting from the new dimension of the air over the battlefield. They used glider planes daringly in Belgium and, what is less known, in one instance (at Bardufoss) in Norway.[58] More important was their employment of parachute troops. Hitler recognized the importance of the quick transport of troops through the air. It was he who suggested to

---

[54] To the chief of the Air Staff, October 1941: "Even if all the towns of Germany were rendered largely uninhabitable, it does not follow that the military control would be weakened or even that war industry could not be carried on. The Air Staff would make a mistake to put their claim too high." *GA*, 508.

[55] Wilson, 134–35.

[56] Nor were Charles Lindbergh's projections excusable. In September 1940 Lindbergh lectured American general staff officers with his conviction: England "would soon collapse" before German air power. This was promptly reported by the German Embassy to Berlin, on 18 September 1940. *GD*, D, X, 415, note 6.

[57] In 1939 none of their planes were produced en masse. Contracts for their construction had been given out as political favors during the thirties. On one occasion a "furniture maker obtained a contract for an all-metal aircraft." In the fall of 1939 secret papers of the Air Ministry were stowed away in an experimental wind tunnel in the suburbs of Paris. The planning bureaucrats forgot to notify the personnel of the station. One day the wind tunnel was started and the papers were "scattered over an entire Paris suburb . . . and this was the first breath of fresh air that ever blew through the French Air Ministry." J. Jalbert, *Les erreurs fatales du Ministère de l'Air* (Paris, 1941), cited in Wood-Dempster, 91.

[58] The condition that Germany had been forbidden to train an air force after 1919 may have stood them in good stead: After 1932 they drew on the experiences of hundreds of glider pilots.

General Student that the latter's parachutists might be used against certain Belgian forts on the Albert Canal, including Eben-Emael, where 580 German parachutists turned the trick. The image of the German parachutists (as well as the screaming sirens of the Junkers 87 dive bombers) helped to induce panic. On 21 May 1940 the Dutch Foreign Ministry in London announced at a press conference that German parachutists had descended in Holland dressed as nuns, monks, and streetcar conductors.[59] The most important, and revolutionary, employment of parachutists was that of the German landing in Crete. There it was General Student who had to convince a reluctant Hitler of the practicability of such an operation.[60] Flying from airfields in southern Greece, the Luftwaffe succeeded in maintaining a close blockade of the entire island from the air, proving that sea power without air cover had become ineffective. Still, the Germans suffered large losses in Crete: Had it not been for the poor communications and the feeble armor of the British forces (the British had only six tanks on the island), the Germans could have been wiped out, as they almost were. Hitler recognized this. On 2 June 1941 he told Mussolini that Cyprus could not be taken, for the conquest of Crete from the air had been a unique experience that could not be repeated.

As the war went on, more and more modern airplanes appeared. In 1939 the fighter planes of some nations still resembled those of the late phase of the First World War; there were biplanes and high-wing monoplanes still in active service, among which the slow-flying British Swordfish was effective as late as in November 1940, when a squadron successfully damaged Italian warships at Taranto. The last biplane mass-produced was the Russian Tchaika in 1939, a disastrously bad model.[61] By 1940 the low-winged plane had become universal. Contrary to general belief, the German fliers' experiences during the Spanish Civil War had taught them little, save for one thing: They discovered the advantages of abandoning close formations such as the classic "V"; instead, they were flying more and more in loose pairs (*Ketten*). The Messerschmitt 109 was, without doubt, the best mass-produced plane of the war. The British Spitfire was not its equal, though a fair match for it sometimes.[62] By 1939

---

[59] What was true was that certain Dutch Nazis, resident in Germany, had landed wearing Dutch uniforms.

[60] Hitler to Student, 21 April 1941: " 'It sounds all right, but I don't think it is practicable.' But I managed to convince him in the end." Student to Liddell Hart, cited by Stewart, *Crete*, 44.

[61] The Germans were ahead of their enemies not only in their design of fast fighters but also in their recognition of the importance of slow and low-flying courier planes, among which the Fieseler "Storch" served them especially well throughout the war.

[62] The first Spitfire prototype was flown on 5 March 1936.

German designers had made great progress, but some of their more daring designs were not translatable into serial production. The first jet plane in the history of the world, a Heinkel 176 prototype, flew on 20 June 1939; a fortnight later it reached the then unheard of speed of 550 mph for a few minutes; on 27 August the first Heinkel 178 jet plane took to the air. A Messerschmitt 263 was the first plane to fly faster than 600 mph, on 10 March 1941; the Messerschmitt 262 jet, the most advanced plane of the entire war, was first flown in July 1942; its serial production came too late (in late 1944) to help the Germans much. The Italians flew a prototype jet in early 1941.

The air forces were the instruments of the young, engaging the imagination of millions. The encounters of fighters in the skies also brought back something reminiscent of the old chivalry of individual combat. Yet war was still war: Technology may have changed the conditions of combat but not human nature and, therefore, the nature of war. This was not immediately recognized by older people; it also affected, naturally, the judgment of the young. "I have a reactionary Navy, an imperial Christian Army, and a National Socialist Air Force," Hitler said on occasion. In the Luftwaffe at the age of twenty-five a young German could become a major.[63]

Still, the most radical changes in warfare took place on land. One of these was the rapid movements of armor and of motorized troops along the roads; another, perhaps more important, was the appearance of armed civilians. The army represents that state. The people represent the nation. Until the Last European War, in the history of modern Europe the acceptance of defeat by the army meant the end of the war. After 1939 the surrender of the army, and thereby of the state, no longer necessarily meant the surrender of the people, and therefore of the nation. This was less evident in Western Europe in 1940 than in Eastern Europe in 1941. But by that time even in France and in the Lowlands a national and popular resistance was beginning to emerge. The end of the military phase of the war did not mean the end of the war. The Germans were pained by this. Even in retrospect they write about this kind of warfare with a kind of self-conscious regret, deploring the barbarism of this kind of warfare, unwilling to attribute to guerrillas, resisters, and partisans the respect that, in their opinion, was more or less due to the military par-

---

[63] Nearly every general officer during the Second World War had had some combat experience during the First; but few of the general officers during the First World War had command positions during the Second. Significant exceptions include General Falkenhorst of the German Army; Admiral Tovey of the British Navy, who hunted down the *Bismarck* in 1941, had fought at Jutland twenty-five years earlier.

ticipants of *Normalkrieg.* Yet the Germans were themselves responsible for this new kind of war. In the past, conquered populations almost always breathed easier whenever the military government ruling them relinquished its authority to a civilian administration. During this war the opposite was true. The German military were almost always preferable to the German civilian authorities. Even a rigid and unimaginative Prussian general was better than the usually unscrupulous Nazi chief who came in his stead.[64]

Continuing war: war between armies and peoples; this was a phenomenon appearing first in 1940–41, of potentially great importance for the future. There were at least four kinds of armed civilians:

1. forces of armed civilians, organized by the government, to be left behind in the land under enemy occupation. Principal examples: Britain, Switzerland.
2. groups of armed civilians, arising more or less spontaneously, sustained by their governments in exile and by allies abroad, with the purpose of sabotage, and of increasing harassment of the occupying power and of its collaborators. Principal examples: the budding resistance movements of Western Europe.
3. bands—patriotic, communist, or otherwise—roaming over considerable portions of a countryside that the occupying enemy, because of the limited number of its troops available for occupation duties, could not entirely control. Principal examples: the nationalist and communist guerrilla armies in Serbia and Greece.
4. auxiliary forces of the occupation armies.

Of these categories much is known about (2) and (3), less about (4), little about (1). These categories are necessarily incomplete and inaccurate: The four kinds overlap. The brave Polish Home Army, for example, combined the functions of (2) and (3). The Soviet partisan forces were something else again: Mostly fitting the description of (3), they had something of (1), dependent as they were (though not always) on the directives of the central government.

In Britain in 1940 a nationwide resistance network was in the making. Much of its organization is a secret even now; it has been described in a short book by David Lampe in 1968. The interest in this book lies not only in its author's description of the clandestine manner in which these armed civilians were being trained but also in his description of how the British resistance had been conceived. In June 1940 General Andrew

---

[64] In October 1939 Hitler declared that the army should get rid of the task of running Poland. In May 1940 he ordered the end of the military administration in Holland and in Belgium.

Thorne, the former British military attaché in Berlin and commander of the 48th Division at Dunkirk, was put in charge of the XII Corps area in southeastern England, preparing for an eventual German invasion. He found the troops at hand few in number and woefully unprepared. "And then,"

> he remembered something that he had seen in East Prussia six years earlier. The principal of the Charlottenburg High School, a military training college in Berlin, had shown him around his family's estates in East Prussia. The land had been given to an ancestor by Frederick the Great on condition that a private army be provided to protect it against invasion from the east. When Thorne visited the estates in 1934 some of the descendants of the original peasant soldiers were digging new defences on the crests of hills, and these were being stocked with arms, ammunition and food. The peasants would not be able to stop a modern invading army, Thorne's friend explained, but when it had passed over they would be able to play hell with its supply and other supporting units. Why not, General Thorne asked himself in Kent that summer 1940, prepare the same sort of civilian 'stay-behind' troops in XII Corps' coastal areas?
>
> He got in touch with General Ismay at the War Office and was told that an officer would be sent along to raise and to train just such a body of civilians who would be known as the XII Corps Observation Unit. . . .[65]

There is a strange unreality to General Thorne's East Prussian story, for it is the only account we have of such activities in East Prussia in 1934 or, at that, afterward. What matters, however, is that this British general asked himself the right question and did the right thing about it. Soon the result was that "alone among the countries that opposed Germany in the Second World War, Britain had a complete resistance organization—trained, armed and waiting more or less patiently for German invaders to arrive. . . ."[66] (An exaggeration: perhaps not quite *alone*, not quite *complete*: still, almost so.) Apart from Thorne, a small group of officers in British Military Intelligence Research had begun to study and organize clandestine operations by armed civilians as early as 1939. It was eventually led by Major Colin Gubbins, a remarkable man[67]

---

[65] Lampe, 2.
[66] Lampe, 62.
[67] In 1939 Major Gubbins was writing booklets with titles such as: *Partisan Leader's Handbook* and *The Art of Guerrilla Warfare*. This should dispose of the legend that partisan and guerrilla warfare in Europe arose from an imitation of Russian and communist practice in 1941 and after.

who set up the "auxiliary units" (much about their organization remains secret even now).

These elite resistance groups had to depend on the support of the entire population; but, then, this was a foregone conclusion of Churchill's government. In June 1940 the "Stand Firm" notices and leaflets posted up in certain places of southern England said that the civilian population is not "expected to adopt a purely passive role."

> On the contrary, the Government has always expected that the people of these islands will offer a united opposition to an invader and that every citizen will regard it as his duty to hinder and frustrate the enemy and help our own forces by every means that ingenuity can devise and common sense suggest.

The army of common sense was the Home Guard, a veritable people's army, which was announced in a broadcast by Eden on the evening of 14 May 1940; the broadcast was not yet over when the first volunteers arrived to register at police stations.

Similar to these English preparations were those of the Swiss. They, too, organized something like a national mobilization; in 1939, alone among the nations of the world, they raised the age limit for compulsory military service to the age of 60. Their commander-in-chief, General Guisan (unlike their commander-in-chief, General Wille, during the First World War) soon became immensely popular; we have seen the preparations he and his staff had made for a resistance of hard-core fighting in the south-central Alps of Switzerland. Like the British, the Swiss also had a Home Guard of their own, *Ortswehren*, called into existence by Guisan in May 1940. By the end of the summer they numbered nearly one hundred thousand.

It is both inspiring and satisfactory to record that the most extensive national preparations for a patriotic and popular struggle to the death existed in Britain and Switzerland, in these old, liberal, comfortable democracies of Western Europe. Of course, the invasion never came: We do not know how these civilian armies would have stood their ultimate test.[68] Neither the Home Guard nor the *Ortswehren* figured in the German invasion plans of their respective countries; still, there is reason to believe that the Germans would have had to pay dearly for this kind of oversight. They were aware of the spirit of widespread patriotism both in England and in Switzerland; this awareness probably contributed to

---

[68] They were, of course, poorly armed, especially in the beginning. In the Imperial War Museum in London one can see coshes and sawbacked swords issued to the Home Guard in 1940.

Hitler's unwillingness to invade these countries. Again, there was something ancient and atavistic in the reactions of these peoples; again, one of the most revolutionary changes in war was due to the reappearance of a very ancient kind of fighting practice. Had the Germans invaded these countries, the clock would have been turned back five hundred or six hundred years.

The clandestine partisan and guerrilla forces that came into being in Greece, Yugoslavia, and Poland in 1941 were inspired by national traditions that were less distant in time, especially in the Balkans, where patriotic guerrilla activity was often difficult to distinguish from tribal banditry. Its function after 1941 was made possible by the small number of German troops available for occupation duties, as well as by the new conditions of land warfare, whereby German control was often limited to towns and the roads. Thus a few weeks after the capitulation of the Yugoslav Army it appeared that the Germans exercised little or no control over large tracts of Serbia, Macedonia, Slovenia, and Montenegro. Much of the same was true of Greece, and to a lesser extent even of portions of Poland and France.

The appearance of the partisans in the Soviet Union was different. There the sabotage by armed people behind the German lines was planned and prepared by the government to some extent; but not too much should be made of the official Soviet claims. "A native love of banditry rather than any affection for communism"[69] stimulated the first partisans into action. They did considerable harm and damage to the Germans, especially after the fortunes of the war had turned against the latter. Yet the motives of the partisans, especially in 1941, were probably mixed, while their purposes were far from clear, probably not even to themselves. They were mostly active in southern Byelorussia and in the central Ukraine—regions where the comportment of entire populations was mixed, at least in the beginning of the war, since the majority may have been amenable to collaboration with the Germans.[70]

By late 1941, all of Hitler's expressed inclinations to the contrary notwithstanding, the Germans began to collect and organize auxiliaries in Russia and in the Ukraine. These *Hiwis* (*Hilfsfreiwillige*)—more than 200,000 in German service by the end of 1941—were different from the satellite troops and the non-German SS units. Their function and their organization is definable only with difficulty, even in retrospect. Their

---

[69] Reitlinger, *House*, 230.

[70] In the town of Borisov, 7,620 Jews were massacred in October 1941; the Germans recorded that many of the most eager local murderers were former Communists.

presence did not become important until 1944, beyond the confines of this book. In the beginning they received only few arms from the Germans. Yet they were clothed in a kind of German uniform. Again, the general term of armed civilians, no matter how imprecise, fits them best. By the end of 1941, on the Eastern Front, it was difficult for the unexperienced eye to distinguished between soldiers and civilians. Virtually everyone wore some kind of uniform. But this condition reflected not the increasing militarization, or Prussianization, of that world, rather the contrary: It signified the increasing democratization, including a certain kind of individualization, of warfare. *Hiwis*, satellite soldiers, varieties of armed civilians as well as regular soldiers, made up a considerable portion of their uniforms; they did this not only out of personal vanity or calculation but also responding to practical needs.[71] This kind of democratic indiscipline spread. It was typical of the British and French and German airmen who already in 1940 often bedecked themselves in flamboyant fashion. This was the beginning of a new and vast phenomenon whose end is not yet: the erosion of the distinction between combatants and noncombatants, between the military and the civilian areas and forms of life. Professional and amateur soldiers were becoming less and less distinct; only experience counted, and that, too, could be acquired rapidly. When the German Labor Volunteer Force, the "Todt Army," was marching and presenting arms with shovels on their shoulders, some of the French spectators were inclined to laugh. Soon they were to learn that the Todt Army could produce as effective soldiers as any.

The volunteer in the French underground who got his first pistol in 1941 may have toyed with it with a kind of nervous interest, and he may have cut less of a figure at his first clandestine instruction meeting than had the recruit of a national army at his basic training; but the former could be trained for the exigencies of the Second World War at least as fast as the latter. Some of the modern weapons contributed to this: The machine pistol or the submachine gun required far less training in marksmanship than the classic infantry rifle. And thus again the war brought back conditions that were very old; land warfare, involving entire populations, returning to some of the brutal conditions of early modern or late medieval Europe, especially in the eastern half of the continent: a rising specter of guerrilla, with every native a potential combatant and, therefore, a potential enemy: *homo homini lupus.*

---

[71] By December 1941 the German soldiers had learned how their tight boots with their steel hobnails, no matter how thick and strong the leather, would cause them intolerable pains of cold and frost. They learned then how to wear loose boots, or layers of woolen socks stuffed with paper; thus, at least in their footwear, they began to imitate their Russian enemies.

## THE MARTIAL QUALITIES

¶ The morale of an army, Napoleon said, counts at least two thirds; its organization and its equipment are the rest. This remained true during the Second World War, all of the mechanization and the technology of warfare notwithstanding, with one important distinction: The morale of the organized armies closely reflected the morale of the entire nation. Napoleon could wage brilliant campaigns with a brilliant army that had been drawn from the large but in many ways disunited French people. During the Second World War this was no longer possible. The democratic development of nations welded them together. When national purpose was wanting, the army fell apart. During the First World War the multinational Austro-Hungarian Army held together, almost until the very end. In 1941, the multinational Yugoslav Army fell apart at the first German blow: The Croats deserted the Serbs.

In one sense the traditional acceptance of leadership was even more important than in the past when, for example, cavalrymen in battle or in pursuit had been largely on their own, since their leaders could not communicate changing orders to them. Good leadership: good soldiers. As the German military were wont to say: *Die Truppe das Spiegelbild ihrer Fuehrer* (The troop reflects its leaders). This explains much, though not all, of the amazing performance of the German Army. There was the usual, and deeply embedded, German inclination to respect and obey authority; there was the excellence of traditional German training, combined with the modern German aptitude for mechanics; there was a sense of national self-confidence that grew in German minds after their triumphs, a belief that a German soldier was worth two enemy soldiers in battle, a belief comparable to that of the English sailor in the eighteenth century. Because of the survival of these traditions German general officers performed well even when they were not National Socialists. Indeed, sometimes the Army was a kind of non-Nazi enclave within the state, one of the last respectable places for conservatives. In this respect there was a certain similarity in the role of the army in Hitler's Germany and in Stalin's Russia. Many Russians still remember—and the last poignant chapters of Pasternak's *Doctor Zhivago* record this feeling—how, in spite of its looming perils and tragedies, they reacted to the outbreak of their war in 1941 with a feeling of liberation, of great inner relief; the atmosphere of danger and death was like a gust of the cold and clear air of patriotism, driving out the miasmatic fear of the oppressive terror of the regime. In Germany, too, for some men their career in the Army was a kind of *innere Emigration,* a flight from the dreadful commonplace world of Nazidom into a higher and, they felt, more traditional national enterprise.

To some extent this kind of psychic release was universal: Sensitive Englishmen and Frenchmen remembered how the war, with all of its terrors, gave them a kind of vacation, a welcome break from the soullessness of their commercial or bureaucratic existence. Their memories, in retrospect, enhanced this charm of the adventurousness: Many men and women found a new outlook, perhaps even a new purpose in life, during their perils through the bombardments of the war. Yet, as we have seen, these inner experiences developed during the war, rather than at its outbreak, as in 1914. In 1939 the peoples of Europe had responded to the war with a kind of sullen discipline, without any of the popular enthusiasms of 1914.

Poland may have been the only partial exception to this. But the Poles misled themselves. They underestimated the German Army, while they overestimated their Western Allies. The inadequate preparations of the Polish Army corresponded with this political state of mind. The Army was poorly equipped, its highest leadership far from adequate. (The Polish pilots were fine fliers. Despite the inferiority of their machines, they destroyed 160 German planes in September 1939. During the Battle of Britain the 303rd Polish Air Force Squadron led in the number of German planes shot down.) Many of the Poles' tactics were outdated; they relied on the experiences of the successful war that Poland had fought against the Soviets in 1920, just as they relied on the traditional meaning and the effects of their Allies' declaration of war. But the British and French declarations of war on Germany in September 1939, no matter how traditional in form, meant little in practice. When the Polish ambassador to France asked for a French air attack on Germany on 2 September, Bonnet told him: "You do not expect us to have a massacre of women and children in Paris!" After about a week the French moved a few patrols forward in the no-man's-land on the German border. This kind of cautionary warfare simply confirmed the impression in Hitler's mind that he had for many years: The martial qualities of the French Army were worth little or nothing, while the British did not have their heart in the war. The Poles fought on with great bravery in many places. At least in 1939 the middle ranks of their command—one-star generals, colonels, majors, captains—gave a better account of themselves than had their high command. Their epic defense of the Westerplatte, their resistance even when encircled by large German units, the discipline with which tens of thousands of their troops retreated and crossed under difficult conditions into Romania or Hungary and then made their way eventually to France, suggested the endurance and the flowering of their martial qualities on alien battlegrounds later during the war.

[269]

A few days after the Russians struck Poland from the back, German and Soviet troops met along the demarcation line. In Brest-Litovsk there was a curious parade: Soviet troops marching past a line of German and Russian high officers. The former were not impressed with the discipline and with the equipment of the Russians—an impression that contributed to their general underestimation of the Russian Army in 1940 and in 1941. In 1939 the opinion of military experts in almost every country was nearly unanimous: The Russian Army was woefully weak in command. There was every reason for holding such an opinion. We know now that at least 1 of every 2 higher officers of the Red Army were either dismissed or executed during the 1936–39 purges: 3 out of 5 marshals, 13 of 15 army commanders, 57 of 85 corps commanders, 110 of 195 division commanders, 220 of 406 brigade commanders. The sorry performance of the Army during the Winter War with Finland further contributed to this low impression.[72] The Soviet Air Force was ineffective, the command was poor, and the troops ignorant, sometimes to an astonishing degree. Stalin and his circle did not think that the Finns would fight. Voroshilov and Mekhlis were responsible for the poor general planning of the campaign. At Suomossalmi a determined Finnish colonel, Siilasvuo, outmaneuvered and outfought two Soviet divisions with a handful of units.[73] Yet is is true that the Russians had mobilized but one military district (Leningrad) at the start of the campaign; and, once they pushed large numbers of units and artillery forward to the Karelian front, their superiority began to tell. Through massive attacks, including the massed employments of tanks[74] and armored sledges, they broke through the Karelian defenses. By the end of the campaign they had brought up 1 million soldiers against Finland. This was not lost on the Finns. In 1941, during the second round of their war with Russia, they were cautious: Even though they had experienced the inferior mettle of the Soviet Army, they had a higher opinion of the endurance of the Russian soldier than had the Germans—or, at that, most of the British and the American experts—in 1941.[75]

---

[72] The so-called Molotov cocktail was, contrary to general belief, not a Communist invention but the name given by Finns and their friends to a handmade weapon used against Russians during the winter war.

[73] Erickson, 565.

[74] Infantry and tanks of the Red Army, including early T-34 models, fought well against the Japanese at the frontier battles of Mongolia, near Nomonhan, in August–September 1939. Still Stalin chose to disperse tanks among infantry units, because of poor advice; see above, p. 254.

[75] While not underestimating the Russians, the Finns overestimated the power of their German allies—who, it must be said, treated the Finns with great consideration. In January 1940 the French gave to Finland certain guns dating from

The British campaign in Norway, Hitler said, "can only be described as frivolous dilettantism." Their intelligence was stodgy, and full of holes, to begin with.[76] Chamberlain's unfortunate statement, shortly before Hitler's daring invasion of Denmark and Norway: "He [Hitler] missed the bus," was but a little more foolish than Churchill's statement, less well known, that the latter made after the news broke: "We have the Germans where we want them."[77] Churchill was responsible for much of the "frivolous dilettantism" of the Norway campaign. For once his intuitive grasp of events failed him: He did not foresee what the Germans were about to do, whereas the Germans assessed the British plans far better. As early as 26 March, Raeder told Hitler that the British would mine the Norwegian coastal waters in hope for a German reaction that then would furnish the pretext for a British landing in Norway. Churchill's plan for mining the Leads (Wilfred) started slow and late and petered out in foggy confusion at sea. Denmark had nearly 15,000 men under arms, but she gave up without a fight: At the Schleswig frontier the guards were asleep; there was but the symbolic firing of a few shots by the Royal Guards at Amelienborg Castle. In Norway the period of compulsory military training had been the shortest in Europe, a mere thirteen weeks: One half of the 13,000 Norwegian troops was in the Far North because of the anxiety of the government about Russia. Their equipment was inadequate, in any event. One of the Norwegian warships in service had been launched in 1858. Still, the Norwegians' reactions were faster than those of the British, who were slow, ineffective, and scattered. Again, it was not only the case of old-fashioned tactics against a thoroughly modern and aggressive enemy; the Germans knew better than the British how to draw upon past experiences, too.[78] Twenty thousand Allied troops

---

the Crimean War. In late 1941 the Germans gave the Finns some of their newest Messerschmitt 109 fighter planes.

[76] As the excellent British official historian of the campaign put it: "The geographical position of Norway and the character of its terrain still encouraged the dangerous belief that 'The country is easy to defend' (*Norway Year Book, 1938*)—a statement which probably refers not only to the supposed invulnerability of the mountaineous hinterland but to the comfortable belief (not confined to Norwegians) that recent developments had made no difference to the traditional and almost automatic protection of their coasts by the British Navy." Derry, 6.

[77] Also, Churchill on 27 January 1940; "Hitler has already lost his best chance." Eden on 25 October 1939: "Already Herr Hitler has lost the initiative."

[78] Hitler read and esteemed the thesis of Admiral Wegener (*Die Seestrategie des Weltkrieges* [Berlin, 1929], in which this author had berated the German

against 24,000 Germans were at hand in Norway: surely not a hopelessly outnumbered force. The French fought better in Norway than the British; their generals, such as Bethouart, were models of bravery compared to the British General Mackesy. At Narvik it was the French Chasseurs Alpins and the Poles who turned the balance against the Germans, whose daring commander, General Dietl, was considering giving up the town as early as on 23 April; the town fell to the Allies only a month later.[79] The Norwegian commander-in-chief, General Ruge, was bitterly disappointed with the British. On the afternoon of 20 April, at the dark and cold mountain town of Slagbrenna, British and German troops met face to face for the first time in the Second World War. The British retreated. This was typical of the entire campaign. Their morale was also low, as General Auchinleck's report in 1941 admitted.

This passed soon. During the six weeks of war in Western Europe the British fought better than the French who, during the entire Second World War, fought better for their country abroad than on their own soil.[80] When on 16 May Churchill asked Gamelin about the state of the French Army, the latter shrugged his shoulders: "inferiority of numbers, inferiority of equipment, inferiority of method."[81] He should have added: inferiority of morale. On the Meuse the third-rate 71st and 55th divisions had melted in an instant; their general (Baudet) also seems to have lost his head. General Beaufre recorded the following terrible scene at the military headquarters of the armies of France, at La Ferté-sous-Jouarre, at

---

Navy for not having taken advantage of the "wet triangle" between Germany, Denmark, and Norway, where German naval supremacy might have been decisive. General Falkenhorst, the German commander in Norway, had been chief of staff to Von der Goltz in Finland in 1918 (whose memoirs Hitler read). It did not occur to the British, on the other hand, to study some of the amphibious and supply lessons on their own landing at Murmansk and Archangel in 1918. British air attacks failed in Norway not because of German opposition but because of the British inability to find the targets: The town plans of Norwegian cities were unavailable. "It appears that our main resource was the town plans in Baedeker's *Scandinavia* (revised 1912)." Derry, 54.

[79] The French, with a courteous gesture, allowed the Norwegian battalion to enter Narvik on 28 May. Ten days later the town was evacuated, as the Allies were abandoning all of Norway because of the tremendous events on the Western Front.

[80] There were a few exceptions to this. The left wing of the French Army, which had entered Holland, fought poorly from the beginning; it was incapable of retaking the islands around Dordrecht that had been captured on 10–11 May by a handful of German advance troops.

[81] Churchill, *FH*, 49.

the crucial moment of 3 A.M. on the morning of 14 May, when the Germans were crossing the Meuse:

> when we arrived at about three o'clock in the morning all was dark except in this room which was barely half-lit. At the telephone Major Mavereau was repeating in a low voice the information coming in. Everyone else was silent. General Roton, Chief of Staff, was stretched out in an armchair. The atmosphere was that of a family in which there had just been a death. Georges got up quickly and came to Doumenc. He was terribly pale. "Our front has been broken at Sedan! There has been a collapse." He flung himself into a chair and burst into tears. He was the first man I had seen weep in this campaign. Alas, there were to be others. It made a terrible impression on me.[82]

Beaufre also remembers the last dinner with Gamelin, on the twentieth: "An enormous confection covered with spun sugar" was brought to the table. "It was grotesque and pathetic. I felt like weeping or hoping that the ceiling would fall on us."[83]

Weygand was hardly better. After the smooth, political Gamelin, indecisive and cautious to the point of cowardice, came the rigid, small Weygand, outwardly a prototypical representative of the old conservative general officerdom of France, yet even more grandiloquent than his incompetent predecessor:

> You are asking my opinions of the French Army. I tell it to you frankly, with a single-minded regard for the truth, which shall not hamper me. I think that the French Army is more battleworthy (a une valeur plus grande) than any time before in its history. She possesses material of first quality, fortifications of the first order, an excellent morale, and a remarkable high command. . . . If we're compelled to fight for another victory, let me affirm: We shall win again![84]

This was Weygand who less than a week after he had assumed command was the first Frenchman in a responsible position to suggest that an armistice (that is, capitulation) might be inevitable. Having ordered his armies to retreat everywhere, Weygand would still relapse into grandiloquence. In a memorandum on 10 June he said "our troops fought heroically"—in order to sweeten the pill of his advocacy of capitulation. He also said at the same time that "in many instances the sense of discipline and duty has been wanting"—but only in order to buttress his po-

---

[82] Beaufre, 175.
[83] Ibid., 188.
[84] In July 1939. Destrem, 47.

litical inclinations: "We are paying for twenty years of lying and of demagoguery. . . . We have nothing comparable to oppose the Germans. There is neither initiative nor real discipline among our troops." "The situation gets worse every day," Baudouin added. The new Under-Secretary of Defense spoke up. "If the situation gets worse it is because we allow it to do so." This was De Gaulle, about whom Weygand said at the end of this meeting, behind his back: "He is more of a journalist than an officer."[85]

That day the French Cabinet had decided to leave Paris, which Weygand declared an open city. He gave detailed orders not to defend Paris.[86] In his memoirs he later wrote: "To this decision, which is personal to myself, Paris, almost alone of the great European capitals, owes it that, in this first peril, it maintained its beauty intact." Spears' comment upon this is true and just: "There may be amongst future generations of Frenchmen those who think that a few ruins in Paris would have been more becoming to her fame than her unscarred beauty."[87] But, then, Weygand was but one among the party of the defeatists. "To make Paris a city of ruins will not affect the issue," said Pétain. He was right. Only this conservative should have recalled what once a brave and saintly French patriot, Péguy, wrote Sorel: "You are right, but one has no right to be right unless one is willing personally to pay the price of demonstrating the rightness of the truth." In 1940 Pétain paid no price; on the contrary, he was rewarded for his convictions. (He paid the price in 1945.) It is hardly surprising that with such commanders-in-chief the French fought so badly. In June 1940 in Cherbourg (the same place where the Germans held out for weeks in 1944) thirty thousand French soldiers surrendered in a matter of hours. They fought badly on land and in the air, though they showed some resolution at sea. The Germans found large numbers of unused guns, trailers, carriers in armament depots; the French made few attempts to destroy anything; even gasoline dumps were left awash where a single strike of a match would have set them ablaze. One of the first bitter volunteers of what would become eventually the resistance, Guilleaume de Benouville, described his fury at seeing soldiers who begged cigarettes from the Germans along the roads. The cowardice of some of the soldiery reflected that of the population. On 11 June, when the French Navy made a brave sortie to shell Genoa from the sea, the populace in the South prevented French and British bombers, ready to at-

---

[85] Baudouin, 94.
[86] Two days later, in his letter to Roosevelt, pleading for help, Reynaud repeated Clemenceau's phrases: "We shall fight before Paris; we shall fight behind Paris." (He did not say "We shall fight in Paris.")
[87] Spears, II, 148.

tack Italian towns, from taking off on certain airfields.[88]. The performance of the armistice army was no better.[89] It was not only wanting in equipment[90]; but, notwithstanding the often valiant efforts of some of its general officers (Generals De Lattre, Armengaud; Colonel Schlesser), its discipline and morale remained low.

There were exceptions—almost always due to bravery in leadership. This was the case of the heroic defense of the Loire bridge by the cadets of Saumur, of De Gaulle's two armored counterattacks, of the French defenders of Boulogne who held out even after the British, and of many of the French defenders of Dunkirk, even after they had to be left behind.[91] Contrary to the general belief, most of the units in the Maginot Line positions maintained their fighting spirit to the end (the most commendable was the XLIII Army Corps, led by General Lescannes, who refused to capitulate, even on 22 June). The fort of Pepinster, outside of Liège, commanded by the Belgian Captain Devos, held out until 28 May. Compared to some of the Belgians,[92] the Dutch fought poorly. Their famous cyclist units were wholly ineffective for the exigencies of modern war.

Against the Italians, the French excelled; far inferior in numbers, the French commander (General Olry) held the Italians almost everywhere for fourteen days. At the coastal station on the Riviera highway outside

---

[88] The ironic Galtier recorded two contemptible examples of civilian abjectitude. Around 16 June French colonial troops tried to make a stand at the outskirts of a village in the department of Seine-et-Marne. The mayor tried to convince them that they had better surrender: Otherwise the Germans would burn the village down. The Senegalese refused: They had been told that the Germans were killing all blacks. The *maire* then led them to a patch of forest where they could take refuge, and consequently directed the Germans to the forest himself. Galtier, 43. The other story told of a French prisoner who escaped from Germany in January 1941. After his rent had accumulated six months in arrears (because of his clandestine status this escaped prisoner could find no work), the landlord denounced him to the German authorities. Ibid., 46.

[89] On 14 July 1940 Baudouin recorded: "Mass at 9 A.M., and at the elevation of the Host the marshal knelt. It is a long time since the Head of the State did this. We went on foot to a meagre review, the first since the disaster; and I came away very upset at the miserable appearance of the few companies which marched past. The men were sickly, yellow, and small. . . . Have we fallen so low?" Baudouin, 168.

[90] One ninth of it was motorized, eight ninths horse-drawn. Paxton, passim.

[91] This was acknowledged by the official British historian. Ellis, 245.

[92] The small Belgian unit, led by General Gilliart, and the small Free French unit, led by Monclar, fought very well in the East African campaign; the Italian General Gazzara surrendered on 4 July 1941 on the Sudanese frontier to these Belgian troops.

Menton, a French sergeant and a few soldiers held up the Italians for twelve days. Perhaps not too much should be made of the two elements to which the feebleness of the Italian martial qualities during this war is usually attributed: to their national character and to the unpopularity of Fascism among them. When the Italians were bravely and competently led, they fought well: in East Africa, for example.[93] Nor must it be overlooked that in November 1940 the Greek Army in Epirus outnumbered the Italians advancing from Albania at a rate of nearly three to one. Yet Mussolini who, at times, could be a superb political realist, and whose experiences as a common soldier during the First World War were comparable to Hitler's, lacked the latter's grasp of military realism. Mussolini's decision to attack Greece did not only turn out to be a large strategical blunder; it was also an enormous tactical blunder from the beginning. Impressed as he was with Hitler, who took over entire states within hours in successive *coups*, in 1939 Mussolini tried (and, at least in the beginning, succeeded) to do the same thing with Albania. In the summer of 1940, he thought that he would do with Greece what Hitler had done with, say, Denmark or Holland. The Italian ultimatum to Greece was even more brutal, the attack even more unprovoked and treacherous, than were Hitler's surprise moves. But Mussolini had no motorized infantry, few tanks, no gliders, no parachute troops—in sum, little or nothing to provide for the swift strikes of the new kind of land warfare. This was the principal reason why the Italian offensive in Greece bogged down after a day or so; and Italian morale sank with it. On the other side of the hill, for the Greeks, this was yet another national war: They responded with courage, though not without cunning. The inspiring impression they made on the world (including Hitler) in late 1940 ought not obscure the fact that once the Germans attacked them in April 1941, they folded fast. Calculation and treachery rose to the surface among their political generals, who thought that by surrendering to the Germans they could make a deal for their country and for themselves.

Certain clichés remain very true. The finest hour of the British came when their backs were to the wall. I am not only thinking of the pickax handles distributed among the first Home Guard recruits, or of the three-hundred-year-old howitzers brought out from museums. The spirit of a last-ditch battle began to appear among the English in France already during May 1940, that searing time of demoralization and defeat. There were the early RAF bombing squadrons in the valley of the Meuse, every second plane plunging to its death; there was the defense of Calais, where the

---

[93] More Italians fell in the East African campaign of 1940–41 than during the entire Ethiopian War of 1935–36. Their last units did not surrender until 18 November 1941, at Gondar.

1: *Hitler triumphant, 12 March 1938:* "In the evening he drove from Leonding to Linz. There he was received by a crying and cheering mass such as … Linz or, indeed, Austria, had never seen." (Photo courtesy United Press International)

2: *The Quatorze Juillet, 1939:* "… the Republic arranged a military display which impressed the foreign military attachés, including the Germans: The sun was dazzling, the equipment was new, there was a contingent of the Scots Guards marching down the Champs-Élysées … an unforgettable day…." (Photo courtesy Wide World Photos)

3: *Paris (as a matter of fact, the Café de la Paix), 3 September 1939:* "...they sensed that this would be a curious war. By early afternoon the boulevards and the Champs-Élysées were filled. In the crowded cafes people sat, rather quietly." (PHOTO COURTESY U. S. INFORMATION AGENCY)

5: *Spring 1940: The French-Swiss frontier.* (PHOTO COURTESY U. S. INFORMATION AGENCY)

6: *Dunkirk:* "*Les parfums du printemps le sable les ignore: Voici mourir le mai dans les dunes du Nord.*" (PHOTO COURTESY WIDE WORLD PHOTOS)

4: *The first morning of the war: 4 September 1939, along the Champs-Élysées.* (PHOTO COURTESY WIDE WORLD PHOTOS)

7: *Hitler in Paris, 23 June 1940:* "... [he] made a strange, furtive and restless visit to a Paris washed by the rising sunlight of a summer dawn, surrounded by those who were closest to him, including Speer and the sculptor Arno Breker." (PHOTO COURTESY UNITED PRESS INTERNATIONAL)

8: *London, May 1940:* "On the evening of 14 May Eden called for Local Defence Volunteers. (Soon they were re-named Home Guard.) Within a day 250,000 men presented them-selves." (PHOTO COURTESY UNITED PRESS INTERNA-TIONAL)

9: *September 1940:* "Soon it became evident that London could take it." (PHOTO COURTESY U. S. INFORMATION AGENCY)

10: *Molotov in Berlin, November 1940:* "...this unimaginative bureaucrat, with his cold slab of a face..." (PHOTO COURTESY THE NATIONAL ARCHIVES)

11: *29 December 1940, Sunday evening:* "The Second Great Fire of London, 274 years after the first." (PHOTO COURTESY U. S. INFORMATION AGENCY).

12: *The Vichy government:* [To Hitler] "Vichy France, all of its authoritarian rhetoric notwithstanding, was nothing but the remnant of an old and corrupt republic. The photos of Pétain's Cabinet showed dwarfish gnarled little men, with rundown mouths and mugs." (Photo courtesy Wide World Photos)

13: *Westminster Cathedral, Polish Army Mass, 1941:* "London . . . this proud and blackened city . . . was the capital of traditional Europe, of a free Europe. She was the focus of hope . . . a memory that later faded, but that, in retrospect, commands respect. . . ." (Photo courtesy Radio Times Hulton Picture Library)

14: *Russian peasants, autumn 1941:* "They believed that the Germans were winning, that they were to be the new masters...." (PHOTO COURTESY NATIONAL ARCHIVES)

15: *Russian mud, October 1941:* "The Germans . . . cursed and prayed that frost would come, making the roads and the fields passable again. Soon they would get all the frost they wanted. . . ." (PHOTO COURTESY NATIONAL ARCHIVES)

16: *Late November 1941:* "Villages in flames, some of them . . . less than thirty miles from the outskirts of the sprawling Russian capital." (PHOTO COURTESY NATIONAL ARCHIVES)

17: *Resettlement, 1941:* ". . . the German peasants from Bessarabia and Bukovina who trekked westward, in wagon trains . . . reminiscent of certain engravings of the American frontier era . . ." (PHOTO COURTESY NATIONAL ARCHIVES)

18: *Vichy, 1941: The Hotel du Parc, Pétain's "seat"*: "This new 'capital,' this seat of government, with its rattan chairs, and grand-bourgeois 1900 hotels . . ." (PHOTO COURTESY WIDE WORLD PHOTOS)

19: *Ciano and Ribbentrop, 1940*: "In 1940 Ribbentrop decided to adopt a ridiculous uniform for the diplomatic service of the Third Reich; this was soon imitated by Italy, Hungary, and certain German satellites, for a while even by the Soviet Union...." (PHOTO COURTESY ACME PHOTO)

20: *Hitler and the Volkswagen*: "Hitler had an interest in cars throughout his life.... One of the few photos that show Hitler smiling survives from 1938; Hitler contemplating the Volkswagen...." (PHOTO COURTESY WIDE WORLD PHOTOS)

21: *The German liberators:* "In many of the villages and towns of Lithuania … the western Ukraine … the people greeted the Germans with flowers, sometimes resuscitating ancient ceremonies such as the presentation of bread and salt, the kind of folklore show that would impress these powerful armed tourists…." (Photo courtesy United Press International)

22: *Paris, summer 1941:* "… streets without cars, the reappearance of bicycles and horse cabs … there were also velo taxis, pedicabs: they were vilely expensive…" (Photo courtesy Wide World Photos)

23: *Entrance to the ghetto in Lublin, 1941:* ". . . tenements dark with grime and soot, keeping the narrow streets in their eternal shadow, blocking sunlight out even when the rest of the Polish plain was warmed by summer . . ." (PHOTO COURTESY WIDE WORLD PHOTOS)

24: *The Cracow ghetto in winter 1940:* Jews loading coals from a sled. (PHOTO COURTESY WIDE WORLD PHOTOS)

25: *Berlin, 19 September 1941:* "For the first time the Jews of Germany were ordered to wear the yellow star on their clothes." (PHOTO COURTESY WIDE WORLD PHOTOS)

26: *The encircled and famine-ridden city of Leningrad, October 1941:* People drawing water from a broken main. (PHOTO COURTESY SOVFOTO)

27: *A Swiss peasant family, 1941:* "The Swiss idea was simple common sense...they reduced the production of fodder and increased the surface of arable land, no matter how poor ... producing surprisingly large amounts of foodstuffs for large numbers of people." (PHOTO COURTESY U. S. INFORMATION AGENCY)

28: *The continuity of life:* Cafe in Brussels, 1941. (Photo courtesy The National Archives)

29: *The continuity of life:* "The staircase of the Paris Opera at the occasion of a gala performance for the Secours National (in December 1940) ... the elegant silvery gowns and evening clothes, glistening under... the chandeliers, indistinguishable from any picture taken from a gala before the war..." (Photo courtesy Illustration)

30: *Madrid, Estación de Norte, 1941:* Spanish volunteer workers leaving for Germany. "The Germanophilia of the lower classes..." (PHOTO COURTESY WIDE WORLD PHOTOS)

31: *London, October 1940:* "The crowds sheltering in the tube stations." (PHOTO COURTESY U. S. INFORMATION AGENCY)

32: *Somewhere in England, July 1940, Home Guard rifle practice:* "George Orwell: 'The bulk of the middle class are just as anti-Hitler as the working class, and their morale is probably more reliable...the patriotism of the middle class is something to be made use of...." (PHOTO COURTESY UNITED PRESS INTERNATIONAL)

33: *De Gaulle and George VI inspecting the Free French, August 1940:* "... More substance than shadow. With all of his skepticism and suspiciousness... De Gaulle still knew that [the British], unlike Hitler, were unwilling to treat [their] smaller allies as wholly expendable, no matter how [they] would be tempted to do so on occasion..." (PHOTO COURTESY UNITED PRESS INTERNATIONAL)

34: *England the refuge of free Europe:* Churchill flanked by Generals De Gaulle and Sikorski, early 1941. (PHOTO COURTESY WIDE WORLD PHOTOS)

35: *General Guisan, the Swiss commander-in-chief:* "... with his severe but kindly blue eyes, with the seamed face of a patrician general-citizen ..." (PHOTO COURTESY UNITED PRESS INTERNATIONAL)

British Brigadier Nicholson answered the German invitation to surrender: "The answer is no as it is the British Army's duty to fight as well as it is the German's." And yet after the Battle of Britain, a climate of weariness, of slackness set in. Long after the war (in 1952), General Templer said to Churchill in private: "There was something wrong with the British soldier in the last war; he would not have stood up to what happened in the First War."[94] The British could rout the Italians even when they were outnumbered one to four; but when the Germans appeared in North Africa, the British retreated before them, even on occasions when they had outnumbered them two to one. Nor was this a question of inferior equipment; we have seen that Britain had more tanks and more airplanes than Germany in 1940 and in 1941.[95] Churchill himself set an angry minute to General Auchinleck in November 1941: "Feeling here has risen very high against what is thought to be our supine incapacity for action."[96]

One example of this "supine incapacity" was Crete. There was the usual slowness and mix-up in instructions passing down the chain of command, perhaps more typical of the British than of many other armies. "At no moment of the war," Churchill himself wrote later, "was our Intelligence so truly and so precisely informed."[97] Well before the German invasion, Churchill instructed the commanders that a German attack was due: "It ought to be a fine opportunity for killing the parachute troops.

---

[94] Moran, 387. On 11 February 1942 Churchill talked to his old friend Violet Bonham Carter, ". . . for the first time in their long friendship she had found him depressed . . . underneath it all was a dreadful fear, she felt, that our soldiers are not as good fighters as their fathers were. 'In 1915,' said Winston, 'our men fought on even when they had only one shell left and were under a fierce barrage. Now they cannot resist dive-bombers. We have so many men in Singapore, so may men—they should have done better.' It is the same, of course, in Libya; our men cannot stand up to punishment. And yet they are the same men as man the merchant ships and who won the Battle of Britain. There is something deeply wrong with the whole morale of our Army." Nicolson, II, 211.

[95] This was the case of Operation Crusader in 1941; see above, p. 162, n. 3.

[96] See also his memorandum about Army morale at home, to the Secretary of State for War on 5 October 1941, a memorandum with the sound of shining trumpets: "Parades, exercises, and maneuvres, the detailed development of the individual qualities of sections, platoons, and companies, continual improvement and purging of the officers of middle rank, courses and competitions of all kinds, should occupy all ranks. There should be plenty of marching with bands through towns and industrial districts. . . . We need regular units of the highest type, and not a mudstained militia that is supposed to turn out and take a hand in the invasion should it come." Churchill, GA, 503–4.

[97] Churchill, GA, 240.

The island must be stubbornly defended." More than three weeks passed before the Germans came: Yet when they descended they were met with confusion, weakness, and disorganization, together with what was perhaps the worst facet of British command at its most mediocre, with a kind of indecisiveness.[98] The morale of the British and Commonwealth troops was mixed. Even before the German invasion there were many deserters. At night they would come down from the hills to drink in the villages, "and shouted and fought in the cafes. The nights had begun to ring with shots and cries. Several of the Greeks had been injured, and at least one killed."[99] The Greeks fought better than any of the British; their defense of the village of Alikianou was magnificent. Contrary to the usual virile claims from the Antipodes, there was not much difference between the Limeys and the Diggers, once things had turned really bad. The very brave and intelligent New Zealand General Freyberg wrote with great frankness in his report about the last stage of the retreat across Crete: "a disorganized rabble. . . . Never shall I forget the disorganization and almost complete lack of control of the masses on the move as we made our way slowly through the endless stream of trudging men."

Still these sorry examples were not typical of the British fighting spirit. What remained typical was the cautiousness of their command. A symbolic episode, reflecting perhaps in a microcosm the entire history of Britain and of Europe during and after the war, was the British commando raid and its temporary liberation of some of the bleak Norwegian Lofoten Islands in late December 1941. The population was euphoric, After three days the raiders left. There returned darkness, bitterness, and gloom.

No exile army showed the spirit and the bravery of the Poles in 1940; near St.-Valéry-en-Caux, Polish troops fought with great bravura, even in the days before the French surrender. In England the government had

---

[98] Stewart, *Crete*, 337—about the British and New Zealand officers: "Their anxious hesitancy had contrasted with the bold and thrusting opportunism of Gericke, Heindl and Ramcke."

[99] Ibid., 53–54. The behavior of certain Air Force units was especially reprehensible: ". . . a mile above (an especially important) bridge a forward platoon of 21st Battalion lay concealed in the river bed. There remained, in mounting apprehension, a mixed collection of Fleet Air Arm and RAF troops, 339 officers and men in all. Few showed much enthusiasm for their prospective role as infantry. An effort was made to coax them into learning something that might help them to defend themselves the New Zealanders offered to instruct them in musketry. But 'they did not want to learn.' Of all the specialists in Crete they continued to be the most disdainful of the cruder forms of fighting. In their quarters, along the east bank of the river above the bridge, they played cards and hoped for the best." Ibid., 126.

some troubles with Polish soldiery due to some of their political manifestations and occasional indiscipline; but their bravery on land, sea, and air
were impressive in nearly every engagement. The Poles demonstrated that
strange compound of continuity and change that was characteristic of the
Last European War: old traditions, new brutalities. The traditional martial virtues coexisted with the grim and unconditional hatred of the
enemy.

"Compared with the old Imperial army, the troops of the Nazi
regime have the appearance of being far more 'democratic.' . . . The gulf
between officers and men seems now to be less unbridgeable. . . . From
highest to lowest there is a more clearly marked participation by all ranks
in a general atmosphere of goodwill. . . ." Several Frenchmen who knew
the Germans during the First World War noted this, as had Marc Bloch,
who found it important enough to record it in 1940.[100] For a while the old
traditions survived, here and there; and then they disappeared under the
oceanic surge of the new brutalities. Admiral Canaris, the head of the
German counterintelligence, opposed Heydrich's plot for outfitting men
with Polish uniforms for the faked attempt on the German radio station at
Gleiwitz the night before the war was to begin; but then Canaris gave in.
In the Polish campaign in September a group of SS men were court-mar-
tialed on the orders of General Blaskowitz for their murder of 450 Jewish
civilians; but they were amnestied almost immediately.[101] In October
1939 an SS circular, printed in *Das Schwarze Korps* in January 1940,
suggested that certain German women ought to consider offering themselves to the SS for higher racial purposes: A Lieutenant General
Groppe attacked this in a scathing speech, which he distributed among
his officers; Groppe was then transferred to another unit. When Colonel
Sas, the Netherlands military attaché, told his chiefs in March 1940 that
German military informants were warning him about the coming German invasion, General Winckelmann said that such a German officer
must be "a miserable wretch."[102] This Dutch worthy, shocked by the
departure from military tradition, did not know that the first German
unit breaking into Holland a few weeks later was to be disguised by
wearing Dutch helmets and Dutch military greatcoats over their German uniforms.[103] We have seen that the Belgian and the Dutch popula-

---

[100] Bloch, 92.

[101] Hitler criticized Blaskowitz' "Salvation Army" concept. Broszat, 41.

[102] Deutsch, 100.

[103] It must be noted that on a few occasions the British, too, would resort to
this wearing of enemy uniforms for purposes of disguise. In Crete a Sergeant
Hulme (later posthumously awarded the Victoria Cross) fought and killed a
number of Germans, having first acquired a German parachute uniform from
one of his dead enemies. In the same period of the war (May 1941) the Ger-

tions were generally impressed with the correctness of the German military.[104] On the day of the French armistice, even the rigid and unimaginative Keitel seemed moved and showed a certain kind of courtesy to his French counterparts; the Italian command, especially Badoglio, treated the French armistice delegation with great civility. The names of certain honorable German general officers (such as that of General Vogl, who served on the Franco-German Armistice Commission in Wiesbaden) ought to be recorded for posterity. When the Duke of Aosta, the commander of the Italian armies in East Africa, died in captivity, the British commander put flowers on his grave.[105]

Nonetheless, it would be a mistake to establish two clear-cut categories, the traditionalists as compared to the Nazi villains. Few of the German generals had the courage to oppose Hitler, just as few of the Russian generals had the courage to oppose Stalin. Some of the best German generals, such as Model or Reichenau, were convinced Nazis. No German officer spoke up against the *Kommissarbefehl*. Let me repeat: There was little European *Normalkrieg* even before June 1941.[106] After the brave British defense of Calais on 27 May 1940, the Germans murdered ninety British soldiers of the 2nd Battalion of the Royal Norfolk regiment at Le Paradis, in cold blood. Some of the bitterest enemies of Hitler were to be

---

mans found that the French vessel *Oued-Grou*, sailing on a lone course in the Mediterranean, was in reality the British *Paracombe*, bound from Leith to Malta.

[104] In his war notes Ernst Juenger recorded the words of his commanding officer, who was paying for straw bought from French people in the town of Neufchâteau on 25 May 1940: "We must remain gentlemen, otherwise we won't succeed." (*Meine Herren, wir wollen doch Kavaliere bleiben, sonst kommen wir nicht weit.*) Juenger, 153.

[105] The Italians generally treated their British prisoners well. In December 1940, officers among the latter communicated this to the papal nuncio. *VD*, 4, 320.

[106] The German treatment of British and of Eastern European (especially Soviet) prisoners reflected a discrimination of kind, and not merely of degree. Moreover, behind it there was a kind of crude calculation. Throughout the war the Germans tried to impress captured British officers with the traditional chivalries of their treatment. Goering and his ilk made special theatrics about this when it came to the reception of British pilots shot down, especially in 1940–41. In one instance they signaled to the British to send a plane over, which would then drop the artificial leg of Commander Bader, the RAF's ace hero. The British indeed sent a plane, and dropped Bader's spare leg, together with a cluster of bombs. Even ten years after the war, the German ace Major Galland recorded this with pained sentiments of rectitude spurned: "This was not a very friendly reply to our well-meant proposal." Galland, 92. (This was not how the Germans treated captured Soviet pilots, either.)

found in Canaris' *Abwehr*, the counterintelligence branch of the German services; yet the bitterest of enemies were not always the most determined opponents, and not all of them were honorable men.[107] What remains true is that the German military were more cautious than were the Nazis or the leaders of the SS: more cautious because they were less committed to the cause of National Socialism and of the Third Reich. On one occasion Napoleon had said that his marshals were like bloodhounds: He had to keep them on a leash. Hitler often said that he wished his generals acted more like bloodhounds; he had to urge them to go ahead.

Lieutenant Estienne d'Orves, a young French marine officer of rightwing persuasions, was one of the first heroes of the French resistance. On 24 May 1941 he was condemned to death by a German military court, which treated him with respect. "The Tribunal," its commanding officer (General Keyser) said, "had a difficult task. The accused is a person of great merit, of great strength of character, who acted for the love of his country."[108] At dawn on 29 August Estienne d'Orves was executed at the Mont Valérien. He spoke to Keyser: "Monsieur, you are a German officer. I am a French officer. Both of us did our duty." And they put their arms around each other. Then Estienne d'Orves cried, "*Vive la France!*," and he was felled by the execution platoon. There was nothing like this during the First World War. On that day, 29 August 1941, three thousand Jewish men, women, and children were machine-gunned by SS units in the suburbs of Minsk and Mogilev. The German military stood by. There was nothing like this, either, during the First World War.

---

[107] The *Abwehr* would employ even German Jews in their capacity of confidential agents as late as 1942 (for example, one G. Ascher in Rome). Some of its principal intelligence officers, deadly and efficient enemies of the resistance, such as Majors Giskes or Bleicher in Holland and France, were acquitted after the war by French and Dutch military courts.
[108] Duquesne, 117.

# 3 . The movements of politics

IN 1939 war was still the continuation of politics by other means. But the reverse of Clausewitz' maxim had also become true: Politics was the continuation of war. Indeed, Hitler was better at waging politics as if it were war than at waging war as if it were politics. Most people still think of him as a military bungler, as the amateur at war—forgetting Napoleon's vulgar little witticism about amateurs who are better than professionals in two fields, in prostitution and in war—a witticism which, however, loses its sting when it is applied to politics, and especially to the propagandistic manipulation of masses of people in the twentieth century by professional politicians. But I am not writing here of professional politicians; I am concerned with the movements of political thought, including sentiment. During the Second World War, I wrote earlier, the thinking of far more people was affected than during the First World War; and, especially between 1939 and 1941, "the mental earthquake was bigger than the physical one." The dramatic and unforeseen events of 1940 and 1941 not only affected the minds of nearly everyone; they changed the minds of many millions. The fabulous successes of the German armies surprised even those who had inclined to sympathize with Germany and National Socialism; they crystallized the political beliefs of some people, they helped to crystallize the convictions of others, they exaggerated the expectations of yet other millions who, in many countries of Europe, thought that they were witnesses of the end of an old political and social order and of the beginning of a new one. But those millions, too—probably the majority of the inhabitants of Europe—who had few such ideological inclinations were influenced by the dramatic spectacle that they witnessed, either directly or indirectly, through the news, radio, pictures. They, too, felt as if the old European order—or disorder—that they associated with liberalism, parliamentarism, political democracy, and bourgeois society was disappearing for good, especially after the collapse of the French.

This change of opinions may have been temporary. After 1941 the notion of the invincibility of the Germans faded; with it went some of the beliefs in a revolutionary new order of Europe. Still, the movement of political opinions in 1940 and 1941 had not been altogether superficial: It left enduring, though more than often suppressed, scars on the memories of an entire generation in Europe. For the mental earthquake of 1939–41 was the result of experience, it was not merely the result of the mass manipulation of minds through propaganda. Nor was the change of opinions always conscious: It could be opportunistic, in the broadest sense of that adjective. As a wise old-fashioned English scholar, H. C. Allen, wrote more than a generation ago, in his fine book *Sixteenth-century Political Thought* (1928): "Men are constantly engaged in an, on the whole highly successful, effort to adjust circumstances and also in an effort, very much less successful, to adjust circumstances to their ideas." This is even truer of wartime than of peace: It was certainly true during the Second World War.

It makes the task of the conscientious historian more, not less, difficult. During the Second World War there was this evil cause: Hitler's cause. For nearly two years it seemed that Hitler and the Germans' cause was the winner. Millions of not very articulate (and also hundreds of thousands of very articulate) men and women adjusted their ideas to this development. Later most of them changed their minds again. How did they do this? and why? How to distinguish the conscious from the unconscious opportunist, the conscious from the unconscious machiavellian? Even novelists, who are often better in dealing with such things than are academic historians, have done little to illuminate these questions.[1] They are nevertheless of the greatest importance: First, because what people think and feel is the basic matter of history, surely in the long run, and often in the short run, too; second, because in the twentieth century, with its large masses, the "climate of opinion" is no longer the near monopoly of a small educated class; third, because the pervasive presence of propaganda and publicity makes it very difficult to distinguish solid opinions and enduring beliefs from their transitory reflections and ephemeral articulations. I have dealt with some of these problems in my book *Histori-*

---

[1] There are a few stabs at this by Anthony Powell and Evelyn Waugh: But the latter's satiric trilogy about World War II suffers from the condition that the opinions represented by his main characters are static: He offers a typology of characters. A more successful effort is the protagonist villain of Jean Dutourd's *Au Bon Beurre* (Paris, 1952): While penning a lighthearted satire of a social type who flourished during World War II, Dutourd was also sketching a typology of opportunism involving acts as well as opinions, worthy of the tradition of Flaubert's *Bouvard et Pécuchet*.

*cal Consciousness;* but my awareness of them was the result of my having lived through, and witnessed, the last war in the middle of Europe.

There is another difficulty for the historian who wishes to deal with the political history of the Last European War. To some extent—but only to some extent—it was an ideological war. In 1939 the political geography of Europe reflected an ideological pattern. Parliamentary democracy was the governmental form of the states of Western and Northern Europe; authoritarian and totalitarian governments ruled the peoples of Central and Eastern Europe; communism reigned in the Soviet Union. In many ways these differences reflected different phases in the evolution of Europe's peoples. Yet often these important differences were not decisive. Hitler's allies included Scandinavian democracies such as Finland; his opponents included authoritarian dictatorships such as Greece. There was nothing very new in this. Geography mattered more than ideology, the interests of states more than their professed and official philosophies. In 1652 Cardinal Mazarin had sent a M. de Bordeaux to serve as French envoy to the England that was ruled by Cromwell and his Puritan dictatorship. "The connections which should exist between neighboring states are not determined by the form of governments," said this envoy upon his arrival in London—a phrase that could be uttered (and, on occasion, was uttered) in 1939 or in 1940 by Ribbentrop in Moscow or by Molotov in Berlin, or even by Sir Samuel Hoare in Madrid. It surely corresponded to the political philosophy of Churchill and to the political pragmatism of Stalin—sometimes even to the political ideology of Hitler.

Still, the existence of ideological affinities provided for a new element in the history of Europe's nations. Every nation now harbored many men and women who wished for the defeat of their state (though not necessarily of their nation) and for the triumph of the enemy of their state. This, too, was not something entirely new: To some extent it marked the reappearance of an old phenomenon from the wars of religion of the sixteenth century. On the other hand, political ideology, in the twentieth century, had become a substitute for religion. There was nothing like it even during the First World War. Except for a handful of revolutionaries, few people had looked forward then to the collapse of their own state with anything like anticipation. During the Second World War there were many people who would commit espionage or treason, propelled by ideological sympathies, without having given this a second thought. With the change in the nature of war and of peace there came a change in the personal sense, deeper than in the legal meaning, of loyalty and of treason.

This meant the beginning of a profound mutation in the traditional relationships of peoples with their governments. I touched on this when I wrote about the black markets; I shall have to return to other manifestations thereof, in the resistance movements, for example. This sea change rose slowly; but it was oceanic enough to wash away much of the accumulated debris of Right and Left. Here is another difficulty that the political historian has to face during the Second World War: The political struggles often did not conform to the accustomed categories of Right and Left. At the time of this writing our political thinking is still encumbered—sometimes hopelessly—with their antiquated vocabulary, even as we should have heeded Tocqueville's warnings long ago: A new science of politics was necessary to the understanding of a new world. By 1939 it was already too late to sort out the proper meanings. Compared to Franco, for example, was Hitler a Rightist or a Leftist? During the Second World War there were "conservatives" who hoped for revolutionary upheavals of the state; there were "nationalists" who hoped for the victory of the Germans, sometimes at the expense of the independence of their own nation. The opposing sides were not those of Right and Left; certainly not before the entry of the Soviet Union and of the United States in the war. This poses certain problems to the historian in retrospect; which is why we must sort out certain realities in the movements of politics of the time.

We shall see, for example, that before 1941 (and in many instances also later) the principal struggle could be seen as that between two Rights, not between Right and Left. This alone should prove instructive, since the history of the Right, all present intellectual fashions notwithstanding, is generally more interesting than the history of the Left: The Right varies from nation to nation more than does the Left. This has much to do with modern nationalism, surely the principal political phenomenon of the past one hundred years, at least. It was overlooked by Marx; with far less excuse, it has been underestimated by his followers. For 1939–41 marked not only the temporary collapse of the Left in Europe; it marked for the second time the nearly universal failure (the first time was in 1914) of the Marxian theory of politics. No matter how cruel, no matter how vulgar, Hitler had a more profound understanding of human nature than had Marx; and national socialism (of which German Nazism was but one variant) proved to be more viable than international socialism. In the broadest sense of the term, National Socialism, the conjunction of nationalism with socialism, was far more than a passing phenomenon—indeed, it may have proven to be the principal political configuration of the twentieth century.

All of this appeared during the Last European War. History and politics were not the same: In this respect the maxim of the great Victorian political historian J. R. Seeley—"history is past politics and politics present history"—was out of date. Nor did history consist mainly of the relations of states, as Ranke had conceived it; it consisted now of the relations of entire nations. The older, more classical, wisdom of Bolingbroke (who had borrowed the phrase from Dionysius Halicarnassus) was truer, and it is still true: History is philosophy teaching by example—or, rather, by examples that really existed and lived; that were *real*. This is why the events of that last war may still teach us something about the nature of politics—and, through that, perhaps even about human nature.

# The split Right

¶ *Revolution von Rechts* (Revolution from the Right) was the title of a significant book by the German cultural historian Hans Freyer in 1931, two years before Hitler came to power. During the next decade Europe moved toward the Right: and 1940 was the dramatic culmination of that movement. The tendencies of the mass political movements that came out of the Depression were Fascist or National Socialist, rather than Communist. This was true not only of Germany but also of most of the nations of Europe (and even of the United States, where people such as Huey Long and the Reverend Charles Coughlin represented the only serious challenge to the popularity of Franklin Roosevelt). This popular eclipse of the Left has been often obscured by the terminology of the political commentators and confused by the vocabulary of the intelligentsia; I shall briefly return to the latter.

The terminology of Right and Left dates back to the French Revolution; the collapse of France in 1940 suggested to many people not only the defeat of a state but also the defeat of the ideals that this state had incarnated, the end of an epoch that had begun with the French Revolution. This was what the Nazi ideologists proclaimed: 1940 marking not only the end of the Europe of the Treaty of Versailles but also of the Europe of the spirit of Paris, not only the end of the era of 1919 but also of the era of 1789. There was a certain reality to this. The deputies of the French people, for instance, responded to the defeat of their Republic in July 1940 rather as the freely elected deputies of the German people had responded to the end of their Republic in March 1933. The similarity in the proportions of the largely constitutional[2] votes abolishing the republican structures and transferring powers to a national dictatorship is interesting. In Berlin in 1933 the vote was 441 to 94, in Vichy in 1940 it

---

[2] Largely, but not entirely: In 1933 in Berlin and in 1940 in Vichy the Communist deputies were excluded.

was 569 to 97[3] for the respective enabling acts of Hitler and of Pétain, for the cancellation of an entire democratic era. There are reasons to believe that these proportions of the parliamentary votes were more or less accurate indices of the sentiments of the respective nations at the time.

This was not only true of the Germans and of the French. Throughout Europe there were many people who welcomed the collapse of the old order; there were many more who, like Maurras, welcomed at least the opportunity that the catastrophe offered for thoroughgoing reforms of society and of politics[4]; there were yet more, probably the majority of the peoples of Europe who, even as they regretted the German domination of the Continent, realized the shortcomings of the liberal and democratic philosophy of government together with the fatal debility of the institutions and the states that incarnated it. The defeat of France broke the confidence of old republicans in the republican institutions. In Holland a neoconservative movement, *Nederlandse Unie*, gathered nearly 1 million members after July 1940.[5] Even in England, where democratic institutions continued to exist, Churchill's dictation of the war and of the austerities of wartime life were very popular throughout 1940 and 1941. He said that he had nothing to offer but blood, toil, tears, and sweat. Across the Channel a very different man in a very different situation, the aged marshal of a defeated France, chose a similarly austere and atavistic motto for his new state—*Travail, Famille, Patrie* (Work, Family, Land) —to replace the antiquated abstractions of Liberty, Equality, Fraternity. The peoples responded.[6] In France eventually the response ran out of

---

[3] A total of 80 voted against; there were 17 abstentions. In Berlin in 1933 the Social Democrats were alone in voting in a bloc against the enabling act given to Hitler; in 1940 the voting in Vichy cut across party lines.

[4] On 20 June 1940 Maurras, in the South of France, wrote the later famous, or infamous, words: "a divine surprise." This was misunderstood later. Maurras welcomed not the defeat of France but the fact that Pétain was in charge of the destinies of France and that Pétain's first radio address suggested an authoritarian course of government.

[5] It stood for a loyal attitude toward the occupying power, but not more. In 1941 the Germans ordered its dissolution nevertheless.

[6] There are innumerable evidences of this for France. The participant and close observer of the early Vichy months, Du Moulin de la Barthète, 186: "Never was the sense of national solidarity so vivid, so evident, than during the first months of Vichy." A young American historian in retrospect: "The fervor, the catholicity . . . of the Pétain cult has no twentieth-century parallel in France." Paxton, 154. On New Year's Day in 1941 Lebrun, the last President of the Third Republic, sent his best wishes to Pétain, wishing him all the best "for the accomplishment of your high mission." As late as in May 1941 the first resistance pamphlets in Vichy France refrained from attacking Pétain; they attacked his "entourage."

steam, later in 1941; because of the feebleness of the government, rather than because of its original ideas. For a while Pétain had some first-class conservative speechwriters.[7] On 10 October 1940 Pétain addressed the French people: "History alternates between periods of [excessive] authority degenerating into tyranny and of periods of [excessive] liberty degenerating into license. The hour has come for France to put an end to these painful alternations and to find a harmony between authority and liberty. . . . The hierarchical character of the new regime is inseparable from its social concerns." These—unfortunately largely rhetorical—terms were unexceptionable for most thinking Europeans at the time. They also corresponded to the inclinations of governments and peoples from one end of Europe to the other, including the conquered and the still free and the neutral nations, from Portugal to Greece[8] and from Romania to Switzerland. When among the neutrals, traditionally democratic peoples such as the Swiss or the Swedes, the authority of the government was strengthened and some of the democratic liberties curtailed, this met with the approval of what evidence suggests was the majority in 1940.

In this respect, too, 1940 marked a turning point: a widespread disillusionment with what was thought to have been the old order of things. I write "old order" and "new order" because these words were a key to the then existing political sentiments. To most people the institutions and the ideas of liberalism, of capitalism, of socialism, of parliamentary democracy seemed hopelessly antiquated. The title of the book by the French neoconservative Anatole de Monzie, published in 1941, is telling in this regard: *Ci-devant*, a word that French-English dictionaries, necessarily imprecisely, translate as "before, formerly, -ex."[9] *Ci-devant*, in French, had meant the epoch of the old regime and of the era of the aristocracy before 1789. After 1940 this seemed to be the right word, indeed, the *mot juste* for the ancient and corrupt democratic and parliamentary regime of the Third Republic. In 1931, revolution from the Right had been still ahead of most of Europe; by 1941 it was accomplished, and the reign of the democratic Left was past: *Ci-devant*. Men such as Henri de Man in 1940 referred to the latter as the *ancien régime*[10] (in 1944 he would refer to the return of the exiled regimes from London as a *restoration*).

---

[7] In June 1940 these even included Emmanuel Berl, the excellent French Jewish writer and philosopher.

[8] "The English," wrote the Greek leader General Metaxas in his diary on 18 April 1940, "support the antiquated ideas of liberalism. This is a pity." Cited by D. Kitsikis, "La Grèce entre l'Angleterre et l'Allemagne de 1936 à 1941," *RH*, (October 1968).

[9] About "ex-people" in 1940, see above, p. 219.

[10] From his diary on 28 May 1940: "This war is in reality a revolution. The old

This widespread view, amounting to a conviction in the minds of millions, was not, I repeat, the propagandistic monopoly of Nazis or Fascists. Even before the French collapse, in the early days of June 1940 Spears recorded a conversation with Georges Mandel, the former secretary of Clemenceau, French Minister of the Interior, an incorruptible democrat, who "indicates his contempt for the many modern politicians to whom democracy meant just that, a speech, an interpellation, a parliamentary row, the dreary, shoddy trappings of popular representation, the whole divorced from reality."[11] "Democracy has for a long time been lacking in foresight and audacity. The idea of the fatherland and of military valor has been too long neglected. . . ." These words were broadcast not by Pétain but by Reynaud (on 6 June 1940). These sentiments went deeper than if they had been but the ephemeral reactions of people to the suddenly looming tragedy of their defeat. In his study of the evolution of public opinion in Belgium during the occupation, Paul Struye noted that in the winter of 1940–41 (that is, at a time when the prospect of a German victory had begun to fade), public opinion was convinced "of the necessity of deepgoing reforms of the old political and social system," that "the abuses of parliamentary democracy" ought to be elminated in the future. Opinions such as these were, thus, neither the inventions nor the monopoly of the partisans of a New German Europe, or of Fascists, or of authoritarians, or even of conservatives. They were shared by many of the earliest, and bravest, opponents of the Third Reich,[12] and by most of the early resisters.

For the principal struggle in the politics of Europe during 1939–41

---

social order, the old political regime are collapsing. Hitler is a kind of elementary or demoniac force, he accomplishes a kind of destruction that has in all probability become necessary. . . ." De Man, CS, 259. Pierre Laval's great speech in Vichy on 5 July 1940: "We are now paying for the fetish that has chained us to the idea of democracy, delivering us to the worst excesses of capitalism, while around us a new Europe has been forging a new world, animated by new principles." Bonnefous, VII, 274.

[11] Spears, II, 30. The occasion was the behavior of a deputy, the mayor of Suresnes, after the first German bombing of Paris on 3 June (an event that the Parisian population had taken in its stride with surprising calm), who "went about the lobbies, screaming: "I will interpellate the government on this outrage as soon as the Chamber meets."

[12] The Communist (though anti-Stalinist) Willi Münzenberg during the Reluctant War: "Democracy and dictatorship have a bad sound among the masses of the people. 'Democracy' reminds everyone in Germany of Weimar, 'Dictator' of Hitler and Stalin. . . ." In the émigré journal Zukunft (Paris: 5 January 1940), cited by Gross, 325.

and in many ways even afterward, was not so much a struggle between Right and Left as it was, rather, a struggle between two Rights. That, too, was not something entirely new. It existed throughout the thirties, even though it was (and still is) obscured by the accepted superficial interpretation of events. In Germany in 1933 the only possible political alternative to Hitler was a military-conservative regime supported or even formed by leaders of the Army. Later the first tentatives of a resistance plot against Hitler, in 1938 and in 1939, were made nearly exclusively by men of the Right, by generals, officers, Catholics, and conservatives. In Austria the partisans of Hitler had to wage a murderous struggle against their principal opponents: the Austrian clericals and the Austro-Fascists.[13] In Italy the only two possible counterpoles to which Mussolini's opponents could gravitate were the monarch and the Pope. In Spain the existence of the traditional upper class and of the Church compromised the prospects of a full-fledged Spanish Fascism, and helped to keep the Franco regime at an arm's length from a full-fledged alliance with Hitler.[14] In Portugal and Greece and Hungary and Bulgaria and Romania and Yugoslavia and Latvia and Lithuania and Estonia (a long list to which I might as well add etc., etc.), the presence of a conservative dictator or of a regent or of a monarch were the principal obstacles in the way of the radical, and often fanatical, movements that during the thirties were attracted by the philosophy of Hitlerism. The Czech democrats dissolved before Hitler's threats; the nationalist Poles fought him to the bitter end—indeed, even beyond. This tendency of the thirties carried over into the war. It reached its peak in 1940, when the principal figures of the European resistance against Hitler became Churchill and De Gaulle, the first in the fullness, the second at the beginning of their great political careers. Churchill and De Gaulle: patriots even more than nationalists, traditionalists even more than conservatives; they were men of the Right.

In the burning summer of 1940 the resistance against the Third Reich flared first among patriots rather than among socialists; among conservatives rather than among radicals; among nationalists rather than among internationalists. This was the pattern in nearly every country across the Continent. The few significant manifestations of opposition in Germany, too, involved mostly Catholics and conservatives.[15] In Russia, too, Hitler

---

[13] The principal organizer of an Austrian Fascism, Prince Starhemberg, entered the French Army as a volunteer in 1939.

[14] The Falangists in Spain were pro-German, the Carlist *Requetés* (reactionary-traditionalist of the extreme Right) were pro-English in 1940 and 1941. In the Vatican, too, the most determined opponents of the Third Reich were cardinals such as Ottaviani and Tisserant—the "reactionary" *bêtes noires* of progressive Catholics two decades later.

[15] Evidences of this are in the secret public-opinion reports of the Reich secu-

was more anxious to repress nationalism than communism.[16] From England, France, and Western Europe, the various German intelligence agencies reported that their principal opponents were to be found among traditionalists of the upper classes rather than among the Socialists and Communists of the working class.[17] We have seen how strong were sentiments of monarchism in Western Europe[18]; we have also seen that George Orwell had been honest enough to admit that often he was more impressed with the patriotic dutifulness of the English upper and middle classes than with either the socialism of the intellectuals or with the reactions of the working class. The reactionary patriotism of the old conservative bourgeoisie (or what had remained of the aristocracies) were the strongest obstacles to the Hitlerian ideas of a new Europe. Their willingness to endure the opprobrium of being called "reactionary" was expressed clearly as early as in 1933[19] in a remarkable little book by the Swiss Albert Oeri, editor-in-chief of the conservative-liberal newspaper

---

rity organization (*Meldungen aus dem Reich*). They are especially interesting in the years 1939–41. The quality and the purpose of the reporting deteriorated later in the war. A few random examples: RSHA file 0040, 9 October 1939: "strong antinational socialist attitude of Catholic priests" in Karslbad. File 0124 (23 October 1939): Leaflets in Vienna: "Long live the Emperor Otto." On All Souls' Day the graves of Dollfuss and of Seipel "demonstratively covered with many flowers and wreaths."

[16] Two examples: Hitler to his High Command on 30 March 1941; "A primitive socialist intelligentsia is all that is necessary to be allowed to function in the conquered lands of Russia." On 2 August 1941: "As for me I find our Communists a thousand times more sympathetic than, for example, a Starhemberg." *Hitler TG*, 28.

[17] Hitler appreciated this till the very end. On 14 February 1945: "Our obvious course should have been to liberate the working classes and to help the workers of France to implement their revolution. We should have brushed aside, rudely and without pity, the fossilized bourgeoisie. . . ." On 15 February 1945: "By not liberating the French proletariat at once in 1940 we both failed in our duty and neglected our own interests . . . the [French] people have shown much more common sense than their self-styled elite. . . ." *Hitler-Bormann*, 60, 67.

[18] In Holland, Belgium, Luxembourg, and Denmark, the first demonstrations against the New Order were those by people who asserted their demonstrative allegiance to their royalty. The first Socialist demonstrations against the local Nazis occurred in Amsterdam in February 1941, and in Brussels in March 1941.

[19] In the year when the "Horst-Wessel-Lied" resounded triumphantly across Germany, one of its lines exalting the comrades who fell in the battle against "Reds and reactionaries."

*Basler Nachrichten.* Oeri wrote that he did not mind belonging to *die alte Front* (the old order): "Let us admit that we, with our democratic conservatism, reject once more our opportunity to ride the wave of the future.[20] This has happened to the Swiss in the past. So be it."[21]

This, then, is one side of the story of the Right—a side that I had to sketch with what is perhaps exaggerated emphasis, because it has been obscured so often. There is, however, another side to the story of the Right: that of the conservatives who went along with Hitler and Mussolini. Fortunately it is not too difficult to sort out the differences between the two sides. There was a pattern to this split of the Right, and it was relatively a simple one: The key was anti-Communism, fear of the Left. This, too, was not a new pattern altogether: It appeared after 1848 in France, when the fear of the radical Left in France, had driven hordes of people, including many conservatives, to support the dictatorship of Louis Napoleon. This pattern reappeared often since that time. In Germany the distrust of the Left and the hatred for Communism had made Hitler acceptable to many conservatives. By the 1930s this had become a worldwide phenomenon. A man such as Quisling, for example, would be attracted to the cause of Hitler and of Germany because of his hatred of Russian Communism. Elsewhere in Scandinavia a democratic monarch such as Gustav V of Sweden (who had a soft spot in his heart for Goering) favored a peace between Britain and Germany in 1940[22]; and Marshal Mannerheim in July 1941 justified to himself the Finnish alliance with Germany for the purpose of eradicating Bolshevism once and for all. But some of the most instructive (and, in retrospect, the sorriest) examples of this narrow-minded conservatism were to be found in France.[23] A kind of paranoid (or call it arteriosclerotic) anti-Com-

---

[20] About "the wave of the future," see below, p. 315.

[21] "So Switzerland missed the wave of the future in the seventeenth century when she could have become a Great Power. She missed her chance of becoming involved in the Thirty Years' War. After 1848 she missed becoming involved in the general European reaction. . . . If [we] now keep our democracy and resist the pull of the wave toward a dictatorial regime, this may seem uninspiring and even boring . . . but it may surely be better for [our] national life in the long run." Cited by Wolf, 181.

[22] "He did not agree with the [British Minister's] suggestion that, if the Russian danger ceased to exist, Germany would remain a menace for Europe." FO 371:N 7786/1818/42; N 220/124/42; also Woodward, I, 54–55.

[23] The "rather Hitler than Blum" slogan, attributed to the French Right at the time of the Popular Front, was a canard perpetrated by Leftist journalists. There were few Frenchmen, even on the Right, who before 1939 sympathized with Hitler. "Rather Fascism than Socialism" would explain their inclinations more correctly.

munist and anti-Leftist obsession made many conservatives eventually the conscious or unconscious accomplices of Hitler. On the morrow of Hitler's occupation of the Rhineland, on 8 March 1936, Maurras, the spokesman of French nationalism, wrote in *Action Française:* "We must not march together with the Soviets against Hitler." In *Le Journal* of 30 April 1936, Pétain attacked the Franco-Soviet Pact[24] because of its "introduction of Communism"—an early clear indication of his political inclinations in retrospect.[25] At the time of Munich most French conservatives were adamant against their country going to war on the side of the Czechs and the British and perhaps the Russians—because, as Thierry Maulnier of *Action Française* wrote in the November 1938 number of the magazine *Combat*, not only was the defeat of France in such a war a possibility, but even more because the "defeat of Germany would have meant the collapse of those authoritarian systems in Europe that form *the principal bulwark against Communism and perhaps the immediate Bolshevization of Europe*" (his italics). By 1940 even old-fashioned nationalists such as Ybarnegaray became full-fledged supporters of the Pétain policy.[26] The Germans were aware of these inclinations, on

---

[24] The signing of this pact marked Stalin's—temporary—adoption of the policy of a Popular Front (meaning Communist willingness to collaborate with all kinds of anti-Fascists), and his—more permanent—inclination to hope for a Second, Western European, Front in an eventual war with Germany. A Franco-Soviet communiqué had been issued (upon Laval's insistence) on 15 November 1935: "Stalin understands and fully approves the policy of national defense, drawn up by France to maintain her armed forces at the necessary level for her security." This was supposed to convert the French Communists into nationalists, a task that did not prove to be too difficult. What was more important, it surely converted many French nationalists into pacifists.

[25] For one of the principal, if not *the* principal, elements in Pétain's political philosophy was a kind of middle-class anti-Communism that was more ideological than patriotic, similar to that of a Papen in Germany or of a John Foster Dulles in America. It was, after all, the so-called anti-German and non-Nazi and pro-American Pétain who told Leon Noël in the winter of 1941 that he was beginning to feel that the Germans might not defeat the Russians, "and this disturbs me."

[26] Anti-Communist memories played a part in this. Together with Pétain, Ybarnegaray played an important role in 1917 in quelling the radical mutinies on the French Front, and he remembered vividly the influence of Bolshevik propaganda among the two Russian divisions that had been stationed in France at that time and that had to be sequestered in detention camps. In 1930 Ybarnegaray called for a break in France's diplomatic relations with the Soviet Union. (Congressman John W. McCormack in January 1940 proposed an amendment to the budget of the Department of State, cutting out the annual

the part of Pétain as well as on that of Leopold III of Belgium,[27] who even-tually would capitulate to them in 1940. General Weygand, the French commander-in-chief and a political conservative, raised not only the specter of a necessary "armistice" as early as on 26 May 1940; he also spoke at that time of his fear of "a revolutionary movement in Paris."[28] In Vichy, Weygand proclaimed that the first priority of the French Army after the defeat was "to prevent a social revolution." Just as Wey-gand's "armistice" was tantamount to capitulation, in this instance "social" was a euphemism for Communism. It reflected a situation during the Last European War where the defeatists were often men of the Right and not of the Left, obsessed as they were with the alleged powers of the enemy *within* their own country rather than with the foreign powers, the enemy *without*—a typical aberration of nationalism.[29]

This cleavage went through the Right, a cleavage essentially between those who regarded Hitlerism as a lesser evil than Communism and those who refused to do so.[30] In this respect there was a difference between Eastern and Western Europeans. Most peoples of Eastern Europe, except perhaps for the Czechs, feared Russian domination more than German domination. They had every reason to do so. But this was a reasonable preference only for those peoples who were threatened by their subjuga-tion by the Soviet Union. There was no such danger in Western Europe; nor was there any danger of a Communist, or a Communist-inspired, social revolution. Yet the fear of Communism explains much of the politi-cal inclinations not only of the French[31] but, farther to the west, of the

---

salary of the American ambassador to Moscow, an amendment that was defeated by only three votes in the House of Representatives.)

[27] See, for example, Bülow note to Ribbentrop, *GD*, D, VIII, 675.

[28] Baudouin, 56.

[29] During the political crisis of March 1940 (see above), the French govern-ment found it more important to placate the French Right than the Left. At the end of May Daladier told the British ambassador that if there was even a minimal chance to approach Mussolini this was worth trying: "French public opinion would expect such an attempt." Woodward, I, 239. "On June 3, Sir R. Campbell reported that M. Reynaud was thinking of a broadcast to influence French public opinion which did not understand why Italy was on the point of coming into the war." Ibid., 240–41.

[30] The former nurtured for the latter a hatred that persisted for a generation, as for example in France, where no one hated De Gaulle with the passion of former Pétain supporters.

[31] Pétain's handwritten notice on 23 June 1941: Nazism and Bolshevism. "Bol-shevism is the greatest danger for Europe. Therefore we, Europeans, should not object to the blows it is now getting" (from the Germans). Cited in Bourget, 223.

Chamberlainites (Chamberlain's private papers are full of evidences of his "profound distrust" not only of Russia but also of any kind of alliance with her) and of the American isolationists in 1939–41.[32] This kind of nationalist fear of Communism in England was of long standing; it led press magnates such as Rothermere to sympathize with Hitler—a trend that in Britain then petered out for good in the summer of 1940.[33]

Thus on the one side there were the Chamberlains and the Pétains (and across the ocean, the Taft Republicans), and on the other, the Churchills and the De Gaulles (and across the ocean, old New Englanders such as Stimson or Knox). For once the cleavage in England was not untypical of the entire Continent. What we must recognize, then, is that the political and historical philosophy of a Churchill was more Rightist than that of a Chamberlain; in many ways the same thing was true of De Gaulle and Pétain. But this is not merely a categorical distinction among shades of conservatism, a question of political semantics. Like everything else in human life, it involves tendencies, inclinations, movement. In this case the marvelous illogic of the English language may assist us, since the sequence in which certain words, including adjectives, are expressed in English influences their meaning. The difference between a De Gaulle and a Laval, or between a Churchill and a Chamberlain, may have been the difference between Leftist Rightists on the one hand, and Rightist Leftists on the other—the second of these pairs of adjectives being the dominant qualifying one, as indeed a bad good poet is more of a poet than a good bad one. The magnanimity of Churchill's patriotism would make him a populist, or an ally of Stalin, when the occasion demanded it. Chamberlain, on the other hand, was a product of the Victorian middle class.

---

[32] Consider, for example, Senator Taft's radio address on 25 June 1941: "The victory of Communism in the world would be far more dangerous to the United States than the victory of Fascism. . . ." This was different from the statement of the then Senator Harry Truman on 24 June: "If we see that Germany is winning we ought to help Russia and if Russia is winning we ought to help Germany . . . although I don't want to see Hitler victorious under any circumstances." Latent in this difference is the issue of the political struggle between Taft's and Truman's versions of anti-Communism during the crucial period after 1945. Charles Lindbergh in July 1941: "I would a hundred times rather see my country ally herself with England, or even Germany with all her faults, than with . . . the Soviet Union." John T. Flynn: "If Russia defeats Germany, Germany will go Communist. If Germany wins, Russia will go Fascist." Cited by Dawson, 82–83. The second half of this half truth was possibly true; the first was not.

[33] But not entirely. For a few weeks the majority of the Chamberlainite conservatives "in some cases carried their mistrust [of Churchill] as far as loathing." Calder, 85. See also above, pp. 94, n. 43; 97.

His famous father had moved from the Left to the Right, becoming a conservative imperialist, and rising in the world. As Christopher Thorne put it about the British conservative appeasers: "Hitler was faced by the heirs not of Chatham but of Bright . . . ," the thirties were "the Indian summer of the heirs of mid-Victorian England, with their Birmingham social conscience and their Gladstonian international high-mindedness, their dedication and their cant." So at a high dramatic moment in the history of the British Parliament, on 2 September 1939, the Tory Leo Amery, fearing another Munich ploy, knowing his fellow Birminghamite Chamberlain only too well, shouted across the aisles to the spokesman of the Labor opposition: "Speak for England!" So in France a Rightist such as Henri de Kerillis, who until 1936 was an *Action Française* member, after which (very much like De Gaulle) he became a spokesman of France's alliance with Britain and Russia, would tell General Spears in November 1939 that the Communists, while bad, were not as serious a danger as "treachery on the Right. There are people on the Right who are far cleverer than the Communists and far better placed to undermine France's war effort." So in Switzerland military officers of the Right, such as General Guisan or Captain Hausamann, convinced and determined anti-Communists, were the animators of a policy of national resistance against Germany, while not only conservative liberals such as President Pilet-Golaz but also conservative political thinkers such as Gonzague de Reynold suggested the necessity of a Swiss accommodation to the "realities of a New Europe"; so in Hungary Regent Horthy, who had come to power in 1919–20 on the wave of the anti-Communist counter-revolution, in 1940 listened to the advice of his old anti-Communist friends, men such as Counts Bethlen and Teleki, who were convinced that Hitlerism represented a greater danger than Communism, both within and without the Hungarian state. So the profoundly conservative Salazar was more deeply opposed to the Third Reich[34] than the superficially conservative Franco (who in 1931 had sided with the Spanish Republicans against the monarchy). The archenemies of Germany and of its friends in Spain and Portugal were the archreactionary Archbishops Segura and Cerejeira: In 1941 they refused to give any support to the cause of the anti-Bolshevik crusade. This pattern appeared in every country, across the Continent. The older, more traditional kind of patriotism was still prevalent. It was different from the ideological kind of nationalism, a symptom of which was the hatred of the Left.

---

[34] Salazar to the Italian Minister Bova Scoppa on 12 June 1940 (the date is significant): Hitler represents a greater danger than Napoleon: He would paganize and Germanize Europe. *DDI*, IX, V, 10.

## THE FAILED LEFT

¶ Few political thinkers have been proven as wrong by events as Marx. He prophesied the advent of violent revolutions. What followed his lifetime were great wars, not revolutions. He foresaw vast struggles of classes, because of their conflicting economic motives. Instead, the wars of the twentieth century were national wars, the struggles not of classes but of entire nations. Contrary to his predictions, the class differences of the nineteenth century began to dissolve; the national states became more homogeneous, not less. Marx failed to see that already during his lifetime nationalism was the main force, that it was one of the results of the mass democratization of the world, that the national characteristics of peoples were not only more enduring but far more important than their transitory economic structures of their changing structures of classes. Even the Russian Bolshevik Revolution of 1917 was no exception to this. What happened in Russia after 1917 was something quite different from what Marx had been able to envisage. Its historical importance, too, was less than that of the French Revolution of 1789. The French Revolution caused a series of great wars all over Europe and even in America. The Russian Revolution was the consequence of a great Europen war, not the cause of it. No revolution in 1789, no Napoleon; no war in 1914, no Lenin. In any event, the year 1914 saw the first worldwide evidence of the vast failures of Marxism. There existed then, for the first time in history, a politically conscious proletariat in many nations; the workers had their Socialist parties, their newspapers, they knew how to read and write and vote and protest. In 1914 the effect of this was that of a cold pat of margarine in a hot skillet; or, to use another image, the currents of Socialism were swallowed up by nationalism as rivers are swallowed up by the sea.

Much of the same was true in 1939, too, but with a difference. Many people, including intellectuals, went on believing in Marxism, in spite of (or, perhaps, because of) its real shortcomings. The reason for this was (and still is) complex; its explanation does not belong in this book. It has much to do with something that I mentioned earlier in this chapter: with the everlasting tendency of people to adjust and readjust their ideas, in plain English, to believe what they want to believe and, among intellectuals, to think what they think they ought to think. Yet, even as a discussion of the mental mechanisms of this kind of unreason does not belong here, its manifestations cannot be ignored; for history must deal with the opinions and sentiments of people, no matter whether they were right or wrong. There are two stories that the historian must tell: the success or the failure of an idea in retrospect, together with its appeal to contemporaries at a certain time. By 1939 most of the Marxist predictions had failed; indeed, the Marxist view of human nature was full of gaping holes. Still there remained millions of Communists and Socialists in Europe. We must attempt to describe them. A man may act on false information, but his act is still a matter of historical record. On the other hand, the falseness of his information will eventually catch up with him, modifying his thoughts and his acts; the two stories are not altogether separable. This happened during the 1930s. It was not only that the Marxist predictions made less and less sense. More and more people were inclined to recognize this.[35] By 1939 the Communists throughout Europe were stunned by the German-Soviet Pact, while the Socialists' response to the Nazi danger was not very dynamic either. The radicals of the Left were split, and they lost a not inconsiderable number of adherents to the rising forces of National Socialism.

We have seen earlier that the Marxist parties gained little from the Depression, and that almost everywhere the movement was to the Right, not to the Left. There were few exceptions to this continental tendency, mostly in southern Europe (Greece, Spain, and Serbia), to which I shall return. By the time the war began, the Marxist categories had no relationship to events; rather the contrary. By 1939, Marxism and its principal spokesmen seemed *old*. Especially in Central Europe (Germany, Austria, Hungary, Romania, and Slovakia), the main inroads of Nazism were made among the industrial working class even more than among the middle classes.[36] On the other hand, many of the remaining capitalists, instead

---

[35] Cf. the testimony of a moderate Leftist in 1940: "I have a very great admiration for the works of Karl Marx." Yet "There are admirable men of science who, though in the laboratory they believe in nothing but experimental research, will gayly write treatises on 'Marxist' physiology or chapters on 'Marxist' physics. What right have they . . . to point the finger of scorn at Hitlerian mathematics?" Bloch, 152. "In this matter of the men of the Left, as of the General Staff . . . Hitler was right. There is no getting away from it. Not the Hitler of the full-dress demagogic speeches, but the Hitler who once said to Rauschning when discussing this very question of Marxism: 'We, you and I, know that there isn't any final stability, but only a perpetual state of evolution. The future is an inexhaustible river of infinite possibilities whose source is a creation which is always being renewed.'" Ibid., 153. (The title of this chapter reads: "A Frenchman Examines His Conscience.")

[36] In May 1939 a national election was held in Hungary ( the first on the basis of universal secret suffrage). In the former so-called "Red belt" of Budapest, in the industrial suburbs, the Hungarian National Socialist Arrow-Cross party

of being warlike and profit-hungry, were among the principal pacifists in 1939 and, in some places, even afterward.[37] We have also seen that in 1940 the resistance of the working classes in Western Europe was feeble.[38] On one occasion even Churchill missed the significance of this general falling apart of the Left. Soon after his assumption of power, he made what was perhaps his most disastrous appointment: that of Stafford Cripps for British ambassador to the Soviet Union.[39] This English Puritan and Socialist worthy made a series of egregious diplomatic mistakes in Moscow. Eventually it took a capitalist such as Beaverbrook to get along spankingly with Stalin.

Were the rulers of the Soviet Union aware of the meaning of this failure of the Left? It is difficult to tell. There are reasons to believe that in this respect, too, Stalin stood out from his underlings, that he consciously discounted the importance of the European Left while he maintained a healthy respect for the men and the forces of the Right; evidences and expressions of his inclinations in this regard may be found throughout the record of his talks with certain foreign visitors. On the

---

made its greatest gains: 41.7 per cent of the total vote. The nationwide vote was 18 per cent.

In October 1940 a miners' strike in Hungary was organized by the Arrow-Cross. The only strike during the war, it frightened the government. No mention of the strike was allowed in the newspapers.

[37] Late in 1939 certain men of the German opposition against Hitler approached certain former Socialist union leaders. "Somewhat ironically, it was an industrialist, Walther Bauer, who furnished the money to pay the expenses for missions whose goal it was to forge that most fearsome of labor's traditional weapons against capitalism, the general strike." Deutsch, 67. The author should have added that the German workers would have done nothing of the kind.

[38] Here is another example: In Belgium the coal miners of Limburg resumed work a few days after the German occupation (as early as on 25 May 1940). By July coal production in Belgium—at a time when nearly one million Belgians were outside of their country, in France—was already over 50 per cent of the production before the German invasion.

[39] About some of the Cripps' mistakes, see below, p. 330, n. 6. "Among the most novel and encouraging innovations of the Churchill regime are the care that is now being taken to fit the right man to the right job—typified by the selection of Sir Stafford Cripps for the Moscow mission," Mollie Panter-Downes in "Letter from London" in *The New Yorker*, 2 June 1940. It must be added that the Cripps appointment was not Churchill's original idea. On 20 May 1940 the British suggested that he be sent to Moscow on a special mission, after which a new British ambassador would be appointed. The Russians refused this suggestion, and suggested that Cripps be appointed as the ambassador. The British deferred to this suggestion and sent Cripps.

other hand, there are evidences, too, of his continuing obsession with different sectarians of the Left: What other explanation is there for the Soviet agents' murder of the German anti-Stalin Communist Münzenberg in June 1940 in France or of Trotsky in August 1940 in Mexico? Stalin probably felt an increasing disregard, if not contempt, for Marx, while he had a certain kind of admiration for Hitler: Stalin's Germanophilia, his anti-Semitism, and his inclinations toward a national kind of socialism may have played a part in this. Still, Stalin made no attempt to square the official ideology accordingly. He had brought about a nearly complete change in the composition of the ruling class of the Soviet Union and of the Communist party.[40] But this vast new kind of Byzantine bureaucracy, loyal to him, went on employing the Marxist-Leninist rhetoric, no matter how unrealistic this was; they knew not how to think or talk otherwise, unless their chief were to tell them so. Thus, for example, Soviet political propaganda in the war against Finland was primitive and senseless to the point of being laughable. The Soviet radio and propaganda directed at Germany and the latter's allies after June 1941 was not much better. After the Soviets had captured 15,000 Polish officers and NCOs in 1939, they tried to convert them to Communism, using methods of propaganda, pressure, and bribery with food and comforts—a powerful instrument in dealing with perpetually hungry men among the misery of the prisoners' camps. They succeeded with about 400 out of 15,000: less than 3 per cent. In September 1941 Vishinski told the Polish ambassador, Kot, that Hitlerism was "opposed not only by Rauschning and Strasser, but by the peasants, workers, and millions of the people, who will take up arms against Hitler and finish off the military defeat. That is not an illusion but a realistic view. . . ." Did he believe what he was saying? It is difficult to tell. On the other hand, when the Bulgarian Communist Dimitrov, during the difficult days of October 1941, suggested to Stalin that the Comintern direct a proclamation to the German soldiers and workers, Stalin—in Dimitrov's words—"agreed, though he felt that no good would come of it."[41]

In any event, the Stalin-Hitler pact of 1939 had thrown the Commu-

---

[40] There is some reason to believe that Stalin had been impressed with the swift success with which Hitler in June–July 1934 had purged his own revolutionaries. When the Eighteenth Congress of the Communist party of the Soviet Union met in March 1939, less than 2 per cent of the rank-and-file delegates had attended the previous Congress, in 1934; of the 1,966 delegates in 1934, 1,108 had been arrested during the 1936–39 purges.

[41] Djilas, 38. After Stalingrad, Stalin told the then Polish ambassador, Romer: The Germans do not surrender; they " surrender only when they are in circumstances beyond their control, and not because they sympathize with the Soviet state!" *DPSR*, I, 490–91.

nists of the world into disarray. This made little difference in Eastern Europe, where the Communist parties were weak and unpopular (precisely because of the popular association of Communism with Russia).[42] In Western Europe the evolution of the Communists from 1939 to 1941 was more significant. It was not as simple as the standard accounts of their opponents suggests, that is: slavish and automatic adjustments of the party line overnight, involving two enormous extreme zigzags, one in August 1939 from extreme and militant anti-Germanism to pacifism and pro-Germanism, the other move in June 1941 in the diametrically opposite direction. In reality it took time until not only Communist voters but also party leaders convinced themselves that they had better follow the Soviet policy line. There were also evidences of the beginnings of Communist resistance to the Germans a few weeks or, in a few instances, even months before Hitler's attack on the Soviet Union.

Before 1939 the Communists were the most assiduous propagators of a kind of Marxist thinking that was wishful to the point of imbecility. On 19 February 1938, for example, their leader André Marty said at a great rally in Paris: "Hitler cannot wage war. For military and economic reasons. He no longer has qualified people. . . . Economically, Germany is on the verge of bankruptcy. . . . She does not have the necessary raw materials to wage war. . . . Hitler does not dare to give arms to ten million workers. . . . Germany cannot wage war with her working class at her back. . . ." There was probably not one leading Communist in Western Europe who knew of the Stalin-Hitler pact before he read about it in the capitalist papers or heard of it on the radio. Thereafter their policy was one of temporizing and hesitation. On 2 September 1939, the Communist deputies in the French Chamber voted for the war credits. Their leader, Thorez, entered the Army; he did not desert for Moscow until October. Still, Stalin's pact with Hitler had made the Communists unpopular. In France the government ordered the dissolution of the Communist party on 26 September 1939—mainly in order to curry favor with the anti-Communist Right. In the Chamber of Deputies nearly everyone voted in favor of this order, including the Socialists. The police ordered the Communist deputies to report for their arrest. With two exceptions every one of them surrendered meekly. This pattern was typical of the rest of Western Europe.[43] In Belgium and Holland on the day of the

---

[42] The exceptions (that nonetheless prove this rule) were Yugoslavia, Bulgaria, and Greece.

[43] More than two decades later a member of the Communist party in Britain recalled "having to flee for his life when he tried to sell the *Daily Worker* in a London working-class suburb" in early 1940. Thompson, *1940*, 21. On the other hand, Spears about April 1940 (I, 114): "Some of us pondered with anxi-

German invasion the police swooped down on Communists and the Nazi sympathizers alike. The Socialists of Switzerland voted four to one to exclude Communists from their ranks.

By early 1940, Communist propaganda was synchronized, by and large, with the strategy of the Soviet Union. The Communists were anti-Allied rather than pro-German; still, they played into the hands of the latter by their incessant propaganda: Down with the War! June 1940 marks the high point of this Communist collaboration with the masters of the Third Reich. Within Germany the former Communist deputy Torgler (Goering's protégé) helped in writing scripts for a secret "pro-Communist" radio station run by Goebbels' Propaganda Ministry for the purpose of propagating surrender among French workers in the French Army.[44] Four days after the Germans had marched into Paris, a French Communist delegation appeared at the German Kommandantur with the request that the Germans permit the publication of *L'Humanité*.[45] The Germans were inclined to give such a permission; but in the end they decided against it, principally because of the excited reproaches of some of their French sympathizers, including Doriot.[46] Consequently *L'Humanité* appeared illegally, a mimeographed sheet; but the Germans had no reason to be troubled with its contents. Its first number, on 13 July 1940, carried a lead article entitled: "*Fraternité franco-allemande.*" "The workers of Paris and the German soldiers get along very well. Their friendly conversations multiply. We are very glad of this. Let us know each other better."[47] *L'Humanité* would also say that De Gaulle was a British agent. In Holland and in Belgium the workers were at first neutral

---

ety the curious fascination Russia had for so many British workers, their strange lack of enthusiasm for the war and reluctance to put their backs into it, reported from some centers of war production."

[44] Boelcke, 375, 377, 381. There is, however, no evidence that Torgler and his colleagues acted upon Soviet instructions. In January 1940 Ribbentrop had sent a trusted official, Rost, on a secret mission to Russia: "He is to prepare an investigation of whether it is possible to bring influence to bear on the French Section of the III International and whether Soviet informational files on French Communists could be inspected." The Soviets were not interested in this. *GD*, D, VIII, 597–98.

[45] In Belgium a pro-Communist paper, *Liberté*, was permitted by the Germans to appear in June 1940; in Holland they gave a license for the Communist newspaper that existed for a few weeks.

[46] The French police arrested Maurice Tréand, one of the members of the Communist party Central Committee, who had gone to negotiate with the Germans; he was subsequently freed on the Germans' orders. Lecoeur, 94–95.

[47] Cited in Lecoeur, 89. In 1944 the French Communist party made frantic efforts to destroy copies of this issue.

toward the Germans; the Communists encouraged this. From Bohemia and Moravia, Heydrich reported that German rule was least unpopular among the workers who were profiting from some of the social reforms decreed by the Germans; and in spite of the extreme German sensitivity to pan-Slav tendencies, Communists in Bohemia and Moravia were not imprisoned by the Germans until February 1941. Then, in one fell swoop, the Germans picked up nearly the entire Central Committee of the underground party.

By this time—the spring of 1941—the Communist parties began to turn, cautiously, against the Germans. This was especially true in the Balkans; but in Holland, Belgium, and France, too, the first participation of Communists in strikes and resistance activities occurred in the spring of 1941. Many of the activities of the Communists were directed not against the Germans but against the local followers of the latter, as in Belgium, for example, where they would attack Rexists and tear down their posters on occasion. There is some evidence that—as in the case of the French and Belgian miners' strikes in May 1941 (in Belgium involving nearly 100,000 miners)—ordinary party members gave the lead, while some of the party officials followed after considerable hesitation. It seems that certain anti-German directives were beginning to pass down from Moscow to certain party leaders in certain countries, for example in Slovakia, as early as in May 1941.[48] On the morrow of Hitler's attack on the Soviet Union, then, the Communists in the conquered nations of Europe and in Britain breathed with a great relief: No longer would they be considered as traitors by many of their fellow men. Thereafter many threw themselves into the cause of the national resistance with enthusiasm, and sometimes even with a kind of patriotic—patriotic rather than Communist—heroism. In August 1939 Stalin had made his pact with Hitler, and it took some time for the Communists across Europe to align themselves with the foreign policy of the Soviet state. In June 1941 the opposite was true: The reactions of the ordinary Communists ran ahead of those of the officials of the Soviet state, who were thunderstruck rather than relieved, and whose first reactions to the German attack were marked by incredulity, confusion, and despair.

The Socialists were better off than the Communists. They were more respectable; untainted by the Nazi-Soviet Pact, they represented the Left variety of parliamentary democracy rather than the Right variety of

---

[48] It was in May 1941 that in Belgium, for example, the Germans completed their files on local Communists, whose mass arrestation took place on 23 June, two days after the German invasion of the Soviet Union.

Marxism. On the other hand, this very respectability could be their undoing. For twenty-five years the Socialists of Europe were plagued by the desertion of some of their more brilliant men, to the Right rather than to the Left. Mussolini was a prime example of this. In Stresa in 1935 he conferred with the Prime Ministers of Britain and France: Mussolini, MacDonald, Laval, three renegade Socialists, among which the last two admired the first, whose break with Socialism had been the most outspoken and radical. The most respectable Socialist in Europe who was not a renegade was Léon Blum, whose very appearance was somehow reminiscent of the world before 1914, someone out of a novel by Romain Rolland, with his dependent mustache and glasses, and with his dependence on the categories of Cartesian humanism. The antiquated appearance of Socialism made it unappealing. "Look at a Socialist Congress," wrote Drieu la Rochelle in 1937: "All these beards, pot-bellies, reeking of tobacco, they're all anxiously waiting for the hour of the apéritif."[49] Drieu's hero was Doriot, the ex-Communist, now a National Socialist, who stood for a rejuvenated France: *"Doriot est notre champion contre la mort."*[50] Across Europe hundreds of thousands of former Socialist voters had become National Socialists by 1938, in Austria, Hungary, Slovakia, and elsewhere. In Belgium, Henri de Man (who had been instrumental in 1917 in persuading Lloyd George to release Trotsky from British internment) had become a neo-Socialist (a term that was a euphemism for a national, as distinct from an international Socialist). An adviser to the King, De Man was favored by the Third Reich for a while; he tried to rally the entire Belgian Socialist party to his side in July 1940, with little success. In Holland the brilliant Socialist economist Rost van Tonningen chose a similar role. There the Germans at first assured leaders of the Socialist trade unions (NVV) that they would not interfere with their activities; in July 1940 the Dutch Nazi Woudenberg was appointed as head of the trade unions, whose leaders agreed. In Belgium the workers were at first neutral toward the Germans; their union leaders even helped to organize the first voluntary workers' transports to Germany.[51] In Denmark

---

[49] Drieu, *CRP*, 53. Writers such as Drieu would make much out of the youth and appearance of Fascist leaders; it is true that men such as José Antonio Primo da Rivera, Codreanu, Degrelle, Mosley, etc., were often young and handsome.

[50] This champion of life over death, however, was puffy and bespectacled, an ugly mug.

[51] The Belgian elder statesman Alexandre Galopin wrote in a confidential memorandum in July 1940: The working class "has been largely favorably impressed by the correct behavior of the enemy troops." Cited by Gerard-Libois, Gotovitch, 351. The secret German situation report (*Lagebericht*) on 2

the Socialist party continued to function under the German occupation. Prime Minister Stauning said after the German invasion that the government would function in a respectable manner; Danish Social Democrats such as Stauning and his Foreign Minister, Scavenius, would, under German pressure, sign the Anti-Comintern Pact in November 1941. (The first significant figure of Danish opposition to Germany in the cabinet was Ch. Møller, a conservative, who resigned in July 1940 in protest.) In April 1940 certain leaders of the Norwegian trade union were willing to cooperate with a Quisling government. In Finland Tanner, the principal figure of the Socialist party, was the leading spokesman for fighting Russia and even Britain, if must, on the side of the Third Reich (he was opposed by Paasikivi, an Agrarian-Conservative). Even before September 1939 a significant minority among the French Socialist leaders had deserted them for the Right: Déat, Paul Faure, Spinasse. On 6 July 1940 Spinasse, a former member of Blum's Popular Front government, stood up in the Vichy Assembly and assured Pétain of his full collaboration, in emotional tones; his speech was followed by that of Xavier Vallat, later the Commissioner for Jewish Affairs, who congratulated Spinasse across the aisles. The Congress of the CGTR (the Socialist trade unions) in Toulouse on 20 July 1940 accepted the new slogan of *Travail, Famille, Patrie* and chose to send a sympathetic delegation to Pétain and Laval. As the Belgian Liberals, the majority of the Belgian Socialist deputies who during the May panic had voted unanimously in Limoges to censure Leopold III for having capitulated to Germany, on 14 September 1940 signed a letter asking for his "forgiveness" and understanding.

This was the all-too-human accommodation of people to a new set of circumstances, of people who were not made of the stuff of martyrs or heroes; we should not ridicule or condemn them all too easily out of hand. On the other hand, there can be little doubt that the then weaknesses of certain Socialists were to a great extent due to the then weaknesses of their beliefs, of their ideological categories. As early as in 1937, George Orwell wrote in *The Road to Wigan Pier:* "We have got to admit that if Fascism is everywhere advancing, this is largely the fault of Socialists themselves. . . .

> With their eyes glued to economic facts, they have proceeded on the assumption that man has no soul, and explicitly or implicitly they have set up the goal of a materialistic Utopia. As a result Fascism has been able to play upon every instinct that revolts against hedonism and a cheap con-

---

December 1940 noted that during the patriotic manifestations on Armistice Day, 11 November 1940 (the first significant resistance activity), "the working class took no part in these manifestations." Ibid., 374.

ception of "progress." It has been able to pose as the upholder of the European tradition, and to appeal to Christian belief, to patriotism, and to the military virtues. . . . For a long time past, certainly for the last ten years, the devil has had all the best tunes. We have reached a stage when the very word "Socialism" calls up, on the one hand, a picture of aeroplanes, tractors, and huge glittering factories of glass and concrete; on the other, a picture of vegetarians with wilting beards, of Bolshevik commissars (half gangster, half gramophone), of earnest ladies in sandals, shock-headed Marxists chewing polysyllables, escaped Quakers, birth-control fanatics and Labour Party backstairs-crawlers. Socialism, at least in this island, does not smell any longer of revolution and the overthrow of tyrants, it smells of crankishness, machine-worship, and the stupid cult of Russia. Unless you can remove that smell, and very rapidly, Fascism may win.[52]

Well, "Fascism" did not win in the end—or, rather, it did not win the war—and its defeat was due to a large extent to Russia and airplanes and Americanization, things that Orwell abhorred. Still, there is a great deal of truth in the above passage; it reflects much of the climate of the late thirties, when the Left was not merely split but feeble, decaying, to a large extent unsure of itself. Eventually the Left recovered during the climate of the war. In the previous subchapter I emphasized that the earliest inspiring examples of resistance at the high noon of Nazi triumphs had come from the Right, while there was another kind of conservatism that would collaborate with Hitler. In this subchapter I must make a similar distinction: Having emphasized the weakness of the Left, I must state that this pattern of spiritless debility did not become dominant in the end. After everything is said, the renegades and the collaborationists among the Socialists turned out to be a minority—though a significant one, to be sure. Eventually the Socialists were to play respectable parts in the resistance of every European nation—though seldom before 1941.

By that time the ancient designations Right and Left[53] were losing much of their meanings. As the wrathful pro-Nazi Lucien Rebatet wrote in late 1941: How strange it is that now "the bankers of France put their hopes in Stalin, and the workers of France in the plutocracy of England." During the late 1930s Right and Left had split in France along the line

---

[52] Orwell, *Wigan Pier*, 246, 248. In early 1940 Orwell wrote in his diary: "W. says that the London 'left' intelligentsia are now completely defeatist, look on the situation as hopeless and all but wish for surrender. How easy it ought to have been to foresee, under their Popular Front bawlings, that they would collapse when the real show began." *Orwell*, II, 362.

[53] Drieu la Rochelle in 1937: "The 'Right' and the 'Left': two of the most outworn, of the least truthful, the stupidest of words."

that separated those who were willing to fight Hitler, if necessary together with the British and the Russians, from those who were opposed to such a war. We saw the split on the Right; but the Center was split, too, with people such as Reynaud or Monnet on one side, Piétri or Montigny on the other; and so were the Socialists, Blum or Auriol for resistance, Paul Faure and Spinasse for Pétainism. There was nothing very ideological in this. The traditional definitions of Right and Left would not help in explaining these divisions. Laval, who opted for a policy of collaboration with Mussolini and Hitler, may have been a renegade Socialist, but he was not a Rightist. De Gaulle, who favored a French alliance with the Soviet Union and with Czechoslovakia and who thought that France should have supported the Spanish Republic, broke with the nationalists of *Action Française;* but he was not a Leftist. Right and Left meant little in the confrontation of the two protagonist nations: Was Britain to the Left, or to the Right, of Hitler's Germany? The national mobilization of the British people in 1940, ordered by Churchill and by Chamberlain,[54] reached an extent to which Hitler and Himmler resorted to in Germany only in 1944. On the other hand, Hitler and Himmler were not only suspicious and hostile to the "old elites"; not only was "reactionary" the most damning word in their political vocabulary; they also went ahead in abolishing many of the symbols of traditional German nationalism, including popular dialects or the Gothic lettering of German script. Of all the states in Europe, Hungary was among the most "Rightist," not only because of surviving feudal elements in its social structure but also because her government was the first that had been erected on the basis of anti-Communism in 1919–20. Yet Hitler disliked the Hungarians. As Goebbels would say in July 1940: "The construction of the Hungarian state is diametrically the opposite from ours."[55] Oddly—or perhaps not so oddly—these very arguments about the "reactionary" nature of the Hungarian regime were held against the latter by spokesmen of the English and American Left, too.

"This is a war of faith," said the bishop of Chichester in 1940, "in which the nations themselves are divided." So were their classes, so were their parties. Still, in the end, the national element proved everywhere stronger than class or party or even ideology. There are at least two general kinds of evidence for this. First, until at least 1941, the conversions flowed in one direction: Many international Socialists or even Commu-

---

[54] As early as October 1939, the Chamberlain government established a national register for all citizens, including a national identity card.
[55] Boelcke, 430. Excerpts from a secret report of Heydrich in June 1940 of a similar nature in Paikert, 162. After 1940 these German criticisms of Hungary multiplied.

nists had become National Socialists, not the reverse. Second, more numerous than these renegades of the Left were those Socialists and Communists who, while not denying their earlier allegiances, discovered that they were convinced and committed patriots.[56] Instead of international Socialism, among the peoples of Europe we find ever newer variants of national socialisms. But this opens up a new set of problems, part of which is terminological.

## NATIONAL SOCIALISM

¶ The chief political reality of the first half of the twentieth century—and perhaps of an entire century beginning with 1870—was national socialism. This has been obscured by a confusion of terminology, a confusion introduced deliberately by Communists and their sympathizers. As early as 1932 the terms "National Socialist" and "Nazi" were forbidden in the Soviet Union. The Nazis were to be called "Fascists" or "Hitlerites"—in all probability because Stalin himself may have recognized how "National Socialism" might fit his increasingly nationalistic regime. This usage was perpetrated by the Left during the 1930s and unthinkingly accepted by intellectuals and journalists, especially in Western Europe and in the United States. It has persisted until this day, when millions of people say "Fascist" with hardly any knowledge of what Fascism was, and when "Fascism" has become the accepted term for all Rightist dictatorships (indeed, in the minds of certain idiots, the synonym for all non-Leftist regimes). This renewed employment of the word "Fascist" has been projected back to the past, so that by the 1960s even serious historians were writing about past phenomena such as the National Socialist Third Reich as if that had been but a variant of Fascism.[57] During the Second World War people saw more clearly. Few

---

[56] Or not so suddenly. The reason why, alone in Eastern Europe, Communism in Bulgaria and Yugoslavia maintained a certain appeal even in 1939–41, had nothing to do with Right and Left: It had much to do with traditional Russophilia; in the minds of these Balkan peoples, Communism was associated with Russia.

[57] This is true of the serious work by Ernst Nolte, *Three Faces of Fascism* (New York, 1965). Uneasy about the problems of his terminology, Nolte in his Appendix (A) tries to explain the reasons why he put the three movements that he studied in depth—the French *Action Française*, Italian Fascism, and German National Socialism—under the covering name of "Fascism." His reasons amount to not much more than the demonstration that Mussolini had

people, except for the Soviets, thought or spoke or wrote about Hitler and the Germans as Fascists.

The origins of National Socialism may be found in the nineteenth century; the origins of Fascism are more recent.[58] Marx failed to recognize the force of nationalism during his lifetime. His followers did not see—because they did not wish to see—the inevitable presence of nationalism within the hearts and minds of the working classes. They ignored not only the growing reality of nationalism but also its unavoidable penetration into socialism. Eventually Nationalist Socialism was to become the new synthesis: anticapitalist as well as anti-Communist. This fusion of nationalism with socialism was becoming evident here and there, even before 1914. The First World War provided the general, as well as the particular, examples of the failure of a Marxist internationalism that was unreal and abstract. The general example was the enthusiastic reaction of the masses of Europe's nations, including their working classes, to the call to war. The particular example was Benito Mussolini's announcement of his conversion to the cause of Italian nationalism.[59] In October 1914 this radical young leader of the large Italian Socialists broke with the party and with the cause of international socialism as he recognized the abstract utopianism of the latter. Thus Mussolini became a national socialist in 1914 even before he was to proclaim the ideology of Fascism in 1919—another example of the shortcoming of the kind of political analysis that accepts the "Fascist" adjective as the common denominator of Mussolini and Hitler, simply because Mussolini assumed power in Italy a little more than a decade before Hitler assumed power in Germany, or because Hitler admired Mussolini at the time.

Fascism and National Socialism had certain things in common: They were anticapitalist as well as anti-Communist, antiliberal as well as anti-Bolshevik, though to different degrees. On the other hand, their ideology, their philosophy, their aspirations, and their style were not the same. In certain places—England, Ireland, Spain, and Holland—the Fascists and the National Socialists were, by and large, the same people, belonging to the

---

preceded, and therefore to some extent influenced, Hitler. This is not very convincing.

[58] This is not the place to discuss the intellectual pedigree of these movements. Still, we ought to note that the word "Fascism" was made current by Mussolini and by his political followers only around 1919 (the earliest antecedent of the word was that of a Sicilian populist grouping around 1892). The first combinations of National and Socialist appear in Europe as early as in the 1870s, in some instances even earlier; by 1900 there were small National Socialist parties in Central Europe, particularly in Bohemia.

[59] It is perhaps symbolic that Mussolini was born in the year Marx died.

same party. Elsewhere—in France, Belgium, Austria, Slovakia, and Hungary—Fascists and National Socialists were not the same people. There were many men and women, including some in Germany and in Italy, who liked Mussolini while they feared and hated Hitler.[60] Until about 1936 certain conservatives, certain liberals, even Churchill, would maintain a great deal of respect for Mussolini, in the practices and ideas of whom they saw—and not altogether without reason—those of a national leader within the general tradition of Western civilization, whose construction of a new political and social order might provide a workable and attractive alternative to broken-down parliaments or to the violence of the class struggle. Hitler admired Mussolini; and yet, in 1934, Fascism and National Socialism stood apart. Italy was the only European power that took a strong stand against the Nazi *coup* in Austria that year. Differences in ideologies were involved, too; within Austria the main opponents of the Nazis were often Austro-Fascists. In 1934 Mussolini, at least implicitly, criticized German racist ideology in a speech in Bari; there were open polemics between Fascist and National Socialist ideologues within Italy[61]; there were even divergences in the official Nazi attitude toward modern Italy within the Third Reich.[62] But by 1936 Mussolini had reached the conclusion that there was nothing to be gained for Italy by

---

[60] "Even during the war many Italians remained Mussolinians while, at the same time—obviously not in a very active manner—they were anti-Fascists." This intelligent distinction by De Felice, *EP*, 221. Nothing like this existed in Germany: there, indeed, in many instances the opposite was true.

[61] The principal anti-Nazi personage in Italy was the popular Marshal Balbo (who was to perish in June 1940 in an airplane accident). His newspaper, the *Corriere Padano*, throughout 1934 waged a strong polemic against the periodical *Il Tevere*, run by Interlandi and Preziosi, calling the latter "the official organ of the social-nationalists in Italy, which took upon itself the grave burden of serving Hitler." De Felice, 163. A book attacking German racism— Mario Bendiscioli, *Neopaganismo razzista*—was published in Brescia as late as in 1937. As late as 1940 and 1941, Ciano tried to struggle against the pro-Nazi and anti-Semitic Farinacci and the latter's newspaper; see, for example, Ciano's interview with Monsignor Montini (later Pope Paul VI), *VD*, 4, 540–41.

[62] An exhibition of modern Italian art opened in Berlin in March 1934. There ensued a bitter struggle between two wings of Nazi philosophers. Rosenberg and his friends attacked Italian futurism in the *Voelkischer Beobachter*. Other periodicals, such as *Kunst der Nation* and *Weltkunst*, called the exhibit priceless. Goebbels quietly supported the latter. Brenner, 78–79, 82–83. Hitler took a middle position; in a subsequent party speech he attacked cubism, futurism, and Dadaism, as well as the "reactionaries" of a "folkish-bourgeois renaissance."

opposing Hitler[63] on the side of the Western democracies. In 1938 Mussolini ordered the Fascist party to conform not only to an alliance with the Third Reich but also to adopt some of the practices of Hitler's National Socialism, including anti-Semitism. The result again proves the faulty nature of the overall designation "Fascist": It was not Fascism that produced National Socialism, but it was National Socialism that thereafter began to absorb Fascism.

In other words, the rise and decline of Fascism simply reflected the rise and decline of Mussolini's Italy, just as the rise and fall of Nazis reflected the rise and fall of Hitler's Germany. Again, political ideas followed power, not the reverse. This was often an unconscious process, but it is instructive to recall certain correspondences. In most European nations the Fascist parties reached the peak of their attraction in the early 1930s; this is indicated by certain electoral results.[64] After 1936, generally speaking, the Fascist parties declined, while a newer type of National Socialism was emerging, just as after 1936 Germany was rising, eclipsing the image of Italy before the eyes of the new radicals. In France the appeal of the ex-Communist and National Socialist Doriot was beginning to eclipse the appeal of the ex-Socialist and Fascist Déat.[65] In Romania the National Socialistic Iron Guard in December 1937 got 16 per cent of the national vote in an election, even as it was rigged against them by the government; at the same time the more or less Fascistic (though anti-Semitic) Christian Nationalists led by Goga received 9.2 per cent of the vote. In May 1939 in

---

[63] Mussolini's dislike for France and England was stronger than his liking for Germany. The French and British conservatives missed this: The Chamberlainites and the French Right went on appeasing Mussolini, hoping that he would thereafter join with them against Hitler. Drieu la Rochelle pointed out the vain hopes of this as early as 4 March 1938, before the Anschluss: If Mussolini were to ally himself with France and Britain against Germany, he would be contributing to the defeat of world Fascism. "This is impossible." Drieu, *CRP*, 114.

[64] The parties of the radical Right gained their largest number of votes in Switzerland in 1933–34, in Holland in 1935, in Belgium in 1936, and in Finland in 1931–32. In Britain "up to 1934 the Fascist advance was breathtakingly rapid, so rapid that during the period of Rothermere support (the *Daily Mail* was favorable to Mosley) there was a possibility that it would gather enough momentum to take Mosley to 10 Downing Steet. As, however . . . the Movement became associated with violence and with developments in Germany, the Movement's path after 1934 was uphill with every step a battle." Cross, 132.

[65] Doriot opposed the French alliance with Russia and called for a friendly relationship with Germany even before Stalin announced in favor of French rearmament in May 1935; Déat, on one occasion, supported the then colonel De Gaulle's argument for an *armée de métier*, before 1936.

Hungary, the National Socialist parties emerged as the second-largest group, with over 18 per cent of the votes. Finally, in 1940, pro-Nazi sympathizers came out into the open everywhere. Perhaps "pro-Nazi" is not the *mot juste*. "Pro-German" would be better—an adjective that, of course, includes all kinds of opportunists who simply discovered the virtues of the Germans when the latter seemed triumphant. But there was more to this. The pro-Nazis and the pro-Germans were those people who were attracted by some of the qualities of the Germans. They included military men who admired the Germans' martial efficiency; technicians who admired their weapons; adolescents who admired their uniforms and their motorcycles; intellectuals who admired their philosophy; anti-Semites who admired the way in which the Germans dealt with the Jews. I shall have to devote an entire chapter of this book to this relatively novel factor in the relations of peoples, to the attraction that the image of one nation has for certain people of another nation.[66] Few historians have devoted sufficient interest to this in the past. Among them was Burckhardt, who said in one of his lectures that "Calvinism was the Reformation of those peoples who did not like the Germans." So during the Last European War, Nazism rather than Fascism was the radical new ideology attracting certain peoples whose cultural forms were Germanic rather than Latin; a few Northern Europeans, and many Ukrainians, Russians, Lithuanians, Hungarians, Slovaks, Croats. So the forms of Fascism rather than those of Nazism were attractive to certain people among the Latin and southern peoples of Europe. By "forms" I mean not only institutions but also rhetoric: certain ways of speech expressing certain kinds of thought. One word may illustrate the differences of Fascism from Nazism: It is the adjective "fanatic." Hitler and Goebbels evoked often the desirability and the presence of *fanatische Nationalsozialisten* (fanatic National Socialists)—an adjective which would not be approbatory in Italian, and certainly not in French.

In any event, by 1940 Fascism was in eclipse because, compared to Germany, Italy was in eclipse; because, compared to Hitler, Mussolini was in eclipse. It had become obvious that, just as the performance of Italy was not comparable to that of Germany, Fascism was less dynamic and less radical than National Socialism. This was no surprise to the Germans, and not even to Hitler, who disliked the Italians while he liked Mussolini; and who—an important point, this—admired the latter's personality rather than his political ideas.[67]

---

[66] See below, p. 383 passim.

[67] This is significant, since of the three principal dictators, Mussolini may have been the most original thinker; he was the creator of Fascism, whereas National Socialism had existed before Hitler, and Communism before Stalin.

And now we come to the second terminological problem. We must make a distinction not only between Fascism and National Socialism, but also between German National Socialism and other national socialisms.[68] Let me repeat the earlier argument once more: Fascism tried to bring about a nationalist kind of socialism; but it was not like German National Socialism. The Fascist ideal was a neo-Renaissance one, not altogether incompatible with Catholic Christianity; the Hitlerian dynamic was reminiscent of the anti-Renaissance fury of Luther, with a powerful populist appeal, and anti-Catholic. Heine in 1834 sensed this latent barbarism among the peaceful Germans of his day; the decline of Christianity in Germany, he wrote, will be followed by a new outburst of wild fury; the old stone gods will emerge from the dust and rubble; Thor with his giant hammer; the French better watch out; it will come with a thunder unheard before in the history of mankind. "A drama will be played out in Germany, compared to which the French Revolution will look like a harmless performance."[69] As early as 1911 Thomas Mann wrote: "The Germans must choose: Goethe or Wagner. The two will not go together. I fear that they will say Wagner." One hundred years after Heine wrote the above, Malcolm Muggeridge visited a German colony in southern Russia in 1933. He saw things with a certain kind of insight:

> The Germans showed him their settlement. They walked with him through pig-sties, stirring up one fat pig after another. They caught sheep between their legs and parted the wool to show him its thickness. They spread grain over the palms of their hands, and gingerly opened the stables of horses and bulls. Their scarred faces, cruel and clumsy, were sensitive to the nature of fertility. They brought the smell of fertility to his nostrils. Barbarians, too, he thought; but belonging to the earth. The barbarity . . . of the Dictatorship of the Proletariat was abstract.
>
> In the evening the Germans put a military march on the gramophone. They all stood up; stiffly, absurdly, spurred heels clicking together, faces obtusely solemn. A barbarism, Wraithby thought, that may, and probably will, make war on civilization. Not, like the Dictatorship of the Proletariat, on life.[70]

---

[68] Or between Nazism and other national socialisms. This somewhat grotesque and not very euphonic word "Nazi" (pronounced "Naatsi" in German, "Nahzi" in English) usually refers to the German variety, deriving from German slang in the twenties, an abbreviation of an abbreviation: the "Nazis" were the National Socialists, *die Nazi-sozi*.

[69] *Heine, SW*, IV, 294. ("*Zur Geschichte der Religion und Philosophie in Deutschland*.")

[70] Muggeridge, *WM*, 245. ("Wraithby" was Muggeridge.) See also the same episode in Muggeridge, I, 259–60.

Mussolini in 1931 said that the twentieth century would be the century of Fascism (he also said later that Fascism was not an article of export). For Hitler this century was to be the century of Germandom, not of National Socialism. In November 1938 he told the South African Pirow: He was "exporting only one idea, and that is not the idea of National Socialism. It is the idea of anti-Semitism." This was largely accurate. Throughout his career, and throughout the war, Hitler regarded the anti-Semitism of other people as the litmus paper of their reliability. Yet this does not mean that Hitler had no political philosophy besides anti-Semitism, that he was merely an opportunist and a nihilist—the shallow and intellectually fashionable interpretation by many of his biographers. Hitler's own conception of the necessary synthesis of nationalism and socialism is apparent from many fragments of his speeches and remarks. It was clearly expressed in one of his more significant wartime speeches to the German nation, on 30 January 1941. After the collapse in 1918 the Germans were in want of a unitary conception, of a powerful appeal to their idealism, he said. This strong appeal to idealism

> was to be found only in two camps: in the Socialist and in the Nationalist one. Just the two camps who were waging a mortal struggle against each other. They had to be fused together: into a new kind of unity.

Hitler was a National Socialist: No doubt about that. What he and his followers did to the German state and to the German people is another story, the terrible consequences and some of the details of which have now been amply described, mostly by conscientious German historians. But in this book I must deal with the general phenomenon of National Socialism rather than with its peculiar German variety, just as I am attempting to deal with the history of Europe in 1939–41 at large rather than with the evolution of the Third Reich during those two years (a necessary shortcoming, since the latter topic remains an instructive one).

National Socialism had many followers and imitators outside Germany. For a passing moment in the history of mankind it seemed to have given form to a new universal development marking an entire century. We have seen that it had a powerful appeal to masses of people, especially to the young, in certain nations of Eastern Europe, and that it had a transitory chance of enlisting the sympathies of certain groups of people even in Western Europe. Nor must it be thought that this appeal was merely to the half educated. Besides certain opportunists, people of high intellectual achievement who sympathized with Hitler in 1940 and after included great writers, great artists, great musicians, European luminaries: major writers such as Céline, Knut Hamsun, Drieu la Rochelle, Giovanni Papini, Wyndham Lewis, Ezra Pound; minor poets and artists such as Jakob

Schaffner, Jon Knittel; musicians such as Mengelberg and Dohnányi; philosophers such as Giovanni Gentile and Bernard Faÿ—an impressive list. The list of respectable European artists and scholars who sympathized with Fascism at least would fill several pages. On a less exalted level American neo-machiavellians such as James Burnham and neo-idealists such as Charles Lindbergh and his wife saw in National Socialism in 1940 the wave of the future (the title of Mrs. Lindbergh's best seller in 1940).

By the end of 1941 this belief in the wave of the future was weakening.[71] But the hard core of European nationalists remained. They were mostly Germanophiles. This is one of the most curious political phenomena of the twentieth century. The adjective "national" meant pro-German. Thus, for example, the "nationalists," the "National Front" in Austria in 1938, in Switzerland from 1933–45, in Bulgaria, in Hungary, in Romania, and also everywhere, designated those movements and those politicians who would prefer, *in extremis*, that their state be conquered by the Germans. Their nationalism was ideological, not patriotic.[72] Germanophilia, as we shall see later, was the key to the inclinations of men such as Knut Hamsun or Sven Hedin, who disliked the English and preferred the Germans already during the First World War. The studies of the Dutch De Jong about the so-called fifth columns, at least in Western Europe, revealed that the most dangerous, and often the only effective, clandestine military pacemakers of the Germans were the people of the German-speaking minorities in the neighboring states of the Reich. In Belgium the early collaborationists were Flemish; with few individual exceptions, the National Socialist movement in Switzerland was German-Swiss in composition. There were, however, millions of people, across the Continent, who were National Socialists not because they had German blood or because they felt related to the Germans, but because they were political and cultural Germanophiles; conversely, there were millions of others who were Germanophiles because they were National Socialists.

For a short time in the summer of 1940 it seemed that the victory of Germany meant the victory of the National Socialists across the Continent, and that the Germans would treat them as their allies, just as a century and a half before the French Jacobins had treated other European revolutionaries as their natural allies. This was the natural belief of all German collaborators, ranging from local National Socialist leaders such

---

[71] Soon James Burnham would be busy typing articles to the effect that the wave of the future was represented by Stalin, not Hitler. As Orwell pointed out in 1944, Burnham was typical of the intellectual who acquired his reputation by predicting the continuation of whatever seems to be going on.

[72] So was the young Hitler's, who remembered his youth in *Mein Kampf*: "I was a nationalist; but I was not a patriot."

as the Dutch Mussert or the Norwegian Quisling to the Hungarian Szálasi or the Romanian Horia Sima. Yet these people did not get what they wanted. For, while Hitler and his cohorts *within* the Third Reich generally speaking, sought fanatics rather than collaborators, they would prefer collaborationists rather than fanatics abroad. Hitler had no particular wish to encourage different national socialisms among the different nations of Europe. His aim was the domination of Europe by Germany, not a European National Socialist revolution. There was a certain amount of pragmatism within this policy: The Third Reich needed subservient governments and people who would produce what Germany needed rather than states whose energy would be consumed by revolutionary upheaval.[73] Hitler and Goebbels and Himmler may have disagreed on the relative virtues of different occupation policies, but they were in agreement on one thing: The New Europe would mean a German-ruled Europe, simply and squarely, not a whit more or less.

This would disappoint their most ardent collaborators. Many of them remained loyal to the cause of the Third Reich to the death. We know of their disappointment in retrospect. The first to be disappointed were leaders among the Austrian Nazis who, in many ways, had been the true originals. Hitler cared little for them. Captain Leopold, the leader of their radical wing, wrote bitter letters to Hitler in 1938 and in 1939; banished in 1941, both Leopold and his only son died in the Russian campaign. The Czech, the Danish, the Dutch National Socialists were frustrated and embittered people; the conquering Germans would not allow them authority in their own country.[74] Even Quisling was not allowed to form a government until 1942.[75] In Belgium the Flemish National Socialist party (VLAG) was generally disregarded by the Germans, who favored the more moderate Flemish VNV. In Hungary, notwithstanding Hitler's distaste for the ideology and the composition of the regime, he chose not to promote the local Arrow-Cross fanatics to power, at least not until 1944, the end of the war: He needed order in Hungary. The most

---

[73] Mussolini, too, did preciously little to encourage Fascism among Albanians; Stalin throughout his career favored people who were loyal to him and to Russia, rather than Communists with a long record of revolutionary agitation.

[74] The panicky Dutch government had arrested 10,000 suspected Dutch Nazis on 10 May 1940. A few days later the victorious Germans freed most of them, including their leader, Mussert. The Germans refused to let him make a broadcast. He wrote in his diary next day: "Not a trace of goodwill toward me by the Germans. This Sunday is one of the most unpleasant ones in my life."

[75] A note by Rosenberg on 6 July 1940: "To me, Quisling's attitude is that of an upright Germanic man devoted to the Fuehrer who ought *never* be treated in this manner." *GD*, D, X, 141.

significant example of this German preference for relatively orderly and subservient governments occurred in Romania in January 1941. Four months earlier, King Carol had been swept out of the country by a nationalist revolution that, with the help of mass demonstrations and the Iron Guard, brought the pro-German Marshal Antonescu to power. Hitler was favorably impressed by the latter; indeed, Antonescu was one of his favorite allies until the end (1944). The Iron Guard was probably the most fanatical and murderous mass movement of all National Socialists in Europe: Its members prided themselves by hanging Jews on butcher hooks in November 1940 and torturing their political opponents (such as the aged and eminent Professor Iorga) on their deathbeds. In January 1941 the Iron Guard element in Antonescu's nationalist coalition tried to rise to power. The Romanian Army crushed their rebellion after three days of fighting, on occasion with the help of German troops and tanks. Antonescu had been assured of the support of Hitler, who told him a week before these events that "co-operation between Germany and Romania does not depend on the existence of Romanian National Socialist party or organization. If that were a prerequisite, in many instances Germany's co-operation with other states would not be possible."[76] And thus the Romanian events were but the most dramatic manifestations of a policy that would be applied all over Eastern,[77] and even in Western Europe, where the Germans would try to work with Pétain and with Darlan and Laval rather than with Doriot and Déat.

---

[76] A few months before, the roving German ambassador, Neubacher, from Bucharest on 19 November 1940: "My main pedagogical task consists in making it clear to the Guardists that there is no place in the new Europe for an isolated revolutionary laboratory. . . ." GD, D, XI, 629. It is interesting to note that in Spain the Falangist newspapers were strongly sympathetic to the Iron Guard in January; Falangist youths demonstrated before the Romanian Legation in Madrid, in favor of the Guardist Minister, who then resigned; their newspaper Arriba wrote that the Falange would not be dealt with in Spain as the Iron Guard was treated in Romania. Ribbentrop's oral recommendations to Antonescu at the end of the revolt are significant because of their terminology: "Marxists to be executed. Idealists to be exiled to Germany." GD, D, XI, 170. The Guardist leader Horia Sima went into exile in Germany, where he was treated indifferently until August 1944. Then the Romanians, including most of Antonescu's people, deftly turned on the Germans and surrendered to the Russians; after that Horia Sima became the head of a phantom Romanian exile government.

[77] The Czech National Socialists had a small foretaste of this. In August 1940 their Storm Troops, the Svatopluk Guard, attacked buildings of the Czech government in Prague; they were forcibly turned back by German troops (though the local SS units did not intervene).

In Western Europe the courage and the idealism of the early nationalist revolutionaries were often of a high order. An early prototype of such a revolutionary was José Antonio Primo da Rivera, the founder of the Spanish Falange (killed by the Reds in 1936). When the Rightist Bernanos turned bitterly against the Franco regime in 1937, accusing it of the worse of cruelties, he had some good words for the Falangists (his son Yves was a member of the Mallorca Falange for a while).[78] In France the National Socialist and ex-Communist Doriot, who in 1938 had insisted "We are the *real* revolutionaries," supported the war in 1939 and fought bravely on the Loire in June 1940.[79] More curious, and tragic, was the career of Joseph Darnand. One of the highest decorated French soldiers in the First World War, an ardent nationalist, he distinguished himself during the reluctant war by one of the few inspiring acts of military bravery among the French: On 8 February 1940, in the frontier woods of Forbach, he and another French infantryman captured an entire German patrol. In June 1940 Darnand stood ready to join De Gaulle; but an interview with Pétain persuaded him to stay in France. Eventually Darnand became the brutal and feared chief of the Milice, hunting down and killing Jews and resistants.

Together with Doriot, the intellectual National Socialists—Brasillach, Rebatet, Drieu—hated the Vichy regime, because it was insufficiently committed to the cause of a German victory in Europe; even more, because the Vichy atmosphere exuded a kind of antiquated conservatism of the Maurras school, which had been bypassed by events. Already in 1934 Drieu wrote: "We need a third party which, while being social, knows also how to be national—and, while being national, knows also how to be social."[80] In late 1941 Lucien Rebatet wrote a chapter in *Les décombres* attacking Vichy, the heading of which could have been written by a Gaullist: "The Parody of a State":

> While a young Europe was being born amidst the glorious pains of a healthy and virile order, Vichy France reminds one of an aged dowager, surrounded by the junk of the previous century, smelling faintly of catpiss, clouded from the shout and tumult of life, ending her existence away from Paris, in a pettifogging boardinghouse, arranging endlessly

---

[78] Bernanos: I knew "a handful of young Falangists, full of honor and bravery, whose program I did not wholly approve but who were animated, as was their noble chief, by a violent sentiment of social justice." Bernanos, *GRC*, 91.

[79] He criticized the ex-Socialist Déat, who agitated against "dying for Danzig" in 1939 (in 1941 Déat would agitate in favor of a French volunteer legion on the side of the Germans, in favor of dying in Russia).

[80] Drieu, *CRP*, 14.

the old and dusty bric-a-brac around herself; a bigoted old bag, accustomed at being shortchanged by crooks wearing cassocks.[81]

To be sure, the style of Vichy was not very inspiring—when, for instance, in December 1940 Pétain was persuaded to move against Laval. This miniscule and comic *coup d'état*, engineered by Du Moulin de la Barthète among others, began to unfold in the latter's office, on the desk of which reposed Pétain's letter to Hitler, explaining Laval's forthcoming resignation in advance. Laval tried to look at the letter, which Du Moulin quickly slid under the blotter. Subsequently Laval was taken to Pétain, in order to receive his sentence of dismissal. Pétain's closest collaborators were eavesdropping breathlessly. They were watching the scene through the large keyhole of the Vichy hotel room, an opening that no doubt had served other interesting purposes in the past. Eventually Pétain caved in. Déat, who had been arrested by the French police in Paris, was let free upon the Germans' demands; so was Laval released from his interment in his château. "Beautiful!" said Laval to Du Moulin, who had been ordered to fetch him. "You arrested me. You put me in a box. . . . That big sausage of a Flandin (*ce grand dépendeur d'andouilles*) . . . I have never met such shit. The socialists of Aubervilliers, all the communists, the steelworkers, the factory gangs, all of these types are *grand seigneurs* compared to this kind of dung."[82] In December 1941 Doriot, on leave from the Russian Front, called on Darlan, pleading for the creation of a French dictatorial state, as had Drieu and Déat pleaded for one French national party in July 1940, in vain. Darlan yawned and kept his eyes half closed through the interview. Doriot left him in a state of fury. This was the Vichy that had proclaimed *La revolution nationale!*[83] The French Na-

---

[81] Rebatet, 639. In this interesting work, published in German-occupied Paris, there occurs at times a curious streak of true (as distinct from ideological) French patriotism: "A truly patriotic sentiment, even if derouted horribly, forces our respect. Let's not forget that the *fighting* Gaullists, even if they number among their ranks the lowest kinds of crooks and mercenaries, include brave men who follow the call of their blood. Allow me to prefer them to the old softies [the Vichy troop] . . . too cowardly to join De Gaulle." Ibid., 591.

[82] Du Moulin, 80. The Pétain government had already arrested some of the leading figures of the Third Republic: Blum, Daladier, Reynaud, etc. In 1942 they were tried before a court in Riom. The trial had to be suspended on German demand.

[83] The term *revolution nationale* was put into currency by Georges Valois, who was a French Fascist in 1925 (and a Gaullist in 1940). Maurras, whose philosophy claimed to be antirevolutionary, went along with it. The term was employed by Pétain in a speech on 11 October 1940, a speech written by Gaston Bergéry, who in July 1940 had proposed, together with Drieu, the creation

tional Socialists were deeply disgusted with it,[84] as they were to be disgusted with Pétain, who was no Hitler, to be sure, no matter how some of his followers tried to create the cult of the national leader.[85]

Thus, partly because of Hitler's disinterest, partly because of the general disinterest of their own peoples, the National Socialists failed. Yet while National Socialism was seldom widely popular,[86] we must not forget that history is more than often made by determined minorities; and in the summer of 1940 these determined minorities had their chance. Most people in Europe were resigned to a new order. But the Germans did little about this. Even at the end of 1940 National Socialists, such as the Belgian Degrelle, were full of hopes[87]: On New Year's Day in 1941 he publicly proclaimed the greatness of Hitler and the necessary "annihilation" of Britain. Five days later six thousand of his supporters paraded in Liège. There were scattered jeers. In February another Rexist parade was attacked by some spectators. By May Degrelle would admit that "the majority of my compatriots are blind"; and the collaborationist newspapers complained of "the collective aberration of pessimism among most of our

---

of a single French national party. On 31 December 1940 Pétain spoke again about his "government of the national revolution." (As Anatole de Monzie wrote in *Ci-devant*, "the constant ambition of reactionaries is to resemble revolutionaries.")

[84] In August 1941 an attempt was made to kill Laval and Déat (it failed). The Parisian National Socialist press said that the attempt was made by *Action Française* adherents. The Vichy press said that the perpetrators were Communists.

[85] Five million photographs of Pétain, at 25 F apiece, were sold by January 1941. Many Frenchmen still remember the Youth Song of 1940–41:

> *Maréchal, nous voilà!*
> *Devant toi, le sauveur de la France*
> *Nous jurons, nous tes gars*
> *De servir et de suivre tes pas.*

[86] Quisling's right-hand man Hagelin was probably correct when Hitler asked him on 13 April 1940, "absolutely frankly," how large a following Quisling might have among the Norwegian people: Hagelin said 15 per cent.

[87] See, for example, his memorandum to Hitler on 20 October 1940: "(1) National Socialist Germany should prepare, beginning immediately, a complete plan for bringing order to Europe. (2) This order is not conceivable unless the German Army assures it throughout . . . Europe. . . . If Germany withdrew militarily from the former parliamentary countries, still terribly riddled by British democratic propaganda, revolution with anarchy would inevitably follow. . . ." *GD*, D, XI, 339.

peoples."[88] Then came the war in Russia for which Degrelle, too, volunteered, in an SS unit.[89] On 4 September 1941 he said: "We are one thousand. We want to be many thousands. To win other thousands, we have to make ourselves into something greater through hardness and suffering. . . . To become the invincible army on the day when, having conquered Moscow, we shall conquer Brussels." Degrelle was thinking like Hitler, who wanted to conquer Moscow in order to conquer London (the same Hitler who near the end of the war told Degrelle that if he, Hitler, had a son, he'd want him to be like Degrelle). In another sense this was nonsense; to Brussels through Moscow, a National Socialist detour comparable to Lenin's forced detour in 1920 when the latter, unwilling to admit the failure of international Communism in Europe, was supposed to have said that the road to Paris leads through Peking.

For us there remains one last distinction to make. After 1941 the National Socialists of Europe were going down to defeat because of their association with Germany. In 1945 German National Socialism was destroyed. Yet national socialism lived on. Let me, for the last time, sum up some of the distinctions of this subchapter. There was German National Socialism: a thing in itself. There were the National Socialists in other countries of Europe—almost always anti-Semitic, usually but not always pro-German. Finally, there was, and there still is, national socialism in the broad sense of the term, covering the general conjunction of nationalism with socialism. The three terms, and the phenomena they describe, were and are not the same: Just as not every National Socialist was German, not every kind of National Socialism was, or is, totalitarian. For this conjunction of nationalism with socialism was more than a passing phenomenon; its protean development may have been the principal political configuration of a century. During the nineteenth century the governments and the principal political ideas in the Western world were a mixture of conservatism and liberalism. After 1870 this dialogue and its dialectic began to lose meaning. For the past one hundred years the principal forms of government and the different ideologies—and not only in the Western world—have been different mixtures of nationalism with socialism. This has been obscured for a long time by the prevalence of an outdated political terminology. Yet it takes little imagination to see how such different men as Castro, Mao, Perón, Nasser, Tito—and, in a broader sense, many of the leaders of the democracies of the second half of the twentieth century—have been representing different variants of National Socialism.

Still, even an elementary description of this protean movement

---

[88] Struye, 36.

[89] So did the Flemish nationalist leader Tollenaere, who fell in Russia in 1942.

would carry us beyond the confines of this book. Here it may be sufficient to conclude the argument by pointing out that the principal dictators of the Second World War, too, turned out to have been national socialists. It is obviously nonsense to call Mussolini a Communist or Stalin a Fascist; yet the national socialist adjective somehow fits them both. Nor is this merely the discovery of a convenient terminological box. National Socialism was, and is, no static phenomenon. The movement toward national socialism was dynamic. There is much evidence to the effect that Hitler's example influenced not only Mussolini but also Stalin who, as the war went on, turned more and more nationalist and anti-Semitic.

At least in the short run, the German example was powerful—no matter how much it may have fallen into disrepute after the war. And by the German example I mean not only the peculiarly crude German variant of nationalism, which, as we have seen, turned many people against the Germans; I mean the German variant of socialism that Hitler had created and that was in evidence for most Europeans during the war. In that respect, too, Hitler produced a new kind of synthesis. As I wrote before, it made little difference whether Krupp under Hitler was socialized or not. This was something new, this dissolution of the boundaries separating "private" from "public" enterprise, institutions, and behavior; it was part and parcel of the great social development of this century, of which so-called capitalist democracies such as the United States have not remained exempt. Hitler was not a capitalist; and he did not fear socialism. The European National Socialists understood this. In November 1941 a new collaborationist newspaper in Paris appeared, with the name *La France socialiste*. A month later the collaborationist Luchaire bitterly complained: "A conservative and clerical France will never obtain a real hearing from the new socialist Germany."[90]

Certain people among the opponents of Germany understood this too. Among them Orwell already in 1936 felt compelled to say that "Fascism" was dangerous precisely because it contained good elements as well as bad ones. "It is far worse than useless to write Fascism off as 'mass sadism,' or some easy phrase of that kind." People ought not pretend that it is "merely an aberration. . . . The only possible course is to examine the Fascist case, grasp that there is something to be said for it, and then make it clear to the world that whatever good Fascism contains is also implicit in Socialism."[91] Having returned from Germany, Nevile Henderson wrote in the winter of 1939–40: "Few people in the twentieth century

[90] Duquesne, 107.
[91] Orwell, *Wigan Pier*, 235.

would deny that with all its horrors and in spite of the ills of the Napoleonic epoch, the French Revolution left behind it theories and systems which were of lasting benefits to mankind. National Socialism is no less a revolution; and, however odious its ideology may today appear to most of us, just as did the French Revolution to our forebears at the end of the eighteenth century, it would be foolish to assume either that there is nothing to be learned from it, or that it will vanish in all its forms, 'unwept, unhonoured and unsung,' from this earth."[92] In 1941 Salazar told Roosevelt's representative Myron Taylor, who was passing through Portugal that, in his opinion, National Socialism would survive the war.

In our times, when the basic political principle is the greatest happiness for the greatest number, it is curious to note that most people—and often the most vocal propagators of the above desiderata—still rate Stalin's Communism higher than Hitler's National Socialism, even as there can be no question that the great majority of the German people lived better and fared better under Hitler's National Socialist regime than had the Russians under Stalin's Communism. There was the relatively high standard of living in Germany where, as we have seen in an earlier chapter, not only guns but also butter was available for a long time, and where the working masses fared immeasurably better under Hitler than had the workers and peasants of the Soviet Union under either Lenin or Stalin. There was, except for Jews, far more individual and political freedom in National Socialist Germany than in Communist Russia; a greater variety of publications in the sciences and in the arts, more elbow room for individual endeavor, even some original and positive achievements in architecture.[93] Moreover, as one reads the reconstructions of the different German opposition movements against Hitler, one must be struck by their relative liberty of movement within such a police state: how relatively easily the Hassels, the Müllers, the Popitzes could flit back and forth in 1939 and 1940 between Berlin and Rome and Switzerland. . . . In February 1940 Ulrich von Hassell would invite the American chargé

---

[92] Henderson, 16.
[93] As the principal historian of artistic and cultural politics in the Third Reich, Hildegarde Brenner, put it: "During the years 1934 to 1940 . . . one cannot deny the 'historical uniqueness' . . . in architecture. In this field National Socialism succeeded in reaching a form of self-expression that cannot be doubted." Brenner, 118. In support of this summary statement, H. Brenner also cites Bruno Zevi (*Poetica dell'architettura neoplastica*, Milan, 1953) and Nikolaus Pevsner (*Europaeische Architektur*, Munich, 1957), two of the most eminent European architectural historians—incidentally, both of them scholars of Jewish origin.

d'affaires for breakfast, trying to convince him that Roosevelt's emissary Sumner Welles, during his coming visit to Germany, should be brought together with certain leaders of the German opposition, Popitz, Planck, and himself. This kind of behavior would have been inconceivable in the Soviet Union or, indeed, in any "100 per cent" police state.

But, then, National Socialist Germany was not quite a police state—at least not in the usual sense of the word. The brilliant and unscrupulous Carl Schmitt, the principal legal scholar of the Third Reich, wrote in 1935 that the National Socialist regime meant the end of the old Prussian *Beamtenstaat*, with its Hegelian conception of a state governed by officials. . . . It was, instead, a *Volksgenossenstaat:* "The state is the instrument of the people." The German working class, among others, felt something of this: The steelworkers of Krupp were even more reliable followers of the Fuehrer than some of the old Prussian civil servants. As late as in March 1945 Speer was driven to despair as he overheard the talk of German workers who, unlike himself, were still full of confidence in the final victory.[94]

*Volksgenossenstaat* and *Beamtenstaat:* In reality, the Third Reich was a mixture of both.[95] In the end, the first absorbed the second, producing a new brutal kind of police rule,[96] in the form of the SS state. For, just as National Socialism, like Fascism, was a post-Marxist phenomenon, the SS state, at the latest by 1944, was a post-Fascist phenomenon. Almost all of the liberties that still existed in Germany in 1941 were survivals from the past. As the danger of defeat rose for the Third Reich, they would be eliminated brutally. This is one of the reasons why Ernst Nolte's lumping together of the *Action Française*, of Italian Fascism, and of German National Socialism under the title *Three Faces of Fascism* is mistaken. The *Action Française* people were looking to the past; the National Socialists to the future. The *Action Française* was pre-Fascist, the SS was post-Fascist.

---

[94] "My country right or wrong"—during the Second World War this no longer rang true. After the First World War Churchill could still admire a young German student who stood up for his country during a debate at Oxford. It is difficult to admire a German who would defend the Third Reich through thick and thin.

[95] "The sheer survival of the state was an important victory for the conservatives, with whom the *Beamten* were nearly synonymous." Peterson, 438.

[96] Even apart from the Gestapo, the German authorities made a policy of trying to enlist chief police officials to their sides in the conquered countries. They did not always succeed, but there were many instances where local police chiefs would collaborate with them willingly: Chiappe in Paris, Hain in Budapest, Pelvig of the Aliens' Department of the Danish state police. In Holland, on German instigation, a day in November 1941 was proclaimed for the "Day of the Netherlands Police."

The SS state was not an old-fashioned police state carried *in extremis* but a new kind of unscrupulous tyranny run by soldier toughs, even including criminals, something that may yet appear again at the last stages of the dissolution of Western civilization, just as it appeared during the last stages of the Third Reich.

In the end, the criminal cruelties of the National Socialist Third Reich were worse than those perpetrated by the Soviet Union, even as the aggregate number of those murdered and imprisoned under Hitler may have been less than the number of those who were murdered and imprisoned under Stalin. But, then, the history of the human race is not made up by numbers, and the history of politics, too, deals with something else than with the aggregate welfare of inhabitants, the greatest "happiness" for the greatest number, whatever that may be. Compared to the untruth of Stalin's Communism, Hitler's National Socialism may have been a half truth; but, as St. Thomas said, a half truth may be more evil than a lie. For this, too, involves a mutation of quality that transcends the quantitative categories of arithmetic. A half truth is not equivalent to 50 per cent of the truth. It means, instead, a 100 per cent truth compounded with, and subordinated to, a 100 per cent untruth, the result being an especially dangerous corruption of the truth.[97] In mathematics 100 plus 100 results in 200. In real life, with its many dimensions, there are many instances when 100 and 100 results in something else, on another level, in *another* kind of a 100.

The brutalities of the Third Reich were beginning to compromise the cause of National Socialism during the war for some of its believers. Even the bravery of the German soldiery was losing its effect. With great prophetic words, Georges Bernanos foresaw this as early as 1938, Hitler's year. "Hitler!" he wrote. "The kind of heroism that you are forging in your factories is made of good steel, we don't deny it. But it is a heroism without honor, because it is unjust."[98]

---

[97] The German aristocratic opponent of Hitler, F. Reck-Malleczewen in 1940: "But we must be completely clear. . . . If nationalism is truly the hallmark of a people in the prime of its youth and energies, how does it happen that under its aegis morality decays, ancient customs die out—that men are uprooted, the steadfast derided, the thoughtful branded, the rivers poisoned, and the forests destroyed? Why, if this is a high watermark of our national life, has our speech been vulgarized in this unprecedented way?" Reck-Malleczewen, 110.

[98] "You do not see this yet, because you are now squandering the last resources of honor in Germany, the honor of free German men. The totalitarian idea is still freely served by free men. Their grandchildren may not know anything else but totalitarian discipline. And then the best among you will turn their eyes towards us, they will envy us, no matter how disarmed and defeated we

might be. This is not all a simple calculation of intellect, Hitler. You are justly proud of your soldiers. The moment approaches when you won't have anything but mercenaries, working at their job. The abject, the pitiless war through which you think you can dominate the world is no longer a war of warriors. It will debase consciences so deeply that, instead of war being the school for warriors, it will be the school of the vile." Bernanos, *GRC*, 324.

# 4 . The relations of states

ABOVE ALL POLITICAL MATTERS stood the relations of states. The war was not a war of classes: It was a war fought by states, rather than by ideologies; it was a war fought by Germany and France and Britain and Russia, not by Democracy and Fascism and Communism. Hitler, Mussolini, Stalin, Churchill, De Gaulle were statesmen first of all. They subordinated their philosophical and political preferences to what they thought were the interests of their states. Hitler wanted to make Germany, rather than National Socialism, dominant over Europe. Churchill fought to save Britain; De Gaulle fought for the survival of France; Stalin, for the survival and for the security—interpreted, to be sure, with a brutal and tyrannical kind of possessiveness—of his Soviet Russian empire. This primacy of state interests above everything else appears clearest in the then history of the Soviet Union, of a state that millions still consider to have been dedicated first and foremost to the cause of world revolution. The history of the foreign policy of the Soviet Union in 1939–41 is interesting and instructive, and it should be of exceptional interests to students of contemporary history and of international affairs, as it reveals the real purposes of a dictator such as Stalin, no matter what his professed ideology might be. It reveals his real matters of interest: security, not revolution; territory, not ideology. Stalin cared not a fig for the Communists of Europe or, at that, of the rest of the world. Their activities, including espionage, in the interests of the Soviet Union was merely a fringe benefit: unimportant, secondary, unworthy of serious thought. At times it was hardly more than a lunatic-fringe benefit, sometimes it was more than that; but Stalin knew that no one could pull the rug from under Hitler by tugging at the fringe. In 1921 Lenin went through all kinds of tortuous motions to isolate the handful of Americans who had gone to Russia in order to distribute vast amounts of food during the famine. In 1941 Stalin said that he would welcome the presence of British or American divisions in Russia under their own commanders. If the price for the survival of the

Russian state was the presence of foreign imperialist armies on its land, with all of the prospects of capitalist contamination, so be it.

Such were the facts of life. By 1939 the official Soviet vocabulary reflected this. Terms such as "state matters," "state politics," "state interests" became sacrosanct, in a stiff parvenu sense. When Stalin or Molotov would employ them it was instantly recognized that *these* were the matters of the highest importance, while references to the class struggle or the cause of the revolution belonged to the older category of accepted pieties. On the one hand, Napoleon's dictum about a certain ineluctable constancy remained largely true: "The policies of all the powers are inherent in their geography." On the other hand, it is also true that state interests are what the statesmen think they are: Stalin's—or Hitler's, or Mussolini's—idea of "state interests" were not quite the same as those of a Sazonov or a Bismarck or a Cavour had been.

During the Second World War the relations of states were a compound of practices old and new. Before describing some of them, I must say something about their practitioners: the officials in charge of relations with other states. In 1939 many of the traditions of diplomatic practice continued to exist. Diplomats and the personnel of foreign ministries were generally regarded as the highest kind of people; Foreign Ministers, with few exceptions, were regarded as the most important members of governments after Prime Ministers. More than any other branch of state service or private occupation, the diplomatic career was still a kind of reserve for members of the nobilitarian aristocracy, or at least of the high gentry. This was true of most of Europe, including Britain; it was still partly true of Hitler's Germany[1] and of Fascist Italy, though not, of course, of the Soviet Union. In 1940 Ribbentrop decided to adopt a ridiculous uniform for the diplomatic service of the Third Reich; this was soon imitated by Italy, Hungary, and certain German satellites, for a while even by the Soviet Union—a silly practice that was later abandoned. In France, Switzerland, in the Northern European democracies, and in Greece, the diplomatic careers were often filled by the patrician bourgeoisie. Where there were few, the state drew on certain intellectuals, as in Slovakia and Yugoslavia, for example.

The diplomatic immunities—ranging from travel facilities through legal and financial exemptions of the host state to things such as the

---

[1] In 1914 nine out of ten of the principal German and Austrian ambassadors were aristocrats; in 1939, three out of six. The Hungarian Foreign Ministry list of 1939 shows that *every* Hungarian Minister was either an aristocrat or a descendant of the landed gentry, with the "de" French *particule* attached to his name; but this was unique.

coveted CD on the automobile license plate—were not merely what sociologists call status symbols; they were status itself, with all of its attendant privileges. A recognized foreign diplomat, compared to other people, was a person more privileged than perhaps ever before in the history of Europe: a large order, this. He may have had little power or influence over the institutions of the host state, but he was largely immune to them. This alone put him way beyond the social stratosphere, into a kind of privileged heaven—in Moscow, for example, where in this respect foreign diplomats stood above the ordinary Soviet citizen as the Pharaoh's priests had stood over the ordinary inhabitant of ancient Egypt. The principal cause of this was not so much the survival of traditions of diplomatic immunity—these were beginning to erode—as the overwhelming authority of the state. During the Second World War the possession of a Swiss or a Swedish passport—that is, recognizable proof of citizenship in a neutral state—was worth more than a papal letter five hundred years ago exempting one from the Inquisition. Now the world was ruled by vast state bureaucracies, and for them there existed no authority above the state.

In other words, many of the traditional practices of the relations of states and their traditional kind of practitioners continued side by side with new and revolutionary and often shocking practices of state relations and with a new kind of state personnel. By and large, the performance of the traditionalists was better than those of the revolutionaries: The Halifaxes did better than the Ribbentrops. At the summit of events Churchill knew more of the world than what Hitler knew; Churchill understood Hitler better than Hitler understood him; Hitler's powerful shafts of insight were not enough to compensate for this. As A. J. P. Taylor wrote, Hitler "rarely listened to his foreign Minister" (true) "and never read the reports of his ambassadors" (not always true). "He judged foreign statemen by intuition. He was convinced that he had taken the measure of all *bourgeois* politicians, German and foreign alike, and that their nerve would crumble before his did. This conviction was near enough to the truth to bring Europe within sight of disaster."[2] Hitler's intuition was powerful: but not always sufficient. There was, after all, some advantage to being a man of the world in the older, traditional sense. All of the Kings and Queens of Europe, regnant or exiled,

---

[2] Taylor, 71–72. For an opposite (and wrong) view by another English historian, Robertson, 1–2: "That [Hitler] could . . . so often apprehend and successfully exploit the weakness of foreigners, despite his notoriously absurd ideas about them and despite his tactical blunders, is frankly atonishing." Why? Also, ibid., 9: "Hitler was the liar speaking the truth." When a liar speaks the truth he is not a liar.

including temporary allies of Germany, knew even in 1940 that Hitler couldn't win.

Among the Foreign Ministers of the Great Powers, few shone: Eden's good looks obscured his weaknesses, Halifax was reliable at best, Ciano was weak, Ribbentrop a poltroon, Molotov a wooden dolt.[3] Much of this had to do with the condition that heads of governments preferred to act as their own Foreign Ministers, keeping the latter sometimes on the tightest of leashes. There were few exceptions to this. One of them was Sweden, where Sandler, the Prime Minister, favored helping Finland during the Winter War; his Foreign Minister, Gunther, was more cautious, and his advice prevailed. A more glaring exception was that of Poland where Beck, the Foreign Minister, had a nearly undisputed authority over high affairs of state through 1939.[4]

During the Second World War the most intelligent ambassadors were traditionalists, more or less[5]: the German Schulenburg, the Italian Rosso, the Romanian Gafencu, the American Steinhardt in Moscow,[6] the

---

[3] About Molotov, of whom John Foster Dulles said that he was the ablest foreign stateman he had ever met, Sir William Seeds (the British ambassador to Moscow) to Halifax on 30 May 1939: "It is my fate to deal with a man totally ignorant of foreign affairs and to whom the idea of negotiation . . . is utterly alien." The Polish Kot: "Molotov was the most important authority in the [Soviet foreign ministry], yet he was the least interesting. Wooden and unctuous, constantly repeating the same phrases, always inflexible, he was the incarnation of banality." Kot, xviii. About Molotov's ineptitude vis-à-vis Hitler, see above, p. 120.

[4] The Poles had some charming and intelligent representatives abroad (Raczynski in London, Ciechanowski in Washington)—still there was something in the Polish national character that kept even their most knowledgeable and cosmopolitan diplomatists from becoming cold realists. One of the most amazing shortcomings in diplomatic foresight was the inattention and the nonchalance with which Polish diplomacy treated the prospects of a German-Russian alignment in the summer of 1939.

[5] "Traditionalist," in this sense, means conservative rather than professional. Nonprofessional conservatives such as Grandi in London or Hoare in Madrid did rather well.

[6] Almost completely isolated, these diplomatists in Moscow turned in a most creditable performance; they were the best-informed people in the Soviet Union—because of their knowledge of people and their closeness to the powerful rulers of that state. They excelled in comparison with a Cripps, who complained that it was "impossible to have any contacts with any Russians and thus to obtain any reliable information as to what is going on in the country. The most that one can get is an occasional piece of gossip through Russian chauffeurs or *dvorniks,* or possibly through foreign journalists." Woodward, II, 28.

British minister, Sir David Kelly, in Berne, the Spanish Duke of Alba in London, the German Blucher in Helsinki; their dispatches and their suggestions would have been approved by Talleyrand or Bismarck. Yet their influence on the decisions of their masters was less than before. Hitler listened to a Schulenburg even less than Napoleon had listened to Caulaincourt or to Lauriston. Besides these obvious limitations of ambassadors working under dictators, there was the additional devolution of diplomatic practices. One of them was their limited leeway of negotiation. The above-mentioned paragons of the ambassadorial craft stand out because of their intelligent reporting of events and tendencies, and because of their suggestions of policies—which does not mean that their suggestions were being listened to. The occasional excellence of the French, the cleverness of the Italian, and the sometimes impressive ability of German diplomacy at its highest levels availed them little in the long run, and sometimes not even in the short run. At the same time, a powerful state, such as the Soviet Union, could afford to be represented by stiff police-state minions, with little imagination and even less knowledge of the world. In short, power could be enhanced by brilliance; but brilliance was no substitute for power.

Within these limitations—admittedly large ones—the traditional apparatus of diplomacy still continued to function, sometimes surprisingly well, even during the most cataclysmic of times. Of all departments of the British government, the record of the Foreign Office was among the least exceptionable. During the high critical months of 1940 it performed very well; Woodward recorded "the absence of panic and despair." Often Churchill trusted the Foreign Office more than he trusted his generals and admirals: with every reason. The French diplomatic service, so often the finest in Europe, and one that often served the republic well in times of trouble, did not distinguish itself either during the thirties or during the war. Often the habitual intelligent realism of the French failed them: Coulondre in Berlin thought in the last days of August 1939 that Hitler had maneuvered himself into a dead end; in April 1940 Alexis Léger thought that the mining of the Norway Leads would produce no German reaction; in May he was largely responsible for the panicky burning of the archives of the Quai d'Orsay. Only one of the principal French ambassadors, Brugère in Belgrade, resigned spontaneously in June 1940. Among Pétain's appointments, few ambassadors shone; among his Foreign Ministers—Baudouin, Flandin, Darlan, Laval, each very different from the others—none could show much of a success. There were few convinced Fascists in the Italian diplomatic service. One of the best Italian ambassadors, Attolico in Berlin (wherefrom he had to resign in May 1940) was an anti-Nazi. He had many contacts with the surviving conservatives in

Hitler's foreign service: He worked with them closely, including the State Secretary Weizsaecker, trying to avoid the worst.[7]

But at this point our earlier distinctions no longer serve. The two categories of traditionalist and totalitarian, conservative and nationalist, diplomat and state official are too crude—they correspond to reality only in part. The career and the character of Ernst von Weizsaecker is an example of this. There are many evidences of his sympathy toward those who were trying to oppose Hitler, and of his inclinations to counter some of Hitler's moves that he saw leading to disaster. Yet in most instances his opposition was potential, not actual. He continued to serve Hitler until the end. Much of this was due to the native slyness and suppleness of this Swabian gentleman—slyness and suppleness at the expense of a certain strength of character. Much of this was due, too, to the very traditions of state service. Some of the gravest faults of men of the traditional *carrière* were inherent in their deeply embedded and unquestioning sense of professional loyalty. This, for example, explains the almost unanimous choice of the French diplomatic service to continue under Vichy after the armistice. They would not turn against the highest authority of their state, and they would justify their continued service by convincing themselves (and their conversants) that they were remaining at their posts in order to mitigate worse to come. At times this kind of self-justification could serve honorable purposes; at times it was hardly more than personal opportunism. When Hitler became Chancellor there were virtually no National Socialist party members in the German Foreign Ministry. By the time Ribbentrop became Foreign Minister, more than one third of the personnel had joined the party; by 1940 the majority were members of the NSDAP. There was a small and dwindling minority of oppositionists, including men such as Ulrich von Hassell, who resigned from the service, and others who were told to resign after they were no longer useful, such as Zech, the German minister to the Netherlands, or Heeren, the minister to Yugoslavia. There was a rising minority of Nazi or pro-Nazi newcomers, usually recruited from outside the traditional services. There was, finally, a large floating majority in the middle who continued to serve—to serve under all circumstances, for all kinds of causes—Papen, for example,

---

[7] A list of those foreign diplomats whose stay in Berlin influenced them in the direction of the Third Reich would be interesting. Unlike in Moscow, there were a few neutrals and nonbelligerants who came to lean this way: the Japanese Oshima, the Turkish Gerede, the Spanish Espinosa de los Monteros, the Hungarian Sztójay. Few of the foreign diplomats who had served in London became Anglophobes. Two exceptions were Ribbentrop and the later Hungarian Prime Minister Bárdossy.

that inept and dangerous intriguer in domestic German politics, about whom it must be said that he made an excellent German ambassador in Turkey throughout the war.[8] The exception to this was the Soviet Union, where a decade after the sovietization of the state apparatus, Stalin's recruitment of a new state service eliminated the last traces of the old order. Some of the older Bolshevik diplomats of the mid-thirties, associated with the image of the anti-Fascist Popular Front period, survived: Litvinov,[9] Maisky, Oumansky, Madame Kollontay. Many people claimed, and still claim, to see in them more sophisticated types of Soviet diplomats. This was yet another Leftist legend. Oumansky was a boor; the blandness and the falsifications in Maisky's memoirs reveal the third-rate mind of this popular Soviet ambassador[10] in London. No Soviet diplomat would talk in any way comparable to the relative freedom with which, say, a Weizsaecker would talk to an Attolico or to a Carl Burckhardt. Nor were Stalin's newer appointees exceptions to this rule: Dekanosov in Berlin, who had begun his state career under the wings of the secret policy (he was a Georgian and a protégé of Beria), was ignorant as well as incompetent.[11]

The changing conditions in the relations of states were not only manifest by new and untrained representatives who were ignorant of many things, including the traditional practices of diplomacy.[12] The most important change was that foreign relations were now conducted on a multiplying variety of levels—a development that had begun to burgeon during the First World War. Relations between states now involved such broad areas that they could no longer be restricted to the competence of the traditional foreign services. The democracies as well as the dictatorships were affected by this. The British and the Swiss governments succeeded, by and large, in maintaining the hierarchical authority of their

---

[8] Foreign Office specialists on occasion were attached to the armies; they played an important role in the clandestine preparations for the German move into Yugoslavia, Greece, and Bulgaria, Operation Marita.

[9] He arrived in the United States the day after Pearl Harbor.

[10] His bust adorns the Imperial War Museum in London. I wonder why.

[11] Having accompanied Molotov to Berlin in November 1940, Dekanosov—probably on Stalin's wishes—was appointed Soviet ambassador to Germany at once. Moscow requested his *agrément* from Berlin with unusual haste. He knew no language besides Russian and Georgian. On one occasion he told the papal nuncio in Berlin that most Catholics in the Soviet Union were living in the Caucasus. *VD*, 4, 330–31.

[12] Schulenburg in Moscow, for instance, insisted that his own staff translate all official communications from German to Russian before the presentation to the Soviet authorities, simply because he had found that the Russians' own translations were often bad and full of inaccuracies.

foreign services over the other departments. Yet even in Britain the Board of Economic Warfare, the Ministry of Information, different intelligence and clandestine services and, on occasion, the powerful office of the Prime Minister himself would work at cross purposes with the Foreign Office. In Switzerland there were occasional conflicts in the purposes of the Foreign Ministry and that of the national police authorities. The government of the Third Reich under Hitler not only conducted foreign policy on various levels, it also allowed the functioning of three or four organizations dealing expressly with foreign relations. There was the "Dienststelle Robbentrop," the latter's private preserve; there was Rosenberg's *AuAmt*, the "Foreign Policy Office" of the NSDAP; there was Bohle's *AO (Auslandsorganisation)*; there was Himmler's *VoMi (Volksdeutsche Mittelstelle)*, later blossoming (if that is the word) into what became the Foreign Ministry of the SS state, RSHA (the Reich Security Office); there was Goebbels' *ProMi*, the Propaganda Ministry, whose influence on occasion extended way beyond the field of propaganda. As the French Germanophile Benoist-Méchin, otherwise full of respect and admiration for the efficiency of the Third Reich, wrote at the time: "After a federation of states, Germany has become a federation of administrations."[13] Ribbentrop[14] was neither intelligent nor strong enough to assert his authority over this welter of totalitarian bureaucracy, which often worked at cross purposes.[15] Yet after all is said, these cross purposes of competing

---

[13] Cited by Hytier, 110.

[14] Hitler made Ribbentrop Foreign Minister in January 1938 for two reasons: because he knew that Ribbentrop was a cypher, and also because he knew that Ribbentrop was unquestioningly loyal to him. (An additional—minor—reason for Ribbentrop's appointment was Hitler's indebtedness to him. It was in Frau Ribbentrop's Dahlem house in 1932 that Hitler was introduced—he was made *salonfähig*—in Berlin, and it was there that the groundwork was laid for his deals with the nationalist conservatives.) Ribbentrop was one of the few people who remained completely under Hitler's sway till the end, indeed, beyond Hitler's death: His memoir of Hitler, written in prison, reflects a kind of uncomprehending—uncomprehending, rather than incomprehensible—admiration. Ribbentrop's loyalty superseded his occasional disagreements with Hitler, most important of which was Ribbentrop's willingness to come to terms with the Soviet Union.

[15] Here are a few examples. On one occasion, in 1939, Ribbentrop forbade members of the Ministry to talk directly with Papen (*GD*, D, VIII, 330)—yet Papen continued to function under Hitler's protection. Bräuer, the German minister to Norway, had not been told of his government's plan to invade that country; Hitler was distrustful and critical of him, and said so on one occasion to Quisling, even after the German occupation (*GD*, D, X, 493). Even *AuAmt* would supersede the Foreign Ministry on occasion, as for instance in German dealings with Afghanistan in 1940 (*GD*, D, VIII, 525). On other occasions the

bureaucracies influenced German foreign policy relatively little, because of the unquestionable and unquestioned authority of Hitler.

Thus the relations between states were now conducted by a variety of people along lines that were both traditional and revolutionary.[16] On the one hand, diplomatic immunities and privileges, amounting to traditional courtesies, were still observed on occasion: Thus, for example, after declarations of war, diplomatic personnel were exchanged according to traditional practices. In April and May 1940 the Germans acted with formal courtesy in allowing the repatriation of the British and the French ministers from Denmark and Belgium. Even in June 1941 the German and Soviet diplomatic personnel were transported home safely from Moscow and Berlin—in the latter case sealed trains carrying trained seals, one is tempted to write. On the other hand, more than 50 per cent of the Polish diplomatic staff in Germany were either executed or died in concentration camps during the war. The Yugoslav minister to the Vatican was arrested and mistreated by the Italians in 1941; the French treated the departing Italians in a singularly rude manner in 1940. There were diplomatic receptions in neutral and even in German satellite capitals where German, American, Canadian, Japanese diplomats appeared together. When, in response to Stalin's demands, Great Britain declared war on Finland and on Hungary in December 1941, the farewell tendered to the remaining British representatives was accompanied by many social and semi-official expressions of courtesy and regret, reminiscent of another era. In most European capitals, including Vichy, American and South American representatives were the social lions through the awesome year 1941.[17] On other occasions, however, British representatives were humiliated and mistreated by Romanians and Bulgarians. The German and Soviet secret police were, of course, equal to the task of arresting or mur-

---

Foreign Ministry was more radical than Ribbentrop: the German consuls general in Prague and Tirana were outspokenly, and disagreeably, anti-Italian in 1940.

[16] A glaring example of ideological zeal amounting sometimes not only to incompetence but also to disloyalty to one's own government was that of Japanese Ambassador Oshima in Berlin. At the end of August 1939 he had been instructed by Tokyo to lodge a mild protest against the German-Russian Pact in view of prior German-Japanese agreements. Oshima told his government that he had carried out these instructions. In reality he did not; and he found it proper to boast of this to Weizsaecker. Like his Foreign Minister Matsuoka, Oshima was a stupid intriguer.

[17] A starry event in the Vichy social calendar in December 1941 was the marriage of the actress Danielle Darrieux to Porfirio Rubirosa, then attaché of the Dominican Republic.

dering foreign officials, including those of their allies, when this was deemed necessary for "state interests."

This compound pattern characterized, too, the opening and the cessation of hostilities. The British, the French, and a host of other governments would still observe the traditional forms of declaring war. Italy formally declared war on Britain and France in June 1940; indeed, Mussolini made a production of this. On the other hand, the Italian ultimatum presented to Greece on the dawn of 28 October 1940 was one of the most cynical and brutal instruments in the history of modern statecraft. Hitler's reluctance in declaring war is worth noting. Aware of the existence of mass sentiments, he acted in line with the peculiarly democratic practice of claiming the argument of self-defense, announcing to his people that their country was about to be attacked. Thus on 1 September 1939 he cried to the Reichstag: "Since 4:45 A.M. we are firing back." (He had allowed his police officials to arrange the fake Polish "attack" on the radio station of Gleiwitz the night before.) He did not declare war on Denmark, Norway, Belgium, Holland, and Luxembourg. In the case of Holland, he and Ribbentrop tried a trick that failed. They planned to send a subordinate diplomat, Kiewitz (he had transmitted the German ultimatum to Poland on 31 August 1939), to Holland, together with four respectable colleagues, a few days before the German invasion. A few hours before the invasion these worthies were to present themselves to the Queen, to convince her that she ought to issue an order to the Netherlands Army not to resist the Germans. Since Dutch intelligence was aware of the pending attack, the Dutch authorities did not allow the Kiewitz "mission" to cross into Holland. In the case of the Soviet Union, Hitler did not only refrain from a declaration of war, he did not even present an ultimatum to Stalin—no doubt because of the risk that, no matter how humiliating its conditions, Stalin might choose to accept them, after all. Perhaps Hitler was right: We have seen how Molotov and Dekanosov were squirming that fateful morning, hoping against hope, trying to exact some statement from the Germans that the German bombing and invasion of the Soviet Union might not amount to a full declaration of war. In November 1939 the Soviet Union pretended that it had not gone to war with Finland. In June 1941 the roles were reversed; now the Finns hoped that the Russians would attack them in some way that would make their declaration of war on the Soviet Union plausible. By bombing Helsinki, the Russians performed this service for the Finns, for what reason God alone knows. After 22 June 1941 the Soviet Union began to allude to traditional practices, from which it tried to profit: Its repatriation of the Axis diplomats was largely correct; in early July 1941 Moscow informed the German government through Sweden that in waging war it would agree strictly to the Hague Convention of 1907. The Germans did not deign to answer, for reasons that are only too well known in retrospect. Yet Italy, Slovakia, and Romania informed the International Red Cross in Geneva that they would treat Soviet prisoners in line with the Geneva Convention of 1929.

These things meant little to Hitler. The formalities of separating war from peace were unimportant. I have referred earlier to the Hitler who practiced Clausewitz in reverse, so to speak: War was not only the continuation of politics, but politics was a kind of continuation of war. There was more to this than the aggressive nature of a fanatic. To Hitler, as to the great Victorian historian Sir John Seeley, politics was present history, while history was past politics.[18] At the same time Hitler, with all of his insistence on the primacy of politics, went beyond thinking about the relations of states: He thought in terms of the relations of entire nations. For Hitler, unlike for Bismarck, the power of the state was not an end but a means: The end was the power of his nation—something that was dynamic, not static.[19] This explains, to some extent, Hitler's ruthless plans for the subjugation of European Russia, leaving little leeway for the existence of Slavic states. In 1940 he told Antonescu that "no frontier on the Continent is definite . . ."—they were temporary in nature. Throughout the entire history of the Third Reich, Hitler never concluded a peace treaty. At the surrender of an enemy his state and Army representatives would sign an armistice,[20] the terms of which were something like those of a preliminary treaty; beyond this he would not commit himself.[21]

Hitler understood that the Second World War was a war of nations. Yet he often drew the wrong consequences of this: He wanted to subjugate entire nations by means of the apparatus of his powerful Third Reich state. All of its propaganda and ideology notwithstanding, he made few attempts to gain the adherence of peoples. This was a mistake, for the peoples of the various nations and states were less passive than in the past. True, their potential collaboration or opposition seldom became so impor-

---

[18] Politics was "history in the making" (*werdende Geschichte*); and history was the "hardened monument" (*versteinerte Wiedergabe*) of politics. Hitler, *MK* (1925 German edition), 467; also *Hitler ZB*, 46, cited in Jaeckel, 113–14.

[19] Consider how this corresponds to the evolution of *Beamtenstaat* to *Volksgenossenstaat*, above, p. 324.

[20] On 20–21 April 1941 in Salonika the Germans actually signed *three* armistice instruments with Greek military and political delegations, one of which had to include the Italians.

[21] This increasing sameness of armistice and peace terms has been, however, typical of the twentieth century. In 1918, the armistice lines imposed upon the defeated Central Powers resembled closely the conditions imposed upon them by the subsequent peace treaties; the same was largely true of the peace treaties after the Second World War, in 1945–47.

tant as to be actually decisive. Yet the relations of states now encompassed many fields; it has become increasingly complex in part because of the vast development of communications.[22] Hitler understood their importance: He would, for example, threaten neutral states because of the attitude of their press—as, for example, Switzerland in 1941—in part because he believed that the attitude of the newspapers reflected the attitude of the government, in part because he knew that the press was capable not only of influencing but also of forming national opinion.

At the beginning of the century, Lord Salisbury said that "the diplomacy of nations is now conducted as much in the letters of special correspondents as in the dispatches of the Foreign Office." Forty years later, entire sections of Foreign Ministries and intelligence offices would scan the press of another nation as much in order to gather information as to find a clue to certain inclinations of state or national opinion. In turn, there was often as much calculation and clandestinity in the management of the press as in the management of intelligence, high diplomacy, or espionage; yet little of this may be found in the record of the documents. I have referred earlier to the influence of the News Department of the British Foreign Office during the crucial period of late March 1939; there are many such examples.[23] In February 1941, the friendship treaty concluded by Turkey and Bulgaria included a clause expressing hope that the press of each country would be motivated by mutual trust and confidence. And it was the totalitarian Soviet Union that used the press unashamedly as a diplomatic instrument, suggesting state alignments of the first order of importance[24]—a classic case of which was the eventually fruitless TASS communiqué of 13 June 1941, suggesting the overwhelming willingness of Moscow to accord with Berlin's wishes.

Thus while the balance of powers, often circumscribed by their geo-

---

[22] This was reflected in the daily work of foreign services also. The number of telegrams increased in volume—though, oddly enough (or perhaps not so oddly), fewer people in charge were reading them. In 1935, the French Foreign Ministry registered twice as many incoming cables than in 1932; by 1939, there was another geometric increase.

[23] In the winter of 1939 the Swedish minister to London "called Lord Halifax's attention to an article in *Le Nord* of November 1939, saying that the supply of scrap iron was more important to the Germans than that of iron ore. The writer of the article later admitted to Swedish friends that he had written it at the request of the Swedish Foreign Minister in order to divert Allied interest from the ore traffic." Woodward I, 70, note 2.

[24] Schulenburg about the Soviet usage of press communiqués on 14 January 1941: "This kind of communiqué, which the Soviet Government has for some one and a half years made a peculiar auxiliary instrument of its foreign policy . . ." *GD*, D, XI, 1,100.

graphical situation, remained as important as before, newer elements, such as the ideological tendencies of regimes, including neutral governments, the existence of volunteer forces, of exile and satellite governments, the foisting of intelligence, open international propaganda, and secret communications, introduced increasingly complex elements in the structure of the relations of states, to the discussions of which I must now turn.

## THE BALANCE OF POWERS

¶ When Germany set out to rule Europe, certain other powers, including Britain, would not reconcile themselves to this. Thus in 1939 the Last European War began; in 1941 it developed into the Second World War of the twentieth century. Hitler wanted to eliminate whatever counterweight to his power existed in Europe; eventually this would have laid the foundations for a new balance of power in the world. These simple statements sum up the history of the years 1939–41, in more than one way. I had to resort to this bland repetition of the obvious in order to insist that "the balance of power," this often condemned and misunderstood phrase, is as good, if not better, as any, to explain these events. For the relations of states do not merely *represent*, in many ways they *are* the relations of power—of power that is actual as well as potential, of power involving the element of prestige, that is, of reputation, of its reality as well as of its image. This does not mean that during Hitler's war the balance of power functioned in the same inexorable ways as at the time of Bismarck or of Louis the Great or of Elizabeth. To the contrary: even more than a mechanical reality, power exists in the minds of people, and during the twentieth century more and more people were thinking of the image of the power of other states.[25] Like courage or fear,[26] the image of power is not merely an external reality; it exists within ourselves.

By the time of Munich, Germany was the dominant power of Europe. At that time the other powers were as yet unwilling to contest

---

[25] In his memoirs, Francois-Poncet, then French ambassador in Rome, recalls how in April and May 1940 sympathetic Italians, including Ciano, suggested to him that there was but one way to halt Mussolini from entering the war on Hitler's side against the Western democracies: "Bring us a little victory!" (*una piccola vittoria*).

[26] Hemingway: "Courage is grace under pressure"—a blast of guff that John F. Kennedy found worthy enough to cite in the Preface of his *Profiles in Courage*. No. Stendhal: "Fear is never in the danger itself, it is in our own selves."

this. Instead, they were readying themselves for the eventuality of a war for which they were unprepared in 1938. This eventuality would come about if Hitler, not content with Germany's status as the dominant power of Europe, would attempt to transform his potential domination in his actual conquest of much of the Continent. For a while after Munich, Britain and France seemed to reconcile themselves to the prospect of Germany's dominant status over much of Eastern Europe. They thought that this might give them some time to rearm, after which time the balance of power might be more favorable for them. That Hitler's expansion in Eastern Europe might lead to a German war with Russia, in which event the Western European powers could profit from their relative neutrality, was a reasonable assumption in line with classic calculations of the balance of power. In reality, the Western leaders gave little thought to this: They feared, rather than encouraged, further German progress toward the borders of the Soviet Union.

The events of March 1939 revealed that "dominant" to Hitler meant a kind of near-absolute domination, and not some kind of Bismarckian preponderance. The British and the French statesmen now feared that Hitler would occupy the smaller states surrounding the Third Reich, one by one. They thought that the best way to avoid this was to tell him that in certain cases, such as in that of Poland, this would mean war with the Western democracies. They were right in thinking that the balance of power was, at last, beginning to turn in their favor: Their rearmament, no matter how slowly, was proceeding, and the United States was beginning to move in their direction. They were wrong in thinking that the Soviet Union, too, would associate itself with them in establishing an overwhelming balance of powers against Germany. Instead of reconstructing the balance of power against Germany, the Soviet Union, harassed by Japan on her Far Eastern flank, opted for a cautious friendship with Germany, in exchange for which she received territories with the consent of the latter.

Hitler, who constantly thought in terms of the balance of power, believed that his sensational success of a pact with Stalin destroyed the attempt of the British in constructing their own balance of power in Europe; in this he was right. He believed that consequently the British would reset their sights and not go to war over the occasion of Poland; in this he was wrong. After his conquest of Poland he thought again that the British would reconsider, and that they would opt for a balance-of-power arrangement with him. He was wrong again. He knew the balance of power; he did not know the British. The latter, who had been supposed to have invented the principle of the balance of power in Europe, no longer cared much for it. They cared less for the balance of power than for getting rid of Hitler. In this sense Hitler was the traditionalist, and the British the ideologues. Yet in a profounder, and real sense, the British acted thus not because they were ideologues but because they felt that the very nature of Hitler's regime stood in the way of any kind of a reasonable balance of power; in short, he could not be trusted, and this was reason enough for the war against him. During the Reluctant War the British Government paid much interest to possibilities, no matter how slight, of an anti-Hitler or even of a non-Hitler government in Germany. From such a government they would have accepted terms—including continued German rule over Austria and Czechoslovakia, possibly even parts of Poland—that they would not have accepted from Hitler. In other words, the composition of government, and thereby the character of states, counted more than the balance of power.[27]

The French were not much interested in this. Curiously enough, it was the French people, rather than the government, who kept instinctively thinking in terms of the balance of power. During the reluctant war the government wanted, first of all, to keep the war away from the national territory. After the German invasion of their country, it tried to buy Italy off with ignoble concessions, in vain. After the fall of Paris, rumors whirled up among the French populace about Russia having entered the war against Germany. Of all the peoples of Europe in 1941, it was the French who were most pleased with the outbreak of the German-Russian War, though it was the British who profited from it the soonest.

After the fall of France, even more than after the fall of Poland, Hitler offered a world balance-of-power agreement to the British. The two alternatives before Churchill were these: to make a deal with Hitler and preserve the Empire; or to fight and eventually defeat Hitler, at the cost of becoming dependent on the United States, at the expense of the Empire. Most European statesmen believed that the British were pondering them seriously. In reality, they didn't give it a thought. The French feared that the British would deal with Germany at their expense. Mussolini feared that Hitler would deal with France at Italy's expense. Of all statesmen, the ones on the edges of Europe—Salazar, Franco, the Turks, and Stalin—saw things more clearly. They saw that as long as the United States supported them, the British would fight on.

Hitler could neither make peace with Britain, nor could he conquer her. This meant a temporary stalemate—not so much in the conduct of the war as in the developing world balance of power. There were the English-speaking democracies, drawing closer and closer together. There was Germany, with her minor allies, among whom Italy was sliding down to the level of a large satellite, not much more.[28] There remained three

---

[27] After 1940 this changed. With Churchill, the British thought that, whatever the outcome of the war, Germany must be destroyed as a great power.

[28] Even before the attack on Greece, the Italians, to assert their independence of action, started to negotiate with the Soviet Union for a balance-of-power

great world powers outside the Continent: the United States, Russia, and Japan. Hitler thought that bringing Japan into his alliance system would restrain the United States; he was wrong. He also thought that the United States and Russia were the principal hopes of Britain; he was right. Unless and until he could split the Anglo-American alliance, which was becoming more and more *de facto* by the day, he had but two alternatives. One was the building of a giant continental and Eurasian bloc: Germany and Italy and Russia and Japan against the Anglo-Saxon democracies of the West; land vs. sea powers, the splitting of the world into two enormous strategical hemispheres. This was what Ribbentrop and perhaps the majority of the German hierarchy would have preferred, all of their so-called conservatism and anti-Bolshevism notwithstanding. Hitler gave it little consideration; and after Molotov's depressing visit to Berlin in November 1940, this prospect definitely vanished from Hitler's mind. The other alternative was to establish this giant Eurasian bloc not together with Russia, but at her expense. If Hitler were to invade and destroy the European Russian state, his rule over the Continent would be invulnerable, and sooner or later the British, or perhaps even better, the Americans, would have second thoughts about carrying on a futile war against him.[29] As I wrote in Part I, this was the method within his so-called madness in attacking Russia; and he came close to success.

He failed not only because he could not defeat Russia, he failed also because of his miscalculations regarding Japan. He should have encouraged the Japanese to move north, not south; against the Soviet Union, not against the United States. Again he misled himself by his ideas about the balance of power. His alliance with Japan, and the latter's prospective war with the Americans in the Pacific, encouraged Roosevelt instead of deterring him. It did not diminish the increasing American presence in the Atlantic. Also, in April 1941 Japan and Russia signed their nonaggression pact, making it possible for both of them—in this they were unique among the great powers during the Second World War—to fight a war

---

and interest-sphere division in southeastern Europe. These negotiations, developing in two stages in 1940–41, came to a halt because the Germans did not want them to develop, just as they would have stopped the Italian attack on Greece had they known about it early enough.

[29] There was a third alternative. He could have split the developing Anglo-American alliance by making a true compromise peace with Britain. This would have led to a new European, instead of a world balance of power. It would have meant that he would have to relinquish at least some of his Western European conquests for the sake of eliminating Britain as his enemy, just as he had to relinquish a portion of Eastern Europe in 1939 for the sake of eliminating Russia as a potential enemy. It was not an alternative that a man such as Hitler would consider seriously in 1940.

on one front only. In 1945 Hitler would complain to his confidants of how much the alliance with Italy had cost him. His alliance with Japan cost him even more.

Before his invasion of Russia Hitler felt compelled to put an end to whatever balance of power remained in the Balkans. Hungary and Romania had become his allies or satellites; Italy possessed Albania; Britain was now on the side of Greece; Yugoslavia and Turkey tried to remain neutral. So did Bulgaria, especially as Russia wanted to be included in this Balkan balance of power by getting that small Slav kingdom under her sway. This is what Molotov attempted to get for Russia in Berlin: a Baltic and a Balkan balance of power. In the Baltic, Germany would have Norway, Russia would have Finland within her sphere, with a Swedish neutral buffer state in the middle. In the Balkans the Germans could have Hungary and Romania, if the Russians could have Bulgaria, with a neutral Yugoslavia in the middle. Hitler was not interested. In the spring of 1941 he did with the Balkans what he had done with most of Europe before: He conquered most of it. This impressed Stalin far more than it impressed Churchill or Roosevelt. Stalin would now accept the German domination of all of Europe, up to the very frontiers of the Soviet Union, perhaps even beyond. He would become an ally of Germany, if that is what the latter wanted, if this were the price for Russia to be let alone. Germany, Italy, Japan vs. Britain and the United States: At best, Stalin wanted to be out of it; perhaps he wanted to wait and see which way the balance of powers would turn in the end. At second best, he would have preferred an alliance of some kind with the Germans rather than with the Atlantic democracies.

He did not have a choice. Hitler did not want to have Russia on his side. (He even dropped, as we have seen, his earlier ideas of the establishment of satellite states on the territory of the erstwhile Soviet Union. He would destroy the possibility of any Russian state on the European side of the Urals.) So Stalin had no choice but fight, on the side of the British and the Americans. His principal object was to save the Soviet state, if necessary, at enormous costs. Even after June 1941 he may have had strong inclinations to consider another deal with Hitler. The two tyrants had considerable respect for one another. But Hitler would not give him this opportunity—not only because, as most serious historians (for example, Hillgruber) explain that Hitler's war on Russia was something entirely new, a war of extermination, total war, a *Ding an sich*—but also because he was again captivated by his own vision of a world balance of power. He thought that the alliance between the Soviet Union and the Anglo-Americans was, by nature, incomplete and impermanent. He tried to break it, first, by eliminating the Soviet Union. By December 1941 he failed, not only militarily but also politically, because after the formal entry of the United States in the war, Stalin had more than ample reasons to fight on. Among Hitler's allies and fair-weather friends Mussolini urged him to break up his enemies by making an armistice, or even peace, with Russia; others, such as Franco, hoped that Hitler would make peace with the British and/or the Americans, while keeping the Soviet Union at bay. Hitler would not do either: He was sure that the Anglo-American-Russian coalition would sooner or later break apart. It eventually did, but too late for him. The Anglo-American alliance with the Soviet Union had but one thing in common: their agreement that the destruction of Hitler's Germany was the prime object of the war.[30] Hitler failed to understand that Britain and the United States would prefer Russian domination over half of Europe over German domination of all or most of it. He thought that the most elementary rules of balance of power would make Britain and the United States think twice before they let Russia establish herself near or in the middle of the Continent, that they would rather seek some kind of accommodation with the German Third Reich. He was as wrong about this at the end of the war as he was at the beginning. The British, those supreme realists, were troubled less by the imbalance of power than by the nature of the Hitlerian German state. Hitler, the fanatical ideologue, went to ruin, among other things, because of his undiminished belief in *Realpolitik*, believing until the end that his opponents were thinking in terms of a balance of power in Europe, too. Such is the irony of history—or, rather, the discrepancy between reality and realism, so-called.

In reality, by 1941 the European balance of power was destroyed. A world balance of power had come into being, with components such as the United States, the Soviet Union, Japan, and China, whose interests in a European balance of power was, at most, partial. This did not mean that the alignments of European states ceased to have importance or that the balance of power was no longer the principal concern of states. There were many examples of this concern, also among the smaller states of Europe. Each state was seeking counterweights against its actual or potential opponents; in other words, a balance of power favorable to her ambitions or interests or to the status quo. Thus Hungary would successfully or alternately seek the support of Italy, of Germany, of Russia, of Britain, of the United States in her quarrel with Romania; Finland would alternately seek the support of Britain, of France, of Sweden, of Germany, of the United States against the Soviet Union; Bulgaria would draw closer to Yugoslavia or Turkey as the occasion of the shifting balance of power would seem to demand. There was nothing new in this. When two

---

[30] Already in 1940 the British indicated to Stalin that they would be willing to go along with Russia's domination of Eastern Europe if this be the price of denying the Germans the opportunity of ruling the entire Continent. See above, pp. 104, n. 71; 167.

children quarrel they welcome the support of a third. It is a condition of human life. What changed during the Second World War was not this condition but some of the elements that made up its principal components —the sovereign state, which, despite its centralized and often tyrannous power, was becoming less sovereign, not more. What was destroyed during the Second World War was not the balance of power but its uniquely European function: After 1941 it was no longer European. Before 1941 the predominance of non-European elements in the balance of power was an exception; after 1941 it became the rule.

## STATES AND IDEOLOGIES

¶ History was still principally the history of states. We have seen that Hitler gave scant help to the local National Socialist leaders in the conquered countries, to the bitter disappointment of those leaders, even as most of them remained loyal to Hitler's cause until the end.[31] Mussolini was even more consistent. When he said that Fascism was not an article of export, he meant it. He favored pro-Italian agents over local Fascists. Stalin, even more than Hitler, was convinced of the weakness of his ideological supporters outside his own country. Like Hitler, he would pay scant attention to them even in places where their presence was considerable—in Bulgaria or Serbia, for example.[32] Unlike Hitler, he wanted the security that territory gave—or seemed to give. Hitler, all of his *Lebensraum* and Blood-and-Soil ideology notwithstanding, showed rela-

---

[31] He was, of course, right in thinking, as in the case of Romania, that Antonescu's military and nationalist government would serve German purposes more efficiently than would a revolutionary regime with fanatics in charge. Yet people within the Antonescu government were beginning to abandon the German cause from 1942 onward. In August 1944 Romania turned on the Third Reich, and the few Romanians that stuck with Hitler were those Iron Guard leaders whom he had abandoned in 1941. It was another defeat for Hitler the *Realpolitiker*. Had he made it clear in 1940 that in each nation he depended, first and foremost, on the local National Socialists, he may have been more successful. He admitted some of this in his talks, recorded by Bormann, in 1945.

[32] In 1940 Moscow insisted that in the event of a closer Russian association with Bulgaria, including the presence of a Soviet naval base in that country, it intended to respect the regime and the unquestionable authority of the—anti-Communist—Tsar Boris. In Yugoslavia the first Soviet ambassador, Plotnikov, paid a demonstrative visit to the grave of King Alexander I, patron of Tsarist Russian refugees, in July 1940.

tively little interest in territorial annexations during the war. Stalin, the chief representative of an ideology according to which states were mere forms superimposed upon the true reality of class structures, and the master of the vastest land empire in the world, greedily pursued the prospect of every morsel of territory he could gain for his state, the sooner the better. Thus in June 1940 he irritated Hitler needlessly by going beyond their agreed partition line in Bukovina. In January 1941, after wrangling for months, Stalin's diplomats obtained from Germany, again at the risk and cost of irritating Hitler, a small pocket of territory near the Polish-Lithuanian town of Suwalki. There for a few muddy acres the Soviets paid the Germans the sum of 7.5 million gold dollars, more than what the Tsar's Empire had been paid for all of Alaska.[33] In September 1939 Stalin, this crafty and cunning Khan, was in a fret as he feared that the German armies in eastern Poland might not pull back to the demarcation line he and Ribbentrop had agreed upon; he told the German ambassador his fears of "the well-known fact that all military men are loath to give up occupied territories."[34] In December 1941, when the German guns were still audible in Moscow, Stalin insisted that the visiting Eden talk territory with him: He wanted a territorial agreement with the British, "not a declaration." Hitler wanted to make the German *nation* sovereign over much of Europe, especially in the East. Stalin wanted to make the Soviet *state* sovereign over the tracts that would belong to him. In this respect Hitler was a more modern statesman than Stalin, who was a kind of Caucasian Mazarin, whereas Hitler's politics had little resemblance to those of a Richelieu or even to those of a Bismarck.

It would be, for example, practically impossible to draw up a precise map of German-controlled Europe during the Second World War. Certain territories were annexed to Germany: a portion of Poland ("Wartheland," Polish Silesia, part of the province of Bialystok, etc.); the small enclave of Eupen-Malmédy-Moresnet from Belgium; a part of Slovenia from Yugoslavia. Other territories, such as Alsace-Lorraine and Luxembourg, were annexed *de facto*, without any international legal reference to their transfers. There were administered territories, such as the "Generalgouvernement" of Poland, protectorates such as Bohemia and Moravia, protectorate states such as Slovakia, occupied states, zones of occupation, etc. In the conquered portions of Russia, matters were even

---

[33] Another fretful Russian insistence on border rectifications of a minor kind developed in November 1939. *GD*, D, VIII, 428–29, note 4.

[34] In regard to the German Army his usual political discrimination escaped him, on 22 June 1941, when he said to his government that the German attack may have been arranged by provocative elements within the Wehrmacht. He thought that the German Army was more anti-Soviet than was the National Socialist party; the opposite was true.

more complicated, partly because of the multiplication of German authorities. Hitler preferred to leave the status of most of the conquered territories undefined. He could be vague on purpose. In certain instances he may have wanted to keep his hand free for potential negotiations in the future.[35] More important, he seldom wanted territory for its own sake. He was, I repeat, thinking in terms of nations, not of states; of people, not of territory.[36] He wanted a very large Greater German Reich, but his concept of such a state was not circumscribed by the traditional limits of territorial sovereignty. He understood and practiced state sovereignty in ways that had hardly any precedents. On the one hand, the sovereignty of the Reich would be absolute within its domains. On the other hand, not only her influence but her very sovereignty would emanate beyond its frontiers in novel and unprecedented ways. On the one hand, Hitler, who had little respect for concordats and canon laws, continued to press the Vatican in order to have the recognition of the authority of German prelates in certain dioceses in the territories annexed by the Reich. On the other hand, he took it for granted that the German minorities living in Hungary[37] or Slovakia or Romania should possess certain privileges exempting them from the authority of these states, privileges elevating these Germans above the majority of the native population.

There were territories under German military administration (such as Denmark, France, Serbia, Greece); territories ruled by a Reich Commissar (Holland, Norway, parts of Russia); territories under a civilian *Gauleiter*, on their way toward incorporation into the Third Reich

---

[35] In Belgium, for example, Hitler gave less support to Flemish separatism than had the imperial German government during the First World War, perhaps because he wanted to keep Belgium as a pawn for some future peace negotiation with Britain.

[36] Again, I must insist that Hitler thought primarily in terms that were *folkish* rather than *racist*. For example, in October 1940 he said that there were three alternatives for the future of the Czech protectorate: continuation of limited autonomy; resettlement of the Czechs and their replacement by Germans; or assimilation of the Czechs through their Germanization. "The Fuehrer decided in favor of the third possibility." *GD*, D, XI, 266. Assimilation, however, is not an altogether racist policy. What racist in the American South has ever believed that the "solution" lay in the assimilation of the blacks?

[37] A German-Hungarian treaty of 30 August 1940 (in exchange for the arbitration whereby Hungary was awarded northern Transylvania from Romania) established, for example, that "the Royal Hungarian government will guarantee the members of the German community the possibility of preserving their German ethnic heritage without any restrictions." The authorities of the Reich could recruit them for service in the armed forces, the SS, for instance. (The German minority in Hungary in 1941 was proportionally the largest in Eastern Europe, about 720,000, nearly 5 per cent of the entire population.)

(Alsace-Lorraine, Luxembourg). This categorization, too, is full of holes. A Reich Commissar ruled Norway and another one the Ukraine; but the realities of German rule in the two places were very different. German "civilian" administration was almost always harsher than military administration—another difference from the past. The most damning evidence of Hitler's ideas about the future fate of the occupied nations comes from his own words. In his closest circle he declared that he did not ever intend to withdraw from the occupied states. On 16 July 1941 he said:

> What is essential is this. We need not publicize our purposes to the whole world. The main thing for us is to know what we ourselves want. . . . Here [in Russia] we must do exactly what we did in the cases of Norway, Denmark, Holland, Belgium. We did not say anything about our purposes and we shall be wise enough to do likewise. So we will emphasize again that we had been forced to occupy a land for the purpose of its order and security; that in the interest of its inhabitants we must provide for its pacification, food, transport—hence our regulations. It should not appear that we are thereby preparing a final solution! (*eine endgueltige Regelung*) . . . We must be clear in our own minds that we will never withdraw from these lands ourselves. . . .[38]

He would never restore their freedoms. He said at his table talk, on 3 February 1942: "Once I conquered a country should I ever restore its freedom? What for? Whoever spent his blood has the right to rule." He wanted vassalage, not territory—or, rather, vassalage rather than territory. We have seen that before the war, in the case of Austria, Czechoslovakia, and Poland, he wanted to establish a condition that was more important for him than Danzig or the Ore Mountains: a complete conformity of these states to the dictates of German foreign policy—meaning the gradual extinction of their sovereign independence. Under such conditions their domestic independence, too, would wither. An example of German official thinking survives in a memorandum by the German minister to Slovakia, a fortnight after the German-sponsored establishment of the "independent" Slovak state in 1939. "The Slovak Republic has undertaken in Article 4 of the Treaty of Protection to conduct its foreign policy at all times in agreement with the German Government. This presupposes merely as a matter of course that developments in domestic politics have to be made consistent with the foreign policy laid down by treaty."[39] One year later the Germans demanded that the Slovak government dismiss the conservative minister Durcansky. Again the memorandum of the German minister is telling. In 1939

---

[38] Cited in Kwiet, 62, note 89.
[39] Bernard memorandum. *GD*, D, X, 268.

. . . Slovakia was the calling card that we were holding out to the small countries of southeastern Europe and particularly the Slavic peoples: This is how independently a small country can live that places itself under the protection of the Greater German Reich. . . .

The new political situation permits us to withdraw our calling card, which we have been holding out for so long that it has become known. The time has now come to make it perfectly plain once again, particularly with reference to the countries of southeastern Europe, that Slovakia is in our *Lebensraum,* that is, that our wishes alone count.[40]

This preference of vassalage over territory was typical of much of the Second World War. (The principal aim of Japan, too, was not the territorial conquest of most of China but the installation of a pro-Japanese government there.) Mussolini's ultimatum to Greece revealed what he wanted: The reduction of Greece to an Italian satellite, rather than definite transfers of Greek territories to Italy. The nature of vassalage would vary, especially as the Germans practiced it. They treated Danes better than they treated Poles. Under Bismarck they had done the same. There was nothing new in these variations. What was new was their attempt to destroy Polish cultural and intellectual life. Unprecedented, too, was the extent of their concern with the printed and the spoken word. The Germans scanned the newspapers of their satellites and allies in great detail, regarding the slightest divergences from German policy as matters of state. In short, if the principal purpose of their statecraft was the establishment of vassalage, this required conformity not only in the acts but also in the words and in the thoughts of the vassal nations.

There arose, consequently, the question of the future of small states, the existence of which has been typical for the history of Europe. In the political philosophy of German *Grossraumordnung,* there was little or no place for them. Mussolini and Stalin, too, would talk often in a derisory tone about the small states. For a while such geopolitical speculations had an effect in the English-speaking world also: E. H. Carr, in his political best seller *Conditions of Peace,* composed in 1941 and published in early 1942, proclaimed that small nations and small states belonged to the past, they had little or no function in postwar Europe.[41] Fortunately things did not at all turn out to be this way in the long run. The rising importance of nationality, above and beyond the traditional importance of the sovereign state, works often in favor of small national states rather than in that of larger ones. In the short run, however, in 1939–41 the small states were

---

[40] Bernard memorandum, 25 June 1940, *GD,* D, XI, 16–18.
[41] Unbeknownst to Carr, his arguments were very similar to those of the "peasant genius" Christoph Steding, a pro-Nazi young German philosopher of history, who had written in the same vein in 1938.

often treated as expendable pawns by the great powers, including even Britain on occasion. "Small nations," said Churchill at a Cabinet meeting in December 1939, "must not tie our hands when we are fighting for their rights and freedom."[42] We have seen that the British secret peace tentatives to the German conservative opposition in the winter of 1939–40 suggested that Britain might not insist on the restoration of Austrian, and perhaps not even of Czechoslovakian, independence; that in 1940 the British intimated to the Soviets that they would favor a Soviet sphere of interest in the Balkans; and that by the autumn of 1941 it became evident that they would not endanger their alliance with Russia for the sake of Poland. Nor were the British above bribing smaller states with the prospect of their future gains at the expense of other states. At the Argentia conference, Alexander Cadogan admitted to Sumner Welles that before the Belgrade *coup* in March 1941 the British minister to Belgrade said "that at the conclusion of the war the subject of the jurisdiction over Istria (then a part of Italy) was a matter which might well come up for reconsideration."[43] Churchill had cabled to the British minister before the *coup*: "Continue to nag, pester, and bite." He might have added "bribe"—which was, among other things, what Sir Ronald Campbell was doing. Still it was Churchill, among all of the statesmen of the Second World War, who best understood and respected the importance of independent small states in Europe.[44]

In December 1940 the old Pétain said in Toulon: "When I speak of the termination of the war I mean an honest and honorable conduct on the part of France until the time of the peace treaty to which all of us are looking forward"—a statement that shows how unreal and antiquated was Pétain's view of politics, how he failed to understand the purposes of the new rulers of Europe. He did not know that Franco, whom he so much

---

[42] Butler, II, 97. The words of a Norwegian *aide-mémoire* to the British on 19 January 1940 is instructive in this respect: "The circumstance that Great Britain is fighting for its life cannot give it a right to jeopardize the existence of Norway." Woodward, I, 74.

[43] Istria, including Trieste.

[44] His policy bore certain important results in the long run—as, for example, in the case of Belgium and even of Greece. Critics of his fateful decision in 1941 to rush to the help of Greece at the cost of abandoning the British gains in North Africa forget that, no matter how ineffective this was in the short run, the presence of British armies in Greece in 1941 provided a boost in morale for the Greeks and a bond between the Greek and British nations. In 1944 the British returned to Greece in order to help the government and the people in suppressing a native Communist insurrection. Would they have had the support of the majority of Greeks in fighting against their native Communists if they had let them down unaided against the Germans three years earlier?

admired, had suggested to Hitler vast territorial annexations at the expense of France; that Mussolini was doing the same; and that Hitler wanted to reduce France to a perpetually enfeebled state, beyond territorial aims that included not only Alsace-Lorraine but also future German bases at Agadir and Casablanca. Pétain did not understand that armistice and peace were now something entirely different from the practices of the past: that defeat now meant the prospects of vassalage, the loss not so much of territory as of independence.

## SATELLITES AND EXILES

¶ Let us now attempt to sort out the status of the governments of the states of Europe in 1941. Here is a general list of their whilom status, ranging from the dependent allies of the Third Reich to its determined opponents:

*Germany's allies* were, in chronological order of their accession to the German alliance: Slovakia, Italy, Hungary, Romania, Bulgaria, Croatia, and Finland.

*Under partial German occupation* was France, with her government in the unoccupied portion having a limited, and dwindling, kind of sovereignty.

*Under full German occupation* Denmark could maintain a considerable extent of domestic independence.

*Collaborationist shadow governments were allowed by the Third Reich* in Bohemia-Moravia, Serbia, and Greece (Norway in 1942), without any marks of sovereignty; they were not recognized abroad, not even by Germany's allies.

Poland, Luxembourg, Belgium, and Holland *had not even shadow governments* under the Germans; nor had Lithuania, Latvia, and Estonia after the Germans had driven the Russians out of these countries.

Spain was a *"nonbelligerent"* according to her government, which was insisting that she was not "neutral" but a "spiritual ally" of Germany and Italy. (Later in the war Spanish neutrality grew and her "spiritual alliance" faded, at a measure exactly apace with the retreat of Germany in the field of war.)

Sweden's *neutrality* was partially compromised by her consent (given in 1940 and withdrawn in 1943) to the transport of a limited number of German soldiers (not in uniforms) through Swedish railways.

*Truly neutral* throughout the war were Switzerland, Ireland, Portugal, and Turkey (the latter in spite of a formal alliance concluded with Britain and France in 1939). Greece was neutral until October 1940 and Yugoslavia until March 1941. (Note that, except for Switzerland, all of these states were on the edges of the Continent; their neutrality was made possible by geography.)

*Exile governments,* stationed first in France, then in London, were those of Poland, Czechoslovakia, Norway, Luxembourg, Holland, Belgium, Yugoslavia, and Greece.[45] All of them were active belligerents, furnishing men and vehicles of war to Britain and to other allies. By 1941 at the latest they were recognized by all of the Allied powers and by most neutrals. The status of the Free Danes and of General de Gaulle's Free French was ambiguous as late as December 1941, even though the latter were among the more active Allied combatants.

To most of Germany's allies the general term "satellite" is applicable to some extent. The governments of these states had not allied themselves with the Third Reich solely under duress. Unlike the European satellites of the Soviet Union after the war, in 1939, 1940, and 1941 the majority of these peoples were not opposed to their alliance with the then master state, Germany. Subordination to Germany did not mean a purge of the state apparatus comparable to what subordination to the Soviet Union was to mean after the war. On the highest levels of government these states depended often on the services of a kind of conservative and cosmopolitan civil servant who was skeptical of Germany's chances of ultimate victory. Some of the Hungarian, Romanian, and Bulgarian civil servants and diplomats would later in the war establish secret contacts with the Allies. Some of these divergences were open, others were clandestine. A few days after the war broke out a minor crisis occurred in the relations between the Third Reich and Hungary (her first ally in many ways): Ribbentrop was angry because the semi-official Budapest newspaper *Pester Lloyd* had written in an editorial that it was "difficult to decide the responsibility for the outbreak of the war"; a few days later the Hungarian government attempted to avoid giving way to a German request that German troops be allowed to pass through northern Hungary against Poland (this request was then dropped because of the rapid advance of the German armies across Poland). In the spring of 1940 the Prime Minister, Teleki, established clandestine channels for funneling secret Hungarian funds abroad for an eventual exile organization in the event that the Germans would forcibly occupy Hungary. A year later, as we have seen, Teleki shot himself in protest against the Germans' forcing Hungary to join them in the attack on Yugoslavia.

Hungary provides but one example of the often small but significant

---

[45] The seat of the Greek government was first Capetown, then London, then Cairo in Egypt; the Grand Duchess of Luxembourg and her son lived in Montreal during the war.

divergences in the external relations of Germany's allies.[46] Among Germany's allies Bulgaria was not at war with the Soviet Union[47]; Finland not with the United States—with German consent, we must add. At least on paper, Croatia was an Italian, not a German protectorate.[48] In reality this meant little or nothing. Also, the Croatians were pro-German and anti-Italian. In June 1941 Hitler was not especially interested in having his satellites participate in the war against the Soviet Union, except for Romania and Finland on the southernmost and northern flank of the advancing German armies. Still Italy, Slovakia, Croatia, and Hungary joined the "crusade" with a certain enthusiasm.[49] The actual sequence of events leading to Finland's entry in the "crusade" was somewhat obscure, though her government's intentions were not. For all practical purposes a secret alliance between Germany and Finland existed in June 1941. The Finnish troops and Air Force received combat-readiness orders even before the Germans. Somewhat prematurely Hitler referred to "our Finnish comrades" in his war speech on 22 June. Three confusing days followed before Finland entered the war officially on Germany's side. She was a willing ally of the Third Reich against the Soviet Union; yet, unlike other German allies, she could maintain a large extent of domestic and even diplomatic independence. Pressed by Stalin, the British government reluctantly declared war on Finland (and also on Romania and Hungary) in

---

[46] On certain occasions the Germans profited from these divergences. They used their satellites for higher diplomatic purposes, including contacts with certain of their enemies. In December 1940 the Hungarian and the Greek ministers in Madrid were engaged in a significant attempt to put an end to the Italo-Greek war. Unlike Stalin, whose suspicions so often got the better of him, Hitler did not always insist that Germany's satellites break diplomatic relations with her enemies. In September 1941 the German minister to Romania was instructed to tell the Romanian Foreign Minister that Bucharest avoid breaking relations with Britain "for the time being" because of the danger of consequent British air attacks on the Romanian oil fields. *GD*, D, XI, 666, note 2.

[47] Bulgaria did not attack Yugoslavia and Greece until late in the campaign (when the Greek government was leaving Greece).

[48] Aimone, the Duke of Spoleto, was declared King of Croatia by the name of "Tomislav II" in May 1940. He never occupied his throne or visited "his" country.

[49] Circumstances leading to the actual Hungarian declaration of war on the Soviet Union were complicated; some of them remain obscure. See above, p. 142, n. 6. Romania announced "a holy war" against the Soviet Union, a fact that did not deter Antonescu from suggesting to the American minister in November 1941 that, like Finland, Romania would not push beyond a certain line in Russia.

December 1941.[50] The Finns emphasized their trust and hopes in the then still officially neutral United States. On the other hand, Slovakia and Croatia declared war on the United States without much hesitation in December 1941.

The government of unoccupied France in Vichy maintained a curious twilight kind of sovereignty for some time. Eventually its recognition abroad dwindled apace with her authority over the people of France; she slid down to the level of a mere satellite, after November 1942 even beneath that status. In 1940 and 1941, however, Vichy was still recognized as the principal and sole government of France by all the major powers of the world, including the United States and the Soviet Union. Officially the Germans were represented by one regular consul in Vichy, Krug von Nidda, neither a minister nor an ambassador. There was a German "ambassador," Otto Abetz, ambitious, Francophile, often benevolent—in Paris, where there was no French government. For many months Pétain and his people entertained the belief that the Germans would soon allow them to return to Paris or at least to Versailles[51]; but nothing came out of this. Hitler knew how to remind the French government of its dependence on his goodwill: Wasn't it as early as 27 June 1940, two days after the signing of the armistice, that Pétain had turned to him, asking that the German columns approaching Bordeaux be halted? Hitler was interested in subordination, not collaboration.[52] Alsace-Lorraine was virtually incorporated into the Reich; other *départements* in the North were put under German military administration. The Germans said nothing to Vichy about this, and to all French entreaties in these matters the Germans turned the deafest of ears. The French took some consolation of the condition that many of their government and civil services continued to function through the entire country; that even in the occupied portion prefects and subprefects were appointed by Vichy. This

---

[50] Finnish relations with Britain were broken on 29 July 1941. In August 1941 the Soviet ambassador to Washington asked the United States to tell the Finns that the Soviet Union was prepared to discuss a separate peace, including territorial compensations, with Finland.

[51] As early as 27 June 1940 the French Foreign Ministry drew attention to the historical precedent of 1871, when in agreement with the Prussian government, the Comte de Saint-Vallier had been a French government delegate in Paris during the siege.

[52] Perhaps the first employment of the word "collaboration" appeared in a memorandum by the Vichy Foreign Minister, Baudouin, in early July 1940: "The lasting collaboration that we wish to establish with Germany must not lead us to accept the extension of Hitlerite ideals to France. . . ." A vain hope, this. Baudouin, 182.

served the Germans' purposes for law and order. Otherwise it meant little or nothing.[53]

Anomalous and unprecedented, too, were the relations of Britain and the Vichy government in 1940 and in 1941. In certain places and on certain occasions they waged virtual war against each other. In other places and on other occasions they were involved in negotiations. In the closed continental courtyard of Vichy the British left a window open for themselves by means of a Canadian legation. As late as February 1941 British and Belgian consulates still functioned in certain places of the then French empire—in Syria, for example. In the fall of 1940 the British and the French ambassadors in Madrid (Sir S. Hoare and de la Baume) were engaged in confidential negotiations; yet British and French forces were firing at each other at Dakar and in Syria; French airplanes flew over Gibraltar, dropping a few bombs on two occasions (after Mers-el-Kebir and after Dakar). On other occasions the British allowed French battleships to pass unhindered before the guns of Gibraltar. In May 1941 the British, while still maintaining nearly normal consular relations with the French authorities in Syria, bombed Syrian airfields that were temporarily infested with German and Italian planes. Two months later, after the British and their Gaullist allies had invaded Syria, the former would accord the French authorities there the honor of the formalities of an armistice.[54] Gradually in 1941 the British abandoned their last considerations for Vichy and strengthened their support for De Gaulle. In any event, they knew that the Vichy government would not dare to declare war on them.

Even more curious, though in a different manner, was the status of Denmark. Hitler considered it as a model protectorate. He would allow the Danes an unusual amount of domestic independence as long as their foreign policy would entirely conform to that of the Reich. Yet a state deprived of its independence in its foreign relations cannot be independent in domestic matters. It was because of her relative independence in foreign affairs that Finland remained independent in her internal affairs.[55] On the morrow of the German occupation of Denmark the Germans promised not to interfere in domestic affairs; they even presented a statement to that effect to the Danish government, the so-called Thirteen

---

[53] The Germans allowed a special government train, consisting of five Pullman cars, to travel between Paris and Vichy. This satisfied the *amour-propre* of some of the French officials; otherwise it meant nothing.

[54] Signed on the fourteenth of July in 1941 at Saint-Jean d'Acre, by Sir Henry Maitland Wilson and General de Verdilhac.

[55] Alone among Germany's allies the Finnish government passed no restrictive measures against Jews. Jews in Denmark, living under the German shadow, were relatively unharmed until 1943.

Points. Soon they were demanding Danish anti-aircraft guns, Danish help in the building of airfields, and increasing conformity from the Danish press. The cumbrous coalition government of Denmark waddled on during the dramatic early summer of 1940. In the first days of July the government, in agreement with King Christian X, was reformed, with the Germanophile Scavenius as Foreign Minister. It was not altogether a pro-German lineup, since it included such men as the Conservative leader Møller, who was soon dropped from the Cabinet (the Germans also demanded his expulsion from the Danish parliament and from his own Conservative party). Scavenius was now the most important personage in Denmark. He believed in a policy of accommodating Germany, within reason; on 31 July 1940 he was the principal draftsman of a Danish government memorandum:

> The Danish Government declares that it is willing in principle to enter into negotiations immediately with the German government about the conclusion of an agreement on an economic community under which the independence of Denmark would be fully maintained.[56]

Nothing much came out of this. Denmark lived on, with the outward forms of her political democracy intact, under a reigning King, with a Socialist heading her government, yet completely under the shadow and power of the German occupants.[57] These remnant forms were losing their meaning in 1941 when the Danish government agreed to all kinds of German requests, including the delivery of certain Danish torpedo boats to the German Navy, a ban on the Danish Communist party, imprisonment of numerous Communists, and the recruitment of a Danish Free Corps for the "crusade" in Russia. In November 1941 Scavenius signed the Anti-Comintern Pact in the name of Denmark. The accompanying declaration said that Denmark would collaborate "positively and loyally in the new continental Europe directed by Germany." Thereby vanished the last shred of the Danish government's independence in foreign relations. Before this time the situation was anomalous: Denmark was represented by ministers and consuls in the capitals of the entire world, including all the warring camps. Especially curious was the position of her minister in London, Count Reventlow, who maintained the claim of the legality of the German-held government in Copenhagen and who in 1940 and in 1941 opposed the idea of any kind of exile government and of any form of organized resistance. Kauffmann, the Danish minister in Washington,

---

[56] *GD*, D, X, 384.

[57] As late as in the spring of 1943 the Germans allowed a free election in Denmark, a unique event in the history of German-occupied Europe. The Danish National Socialist Party received 3 per cent of the vote.

felt free to announce his independence from the home government. On 9 April 1941 he agreed to the American occupation of Greenland.[58] Later in the war there would be Free Danish detachments fighting under British command (and, of course, numerous Danish merchant ships sailing in Allied convoys). Yet in the case of Denmark an exile government did not exist. The authority of the home government remained recognized, at home and abroad, throughout the war.

This was not the case of the collaborationist governments of Czechia, Serbia, Norway, and Greece. Some of these sprang into being more or less spontaneously—the Norwegian Quisling had a number of counterparts—yet their authority was minimal. Some of their personages were poltroons, others were patriots; the motives and purposes of most of them were mixed. There were clandestine contacts, on occasion, between some of these avowedly pro-German collaborationists and their self-exiled combatant compatriots abroad. The relations between some of the Greek collaborationists and the conservative royalists in the Greek exile government were complicated and Byzantine; probably they will never be unraveled by historians.[59] Some of the communications between the unfortunate Czech "government" of General Elias (executed by the Germans in the fall of 1941) and the Benes group in London are now known.[60]

The government of the Netherlands, foreseeing the possibility of enemy invasion and occupation, as early as 1937 prepared instructions for its highest civil servants, the General Secretaries, to remain in the country in order to provide for the needs of the civilian population. The Germans tried to profit from their presence: Soon, however, collaboration, even in technical matters, between the General Secretaries and the German authorities became cumbrous and difficult. Yet it was in Holland, somewhat like Denmark, that in 1940 "a *political* solution of a situation under German hegemony, pursued strongly by the German side, seemed the likeliest."[61] The failure of such a "political solution" was entirely due to the German side. The Dutch people, in the summer of 1940, were not altogether unwilling to go along with a national policy of moderate cooperation with Germany; but, then, Hitler was not really interested in a "political solution."

Similar, yet not analogous, to the Holland situation was that of Belgium. Hitler left the future of that state, too, intentionally vague. There,

---

[58] Iceland (a Danish island before 1944) and the Faeroe Islands had been occupied by small British detachments in 1940.
[59] Like the secret contacts between some members of the Mafia and their American connections before the invasion of Sicily in 1943.
[60] They have been described by Mastny, 154–55, 190–91, 225.
[61] Kwiet, 11.

too, in the summer of 1940 the Belgian people and their highest representatives were seriously seeking an accommodation with the Third
Reich. But while Holland had a functioning government in London,
presided by the undisputed authority of the royal family there present,
the Belgian monarch had elected to stay behind, asking for the armistice
himself, hoping thereby to influence Hitler. A deep breach opened between the King and the exile government. For several months the very
existence of the exile government was in doubt. Fleeing before the German armies, provisionally established in the French town of Limoges, the
government condemned Leopold III for having signed an armistice
without its consent. But soon these Belgian statesmen were caught in the
whirlpool of the French collapse. In Bordeaux the British suggested that
the Pierlot government move on to London. The majority of the government refused. They voted themselves out of existence. Pierlot wanted to
return to Belgium and asked the King for his consent. The King refused
an answer; the Germans refused to permit the politicians' return. The
Pierlot government ceased to function. This seemed to be the end of the
unhappy odyssey of the Belgian politicians. They had dragged themselves
from pillar to post, from Limoges to Poitiers, to Bordeaux, to Sauveterre,
to Perpignan, in the end to Vichy, where most of them dwelled in unease
and misery, in the shadow of the shadow government of France. On 20
August Pierlot wrote an official letter to Leopold III declaring that the
Belgian government existed no longer. But now there occurred a change.
While the Vichy government indicated that they did not welcome the
existence of Belgian exile politicians in their midst, across the Channel the
guns of Britain drummed on and on. There was a break in the government. The majority of the Ministers drafted a manifesto, asking their
countrymen to "unite around the King." Yet two important ministers,
De Vleeschauwer and Gutt, had made their way to London by September; and now Pierlot and Spaak, refusing to sign the manifesto, started
off to England on their own. They left Vichy with Pierlot's seven
children, in two ramshackle automobiles packed to the gills. On the frontier the Spanish refused them a visa. For two days they were stuck in no-
man's-land, living in their cars. Then they were allowed to enter Spain;
they were promptly interned in a provincial hotel. After four anxious and
miserable weeks Spaak escaped, with the help of a compatriot, under the
seat of a truck. He made his way to Lisbon and from there to London.
The odyssey was worthwhile. As in the case of Denmark, the Belgian
minister in the United States had taken it upon himself to establish the
cause of a Free Belgium abroad. While the Comte d'Ursel, the Belgian
minister to Switzerland, sent a circular to Belgian envoys abroad in September, suggesting a cautious policy of accommodation not only with the
King but also with the Germans, Theunis from Washington refuted his

arguments in a brilliant and clear countercircular. By December 1940 there were enough reputable Belgians around Spaak in London to publish another refutation: And thus the Belgian exile government came into being. The chasm between the captive King and the combatant government remained—it would grieve and tear the country for many years after the war—but there was unity among the Belgians abroad: They had but one government, the free exile government in London.

During the Second World War these exile governments had more substance than shadow. They played a greater role than had exile governments in the past. Much of this was due to the development of communications. Unlike in the past, millions of people were aware of their existence. The radio broadcasts from London reminded the home people of their presence. The Germans knew this: No matter how contemptuous they were in public about these "phantom reactionaries," they strenuously tried to combat the exiles' influence.[62] The exile governments had considerable freedom of movement; they were recognized by almost all of the neutral states,[63] in some instances even by Germany's allies. The exile governments maintained secret contacts with their homelands, sometimes even with certain people within the German-imposed satellite governments.[64] Conversely, certain personages among the latter tried to maintain contact with the Western Allies through personalities who—at times with the silent consent of the home government—had defected to London.[65]

---

[62] As early as 27 June 1940 Goebbels was preoccupied with the presence of De Gaulle in London. Boelcke, 404–5, 409. On 27 June 1940 Goebbels' instructions to the German press were: "The name of De Gaulle should not be mentioned."

[63] Recognition was not merely a formality. It meant diplomatic privileges, and facilities of all kinds of communications. The Germans knew this. In January 1941, for example, they complained to Vichy about the continued activities of Belgian, Luxembourgois, Dutch, and Czechoslovak consulates in France. The French said that they were willing to strike these off the consular lists. The Germans insisted that they wanted not merely "satisfaction in principle but one in practice." CDA, III, 481. To please the Germans, Stalin in May 1941 withdrew recognition from the Belgian, Dutch, Norwegian, and Yugoslav legations in Moscow; he recognized the short-lived Iraqi nationalist and Germanophile regime of Rashid Ali-el-Quailani.

[64] Bulgaria maintained diplomatic relations with the Soviet Union; Finland with the United States; both of them and Hungary and Romania with Guatemala; unofficial relations were maintained between the Polish exile government and the governments of Hungary, Romania, Bulgaria, and Finland.

[65] The first example of such a defection was that of Sir George Franckenstein, the distinguished Austrian minister to Great Britain, who resigned in March 1938.

Thus, for example, the Hungarian ministers to Great Britain and to the United States, having resigned from their posts in 1940, were officially condemned *in absentia* by the Teleki government, while at the same time Teleki considered them as potential representatives of a free Hungarian government in the future. Even the model German satellite of Slovakia had its dissidents, its ministers to Poland and to Italy, who declared against the German alliance in September 1939.

In sum, it was better to be an exile than a satellite. A handful of Gaullists were able to snatch authority from vacillating officials in a handful of government buildings in the French colonies in 1940. Henceforth the De Gaulle movement presided over vast territories. They were more successful than the British, who through their consuls had attempted to bribe some of the French officials in North Africa at the time of the armistice. The Gaullists were not successful everywhere; they failed at Dakar, their most serious setback in 1940. On other occasions De Gaulle's tug of war with his patrons the British was more successful than were his struggles with his compatriots. With all of his skepticism and suspiciousness in regard to the British, De Gaulle still knew that Churchill, unlike Hitler, was unwilling to treat his smaller allies as wholly expendable, no matter how he would be tempted to do so on occasion.

The relations of the exiles and their Western patrons were, of course, far from smooth or perfect. The first instance of an ugly undercover squabble occurred in late September 1939 with the establishment of the Polish exile government in France. The French intervened in the very choice of the President of Poland.[66] Gieysztor ("Heller"), the first important emissary of this government to underground Poland, sliding secretly into Warsaw in January 1940, gave "a grim account of the conditions in Angers," the temporary seat of the Polish exile government in France, "to which he did not want to return, as in fact he did not. He described the strife, the quarrels, intrigues, and maneuvering to power and office among the émigrés."[67]

At the time of the French collapse the Polish exiles were divided for a day or two, many of them hesitating whether to go to Spain or Brazil or Canada. The British came to their rescue promptly. On the evening of 18 June 1940 the President of Free Poland arrived in London, where the King and Queen of England came to meet him in Waterloo Station. For

---

[66] President Moscicki officially resigned on 17 September 1939, as he left the territory of Poland. He appointed Wieniawa-Dlugoszowski, the Polish minister to Rome, as his successor. The French (because of the pro-Italian reputation of Wieniawa) protested against this appointment. After a week of squabbling, Wieniawa resigned and Raczkiewicz was elected President, having been put forward by the Polish ambassadors to Paris and to London.

[67] Korbonski, 40.

the third time in six weeks Their Majesties stood under the glass canopy of that great and grim railway station, welcoming the exiled head of an ancient European state. Apart from all diplomatic calculations of investment and protocol, it was a high mark of British honor.

Later in the war Britain's relations with the Polish government and Army turned more and more difficult—even more difficult than the more publicized and often openly staged dissensions between the Free French and the British. The shadow of Russia grew into a mountain by 1941 between them: The British knew that their victory, perhaps even their survival, depended on good relations with Russia, necessarily at the expense of their commitments to a Free Poland. The Poles, too, were willful and thoughtless on occasion. Evidences of extreme nationalism and of occasional anti-Semitism in their ranks were eagerly displayed and argued by the British Left in the press and in Parliament. Yet the bravery of the Polish soldiers, sailors, and fliers in the service of Britain as well as in the underground struggle within Poland was impressive enough to restrain their critics. Through the murkiest days of 1940 and 1941 the British-Polish comradeship in arms kept its gleam through the gloom.

## Neutrals and volunteers

¶ In 1939 there were more than thirty European states. Six of them remained neutral at the end of 1941, in addition to the Vatican State and to the minuscule mountain coprincipality of Andorra. The Germans respected some of these conditions, including certain traditional privileges of neutrality, when it was in their interest to do so. The peoples of the neutral states shared many of the material privations of their warring neighbors. Curiously enough, they were better off during the Second World War than during the First, when neutral Holland and Norway had suffered food shortages even worse than had some of the nations at war. Even more curious was the condition that landlocked Switzerland was the continental state least deprived of food imports and raw materials and luxury goods, whereas Spain, open to an ocean and a sea on the western edge of the Continent, suffered vast inadequacies and a near famine in 1940–41.

Air communications were a new element. The neutrals benefited from them in certain ways. Air transport diminished the effects of the sea blockade. By 1939 a Pan American Clipper service was flying weekly between Lisbon and the Americas. Airplanes brought a trickle of valuable goods to landlocked Switzerland. Other planes dropped deadly cargoes of bombs on neutral lands by mistake. The Germans dropped bombs on

Switzerland and Ireland, Italians on the—then neutral—Serbian town of Pec, British (and later American) planes on Swiss towns. In 1940 the Swiss sought safety in remaining an island of light in the midst of a blackened-out Europe. In 1941 they had to conform to German wishes and extinguished their lights at night, becoming indistinguishable from the rest of the Continent. (Turkey had decreed a partial blackout of the country in late November 1940.) Another novel problem of aerial communications was the one posed by clandestine shortwave radios. During the First World War Lenin and his cohorts had no radio transmitters or receivers; still the Swiss were glad to get rid of them in 1917. In 1941 there were at least six clandestine spy networks operating in and out of Switzerland, two of them pro-Soviet (assisted and abetted by the British).

Almost without exception, the neutrals were less willing to receive refugees than they had been in the past. The Swiss decided as early as 1933 not to add to the burdens of their unique democracy by encouraging the arrival of hundreds of thousands of refugees, mostly Jews, from Germany and from other portions of Europe. In 1940 and thereafter the Swiss would not expel those refugees, particularly those coming from subjugated France, who succeeded in making their way to their safe territory; but their authorities tried their best—and a very bad best it could be, on occasion—to discourage them. In 1940 the pseudo-Fascist state of Franco Spain was more generous in admitting refugees (at least in transit) than was Switzerland. Among the neutrals the record of the Portuguese and of the Swedes was relatively most humane, that of the Turks the least. Germany's ally Hungary accepted and succored many thousands of Polish refugees in September 1939 and after.

The neutrals did not want to irritate Hitler. They felt that they had to resort on occasion to compromises in order to preserve the essential and minimal conditions of their neutrality. Thus the government of Sweden in late June 1940 chose to agree to the German request that limited numbers of German troops, not in uniform, be permitted to travel on Swedish trains to and from northern Norway. There was nothing new in this.[68] Neutrality was not a fixed state: There were gradations to it. The attitudes of the neutral states waxed and waned as their governments adjusted their state policies to the changing fortunes of the war. Relatively new was the ideological factor. The governments and the peoples of the neutrals, with the exception of Spain, did not wish the Germans to win. Hitler knew this: Whereupon he demanded, at times successfully, at times in vain, that the neutrals conform not only in their acts but also in

---

[68] In February 1940 the British-French Supreme War Council considered that Allied forces on their way to Finland "might be disguised as volunteers, after the example of the Italian 'nonintervention' in Spain." Butler, *GS*, II, 107.

their words, that the presses and the radio and the film industry of the neutral states refrain from publicizing anti-German materials. The appearance of a pro-English cartoon in a newspaper would irritate him more than the delivery of an important batch of raw materials to England. Of all the neutrals, Switzerland's problems with the press were the most acute. In 1939 the people of this small country were among the most literate in the world: Switzerland had more than four hundred newspapers. The government was sensitive to German demands. It cut down the employment of German refugees in the newspaper industry. In February 1940 it banned the publication of Rauschning's book on Hitler. Before the fall of France most Swiss newspapers printed the French and British war communiqués before the German ones; the Germans protested, with some effect.[69] After the fall of France there was, as we have seen, a temporary surge of sentiment in Switzerland among many people who were in favor of a cautious accommodation with the triumphant Germans. This was manifest in the slogan *"Mourir pour la presse?"* (Why die for the press?). This wavering fear passed. In the history of wartime Switzerland the conference in the rooms of the *Neue Zürcher Zeitung* on 1 July 1940 merits at least a footnote below that of the military assembly on the Rütli later that month.[70] This newspaper, said Bretscher, its editor-in-chief, will not conform to the new order in Europe. The government was aware of the acute German attention paid to the Swiss press. On 17 July it passed on to the editors of the newspapers an unusual directive, suggesting that they be prudent and trim their generally pro-British attitudes. Later this overcautious directive was balanced by another government warning, this time against the tone of defeatism in certain papers.

In matters of the press, Spain stood on the other extreme. Franco's ill repute with the democracies was enhanced by the shrill and often brutal rhetoric of much of the Spanish press during the war. Its exaggerations and its venom at times would surpass the tone of the German press itself. On the other hand, illiteracy in Spain was high; unlike in Switzerland, the effect of the press on public opinion and popular sentiment was limited. In the international relations of Spain the press counted little. Franco was, by nature, a cautious temporizer.[71] Yet his neutrality was the result less of

---

[69] Albrecht, K., *Neutraelitaet und Presse*, Dresden, 1942, cited in Hartmann, 27.

[70] See above, p. 106. It was by no means certain in July 1940 that the resistance manifested by General Guisan would carry the day. A memorandum by the popular and pro-German Colonel Däniker asked for the replacement of Guisan. As late as June 1941 certain Germanophile Swiss officers were talking about a "march on Berne." But nothing came out of it. A few Swiss representatives abroad were pro-German, including Steiner, the Swiss minister to Yugoslavia.

[71] This was typical of his political career before 1934, and also of his military management of the Civil War.

virtue than of necessity. After three years of a murderous civil war, Spain was bled white and weak. Franco and his cohorts were tempted to cast the lot of their impoverished country with the Axis in the summer of 1940; but their temptation passed fast.

Unique for Spain was the great influence that three other neutrals had on the nonbelligerent state in the crucial period of the war: Portugal, the United States, and the Vatican. The restraining influence of the Portuguese neighbor on Spain was considerable. No matter how authoritarian and anti-Communist, Salazar did not waver in his dislike for Hitler and in his respect for Britain. When on 30 July 1940 Spain and Portugal signed a pact of friendship,[72] this at first pleased the Germans, who wanted to move Portugal away from Britain in the direction of Spain. Very soon it became evident that the opposite was happening; it was Salazar who was quietly pulling Franco away from the German side. The United States loomed even larger than Portugal in Franco's mind. As early as September 1940 he approached the United States with the harebrained scheme of trading huge amounts of Spanish olive oil against American shipments of wheat. Roosevelt's answer was a not very chivalrous suggestion of Black Mail wrapped in a Red Cross. The American Red Cross would send a shipload of wheat to Spain if that was to be unloaded under American Red Cross supervision, and if (a big if, that) Franco would stay out of the war. Franco opened his sleepy eyes; Roosevelt pulled back when Franco went to meet Hitler at Hendaye; eventually in November the wheat shipment came through. Thereafter American-Spanish relations gradually improved, in spite of the furious anti-Franco tone of the American press and the nearly impossible relationship between the American ambassador Weddell, and Serrano Suñer.

Certain other neutrals, South American states and the Vatican, were instrumental in mediating between Madrid and Washington.[73] In the winter of 1940–41 Franco, who met Pétain in Montpellier and Mussolini in Bordighera, was thinking of a "Latin bloc"[74]—Spain, Portugal, Vichy France, Italy, the Vatican—a kind of "Rome-Madrid axis"—ideologically and politically balancing the preponderance of the Third Reich; but nothing much came out of this, save a little rhetoric and a few editorials by Maurras. At the same time Spain gave facilities to German officers around

---

[72] About some of the anti-Portuguese intrigues of the Franco people in 1940, see above, p. 113.

[73] In spite of the condition that many South American states kept officially recognizing the Republican Spanish exile "government." In July 1940 Spain and Chile broke their relations. These were restored three months later due to mediation extended by the Vatican and by Brazil.

[74] With encouragement from the Vatican. *VD*, 4, 168–69.

Gibraltar; German ships and submarines were permitted to make secret use of Spanish ports; German intelligence and radio networks were functioning in many places in Spain. In June 1941 bands of Spanish Fascist youths stoned the British Embassy in Madrid, and Franco joined Hitler's Anti-Bolshevik Crusade—at a safe distance from Russia, to be sure. The so-called Blue Division, amounting to a volunteer force of more than 17,000 Spaniards, went off to fight on Hitler's side in Russia, wearing German-issue uniforms.[75] In 1942 Franco would begin to trim his sails according to the prevailing winds in the fortunes of the war, again particularly with the United States in mind. Still the Spanish government was the only one among the neutral states of Europe wishing, in its way, for an Axis (Axis, rather than entirely German) victory during the first one or two years of the war, and which later publicly regretted Germany's defeat.

Sweden's chance for neutrality was enhanced not only by her prestige and by the reputation of her unusually well-equipped Army and Navy but also by the interest that certain great powers had in her neutrality. Thus on the morrow of Germany's invasion of Denmark and Norway[76] (for which Molotov congratulated the Germans), the Soviet government also informed Berlin that it regarded Sweden's neutrality as desirable. During the campaign in Norway the Norwegian minister Mowinckel came up with an unprecedented plan for the neutralization of northern Norway, involving an unoccupied zone supervised by Swedish troops. The plan had a certain appeal to Stockholm but not to Berlin, since the Germans were on their way to conquering all of Norway by the end of May. In the fall of 1940 Sweden and Finland (with American support) advanced cautiously another plan of northern neutrality, an eventual close union of the two countries for the duration of the war. The Germans and, foolishly, the Russians, reacted violently against this plan, which might have secured Finland's neutrality for the rest of the war. By and large the Germans were respectful of Swedish neutrality. In turn, the Swedish government felt that it had to consider certain German requests: In addition to the June 1940 transit agreement it allowed the Germans to set submarine nets in the Swedish territorial waters of the Øresund. On 25 June 1941 the Swedish government permitted the transit

---

[75] The first volunteer unit composed of men of a nonbelligerent state was that of Swedes during the first Winter War, when 9,000 Swedish volunteers, including an entire volunteer unit of their Air Force, fought on Finland's side.

[76] It is often forgotten that Norwegian neutrality was compromised during the First World War, when the British blockade rendered the country nearly helpless. By 1918 the maritime—as distinct from the formally diplomatic—policy of Norway had lapsed from her original neutrality to practices that favored the British unilaterally.

of an entire German division across the North, to Finland.[77] During the First World War most Swedes were pro-German. During the Second World War most Swedes were anti-German and Anglophile. Their ambassadors in Moscow and Washington were correct in assessing the prospect of Germany's defeat in the fall of 1941. In September 1941 there were some signs that the Germans might invade Sweden (as a counterstroke, perhaps, against the British plans for a precipitate landing in Norway).[78] The Swedish General Staff discreetly approached the British about a concerted plan to march on Trondheim. After a fortnight, however, the signs of a German invasion disappeared.

The government of the Irish Republic was not Anglophile, of course; but it was not pro-German either. In June 1940 there were unusual secret contacts between the Irish and British command staffs toward the eventual formation of an all-Ireland Defense Council. Lord Craigavon, the rigidly anti-Catholic Prime Minister of Ulster, was influential enough to kill the idea. In the autumn and winter of 1940 Churchill hoped that American pressure would make the government of De Valera open some of the southern Irish ports for the British, but De Valera refused, even in the face of subtle—and some not so subtle—American pressures.[79] On the other hand, the number of Irishmen who had volunteered for the British forces remained considerable during the war.

On the other edge of Europe, the Turks—a race whose prowess in the past was usually military and seldom political—showed great diplomatic ability during the Second World War. In October 1939, they signed a sort of alliance with Britain and France, which they let lapse judiciously in 1940. During the winter of 1939–40, the Turkish Foreign Ministry elaborated an intelligent and workable plan for a Balkan entente, a neutral bloc including Greece, Bulgaria, Yugoslavia, Romania, and Turkey; it was not the latter's fault that this did not come about. The Germans' cause was assisted in Ankara by Papen, the German ambassador,

---

[77] Sweden put an end to these German transit facilities in 1943.

[78] See above, pp. 149–50.

[79] Irish relations with Germany were correct throughout the war. This was in part due to the judicious behavior of the German minister in Dublin. Unlike in 1916, there was little collusion between Irish extremists and Germany. In the summer of 1941, however, certain IRA members as well as certain Irish politicians engaged themselves in conversations with a German agent, Goertz. The latter was respected and liked by his Irish conversants (he was buried in Ireland, with a swastika on his grave, in 1947). During the same year the Nazi diplomat Veesenmayer (later he became Hitler's envoy to occupied Hungary, in 1944) was involved in inconclusive negotiations with the Irish about eventual German support to Irish guerrillas in the case of a British occupation of southern Ireland.

a curious example of that rare thing, a failure in domestic politics who ends up by being an excellent diplomat.[80] In the summer of 1941 Turkey was tempted to join in the war against her ancient enemy Russia. The British presence in the eastern Mediterranean was instrumental in dissuading the Turks who, perhaps for the first time in their modern history, were learning quickly how to profit from neutrality. On the russet Anatolian plain, Ankara by 1941 had become, like Lisbon, a sophisticated capital city at the tail end of the wartime Orient-Taurus Express, pullulating with all kinds of agents and spies (including purchasing agents).[81]

There remains that most august and unusual neutral state of the Vatican. Its influence during the Second World War was very great, far greater than during the First World War; indeed, greater than at any time in the modern history of Europe. Among the war leaders Hitler and Roosevelt recognized this. Oddly enough, the Pope, Pius XII, was less confident of his potential influence than were some of his opponents. Since this potential influence was spiritual rather than temporal (or, rather, spiritual with potential temporal effects), most of the survey of this phenomenon—a profound and complicated one, to be sure—belongs later in this book, to a subchapter on religion,[82] rather than to the present one of neutral diplomacies. Still the place, and the function, of the Holy See was temporal as well as spiritual. Its physical presence, a neutral state in the center of an Italy at war, was important in itself. Mussolini, who had confirmed this papal sovereignty and independence in the Treaty of the Lateran in 1929, abided by its provisions during the war. So here was a sovereign state in the midst of the capital of Hitler's principal ally, receiv-

---

[80] The Germans and the Turks liked each other. The latter had a great respect for Papen, whose prestige was deemed sufficiently dangerous for Moscow. A Soviet agent was sent to assassinate him in 1942; the attempt failed. Hitler, too, respected the Turks. In March 1941 he sent a special message to the President of Turkey: The German troops entering Bulgaria would not approach the Turkish frontier closer than 30 kilometers. The Turks told the British that in the reply of their President to Hitler the former regretted "that the Germans had not carried out their previous undertakings not to enter the Balkans." In reality, this sentence did *not* figure in the President's message to Hitler. Woodward, I, 582, note 1.

[81] The British, who failed in trying to bring in the Turks on their side in 1943 and in 1944 (they were represented there by an unusually inept ambassador, Sir H. Knatchbull-Hughessen), were able to restrain Turkish inclinations toward Germany in 1940. It was also one of the rare instances of effective economic warfare. Germany had been Turkey's principal trading partner before 1939. Between July 1940 and June 1941 the British succeeded in reducing the German share of Turkey's foreign trade from about 50 per cent to 10 per cent.

[82] See below, pp. 455–78.

ing and dispatching foreign representatives, broadcasting from its own radio station, printing its own newspaper—in sum, possessing significant and on occasion very important independent privileges of its own. Mussolini felt that he had to agree to the passage of British ambassadors and of American envoys through Rome. The most important of these was Roosevelt's personal emissary, Myron Taylor, who traveled across Italian territory, crossing Rome into the Vatican, several times,[83] carrying in his breast pocket Roosevelt's messages to the Pope, trying to induce the latter to bless the struggle against Hitler. The British minister to the Vatican was allowed to leave for and return from London in 1942: Italian sentries saluted him on his way, with a few officious agents, in their customary black suits, plodding around his car. The envoys of lesser powers to the Holy See could not always count on such a respectful treatment by the Italians. In July 1941, the Italian police removed the Yugoslav minister to the Vatican, in violation of the Lateran Treaty of 1929.[84]

One of the principal problems of Vatican diplomacy involved the recognition of new regimes and of territorial changes. Its traditional policy was to refuse recognition of territorial changes prematurely. On the other hand, this often meant a series of troubles involving the jurisdictional authority of certain bishops.[85] Beyond these—often not unimportant—formalities of juridical recognition, these difficulties involved the very conditions of neutrality. A Polish bishop was, after all, a Pole; a nuncio of Italian birth was an Italian (the British tried to have the Vatican remove the nuncios from Malta and Egypt)—men often influenced by their own national sentiments. The principal diplomatic officials of the Holy See were, of course, prelates who had been trained to rise above their national and social origins. Some of them acquitted themselves honorably and well. The dispatches of certain nuncios such as Cicognani in Madrid or Godfrey in London, the minutes and the instructions of the two principal secretaries, Maglione and especially Tardini in Rome, reveal the workings of first-class minds and of excellent characters. There were nuncios (Valeri in Vichy, Orsenigo in Berlin) whose performance and judgment were often poor. Monsignor Roncalli, later Pope John XXIII,

---

[83] Myron Taylor visited the Vatican three times during the crucial years of the war: 27 February–22 August 1940; 5–21 September 1941; and 17–28 September 1942.

[84] *VD*, 5, 118, 287.

[85] Examples of these included the jurisdictional authority of a Slovak bishop over the small mountain enclave of Spis, which Slovakia claimed to have annexed from Poland; the continued existence of the Polish archbishop in Vilna after the Lithuanian annexation of the latter, the cautious support that the Vatican extended to certain Croatian bishops, etc.

the nuncio in Ankara, who later in the war showed a kind of diplomatic capacity that enhanced his large-hearted human qualities, was not always judicious; he was often unduly influenced by Papen's staff in Ankara.[86] Nor was the secret intelligence of the Vatican always first-rate.[87] Yet the influence of the Holy See was great, increasing steadily through the war. It involved the interests not only of millions of Catholics throughout the world but also those of the people of Rome and of Italy on important occasions. Thus, for example, the Vatican was instrumental in arriving at a tacit agreement in October 1941 to the effect that the British would not bomb Rome if the Italians and the Germans would not bomb Cairo.[88]

This deal was reached through the envoy of President Roosevelt. It was typical of the fast-growing influence of the United States. From the very beginning of the war until December 1941, among all neutrals the influence of the United States was the greatest. But this respect for the United States, and of its representatives,[89] not only in the democratic but also in the neutral and in the German-occupied states of Europe, is another story, to which we shall have to return.[90]

## COMMUNICATIONS AND INTELLIGENCE

¶ Diplomacy consists of the communications of authorized representatives of states. The record of these communications is the material for the history of diplomacy. During the twentieth century the volume of these communications has grown, sometimes to an unmanageable extent. The representatives of governments have been multiplying, too, on all kinds of levels, often in unprecedented manners and ways. The result of this

---

[86] On several occasions Papen attempted to use the nuncio for peace feelers. On the latter's dispatch, reporting a significant conversation with Papen on 16 April 1942, Monsignor Tardini minuted: *"Non essere troppo caldi."* (Watch out). *VD*, 5, 543.

[87] As late as 1 May 1940 the nuncio to Italy, Borgongini Duca, reported that while Italy's entry into the war was now inevitable, this would be confined to an Italian occupation of Croatia. *VD*, 1, 443.

[88] *VD*, 5, 307.

[89] This was not only a matter of state relations. See, for example, the memoirs of Cyrus Sulzberger, Jr. (Sulzberger, passim). In 1940 and 1941 this young American newspaperman, of Jewish ancestry, could travel across Europe, including Germany's allied states, like a privileged prince of the Renaissance. It must be added that he made good use of his advantages and provided intelligent reports for the New York *Times*, owned by his family.

[90] See below, pp. 496–512.

is obvious. The diplomatic documents are an ever smaller part of the record of the relations of states, let alone of the relations of entire nations. Some of the most important communications remain unrecorded, while the historical value of the inflated volume of the recorded communications is usually inferior to that of the diplomatic papers of the past.[91] Moreover, one must know how to penetrate beneath the often verbose and opaque language of the bureaucracy, especially of that of a totalitarian state; one must know how to detect a variety of nuances; one must be skeptical of the authenticity of a document, of the literal meaning of the record itself.

Hitler did not like to write or even to dictate. He did not mind using volunteer agents, unofficial intermediaries on occasion, people whose acts and words were seldom recorded for posterity. The Swedish Dahlerus, Goering's friend, tried to prevent the break between Britain and Germany in August 1939. Sven Hedin was another Swede whom Hitler regarded highly: He used Hedin to suggest certain matters to London and, perhaps on one occasion, even to Moscow.[92] In 1940–41 Hitler used a Yugoslav journalist, Gregoric, in his complex diplomatic game in trying to lure Yugoslavia into the Tripartite Pact. There are, as we have seen, some indications that Hitler tacitly accepted Hess's idea of flying to England (he certainly knew of Hess's first attempt to establish contact with English personages in September 1940). It is even possible that Hitler had a secret personal connection to Stalin; we do not know.

Churchill communicated with Roosevelt privately. Soon after Churchill's assumption of power, he found that he could not even use the American Embassy in London for this purpose.[93] Chamberlain used a

---

[91] See Bibliographical remarks, below.

[92] In early March 1940 Hedin was in Berlin, trying to intervene in favor of the Finns. The Soviet Embassy was informed of his presence and of his talks. (*Hedin*, 102). On other occasions Hitler told Hedin matters that he wished to transpire to London and Washington. (Ibid., 177). On 5 December 1940 (the date is significant—it was the day when Hitler spoke to von Bock and other generals of his decision to attack Russia), Hitler told Hedin: ". . . I can tell *you* in the strictest confidence that Molotov came to Berlin with very far-reaching demands on Finnish territory, and that it was Russia's intention to occupy the whole of Finland, but I gave Mr. Molotov to understand very clearly from the start that further Russian occupation of Finnish territory was not in accordance with Germany's wishes. Never forget, Herr Doktor, that this information is intended for you alone. . . ." Ibid., 177. Only a fraction of Hedin's wartime papers were published in English, in an obscure edition in Dublin.

[93] There were two reasons for this. One was the presence of a code clerk, Kent, an obsessed American isolationist and consequently a Germanophile, whom the British arrested on 21 May 1940 for filching messages for private

THE RELATIONS OF STATES

minor Italian official by the name of Dingli as his intermediary with the Italian ambassador, Grandi, in 1938 and 1939. The name of Sir Joseph Ball appeared in Grandi's dispatches as the secret intermediary; Dingli's name turns up in the papers of the Hungarian Legation in London. The secret contacts between Vichy and London in 1940–41 involved a number of men who were not diplomats: Professors Rougier and Chevalier, Colonel Groussard, etc. The names of unofficial (and often, alas, undiplomatic) intermediaries between the warring states of Europe during the Second World War would fill a directory—a kind of neo-Gothick Almanac.

But at this point we must make a distinction—not an absolute or precise one, to be sure, but the kind of distinction that does make a difference—between communications and intelligence. They must not be equated. Our entire civilization is weighed down by the cancerous growth of communications—and by a decline of intelligence. This was true of the Second World War, even in the limited sense of political intelligence. Enormous bureaucracies had come into being, involved in communication and in intelligence.[94] Yet most of the sensational spy stories notwithstanding, secret intelligence about enemy operations had few decisive effects during the Second World War. The statesmen talked much; few of them knew how to listen. Stalin misread the evidence of Hitler's intentions, no matter how massive the evidence. Hitler and Churchill made similar mistakes.[95] The Dutch, the Belgian, the Yugoslav governments knew when

political purposes. The other was the ambassador, Joseph Kennedy, Sr., whom Churchill and Roosevelt (about the latter and Kennedy, see above, p. 112, n. 10) had every reason not to trust. "The Foreign Office also considered that, owing to Mr. Kennedy's openly expressed defeatism, the United States Embassy was an undesirable channel." FO 371 A 3261/1/51.

[94] A good example of their overlapping is that of the case of the German newspaperman Fritz Hesse. A protégé of Ribbentrop, stationed in London, Hesse was instrumental in confidential contacts with the Chamberlain people in London before the war, and for certain significant diplomatic tentatives during the war. Consequently his memoirs contain material that is not always to be found in the diplomatic records. Yet Hesse, who considered himself to be an important agent of German foreign policy, was, in reality, an agent of communications and not of intelligence. In plain English, through all of his important contacts Hesse told much and learned little that was worthwhile.

[95] Hitler, who seldom read his ambassadors' dispatches, was nevertheless much interested in secret information culled from spies, especially on two crucial occasions. In early July 1940 he wanted to read *all* reports of all kinds of agents and the transcripts of monitored telephone conversations from London. In the spring of 1941 he wanted and got a series of confidential reports gathered by agents working within the Soviet Embassy in Berlin. Much of this involved

the Germans would attack; yet their defenses broke on the first day. The Germans, the Italians, the British, the Swedes,[96] and the Hungarians had broken radio codes and read it. None of this made much difference, even when the information was reliable. A former employee of the British Embassy in Rome kept selling secret material to the Germans for years. In Moscow the Germans had the record of the conversations between the Yugoslav and the Greek ministers in 1940. The Germans would spy on their allies and satellites; they read *all* of the code communications of the Hungarian Legation in Berlin after 1938. They got copies of some of Cripps' letters to the Soviet Foreign Ministry as late as in the spring of 1941. They had their informants in the Vatican. In at least three instances the phrase appears in the published Vatican documents: Care must be taken because *Il Sig. Menshausen sa tutto.* (Menshausen [the German chargé] knows everything). Yet to know "everything" is the beginning of wisdom, not the end of it. The top echelons of the military intelligence, beginning with Admiral Canaris, were seldom in sympathy with Hitler's plans. More important, the Germans—and especially Hitler —were far from immune to the usual temptation of gathering and using intelligence for preconceived purposes, to confirm their own ideas after their minds were made up.

The term "fifth column" came out of the Spanish Civil War. In 1936 General Mola told journalists that, in addition to the four Nationalist columns converging on Madrid, there was a fifth column in Madrid itself. So there was: But Madrid did not fall for nearly three years. The fifth column did not rise until the end: what happened then was that hundreds of men and women, dust-laden, were coming up, with halting steps, from the cellars of neutral embassies, with eyes blinking in the unaccustomed sunlight. Yet the term caught on. In 1940 the notion of a fifth column fed the fires of the panic that swept the states and nations of Europe as the Germans were bearing down on them. Yet cases such as the handful of Dutch Nazi soldiers in German uniforms, or the few Quislingite Norwegian officers, were few. Professor De Jong, the principal Dutch historian of the war, made a judicious assessment of the fifth columns in retrospect. Their importance was vastly exaggerated. Unlike Arthur Koestler and Peter de Polnay,[97] Professor De Jong admitted that he had been wrong.[98]

---

trivia, but Hitler was acutely interested. See *GD*, D, XI, 980–81, especially note 5; also 1,985–86.

[96] They broke the German military code for several months in 1940–41.

[97] Koestler and Polnay about Paris in May 1940: "Everywhere in Paris I saw morse signals. The men of the fifth column were at work." Cited by De Jong, *D5K*, 14.

[98] "I, too," wrote De Jong, "had been a victim of the panicky fear of the fifth column. Many, whose statements (cited by me here) proved to have been

His respect for the truth must command our respect, in turn. In Eastern Europe conditions were slightly different: The German populations, bristling with aggressive pride, would sometimes function as advanced agents of the German armies. But this was something that their enemies knew—hence, for example, the harsh and cruel treatment inflicted on the German minority by the Poles in August–September 1939.

The history of Soviet intelligence in 1939–41 is especially murky and complicated. Few documents survive; their evidence is ambiguous as a matter of course. In the 1960s there was a sentimental tendency to exalt the efficiency and the heroic self-sacrifice of Soviet and pro-Soviet agents in 1941, together with the semi-official recognition within the Soviet Union that Stalin had paid little heed to the information they were furnishing. Yet the effectiveness of Soviet intelligence in 1939–41 is far from impressive.[99] True, there existed a reservoir of people, international Communists and fellow travelers, ranging from dedicated revolutionaries (they were few) to the shadiest kind of Eastern European refugee, people who would offer their services to Soviet intelligence. It is not generally known that their networks existed side by side with another Muscovite network, directed usually by Soviet engineers and journalists abroad. The two networks were seldom co-ordinated. The members of the first were mainly Jews, of the second Great Russians and Ukrainians, often anti-Semitic; all in all, an unattractive bunch. German pressure, and all too often a little Nazi cajolery, led to mutual betrayals on all levels. Possibly the most useful source of Russian intelligence came from Switzerland, where a German émigré, Roessler, furnished items of information to Mos-

---

groundless, though understandable at the time, will be pleased to know that I myself had written in the year 1941 about the 'masterful organization' of the fifth column in my native city of Amsterdam. . . ." De Jong, *D5K*, 12, citing himself: De Jong, *Holland*, 41.

[99] This includes the now legendary Richard Sorge in Tokyo, whose activities, strictly speaking, do not belong to the compass of this book. Taking advantage of his excellent contacts at the highest level of the Japanese government, Sorge radioed to Moscow that the Germans were about to attack on or about 22 June 1941 and, later, that the Japanese were about to move against the United States and Britain in the Far East, not against the Soviet Union. Much of this information was available from other sources. Sorge merely confirmed what the British and the American government knew, and what their leaders were letting Stalin know, in turn. On the eve of Hitler's attack Stalin was no more inclined to listen to Sorge than to Churchill or to Roosevelt. In October there was not the slightest sign that the Japanese might attack in Siberia. What Sorge funished was yet another piece of information, not the missing piece of the puzzle—the metaphor dear to intelligence romanticists and to the writers of spy stories.

cow that also went to the secret Swiss military intelligence "Bureau Ha." There is reason to believe that most of this material had been fed to Roessler & Company by the British. In any event, this important source of intelligence for the Soviets could operate only with Swiss consent, at a time when it was in the interest of the Western democracies (including Switzerland) that Russia should hold out against Hitler.

Most of these intelligence networks worked through shortwave radios, involving a new kind of technology in the transmission, concealment, falsification, and pinpointing of signals. In other instances, spying and smuggling still depended on the old ways: Wartime life in the valleys of the Pyrenees, along the Swiss-French frontier, in the forests of the Jura or on the rocky paths of Andorra had a touch of earlier centuries, with smugglers shepherding small groups of weary wanderers across the border. The frontiers were not closed everywhere. As late as February 1941 thousands of Belgians crossed the French frontier every day to work in factories and mines. Generally speaking, however, technology eroded many of the previous conditions of sovereignty and of neutrality. Thus, for example, in November 1940, months before Bulgaria chose to sign her pact with Germany, her government agreed to allow the entry of German teams of a few hundred specialists who were about to set up air observation stations. As early as 1 October 1940 Hitler permitted the special "Rowehl" air reconnaissance unit to fly over the border at great heights and intrude as far as 160 miles into Soviet territory. The Spanish government in 1940 allowed German staff officers to traverse Spanish territory and study various possibilities for attacking Gibraltar; the Spanish also agreed to fuel German tankers and submarines in the smaller bay harbors of Spain.

The British intelligence services could count on a large number of dedicated patriots and anti-Nazis across the Continent. During the Chamberlain period the British made little use of their services: British intelligence depended on its traditional ways, not always effectively.[100] When the British government tried to cultivate contacts with the German opposition they were principally interested not so much in the cultivation of opposition to Hitler as in gathering scraps and bits of information from these people: in intelligence rather than in communications. Much of this changed in the high summer of 1940. The British government under Churchill decided that one of its principal weapons against Hitler would be its support of anti-German resistance across the Continent. On 19 July

---

[100] As early as March 1940 a small group of British intelligence officers were working in Norway, reporting to the naval section of Military Intelligence in London; still it was the British, not the Germans, who were taken by surprise, and bumbled in Norway a month later.

1940, the very day when Hitler broadcast his grand peace offer to the British Empire, in London SOE, "Special Operations Executive," the British agency for subversive warfare, was established, with its headquarters on Sherlock Holmes' Baker Street. Like Gestapo, Abwehr, RSHA, and SS in Germany, in Britain SOE and the traditional intelligence services were often at odds with each other. Their divergences were probably less harmful for the Allied cause than was the bitter clandestine infighting between a Canaris and a Heydrich for the Germans. The British were slow in tuning and turning their networks up to a taut and high kind of efficiency.[101] Yet by the end of 1941 tens of thousands of men and women in nearly every country across the Continent were ready to risk their lives for the victory of Britain.

## INTERNATIONAL PROPAGANDA

¶ We have now seen that by 1939 the relations of states have become much more complicated than before. This growth in their complexity was only partially attributable to technology. Much of it was due to the growth of government itself, to the increasing bureaucratization of life—which, in turn, was a consequence of the worldwide phenomenon of democratization, including the increase in universal literacy. "A war for the minds of men" was a reality during the Second World War, as indeed it always is. A battle is always a battle for the minds of men; in actual combat, too, a battle is lost when one side convinces itself that it is lost. What was relatively new during the Second World War was the extent of the war for the minds of men. Large majorities, entire peoples had to be convinced that a certain side was winning (or losing). More than before, international propaganda had become a prime instrument of statecraft. Hitler and Goebbels were masters in comprehending this in certain ways; Churchill and De Gaulle in other ways. Their approaches, and sometimes their techniques, were different. Both sides, however, employed the press, the radio, the cinema, the theater, and cultural propaganda far more extensively than before. The Germans and the French had their Ministry of Propaganda, the British their Ministry of Information.[102] Beneath and beyond these official state agencies there was the

---

[101] Example: The first steady radio contact between Poland and London did not start operating until 2 August 1941.

[102] In 1939–40 the French director of Propaganda and Information was the writer Jean Giraudoux, famous for some of his plays, including *La Guerre de Troie n'aura pas lieu* (literally translated, The War of Troy Will Not Take

press. We cannot deal with it in detail. A comparative history—that is, an intelligent and excellent analysis of the European newspapers during the Second World War—is a joint task worth the efforts of teams of historians; as yet, little work has been done in this field.

In 1939–41 newspapers were still the principal sources of what are nowadays called "mass communications." People received their information, and often their opinions, from newspapers—especially about foreign countries and international affairs. The newer influences of magazines and of radio were still limited, though growing; television did not exist.[103] In Eastern Europe millions of people were first-generation newspaper readers. The twentieth century, Oswald Spengler had written, produced a dreadful kind of person: the kind of man who actually believes what is printed in the papers. This was a half truth. At least the second generation of newspaper readers learned quickly *how* to read the papers—what to believe and what not to believe. Perhaps the only exception to this was the Soviet Union, whose newspapers were devoid of any nuances, and whose readers—most of them recently liberated from the fetters of illiteracy— showed, as yet, little discrimination. On 26 November 1939 *Pravda*, the premier newspaper of this great empire, wrote that the Finnish Prime Minister was "a scarecrow, a fool, a marionette, a clown pirouetting in the circus ring"—a not untypical example of the political prosody of the Soviet press. The Germans and the Italians allowed—and on occasion even cultivated—differences of nuances in their daily press: *La Stampa* remained different from *Il Popolo d'Italia*, and the *Frankfurter Zeitung* from the *Völkischer Beobachter*.[104] Goebbels tried, and at times succeeded, in employing talented journalists of a non-Nazi persuasion,[105] in order to buttress the influence and the reputation of the Third Reich both within her borders and abroad. In the spring of 1940 he brought together a number of such journalists, and he launched the successful *Das Reich*, a political-cultural weekly that followed, to some extent, the model of the English literary-political weeklies of *The Spectator* type. An even more successful Goebbelsian adaptation was the picture magazine *Signal*, mod-

---

Place). In October 1939 *Gringoire* wrote: "The War of Troy did indeed take place. Let us hope that M. Giraudoux is better informed than that."

[103] Television came to England in 1939, when nearly 20,000 television sets were functioning. In September 1939 the BBC television service closed down for the duration of the war. In the summer of 1940 the Germans used closed-circuit television, showing films to patients in a few selected military hospitals.

[104] In Vichy France the conservative-liberal *Le Jour* and *Figaro* continued publishing until the autumn of 1941. In Paris *Le Matin*, *Le Petit Parisien*, *L'Oeuvre*, and *Paris-Soir* went on publishing under the Germans, as also the daily *Auto-Sport*.

[105] Examples: Margret Boveri, Karl Silex, Ursula von Kardoff, Paul Schiffer, etc.

eled after the American *Life*.[106] The German Ministry of Propaganda tried, on occasion, to buy up foreign newspapers. After their occupation of foreign countries the Germans devoted relatively little interest to the occupied press. The circulation of these papers did not decrease. People read them avidly, since their hunger for information was even greater during the exigencies of the war. Yet the vast majority quickly acquired the knowledge *how* to read between the lines—*intelligence* in the literal sense of the Latin verb: *inter-legere*—they learned what not to believe, even (or, perhaps, especially) when it was printed in these newspapers.

Newspapers, as we have seen before, were employed by governments as instruments of state relations, too, not only in order to influence other people but also to signal matters to other governments: The Soviet Union provided a prime example of this, with its Tass communiqués and *Pravda* and *Izvestia* articles. Elsewhere, too, editorialists in important newspapers would state or suggest certain matters with the hope of bringing this to the notice, not of their domestic readers, but of foreign governments.[107] The press became, on occasion, an instrument not only of domestic politics but also of international statecraft—let us add, not always with propitious results. In other instances newspapers were used by governments to communicate false information in order to mislead the enemy. A minor example thereof was Goebbels' order to confiscate "prematurely printed" copies of the *Völkischer Beobachter* of 16 June 1941, in which number a leading article had appeared, written by Goebbels himself, with the title "Crete as an Example," suggesting that after their success in conquering Crete by air the Germans were preparing a landing in Britain. The very act of the confiscation was meant to impress the British (and presumably also the Russian) governments to the effect that the next German move would come in the West, not in the East. The British themselves would resort to propaganda falsifications on occasion.[108] In most instances, however, the *faux* of the British press were neither governmental nor even intentional. (This writer remembers an

---

[106] In Switzerland alone *Signal* sold 80,000 copies each week in the summer of 1940—a considerable success for Goebbels, even as the price of the magazine was artificially cheap.

[107] Example: In March 1941, even after the Greek government had committed itself to a full alliance with Britain, certain influential Athens papers suggested (*Kathimerini*, on 8 March 1941) that the government and the people of Greece continued to regret the prospects of war with Germany, which they wished honestly to avoid.

[108] Example: publication in British papers of a false letter by Colonel Moelders, shot down in November 1941, a German air ace, a Catholic, full of subtle anti-Nazi passages.

issue of *Picture Post* in 1940 showing a partly burned-out British tank with the caption: "Destroyed Italian Tank.")

Even though they could be disseminated by air, pamphlets played relatively little importance during the war. It took some time for the British to learn that, like most of the bombs, few of the pamphlets would fall on the target areas. The very provenance of the pamphlets made their recipients skeptical. They were, simply, too direct a form of propaganda to impress people.[109]

Far more important, extensive, and effective were the international effects of the radio. Militarily the radio had become an absolutely essential instrument of communication. The swift movements on land and in the air depended on radio equipment; entire battles turned on the adequacy or inadequacy of radio communications. "A hundred extra wireless sets could have saved Crete."[110] Perhaps even more important was the function of the radio in the battle for the minds of people. The Germans recognized its importance early. Hitler's oratorical powers on the radio are well known.[111] In 1939 a considerable portion of the peoples of Europe owned radio sets—perhaps as many as 15 per cent in the western half of the Continent,[112] in addition to a high percentage of the literate classes elsewhere. The capacities of radio transmission and reception had developed to the extent that even a simple set could pick up foreign broadcasts within a radius of a few hundred miles without difficulty. A small but growing portion of radio sets—especially those of radio-phonograph consoles, which had become popular in the late 1930s—had shortwave bands. The reception of distant stations on these was relatively easy, especially during the afternoon and night hours.

The Greater German radio system (*Grossdeutscher Rundfunk*) began to broadcast regular foreign-language programs before the war; in January 1939 it extended its services further; in January 1940 it broadcast daily programs in twenty-two languages, in January 1942 in more than forty. Because of its often blatantly propagandistic nature, German inter-

---

[109] There were a few exceptions. In January 1940 the Germans cast 200,000 examples of a vulgar and humorous soldier's sheet, entitled *Le Journal de Cambronne*, over the French lines of the Maginot. Many of the bored French draftees read them with considerable amusement and interest.

[110] Stewart, *Crete*, 481.

[111] The first *coup d'état* in the history of Europe in which the insurrectionists tried to get control of the state radio was the Nazi stroke in Vienna in July 1934.

[112] In 1939, 23 per cent of the population of Sweden and Denmark, 19 per cent of the British, 16 per cent of the Dutch, and 14.5 per cent of the Norwegian people had radios.

national radio was generally limited in its effects.[113] The great international radio success of the war—its reputation was to survive the war for decades—was that of the British Broadcasting Corporation. The BBC began an extensive and rapidly expanding service of foreign-language broadcasts in the summer of 1939. In 1940 its broadcasts reached all of Europe. Millions listened to them, principally because of the reputation of the accuracy of news from London. By late 1940 in French-speaking Western Europe the term *la poste* meant the radio news from London. At the hour of the customary news broadcasts the streets of cities and towns emptied; everywhere people were hurrying home to listen in darkened rooms to the news from Britain. The Germans passed decrees and laws forbidding the local population to listen to foreign radio broadcasts. Still the prices of radio sets soared. In Belgium they were openly advertised in the newspapers as late as 1941.

*C'est le ton qui fait la musique:* The very tone of radio broadcasts could signal policy changes. Entire populations grew sensitive to such matters. So were their governments. When in October 1940 London and Vichy reached a cautious agreement mostly about blockade matters in Madrid, one of the requests of Vichy was that London tone down its radio criticism of the Vichy regime—which then the BBC did, to General De Gaulle's dismay.[114]

The exile governments' influence on their peoples would have been much more limited without the radio. As Professor De Jong wrote,

> In an occupied country, indeed, the radio comes to have immense importance in men's lives. If you do not turn on your set at all, because you do not wish to listen to enemy propaganda, then it stands as a mute witness of your defiance. But if you are willing to take the risk, you can hear what you wish to hear, and thus choose your own individualistic, nonconformist path. Thus the radio set became more than a means of receiv-

---

[113] Exceptions: German radio broadcasts to Latin America were often popular; in 1939–40 so was their French program beamed from Stuttgart; and—a surprising figure, this—as many as six million people in England may have listened to the broadcasts of the traitor William Joyce, "Lord Haw-Haw," on occasion. (It must be remarked, however, that most of these listeners tuned in to Lord Haw-Haw as a source of entertainment rather than for information. The political effects of his broadcasts were minimal.)

[114] Unlike De Gaulle, Churchill, and Hitler, Marshal Pétain did not write his radio speeches. His radio allocution of 1 January 1942 had a curious history. Drafted by Du Moulin de la Barthète, it included certain subtleties of *attentisme.* Upon the entreaties of others in his circle, Pétain decided to change the text, but it was too late: It had been recorded on the then customary wax discs and was so broadcast.

ing news from the outside world, more than a shield against Nazi propaganda. It was a symbol of the right of each individual to think for himself.[115]

Under such circumstances certain broadcasts from neutral states acquired great importance. They obviated much of the natural jealousy with which some of the suffering nations were wont to regard their more fortunate neutral neighbors, as had happened during the First World War. Norwegians depended on the Swedish state radio. In France the most popular radio, after the BBC, was the French-speaking service (Radio Sottens) of Switzerland; hundreds of thousands listened regularly to the weekly talks of the Swiss journalist René Payot. For the first time in its history the Vatican broadcast extensively during a war. The effects of the broadcasts of this august supernational authority, which had put the word *propaganda* into currency many centuries ago, were insignificant, principally because of their unimaginative nature, usually restricted to the propagation of Catholic religious rhetoric. Its propaganda was often useless: unduly vague, unduly narrow, or both.[116]

Clandestine or "black" international broadcasts had limited effects. In the summer of 1940 as many as five fake English radio stations were set up by Goebbels; their signals as well as their influence were weak. A strong clandestine "German Soldier's Network," "Gustav Siegfried I," operated by the British, had a limited audience among the German garrisons in the West; Goebbels was sufficiently worried about it to order an extensive search for its location; the German triangulators finally pinpointed it in November 1941, about sixty miles northwest of London. The Soviet radio broadcasts were of poor quality: Even Communists would rather listen to London than to Moscow.

For the first time in a European war films played an important role in international propaganda. Goebbels was among the first to recognize this. He had a great admiration for American picture magazines and photographic techniques; he especially admired Hollywood and American films. In the summer of 1939 the French government prevented German

---

[115] De Jong, "Mass reactions to German Occupation," *TW*, 20–21.

[116] Example: In January 1941 a Jesuit, Father Fulst, from Soviet-occupied Lithuania, writing also in the name of his unfortunate bishop, asked the Vatican to stop its bland and often inaccurate anti-Bolshevik broadcasts, beamed in Lithuanian from Rome once a week. Please stop this kind of broadcast, the prelates begged the Vatican, especially its anti-Marxist treatises, etc. "This propaganda is wholly unnecessary, since the best anti-Bolshevik propaganda is what we see every day around us. . . ." The broadcasts "bring us nothing but misfortune and help us not at all." *VD*, 4, 379.

agents from buying the majority of shares of the French newsreel company Pathé-Cinema. Elsewhere, in Hungary and in certain Balkan states, the Germans bought up not only important newspapers but also certain movie theaters, which then became the outlets of German and pro-German films. People would learn about this quickly: *This* was the German theater, *that* was the one that still showed British and American films—as with the different nuancé newspapers, different people frequented different theaters. The German newsreels were very well made; at times their effect was powerful (as the hour-long news films on the Polish and Western campaigns). The British newsreels were less imaginative; they depended too much on American photographers and film companies.

Art exhibitions, music, dancing, sporting events—all played a part in this new kind of international cultural propaganda. We cannot even list its numerous manifestations here. In many ways they were but the consequences of a kind of international publicity that had burgeoned into enormous, and often senseless, proportions during the 1920s and 1930s. One portion of this history—the German appropriation of objects of art in the conquered territories—has been surveyed by postwar specialists in the history of art[117]; the rest belongs to a history of publicity techniques rather than to the history of the Second World War.

A man such as Goebbels understood these new developments in the relations of nations very well. He saw in a publicity campaign a struggle, a battle, in a more or less American manner.[118] But there was even more to this. In April 1940, before the Scandinavian campaign, he told his collaborators that what was happening in Europe was only a repetition, on a larger scale, of the revolutionary struggles of the Nazis within Germany

---

[117] A special office of the Wehrmacht was that of the "military protection of art" (*Militaerische Kunstschutz*), functioning on a more or less traditional level, at times protecting the cultural heritage of certain subjugated nations. Against this worked different task forces, including those of Rosenberg and Goebbels. See below, p. 518, and Günther-Hornis, passim.

[118] One example of his few failures was the "V" campaign in 1941. In the spring of the year the Continent was flooded with badges and posters marked with the letter V, *Victoria*, for Germany. (The letter *V* had a peculiar attraction for the German mind during the Second World War—"V-Manner," "V-Waffen," etc.) Soon the meaning was turned around; "V" was to mean Churchill's victory, later manifest in his V for Victory sign of two fingers; it also referred to Beethoven's Fifth Symphony, the signal of the BBC's European program, signifying Britain as the repository of European civilization. According to Bennett, 41, the V sign had been thought up by the Belgian section of the European service of the BBC, and it was an Oxford don, C. E. Stevens, who "discovered" that the Morse code of the letter *V* corresponded with the rhythm of the opening bar of the Fifth Symphony.

before 1933.[119] A generation and a world war earlier, the young Marcel Proust wrote in a fragment, in 1915: "The life of nations merely repeats, on a larger scale, the lives of their component cells; and he who is incapable of understanding the mystery, the reactions, the laws that determine the movements of the individual, can never hope to say anything worth listening to about the struggles of nations."[120] In this respect this bourgeois French genius was a more precise prophet and a more profound observer than the revolutionary German genius of a Goebbels. Now we shall have to devote an entire chapter in order to show how and why.

---

[119] "We are experiencing today step by step the repetition of events that we had experienced once before. In Europe we are carrying through the very same revolution which we carried through in Germany on a smaller scale. Only the dimensions have changed. The principles, experiences, methods of that time are valid also today. They are equally valid for the struggle among nations." Cited in Hillgruber, *HS*, 593, note 55.

[120] Maurois, *Proust*, 287–88.

# 5 . *The sentiments of nations*

THE STRUGGLES OF NATIONS"—historians and so-called social scientists have hardly begun to study them in depth or in detail. This statement sounds surprising. During this century we have seen an enormous and growing preoccupation with international affairs, international relations, international organizations. A new generation of scholars have addressed themselves to the study of these matters, so that International Relations have emerged as an academic speciality, with entire university departments staffed by experts and professors of international relations. Still, the very word "international" has been used in a superficial and inaccurate and, therefore, misleading way[1]—when we speak of international organizations, international relations, etc., we mean the organizations and the relations of states, not of nations; of governments, not of peoples. Yet states and nations are not the same thing. The development of the relations of nations, of truly international relations, has been relatively recent. Of course, nations have always had some relationships with each other; but it is only recently, with the development of communications, including universal literacy, that the relations of entire nations assume great importance. The mass movement of goods and of people have contributed to this, relatively novel, element in the history of states and of peoples: *to the image that one nation has of another nation.*

The continuous and permanent relations of states in Europe precede the continuous and permanent relations of nations by nearly five hundred years. The study of the former, the modern history of diplomacy, goes back to the Renaissance when, starting from Italy, these relationships began to extend over most of Europe. Now, in the twentieth century, we must progress from diplomatic history to the new and still largely uncharted ocean of international history. We saw in the foregoing

---

[1] It may be significant that the word *international* was formed in English by Jeremy Bentham, surely one of the most abstract political thinkers of the modern age. Smith, *English Language*, 71.

chapter that the relations of states encompass matters that are much broader than the official relations of their governments. In turn, the relations of nations include broader—and deeper—matters than the relations of states.

The historical study of these matters is only in its infancy.[2] One of the reasons for this is the habitual slowness of the academic mind, amounting to near stagnation during the twentieth century, all of the superficial appearances of the "knowledge explosion" notwithstanding. Another reason is the enormous scope of this kind of topic. The source materials for a comparative historical reconstruction of international relations, involving the image that one nation has of another, are extraordinarily scattered, complex, and difficult: The images vary in their intensity and also in their authenticity, since they are, more than often, reflections rather than causes of their public manifestations; and these manifestations, especially in the twentieth century, are protean, so voluminous as to be often virtually unchartable.[3] Still, we must attempt to describe some of these evidences, to try to understand them at some depth. The method of historical knowledge requires accuracy; but the purpose of historical knowledge is understanding even more than certainty. Our inquiry may be superficial by necessity; it will not be shallow.

During the Second World War these international affinities were very important factors. We cannot afford to neglect them. Of course, such relationships, in the shape of national prejudices based on the historical memories of generations, had existed in the more distant past, too, on a kind of tribal level—Turks and Greeks, Poles and Germans disliking or even hating each other: neighbor distrusting neighbor. But during the past one hundred years the images of even distant people had begun to crystallize in the minds of other millions, no matter how far away. In 1840

---

[2] A pioneer work in the field is Rémond, René, *Les Etats-Unis devant l'opinion française, 1815–1852*, (2 vols.; Paris, 1962); see especially the introductions by Rénouvin and by Rémond, setting out the novelty and the scope and the difficulties of this kind of study.

[3] They must, for instance, include such matters as the number of visitors from one country to another, their volume of mail, their volume of trade, translations of books from one language to another, school and university programs, guest performances, references to the other nation and its people in the literature, press, theater, movies, magazines; their athletic encounters, sports events, etc. But these figures in themselves mean little; they must be approached with Pascal's *esprit de finesse* rather than with Descartes' *esprit de la géométrie:* What counts less than the frequency is the tendency and the intensity of the crystallizing or crystallized image; not the volume of trade, for example, but the visibility of the imported product, its popular association with the other nation, the retention of the image of its origins and of its quality, etc.

a Magyar or Romanian peasant had no idea of how an Englishman or a Frenchman looked. By 1940 he had acquired an image of them, often wrong in its details, yet, in a way, real.

We have touched upon this matter earlier, when we noted that in many European countries the higher bourgeoisie was Anglophile, while the rising lower-middle classes were Germanophile; and now we have to deal with such matters in greater detail. We shall have to deal with the attraction or with the dislike that the image of one nation inspired among the people of another nation. This is not a perfunctory matter. A nation—especially in Europe—represents a cultural prototype of sorts. Anglophilia or Francophobia, Germanophilia or Russophobia often represented certain kinds of cultural preferences. In 1939 the ideological factor seemed to obscure this. The existence of states in the form of ideological prototypes—Communist Russia, Fascist Italy, National Socialist Germany—was a relatively novel factor, besides and sometimes above the element of the image of a cultural prototype; but we must be careful to sort out certain priorities.[4] Not every Germanophile was a Nazi, not every Anglophile was a democrat. Fascism was one thing, Italophilia another. On the other hand, millions were sympathetic to Germany because of their political sympathies for National Socialism, while others made allowances for Hitler because of their cultural sympathies for Germany. For a while ideological preferences seemed dominant. But only for a while. In 1936 the Spanish Nationalists, because of their admiration for Italian Fascism, would often call their Republican opponents by the derogatory term *Abisinos* (Abyssinians).[5] Yet in less than a year this Italophile fashion disappeared from the Nationalist ranks, mostly because of the poor performance of the Italian volunteers. On the other hand, ideological fanaticism could, on occasion, obscure nearly everything else. Even the traditional Spanish jealousy for their French neighbors, together with the Spaniards' consequent traditional admiration for the Germans, could hardly account for the remarkable sentence by one editorial writer in the Falangist *Arriba*, who in January 1941 described Hitler as "the most human personage that history has known." Ideological inclinations would obscure realities even in the minds of people who ought to have known better, as when on 31 May 1940 Darlan told Churchill that the

---

[4] This is exactly what Communist intellectuals conveniently overlooked, and this is exactly what led to their disillusionments. Obsessed with the *ideological* prototype of the Soviet State, they refused to see the *national* and cultural characteristics of Russia. Their illusory image of the Soviet political ideal left no place for their consideration of Russian barbarism.

[5] Eby, 114. "Admiration for the Italian brand of nationalism was reflected even in the style of the beards the [defenders of the Alcázar] cultivated, the bushy spade of the Italian aviators being the favorite."

Italians were much better soldiers than they had been in the last war. In Italy proto-Nazis such as Farinacci had been Germanophiles from the beginning; they became Nazified anti-Semites only consequently. On the other hand, the Romanian radicals of the Right, who in the past had been influenced by some of the ideology of the *Action Française*, became violently pro-German by 1937; their admiration for Germany was largely consequent to their hatred for Jews and for liberalism. In a confidential report to Vichy, the prefect of the *département* of the Nord in June 1941 said that Communists had had a hand during the recent strikes (this was before the German attack on Russia), and yet "the immense majority of the population of my *département* is of pro-English sentiments."[6]

"Pro-English": By 1939, at the latest by 1940, this adjective would encompass many things: liberal, democratic, humanist, pro-Jewish, even *Catholic* on occasion,[7] anti-Nazi in every case: a multitude of virtues. Often this was more than a transitory attribution of virtues to a nation that seemed to incarnate the opposition to Hitler. Traditional memories played a part in these attitudes, as indeed they did in the renascent Russophilia among some of the Orthodox and Slavic peoples of the Balkans in 1940, sometimes against all evidence, since Russia and Germany were close partners at the time. As early as 1937 Rebecca West asked a Montenegrin peasant: "How many of you are there?" "With Russia, 180 millions." "Yes, but how many without the Russians?" "We will never desert the Russians."

Hitler understood this kind of thing very well. On 28 April 1941 he told his ambassador to Moscow that the British pulled the strings in the Belgrade *coup* of a month before, "and yet the Balkan peoples all had the impression that Russia had been behind it."[8] Hitler's insight into certain national attitudes, often based on little more than instinct, seldom deserted him. On the other hand, his instinctive insights of this sort often stood in the way of a higher realism: He would, for example, attribute ideas to the English that the latter did not have. Still, Hitler was not a prototypical ideologue: He thought much more in terms of nations, of cultural prototypes, than in terms of ideological prototypes and states.[9]

---

[6] *CDA*, IV, 596.

[7] Here is an extreme example: Among the German-Swabian peoples in the Danube Valley, the non-Nazi minority was often called by the majority, in a derisory manner, "*Madjaronen*," "*Katholiken*," "*Englaender*."

[8] *NSR*, 331.

[9] At this point I wish to draw attention to one of the components of Hitler's thinking that has been generally overlooked by students of his life. This was his traditional, contemptuous, and hate-filled Francophobia. I write "traditional" because Hitler came from a part of Austria where people did not only have strong and natural affinities with their German brethren across the

Scholars and intellectuals, I repeat, have hardly begun to study the evidences of these kinds of inter-national relations, involving the image of the culture and of the prestige of one nation on another, on all kinds of levels. This kind of national prestige, often necessarily on vulgar levels, appeared at times in international sporting events. Goebbels recognized this—indeed, he was sometimes unduly sensitive to it.[10] In April 1941 he said that he would ask the Reich Sports Commissar not to allow inter-national matches if there was the slightest chance that Germany might lose (this two days after the Swiss national soccer team beat Germany 2–1 in Berne.)[11] Other governments, too, were sensitive to this kind of international relations. In November 1940 Moscow tried—in vain—to have one of its best teams invited to play in Sofia. The Bulgarian government, fearful of certain pro-Russian sentiments among the people, declined.[12]

---

border, but also where dislike for the French was a long and deep tradition. It was in the small village of Braunau, Hitler's birthplace, that the Nuremberg bookseller Johann Philipp Palm was shot in 1806, after he had published his anti-French pamphlet *Deutschland in seiner Tiefsten Erniedrigung*. In any event, a careful reading of *Mein Kampf* ought to reveal that Hitler's hatred for the French and his passion for a Greater Germany were parallel growths. There is his early memory of the German picture book depicting glorious scenes from the Franco-Prussian War; there is, too, an important passage about the anti-Semitic *Deutsche Volkszeitung:* "The disgusting veneration which the press even then expressed for France got on my nerves. One had to be ashamed of being a German when seeing these sweetish hymns of praise to the 'great culture nation.' More than once this wretched wooing of France made me put down one of these 'world papers.' I turned more and more to the *Volksblatt. . . .* I did not agree with its sharp anti-Semitic tone, but now and then I read explanations which made me stop to think." Hitler, *MK*, 71. To these evidences I may add that Hitler failed French in high school, and he had to take a repeat examination in it. At the end of his life: "I never liked the French race and the French." *Hitler-Bormann*, 68, also passim. See also below, p. 441, n. 150, Hitler on Churchill's Francophile reputation.

[10] Goebbels' instructions on 22 April 1940: During the popular national music broadcast on 5 May (*Wunschkonzert*) "there should be a transmission of the Germany-Italy [soccer] match but only if Germany is leading." Boelcke, 325. It is pleasant to record that Italy won, 3–2.

[11] This does not mean that the results of international athletic competitions were unrelated to the real strength of certain nations. In 1940 Montherlant recalled a boxing match between French and German university students in 1937. The Germans won every event. In July 1939 Germany beat France 105–48 in an international track meet; the French won only one event. (In August the French did win the world championship—of archery.)

[12] In the fall of 1941 the Spanish government decided to cancel international Spain-Portugal matches during the foreseeable future: There had been fights

On a deeper level, then, we must observe that, as Proust had noted in a kind of intellectual shorthand, there exist considerable similarities, though not analogies, between the psychic reactions of persons and those of modern nations. "We must, of course," I wrote several years ago in *Historical Consciousness,*

> be careful not to indulge in drawing biological parallels between nations and persons: We must not attribute "souls" to nations. . . . But not only do national characteristics, such as "mercurial," "temperamental," "steady," "solid," "imaginative," "unimaginative" exist; some of the functions of these characteristics do resemble certain functions of personal characteristics. A community, like a person, may be "humiliated," "downcast," "ashamed"—metaphors which cannot be applied to economics and rarely to civilizations. And this is a condition which reflects not only superficial appearances but deeper reactions, too: It may not be unreal, for example, to suggest that on certain occasions the military conquest of a nation by another nation may result in psychic conditions which, without being analogous, may resemble the results of a sexual conquest, since the sexual act does mean the imposition of the will of one participant on another, involving at least a partial acquiescence or even the collaboration of certain elements within the latter, and, as even Freud would say late in his career, the temporary creation of a community between two. . . .

This, I suppose, applies to the reaction of some Frenchmen (and not only of Frenchwomen) to the conquest of France by the Germans—the reaction of which writers such as Brasillach would cruelly remind his countrymen later in the war: No matter what you say now, remember, *we slept with the Germans.*[13] (And, he would add, in a less brutal and more suggestive manner: We liked some of it; and we will not forget it—certainly, let me add, not in the national subconscious.)[14]

Such a reaction of entire peoples to the power of the enemy was not

---

among the spectators, and the two neutral neighbor peoples disliked each other too much—a fact recounted by no less of a conservative personage than General Moscardó to Hitler in December 1941.

[13] Many French prostitutes remembered the Germans: They were not only good customers—they were *kinder* than the Americans in 1944 and after. Marie Thèrése, *passim.*

[14] It may not be farfetched to suggest that this was why, during the chaotic days of the Liberation, in many French towns Frenchwomen who had consorted with Germans during the occupation were driven through the streets naked, with their heads shaved—a brutal and desired transference of the feeling of national shame.

merely a prototypical reaction of the prototypically "overrefined" or "feminine" French. Note the more primitive, and perhaps therefore even more primal, psychic elements in the reminiscences of ordinary Russians from the time of the great Moscow panic in October 1941 when, for once, the political-military metaphor is both telling and precise, since the city *lay open for the Germans for the taking:*

> [Most people] . . . preferred to remain at home and await the arrival of the Germans . . . some people were "almost happy" at the expected German occupation. He recalled that they "sat around just waiting, the women talking about the number of times the Germans would rape them."[15]

The word "shame" recurs frequently in these memories. Even more significantly,

> With the end of the crisis, the attitude, at least of some elements of the population, toward the Germans appears to have undergone a radical change. . . . In a rather irrational way, the population was angered and disappointed by the failure of the Germans to enter the city. They lost some of their respect and fear of German might. As one informant put it: "The Germans behaved like a beloved woman who had become unfaithful." [*I would rather put it: like an expected man who had failed to appear.*] The Germans were no good because they had failed to do what *some* people *had wanted* and what *so many had expected.*[16]
> In a sudden reversal of mood, the people had shifted from almost hopeful expectance in some cases, and resignation in others, to a rigid determination to resist. . . .[17]

One need not be a Freudian to recognize certain significantly sexual elements in these attitudes. Yet not too much should be made of the sexual factor in this reaction of entire national masses to the power of the enemy. It rather seems that, just as Proudhon was a deeper seer than Marx ("People react to the realities of power rather than to ideas about social contracts") and Adler (and Jung) deeper than Freud, in these interna-

---

[15] Goure, Dinerstein, 211. About the Moscow panic, see above, p. 151. "A common phrase had it that Hitler had sworn 'to drink tea in Moscow on the 16th.'" Ibid., 209.

[16] My italics.

[17] Goure, Dinerstein, 220. The Polish ambassador, Kot, to Sikorski on 12 October 1941: ". . . I decidedly consider your visit here as purposeless at the moment. It can have no effect in reinforcing the Russian masses, since they live in the secret hope that the regime will fall, and they dislike the Poles. . . ."

tional affinities or antipathies sentiments of relative inferiority or superiority are more deep-seated than the sexual element. Consider, for example, this passage from Mussolini's letter to Hitler on 24 August 1940:

> *France*. I feel sure that you cannot have failed to note the extraordinary psychological phenomenon, so typical of the indomitable (?) pride of the French, that *France does not consider herself conquered*. . . . [Mussolini's italics.]

On 9 November 1940 Mussolini said to the nuncio in Italy, Borgongini Duca: "The French are the worst, because they do not only hate us, they have a contempt for us (*ci disprezzano*)."[18]

Hitler and the German people were not exempt from such feelings. The superman and super-race attitude of the Germans may have been often a kind of national compensation for a deep-seated feeling of inferiority in regard to the older, and often more deeply civilized, nations of Western Europe.[19] That, however, is necessarily a hypothesis. What is not hypothetical are the evidences of Hitler's curious psychic relationship to the English. One of its most telling expressions may be found in his speech at Saarbruecken, on 9 October 1938, after Munich:

> It would be a good thing if in Great Britain people would gradually drop certain aims which they have inherited from the Versailles epoch. We cannot tolerate any longer *the tutelage of governesses,*

a metaphor which Churchill must have regarded as sufficiently significant to print it in italics in his war memoirs.[20] On 4 June 1939, in Kassel, Hitler said:

> I can never admit for a second that anybody in the ranks of our western opponents has the right to look upon or imagine himself as superior to us Germans. Nor do I, on that account, suffer in the least from any sort of inferiority complex!

---

[18] *VD*, 4, 237.

[19] One interesting sidelight on the Third Reich is how, all of its racial nationalism notwithstanding, the Germans' sentimental predilection for exotic women, with foreign names, continued strong. In the same Reich whose people gave their daughters pagan Germanic names—tens of thousands of baby girls received names such as Gudrun after 1933—the stars of Goebbels' film industry bore names such as Lida Baarova, Olga Tschechowa, Lil Dagower, Maria Tasnady, Christina Söderblom, Rosita Serrano, etc.

[20] Churchill, *GS*, 329.

The italics in the earlier passage were Churchill's. The exclamation point in this speech was Hitler's. Both are telling.

There is no need to string out further the many examples of Hitler's admiration for the British, together with his consequent and often unrealistic expectations.[21] It was, at any rate, a typical characteristic of his mind, and it was not untypical of the ambiguous relationship of many German people toward the English during the war, evidences to which I shall refer in this chapter, even as we must recognize its variations, including the very condition that, curiously enough, Hitler may have been more pro-English than were the majority of Germans.

In any event, Anglophobia and Anglophilia, Germanophobia and Germanophilia were not ephemeral phenomena, the mere adjustments of people's ideas to the circumstances of the war. The roots of these international affinities were deep and long-standing, and their manifestations were protean. They had, in turn, much to do with the persistence of national characteristics. Conveniently ignored and dismissed by modern social scientists, with their Marxian categories, these national characteristics were in evidence, vital, strong, and persistent during the Second World War, all of its ideological movements notwithstanding. The problem of the presence of the Jews in the midst of Europe's nations was so intertwined with this condition that we shall have to attempt to describe the sordid and tragic story of their persecution and destruction from such a viewpoint, from a perspective that must necessarily be slightly different from the usual practice that treats the story of Jewry during the Second World War as if it had been but another recurrent chapter in the long history of anti-Semitism and Judeophobia.

---

[21] I write "expectations" because sometimes it is not easy to ascertain the purpose of Hitler's frequent protestations of his goodwill for the English. In conversations such as he had with Sven Hedin (see above) and others, the wish to let the British know of his inclinations was certainly present, probably even in his conversation with the Hungarian Prime Minister, Teleki, in Vienna on 20 November 1940: ". . . he was sorry for the many fine people and the beautiful cities that were being demolished in England in this way—sorry, especially because everything was happening only because of a few incompetent politicians." GD, D, XI, 635. Hitler knew that Teleki was a conservative, and it is at least possible that this statement, too, was intended to reach the ears of the British minister in Budapest, O'Malley, who had been designated by Haushofer to Hess two months before (see above, p. 110, n. 8) as a possible British diplomat liable to lend an ear to German peace suggestions.

## INTER-NATIONAL AFFINITIES

¶ Not every Germanophile was a Nazi. After 1870 Germany was the most important nation on the Continent. Her dominant position was not merely political, military, or economic. German, not French, was the second language of millions, not only inside but also outside the German-speaking monarchies; it was the language of commerce in at least one half of Europe, from Russia to northern Italy. German modes of education, from the middle schools to the universities, had been adopted by nearly all of the states of Eastern and Northern Europe. The prestige of German universities was very high. German forms of thought, and of philosophy, were fundamental in the intellectual development of entire generations; their appeal extended to peoples who in the past had been unaffected by German culture—to Spaniards, Italians, Greeks, Turks. At its best, this German culture had produced thinkers who revitalized the European mind by providing an alternative to the ossified rationalism of the French eighteenth century. Much of this German cultural prestige was to be destroyed by Hitler, and, at the latest by 1945, the defeat of Germany marked also the end of a chapter in the intellectual history of Europe, indeed, of the world.[22] Some of this German prestige was beginning to erode immediately after his assumption to power in 1933; yet its impact was still powerful in 1939, when it was reinforced, temporarily, by the enormous surge of German power across the Continent.

On the highest levels of European culture and society the Germanophile impact was limited, but it was far from insignificant. There were thinkers, writers, and artists who were no longer attracted by the rationalism represented by the French, and who were indifferent to the slow pragmatism of the English, tradition. They were inclined to think that Germany was the nation that could revitalize Europe, and perhaps the entire civilization of the West. In Scandinavia, especially in Sweden, there were many people who were Germanophiles without being Nazis; some of them, like many American midwestern isolationists of the period, could reconcile their faith in democracy—populist, not liberal, democracy—with their Anglophobia and Germanophilia. In Latin Europe, on the other hand, there were convinced Fascists such as Papini in Italy or French Fascists and National Socialists who despised democracy even as they had no particular love for the Germans. We have seen, too, how the fear and

---

[22] See above, pp. 6–7; and below, pp. 525–26.

hatred of Communism produced a veritable split on the Right, dividing patriots from nationalists, reinforcing the Germanophilia of the latter, since they were inclined to believe that Germany alone could serve as a bulwark of European civilization against Russia and Communism. There was an element of conservative Germanophilia in the political and cultural inclinations of men such as Pope Pius XII, King Gustav V of Sweden, and Leopold III of Belgium, who otherwise had little interest or sympathy for the ideology represented by the Third Reich.

Too much should not be made of this kind of conservative Germanophilia. It was a predisposition rather than a definite preference. To some extent it repeated the pattern of the First World War when, too, many Swedish, Spanish, Swiss, Romanian, and Greek conservatives, including the dominant conservative group in the Vatican, were Germanophiles. During the Second World War, however, the excesses of National Socialism filled the aristocracy and the patricians and the conservative bourgeoisie of most of Europe with aversion. In 1914 the conservative elements of society in Switzerland, Sweden, and Greece were usually pro-German. In 1939 they were not.[23]

The obsessed Germanophiles were, generally, revolutionaries and radicals, and, as we have seen, they had risen from other, newer, classes of society.[24] The rising lower-middle classes, rather than the upper-middle classes, including first-generation university students, were Germanophile: They were impressed with the virility, the technical achievements of the Germans. Their very distrust and envy of the older, more patrician classes played a certain role in their preferences. The former disliked the latter, culturally self-confident as these were, with their Anglophile and Francophile preferences. This kind of division within the middle classes was not only a European phenomenon, it was also global: It

---

[23] An eminent example is the Greek Metaxas, who had hoped for and believed in the justice of a German victory during the First World War, when Germany seemed to represent the conservative and authoritarian opposition to the egalitarian principle. Yet he proved a brave opponent of the Axis in 1940–41. His patriotism and his monarchism were dominant. Unlike Mussolini, he was not an ex-Socialist; unlike Hitler, he was a monarchist.

[24] Thus, for example, in Romania the kind of Iron Guard intellectuals whose anti-Semitism and anti-Communism had been formerly nourished by articulate French political writings of this kind, of the anti-Dreyfusard and Maurrassian tradition, by the middle of the thirties became violent Germanophiles and Francophobes; not even such events as the loss of northern Transylvania to Hungary by way of a German-Italian "arbitration" would shake their faith in Germany. In Croatia the National Socialist leader Kvaternik's grandfather had been a follower of Napoleon III.

existed in such diverse places as the United States, Argentina, Japan, and the Near and Middle East.[25]

Often this was a nearly automatic reaction: People came to like the Germans because they disliked the English; or, in many instances, the reverse. We cannot probe deeper into the roots of these preferences; it is enough to register their existence. In Eastern Europe at least the pattern was simple: Most peoples simply preferred the Germans to the Russians. The exceptions to this were certain Bulgarians, most Serbians, and, to some extent, Czechs, partly because of their atavistic pan-Slavic and Orthodox memories, and also because these peoples at that time were still fortunate, they had few experiences with the Soviet Union, which was still far away: They could nurture their Russophile illusions without an admixture of fear.

So much about the general predispositions to the Germans. Let us now look briefly at the reactions of peoples, especially in Western Europe, to their sudden and shocking experiences with the conquering Germans. Their first reactions were, generally speaking, positive, in a surprising way. The Germans were not as barbaric or brutal as had been feared, certainly not as anti-Nazi press propaganda had depicted them. As De Jong noted in Holland, ". . . the Germans were not so bad, after all," people said. "You could not deny that some of their ideas were quite sensible. . . ."[26] The occupation, noted Struye a few weeks after the tragic event in Belgium, "was welcomed,"

> if not like a deliverance, at least with a feeling of physical relief. This impression was reinforced by the first contact with the soldiers of the enemy. Their look as well as their behavior . . . was a revelation to many of our compatriots. The athletic and correct aspect of their soldiers no longer conformed to the images and memories they had of the Kaiser's Army. . . . In effect, the occupiers gave an example of order and discipline—of a discipline which seemed to have been accepted willingly—of a social sense, of responsibilities, of democratic solidarity.

---

[25] Even after the war, Germanophilia remained strong outside of Europe. For example, there was more to the Germanophilia of the rising Arab middle classes than a mere reaction to their fear and hatred of Jews; the Germanophilia of the Afghans, for example, represented and represents more than a natural political reaction of their fear of the neighboring Russian and British empires. In 1937 and 1938 secret treaties had been reached between the Afghan and German governments. The Afghan ambassador in Turkey to Papen in 1940: "Germany has many friends, more than she thinks: They wait for her to show the way to a new order of the globe."

[26] De Jong, *TW*, 1.

This attitude stood in contrast with the anarchy of disorder, of selfishness, of abandonment, of egoism and of panic that had characterized the first days of the war in Belgium.[27]

Fabre-Luce put it in this way for France: "For a moment Germany stood as an incarnation of order before a hysterical nation." We have seen that in the popular quarters of Paris the Germans were admired and, in some ways, even welcomed on that ominous day of shame, 14 June 1940.[28] Elsewhere in France, too, it was apparent that the reaction to the Germans was different from that of the last war. The popular language reflected this. *Boche* was not used much during the Last European War. The somewhat more patronizing *les Fritz, les Fridolins,* sometimes *les Frises,* referring to their Prussian crew-cuts, replaced the earlier and more contemptuous nickname.

We have seen that by the autumn of 1940 the populations of the conquered Western European nations were beyond the first mental shock. They were no longer inclined to believe in the inevitability, let alone the desirability, of the German victory. By December 1940, according to Struye, only a small minority believed in a German victory, a larger minority believed in a British victory, and the majority in some kind of a compromise peace. Many evidences indicate that this was true of other peoples too. It had much to do not only with the failure of the Germans to win the war against England; as time went on, the cruel selfishness of the Germans' new *German* order was becoming more and more apparent; it was, in any event, something different from the latent hopes for a new *European* order. Still, a kind of admiration for the Germans remained. In May 1941 André Gide himself wrote in his *Journal:*

> If the English succeed in driving the Germans out of France (a somewhat premature assumption, this) a party will form in our country to balk at that deliverance, to discover that the recent domination had something to be said for it, since it at least imposed order, and to prefer it for the disorder of freedom.
> A freedom for which we are not yet ready and which we do not

---

[27] Struye, in Delandsheere, Ooms, 17. A Belgian bourgeois told Henri de Man: "I had expected them to be ruffians and I found Boy Scouts in search of good deeds!" De Man, *CS,* 251.
[28] See above, p. 84. In 1952 a French chauffeur in Cannes said to the German actress Hildegarde Knef: "I could tell you were German right away—I really love them—those were the days when we had a bit of law and order around here." The marvelous Miss Knef adds in her memoirs: "a model example of how one is often admired by the wrong people for the wrong reasons." Knef, 247.

deserve. Freedom is beautiful only because it permits the exercise of virtues that it is first essential to acquire. . . .[29]

At about the same time Paul Struye noted that in Belgium "the nearly universal hatred for the Germans is not unmixed with respect."[30] The German invasion of Russia changed little or nothing in these attitudes. The Germans received little support from Catholics and conservatives. Yet, as their ultimate defeat became more and more obvious, the respect for them continued to exist.[31]

In Eastern Europe the situation was different: Except for Poles and Czechs, nowhere did the national majorities hate the Germans. The respect for the German Army had turned some patriotic Serbs into Germanophiles. A considerable number of Greek officers were pro-German, their admiration for Germany was of long standing, and it was not merely the result of their preference for having been conquered by the German rather than by the Italian Army. In many of the villages and towns of Lithuania, Latvia, the western Ukraine, etc., the people greeted the Germans with flowers, sometimes resuscitating ancient ceremonies such as the presentation of bread and salt, the kind of folklore show that would impress these powerful armed tourist invaders. There was more to the pro-German feeling among these peoples than the gratitude for having been liberated from Russian Bolshevism. At best, these people saw in the Germans the harbingers of European culture: The Germans represented virtues and talents to which these Eastern peoples aspired. At worst, some of these people, including many of the "liberated" Russians, admired not only the efficiency but also the very brutality of the Germans, who were popular not despite but because of their cold cruelty: *They* knew what to do with the Jews.

This kind of latent Germanophilia had a few surprising manifestations among the Russians themselves during the years 1939–41 when the Soviet government had its pact with Germany. Foreign Communists in Moscow, including the then German Communist fledgling Walter Leonhardt, would remember scenes in June 1940 such as the Russian peasant in the Moscow trolley car who smiled idiotically and rubbed his hands at reading the news that Hitler had captured Paris; the other passengers would nod with beaming approval. But, then, the Soviet system

---

[29] Gide, II, 276.

[30] Ibid., 55.

[31] The only pieces of English territory occupied by the Germans were the Channel Islands, off the coast of France, in late June 1940. "At first, the islanders had been as much amazed by the lenience of the Germans as the latter had been by the absence of resistance and sabotage." Calder, 411.

had eliminated the once-powerful influence of the traditionally Francophile Russian upper classes. Among the powerful Soviet hierarchs, Molotov and Stalin would, on occasion, reveal their inclination toward Germany and things German that went beyond the endemic Soviet respect and fear of the latter: an inclination that contained elements of admiration, and of a definite preference for Germany over the Western bourgeois democracies, especially England—a popular attitude that carried over into the war.[32]

In turn, what were the attitudes of the German people toward the other nations of Europe in these years of their triumphant victories? I repeat: It is not easy to ascertain tendencies even as one must attempt to understand them. The evidences for the historian are vague and scant in this field, even as they exist in a variety of sources: remnants of the written and the printed and the spoken word, and the sometimes (but only sometimes) interesting reports of the secret police registering expressions of popular sentiments.[33] Again we must distinguish between the governments and the peoples. The German government and the press would, for example, praise Mussolini's Italians at the same time when the German popular and national attitude toward the latter was rather contemptuous, even before the first Italian defeats in the war. Atavistic and folkish memories played a role in such attitudes, especially among Austrians who had disliked their Italian neighbors for a long time. On the other hand, the careful and detached student of the Third Reich must be struck by the relative lack of response of the German people to the racial propaganda put out in streams by Rosenberg and Himmler. National sentiments of superiority, where they existed among the German people, were cultural rather than racial. This is a subject of enormous significance and delicacy which, for the best of my knowledge, lies largely unexplored. There was, and there remains, a superficially slight but essentially profound difference between a *folkish* and a *racist* type of thinking. The response that Hitler evoked in the German spirit was the result of the former, rather than of the latter.[34]

---

[32] During the October 1941 crisis in Moscow, "A very observant French newspaperman reported his impression that, at the time, most people showed a conciliatory attitude toward the Germans (primirencheskoe nastroenie). . . . The general attitude toward the German was that he was clever, and that he had technical, and organizational ability superior to that of the Russian. . . ." Goure, Dinerstein, 207.

[33] *Meldungen*, op. cit., (In the following pages the references to *Meldungen* are not those of the Boberach edition; the numbers are taken from the microfilms in the library of the Institut fuer Zeitgeschichte, Munich).

[34] One evidence of this in Hitler's own words in *Hitler-Bormann*, especially

Plainly, the German people's tendencies toward the other peoples of Europe were mixed. Their attitude was not that of thorough self-confidence. The dominant self-attribution of a triumphant people was missing. Sometimes popular attitudes differed from those of the regime, as in the case of Italy or Finland during the first Winter War; sometimes they were in harmony, as in the German attitudes toward Czechs and Slovaks; often the attitudes of regime and people both were mixed, as in respect to their English opponents. The majority was blameworthy in the sense that it would more or less willingly ignore their government's treatment of other peoples. This suppression of scruples for the sake of national discipline, rather than a kind of enthusiastic barbarism, was typical of the majority of Germans during the Second World War—a national characteristic that extended to their lack of sympathy for the Jews and for the Poles, to whose evident mistreatment most Germans were rather indifferent until the very end of the war. (There is some reason to think that the Germans blamed the Poles for having provided the pretext for the war.)

Unlike in 1914, in 1939 there was no popular enthusiasm for the war in Germany. This probably explains some of the painful correctness with which the German soldiers tried to behave, especially in Northern and Western Europe in 1940. They acted as if the war had been foisted upon them by Germany's enemies. This kind of behavior did, as we have seen, impress the conquered peoples on occasion.[35] The latter were, however, unaffected by official German acts of agreeableness, including even Hitler's decision to release most of the Flemish prisoners of the Belgian Army, or his decision to return the ashes of the Eaglet, Napoleon II, to Paris, to be deposited with those of his father in the Invalides on 15 December 1940, on the one hundredth anniversary of the grand *Retour des Cendres*. The act echoed in a void. The climate of Paris was arctic and silent.[36] "In the snowy night, in a darkened and deserted Paris,

---

the talk recorded on 13 February 1945. ". . . pride of race is a quality which the German, fundamentally, does not possess." "We use the term of Jewish race as a matter of convenience, for in reality and from the genetic point of view there is no such thing as the Jewish race."

[35] Like the Belgians, the French were especially impressed by the novel democracy of the German Army: soldiers and officers going about together; also by certain personal courtesies, as when German soldiers would give up seats to women in the Métro. Soon, however, these occasional courtesies would disappear.

[36] Re arctic Paris, see also above, p. 109. This sense of the coldness impressed the German occupants. See in the diaries of another anti-Nazi German intellectual, October 1940: "The hopeless, cold, emptiness of the city is even worse

the heavy cortege moves across the city unnoticed, unobserved."[37]

During the Second World War the German people were less Francophobe than were their leaders. At the end of May 1940 Goebbels ordered the orchestration of a propaganda campaign against the French: "The hate against France must be rekindled again . . . the French must be shown to be negrified sadists, and a tireless campaign must be waged so that latest in a fortnight the entire German nation is filled with fury and hate against France, contaminated with corruption and free-masonry as she is."[38] A fortnight later the Germans entered Paris, and we have seen that the hate was largely absent. The Goebbelsian campaign had failed.[39] Yet much of this novel German leniency to the French was due, too, to the condition that, perhaps for the first time in their history, the Germans were sufficiently self-confident in face of them: The French were no longer their opponents of the first rank. The Germans felt that they could do as they pleased. In May 1941 a last summary report from the *préfets* of the occupied zone was sent to the French Armistice Commission. Entitled "Consequences of Nine Months of Occupation," the study said, among other things: "In everyday reality the Germans of all ranks treat France as a storehouse to be emptied, and they treat the immense majority of Frenchmen as potential slave laborers. . . . (*comme des vaincus corvéables*). As long as this lasts it will be difficult to proceed in the way of collaboration."[40]

By that time the number of foreign laborers and prisoners of war in Germany had risen above one million; and one indication of German popular feelings is that of their attitudes toward these unfortunate foreigners in their midst. Voluminous records of the organization during the war of foreign labor in Germany exist. They have been surveyed in a valuable work by Professor C. Homze, which includes a record of the studies undertaken by German industrial psychologists in the winter of 1941–42, who ranked the ability of foreign workers from the best to the poorest[41]:

---

than one had expected." In the spring of 1941: "The climate here is arctic in character." Hartlaub, 34–35.

[37] Fabre-Luce, I, 136.

[38] Boelcke, 370.

[39] On 27 June Goebbels ordered that there should be no sentimental or cultural references to Paris, which must decline to the level of a provincial city (Boelcke, 409). On 10 July: "We must again make France unpopular and Italy popular." Ibid., 422. July 12: "We have but one aim: to keep France in the future as weak as possible." Ibid., 424. July 26: "No sentimentality: Exactly as before, the hate against France must be kept alive, it cannot be allowed to lay dormant." Ibid., 438.

[40] *CDA*, IV, 385–96.

[41] By the (Zehlendorf) Institut fuer Arbeitspsychologie und Arbeitspedagogik,

| Men | Women |
|---|---|
| French | Russians |
| Russians, Greeks, Poles | Poles |
| Yugoslavs | Greeks |
| Dutch, Norwegians | French, Yugoslavs |
| Italians | |

Ill feeling for the Italians ran high from the earliest days of their intervention in the war. On 23 June 1940 Goebbels felt that he had to issue instructions against "the growing sentiments of anger and hate against Italy."[42] The Italian workers were disliked by the Germans ("they view their stay in Germany as a vacation"). The Italian defeats in Greece and in North Africa contributed to this popular sentiment. In turn, the German esteem for the Greeks rose, remaining high through the war. Hitler himself professed admiration for the Greeks: He forbade the bombing of Athens (though not of Piraeus), and on several occasions did not hide his respect for Greece; he would compare Greece to Finland ("two small nations who knew how to defend themselves") on occasion. This respect for small nations did not extend to Switzerland, which he despised.[43]

The description of German popular and national attitudes toward most of the peoples of Europe during the Second World War is a subject that still awaits its serious and careful historians.[44] Many of these attitudes

---

400,000 foreign workers were tested, "similar to the U. S. Army World War I tests for literacy." Homze, 241–42. The different ratings of men and women are of some interest.

[42] Boelcke, 402. On 6 July Goebbels worried about Ciano's coming visit to Berlin: "It is impossible to get enough people on the streets; the danger also exists that the population of Berlin might show its feelings against Italy." Ibid., 417.

[43] To the Hungarian minister Sztójay he said on the day of the German invasion of Greece (6 April 1941) that he felt sorry for the Greeks; he repeated this on the nineteenth; to Schulenburg on the twenty-eighth: "poor little Greece, that small plucky nation." He gave instructions to release a considerable number of Greek prisoners of war.

[44] Such historians will, I repeat, face the methodological difficulty of the enormous variety of evidence, ranging from all kinds of expressions of popular opinions through the mountains of remnant newspapers to the vast assembled archives of the Third Reich. Among the latter he will encounter examples of curious nonsense such as the physiognomical "survey" mounted by Himmler's RSGA in October 1940 concerning the racial typology of Czechs—with whom, after some reluctance, the German authorities permitted Germans to intermarry, but only after the Czech marriage partner furnished "physiog-

were long-rooted, and they underwent little change during the war. We must, however, say something about their curiously ambiguous attitude toward the English. For, while Hitler's hatred and contempt for the French was greater and deeper than the Francophobia of the German people, the reverse was true about the English: Hitler esteemed them higher than had the German people.[45] The common people of Germany disliked the English because of their haughty and aristocratic image and sometimes because of the very qualities to which Hitler would pay tribute on occasion. Much of this transitory but significant sentiment transpires not only from the German press but also from the confidential surveys of popular opinion to which we referred earlier. As early as in October 1939, when these *Meldungen* are scattered with occasional evidences of secret conservative, Catholic, and monarchist opposition to the war, they report "sentiment strong against England." Even in the high summer of 1940, when, in spite of the great victory over France, there was little or none of the national frenzy that had accompanied the German triumphs in the West during the First World War, most Germans, unlike Hitler, were ready to have their go at England. On 20 June, for example: "People wish, sometimes openly, that Churchill wouldn't give up (*dass Churchill hartnaeckig bleibe*), because then, instead of saving their skins by capitulating, the British will really get it in the neck!"[46] One week later: "Overwhelming is the hope that the Fuehrer attack England immediately." A few weeks passed. "What are we waiting for? (*Wann geht es los?*)"[47] By September disappointment was beginning to set in—and the German people continued to blame the English for resisting. One of the more curious,

---

nomical photographs." "A rough estimate of the racial structure of the Sudetenland . . . shows that . . . the racial picture of the Czech people is considerably more favorable today than that of the Sudeten German population." Cited by Mastny, 132.

[45] Goebbels followed Hitler in this respect, too. He ordered the German press to stoke the fires against the French and to dampen the fire against the English. Examples: 12 December 1939: "The press should not be contemptuous of the military worth of the English." (Boelcke, 241). 7 July 1940: Attack Churchill "but never the English people as such." Ibid., 417. The English are good fighters (26 May 1941) (Boelcke, 751). On the other hand, the press should combat the popular belief that "the English are tougher than we are." Ibid., 699.

[46] *Meldungen*, MA 441/2, 1,789. One is reminded of Churchill's comment on Mussolini's words at the time, to the effect that Italy wanted war now. "He need not have fretted himself. He was soon to get all the war he wanted."

[47] Ibid., MA 441/2, 2,057. There emerges, too, an unpleasant kind of Germanic brutality. On 26 June: Switzerland, like the Baltic states, must disappear. "The cheese state (*Das Kaesestaat*) must disappear."

and least attractive, sides of the German psyche, with its compound of brutality and self-pity, appears in the report on popular sentiment at the end of September. "The retaliatory attack on Cambridge evoked the highest approval everywhere among the population, accompanied by universal expressions of hope that more retaliatory attacks would follow"[48]— at the time when for every hundred German bombs cast on Britain one or two British bombs were dropped on Germany.

As the war went on, a certain German respect for Britain rose, mixed with the continuing bitterness for the arrogant unwillingness of the British to consider the merits of the German case in Europe and, later, in their "crusade" against the Soviets.[49] This national ambiguity was also expressed by the often self-consciously traditional and chivalrous manner in which German soldiers, sailors, and fliers fought their British opponents in the Battle of Britain and also elsewhere.[50] The popular slang of the German soldiery reflected different views of their enemies. Across the Channel the pilots of the Luftwaffe called their British foes *die Lords*— a not very imaginative and perhaps therefore significant, nickname. Less than a year later millions of German soldiers would call their Russian opponents *die Iwans*. Lords and Iwans! The primitive nicknames are telling. They reflect the ambiguity, the dual standards of the Germans' image of their enemies; and also their image of themselves, struggling against haughty aristocrats on one front and against primitive peasants on the other. Their attitudes toward the Slavic peoples of Eastern Europe—a mixture of brutality and condescension[51]—was in more than one way typical, not of the Prussian but of the southeastern and Austrian mentality. It was reinforced by their traditional anti-Communism. While elsewhere in Europe the notion of a crusade against Bolshevism influenced relatively few people, within Germany it was more successful. It was a ra-

---

[48] Ibid., MA 441/2, 2,437.

[49] A prototypical expression of this duality is reflected in the text under two photographs in the *Berliner Illustrierte* of 18 July 1940 (p. 707). One shows the bewigged royal herald in the City of London as he reads the proclamation of the war blockade against Italy: "The form and content of [this proclamation] is just as antiquated as are the methods with which England hopes to save herself from the hurricane of a new era." The other photograph shows Anthony Eden: "Elegant as always, he steps past the wire barricade."

[50] Even in the bitter close fighting in Crete, the Germans were often "gallant and chivalrous foes." Stewart, *Crete*, 383. Of all prisoners of war, the British were treated relatively the best in Germany (with the exception of Americans, later in the war). A few prisoner exchanges were made. In September 1941 a handful of badly wounded British pilots were allowed to return to England to die in peace.

[51] Serbs, Croats, and Bulgarians excepted.

tionalization of the people's acquiescence to the invasion of the Soviet Union.[52] On the other hand, acquiescence did not mean enthusiastic participation. The patronizing condescension implicit in the word "Iwan" reflected little of the higher Nazi notion that the eastern Slavs were merely "subhumans." Here was another example where the attitudes of the German government and of the German people were, even though slightly, different.

During the war the inclination of the other peoples of Europe toward the British assumed great importance. The British were, after all, incarnating the resistance to Hitler, they were fighting the Germans alone during an entire year. "England," Pitt the Younger had said at another memorable time in European history, "saved herself by her exertions, and Europe by her example." Now salvation from Hitler was a virtue even greater than salvation from Napoleon had been. There was another difference, too. By 1939 the image of England had entered the minds of millions of people in Europe to whose great-grandparents the word "England" meant but a vague blur. In addition to the more traditional Anglophilia among the European upper and upper-middle classes, there existed a newer kind of pro-English sentiment among masses of people who wanted the English to defeat the Germans. I have referred to this kind of Anglophilia earlier: an attitude that included a respect for tradition, a disdain for demagoguery, a kind of liberal elitism of the spirit.[53] These Anglophile attitudes continued to exist among the upper classes in Germany, too; Goebbels was very sensitive to them. On 7 January 1941, for example, he dictated his instructions: "Proceeding from the certainty that the society ideal in Germany (*das deutsche Gesellschaftsideal*) is widely influenced by the English example, the Minister warns against the further unwitting popularisation of the English Gentleman-ideal."[54]

"For all practical purposes," said the German minister to Estonia to the Estonian General Laidoner in the winter of 1939, "the hardly comprehensible aura which still enveloped England in spite of all past experience continues to delude some countries even now."[55] It had spread to

---

[52] Soviet Union, not Russia: The confidential information sheet of the Party Chancellery on 19 July 1941 insisted in a *Sprachregelung ueber die Sowjetunion* that the terms "Russia" and "Russian" were not to be used. About the support of the crusade against Bolshevism even by non-Nazi German Catholic bishops, see below, p. 464, n. 25.

[53] This writer remembers from wartime Hungary: to profess respect and admiration for England meant an association with a better class of people. (The attitude toward England was one of the principal marks that would distinguish the true snob from the mere opportunist.)

[54] Boelcke, 597.

[55] *GD*, D, VIII, 687.

the four corners of Europe, and it survived the great shock of the German conquest of Western Europe, only to flourish vividly in the minds and the hearts of people once the fact of stubborn British resistance became evident. In August 1940 people in Brussels would fill the space before the British war monument with flowers. The Germans were much irritated by this. In September people in Belgium, Holland, and Luxembourg would astonish foreigners as they spoke freely of their admiration of Britain in the streets and trolley cars. In neutral Portugal many cab drivers flew small Union Jacks, young bourgeois went wild over the few coveted Spitfire badges from Britain, there were primitive Churchill silhouettes in forms of badges, to be worn in buttonholes.[56] The Germans protested. About Greece, then still neutral, Mussolini complained to Hitler in October 1940: "The King is English, the political classes are pro-English, and the people are immature but trained to hate Italy." Scenes of the Greeks' popular devotion to the English were recorded by many observers. "Their women and children, and the old men, gathered in the doorways of their shattered homes, asking only that the British should return. A colonel of the 1st Armoured Brigade described the scene as the long column of battered trucks entered Athens:

> No one who passed through the city with Barrowclough's brigade will ever forget it. Nor will we ever think of the Greek people without the warm recollection of that morning—25 April 1941. Trucks, portées, and men showed plainly the marks of twelve hours' battle, and the hundred and sixty miles' march through the night. We were nearly the last British troops they would see and the Germans might be on our heels; yet cheering, clapping crowds lined the streets and pressed about our cars, so as almost to hold us up. Girls and men leapt on the running boards to kiss or shake hands with the grimy, weary gunners. They threw flowers to us and ran beside us crying: "Come back—You must come back again —Goodbye—Good luck."[57]

The British defeat in the Balkans and in North Africa during the spring of 1941, which had reverberations in the United States, left the Anglophile opponents of the Germans in Europe untouched. The blast of the German onslaught on the Communist Russian empire again did nothing to weaken this kind of Anglophilia; rather the contrary. At the end of June 1941 "the smallest English success is greeted by nine tenths of the Belgians as if it were their own national triumph."[58] Many Dutchmen and

---

[56] "Another badge is a hat and a cigar." Duff, in RIIA Survey 1939–46, 321–22.
[57] Lieutenant Colonel R. P. Waller, *Journal of the Royal Artillery* (July 1945), cited by Stewart, *Crete*, 18–19.
[58] Delandsheere, Ooms, 377–79.

Belgians would say at this time: Better a hundred times a British dominion than to be a German protectorate. On 8 September 1941 in the Belgian town of Hasselt the funeral of a Belgian volunteer with the German forces in Russia took place; it was boycotted by the people, including most of the family of this unfortunate. The next day the people of Hasselt buried a British pilot who had been shot down over the neighboring fields; his grave was covered with masses of flowers. The Germans punished the people of Hasselt. During the winter of 1941–42 Degrelle's pro-Nazi *Pays Réel* wrote in a bitter tone: Why, to the average Belgian, is *"anglophile"* synonymous with *"bon Belge"?* What Paul Struye recorded about the Anglophilia of the Belgian people at the end of December 1941 was true of many millions of other peoples across the Continent:

> People think that there is no other people in the world who stand the test with such self-control and dignity. . . . They are very impressed with the freedom of expression that, in the very midst of a war, is allowed in England to the newspapers and to Parliament. They emphasize the contrast between the frankness with which the British announce their losses and the silent treatment with which the Germans cover up their defeats.[59]

Eventually this European Anglophilia would undergo strains later in the war. The suppressed peoples expected swifter, more daring British moves against Hitler. One of the results of these expectations were the many unfounded rumors about spectacular British triumphs or landings on the Continent in 1940, 1941, and 1942. After Pearl Harbor most Anglophiles thought that the war would end with a British victory by 1943 at the latest. They were to be disappointed with the slowness of Allied strategy. Yet there did exist a brief period in the history of Europe when the image of the British flag, with all of its royal richness and blue elegance, lifted the hearts of Europeans higher than ever before or after. There were symbolic coincidences,[60] and a newly found loyalty crystallizing around the solid heroic figure of Churchill.[61] Their finest hour impressed even people who had feared or disliked the British for

---

[59] Struye, 85.

[60] Gladstone Street 13 was the home of General Simovic, the seat of the anti-German conspiracy that succeeded, with British help, in March 1941.

[61] The British, among other prisoners of war, records Stewart, among others (Stewart, *Crete*, 490), "found themselves marked and honoured for their particular claim to the word that had become universal in all the slave camps of Europe. Frenchmen, Russians, Serbs, Greeks, Dutchmen . . . knowing nothing of each other's languages, held in common the name of 'Churchill,' to pass between them as a 'talisman of hope.'"

long centuries. The Irish, neutral observers noted, were impressed with British resistance in the autumn of 1940. The people of Madrid were impressed by the coolness with which the personnel of the British Embassy reacted to the ugly popular demonstrations before its building in June 1941.[62] "In Spain," the Anglophobe Serrano Suñer told Hitler in November 1941, "there are still *many* Anglophiles." Their number certainly did not decrease.

Let us now pass to the other side. Anglophobia during the Second World War could be a potent factor in the inclinations of many people. Anglophobia, rather than pro-Fascism, was the key of the inclinations of the armistice party around Pétain. France was unique in this respect, for the roots of French Anglophobia were longer and deeper than elsewhere. Pétain himself thought that the English were utterly selfish, that they would, without the least hesitation, make peace with Hitler at the expense of the French. He said so to the American ambassador, Bullitt, on 4 June 1940: The British would probably "fight to the last Frenchman, and then seek a compromise peace." "England," said Pétain to Baudouin on 8 June, "has got us into this position. It is our duty not to put up with it, but to get out of it."[63] A day later, in Briare, Weygand accused Reynaud of excessive loyalty to England; Pétain backed Weygand immediately. Standing in the wings to come forth as the savior of his country, Pétain blamed England for the agony of France, convinced that the salvation of his nation depended, first and foremost, on her breaking away from England.

Besides this ancient and deep-rooted kind of antipathy, there was a newer kind of Anglophobia, of a political rather than an atavistic sort: the Anglophobia of those who believed that the very parliamentary democracy of England proved her being hopelessly decadent. This kind of Anglophobia was frequent among earlier disillusioned Anglophiles.[64] A man such as Drieu la Rochelle became anti-English not by inclination but by choice: He had convinced himself that, by remaining allied with England, France was attaching herself to a dying power. "Why," wrote

---

[62] The crowd shouted itself hoarse: "Gibraltar! Gibraltar!" A British clerk opened the door and told their spokesmen: "What do you want?" "Gibraltar!" "Not here. (Aquí non es.)" Dossinague, 59.

[63] Baudouin, 84–85.

[64] In Spain, for example, José Antonio Primo de Rivera, the brave and intelligent founder of Spanish Fascism, admired not only Mussolini but had also derived much of his ideas for a more disciplined, more self-sacrificing, more athletic Spain from Kipling—as had his intellectual forerunner Ramiro de Maeztu, perhaps the most interesting early Fascist political thinker in Europe, whose Anglophilia had touched Anglomanic dimensions before the First World War (but not afterward).

Drieu as early as in February 1938, "do you think that this people who are falling back before Mussolini and before the Japanese would help us stop Hitler? Think of the steep decline (*la chute verticale*) that marks the attitude of England in front of Mussolini at the time of the Abyssinian affair, when compared to her attitude in front of France at the time of Fashoda."[65] This belief in English decadence was the key to the political course of Pierre Laval during the war.[66]

Soon the Pétain people would have to consider the tares of their Anglophobia. When François-Poncet overheard the belated reading of the German armistice terms regarding the French fleet, to the British ambassador on 22 June 1940, François-Poncet remarked: "They [the English] will never forgive us for this."[67] Still, the men around Pétain would rationalize their Anglophobia. "I have been deceived by my brothers in arms," Darlan exclaimed after Mers-el-Kebir. "They have betrayed the trust I reposed in them."[68] "Trust" was good: If not quite like Cain ac-

---

[65] Drieu, *CRP*, 109. When Mussolini had been visited by Chamberlain in January 1939, the latter told Ciano: These men are "not of the same stuff as Francis Drake and the other magnificent adventurers who created the Empire. They are after all the tired sons of a long line of rich men. . . ."

[66] This intelligent Frenchman, whose political life ended in a sordid tragedy, was neither a typical pro-Fascist nor a Germanophile. Attempting to serve his nation in defeat somewhat like a second Talleyrand, one may detect two principal strains in his political philosophy: his hatred of Communism, and his Anglophobia. The latter is usually attributed to his unfortunate experiences with the British during the Italo-Abyssinian war. (Few historians noted that Laval had been the protégé of the Anglophobe and Germanophile Caillaux, of World War I note.)

One must record, however, Laval's political insights. In August 1940 the French diplomat-writer Paul Morand returned from London to Vichy. He told Laval that the English would hold out and that there would be no German invasion of England. "It's possible," Laval answered. "But this doesn't mean that the English haven't missed their chance. They will not win the war. I have no ill will toward them, but England's day has passed. No matter what happens now, she will lose her empire. Tomorrow, she will become a Holland. She will not gain a foothold in Europe again. She left it forever when she re-embarked at Dunkirk. She did not want to divide the world with Germany and the world is going to get away from her. Everything that doesn't end up by being Russian will be American. . . . It is no longer the English who are going to win the war—the British empire will become an American empire." *Caveat lector:* This Morand interview was given to a sympathetic collector of Laval political memorabilia well after the war, in October 1951. (Hoover, *France*, III, 1,336). It is nonetheless impressive.

[67] Charles-Roux, 88–89.

[68] Baudouin, 157.

cusing Abel, it was at least Claudius accusing Hamlet. In the fall of 1940 Darlan told the American chargé in Vichy that "a German victory is really better for France . . . than a British victory. In any event the British empire is finished."[69] "The British," said General Dentz in a speech in Arles on 13 October 1941, "represent those things which almost destroyed us: democratic-masonic politics and Judeo-Saxon finance. They represent the past, nothing constructive. . . ." Did this ancient and badly battered general believe that he represented the future? At the same time (on 26 September 1941), Pétain told Monsignor Valeri, the nuncio in Vichy, that a "more constructive" American attitude could bring about a compromise peace; and "if England does not accept, she will be destroyed," England, who was "the source of all the evils that had befallen France and for which country he did not have the least speck of sympathy."[70] In this respect we may find the only similarity between the attitudes of Pétain and of Stalin (about whom the American ambassador, Steinhardt, accurately reported a week before the German invasion of Russia that, "while the Soviet Government has little liking for Britain, it has great respect for the United States")—even though the sources of Russian Anglophobia were different from those of the French. For a while this kind of Anglophobia evoked popular echoes. *Gringoire* would campaign to rename the Promenade des Anglais in Nice; patriotic writers such as De la Varende would deliver historical lectures about Joan of Arc and the hateful English and their allies. Yet the spirit of Joan of Arc was represented less by the aged marshal dawdling in the casino spa of Vichy than by the willful De Gaulle in his austere quarters in London. The French people were about to recognize this. Soon the temporary fever of Anglophobia abated rapidly.[71]

It is easier to sketch the inclination of the English (and Scotch and Welsh and Scotch-Irish) people toward individual nations on the Continent. Their attitudes were more homogeneous, because of the insular traditions of the people. Yet significant currents and countercurrents existed among them on occasion. "The currents of appeasement in the country at large still await their historian," wrote the young English historian Christopher Thorne a few years ago.[72] Writing half a decade later, and nearly forty years after the events in question, this writer emphatically agrees. Practically none of the historians of the appeasement pe-

---

[69] *FRUS*, 1940, II, 490.
[70] *VD*, 5, 258.
[71] Remnants of it survived the war. Then, as now, the French dislike of the English was different from their traditional Anglophobia. It was a compensation for their own inferior performance during the war.
[72] Thorne, Introduction.

riod, including those who had devoted special studies of the subject, observed that a certain current of Germanophilia was the common denominator of the often disparate advocates of the policy that Chamberlain personified—the son of the Joseph Chamberlain who another forty years before 1939 had spoken out publicly for an English-German alliance. This thick bundle of Germanophile sentiment was made of many strands: the Victorian (and often Scottish and Liberal) respect for the old German Protestant virtues of domesticity, discipline, patriotic piety, and industry; the attendant dislike of the alleged frivolity, immorality, selfishness, and irresponsibility of the French; the kind of mild racism which, filtering through Carlyle, Froude, and the Kiplingism of the nineties, saw Germans and Scandinavians somehow more congenial than the other continentals east of Calais[73]; the respect for the Germans' fighting qualities during the First World War; the belated uneasiness about the unfair treatment meted out to the Germans at Versailles; finally, there was the element of anti-Communism. We need not analyze or illustrate evidences of this British Germanophilia further in this book, since by the spring of 1939, even before the outbreak of the war, Hitler's excesses made it vanish from the minds of Englishmen for a long time, perhaps forever. While a certain kind of moderate Anglophilia survived on certain levels of German society, Germanophilia melted away in England. In this respect there was hardly any difference between the classes of the English people.[74] Their attitude toward Germany hardened and simplified. There was little of the Germanophobia of the First World War, nothing like the anti-German riots that swept certain English cities in 1915[75]; but this was simply due to the absence of mob feeling, not to any accrued mellowness toward the Germans.

During the first, silent winter of the war, in 1939–40, the British troops in France got along better with the French than they had in

---

[73] As late as in 1937, during the Spanish Civil War, the then governor general of Gibraltar wrote: "There were our sailors of H.M.S. *Hood* and the sailors of the *Deutschland*, going about arm in arm, the best of friends, playing football, and visiting cafés and cinemas together. Our sailors will do that with the Germans, for whom they have the greatest respect, and with no one else." Harington, 197.

[74] It is interesting to record that one of the principal originators of the 1940 Anglo-French Union plan, drafted on 14 June—that is, the day of the fall of Paris—was Leo Amery, the Birmingham Tory, erstwhile protégé of Joseph Chamberlain; Amery turned into a patriotic Churchillite by 1939 and became a principal opponent of Neville Chamberlain. To be a Churchillian meant, of course, to be a Francophile. So had Hitler made Germany the enemy among the Toriest of Tories.

[75] Some Germans (including refugees) were interned in 1940.

1914–18, noted Major Ellis, the official and principal historian of the 1939–40 Western European campaign: "They were chiefly impressed by the friendliness of the French people."[76] The debacle in May 1940 strained these sentiments of mutual friendliness. Many British officers were appalled by the weakness and the incompetence of their French counterparts. Along those sections of the front where British and French troops were struggling side by side, there was little conflict: They were in the same horrid mess together. One exception was the first four days of Dunkirk. There were clashes among British, French, and, on occasion, Belgian soldiers during the retreat into the bridgehead; more ugly scenes[77] and bitterness during the long and terrifying wait on the beach. General Gort had ordered that no Frenchmen should be embarked on British ships; on 31 May Churchill overrode him. On the other hand, the behavior of the English people to the French soldiers in England was exemplary.[78]

In June 1940 King George VI wrote to his mother: "Personally I feel happier now that we have no allies to be polite to and to pamper." This attitude was typical of the British people in their finest hour[79]: a unique and insular kind of bravery. Some of its expressions were recorded and scattered in personal memoirs—in Harold Nicolson's *Diaries*, for instance. It is more difficult to ascertain how the common people felt. About this we get some glimpses of evidence, less from the sometimes fatuous statistics of the British equivalent of the Gallup poll[80] or from the populist reconstruction of the English at war by Angus Calder than from George Orwell's diaries and letters, for the simple reason that this was Orwell's principal interest as a writer: to record how people really felt, what they

---

[76] Ellis, 22.

[77] Such ugly scenes included cordons of Welsh Guards with fixed bayonets holding off French staff cars and troops who were trying to make their way to the embarkation beaches; conversely, the refusal of certain French officers to obey the British rules of assembly and embarkation. Mordal, *Dunkerque*, passim, made much of these dissensions. (This otherwise admirable and precise French naval historian must nonetheless be considered with care: His Anglophobe and Pétainist sympathies show through.)

[78] One exception was the regrettable hand-to-hand fighting between British marines and French sailors in July 1940 when the former boarded French war vessels and submarines in English ports by force.

[79] This was, at any rate, different from the incredibly obtuse and self-complacent statement by Chamberlain's colleague Hudson to the Polish ambassador on 1 September 1939: "How lucky you are! Who would have thought, six months ago, that you would have Britain on your side as an ally?" Raczynski, 77. "Lucky" was good.

[80] Mass Observation.

really thought. On 25 October 1940, for example, he cited a friend: "Foreigners are more frightened than English people during the raids. It is not their war, and therefore they have nothing to sustain them."[81]

The English people were remarkably tolerant to the many foreigners in their midst. Many of the English protested in the summer of 1940 against the internment of all aliens, ordered the government.[82] When Mussolini struck the Allies in their back, there was sporadic violence in the Soho in London[83] and uglier scenes in Glasgow, of all places: but this soon gave way to a kind of amused, and patronizing, contempt. "Help the poor buggers" was the attitude of British seamen to the shipwrecked Italians during the Battle of Matapan; in turn, British sailors recorded how Italian motor torpedo boats would go out of their way to rescue them in the South Aegean after Crete. On one occasion an Italian captain said that their entire Navy "had not forgotten" the chivalrousness of the British at Matapan. In East Africa and the Kenyan internment camps, however, the British treatment of Italian prisoners could be often indifferent to the point of being cruel.[84]

A curious chapter in the international affinities of the British people was their sudden and, in retrospect, exaggeratedly sentimental admiration for the Russians. Let me illustrate this through a contemporary illustrator himself, the excellent Osbert Lancaster:

> Cartoon on 23 June 1941 (the very day after the German invasion of Russia, the drawing must have been made on the twenty-second): Two British upper-class gents trying out greeting each other with their left fists raised.

---

[81] And he added this significant sentence: "I think this might also account for the fact—I am virtually sure it IS a fact, though one mustn't mention it—that working-class people are more frightened than middle-class." *Orwell*, II, 378.

[82] One exception was the preternaturally insular J. B. Priestley—whose broadcasts, according to populist historians, were even more popular than was Churchill in the high summer of 1940. His wartime novel, *Blackout in Gretley*, in which a refined Austrian refugee woman turns out to have been a Nazi agent, was one of his worst.

[83] Orwell's walk through Soho on 12 June 1940: " 'The Spaghetti House' had renamed itself 'British Food Shop.' " Calder, 131, 489, on "anti-Wop" sentiment.

[84] One of the deeply human tragedies of the Second World War was the death of the Duke of Aosta in British captivity. This quiet and reserved royal Italian personage, who disdained the Germans and the vulgar side of Fascism, fought with commendable bravery and self-discipline in East Africa in what he knew was a losing cause against his unwanted enemies the British, whom he respected and who, in turn, respected him.

18 July 1941: Tory gentleman, old-fashioned elegance, reading "Life in the USSR" to bemused friend: "Which are we, Carruthers—workers, peasants or intellectuals?"

17 July 1941: Lib-lab intellectual types in a BBC studio, one at a piano, the other chattering excitedly into a telephone: "Listen! I've found a man who can make the 'Internationale' sound just like 'Home, Sweet Home!'"

30 September 1941: Supervisor to older woman in a tank factory, she painting: 'Kick 'em in the . . .' on a completed tank: "Er, very praiseworthy, Miss Fanshawe, but wouldn't it perhaps be better to write it in Russian?"[85]

With very few exceptions (Catholics were among the latter), the British people reacted to the German invasion of Russia with an emotional attitude that is explainable only partly by the evident relief that this event had for a population that had been plagued by nightly German air attacks, and by the hope that in Russia Hitler would break his neck. Another element in this British Russophilia was furnished by the revived sympathies for the Soviets not only among intellectual Leftists but also among the working classes, a revival of the attitudes of 1920. Yet none of these obvious reactions can explain the Russophile attitude of an entire people—an enthusiasm that at times touched the irrational, reminiscent of the popular delusion of 1914, when hundreds of thousands of Englishmen had believed rumors of Russian troops having landed in the North of England, on their way to the front in France. On the very first day of the Russian war the attitude of the people, as recorded by Orwell, showed a remarkable degree of common sense[86]; but soon afterward an oceanic

---

[85] Lancaster, 19.
[86] June 1941. "Talking to people in the Home Guard, including Blimps and quite wealthy business men, I find everyone completely pro-Russian, though much divided in opinion about the Russian capacity to resist. Typical conversation, recorded as well as I can remember it:

> "*Wholesale poulterer:* 'Well, I hope the Russians give them a bloody good hiding.'
> "*Clothing manufacturer* (Jewish): 'They won't. They'll go to pieces, just like last time. You'll see.'
> "*Wholesale grocer:* 'Damn it, there's two hundred bloody millions of them.'
> "*Clothing manufacturer:* 'Yes, but they're not organized,' etc., etc.

"All spoken in ignorance, but showing what people's sentiments are . . . will be. It is forecast that they will be just like the White Russians. People have

sentiment of Russophilia, whipped up by the press, reached proportions that are uncanny and disturbing in retrospect. They are disturbing because this kind of adulation of a faraway people went hand in hand with what was probably a waning self-confidence[87] of the British in their own ability to carry on the war against the Germans with success. In any event, this British love for the Russians was one-sided and unrequited—as indeed the Anglophilia of millions of Europeans was unrequited; for the English people did not care to give the kind of leadership to Europe that their admirers had expected.

There remains something to be said about the international affinities of the smaller nations. In many ways these had changed but little: Hungarians and Romanians, Albanians and Greeks, Spaniards and Portuguese went on mistrusting and disliking each other, attitudes that sometimes conformed to the political exigencies of their governments, sometimes not. More often than not, these antipathies could be exploited by the greater powers. At times, however, the common fear of a great predatory neighbor would overcome even the most ancient enmities—as, for example, in September 1939, when the Polish commander of the city of Vilna suggested that the Lithuanians move in and take the city, rather than the approaching Soviets; also, the Lithuanians later took relatively little advantage of the sufferings of their enemy and neighbor Poland. In spite of their mutual disappointments, the Scandinavian peoples largely overcame their jealousies toward each other. At the end of June 1940 the Swiss writer C. F. Ramuz wrote in his diary: "Armistice. Something has fallen on our right, on the other side of the Jura. We heard the sound of the collapse. After that, a great silence. Instead of the soft sweet warmth we can expect nothing but the cold from there." The French treated Italians bitterly and cruelly after Mussolini's attack; the Italians, on the other hand, treated the French with exceptional sympathy and kindness.[88] One

---

visions of Stalin in a little shop in Putney, selling samovars and doing Caucasian dances, etc., etc." *Orwell*, II, 405.

[87] It went hand in hand, too, with a kind of superficial pragmatism, the principal mark of which was a typical British unwillingness to think of the unpleasant side of Russian potentialities. As the Polish ambassador in Moscow wrote Sikorski on 3 October 1941 about the visiting Beaverbrook: "He doesn't even want to understand the peculiarities of Russian conditions, and . . . he thinks of the people here as like (sic) western people even in regard to their sincerity and the keeping of obligations. . . ."

[88] This kind of human sympathy was not only extended to the departing French diplomats and later to the French armistice commission arriving in Rome; on the relatively quiet sectors of the Alpine front, near Barcelonnette, Italian soldiers attempted to fraternize with their French opponents. After the Belgian capitulation the French population often turned on Belgian refugees:

exception to these neighborly sentiments came from some of the Spanish. "All the French are cockroaches," said General Queipo de Llano in 1939. After the French collapse the Franco government reached out for a chunk of the French empire, even for a slice of French metropolitan territory. In July 1940 Arab broadcasts on Madrid radio suggested the possibility of a Moslem insurrection in Algeria against the French. In brief, Pétain's (and the French Right's) notorious Hispanophilia was reciprocated by Franco not at all.[89]

But, then, the addled mind of Pétain represented a conservatism that was very different from the radical traditionalism of a Bernanos, who had understood in a flash the perennial element of the sentiments of nations. "I watched the enemies of my country face to face," the latter wrote in 1937 in Mallorca. And these enemies were not necessarily the Spanish "Reds," but all kinds of Spaniards, all kinds of politicians, including Catholics and conservatives. "Listen, imbeciles," Georges Bernanos spoke to some of his countrymen, "France will not be despised by the world except when she loses her pride in herself."[90] He understood the essence of *national character*—the meaning of the noun as well as that of the adjective.


## PERSISTENCE OF NATIONAL CHARACTERISTICS

¶ Henry Adams (a very different man from Georges Bernanos) called national character "the most difficult and most important . . . of all historical problems." Disregarded by Marxists and by abstract ideologues of many kinds, the persistence of national characteristics during the Second World War was (or, rather, should have been) especially significant as well as important. They did not disappear with the rising tide of social democracy; rather the contrary. The nations of Europe had become more homogeneous, not less. This was, I repeat, the consequence—unthought of and unforeseen by Marx—of their social development; but it was also a

---

Their rations were reduced on occasion and their cars requisitioned by local authorities. Conversely, in Belgium, Walloons even more than Flamands would be deeply disappointed and resentful of the French, "to the point of disgust" (Struye)—an attitude that lasted well into 1941–42.

[89] A particularly ugly instance of Hispanic treachery was committed by the execrable Serrano Suñer in February 1941 who, after a cordial and sentimental meeting that Pétain had with Franco (in Montpellier, February 1941), told the German ambassador in Madrid that Pétain was not really pro-German, and therefore not to be trusted, *GD*, D, XII, 62.

[90] Bernanos, *GRC*, 133.

consequence of their political and cultural unity. The latter, for many European nations, was relatively recent. In 1939 the independent national statehood of Czechs, Slovaks, Yugoslavs, Finns, Estonians, Latvians, Lithuanians, Irish, Albanians was less than a generation old; even Germany and Italy had become united less than seventy years before.

The rise of universal education, national bureaucracies, and the development of communications helped to crystallize this consciousness of nationality; they brought about the overwhelming homogeneity of national cultures. So did the cities. Millions of people had left their villages and moved to the cities during the half century before 1939. There their behavior during the Second World War proved Spengler and the conservative critics of modern urbanization wrong. In spite of the drastic difficulties of living under the strains of material deprivations and sieges and bombing, the modern city-dweller proved that he was far from being a rootless proletarian. He was not less patriotic, not less disciplined, possibly even more resourceful than much of the country population.

At the same time, regional characteristics were deteriorating. The neoromantic idealizations of country life, the conservative propaganda of "back to the soil" inspired a few writers and would-be agrarians; it had no effect on the masses. The ideology and the bureaucracy of the Third Reich was wholly opposed to the persistence of regionalism, all of the superficial impressions of its cult of *Blut und Boden* (blood and soil) notwithstanding. Goebbels, for example, wanted dialects to disappear; he ordered the omission of dialect talk on the radio and on the stage, even in light programs. Hitler, of course, saw the function of the Third Reich as an enormous German melting pot, in more than one way. Still, regional differences in the behavior of peoples could be, on occasion, important. In certain instances they would revert, significantly, to older, atavistic patterns. Laval would talk much, on occasion, about the stolid and gnarled characters of his Auvergnats; and indeed there was some evidence that these people of the Massif Central were the thickest of conservatives, supporters of the Pétain regime, while some of the earliest signs of popular resistance arose among the scattered Protestants of the Cévennes, recalcitrants ever since the time of Louis XIV. As late as in December 1941, one third of the Free French forces consisted of Bretons. Discipline among workers in the South of England in 1940 was higher than among the northerners; this curious pattern was reversed later in the war. Studies of these differences in regional attitudes (and not merely of regionalisms), including perhaps even the different performances of troops from different regions, still await their historians.

Before 1933 the cradle of the Hitler movement was in the South, not in the North of Germany, even though his massive electoral strength came from the North. An unusually large number of high-ranking Nazi and SS personages had come from Austrian and Bohemian parentage;

among the two hundred recipients of the Knight's Cross of the Iron Cross order that Hitler awarded in July 1940, a large percentage were Bavarians and German Southerners. On the other hand, evidence suggests that the response of the conservative and Catholic population of the German South and of Austria to the promises of the Third Reich were fading faster than in the North. In September 1941 the decree ordering Jews to wear the yellow star on their clothes evoked numerous expressions of sympathy in Munich, a popular response that, except for Berlin, did not exist in the North. In Bavaria by 1941 even outwardly 100 per cent reliable Nazi party members and civil servants, such as Mayr, the mayor of Augsburg, behaved on occasion with a kind of humane decency that was rarely found in the orderly and partly Prussianized North; and in Austria the attraction of the Great German melting pot was fading even among the earlier pan-German romantics. In other words, the reactions of southern Germans were, generally, more rapid than those of Germans in the North. The older, more traditional attitudes of the southern Germans began to reappear again, submerged though they had been by the ideological enthusiasms of the previous decade.

We are touching here upon one of the deepest and most complex elements in the characteristics of peoples: upon the divergences of their mental habits. And it is here that I must insist that, when speaking about national characteristics, I am speaking about something that is cultural, not biological.[91] A corollary of this is the condition that while habits of speech are obviously the results of mind, the reverse, too, is true. Thus certain national characteristics of mind are both expressions and results of national rhetorical habits[92]—something that becomes increasingly important with the spreading of mass communications, with that verbal flooding of everyday life whereby a kind of national publicity is seeping into the cracks of the private mind. The brutality of Nazi rhetoric, I repeat, both reflected *and* crystallized a national tendency to act brutishly "in the face of certain realities." Immediately after the German conquest of Poland a German satrap, Übelhör, said in Lodz: "We are masters. As masters we must behave. The Pole is a servant and must serve us. . . ." Who else but a German would speak thus, in 1939? A rereading of Hitler's

---

[91] See an explanation of this in Lukacs, *HC*, 199–210.

[92] I believe, for example, that in the vast and growing mass of historical studies of the First World War insufficient attention has been devoted to this problem of national rhetoric. While it is not really arguable that the Germans were more nationalistic than, say, the French or even the English, it is arguable, and indeed demonstrable, that German nationalism was different, partly *because* German expressions of German nationalism were different. In brief, *the Germans spoke uglier.*

speeches, too—his public rhetoric—reminds us of this. In his speeches suggesting peace to the British, he spoke of their Prime Minister in terms that were insulting enough to preclude negotiating with him.[93]

Much has been said about the quality of Churchill's rhetoric. Many years after the war he said that the British people were the lion; he was merely their roar. This is all too modest and misleading. In 1940 he was both lion and roar. The British people were unaccustomed to it; but they liked it. They were unaccustomed to it because no one had spoken to them in such tones for a long time. The tone, the tenor, and the rhetoric were vividly English, and yet English of a kind that had been submerged, though not entirely buried, in the minds of Englishmen. Their response did not survive the war; but in 1940 it was more than enough. It expressed some of the best characteristics of Englishness (Englishness rather than Britishness); it proved the persistence of certain national characteristics. The best of it was that peculiar mixture of racial pride and personal bravery that marks the quality of English patriotism. The English feared defeat more than they feared death. About this there exists an unconscious concordance in the personal records. The sweet Oxford Christian, C. S. Lewis, to Owen Barfield on 2 June 1940: "And oddly enough, I notice that since things got really bad, everyone I meet is less dismayed. . . . Even at this present moment I don't feel nearly so bad as I should have done if anyone had prophesied it to me eighteen months ago." On 10 June 1940, the epicurean Harold Nicolson: "We all feel in a strange way exhilarated by this day of disaster." On 21 September (in the thick of the Blitz), George Orwell, in his diary: ". . . huge areas of London almost normal, and everyone quite happy in the daytime, never seeming to think about the coming night. . . ." Churchill, in his memoirs: "This was a time when it was equally good to live or die." "Equally" is good.

What were the deep sources of this willingness to die, if must? The British people: Were they obtuse because they were brave? Or were they brave because they were obtuse? Probably the former, but it is difficult to tell; and perhaps it is not the historian's task. The British people *were* obtuse—like their unthinking but deeply felt pride, that was an atavistic national characteristic, too. On the dark second day of Dunkirk, "people talk a little more of the war, but very little," Orwell recorded in his diary. "As always hitherto, it is impossible to overhear any comments on it in pubs, etc. Last night [Eileen] and I went to the pub to hear the 9 o'clock

---

[93] For example, in his most important speech of 19 July 1940, offering peace to the British: "This time Mister Churchill won't be able to lie and cheat about the evidence. . . ." Or consider his reference to the Polish state: "a puffed-up scarecrow" (*ein aufgeblasener Popanz*) in the same speech.

news. The barmaid was not going to have turned it on if we had not asked her, and to all appearances nobody listened." Two days later: "Still no evidence of any interest in the war. . . . It is seemingly quite impossible for them to grasp that they are in danger. . . . They will grasp nothing until the bombs are dropping. [Cyril] Connolly says they will panic, but I don't think so."[94] This theme recurs throughout Orwell's diary in 1940 and 1941. "You have all the time the sensation of kicking against an impenetrable wall of stupidity. But of course at times their stupidity has stood them in good stead. Any European nation situated as we are would have been squealing for peace long ago."[95] (Not quite true.) Nicolson on 11 August 1940: "Just as her people are comforted by the feeling that it is all too bad to be true, so in Germany they are disconcerted by the reflection that it is all too good to be true." (Quite true.)

"Blessed be the towers that crown England so fair," wrote the poet Robert Bridges in 1940 in high-Augustan verse. So Churchill, at his imaginative best, would instruct the British minister in the then remote Switzerland in the dark Nazi summer of 1940, isolated in the middle of the Continent, surrounded by the unblessed dark towers of Germandom that shut out the sunlight: The legation ought to seem "very gay and confident and have noisy parties of our own."[96] This was the high aristocratic spirit, so different from the low Chamberlain spirit that still lived on, low not because of its lack of patriotism but because of its lack of imagination,[97] for the obtuseness of the British people could often result not in courage but in lassitude. The intelligentsia were self-centered and silly, as usual[98]; fortunately, they counted little. But masses of English

---

[94] *Orwell*, II, 350.

[95] Ibid., II, 395 (15 April 1941). About English popular reactions to the Blitz, see also above, pp. 133–34; 217.

[96] Wiskemann, 45.

[97] The holdovers of this spirit were there among the military, with the result that certain military operations turned out to be overcautious, unimaginative, and slow. On occasion this was reflected by the very expression of the people in charge. In December 1941, for example, after the all too short British commando raid on the Lofoten Islands, a General Tripp, naval adviser to the Ministry of Information, drafted the communiqué stating that one of the main objectives of the raid was "to destroy stocks of cod-liver oil because of its vitamin properties." Nicolson, II, 151.

[98] This is a harsh statement. But illustrations of it are potentially endless. For example, Stephen Spender to Nicolson on 17 August 1941: "He says that the ordinary man in England does not feel this is his war, but feels it is Mr. Churchill's war. He compares the feeling with that in Spain during the Civil War, when every peasant was raised above himself by faith and excitement

workers, too, were infected with a kind of maddening slowness or even with a recalcitrant unwillingness to do their duty, on occasion. On the night of 23–24 May 1940 the stevedores brought to Calais to help in the loading of ships refused to work under the sporadic German shelling. They skulked and hid in corners; they had to be dragged out by exasperated officers.[99] "British factories did not, as so many Britons today would like to believe, work at a frantic pace throughout the summer and autumn of 1940 in order to replenish the nation's store of arms."[100] Evelyn Waugh, who earlier had written funnily-glowingly of the spirit of Dunkirk on the last page in *Put Out More Flags*, in *Officers and Gentlemen* wrote about the private who on the morrow of Dunkirk demanded Sunday leave from his commanding officers because he and his girl had inscribed themselves for a dance competition. We have seen that in September 1940 there was genuine cause for worry in London because of low morale in the East End; in May 1941 there was another general slump of morale. Fortunately, this did not last: The Germans deflected their attacks to the far end of the Continent, and for the people of Britain the long war flattened out.

The French, unlike the English, feared death more than they feared defeat.[101] But this statement, so cruelly condemnatory at first sight, must be qualified to a certain extent. The English, who had not been conquered by an invader for nearly one thousand years, knew in their bones that their defeat would mean a kind of death for England, that its effect would not be temporary. The French, on the other hand, knew in their heads, if not in their bones, the memory of national defeats together with the memory of their national recoveries. Still they, in 1940, gave up too easily. Worse, most of them would rationalize the inevitability of their surrender—one of the dangerous tendencies of the intellectual strain in the French national character. The mind as well as the flesh of the French were mottled with weakness in 1940. The French unions had gained what they wanted, the three-week paid vacation included—with the result that in August 1938, the month before Munich, there were but seven workdays in France during that entire month. "Yes, long before the war France stank of

---

and hope." Nicolson, II, 184. "Every peasant" is good. So Azaña must have been a more inspiring leader than Churchill. Fortunately the proof of the pudding was in the eating, the commentaries of the dyspeptic dietitians notwithstanding.

[99] Neave, 85.
[100] Lampe, 113.
[101] Labouchère in 1870: ". . . the Parisian is not a coward, but his individuality is so strongly developed that he objects to that individuality being destroyed by some stray shot."

defeat. . . ." wrote Gide in his diary in 1943.[102] "The mud accumulated during decades of moral turpitude and inefficient and often corrupt regimes was coming to the surface in France and bursting in fetid bubbles," wrote Spears about 1940.[103] Spears also saw a kind of "incomprehensible apathy, the lack of any reaction among the people." Were the French affected by a kind of narcolepsy, by a national sluggishness of mind? This is what Marc Bloch suggested in his thoughtful memoir, as he wrote of his experiences in the field, about "certain breakdowns, which cannot, I fear, be denied, [and which] occurred mainly because men had been trained to use their brains too slowly. Our soldiers were defeated and, to some extent, let themselves be too easily defeated, principally because their minds functioned far too sluggishly."[104] But was this not the reaction of Bloch's quick Jewish mind? For this apathetic people knew how to run and flee in 1940; they made up their minds instantly; scores of *préfets* and other officials abandoning their *départements*, towns, offices, driving southward as fast as they could go. As Bloch recorded: "There were cases of officials leaving their post without orders. . . . It was no rare thing, along the roads crowded with refugees, to come on complete local fire brigades perched on their engines. At the first rumor of the enemy's advance, off they had rushed to find safety for their persons and their property. . . ."[105]

The reaction of the armistice party was simply to get through the worst as soon as possible. The French idiom has a marvelous little phrase about being in a difficult fix—as, for example, when someone has to tell his wife that he intends to divorce her, after all—*un mauvais quart d'heure* (a bad fifteen minutes). When in 1940 someone such as Weygand was speaking of the *dernier quart d'heure*, what he had in mind was a *mauvais quart d'heure*. . . . Perhaps the problems of the French in 1940 were not to be found on the level of obtuseness or bravery, or of quickness or sluggishness of mind. The French *knew* that *they* couldn't win; and, quicker than other people, they drew certain conclusions therefrom. They had been caught on the horns of their own particular dilemma: Having been educated to pay homage to an intellectual tradition that, at its best, exalted mind over matter, in 1940 they were overwhelmed by the evidence of their enemies' power over matter. As Jean Dutourd wrote later: The pen *is* mightier than the sword; but philosophy will *not* stop a bullet. In 1945 Hitler pronounced terrible words against France: She was nothing but a "prostitute . . . a raddled old strumpet," with "incompa-

---

[102] *Gide*, II, 315.
[103] Spears, I, 257.
[104] Bloch, 48.
[105] Ibid., 132.

rable powers of blackmail."[106] Old: yes. Strumpet: no.[107] An old people with all the charms of a Ninon de Lenclos. Hitler, in 1945, exaggerated their mental powers, for where were those "incomparable powers of blackmail?"

In 1940 the French, these exemplary intellectual opportunists (I write "exemplary" not in a pejorative sense, for, unlike other intellectual opportunists, the French often know what they are doing, and they make no bones about it), *knew* that they were defeated—hence the rallying of some of the best among them to the austere patriotic rhetoric of Pétain, a rhetoric that soon proved to have been hollow oratory and little more. And now their intellectual acumen deserted them for a while: Many of them believed because they wanted to believe. Women would curtsy before Pétain as if he were a grand monarch; traveling salesmen would drink to his health in provincial restaurants. There was something cheap and Mediterranean about this regime that did not at all accord with its initial presumption of austerity and asceticism.[108] Darlan, who prided himself for being the cold and austere guardian of what remained of France's patrimony, thought that the fact that Hitler received him on 11 May 1941, on the saint day of Joan of Arc, amounted to a great and symbolic honor. As if Hitler cared (or, probably, as if he knew). At worst, intellectual opportunism among the French degenerated into private hatreds: To paraphrase Pascal, from their hearts came reasons that their reason would entertain at its worst. In few occupied countries did the Germans face such a stream of denunciations as among the French. The complexities of the cramped hatreds and envy of neighbors took precedence over the most elementary demands of patriotism or, indeed, of human decency. Perhaps this was one of the results of the unfettered individualism, of the *culte de soi*, that the French had practiced for so long, and that they preached to themselves on occasion.

Particular examples of French civic bravery were not lacking, not

---

[106] *Hitler-Bormann*, 60.

[107] In certain French towns, including Paris, the Germans put up special signs for brothels serving Germans, distinct from other brothels for Frenchmen. Audiat, 6, recorded that the inhabitants of the *maisons françaises* took a certain pride in these signs, regarding them "as a sign of their patriotism."

[108] The regionalism of the Pétain regime—as indeed that of Maurras—was one-sided, meridional, Hispanic. Drieu la Rochelle was irritated by the cult of Mistral (this good bad poet of the early twentieth century had written verse in the resuscitated Provençal language; Pétain sent an encomium to Mistral's widow in September 1940), and in 1941 Drieu accused Pétain of denying *la génie du Nord*, neglecting the France north of the Loire, by which he did not only mean the occupied zone but also a geographical and cultural side of the French national genius.

even during the dark interregnum of the French spirit in 1940–41. Had the Germans been halted somewhere north of Paris, the Parisians might have stood up to bombing as had the Londoners. On the evening of 3 June 1940 the *Comédie Française* gave a Péguy reading: The theater was full, the sirens sounded, the anti-aircraft guns were firing, but no one in the audience stirred. Later that month the first reactions of the villagers to the refugees were marked by sympathy and kindness; the selfishness developed only later, with the flood of the debacle. The family spirit remained strong and unimpaired during the great exodus: The French would not leave a relation behind. There was a positive side to their intellectualism, to that national characteristic that failed them badly during the twentieth century, too: that Gallic respect for intellect which, on occasion, would supersede whatever was opportune, politic, or fanatic. In no country occupied by the Germans was such diverse fare available in books and in theaters as there was in France. For a while this even extended to Jewish savants and men of letters who had distinguished themselves in the past. In January 1941 official and semi-official France would pay its respects to Bergson at his funeral in Paris; new writings by Maurois (who, at first, defended Pétain from the safety of refuge in America) and by Max Jacob were published in 1941; Céline, in the midst of this frenzied anti-Jewish period, found time to send a witty and sympathetic message to Emmanuel Berl. And beneath—or, perhaps, above—everything there would sparkle, on occasion, the incomparable mocking humor of the French. It would desert them at times but reappear, again and again.[109] A Parisian conversation in September 1940:

A German: For a defeated people you seem pretty cheerful.

A Frenchman: And for a triumphant people you seem pretty gloomy.

When in December 1940 Hitler sent the remains of Napoleon II to Paris, to repose in the Invalides, the irreverent Parisians would say that instead of ashes they'd rather have some coal. But there was more than that in their attitude of indifference: It was a typical example of the kind of calculated indifference shown by the French to foreigners trying to meddle with symbols in the history of France. There was something existential in the patriotism of this people that never quite disappeared, not even

---

[109] Michelet wrote one hundred years earlier in *Histoire de la Revolution*: France "laughed sometimes during the Terror; she was not frozen in fear. There was laughter; there were tears, emotions in both ways: but no frozen sadness (*nullement la tristesse immobile*). This elastic quality of the [national] morale remained intact; this practical superficiality (*la légéreté*) of the national character proved useful, it prevented the national character from being crushed. . . ."

in the worst days of national defeat. What is more important, everyone knew it. Why would the dynamic and pro-Nazi Rebatet dedicate his powerful contemporary book *Les décombres*, in 1941

| | |
|---|---|
| To my mother, | *A ma mère* |
| To my few remaining friends. | *Aux amis qui me restent.* |

In 1941 the Russians fought much better than had the French in 1940; yet one of their best generals would go over to the Germans and offer himself to their side in 1942. During the Second World War there were ugly instances of French cowardice and of French opportunism; yet a French General Vlassov was inconceivable.

The national characteristics of peoples persisted and became readily apparent during the war, regardless of ideologies. Opportunism, grandiloquence, humaneness among the Italians. When the British, having defeated the Italians, entered Asmara, they arranged for a dinner in what was the best hotel of the town, the Albergo Ciano. "Unbeknownst to them, the Italian manager had spent a number of years as a waiter at the Savoy and Piccadilly Hotels in London; when they entered the dining room they were confronted with the menu cards printed 'Fifth Indian Division—Celebration Dinner!'"[110] The grandiloquence of Fascist journalism in 1940–41 was something to behold. Mussolini himself was responsible for some of these ludicrous exaggerations. He let himself be carried away by his own rhetoric to the extent of disregarding the character of his own people—as, for example, in his grandiloquent assertion of Italian virtues, when he insisted that the Italian armament industry construct small tanks (they proved to be useless) because these "were attuned to the quick reflexes of Italian soldiers." As he was soon to learn, these quick reflexes often led to quick capitulations. And, no matter how official was the ideological policy of Fascist anti-Semitism, the humaneness of the Italian people often triumphed over their ingrained opportunism. As early as 1938 the anti-Semitic decrees were unpopular, the first instance of the regime's unpopularity in many years.[111] The Italian occupation authorities protected Jews in Greece, Albania, and Yugoslavia well before it became evident that the war was going against the Axis. In many instances the Italian authorities' behavior to the Jews was preferable to that of the local populations, certainly in Croatia and on occasion even in Greece. Grandiloquence of another kind, allied with both impracticality and cunning, remained a Spanish characteristic. While the totalitarian rhetoric of the Falangist press reached hyperbolic heights, the Spanish exasperated Hitler (and, on occasion, the British and the Americans) not merely because

---

[110] Barker, 182–83.
[111] De Felice, xxxv.

they were crafty but also because their impossible lack of organization made it very difficult to deal with them. Calculation and stubbornness remained characteristic of the Swiss, their peculiar duality that nearly served them ill in the high summer of 1940 but that would serve them well soon afterward. The stubborn neutrality and independence of the Swiss affected even the Reich Germans in their midst: Only about 15 per cent of the German colony were members of the National Socialist party or its organization in Switzerland. In Belgium ideological inclinations would on occasion supersede national differences. "The Flemish nationalists," proclaimed Staf de Clerq in his speech in Antwerp on 2 December 1940, "have always stood for the German spirit against the Latin." Yet this was less true during the Second World War than during the First World War. Only a minority of the Flemish nationalists, and a small minority of the Flemish-speaking people, joined the National Socialist VNV, while some of the most extreme collaborators of Hitler, such as Degrelle, were Walloons. Stolidity, rather than bravery, characterized the Dutch. Their local National Socialists were relatively the most numerous among the peoples of Western Europe; after the war the Dutch themselves felt that perhaps they could have behaved better.

Brave, quixotic, and garrulous were the Poles,[112] self-intoxicated on occasion by their national rhetoric, and often anti-Semitic, as indeed were many Hungarians (among the latter pro-German sentiments were often the results of a cultural background). The hatred of the Jews among certain Eastern Europeans, particularly Romanians, Lithuanians, and Ukrainians, is frightening in retrospect; from these people came forth the first volunteers, offering their services to the Germans in mistreating the

---

[112] Two illustrations from the papers of the Polish Legation in Moscow in the fall of 1941: ". . . The Polish people of whom we get reports and with whom we have contact here in groups during their transit through Kuibishev eastward deserve our admiration. The majority of them are ordinary people, the families of foresters, settlers, workers. They are all emaciated, overworked, but extraordinarily patient, calm, enduring, dignified, making no reproaches. They are all confident of a happy future and are filled with faith that they will get back to Poland. Many of them have tiny savings and refuse aid; they require directions, a kind word, but manage without financial help. Help is asked for families who have been plundered, the seriously ill, mothers with numerous children, or rather, their fellow travellers ask help for them. . . . The moral level is high, cases of bad behaviour are rare, and are condemned by public opinion, the longing for religious life is great. . . ." Kot, 101. "The intensification of a suspicious attitude toward Poles are partly the result of the boundless garrulity of many people, especially officers, who extensively and vociferously proclaimed the necessity to settle accounts with the Soviets. . . . The NKVD agents collected all this sort of boasting talk as proof that it was impossible to cooperate loyally with the Poles." Ibid., 164.

Jews. But once we look at the peoples of the easternmost fringes of traditional Europe, including the Soviet Union, we encounter national characteristics that functioned differently from the ingrained inclinations of those older European nations whose consciousness of their nationality had crystallized centuries earlier. We may even say, in a necessarily shorthand statement, that the opportunism of those Eastern Europeans, and perhaps especially of the Russians who collaborated with the Germans, was emotional rather than intellectual. There was, for example, a mysterious duality—duality rather than ambiguity—in the behavior of the Russian populations during the early portion of the war. Less intellectual than, say, the French or the Italians, one characteristic of their behavior was a certain slowness of mind.

In an important way their slowness of mind served them well. Like the British in 1940, the Russian people in 1941 did not know that they were beaten.[113] On the other hand, their reactions to the German danger could be extraordinarily slow.[114] It took Stalin twelve days after the German attack to gather himself and address his people. On occasion he himself would voice his exasperation, as for example on 20 September 1941, when he burst out in the presence of Cripps: "What is to be done with these Russians? They never are able to do anything in time." A careful study of national behavior among different prisoners of war in German camps remarked that while French and Belgian and other Western European prisoners had been most eager to hear any kind of news about the events of the war, this acute thirst for news had not been shared at all by the Russian and Ukrainian prisoners.[115] Under the name of "inertness" a postwar study of Soviet defectors discussed, perhaps in unduly heavy language, this phenomenon:

> The outstanding trademark of the Soviet citizen is the well-nigh completely instinctive, non-spontaneous adjustments to the "party line" of the moment: inertness. Inertness had made the Soviet national politically disoriented, bewildered and far from self-reliant, maximally susceptible to an action like collaboration with the Hitler regime. And as the effect of inertness, as a rule, was nearly complete within the USSR, so now the emancipation from the external symptoms of inertness was striking and rapid. This great sense of vacuum and their search for new affiliation

---

[113] Was there a difference nonetheless? The British would not entertain the idea that they might lose the war. To the Russians it would not occur. The British would not, the Russians could not speculate about the political contingencies of the future.

[114] About this slowness of oriental reactions (Japan), see also above, p. 163, n. 8.

[115] Maury article in *RH2M* (Jan. 1955).

explain the swiftness with which the Soviet soldiers, only recently paralyzed by inertness, now enlisted in German undertakings and embraced new anti-Stalin doctrines. . . . It is therefore a striking feat of backward projection that many a Soviet exile will bitterly deny and resent any suggestion that his present anti-Stalinism was not full-blown within the USSR and also perhaps not generally shared there. Closer questioning by this writer on many occasions revealed that only following German capture did coherent and compelling anti-Stalin emotions become crystallized.[116]

That is, the Soviet defectors lied. But did they know that they lied while they lied? That is a moot question, perhaps the one at the bottom of most of our problems with Russian rhetoric and Russian behavior. (The prevarications of the Russian bureaucracy and of their propaganda defied reason, as, for example, in December 1939, when the Soviets maintained that they were not at war with Finland, and when their radio announced that Russian planes flying over Helsinki were not dropping bombs, they were dropping bread to feed the poor.)

In any event, it was in the revolutionary Soviet Union, in a state the very existence of which was supposed to represent the decisive break with the previous history of mankind, that the dead hand of the past was a living reality. Stalin resembled Ivan the Terrible[117] more than Hitler resembled Bismarck or Mussolini resembled Napoleon or Pétain resembled Bazaine. To paraphrase Santayana: Those who do not know history are especially prone to repeat it. But did not Stalin know history? In late 1941 his speeches included thunderous evocations of Tsarist hero-generals, Kutusov, Suvorov. In the fall of 1939 he proposed a boundary to the Finns that coincided largely with that of Peter the Great. On 14 October the Finnish Paasikivi told Stalin: "The line your military command has in

---

[116] Fischer, 141.

[117] One characteristic instance was Stalin's xenophobia, which was a natural inclination on the part of the Russians. Its evidences are numerous throughout the war. But already before the war we have one of the few surviving documents of the Soviet secret police, the infamous Order No. 0054 issued in Lithuania, listing potential suspects. "The lists item all former officials of the State, Army and judiciary; all former members of non-Communist parties; all active members of student corporations; members of the National Guard; anyone who had fought against the Soviets (i.e., in 1918–20); refugees; representatives of foreign firms; employees and former employees of foreign legations, firms and companies; people in contact with foreign countries, including philatelists and Esperantists; all clergy; former noblemen, landlords, merchants, bankers, businessmen, owners of hotels and restaurants, shopkeepers; former Red Cross officials." First published in *Lithuanian Bulletin*, it is cited in Conquest, 284.

mind would be quite impossible on economic grounds alone." Stalin: "Soldiers never think in economic terms."[118] He certainly did not think in Marxist terms—a condition which served him well throughout the war.

At any rate, the behavior of nations during the Second World War shows enough evidence to disprove all of the theories of behaviorism, economicism, sociologism, environmentalism, structuralism, materialism, —in short, of the intellectually fashionable deterministic theories, even now. For, ultimately, behavior is the result of mind; and national inclinations are the results of national habits of mind.

On another level we ought to note that their quickness of mind did little good to the French or to the Italians during their national debacles, even though it would serve them well on occasion later in the war. The Latin nations of Europe, with few exceptions, fought poorly; the Germanic nations, with some important exceptions, fought better; and in many ways the Slavic peoples of Eastern Europe showed the greatest capacity for endurance of all.

But if endurance went one way, growing more and more massive as our eyes move from West to East, inhumanity went in another. Hardly any fleeing Jews would (or could expect to) be hidden by Russian peasants or workers, including Communists. Some Jews were hidden and sustained by Germans and by Hungarians. Many Jews were hidden by Frenchmen and by Italians, including Fascists. And this brings us to yet another matter, to the tragedy of the Jews, involving the sentiments of nations.

## THE PROBLEM OF THE JEWS

¶ Entire libraries exist that are devoted to the record of the German attempt to eliminate the Jewish people from most of Europe during the reign of the Third Reich, and particularly during the Second World War. It is good that such voluminous records exist, lest some future generation be led to believe that these crimes were exaggerations or even legends. In addition to the records, there are the later reconstructions of these events and also the accounts of the victims. Almost by necessity most of these accounts are one-sided; they are written from the viewpoint of the victims, of the survivors, of their sympathizers: But a record, for being one-sided, is no less of a record for that. In this subchapter I will, however, attempt to describe something slightly different: the story of

---

[118] Tanner, 29.

the persecution of the Jews during the Last European War, in 1939–41, with an emphasis perhaps less on the acts of the persecution than on the sentiments of nations and on the purposes of Hitler.

Nevertheless, I must begin by summing up first what happened—and attempt to deal afterward with what people, including Hitler, thought was happening.

Hitler's original aim was to expel, not to exterminate; to force all Jews out of Germany rather than to kill them. Such expulsions of Jews occurred before in the history of Europe.[119] Jews were unpopular in many nations in Europe, especially in Eastern Europe; again, there was nothing very new in that. What was new was that the suppression of Jews was now demanded by the principal state in Europe, a very Great Power indeed. This obsession of a powerful state with the interior minorities of other states had few precedents in the Modern Age; indeed, it introduced a new element in international relations. The German government's estimate of the trustworthiness of the governments of its neighboring states (and often not only of its neighboring states) not only included, it often depended on, these governments' attitude toward the Jews who lived under them. If Hitler's trust could be secured by suppressing the Jews, so be it: This was the attitude of many (though not all) bureaucrats within Germany, and of many (though not all) national leaders, especially in Eastern and Southern Europe.

They wished that their Jews, and with them their Jewish problem, would go away. In 1933 the large emigration of Jews from Germany had begun; in 1938 and 1939 many Jews from Austria, Bohemia, Moravia, Slovakia, and a lesser number from Hungary, Poland, Italy, and Romania followed them. They could take a substantial amount of their material wealth with them; this was not with what Hitler and Goebbels were concerned. Before 1939 most of them emigrated to France and Britain (the British alone took in more than 80,000 Jewish refugees during the 1930s). After 1939 those who were fortunate enough to receive entry visas to the United States or to other states of the Western Hemisphere or to Palestine were allowed to trickle through the few remaining neutral sluices out of Axis Europe by the most circuitous routes, via Portugal or Turkey or the Trans-Siberian Railroad. Most of this trickle ceased to flow after

---

[119] Perhaps the principal difference now resided in the extreme rigidity with which Hitler and his government would define, on a racial basis, who was a Jew and who was not, through the so-called Nuremberg Laws of 1935, reaching back to their grandparents. (A number of half Jews and even full Jews who were married to "Aryans" survived the Third Reich in Germany proper.) But the Spanish persecution of the Jews in the late Middle Ages, though established on the basis of religion, was also considerably racial.

November 1941, but a few droplets westward[120] were permitted by the Germans throughout the rest of the war. Had Roosevelt or Churchill announced that they were ready to suspend the war and send their ships to transport the remaining Jews out of Europe, Hitler would have responded in an instant.[121]

This enforced emigration was one side (or, rather, one level) of the story of the Jews during the Last European War. The Germans, in any event, were not the sole perpetrators of it. In December 1937 the anti-Semitic Romanian, in 1938 the less dogmatic but also considerably anti-Semitic nationalist government of Poland were thinking about forcing a mass of Jews out of their countries; they even tried to discuss this with the Germans on occasion, as in October 1938 (the Polish government had been speculating about Madagascar as a receptacle for the Jews of Europe even before the Third Reich had—an odd footnote to this history).[122] Between 1935 and 1939 a number of states in Europe passed laws or regulations restricting their Jewish populations and discriminating against them —Romania, Hungary, Italy, Slovakia—and not always because of German pressures on these states. But by 1939 there came a change in Hitler's attitude, a change that was literally fraught with the most extreme consequences—and this was due to the crystallization not of plate glass[123] but of something in Hitler's mind; of his conviction that if it came to another war with France and England, this would mean a war to the death with the Jews of the world.[124] For it was then, in January 1939, that Hitler convinced himself that the Munich "settlement" was merely a respite, that the British and the French, *because of the increasing prospect of their American support* (a most important consideration, this, to which

---

[120] To this we must add the considerable number of Polish Jews who fled to the Soviet Union in 1941.

[121] People who berate Roosevelt and Churchill for not having done this are blind in their retrospect. They do not recognize that such a deal with Hitler, apart from its practical difficulties, would have played straight into his hands: first, in splitting the Western leaders from Stalin; second, because Hitler then would have had convincing proof for his argument that Roosevelt and Churchill were fighting a world war against Germany principally in the service of Jewry.

[122] On one occasion the Romanians preceded the Poles. In December 1937 the anti-Semitic Romanian Prime Minister, Goga, told the visiting Right-wing Jérôme Tharaud: "There is but one solution: to transport them in mass to some still empty piece of territory . . . to an island from where they could no longer leave . . . to Madagascar, for example." Tharaud, 184.

[123] I am referring to the *Kristallnacht*, the Nazi smashing of Jewish shops, homes, and synagogues in November 1938; see above, p. 23.

[124] See also above, p. 27.

I shall return), were becoming determined to fight the Third Reich. And America, especially Roosevelt's circle, was pullulating with influential Jews. So on 30 January 1939 Hitler put this ominous passage in his speech (it was to be his last speech in peacetime on the anniversary of his assumption of power), the significance of which appears only in retrospect, but it is nonetheless clear for that:

> Today I will once more be a prophet. If the international Jewish financiers *inside and outside Europe* [my italics] should again succeed in plunging the nations into a world war, the result will not be the bolshevization of the earth and the victory of Jewry, but the *annihilation* [my italics] of the Jewish race *throughout Europe* [my italics again].

And so it was almost to be. Almost; because a considerable remnant of Jews was to survive the war. But what we must recognize is the importance of Hitler's announcement; he would annihilate the Jews of Europe, if need be. This policy of annihilation did not become official and definite Third Reich policy until January 1942—another significant date, coinciding with Hitler's belated decision to mobilize the Reich for total war. Yet mass murders of Jews were beginning to occur earlier, in 1941, perpetrated by Germans, with the help of Ukrainians, Romanians, and Lithuanians on occasion. Nearly half a million Jews were killed in the summer and autumn of 1941. Thus we may distinguish between three phases of the Germans' handling of the Jewish problem during the Third Reich:

> *Before the outbreak of the war, 1933–39:* emigration, in increasing measure, from Germany;
>
> *1939–41:* emigration continued, concentration in ghettos in Poland, sporadic mass murders in the East;
>
> *January 1942–November 1944:* systematic extermination, with a minimum of emigration wherever this was still possible;
>
> *November 1944–May 1945, the collapse of the Third Reich:* systematic extermination suspended, but a *de facto* annihilation was still taking its toll through starvation, disease, and continued mistreatment.

We can see that in this respect, too, the Last European War, 1939–41, represented a transition. The emigration of Jews from Europe went on, much diminished, because of the conditions of the war; the emigration was permitted by the Germans, and it was desired by many other states.[125]

---

[125] Mussolini, for example, would facilitate the emigration of Jews from Italy

For the German persecution of the Jews was not governed by the ebb and flow of the dictates of some kind of a fanatic frenzy: Hitler's treatment of the Jews was part and parcel of his general view of the world struggle. It was because of the war that German policy was turning, gradually,[126] in the direction of a more or less "final solution." This gradual hardening of a terrible policy was part and parcel of the gradual hardening of the mental cruelty of the German regime, of its propaganda to describe the Jews as both the lowest and the most despicable of all possible enemies, an attitude that was expressed by the increasing restrictions and the humiliations of the remaining Jews within Germany.

Of the successive stages of this policy the following are but random examples. After the first day of the war, 1 September 1939, Jews were no longer allowed to go out at night. After the end of the Polish campaign (23 September 1939) they were no longer allowed to listen to radios. In October 1939 Jews were transported from Austria and Bohemia and Moravia to Poland for the first time. During most of 1940 there was some hesitation about what to do with the remaining Jews within Germany,[127] just as Hitler did not quite know how to conclude the war. By September 1941 the prospect of imminent war with America stared Hitler in the face; and for the first time (19 September 1941) the Jews of Germany were ordered to wear the yellow star on their clothes.[128] In October 1941, the deportation of German Jews to the East began; emigration from Ger-

---

even by allowing favorable exchange rates for them. By October 1941 6,000 (about one out of seven) Italian Jews had left, mostly for America, together with thousands of foreign Jews living in Italy at that time.

[126] I must emphasize that the implementation of this change of policy was gradual. The German Jews were still hoping: In 1936 and 1937 fewer Jews left Germany than in 1933 and in 1934. We have seen that January 1939 represented a significant turning point in Hitler's attitudes. Yet during that month Schacht was still his special delegate for Jewish emigration matters (even as on 20 January he had been dismissed from the presidency of the Reichsbank). On 24 January, a week before Hitler's above-cited speech, Goering ordered the Interior Minister, Frick, "to promote [Jewish] emigration through all possible means."

[127] The three sporadic deportations in 1940, one eastward, two westward (Jews transported from Stettin to Poland in February, Jews deported from Baden to France in October, French Jews deported to France from Alsace-Lorraine in July) may be seen as having some significance as forerunners of the larger policies that were planned: one, the "solution" of a Jewish reservation in Poland, the other the "solution" of settling the Jews in some remote French colony such as Madagascar.

[128] "It was the hardest day all during those years of Hell." Klemperer, 204.

many was finally suspended; and in January 1942 the systematic extermination of the Jews of all Europe became official German policy.

This was a sequence of events inflicted upon the remaining Jews of Germany. In other countries of Europe this sequence of humiliations and mistreatments was often similar, though often not as systematic as in Germany. In any event, the Jewish population in Germany was now rapidly diminishing. Here is a telling sequence of figures from one German town at random:

JEWS IN THE CITY OF ESSEN

| 1925 | 4,504 |
|---|---|
| June 1933 | 4,506 |
| May 1939 | 1,636 |
| September 1940 | 1,225 |
| October 1941 | 1,039 |
| November 1941 | 795 |
| November 1942 | 111 |

Or: On 29 November 1941, 512 of the remaining Jews of Nuremberg were transported to Riga. Seventeen of them survived the war.

Between 1939 and 1941 Hitler still considered two alternatives to annihilation. One was the Madagascar "solution," which he mentioned seriously several times, even to Mussolini, in 1940.[129] The continuing war with Britain made this unfeasible, to say the least. Yet Goebbels would discuss it with his underlings as late as in the autumn of 1940.[130] On the other hand, there survives a memorandum from Heydrich to Ribbentrop as early as 24 June 1940 (the date is significant: the morrow of the armistice with France, *before* certain officials of the German Foreign Ministry would address themselves to the Madagascar plan[131]; perhaps Heydrich was more realistic about the continuation of the war):

---

[129] On 20 June Hitler spoke about it to Raeder (Hillgruber, *HS*, 245, mistakenly writes: "Hitler's only reference to the Madagascar Plan"). On 1 August Hitler to Abetz: He intended to evacuate all Jews from Europe after the war. *GD*, D, X, 484. On 20 November 1940 to the Hungarian Prime Minister, Teleki: Hitler "regarded the solution of the Jewish question for Europe as one of the biggest problems of the peace. It was his intention in the future peace treaty to give all states within Europe to participate in this solution the possibility of doing so by forcing France to make one of her possessions available." *GD*, D, XI, 635.

[130] Boelcke, 511.

[131] Rademacher memorandum of Madagascar plan, 3 July 1940: "The desirable solution is: 'All Jews out of Europe.'" Madagascar transferred to Germany as a mandate, naval, air bases, German police governor. "This arrangement will

The total problem can no longer be solved through emigration. *A final territorial solution (Eine territoriale Endloesung)* becomes necessary.

This territorial solution was, first, the plan to gather Jews into a ghetto state, a so-called Jewish reservation, near Lublin. Hitler discussed this, too, with Mussolini. There are reasons to believe that Hitler planned to keep such a Jewish reservation as a kind of hostage for eventual deals with the United States, in view of the considerable Jewish population of the latter. But in 1940 this plan was abandoned, too[132]; and the forced concentration of Jews in special town ghettos, such as the one in Warsaw, began. And after the invasion of Russia had started, on 31 July 1941 Goering—who had been a prime mover of emigration, and who did not seem to have had a dominant inclination to inflict systematic cruelties on Jews[133]—used, for the first time, the term "final solution" *without* referring to a "territorial" reservation. He minuted to Heydrich:

> Supplementing the duty that was assigned to you on 24 January 1939 to solve the Jewish problem by means of emigration and evacuation in the best possible way according to present conditions, I hereby instruct you to make all necessary preparations concerning administrative, financial, and material matters for a general solution (*Gesamtloesung*) of the Jewish question within the area of German influence in Europe. . . . I instruct you further to submit to me as soon as possible a general plan showing the measure of organization and for action necessary to carry out the desired final solution (*Endloesung*) of the Jewish question.

There is some reason to believe that, in spite of the ominous language, Goering was not yet thinking of the systematic murder of millions of Jews in gas vans or death factories. Yet he must have known that by that time the sporadic mass killings of Jews in the East had begun, performed

---

prevent the possible establishment of a Vatican state of their own in Palestine. . . . moreover, the Jews will remain in German hands as a pledge for the future good conduct of the members of their race in America." *GD*, D, XI, 3.

[132] As early as 12 March 1940 (before Sumner Welles' visit to Berlin), Hitler said to his "Americanist" expert Colin Ross, who had asked for some "positive solution" of the Jewish question, that this was indeed desirable: But "the Jewish question was a space question which was difficult to solve," the establishment of a Jewish state around Lublin would not constitute a solution, as there would be too many people living closely together there. *GD*, D, VIII, 912–13.

[133] In 1940 he ordered that the expulsion of German Jews to Poland be temporarily suspended; he intervened for a number of individual Jews; in the autumn of 1941 he "obtained a respite of rather more than a year for the families of Jewish armament workers in the Reich" (Reitlinger, *FS*, 17–18).

by the SS and action commandos (Einsatzgruppen). At the end of September in Kiev alone 33,000 Jews were killed in two days. By the end of the year the first gas chambers were erected in Poland.[134] Then the German Army was halted before Moscow, the United States entered the war, Hitler ordered the full mobilization of the German war economy, and on 20 January 1942, in an office in the Wannsee suburb of Berlin, a group among the top bureaucrats and police officers of the Third Reich made the extermination of Jews of Europe official German state policy.[135]

At that moment, according to Heydrich, there remained:

within former Germany: 131,800 Jews;  360,000 had emigrated since 1933
within former Austria:  43,700 Jews;  147,000 had emigrated since 1938
within former Bohemia
  and Moravia:  74,200 Jews;  30,000 had emigrated since 1938–39

Thus one out of four Jews remained in Germany and Austria,[136] three out of four having had the opportunity to flee, by emigrating abroad.[137] This was very different from the rest of Europe, where the Jews who fled before the "final solution" were a small minority, their numbers sometimes minimal.

But after this time, the end of 1941, the fate of the remaining German Jews and that of the Jews of other European states was no longer very different. The Germans now took it upon themselves to extend the "final solution" systematically to all of the territories under their control. Be-

---

[134] The extermination camp in Chelmno started operating in December 1941. Belzec, Maidanek, Sobibor, and Treblinka were erected at that time. Auschwitz-Oswiecim had been set up in May 1940 as a concentration camp for Polish prisoners; the factory of Birkenau (Auschwitz II) was built during the summer of 1941. On 3 September 1941 six hundred inmates were killed by gassing there, the first "experiment."

[135] *IMT* NG-2586, the "Wannsee Protocol." A minimum of selectivity remained. The extermination decree was not yet *total*. The Protocol included reference to a "work force" (*Arbeiteinsatz*) and of the establishment of a "model" camp (*Theresienstadt*) for wounded and decorated Jewish veterans of the First World War.

[136] By the end of 1939 77 per cent of these remaining Jews were over 40 years of age; a very large portion of these were over 65.

[137] Some of these were unfortunate enough to be caught up again by Hitler's minions in France, Holland, and elsewhere. Those who had been fortunate enough to escape to the Western Hemisphere turned out to be the most vocal and the most influential of Germany's enemies (as, for example, the "Jewish Prussian" Emil Ludwig, who said in 1939: All Germans were Nazis, there was no exception, there was no other Germany. Gross, 327).

tween 1939 and 1941 such a direct German policing of Jews was practiced only in Poland, the only place in Europe where the wearing of the yellow star was mandatory for Jews before 1941 (it had been decreed in November 1939). In other occupied territories the Germans often let the local authorities carry out different restrictive measures under German supervision. In their allied states, satellites, and vassalages, the fate of the Jews varied. In some places, as for example in Denmark, their vexations were limited; in other places, as for example in Hungary, their humiliating restrictions were considerable; in Romania,[138] Lithuania, Latvia, and the Ukraine, they were exposed to murderous rampages by local fanatics, by extreme nationalists, and on occasion by common criminals. In Croatia and Romania Jews had to wear the yellow star before they had to do so in Germany. Almost everywhere in Europe the allied and the satellite and the vassal governments would impose anti-Jewish legislation, imitating the Germans at times spontaneously, at times responding to German pressure, in order to curry favor with the Germans.

I have tried to sum up the events afflicting the Jews of Europe from 1939 to 1941 succinctly. Yet a careful survey of the decisions that affected their fate, and even of the successive events that befell them, somehow falls short of suggesting the deeper reality of the physical and mental life of these unhappy millions in the shadow of the scourge that was rising above their heads. They would not put anything past their enemies, the Nazis; yet somehow they could not, and would not, believe that they would be transported away in order to be killed in the mass. In plain English, they could not, and would not, look death in its face. The cause of this was not cowardice; it was their mental attachment to the rule of reason. For one thing, this naturally pessimistic and intelligent race went on to believe that the victory of the Allies and the defeat of Hitler was preordained, that it would happen soon. And this was as true of the wretched poor Jews in their hovels in Podolian villages as of the Parisian Jews who were walking along the Croisette in Cannes in 1941,[139] of Dutch professors of mathematics as well as of poultry handlers in the muddy villages of Bessarabia—because in so many ways life was still going on, in so many ways it still made sense. About their enemies they could believe the worst; about their own fate they could not do so.

---

[138] The Romanians, shamelessly opportunistic, were typical of those who actually wanted the Germans to do this job for them. The language of the Romanian Prime Minister, Gigurtu, to Ribbentrop, on 26 July 1940—note the date—is worth quoting: "Romania could also solve the Jewish question definitely only if the Fuehrer carried through *a total solution* [my italics] for all of Europe." *GD*, D, X, 303.

[139] Cannes=Kahn, said some of their critics.

In any event, the life of the remaining Jews in Europe in 1941 was as yet far from uniform.[140] The signs, however, were more than ominous; and when the turning point of the war came, in the winter of 1941–42, Hitler and his government decided that they would no longer tolerate this lack of uniformity that might, after all, ensure the survival of large numbers of Jews, their mortal enemies, after the war.

In his attempt to eliminate the presence of Jews from Europe, Hitler, as we have seen, had many accomplices, with varying degrees of willingness. Their story is also well known, relatively speaking: It is part and parcel of the pathogenesis of modern anti-Semitism. There is, however, a distinction—ignored by the causal categories of materialism and often obscured by modern medicine itself—between the etiology and the pathogenesis of a disease, of a tendency, of an inclination. Much has been written about the pathogenesis, about the ugly symptoms, about the symptomatic development of anti-Semitism. Little has been written about its origins—a far more obscure, complex, and difficult topic, which I cannot avoid here, when I am dealing with the sentiments of national populations. To many of them the presence of Jews in their midst was an irritant. It is not enough to say that this should not have been an irritant; and it is not enough to recount the often cruel and shabby attempts through which people tried to deal with this irritant. To detect the symptoms of an ulcer is one thing; to follow its treatment is another; to try to find out something about the origins of the ulcer is yet another. The first two involve its pathogenesis, the last its etiology.[141] We know very little about the etiology of ulcers or of headaches or of modern anti-Semitism. Yet we ought to try.

Almost two centuries ago the influx of increasing numbers of Jews out from the western provinces of the then Russian Empire to Europe began. This migration was one of the most extraordinary and consequential events of the nineteenth century; no historian worthy of this story has yet arisen. The Jews were almost the only people who migrated not only from the countryside to the cities of Europe but also from one nation to another. Within a few decades, sometimes within a few years, their numbers would rise from 1 to 4 or 5 per cent of certain national popula-

---

[140] In the neutral states the relatively few Jews lived on, cowed but free. One neutral, Turkey, began to vex its Jews through all kinds of oriental chicaneries in the winter of 1941–42. Among Germany's allies the Finnish government refused to touch its Jews. Every other government in Hitler's Europe passed restrictive and often cruel ordinances against Jews after 1939, almost always on a racial basis.

[141] A discussion of this is in Lukacs, *PMA*, 142–43.

tions, from 5 to 25 per cent of the populations of certain cities, from 10 to 50 per cent of certain professions. They would naturally prosper in the capitalist and early-capitalist societies of the nineteenth century. Many of them became assimilated, civic-minded, determined to be patriotic; a minority of them would intermarry with the national bourgeoisie, sometimes even with the aristocracy. All of this evoked a great deal of envy, and the modern phenomenon of racial anti-Semitism which, in many ways (though not in all), differed from the ancient and largely religious Judeophobia. The liberals believed that this was a temporary reaction, and that with the assimilation of the Jews it would disappear. The Socialists believed that it would disappear with the rise of the working class, mostly due to universal education.[142] They were wrong. The popular hatred would rise against the assimilated Jews even more than against their poor benighted brethren and relatives who still lived in ghettolike quarters in the East of Europe, murmuring their outlandish prayers and wearing their outlandish habits. It was the successful Jewish men and women, prospering in the midst of a national society, who were disliked. Few people understood the consequences of this. Among them were the Zionists and the modern anti-Semites. The first, at the opening of the twentieth century, proclaimed that after two thousand years the Jews should declare that they are a separate people and return to Palestine. The second believed that this would not happen, and that the presence of Jews in the midst of non-Jewish peoples was the chief instrument of the decay and of the eventually disastrous degeneration of the latter.[143]

Before 1914 the influence of these modern anti-Semites was intense, though it was politically limited save in occasional instances and places. During and after the First World War the number and the influence of Jews within the national states of Europe changed relatively little. Yet anti-Semitism became more popular and widespread, especially in Central Europe. One of the reasons for this was the participation of a number of Jews in the Bolshevik and Central European Communist revolutionary at-

---

[142] The German Socialist Bebel about anti-Semitism, 1906: "It is a consoling thought that it has no prospect of ever exercising a decisive influence on political and social life in Germany." Such thoughts, though consoling, are not necessarily wise. Bebel, *Sozialdemokratie und Antisemitismus*, cited by Pulzer, 197.

[143] There were yet another kind of men who recognized that a problem existed: the great thinkers and writers, seers. Nietzsche had written: "Any thinker who is concerned with the future of Europe must keep Jews as well as Russians in mind." James Joyce's prototype of Modern Man was Leopold Bloom, a Central European Jew transplanted to Dublin. (And now to mention strange coincidences: Nietzsche had gone mad in the year Hitler was born. And like Leopold Bloom, Alois Hitler, Adolf's half brother, was living in Dublin in the first decade of the century, married to an Irishwoman.)

tempts after 1917. We have seen that between the wars nearly everywhere in Europe, and especially in the nations neighboring the Soviet Union, the popular tendency was sharply anti-Communist. Another source of anti-Semitism was the repugnance to international capitalism which many of the increasingly homogeneous populations of Eastern Europe professed after the First World War.[144] We have seen that national, and not international, socialism was the main common denominator of most mass movements after the First World War. The modern nationalist was a Socialist of sorts: He was certainly opposed to capitalism as well as to Communism; he was anti-internationalist and consequently often anti-Semitic. After the rise of the Third Reich, anti-Semitism rose again in the 1930s, for the second time after its first wave around 1919. Again we cannot discount the opportunistic element in its appeal, in addition to the potential receptivity of anti-Semitic propaganda on the minds of people who, especially in Eastern Europe, were first-generation newspaper readers. In Western Europe there was another factor, affecting a minority, perhaps especially in France: the crystallizing conviction of those who believed that, were it not for the Jews and for their influence, the Western democracies, and particularly their corrupt parliamentary governments, would not have chosen to engage in a second world war with Germany.[145]

The governments of Europe, including the most democratic or liberal ones among them, were aware of these sentiments. In 1939 there was not one European state that did not discriminate against Jews in one way or another: the British, the French, the Swiss, the Swedes, all of them preferred to receive non-Jewish rather than Jewish refugees from Central Europe, if need be. Their consent to receive Jews at all, and indeed in large numbers, on the other hand, does them honor; and there is no question that while Jews may not have been especially popular, these governments and the majority of their peoples were shocked by the Germans' mistreatment of the Jews. Let me repeat: the visible presence, and the influence, of Jews was more of an irritant than were their numbers, for

---

[144] This was especially true of Germany, where a variety of political and social thinkers proclaimed during the 1920s that the assimilation of the Jews had failed, that people are seeing through the surface and recognize a potentially dangerous Jewish separateness: "A threatening world pogrom hangs over their heads." Hans Blueher, *Secessio Judaica* (Berlin, 1922), cited by A. Bein, *VFZ* (April 1965), 131.

[145] This seems to have been the principal cause of Céline's conversion to an extreme form of anti-Semitism as early as in 1937. Céline to Rebatet in the winter of 1939: "To be screwed because of the Jews, this is the Alsace-Lorraine of this war." (*Se faire enculer par les Juifs, c'est la nouvelle Alsace-Lorraine.*) Rebatet, 249.

after the First World War the number of Jews in Europe hardly increased at all:

JEWS OF THE WORLD

| | In millions | In Europe | In the Americas |
|---|---|---|---|
| 1825 | 3.3 | 83.2% | 0.3% |
| 1925 | 14.9 | 62.8 | 29.5 |
| 1935 | 16.2 | 59.7 | 31.3 |

In 1939 nearly one out of every two Jews of the world still lived in Eastern Europe. In Kaunas, the capital of Lithuania, Jews amounted to 33 per cent, in Warsaw to 28 per cent of the inhabitants. In Poland the Jewish minority was over 9 per cent, in Lithuania over 7 per cent of the population. Yet in most Central European countries and capitals the Jewish population was diminishing: Jews within the frontiers of postwar Hungary in 1910 amounted to 6.1 per cent, and by 1930 only to 5.1 per cent of the population. A total of 8.2 per cent of the inhabitants of Prague had been Jews in 1871, only 4.2 per cent in 1925. The proportion of Jews of the populations of Vienna, Berlin, Frankfurt, and Hamburg all dropped well before Hitler came to power. (The proportion remained largely the same in Poland; it had risen in Romania, where anti-Semitic legislation was introduced in 1937.) On the other hand, the number of Jews in Paris had risen from 30,000 in 1870 to over 300,000 in 1936.[146] Many of them were foreigners, in spite of the relatively liberal French naturalization laws; according to the *préfect* of the *département* of the Seine, in October 1940 of the nearly 150,000 Jews there, only 86,000 were French citizens. Unscrupulous scum, such as the type of a Stavisky or of an Ilya Ehrenburg, merely floated on the surface; yet it was the intelligent, sensitive, and honest Jewish French philosopher Henri Bergson who wrote in his testament in February 1937, well before the war:

> My thoughts have led me closer and closer to Catholicism in which I see the full achievement of Judaism. I should have been a convert—had I not seen for years the rise of a tremendous wave of anti-Semitism coming upon the world (alas, to a large extent provoked by Jews completely devoid of morality). I want to remain among those who tomorrow will be the persecuted ones. Still I hope that a Catholic priest, if the Cardinal-Archbishop of Paris so allows, may say a prayer over my grave.

---

[146] Assimilation, and conversion, made these statistical figures difficult to ascertain with precision. Even in Italy, where the number of Jews was very small: "Contrary to what may be thought, to ascertain the sum-total of the Jewish population is by no means easy." De Felice, *EF*, 5.

It would be a mistake to think that what Bergson saw as the coming tremendous wave of anti-Semitism was the creation of the Germans alone. On the other hand, the impressive rise of the anti-Semitic Third Reich would convert all kinds of people to anti-Semitism who had not given it much thought before. This kind of opportunism was conscious in some instances, hardly conscious in others. As we have seen before, the anti-Jewish legislation of governments under the German shadow was sometimes spontaneous, sometimes opportunistic; it is difficult to disentangle their motives.[147] In 1938 Mussolini's first anti-Jewish measures were spontaneous[148]; so were the first such measures by Vichy in the fall of

---

[147] The case of Hungary was not untypical. Restrictions upon Jews in certain fields was the official policy of the nationalist regime ever since the collapse of the Communist experiment in 1919, whose leadership had been heavily populated by Jews. The number of Jewish students were thereafter limited in the universities (as also in Romania and in Poland). In early March 1938—significantly, *before* Hitler's occupation of Austria—the then Prime Minister, Darányi, announced plans for general legislation limiting Jewish influences in Hungary. The first law was passed a few months afterward, limiting the participation of Jews in certain professions to 20 per cent. (This legislation was supported even by some of the conservative and democratic, that is, anti-German, deputies.) The second, more stringent, anti-Jewish legislation in 1939 reduced this percentage and proceeded toward a racial definition of who was a Jew. In 1941 another decree virtually defined Jews largely in accord with Nuremberg criteria. Yet these laws tell only a part of the story. *De facto*, Jews in Hungary, until 1944, when Hitler chose to occupy the country, were relatively untouched in certain spheres of everyday life. On other occasions, however, Jews were brutally and senselessly humiliated and mistreated by certain authorities; there were also certain occasions of murder perpetrated in the case of alien Jews deported to Kamenetsk-Podolsk in August 1941, of certain conscripted Jewish forced-labor battalions in Russia and in one case involving Jewish men, women, and children, in Ujvidék (Novisad), in January 1942.

[148] In 1932 Mussolini made the Jewish Guido Jung the Italian Minister of Finances (Mussolini said to intimates: "A Jew is needed there."). In 1933 and 1934 Mussolini suggested to Hitler that he moderate his pressure on the Jews. (See below, p. 451, n. 176, about Hitler's counterarguments in his interview with the Italian ambassador, Cerruti, on 31 March 1933; they are very significant.) The first signs of official anti-Semitic legislation in Italy were suggested in the pages of the journal *Informazione diplomatica* on 16 February 1938, that is, *before* Hitler's occupation of Austria. De Felice, *EF*, 410: "There is no evidence to the effect that Mussolini may have decided to suppress [the Jews] because of direct German pressure; thus one must conclude that this was a spontaneous decision on his part. For many years afterward in this application of anti-Semitic regulations he was not in the least influenced by the [German] Nazis."

1940.[149] These were measures of national sanification that men such as Mussolini and Pétain deemed desirable for some time; they were meant to put strong limits upon the influence of Jews in their respective countries. The condition that such legislation would bring them into accord with German practices was a contributory rather than a principal factor in their decisions.

A certain criticism of Jewish influences existed among the most determined enemies of Nazidom. In *The Gathering Storm*, written after the war, Churchill recounted how Hitler had missed the opportunity of meeting him in 1932. The latter's well-bred middleman, "Putzi" Hanfstaengl, spent an evening with Churchill's party in a Munich hotel. Churchill told him that he was willing to meet Hitler, and that one thing that he could not understand was Hitler's obsession with Jewish birth:

> Why is your chief so violent about the Jews? I can quite understand being angry with Jews who have done wrong or are against the country, and I understand resisting them if they try to monopolise power in any walk of life; but what is the sense of being against a man simply because of his birth? How can any man help how he is born?[150]

The great good common sense of this great man shines through these phrases: It illuminates the falsity of much that goes under the philosophy of anti-Semitism in an instant.

I cited this example to show that Churchill, too, could "understand" a certain kind of concern with undue influences exercised by certain Jews on certain occasions. This latent irritation with certain Jews would crop up in England even in 1940.[151] Little of its evidence survives on paper; but there is, again, the diary of that deeply concerned humanist, George Orwell. On 15 October 1940: "Some murmurings about the number of Jews in Baldock—declares that Jews greatly predominant among the people sheltering in the Tubes. Must try and verify this." Ten days later:

---

[149] "Germany was not the source of anti-Jewish legislation by Vichy. This legislation was, if I may say, spontaneous and autochthonous." Du Moulin, 280.

[150] Churchill, *GS*, 83–84. A more detailed, and somewhat corrected, description of this missed encounter—with a significant reference to Hitler's Francophobia ("in any case, they say your Mr. Churchill is a rapid Francophile"), in Hanfstaengl, 184–86.

[151] Spears on Bordeaux, 15 June 1940: "We saw that some men turned into jellies by fear. As Georges Mandel, easily the bravest man in Bordeaux, was a Jew, I can say that some of his co-religionists . . . were so transfigured by fear as to be totally unrecognizable." Spears, II, 260.

The other night examined the crowds sheltering in Chancery Lane, Oxford Circus and Baker Street stations. *Not* all Jews, but, I think, a higher proportion of Jews than one would normally see in a crowd of this size. What is bad about Jews is that they are not only conspicuous, but go out of their way to make themselves so. A fearful Jewish woman, a regular comic paper cartoon of a Jewess, fought her way off the train at Oxford Circus, landing blows on anyone who stood in her way. . . .
Surprised to find that D, who is distinctly Left in his views, is inclined to share the current feeling against the Jews. . . .[152]

Thus a kind of selective anti-Jewish feeling would persist even among the avowed and bravest enemies of Hitler during the war. Patriotic Jews, such as Georges Mandel, felt it to the marrow of their bones.[153] In June Mandel said to his few friends that his bravery no longer served either him or his France, for the very condition that he was a Jew compromised his insistence on continuing to fight the Germans.[154] Charles de Gaulle was reputed to have been bitter that among the few Frenchmen who joined him during the first days in London many were Jews—not because De Gaulle was anti-Semitic, but because he knew and felt that the presence of so many Jews in his small patriotic grouping would make it unrepresentative and unpopular.

"The Jews are rotten soldiers," said Stalin to the Polish General Anders in December 1941; "they are poor soldiers," he said to the Polish minister Kot, it is "not worth discussing them."[155] Alone among the statesmen of the anti-Hitler coalition, Stalin would not care a whit for what was about to happen to the Jews in death camps; it may even be that he admired Hitler for his resolution in dealing with the Jews. (In turn, there is reason to believe that Hitler's inclination to reach an agreement with Stalin in 1939 was fortified by his impression of how Stalin had eliminated many Jewish Bolsheviks during the purges of 1936–39.) Thus

---

[152] *Orwell*, II, 377, 378.

[153] It was under his rule as Minister of the Interior that many alien Jews were interned in the camp of Le Vernet.

[154] Thus the scathing comment of Fabre-Luce on Mandel is especially unjust; "Beneath his nationalism lies his absolute contempt (*mépris*) of France." Fabre-Luce, I, 227. In writing this Fabre-Luce is contemptible, not Mandel.

[155] Kot, 153. It must be admitted that Anders, sensing Stalin's anti-Semitic sentiments, tried to appeal to them: "Many of the Jews who have applied to join are speculators or people who have been punished for smuggling; they will never make good soldiers." He evidently did not want to see too many Jews in the free Polish army formed in Russia. (A that time nearly 30 per cent of the volunteers in the 5th Polish Division within the Soviet Union were Jews.)

dislike of the Jews was not always absent from the sentiments of those who fought the Third Reich during the Second World War—a condition disproving Hitler's argument that he was fighting the joint forces of Bolshevism and Judaism.

There were, on the other hand, many people, including profound and prophetic writers and thinkers who, deeply vexed though they had been earlier with the Jewish presence in the midst of their peoples, turned resolutely against Hitler. Transcending their earlier anti-Semitism, they became lone torch-bearers of Christian resistance. Perhaps the outstanding example among these men was Bernanos, who had written one of his first books in praise of the anti-Jewish prophet Édouard Drumont in 1931. There were other, perhaps less inspiring, examples. But in many instances statesmen and writers who had been anti-Jewish in 1920 were opponents of Hitler in 1940—because they saw Nazism as a greater danger than Communism or Judaism.[156] During his abortive attempt to bring Hitler to meet Churchill in 1932, Hanfstaengl remembered the latter's words: "Tell your boss from me," Churchill told Hanfstaengl, "that anti-Semitism may be a good starter, but it is a bad sticker."

This may have been true in Western Europe. Anti-Semitism in Italy, as we have seen, was unpopular. At any rate—or, rather, at a high rate— honorary "Aryanization" was possible in Italy through the office of a Fascist hierarch, Buffarini-Guidi; it could be bought by heavy sums. Here, as in many other instances, corruption mitigated tyranny. There was more to this than mere greed: We have seen that in Croatia and Greece the Italian military would naturally and spontaneously protect local Jews from the excesses of local fanatics and criminals. After the terrible blow that had befallen them in 1940, most of the Belgians, Dutch, and French were indifferent to the first anti-Jewish measures. This kind of passive attitude remained selective: Many would be indifferent to the fate of foreign Jews in their midst, but few refused at least some assist-

---

[156] Examples of this were numerous in Hungary; for example, the great Magyar historian Gyula Szekfü. Here is another example from the confidential letter of the Regent, Horthy, to Prime Minister Teleki on 14 October 1940: "So far as the Jewish question goes, I was anti-Semitic through my entire life. . . . Perhaps I was first in propagating anti-Semitism in a loud voice, yet I cannot silently look at inhumanity, sadism, purposeless humiliation, when we still need them [the Jews]. In addition for my country I regard the Nyilas [the Hungarian National Socialists] far more dangerous and far less valuable than the Jew. The latter is bound to us by his interest, and he is more faithful to his adopted country than the Nyilas who . . . want to hand our country over to the Germans." *Horthy TI*, 262.

ance to their native Jews. Laval, far more set on a pro-German course than Pétain, was less inclined to favor anti-Semitic measures than was the latter.[157] Yet, in order to curry favor with Hitler, Laval would make a few scathing remarks about Jewish influences during their first interview. This kind of selective anti-Semitism prevailed for a while. The anti-Semitic Scapini succeeded in making sure that Jews among the French prisoners of war in Germany would not be separated from the others. For about a year after the fall of Paris the daily life of Jews there was still largely unvexed, even as a terrible threat hung over their heads. Not all of the French National Socialists and collaborationists were extreme anti-Semites. Fernand de Brinon represented the government at Bergson's funeral. "Even as late as 1942, Marcel Déat distinguished between the Jew who was harmful to the French community and who should be deported, and the Jew who fought and shed his blood for France and who should be acepted as 'an honorable and honored ally.' "[158] Statements such as this may be interesting in retrospect. Yet they had few practical consequences. The anti-Semitism of a Mussolini, of a Laval, of a Déat may have been selective; but in the end these men did little or nothing to save the Jews from the clutches of Eichmann and of his German likes. Again I am reminded of the condition that men will adjust their ideas to circumstances with far more ease than they will adjust circumstances to their ideas; again, I insist that we ought to reverse Hegel and Dostoevsky, et al.: What ideas do to men is important, but what men do to their ideas is even more real.

There was, however, a difference: that between the peoples of Western and of Eastern Europe. There was little or no selectivity in Eastern European anti-Semitism. Let me repeat what I said a few pages earlier: In the Soviet Union avowed Communists would often deliver Jews to their death; in France avowed Fascists would often help individual Jews. The extremist Fascist Roberto Farinacci, an anti-Semite and pro-Nazi, demanded in an article in 1936 that Jews should be "Fascists first, Jews second."[159] Farinacci did not understand that to his admired German allies this would have meant nothing. Rather, the contrary: the

---

[157] Baudouin, 255, 236.
[158] Soucy article in Greene, 289.
[159] Jews in Italy were to be found among the early Fascists; more than two hundred of them took part in the March on Rome in 1922; Fascist volunteers in the Spanish Civil War numbered a few Jews, one of whom (Liuzzi) died in battle; the first officers of the later Israeli Navy had been trained aboard a Zionist ship put at their use by the Italian government in the 1930s; Mussolini favored the Falasha Jews in Abyssinia, and on occasion he speculated about creating a small Jewish enclave there.

more assimilated, the more integrated, the more patriotic, the more Germanized the Jew, the more the Nazis wanted to get rid of him. To his sycophantic Fascist biographer, De Begnac, Mussolini said in October 1941: "The truly patriotic Jew loses the polemical characteristics of his race." Referring to General Pugliese, an Italian Jewish veteran who played an important role in repairing some of the damage in the harbor of Taranto in November 1940, Mussolini added: "I ordered the Aryanization of such fine men." Such an attitude on Hitler's part was inconceivable. In this respect Hitler's Judeophobia was even more typical of certain Eastern European than of certain old-German attitudes. There were people in Eastern Europe (the Iron Guard in Romania, for example) for whom the very cruelty of the Germans to the Jews made the former popular. This was perhaps even true of certain peoples of the Soviet Union, a condition that is usually passed over in silence by those who ought to know better.[160] Among the victims of the Germans, the Czechs were not anti-Semitic but, as Mastny put it, "examples of effective help were rare."[161] It is more difficult to generalize about Poles, among whom anti-Semitism persisted, even as effective help to Jews was not infrequent. There were instances of avowed anti-Semitism among the Polish exiles in England; there was much anti-Semitism current among the Polish refugees in the Soviet Union, where approximately one of three among them were Jews. In discriminating between Jews and Poles, the Poles there sometimes played unwittingly into the hands of the no less anti-Semitic Soviets, who would thereby succeed in reducing the importance of the Polish military units raised in the Soviet Union during the fall and winter of 1941–42. Many of the unfortunate Jews who had fled to the Soviet Union in 1941 were cured of whatever pro-Soviet sen-

---

[160] There is some reason to think that the relative silence of the Soviet government in regard to the German murders of Jews in the western Soviet Union—a silent treatment that stands in noteworthy contrast with the Soviet atrocity campaign accusing the Germans—issued, and still issues, from the consideration of the Soviet rulers to the effect that repeated reminders of how the Germans had treated the Jews would not at all result in increasing Germanophobia among the people; rather, the contrary.

Among anti-Soviet exiles the silence is no less impressive. In the valuable two-volume work of Ilnytzky, *Deutschland und die Ukraine* (Munich, 1956), an extremely detailed documentary of the relations of Germans and Ukrainians during the Second World War, there is hardly a word about the Jews, in spite of the treatment of the latter having been, in many instances, an important element in German-Ukrainian relations.

[161] "Only an estimated 424 Jews survived the war in hiding, a figure believed to be proportional about the same as in Germany or even lower." Mastny, 183.

timents they may have possessed[162]; many wanted to enroll in Polish units, if only to avoid the dubious advantages of Soviet citizenship. In some instances Poles as well as Russians made this impossible for them—especially after December 1941, when a Soviet decree forbade the enrollment of "non-Polish" persons into these units.

Generally, the farther east we look, the less we find the persecution of the Jews alleviated by popular sympathy. In this respect, too, Germany was in the middle of the Continent. The few surviving Jews remembered that on that bitterest of days, 19 September 1941, when they were ordered to wear the yellow star in public, a number of Germans on the streets offered signs and, on occasion, small acts of sympathy to them.[163]

But these variations of attitudes, too, made little difference in the long run: For Hitler's attitude toward the Jews would not change. To solve the Jewish problem: This was the principal purpose of his life, a conviction that he reaffirmed in his testament a few hours before his death. Since he was the protagonist of the Second World War in Europe, I feel obliged to say something, for the last time, about Hitler's principal conviction, inasmuch as this influenced not only the course of his actions against Jews but also his course of action in the war. It must be understood that Hitler was not a typical racist, the kind of person who attributes everything to biological differences and who consequently rationalizes his dislike of Jews or of blacks or of Indians. Hitler's basic conviction was his Judeophobia; his racism was consequential, and secondary,[164] to that. The *motives* of his Judeophobia were, and remain,

---

[162] In 1939 and in 1940 (no doubt in part because of their preference of the Soviets over Germans), a number of Jews played conspicuous roles in welcoming the Soviet incorporation of eastern Poland and certain Baltic states. (See, for example, the dispatch of the nuncio from Kaunas, Monsignor Centoz, to Monsignor Montini [the present Pope Paul VI] on 6 August 1940, in *VD*, 3*, 284.)

[163] "Anti-semitism may be a good starter, but it is a bad sticker." This was especially true of Bavaria. In Munich, once the cradle of the Nazi movement, on 19 September 1941, from the diary of a Jewish survivor: "How does the population react? Most people pretend not to see the yellow star. Very rarely does someone express its satisfaction in the streetcar to the effect that from now on 'the pack of Jews' could be recognized at once. Yet we experienced and continue experiencing many expressions of horror over this regulation, and many expressions of sympathy for its victims. . . ." Behrend-Rosenfeld, 132–33.

[164] His Judeophobia was extraordinary; his racism was rather ordinary and not untypical of a certain kind of German racism. His Judeophobia was rigid and

obscure. This is where psychological categorization usually goes wrong, in spite of its superficial sophistication, because of its primitive attributions of causalities; for there is a difference between motives and purposes, a difference of which contemporary philosophy, including professional historianship, remains painfully ignorant. The two are not always and altogether separable; still, it is the historian's task to describe purposes rather than speculate about motives. There is some evidence to the effect that Hitler thought that his father had been half Jewish.[165] Whether this effect was the principal motive of his Judeophobia is difficult to tell. The latter was a phobia, to be sure, a phobia powerful enough to govern the principal purposes of his life. He may have wanted to get rid of Jewishness within himself; we do not know. What we know is that he wanted to get rid of Jewishness within Germany and within Europe. "Getting rid" is the operative phrase. We have seen that between January 1939 and January 1942 Hitler's policy toward the Jews of Europe developed gradually from expulsion to extermination. "Getting rid" explains much of this, if not all. Hitler, as also other German anti-Semites, kept referring to the Jews as parasites, pests.[166] "Getting rid" of something or of somebody does not necessarily mean that one needs to annihilate him; yet in extreme circumstances annihilation might become necessary.[167]

It is true that a careful scrutiny of Hitler's expressions will show a reference to the extermination of certain Jews that cropped up well before 1939. There is a passage in *Mein Kampf* that perhaps during the First World War, "twelve or fifteen thousand of these Hebrew corrup-

---

consistent, while his racism was inconsistent and flexible. (He sought alliances with Moors, Arabs, Japanese, Chinese. He often spoke contemptuously of Rosenberg's official racist philosophy. About his reservations re the biological concept of races, see also above, pp. 397–98). When in 1940 Himmler began to recruit SS volunteers from among Nordic nations—Dutch, Norwegians, Flemish, etc.—Hitler, as Wright puts it, "remained skeptical about this experiment; more clearly than Himmler, he instinctively recognized the surviving hold of national sentiment even among the Nazis of the conquered land." Wright, 141–42.

[165] His father wasn't. See the most conclusive discussion of this in Maser, 26 ff.

[166] It is significant that the gas used for the mass extermination of Jews was "Zyklon B," used beforehand in exterminating domestic parasites such as bedbugs. "Zyklon" was a household trademark word in Central Europe in 1939. Only after 1945 did it become known for what purposes it was used during the war.

[167] It is typical of the extreme nationalist that he is more obsessed with the danger of internal subversion than of external enemies to his country. (Alfred Duff Cooper: The jingo nationalist "is always the first to denounce his fellow countrymen as traitors.") Hitler, too, was more obsessed with Jews within Europe than with the danger to Europe from other races.

tionists" should have been gassed, rather than hundreds of thousands of the best of Germans on the front. Note, however, that here Hitler spoke of but a small number of evil Jews, not yet of the entirety of Jews in Germany. We have seen that he preferred expulsion rather than extermination,[168] even after he came to power in 1933. We have also seen that during the winter of 1938–39 this policy was suddenly hardening. Now for the first time Hitler's design began to involve the Jews of all Europe. On 24 November 1938 he told the visiting Oswald Pirow, the Germanophile South African Minister of Economy and Defense: "One day the Jews will disappear from Europe. The last thing Judaism wants is to see the Jews disappear from Europe."[169] It is significant that he should speak of Europe at large. On the one hand, it suggests his notion of his European hegemony. On the other hand, it suggests that core of realism that, alas, was seldom absent within his megalomania. He could not lay his hands on America's Jews. He also hoped that the mass migration of Jews from Europe to America would create a formidable wave of anti-Semitism there. "Getting rid" often includes the wish to root out this or that pest and transfer it somewhere else. "Getting rid" of the Jews in Europe meant to saddle America with this problem, if need be.

He also knew that the Jews of America, influential around Roosevelt, wanted his destruction.[170] I suggested earlier that this may have been the key to his change of policy in January 1939. It was the key, too, to his policy of forced emigration during the first two years of the Second World War. On 6 April 1941 he told the Hungarian minister, Sztójay, that the governments of European states must get rid of their Jews. They must emigrate. "Millions of decent Germans, Hungarians,

---

[168] There were, of course, Nazis—and not only in Germany—who spoke of the desirability of extermination before 1939. Few were as outspoken as the British extreme anti-Semite Arnold Leese, who wrote in the February 1935 number of his paper, *The Fascist:* "It must be admitted that the most certain and permanent way of disposing of the Jews would be to exterminate them by some humane method such as the lethal chamber. It is quite practicable but (some would say, unfortunately) in our time it is unlikely that the world will demand the adoption of that drastic procedure." Cited in Cross, 153.

[169] On 21 January 1939 (the date is significant; see above, p. 430) Hitler to the Czech Foreign Minister, Chvalkovsky: "We are going to destroy the Jews. They are not going to get away with what they did on 9 November 1918. The day of reckoning has come."

[170] His enemies knew this too. In 1939 the anti-Nazi Trott in Washington: "the influence of Supreme Court Justice Felix Frankfurter." Deutsch, 152. The French Ambassador in September 1940: "Strong Israelite influences, especially in the Treasury Department." Charles-Roux, 169. Jay Pierrepont Moffat of the State Department on 31 January 1941: "The power behind the throne was . . . Felix Frankfurter." *Moffat,* 349–50.

etc., had to emigrate, traveling in steerage. He sees no inhumanity in emigrant Jews traveling second class." On 30 January 1941 Hitler repeated his warning of two years before. "People should not forget [what I said before] . . . that, *if the other world* will be pushed into a world war (*in einem allgemeine Krieg*) the role of the entirety of Jewry in Europe will be finished, once and for all! They may laugh about this even now, just as they laughed earlier about my forecasts. . . ." Contrary to the still accepted view, Hitler was far from underestimating or dismissing the United States from his mind. To some extent the Jews of Europe were to be hostages, because of the United States.[171] But after Pearl Harbor the role of hostages was played out, it was done with.

I must insist, again and again, on the method within what otherwise must seem Hitler's madness. For him the problem of what to do with the Jews of Europe was integral to the problem of what to do with the war. We have seen that in November 1941 he began to admit the thought that he might no longer be able to win his European war.[172] And now the United States entered the war, an event which, to him, was evidently prepared and facilitated by powerful Jewish influences there. To get rid of the Jews in Europe by expelling them to America was no longer possible. There was now no other way out for them; and, perhaps, for him. The news of Pearl Harbor lifted the hearts of millions of Jews around the world. It was also the death knell for millions of Jews in Europe, even though none of them knew this. Few people know it even now, though much of the evidence points thereto.

The ominous conference at 56–58 Am Grossen Wannsee had been originally called for 29 November; it was then postponed to 8–9 December 1941, and it finally met on 20 January 1942, to set down the

---

[171] Ribbentrop was also aware of this. With characteristic heavy-handedness in July 1941 he instructed the German chargé in Washington that the latter try to suggest to influential American Jews the desirability of keeping the United States out of the war: for, in the case of America's participation in the world war, the influence of Jews in America would diminish, and in the case of setbacks and wartime privations anti-Semitism among Americans would result. (Also, as late as November 1941—that is, *after* the official suspension of emigration from Germany—the German Armistice Commission in Wiesbaden requested that the French give transit visas to those German Jews who were ready to emigrate *from Switzerland* through Vichy France and Spain to America. *CDA*, V, 299.) Until October 1941 the Germans allowed American Jewish organizations (Joint) to ship some food to ghettos in Poland.

[172] See above, pp. 157–58. The principal American historian of Hitler's war aims is quite wrong about this: "It has been suggested that it was precisely because the war was lost that Hitler was determined to wreak this last grim vengeance for his defeat. But this thesis is surely untenable." Rich, 11. By no means.

guidelines of the "final solution." There is no decree, no piece of evidence bearing Hitler's signature that records his assent to the extermination of the Jews[173]; there is evidence that he would still prefer expulsion to extermination[174]; still, there is place for little or no doubt that he knew what was about to begin. He would refer to his 30 January 1939 "warning" to the Jews over and over again in his public speeches, as for

---

[173] Krausnick, 59: "The exact moment in which Hitler made up his mind that the Jews must be physically destroyed cannot be precisely determined by the evidence available." Krausnick thinks that "it cannot have been later than March 1941." (Krausnick, 60). Maser, 334, cites a cryptic entry in Rosenberg's diary on 2 April 1941: "There is something that I shall not put down in writing today, but I shall never forget it." Yet insufficient attention has been directed to the significant passage in Reitlinger, *FS*, 50–51: "The history of the first stage in the deportation of Jewry, the stage that ended in October 1941, shows that the Germans were sensitive to American opinion and until June 22 to Russian opinion. Thus, while the conditions were invariably murderous, deliberate mass murder was not practiced. It is significant that Frank used the words: 'Liquidate them yourselves' nine days after Pearl Harbor and that the first gassings in Poland took place at the end of that year. *It may even be doubted whether the Fuehrer Order to exterminate Russian Jewry would have spread west of the former Russian demarcation line, if the United States had not entered the war on December 7, 1941*" [my italics].

[174] See, for example, his table conversation on 23 January 1942 (again the date is significant): "One must act radically. When one pulls a tooth, the pain quickly goes away. The Jew must clear out of Europe. Otherwise no understanding will be possible between Europeans. It is the Jew who prevents everything. When I think about it, I realize that I'm extraordinarily humane . . . I restrict myself to telling them they must go away. If they break their pipes on the journey, I can't do anything about it. But if they refuse to go voluntarily, I see no other solution but extermination." His Chancery secretary, Lammers, in Nuremberg "gave his version of his non-involvement . . . he had asked Hitler in early 1942 what the 'Final Solution' was; Hitler refused to discuss it, except to say he had given Himmler the order for the evacuation of the Jews. After a March 1942 meeting attended by one of his staff, Lammers prepared a long report, hoping to provoke a discussion, but Hitler refused to talk about the matter and insisted there be no more reports. . . ." Peterson, 30. As late as 1944 Hitler would consent to the emigration of certain Jews; on one instance he spoke of the desirability of their ruthless employment in certain industries (Milward, 128). "Although throughout the war Hitler continued his diatribes against Jewish finance, at no moment did he seriously attempt to stop the Gestapo trafficking in the lives of Jewish property-owners . . . he lost interest in the devilish thing he started. . . . Only toward the end of the war he appears to have become aware of the extent to which his orders had been disregarded and of the scale on which European Jewry had survived. . . ." Reitlinger, *FS*, 4–5.

example on 24 February, 30 September, and 8 November 1942 (he mis-dated the original warning in these speeches, when he kept saying that he had warned the Jews at the outbreak of the war, referring to his speech of 1 September 1939—in which, however, he made no reference to the Jews). Whether this error[175] was voluntary or involuntary, Hitler connected the outbreak of the war with his decision to dispose of the Jewish problem. What he did not say in public he would say to his private circle, near the end of the war: Germany may lose this war, but at least he did cleanse Germany, and Central Europe, of its Jews. And this was one of the principal—perhaps *the* principal—aims of his entire life.[176]

Hitler lost the war against the great powers of the world; but he won his terrible war against the Jews. He went to his death with this belief, and this is the accepted belief even now in a world that despises his name. Yet this is not so; for, in the end, he lost his war against the Jews, too. I am not only speaking of the fact that in 1945 millions of Jews still remained alive in Europe, not to speak of many more millions in America. I am speaking of the "Jewish problem" in the minds of nations and of peoples: For it was Hitler's "final solution" that made anti-Semitism unpopular to the point of it being literally unavowable and un-speakable, nearly everywhere in the civilized world. Let us suppose that the Germans had not decided upon the mass killings of the Jews of Europe after December 1941, even as they would have gone on to coerce, mistreat, humiliate, and expel them. It would not have affected the out-come of the war. After the war millions of Jews, especially in Eastern and Central Europe, including Germany, emerging from these humiliat-ing sufferings with tortured souls, may have demanded revenge, compen-sation, special privilege. This would have turned many people against them (as, indeed, anti-Semitism reappeared in Poland and Hungary im-mediately after the war, under much less excusable circumstances). Stalin and the Soviet Union might have opened the western gates of the Soviet

---

[175] See the discussion of this in Jaeckel, 81–84.

[176] Hitler to the Italian ambassador, Cerruti, on 31 March 1933 (see above, p. 440): Mussolini, whom he admires, does not understand the Jewish question, which he (Hitler) has studied "for long years, from every angle, like no one else" . . . "I don't know whether my name will be held in high repute in Ger-many two or three hundred years from now, no matter what I am hoping to achieve for my people, but in one matter I am absolutely certain: In five or six hundred years the name of Hitler shall be glorified everywhere as the person who once and for all had extirpated the Jewish pest from the world." Cerruti, 150.

empire and let millions of Jews stream westward, in order to cause dissension and trouble. In short, anti-Semitism may have been rampant in Europe and, presumably, in America, too—something that Hitler had often predicted. He could have gone to his grave with the conviction that he had planted the seeds of a formidable wave of Judeophobia. Instead, he believed that he had made a good harvest of the chaff. But he did not only overlook the stubble; his last casting of the seed of Judeophobia—his principal warning in the last paragraph of his testament to his people[177]—fell on arid ground, even in Germany.

There is another, allied, consideration. It is now universally thought that Nazism was much more criminal than Communism. Now this argument, taken for granted by the liberal mind, will stand *only* because of the Jewish issue. The German people were better off under Hitler than the Russian people have ever been under Lenin or Stalin or their successors. It may even be argued that many of the peoples of Europe under German occupation suffered less than some of the peoples of Eastern Europe would suffer under the Russians. Had Hitler and his cohorts not committed their awful deed of a mass murder of Jews, sooner or later thoughtful people might have become amenable to the argument that, after all was said, Hitler and Nazism were less evil and much less cruel than Stalin and Communism. The strength inherent in this argument ought not be underrated. There are millions in Europe, and not only in Germany, who believe this even now. For those who don't, the decisive argument is the mass murder of the Jews. It is because of this sad and horrible deed that Hitler may never inspire the respect that is sometimes the due of a Napoleon. Innocent Jewish children, mothers, old men, young people, together with other millions, vanished without a trace from the earth. Their blood stains our memories, a stain that may have saved later Jewish generations from the scourge of persecution, a stain that is large enough to darken Hitler's place in history, for a long time, perhaps forever.

At the beginning of the twentieth century in Vienna, the Vienna in the atmosphere of which Hitler was to live, an extraordinary young Jewish genius, Otto Weininger, wrote an extraordinary book entitled *Geschlecht und Charakter* (Sex and Character) about women and men, Jews and Christians, the problem of whose relationships consumed his fiery mind. Weininger, who was appalled by the increasing influence of

---

[177] "Above all I charge the leaders of the nation and those under them to scrupulous observance of the laws of race and to merciless opposition to the universal poisoner of all peoples, international Jewry."

what he saw as a new and godless breed among the Jews of Europe, was probably right in foreseeing the rise of a tremendous movement of anti-Semitism. He was wrong in believing that this would be the result of a new, rising Christianity:

> Against this new Jewry a new Christianity comes to light: Humanity thirsts for the founder of a new religion, and the struggle moves toward a decision as in The Year One. Between Jewry and Christianity, between commerce and culture, between woman and man, between earthbound life and a higher life, between nothingness and Godhead mankind will again have to choose. These are the two opposite kingdoms; *There is no Third Reich*.[178]

There *was* to be a Third Reich, a Third Reich that was to be ruled not by the religion of Christianity but by the religion of the folk. As Hitler, the prophet of this religion, said in Salzburg on 6 April 1938: "In the beginning was the *Volk*, and only then came the *Reich*."[179]

Weininger had killed himself in 1903 at the age of twenty-three, it seems because of his disillusionment with Christianity.[180] The cult of the *Volk*, not of Christianity, was to be the principal enemy of Judaism. And where would Christianity stand now in this mortal struggle?

---

[178] Weininger, 288. (*Das sind die beiden Pole; es gibt kein drittes Reich.*)

[179] See above about *Volksgenossenstaat*, p. 324.

[180] On 1 December 1941 Hitler speculated at his table: Were there, are there, any decent Jews? Hardly any, he said. (He would admit the existence of some.) Dietrich Eckart, his early mentor, "told me once, he knew but *one* decent Jew [Hitler's italics], Otto Weininger, who took his own life as he realized that the Jew lives by the decomposition of other nations and peoples! (*von der Zersetzung anderer Volkstums lebt!*) Hitler TG, 36.

# 6 . The convergences of thought and of belief

LOVE, AS PASCAL SAID, is not really blind. When the arms clash, the Muses are not silent. These are not abstract refutations of ancient saws. During the twentieth century more and more people have been thinking more and more (though not necessarily better). Education, technology, and publicity lead to the intellectualization of life. Propaganda, pictorialization, and mass communications flourish during modern war; we have dealt with some of their manifestations and effects: Even though ephemeral and superficial, these effects must be noted by the historian of politics as well as by the historian of culture. In the history of art and music and literature, two or three years, 1939–41, was of course too short a period for new forms to crystallize, even as painters, composers, writers, and poets were far from uninfluenced by what they thought was the development of events in the world. (Had Hitler won the war, the history of European art, and not only the history of European artists, would have been quite different—at least for a while.) In other, perhaps more mundane, matters, the thinking of people did crystallize into recognizable forms. Such various matters include the beginnings of the resistance movements, of a tendency toward European supernationalism, of the Americanization of mass culture, and of the feasibility of atomic bombs.

We must look at the churches, and include religion. This is not an easy task. We know little or nothing of what people believe. It is difficult enough to reconstruct what people did; it is much more difficult to reconstruct what they may have thought; it is nearly impossible to reconstruct what they believed. The historian cannot penetrate the souls of people, most of whom are dead. If he is sufficiently thoughtful, he will recognize that the idiotic categories of psychohistorians and of religious sociologists are of no help to him. Rather, he will keep in mind the wise and profound remark of Dr. Johnson: "Intentions must be gathered from acts." So with beliefs. We know little or nothing of what people believe. We know a little—very little—more about what they think, including at times what they think they believe. All the historian can say is that by their acts and their words people sometimes reveal some of their dispositions. In the next subchapter we shall attempt to say something about the acts and words of professedly religious people, rather than about the categories of their beliefs.

# RELIGION

¶ In 1939 the vast majority of the peoples of Europe, excluding the Soviet Union, were baptized Christians. At least eight out of ten inhabitants of the Continent, again excluding the Soviet Union, were baptized Catholics. These numbers are nearly meaningless. Only a minority were regular churchgoers. The erosion of the power of the churches had been going on for centuries. After the First World War a broad revival of religious sentiment (a phenomenon that had followed the revolutionary and Napoleonic wars and that was to follow the Second World War) did not occur. Shortly before 1939 the prestige of religion, especially of Catholicism, began to increase, mostly among opponents of the new totalitarian philosophies and regimes. This was not a mass phenomenon, however.

Most generalizations are useless, too. There were vast differences from country to country, from one end of Europe to another. In England the cult of a certain morality survived the abandonment of the churches; in Russia it did not. The English working class may have been among the least religious in Europe; it was surely the least revolutionary. Most people went to church in Ireland and in Poland, the fewest went to church in the Soviet Union and in Sweden, peoples with hardly anything else in common. The influence of the churches was stronger in the South and the East than in the West and the North of the Continent. Again, there were many exceptions: Ireland, Holland, Spain. Again, the generalizations do not help us. Influence was one thing; respect, another. In the agnostic France of the 1930s the traditionally popular and intellectual disrespect for religion was beginning to disappear.[1] Among the Greek Orthodox peoples of Eastern Europe the powers of the established clergy were beginning to provoke stirrings of disrespect. In June 1940 Henry de

---

[1] Example: In 1939 it was *bon ton* for certain Catholic families in France to have the required civil marriage performed a few days before the church wedding; and a well-mannered *maire* would tactfully address his congratulations to the bride as *Mademoiselle*—that is, a wife yet to be.

Montherlant, speculating about the dead god Pan, looking out to the sea from the decaying quays of Marseilles, wrote: "I believe that Europe must break away from Christianity for a long time. . . ." This is what radical intellectuals were thinking in Serbia or Bulgaria, not in France, where in 1940 Socialists and atheists were reading Péguy and Bernanos for consolation. The Soviet ambassador to Germany (Skvartsev) told a German diplomat (Woermann) in January 1940 that the Vatican and Catholicism were "dead." He was even more wrong than Montherlant, which should be no surprise. In 1935 his master Stalin had addressed a rhetorical question to Laval: "how many divisions has the Pope?," implying that the latter had none at all.[2]

Our problem is not how many divisions the Pope had but where did they stand, how did they fight, if indeed they stood or fought at all. Our problem is how to ascertain the quality, rather than the extent, of religious influences: *How*, rather than *how much* religion influenced the thoughts and words and acts of peoples. And here we encounter the phenomenon that we met, again and again, throughout this book: the overwhelming influence of nationality in the minds of people. With very few exceptions, people were Hungarians or Danes or Englishmen first, Catholics or Protestants second. A German Catholic thought of himself as a German who happened to be a Catholic, not the reverse. It was as simple as this—or as complicated. There was nothing very new in this—certainly not in the age marked by nationalism. What was relatively new was the influence of nationalism among the consecrated representatives of the churches, especially of Catholics who were (or, rather, should have been) the representatives of a universal and supranational faith.

The most glaring examples of nationalist religion existed in certain places of Eastern Europe. In 1939 and after, entire nations in Central and Eastern Europe found themselves on the side of the Third Reich. Among some of these peoples both the hierarchy and the masses of practicing Catholics welcomed the alliance with the Germans. At least for some time they saw little or no conflict between the principles of their accustomed religion and those of the Germans. The clearest examples of this were in Slovakia and Croatia. They came into existence because Hitler had destroyed the multinational states of Czechoslovakia and Yugoslavia, within which many Slovaks and Croats had felt that they were subordinated by the ruling Czechs and Serbs. Monsignor Tiso, a Catholic priest,

---

[2] This is one of the few witticisms attributed to Stalin. In reality, he had taken it from Napoleon.

became the President of Slovakia in 1939.[3] His populist[4] religion was typical of much of Eastern Europe. He followed Hitler to the end, notwithstanding warnings and admonitions from the Vatican. Among Tiso's grievous errors, his unwillingness to resist the expulsion and the eventual extermination of the Jews in Slovakia stands out—an unwillingness that he shared with the majority of his countrymen.[5] The record of the Croatians was even worse. Encouraged by their own, fanatically nationalist, Catholic clergy (among them the Croatian Franciscans played an especially atrocious role), in the summer of 1941 Croatians massacred perhaps as many as one hundred thousand Orthodox Serbians and Jews.[6] There were priests and monks who prided themselves for having cut the throats of hundreds of Serbians.[7] For the first time in centuries they en-

---

[3] Another priest, the Uniate Catholic Monsignor Volosin, was the President of the short-lived state of Carpatho-Ukraine in 1939. The Vatican was opposed to ecclesiastics assuming high political positions: See the dispatch by Maglione on 21 August 1940 and Tardini's memorandum of 12 November 1939, *VD*, 4, 115.

[4] The Slovak nationalist Catholic party, founded by another priest, Father Hlinka, bore the name People's Party. Its kind of Catholic populism existed in Lithuania, the Ukraine, and Croatia, also in Austria, Hungary, Bavaria, and the United States. It had, with the partial exception of the Flemish, no equivalents in Western Europe.

[5] A typical example of Tiso's Eastern-European nationalist concept of Catholicism may be found in his speech of 7 September 1941, in which he praised German National Socialism, whose doctrine, according to him, was very similar to that of the Catholic Church. He also said that the encyclicals of the Pope, to whom he paid unctuous verbal allegiance, "are His dogmatic teachings, supreme principles, which the Pope allows the leaders of each nation to apply according to their particular conditions." The nuncio remonstrated against this. *VD*, 4, 278; also 301–2.

[6] Both the German and the Italian occupation authorities were appalled. On occasion they would protect Serbs (the Italians both Serbs and Jews) from their killers. The following passage appeared in an article in an Italian newspaper, the Bologna *Resto del Carlino*, about the massacres: "There have been, and probably still are, bands of murderers led and inflamed by Catholic priests and monks. The thing has been proved to the hilt: At Travnik, a hundred kilometers south of Banjaluka . . . a friar who was caught urging on with his crucifix a band of which he was the leader. . . . So we have the Middle Ages, but made much worse by the use of machine guns, hand grenades, tins of petrol and charges of dynamite. . . ." Croatian Franciscans "kill, bury alive, throw the dead into rivers, into the seas, over precipices. . . ." Zoli article in *Resto del Carlino* (18 and 21 Sept. 1941), cited by Falconi, 299–300.

[7] Examples: The Franciscan Father Brzica boasted of having himself cut the throats of more than one thousand Serbs. Other priest-killers were Fathers

forced mass conversions at the threat of death.[8] Their bishops did little or nothing to restrain them.[9]

In Eastern Europe, where these repellent examples of nationalist religion flourished, the adjective "Christian" had had a political and racial connotation for decades. In many places, and among many peoples, "Christian" meant, simply and squarely, non-Jewish. After the First World War, as a reaction to international Communism and to liberal cosmopolitanism, "Christian" acquired the additional connotation of nationalism and of anti-Communism. It had much to do with ideology, politics, and race; it had little to do with the Gospels. Among the younger clergy there were some who saw themselves as the idealist representatives of national populism.[10] Their allegiance to their people counted more than their allegiance to the supranational Church of Rome, with its antiquated cosmopolitan characteristics. They saw themselves as the vanguards of a spiritual renewal among their peoples.[11] Among the peoples who were

---

Filipovic-Majstrorovic, Bralo, Kamber, Djuric, Mogus, Klaric, Vukelic, Medic, Prlic, Pilogrvic, and Cvitan. Laurière, 95 ff.

[8] The populist tendency appears clearly from the letter of the Croatian Ministry of Justice and Cults to the bishops, in June 1941: "The Government desires that priests, intellectuals, managers, businessmen, rich peasants among the Orthodox should not be accepted into the Catholic Church. Only the poor Orthodox population should be converted." After numerous remonstrations from the Vatican the Croatian Bishops' Conference in December 1941 reluctantly forbade further pressures for mass conversions.

[9] Bishops Saric and Zimonic published "Odes" to Pavelic the leader of Croatia, in official Catholic newspapers (*Katolicki Tjednik, Hrvatski Narod.*) Saric was the leader of the "crusade" movement, started in the 1930s in Croatia. "In the service of truth, justice, and honor," he wrote in 1941, revolutionary methods are sometimes necessary. It is "stupid and unworthy of Christian disciples to think that the struggle against evil could be waged in a noble manner, with gloves on." Cited by Falconi, 294. Archbishop Stepinac, imprisoned by the Tito regime after the war, was more moderate; but he, too, did little to restrain the fanatics in the beginning.

[10] The Slovak minister, Tuka, to Ribbentrop in November 1940: The older Slovak priests were conservative, "the younger clergy, however, were already ardent National Socialists." *GD*, D, XI, 698. Pavelic said the same to Hitler in 1941.

[11] Most of these younger priests were narrow, fanatical, and half educated. There were, however, a handful of others, better educated, who would follow the same nationalist ideology, a vision that carried them close to Hitler; for example, two poet-priests, the Hungarian László Mécs and the Flemish Cyriel Verschaeve, the latter eventually the head of the National Socialist Flemish movement in exile, retreating to Germany in 1944.

subjugated by the Germans, a kind of anti-Semitic nationalism continued to prevail. In Poland the record of the clergy and of the hierarchy, otherwise almost unexceptionally patriotic and brave, in regard to Jews and other minorities was mixed. In Lithuania and in the Ukraine it was worse. The bishop of Kaunas, Brizgys, in August 1941 forbade all priests of his diocese "to intervene for Jews in whatever form. He refused the entreaties of numerous (Jewish) delegations who had come to him in person, begging for his intervention with the Germans."[12] Elsewhere the sorriest quarrels arose between Polish and Lithuanian prelates on occasion, even when the shadow of the Soviets was threatening them both.

These were some of the worst examples of religious nationalism. Religious nationalism was, of course, one thing; nationalism as a religion was another: The latter would often assume neopagan forms, as in the Third Reich. This distinction is meaningful only in retrospect. Religion and nationalism were often commingled inextricably in the minds of people, frequently with the result of confusion, uncertainty, and compromise. Religion and nationalism had been, after all, fighting the same enemies for a century at least: Communism, internationalism, liberalism. Most prominent Catholics (and also Protestants) still saw their principal enemies on the Left. France provides the best example of this, a country where the traditional Right and the Catholic Church had been allies for a long time, all of their minor squabbles notwithstanding. This seemed to be the case in 1939, when Pius XII lifted the ban, decreed by his predecessor in 1926, over the ultranationalist *Action Française.* In June 1940 the overwhelming majority of the hierarchy, the clergy, and the churchgoing minority of Frenchmen and Frenchwomen welcomed Pétain's assumption to power.[13] "Pétain is France, and France is Pétain!"

---

[12] *IMT*, No-2849. Later this attitude changed somewhat. In Vilna a Father Gylys bravely intervened for Jews as early as October 1941. The letters to Rome of the spiritual leader of the Uniate Ukrainians, Archbishop Szeptycki, contained many anti-Jewish allusions. (His letter to Cardinal Tisserant, 26 December 1939, in *VD*, 3*, 170.) At the end of this letter Szeptycki asked that Rome order secret prayers of exorcism against the Communists, whose "regime cannot be explained except by a massive possession by the Devil" (ibid., 172–73)—an example of the religious obscurantism residing in one portion of the split mind of this prelate, whose very nationalism ought to have told him that Communism was reigning in Lwow not because of the diabolical teachings of Marx but because Poland had been divided by Germany and Russia again.

[13] Fervent supporters of Pétain were Cardinals Gerlier and Baudrillart (the latter an extreme collaborationist, due to his obsession with Communism), also the Bishops of Grenoble, Arras, Mende, Nice, Nimes, and Aix, also the nuncio to France, Monsignor Valeri, in the beginning even Pastor Boegner, the leader

said Cardinal Gerlier of Lyon, not a collaborationist, in November 1940. Few French Catholics knew, or wished to know, that Pétain (unlike the deeply religious De Gaulle) was not much of a practicing Catholic (he rarely went to Mass, even in Vichy). The allocution of Archbishop Saliège of Toulouse in June 1940 clearly expressed what French Catholics were then thinking. France had suffered a defeat, God had chastised the French people

> for having expelled God from the schools of the nation,
> for having supported a sickening literature . . .
> for the depressing promiscuity in homes, offices, factories
> Lord, we ask your forgiveness. . . .
> What have we done with the victory of 1918?
> What would we have done with a victory in 1940?[14]

This was the same prelate who was to distinguish himself by his assistance to refugees and to Jews; who in 1942 was to defy both Vichy and the Germans by issuing what was perhaps the most inspiring pastoral letter of the entire Second World War in defense of the persecuted.

That was not merely a readjustment of opinions to changing experiences under the Germans, including the changing fortunes of the war. During 1941 the patriotic disillusionment with the Pétain regime involved more and more French Catholics. In January 1941 a priest in Toulouse (Monsignor de Solages) was reported to the police for having said that he preferred a victorious France governed by Léon Blum to a defeatist France governed by the Marshal—an eccentric minority opinion at the time. By December 1941 Monsignor de Solages was no longer a *rara avis* among French Catholics. The older Rightist equation of nationalism and Catholicism, meaning in practice the subordination of the latter to the former, was losing its appeal. The old Archbishop Chollet of Cambrai put his finger on the issue in a letter to the nuncio as early as 18 January 1941. Pétain had just given Cardinal Gerlier the text of a proposed radio speech, dealing with the principles of individual rights in France. "There are excellent things in it. There are deplorable things in it, too, in my opinion." For example: "The citizens owe their labor, their resources, their very life to the Fatherland." "Stalin," the archbishop added, "would gladly sign such a proposition."[15]

---

of French Protestantism. The Bishops of Toulouse, Montauban, Bayonne, and Dax were later among the early resistants.

[14] *La Croix* (28 June 1940), cited also in Vidalenc, 360–61.

[15] *VD*, 4, 354.

The peoples and the churches of many of the subjugated nations, especially in Western Europe, were fortunate in that there was little or no conflict between their patriotism and their religion; both were opposed to the principles and the practices of the Third Reich. The appeal of the churches, especially of the Catholic Church, rose in the latter half of 1940, leading to crowded churches, reconversions, and conversions.[16] Unusually large numbers of people filled the cathedrals and churches of England on 26 May 1940, a National Day of Prayer. The Dutch bishops condemned National Socialism in their pastoral letter of 13 January 1941, excerpts of which were even published in the Amsterdam newspaper *De Tijd*. In Belgium the conservative and royalist Cardinal Van Roey was a leader of the resistance.[17] Degrelle and the Rexists considered the cardinal their worst enemy.[18] The result was that the Catholics of Belgium remained hostile to the New Order. Even the conservatives had no sympathy for the "crusade" against the Soviet Union. Meanwhile, many of the old animosities between Left and Right were vanishing. The church, schools, and the secular schools assisted each other on many occasions, a practice unimaginable a few years before. Many Socialists and Jews were hidden in convents. Not only the Walloon but also the majority of the Flemish hierarchy stood against Hitler, as was the case of the hierarchies of Poland, Denmark, Norway, Luxembourg, Bohemia-Moravia, Serbia, and Greece.

"The sentiment of nationality," wrote Monsignor Tardini in the Vatican, in a memorandum in November 1940, "is more vivid than

---

[16] "Another useful channel for mass consciousness was found in the churches. Here again the people gathered together for an act of worship of which the implications were national as well as religious. When all other forms of assembly were suppressed this was of paramount importance. Collective unity increased the religious spirit, and this in its turn made the sense of unity more powerful, more complete. Even funerals were felt to be moving symbols of mass opposition; in their mourning the people fortified each other against the regime which tried to keep them apart." De Jong, *TW*, 20.

[17] His speech on 20 August 1941 to a group of seminarians deserves citation. "Five centuries ago France had been invaded, as she is today. At that time it was the English. Everyone was a 'collaborationist': Paris, the Sorbonne, the Court, the bishops. Yet a little girl had risen, inspired by God. Against everyone else she fought against 'collaboration.' She said: 'These people must get out of France.' And it was she who was right. We do not have a Joan of Arc. . . . We do not have to wait for one. . . . Good reason, common sense, all suggest that we think in terms of *confidence and resistance*, since we are certain that our country shall be restored and rise again." Delandsheere, Ooms, 427 ff.

[18] Matthys, propaganda leader of the Rex, in May 1941 attacked openly "the filthy clergy . . . the purple of the cardinalate is mixed with the Masonic filth. The totalitarian state takes account of this."

perhaps ever before." And now the national sentiments of an extraordinary number of smaller peoples are being suppressed by the greater nations. But the suppressed are too numerous. "Add up Poles, Norwegians, Danes, Belgians, Dutch, Albanians, Greeks, Austrians, Czechs, Romanians, etc., and one gets an impressive figure. It is impossible that such an enormous mass of peoples should be kept enslaved forever. It is now, because Germany and Italy are organized by an iron dictatorship; but this cannot last long. And the Church knows how to foresee and how to provide."[19]

We have now seen that, generally speaking, religion was often subordinated to nationalism among certain nations in Eastern Europe, while a contrary development took place, on occasion, among certain nations in Western Europe. In this respect, too, the German people were in the middle of the Continent. Only a minority of German Protestant pastors, and not more than a handful of German Catholic prelates and priests, subordinated their religion to the service of the Third Reich in any way comparable to the often murderous fanaticism of Croatians or Ukrainians. Yet, with a few exceptions, the leadership of the churches in Germany was timid and introvert, often to the point of ambiguity. The Lutherian German tradition of obedience to the state played a special role in this, having also affected generations of German Catholics. The autobiographical notes of the infamous Hoess, the commandant of the Auschwitz death factory, show this. He had come from a strict and pious Roman Catholic home. "I can still clearly remember how my father, who because of his fervent Catholicism was a determined opponent of the Reich government and its policy, never ceased to remind his friends that, however strong one's opposition might be, the laws and the decrees of the State had to be obeyed unconditionally."

When the war broke out, on 2 September 1939 the bishops of the Evangelical Church addressed their people:

> Since yesterday our German people have been called on to fight for the land of their fathers in order that German blood may be reunited with German blood. The German Evangelical Church stands in true fellowship with the fate of the German people. The Church has added to the weapons of steel her own invisible weapons from the Word of God. . . . So we unite in this hour with our people in intercession for our Fuehrer and Reich, for all the armed forces, and for all who do their duty for the Fatherland.

---

[19] "*E la Chiesa sa prevedere e provvedere.*" 2 November 1940, *VD*, 4, 214.

The allocution of the Catholic bishops of Germany was hardly less nationalist:

> In this decisive hour we encourage and admonish our Catholic soldiers, in obedience to the Fuehrer, to do their duty and to be ready to sacrifice their whole existence. We appeal to the faithful to join in ardent prayer that God's providence may lead this war to blessed success for Fatherland and people.[20]

A few days before the outbreak of the war, the ambassador of France to the Vatican asked that the Holy See "say a word or make a gesture" in favor of Poland "before she is to enter the great trial which now stands ahead of her." "His Holiness," minuted Monsignor Tardini, "says that this would be too much. One should not forget that there are 40 million Catholics in the Reich. To what things they would be exposed after such an act by the Holy See! The Pope has already spoken, and clearly enough."[21] He had not spoken clearly enough; but this is not the point here. Our point is that the Pope Pius's concern with the Catholics of Germany in 1939 was exaggerated: for Hitler had no intention to aggravate their feelings for the duration of the war.

True, Nazi philosophy was hostile to the established churches, and especially to the Catholic Church.[22] But Hitler, as we have seen before, thought little of the Nazi official philosophy. He was, also, more of a tactical politician than what his often extreme utterances led people to believe. The war broke out and Hitler, together with the Third Reich hierarchy, decided not to stir up the religious situation among the German people. On 9 September 1939 he ordered that "no further action should be taken against the Evangelical and the Catholic churches for the duration of the war."[23] The leaders of the churches went along with the

---

[20] Cited by Conway, 234.

[21] *VD*, I, 256–57.

[22] Example: from a "scholarly" article on the Catholic Church and the Jewish question, in 1939: "In sum we may say: the Catholic Church will never commit herself to a clear and decisive stand against Jewry. It is out of the question that she could ever become an ally of folkish ideology, since thereby she would abandon her own mission and her particular substance. . . . We must face these facts as they are: Jewry itself may be annihilated in Germany; yet the Church, in many ways the extended branch of Jewry, is here. . . ." J. Roth, "Die katholische Kirche und die Judenfrage," *Forschungen zur Judenfrage* (Hamburg, 1939), Vol. 4, 175.

[23] The census of 1939 showed that 95 per cent of the people were either Catholic or Protestant, 1.5 per cent were atheists, and 3.5 per cent were "God-be-

war, often without enthusiasm but without the slightest of protests. Hitler knew what he was doing. In June 1940, at the moment of his high triumph in the war, for example, he decided not to enforce the prohibition of the Jesuits in Austria, "since [the Fuehrer] wanted to avoid during the war all measures, unless definitely necessary, which might cause the relationship of the State and the Party to the Church to deteriorate. . . ."[24] A year later the remaining Catholic newspapers were disappearing; a general policy of suppressing religious institutions had developed. On 22 July and on 3 August 1941 the Archbishop of Münster attacked certain aspects of Nazi policy from the pulpit, a rare instance in the history of the Third Reich. He spoke approvingly of the war against Bolshevism in the worst German-Catholic manner.[25] At the end of his sermon, however, Archbishop Galen assailed the policy of closing down convents as well as the euthanasia practiced by certain state institutions. Hitler chose not to proceed against Galen. On 28 August Hitler ordered that the confiscation of Church and monastic properties be halted immediately. The secret-police reports stated at the time that in places in Catholic Bavaria morale among the people was depressed because of the policy of removing crucifixes from schoolrooms and bells from the steeples of churches. Hitler ordered this stopped; he called his Bavarian *Gauleiter*, Wagner, "stupid."[26]

The attitude of the German Catholic population to the Third Reich and the war was ambiguous. On the one hand, the antireligious propaganda of the Nazis had little or no effect on them; rather the contrary.[27] On the other hand, non-Nazi did not mean anti-Nazi: The

---

lievers"—a statistic that certainly indicates that the efforts of the Nazis to "convert" the German people to a neopagan or "German-Christian" religion were erratic and that their results were consequently feeble.

[24] Lammers to Kerrl (Minister of Education and Religion) (14 June 1940), cited by Conway, 439–40.

[25] "We felt free and liberated from a deep concern when, on 22 June 1941, the Fuehrer and *Reichskanzler* . . . declared the Pact with Russia as liquidated and revealed before the German people the lies and the faithlessness of the Bolsheviks. Day and night our thoughts dwell with our brave soldiers, that God assist them in their struggle against the Bolshevik menace to our people. . . ." Cited in Boberach, *KK*, 570–71.

[26] If "he does anything so stupid again, he would have him sent to Dachau." Peterson, 219.

[27] An example of the intrinsic resistance of the Catholic, compared to the Lutheran, population appears from the following statistic of people who officially declared that they had resigned their church allegiances (these *Kirchenaustritte*, for taxation and statistical purposes, had to be registered officially). In Gau Moselland (with a large Catholic majority), the figures in 1939–41 were these:

Catholic people of Germany and Austria did not resist Hitler and the Reich; save for a few exceptions, there was hardly any difference between their general behavior and that of the non-Catholic population, including their contribution to the war effort. They remained loyal to their priests and bishops. Except in strictly and often narrowly religious matters, they received little guidance from these men or, at that, from the Pope. On 9 March 1939 the newly elected Pius XII had a conference in Rome with the German hierarchy, an excerpt from the record of which sums up much of the attitude of the German bishops. The Pope was talking about forms of address. Cardinal Innitzer of Vienna (who had had troubles with the Nazis a few months before) posed a few anxious questions. Cardinal Bertram of Breslau said: "I told the children: Heil Hitler —that is valid for this world (*das geht auf das irdische Reich*); Praised be Jesus Christ—that is the tie between earth and heaven."[28] No neater formula could be imagined.

German Catholic ecclesiastics who were convinced adherents of Hitler were only a handful: Bishop Rarkowski of the armed services; a Father Keller, who served for a while as a double agent for the secret police. The aristocratic Bishop of Berlin, Preysing, bitter and disappointed with his colleague Bertram, considered resigning his office in June 1940; Pius XII persuaded him not to do so.[29] The Catholic population was

---

CHURCH RESIGNATIONS

| July–September 1939 | | | | April–June 1940 | | | |
|---|---|---|---|---|---|---|---|
| Evangelical | | Catholic | | Evangelical | | Catholic | |
| Men | Women | Men | Women | Men | Women | Men | Women |
| 422 | 157 | 180 | 82 | 103 | 77 | 84 | 47 |

| January–March 1941 | | | | April–June 1941 | | | |
|---|---|---|---|---|---|---|---|
| Evangelical | | Catholic | | Evangelical | | Catholic | |
| Men | Women | Men | Women | Men | Women | Men | Women |
| 188 | 154 | 83 | 50 | 132 | 136 | 126 | 80 |

Heyen, 186.

---

[28] *VD*, I, 433.

[29] *VD*, 2, 143. Preysing was also among the few members of the German hierarchy who protested against the cruel treatment of Polish Catholics in the Warthegau. *VD*, 3*, 305.

notably less confident in Hitler's ultimate victory than were the rest of the Germans; the secret-police reports and records attest to this.[30] There is also evidence that they were less anti-Semitic. With few exceptions, however, the hierarchy restricted itself to helping Catholics of Jewish origin.[31] The Catholic organization Raphaelsverein, functioning until September 1941 with the express permission of the authorities, tried to expedite the emigration of these unfortunates—a policy altogether in accord with Hitler's desiderata. The hierarchy made few protests concerning the terror exercised by the Reich in foreign nations.[32]

In addition to memoirs and reminiscences, we have two main sources of evidence concerning the acts and the thoughts of the professedly Christian people of Germany during the Last European War.[33] One of

---

[30] For example: RSHA *Meldungen* in late 1939: MA 441/2 0040, 0125, 0723 (January 1940: In Bavaria the Catholic people treat Polish prisoners much better than other people treat them); 22005 (July 1940: The Catholic population is less enthusiastic about the triumphs in the war than are the Lutheran Evangelicals, including the clergy of the latter.) On the other hand, the Catholic nationalist Bishop of Speyer, Monsignor Bornewasser, saw a religious portent in the German victory over France. Boelcke, 561. MA 441/2, 2219, 14 July 1940: A Catholic priest in Nuremberg: "What good are two hours of triumphant talk over the radio against the will of God?" Catholic reaction to Jews in November 1941, MA 441/5 5316.

[31] Between 1900 and 1932 in Germany six times as many Jews converted to various Protestant churches than to the Roman Catholic Church. Between 1933 and 1939 the very opposite was true: Eighty per cent of Jewish converts chose Catholicism.

See *VD*, vols. 6 and 8, passim. It is regrettable to note that the assistance to these unfortunates was often extremely limited. On 20 January 1941 Cardinal Innitzer of Vienna wrote an imploring letter to Rome, pointing out the desperate condition of 11,000 non-Aryan Catholics in Vienna—desperate because while the remaining Viennese of the Jewish faith were still receiving various, mostly American, sources of material succor, these abandoned Jewish Catholics had no source of support. Pius XII consented to transmit the paltry sum of $2,000.—*VD*, 8, 79.

[32] In the Warthegau portion of Poland, annexed to Germany, only 3 per cent of the Polish parish priests remained at the end of 1940. More than 300 had been executed. By February 1941 only 45 of the 441 Catholic churches were still open; by the end of October 1941 the remaining Polish priests had been arrested. In 1942 there were 2,000 Polish priests in Dachau alone. Eventually not only Preysing but also Bertram wrote about this to the Pope (*VD*, 3*, 393). In August 1940 the *Gauleiter* of Lorraine expelled the bishops of Metz and of Strasbourg.

[33] The published papers of the Holy See (*VD*) deal mostly, though of course not exclusively, with international ecclesiastical affairs, with little information or evidence about the sentiments of the people.

these sources are the already mentioned secret reports, compiled by RSHA, SD, and Gestapo, often overlapping authorities.[34] The other source is that of religious publications. Here, too, the tone of the Evangelical as well as of the Catholic press is revealing—or, rather, dulling. Restricting themselves to a narrow, though often pretentiously deep, scope of religiosity, the editors of these papers filled their pages with liturgical and philosophical articles that were almost completely irrelevant to the existential problems and dilemmas of life under a totalitarian dictatorship and during a war. Those nuances of divergence and of discrimination that careful and experienced readers could find, on occasion, in certain publications were just about absent in the religious press. The absence of relevance—indeed, of reality—in the latter was cultivated by their cautious editors on purpose. Their conformity did not help.[35] In the

---

[34] See above: Boberach; Boberach, *KK; Bayern KL;* Heyen. The collectors of confidential information were especially active in the fall of 1939; after 1941 both the frequency and the value of the reports sharply diminish. They include various acts of recalcitrance on the part of individual priests and pastors, and also on the part of churchgoers and believers. Their evidence confirms, by and large, the general impression: Save for a few individual instances, conformity with the requirements of the government during the war, ranging from occasionally moderate enthusiasm to occasional sullenness (among certain Catholics).

[35] Examples: The first wartime issue (24 September 1939) of the Bavarian *Kirchenzeitung* (a Catholic publication with a considerable circulation) "carried a vigorous sketch of St. Michael subduing Satan (a note reminding the reader that St. Michael was Germany's patron saint) along with an article which declared: 'Our fathers and brothers are at the Front and we know that they are fulfilling their difficult duty to the ultimate in a spirit of comradeship and readiness for self-sacrifice. But their heroic offering would be an accusation and judgment upon us if we at home were not similarly willing to close ranks. . . . There is now no longer room for petty divisiveness, for selfishness, for indolent comfort, or pleasure-seeking. . . .'" Ibid. (9 October 1939): "In times that demand of men the fullest dedication and ultimate surrender of self, the Catholic turns to the sources of spiritual strength and grace which surmount mere natural powers and perfect the heroism of fighting men. . . ." Titles of certain feature articles in the *Muenchner Katholische Kirchenzeitung:* "Heroic Reflections of Courage"; "We Play Our Part in the War"; "The Unity of Front and Homeland"; "War, School of Sacrifice"; The *Klerusblatt* (6 November 1940): "When the drums roll and the arms are presented over the resting places [of the fallen], then the great flood of German determination and German awareness of common unity, released by sacrifices, bursts forth. As every German says in his heart, they shall not have died in vain!" Ibid. (1 November 1939): "Great is the age in which we live; fortunately its gigantic struggles found a great race to match them." The above are cited in an unpublished paper by Professor Gordon C. Zahn, listed further in the bibliography of Zahn, op. cit.

second half of 1941, officially because of paper shortages, most of the church and religious publications were suspended; except for their editors and writers, their disappearance was generally unlamented.

The Jesuit Delp's *Prison Meditations* and the Protestant Bonhoeffer's *Letters* and his *Ethics* survive among the most poignant, if not the most poignant, expressions of anguished Christians in Europe during the Second World War. They were composed toward the end of the war, in the midst of catastrophe, completed in prison by men who were condemned or about to be condemned to a cruel death. Delp's honest sincerity does not merely shine, it burns through these tragic pages. Yet it was the same Delp, a promising young Jesuit philosopher at the time, who had been made editor of the Catholic periodical *Stimmen der Zeit* ("A Catholic monthly for spiritual matters of the present") in 1939. Continuing in this capacity until the publication ceased to appear in 1941, Delp wrote long theological and philosophical articles during the first two years of the war, articles that were not untypical of the German Catholic mentality of the time. In an article in the April 1940 number, entitled "The War as a Spiritual Achievement," Delp cited St. Thomas, among others: "Just as it is the task of religion to manifest honor to God, it is a matter of duty to manifest honor to one's parents and to the fatherland."[36] In an article in the June 1940 number, entitled "Heimat," Delp found it propitious to quote from the works of Hans F. K. Guenther,[37] a then famous Nazi professor, whose main contribution had been the elevation of the doctrine of race to the level of a science.

"Flight, emigration, or reaction are not the attitudes of a true Christian," wrote Delp in September 1939[38] at the beginning of the war. As the war went on, his attitudes underwent a profound change. The attitudes of many other German (and also of non-German) Christians changed, too, after 1941; what was unusual was Father Delp's martyrdom. He drew the consequences of his convictions; and he paid the supreme price for them. Like his Protestant brother Bonhoeffer, whose meditations were unknown to him at the time, Delp recognized the failure of the churches, and at the edge of the grave he saw the need for a new kind of existential Christianity. He wrote in prison: "But recently a man turning to the Church for enlightenment has all too often found only a tired man to receive him—a man who then had the dishonesty to hide his fatigue under pious words and fervent gestures. At some future date the honest historian will have some bitter things to say about the contributions of

---

[36] Delp, "Der Krieg als geistige Leistung," *Stimmen der Zeit* (Apr. 1940), 209.
[37] Ibid. (June 1940), 283.
[38] Ibid. (Sept. 1939), 450.

the Churches to the creation of the mass mind, of collectivism, dictatorships and so on."[39]

The Cardinal Eugenio Pacelli, Secretary of State of the Holy See,
was elected Pope on 2 March 1939. This saintly and sincere Pope was a
Germanophile.[40] He was a "black" Roman, with a special affection for
German culture. More important, he had been deeply impressed by his
experiences as nuncio in Bavaria and in Germany from 1917 to 1929,
where he had witnessed the dangers and the tribulations of the German
people *in situ.* His election to the papacy was extraordinarily swift, and
there are some reasons to believe that the reputation of his potentially
propitious relationship with Germany played a certain role in his election.
Unlike other Germanophiles, Pius XII had no sympathies for Nazism.
His Germanophilia, however, was manifest not only in his special concern
for the German people, especially German Catholics; it was also part and
parcel of his religious and political conservatism. This had an important
effect on the supranational as well as on the international function of the
Vatican during his reign, and especially during the Second World War.

Pius XII did not protest against the German annexation of Bohemia
and Moravia. He was tardy, cautious, and vague in condemning the German mistreatment of Poland, an attitude that filled with bitterness the
otherwise fervent and loyal Catholics of Poland, especially those in exile.
On 11 March 1940 Ribbentrop visited the Vatican, bringing Hitler's best
wishes to the Pope. Their conversation reveals something about the extent to which Pius was willing to go to assure Hitler of his goodwill.[41]

---

[39] *Delp PM,* 150.

[40] His predecessor, the old Pius XI, was not. Example: His conversation with
the French ambassador on 17 March 1936, after Hitler's reoccupation of the
Rhineland. "If you [the French] had immediately moved 200,000 soldiers into
the zone reoccupied by the Germans, you would have rendered an immense
service to the entire world." Charles-Roux, 447. Pius XII would have never
spoken, or felt, this way. Unlike Pius XI, who was equally anti-Communist,
Pacelli was unable to distinguish between Communism and Russia; see, for
example, his remarks to Charles-Roux, *DDF* (2), III, 637.

[41] Tardini notes, *VD,* I, 384–87. Examples: "Ribbentrop observed that Pope
Pius XI had spoken too harshly against Germany. His Holiness drew attention
to the fact that he spoke kind and good words [about Germany] to a [recent]
group of German pilgrims." Pius told Ribbentrop that his recent praise for
small nations that have been victims to aggression referred to Finland, "in Germany it was thought that he had referred to Poland." He knew that the German people followed Hitler "without exceptions." Pius's remonstrations to
Ribbentrop were restricted to the rights and schools of the Church in Ger-

There was some evidence that in June 1940 the Vatican considered a cautious policy of accommodation to the prospect of a German victory in the war.[42] It favored the armistice party in France.[43] In July 1940 the Vatican tried to convince London to listen to certain German proposals for a negotiated peace. In March 1941 it counseled the Yugoslavs to seek an accommodation with Germany. Pius refused to condemn the German attack on Yugoslavia and Greece.[44] He gave limited recognition to the murderous Pavelic government of Croatia. In April 1941 the Vatican broadcasts halted their references to problems of the Church in Germany. The British protested, in vain.[45] "The Church," as another British note had put it, "will lose her influence if she continues to condemn strongly Bolshevism and Communist atheism, without taking the same strong line against the anti-Christian theories and the menace of Nazism."[46] These admonitions had no effects. Pius XII also refrained from saying anything against the German persecution of the Jews—not because he had any sympathy for these measures but because of diplomatic reasons.[47]

---

many. Ribbentrop was sufficiently impressed to say after the audience: "I see that His Holiness has Germany always at heart." *VD*, 5, 272. On 13 March *Glos Polski*, a Polish newspaper in France, wrote with some bitterness about Ribbentrop's reception. Pius XII became very angry, demanding satisfaction from the Polish exile government (*VD*, 1, 411)—a rare example, this.

[42] It was in June 1940 that, for the first time, blessings to German "soldiers in the field" appeared in Pius's letters to various German bishops: *VD*, 2, 146, 141, 169, 109.

[43] On 8 June the German ambassador reported to Berlin that Vatican opinion was that France "ought to follow the example of Belgium," i.e., surrender. Bergen dispatch, cited by Friedlaender, 62. Cardinal Tisserant was very bitter at the then policy of the Vatican.

[44] The narrowness of his attitude is revealed by his remarks, recorded by Tardini, on 7 April 1941, in response to a British request that the new German invasion be condemned "in some way" (*VD*, 5, 447). "His Holiness wishes to note: (1) We have no [official] relations with Greece. The Greek government had never allowed an Apostolic Delegate. (2) The new Yugoslav king did not bother to inform us about his assumption of the throne." *VD*, 5, 448.

[45] *VD*, 4, 30–31, 541; also 242, 283–84. In September 1940 the British minister to the Holy See had to urge Pius XII to send a message to the King and Queen of England on the occasion of their having escaped injury when a German bomb had fallen on Buckingham Palace. The Pope consented reluctantly, insisting that this routine communication remain unpublished. *VD*, 4, 148–49.

[46] *VD*, 4, 354.

[47] The silence of Pius XII in this regard has been treated in detail by critical writers. An interesting addition to the accumulated record: On 8 September

This is one side of the complex history of Pius XII and of the Vatican in 1939–41. The other side of the story is no less documented and documentable. In spite (and also because) of his special inclination toward German Catholics, the Pope and the Holy See entertained great reservations and few illusions about Hitler and his regime. They lent themselves—with extreme caution, to be sure—to the clandestine contacts between certain German conservative circles and the British government in the winter of 1939–40.[48] The papal nuncio was among those who alerted the Belgian government to the imminent German invasion in early May 1940. The Holy See condemned the German attack on the Lowlands. It tried to influence Mussolini against going to war on Hitler's side, with the result of a crisis in Mussolini's relations with the Vatican in May 1940. Pius XII kept up a correspondence with Roosevelt and nurtured exceptional relations with the United States. The Vatican was influential in keeping Franco at arm's length from Hitler. All of its anti-Communism notwithstanding, it refused to give approval to Hitler's anti-Communist "crusade." Its diplomatic envoys, with few exceptions,[49] were intelligent and humane prelates. They tried to assuage nationalist hatreds, and intervened for internees and prisoners of wars, including Jews, often with success.[50]

The policy of Pius XII was unduly narrow. He restricted himself to the interests of Catholics, often excluding almost any other consideration.[51] Besides this often unduly narrow conception of the functions and the tasks of the Holy See, there was the often unduly broad preoccupation with Communism—an attitude that, as we have seen earlier in this book, was typical not only of a certain kind of Catholicism but also of a

---

1940 Cardinal Maglione, in order to emphasize certain Fascist attacks on the papacy, wrote the apostolic delegate, Cicognani, in Washington: "In its number of the sixth current the *Regime Fascista* [Farinacci's extreme pro-Nazi newspaper] dared to criticize the noble discourse of His Holiness to the leaders of Italian Catholic Action, writing: 'The Pope does not agree with our struggle against Jewry.'" Pius XII struck this passage from the dispatch to Washington with his pencil. *VD*, 4, 143.

[48] Excluding the French, however, toward whom Pius XII maintained a certain kind of distrust.

[49] Orsenigo in Berlin, Valeri in Vichy. (From a dispatch by the latter, 4 October 1940: "As it is, alas, beyond doubt, the Jews contributed as much as they could to the outbreak of the war." *VD*, 4, 173.)

[50] Exemplary, in this regard, was the behavior of nuncios such as Cassulo in Romania and Roncalli in Turkey.

[51] For example, the intervention of the Holy See in favor of Catholics of Jewish origin, including recent converts, was frequent in 1939–41; but such support was seldom extended to persons of the Jewish religion.

certain kind of conservatism throughout Europe, indeed, the world. Pius XII—influenced by his early experiences in Munich—regarded Communism a greater danger than Nazism. The defeat of Germany, he thought, would mean the triumph of Communism *all over* Europe.[52] The Germans knew how to profit from these inclinations.[53] The German ambassador, Bergen, went too far in reporting, in September 1941, about the war in Russia that "In his heart the Pope, I am told, is on the side of the Axis Powers."[54] The pro-German desires and attitudes of those Catholic prelates which were consequent to their frenetic fear and hatred of Communism[55] were not typical of the attitudes of the Pope and of the Vatican hierarchy. Yet there is no question that Pius XII continued to regard Germany as a potential bulwark against the menace of Bolshevism.[56] In this respect his attitude was the very opposite of that of Churchill, and especially of Roosevelt,[57] even as Pius attempted to cultivate profitable relations with the latter.

---

[52] ". . . if the Russians win the war . . . Communism victorious means Communism the absolute master of the European continent." Tardini memorandum, 15 September 1941, *VD*, 5, 215–18. This most intelligent statesman of the Holy See added: "For myself I hope that from the present war in Russia Communism issues defeated and annihilated and Nazism issues weakened and . . . conquerable."

[53] Example: In 1941 they allowed German Catholic choral groups to visit Spain, impressing the Spanish with the joint German-Spanish commitment to anti-Communism. *VD*, 4, 416.

[54] His dispatch from the German Foreign Ministry archives (Microfilm Reel 535, 240042–43) is cited in *VD*, 5, 23.

[55] Examples: The Croatian Archbishop Stepinac on 13 February 1941—that is, *before* the Belgrade revolution in March 1941—asked for Vatican support, criticizing the royalist Yugoslav government because of its diplomatic relations with the Soviet Union. *VD*, 4, 386. The doddery Cardinal Baudrillart in Paris blessed the French legionaries in German uniform: "the best sons of France." The Italian Monsignor Constantini blessed the Italian soldiers going to Russia: "They defend the ideal of our liberty against the Red barbarism." On 29 June 1941 the Ukrainian Catholic apostolic vicars in Jaroslaw and Sanok asked for public Masses for the triumphant progress of the German Army against Bolshevism, etc. At the other end of Europe, the conservative Cardinal Cerejeira of Lisbon instructed his clergy *not* to identify Communism with the Russian people.

[56] For a while the Vatican considered sending Catholic priests into the parts of the Soviet Union conquered by the Germans, for the purpose of the reintroduction and propagation of the faith (Tardini memorandum, 29 June 1941, *VD*, 4, 592). The Germans did not want this. If anything, they favored the autochthonous Orthodox churches.

[57] About the significance of the Pope's relationship with Roosevelt, see below, pp. 505–7.

These attitudes and policies of Pius XII were subjected to much attention, and to acerbic discussion, in the 1960s, after his death and well after the war. The polemical literature, composed before the serial publication of documents of the Holy See, is enlightening in spots but also often compromised by special pleading. Probably the main shortcoming of some of the, often capable and serious, critics of Pius's relationship to Nazi Germany[58] lies in their at times unconscious distortion of their perspectives in retrospect. What they see as subtle designs in Pius's diplomacy were often not more than excessive caution. Pius was unduly cautious in overestimating what Hitler would or could do against Catholics in Germany in the event of a papal condemnation of Nazism during the war. Yet we have seen that Hitler did not wish to add to his wartime burdens by a confrontation with the masses of German Catholics. Pius also overestimated the appeal of Communism after the war. Yet, as events were to prove, Communism was established only in those countries of Europe where the Russian Army was the occupying power.

The shortcomings of Pius's spiritual leadership lay in the restriction of his concerns to the welfare of the Catholic Church. The Pope had to weigh the prospect that his condemnation of Nazism, besides being futile, might endanger the spiritual welfare of millions of Catholic Germans. Yet, if the Catholic Church is the *catholic* church, and if the Pope is the Vicar of Christ, should his concern for the spiritual privileges of Catholics have been so categorical as to exclude his moral concern for the lives and deaths of non-Catholics? Also, Pius XII underestimated the spiritual prestige of his Church.[59] Even if a clear Papal condemnation of Hitlerism may not have assuaged the sufferings of its victims (which is not certain), its potential influence in the long run could have been enormous, not only among Catholics but also among all kinds of Christians, agnostics, Jews in Europe, millions of people whom the experiences of the war made receptive to and even desirous for the kind of spiritual leadership that the traditional and universal Catholic Church could have given.

My emphasis on the Catholic Church and on its adherents in these pages was principally due to the fact that they constituted the great majority among those Europeans who were baptized Christians. It was also due to the consideration that in the course of modern history the Protestant churches became national churches in many places, having gradually

---

[58] Friedlaender, Lewy, Hochhuth, Nobécourt, Falconi, Boeckenfoerde, Amery.
[59] See my article in *Continuum* (Summer 1964).

abandoned many of their claims for universality. Shortly before 1939 this, too, was beginning to change: An interest in international religious co-operation, and in ecumenicism of a kind, was beginning to stir among certain Western European Protestants. This, too, involved but a very small minority, though it was to bear certain fruits toward the end and after the war.

The most extreme example of a Protestantism that was willing not only to subordinate its spiritual claim to the national state, but also to witness its own absorption by the latter was represented by the wing of the German Evangelical Church calling itself "German Christians" ever since 1933, hoping to become the state church of the National Socialist Third Reich. In June 1940, at the height of German triumphs, the bishop of this church proposed to the German Minister of Religion that it transfer all of its possessions to the National Socialist state. "It thereby desires to prove that it wishes to be considered as nothing apart from the State, but rather feels itself bound up with the prosperity of the State."[60] Hitler refused this suggestion. He was more in favor of the toleration of a bland and innocuous religiosity than of the establishment of a state church or of a state religion. He had more respect for the non-Nazi, and occasionally dangerous, wing of the "Confessionals," the *Bekennende Kirche* of the German Protestants, than for those of the "German Christian" wing. The very opposite of the latter German kind of Caesaropapism was expressed in England by George Bell, the Anglican Bishop of Chichester.[61] The Church must remain the Church, he wrote in January 1940. The Church "is not the nation. It is not the state's spiritual auxiliary with exactly the same ends as the state."

The vast majority of German Lutherans opted neither for the German Christians nor for the earnest recalcitrants of the Niemoeller or Bonhoeffer type. Their attitudes were, if not determined, in most cases circumscribed by their particular historical, geographic, and political situation. This was more or less typical of much of the Continent. It is interesting to note, for example, that in Switzerland the situation was opposite to that in Germany: The Swiss Evangelical Church produced the most outspokenly anti-Nazi pastors. In Denmark and Norway the Lutheran churches resisted Nazism from the beginning. In Norway a minority of clergymen would go along with Quisling and the Germans;

---

[60] The minister, Kerrl, died in December 1941. Hitler said at his death: "Kerrl, with the noblest of intentions, wanted to attempt a synthesis between National Socialism and Christianity. I do not believe this is possible. . . ."
[61] Significantly, Bishop Bell was personally acquainted with some of the best German Protestants, opponents of Hitler such as Niemoeller and Bonhoeffer of the *Bekennende Kirche*.

most of these were German clergymen living in Norway, or Norwegian pastors who had received their training in Germany. The Lutheran churches in Finland and in Latvia had strong nationalist, anti-Russian, and, in the case of the former, Germanophile wings. Perhaps the most Nazified of all churches in Europe was the German Evangelical Lutheran Church in Romanian Transylvania: It furnished some of the leaders of the German minority, and functioned as a privileged state within Romania. In Italy, and in certain places in France, Protestants were among the early resistants: They had a long tradition of resisting the oppressive authority of a state church.

We have seen earlier that the most extreme instances of religion serving as a handmaiden to nationalism existed in Eastern Europe. This was not a geographical accident: It was the result of particular historical circumstances, including the powerful traditions of folkish nationalism, which was typical of the Orthodox churches. Far more national than universal, their very organization and spiritual jurisdiction was autocephalous, a condition that increased after the Bolshevik Revolution. In 1939–41 the most revolting examples of a fanatically nationalist religiosity occurred in Romania, where the Iron Guard, called also "the Legion of the Archangel Michael," exacted a religious oath from its followers. Its members had to be Romanian Orthodox, and the installation ceremonies included a recitation of the "Prayer of the Brother of the Cross." Some of these members were Orthodox priests who prided themselves in having taken part in political assassinations.[62] These fiends did not even have the excuse of the nationalist Catholics in Croatia, who had reacted to their earlier suppression by the Orthodox Serbs,[63] since in Romania the Orthodox Church was a privileged corporation of the state. The record of the Bulgarian Orthodox Church was more humane (the Metropolitan of

---

[62] The Fathers Dumineca, Palaghitsa, and Dimitrescu-Borsa, for example; the last two were trained by the SS, which one of them, formerly a member of the elite Death Squad of the Iron Guard, eventually joined.

[63] In July 1935 the Serbian Orthodox Church excommunicated the Serbian Prime Minister and those officials who played a part in the Concordat that Yugoslavia had concluded with the Vatican that year. (The excommunication was suspended in January 1938.) After the collapse of the Yugoslav state, the Germans published a photograph of the Serbian Patriarch Gavrilo, hiding in a cave, "surrounded by a deposit of fine *jambon* to avoid the danger of hunger, and by a rich collection of gramophone records featuring Josphine Baker, to avoid the danger of melancholy . . . thus ended among the Orthodox circles of Sofia, I think forever, ideas of future Balkan alliances of a religious nature." This from a report of the nuncio Roncalli, later Pope John XXIII, reporting on his recent trip to Bulgaria (22 July 1941), *VD*, 5, 94–95. Gavrilo, however, proved to be a distinguished and brave prelate.

[475]

Sofia intervened in behalf of Bulgarian Jews successfully). The Greek Orthodox Church was extremely nationalistic and anti-Catholic. A supreme example of neo-Constantinism occurred in April 1941, when the reputedly ascetic and unworldly Orthodox monks of Mount Athos sent Hitler a scroll, declaring him a successor of the Emperor of Byzantium.[64]

Stalin may have—in 1935—discounted the presence of the Pope's divisions. He certainly did not—in 1939 and after—discount the benefit of religious dividends.[65] While a few anti-Bolshevik bishops among the decaying White Russian émigrés would urge on the Germans to liberate Russia from the yoke of the "Red Devils," Stalin in September 1941 ordered the suppression of the League of Militant Atheists; *Pravda* on 23 September 1941 sprang to the defense of sanctity, assailing "the barbarous Fascist hordes, drunk with blood, ridiculing the religious sentiments of women, Catholic and Protestant, desecrating churches and violating the sacred vessels"—a superb passage. Most Russian Orthodox bishops followed the example, and the language of the Patriarch Sergius, who attacked "Fascist bandits," asked the faithful "to bless our leaders," and in December 1941 designated the Germans as "two-legged jackals" and "depraved monsters." Another Sergius, an archbishop and a younger adviser of the Patriarch, had first been sent by the Soviets to work in the Baltics; in June 1941 he chose to conceal himself in the dark and dusty crypt of the Orthodox Cathedral in Riga. Emerging fresh and ambitious, he rushed to send telegrams of greeting to Hitler[66]—a surviving example of what someone, either Trollope or Sydney Smith, had said in dear old

---

[64] Heer, *Glaube*, 416. Similar were the attitudes of certain Mohammedans. Example: From Persia the apostolic delegate wrote to the Vatican on 29 November 1941 that the population was incensed against Catholics, and the talk of the bazaars is that Hitler was the Twelfth Prophet of Islam. *VD*, 5, 294.

[65] In the beginning of their occupation of the Baltic states, the Soviets' attitude toward the local churches was correct. Gradually they began to favor the Orthodox clergy, including White Russians, and proceeded with the deportation of Catholic priests. One of the truly great and unsung heroes of the Catholic faith was Monsignor Profittlich, the German-born Catholic apostolic delegate to Estonia. He chose to stay in Estonia after the other priests, mostly German, had gone (one exception was that French Jesuit Father Bourgeois, who wrote a small book about these dark times). Monsignor Profittlich asked respectfully that the Pope instruct him whether to stay on, which almost certainly would mean deportation to Siberia. (It did.) The calmness and humility of his letter to Cardinal Maglione (31 October 1940, *VD*, 3*, 320–21) is that of a true and unassuming witness to the faith, suffused with potential martyrdom, shattering in retrospect.

[66] Fireside, 134.

Victorian England: "Everything suffers from translation except a bishop." Elsewhere in the Ukraine and Byelorussia the attitude of many of the Orthodox clergy depended on their belief—on their belief of who was winning the war, Hitler or Stalin.

During the Middle Ages the cult of morality was hardly separable from that of religion. Eventually morality survived the decline of religion, especially in certain Protestant nations. We have seen that in this war, the geography of Europe reflected her ideological division: the radical Right, National Socialism in the center of the continent, between Democracy in the West and Communism in the East. Perhaps in an even deeper sense, the ideological division had certain religious roots. In many ways this was a war of ex-Catholics (Hitler, for example) against ex-Protestants (the English, for example) and ex-Orthodox (Stalin and the Bolsheviks, for example). But there was more to that. During the Second World War certain peoples among whom practitioners of religion were a small minority behaved better than many other peoples among whom a large proportion were regular churchgoers. In plain English, a good pagan was a better man than a bad Christian. There was more to that, too. The enduring decency of most of the English people[67] was not the result of the kind of atheistic humanism that existed elsewhere in Europe, the virtues of which intellectuals had preached, believing that this higher kind of man-made morality would simply succeed the disappearance of Christianity. There is reason to believe that the relatively moral behavior of most people was the, often unconscious, result of tradition rather than of cerebration. There ran a deep spiritual undercurrent in the minds of people who during the Second World War were shocked out of their wits by what they saw around them, not only the disasters of

---

[67] "Mass Observation, in a survey at the end of the war, found that about two thirds of men and four fifths of women, in a London suburb, said they believed in God, and only about one person in twenty was ready to profess atheism. But six out of ten said they never went to church. A third of the under-forties were non-believers. . . . From the Roman Catholic point of view, Britain was steadily becoming not less, but more Christian. The Catholic priests had found converts at a steady rate of eleven or twelve thousand a year in the mid-thirties . . . the estimated Catholic population of Britain increased in the 1940s by over four hundred thousand, to nearly four millions. . . . The Church of England found its supply of ordinands drying up completely, and those exacerbated a chronic fall in the numbers of Anglican clergy. . . . The diocese of Birmingham, a somewhat extreme case, had 178 curates in 1938, and only 38 in 1948." Spinks, 217, cited in Calder, 478–79.

war but also the disasters of the mass mind.[68] For the first time in many centuries a generation of Europeans were freeing their minds from allegiance to the state without, at the same time, becoming antireligious. The respect for the churches, and especially for the Catholic Church, had risen, in spite of the sometimes ambiguous behavior of its representatives. There was a spiritual, and not only patriotic, current animating the early resistance movements, beginning as early as in 1940–41: a new belief in Christian democracy, specifically European, it survived the war.

## RESISTANCE

¶ The history of the various resistance movements during the Last European War must be restricted to a few pages in this book. The militant phase of opposition to the Germans had, with few exceptions (Poland, Serbia, and certain parts of the Soviet Union) hardly begun before the end of 1941. Even after 1941 the contribution of the various European resistance movements to the defeat of the Third Reich was not decisive. Yet their appearance at a certain time in the history of Europe is one of those matters that are more significant than they are important. There is a certain significance to the word "resistance" itself.[69] Less militant than, say, "counterattack," less aggressive than "opposition," "resistance" suggests something that is deep-seated and humane rather than dynamic and progressive. The popular notion, even now, is that Hitler and his cohorts were a group of reactionary madmen, going berserk, to whom the large democratic majority of the peoples were opposed, and that therefore the former were bound to go down in defeat. What happened, in reality, was a vast movement in the history of the Continent, a tide of German triumphs which, at least for a time, brought on a flooding of popular senti-

---

[68] In 1941 the Austrian Jewish writer Franz Werfel, having just escaped through the South of France, and for many years deeply impressed with the strength of the Catholic faith among some of the simple people he had known, dedicated a poignant reconstruction of the story of the little Bernadette Soubirous, to whom the Virgin had appeared at Lourdes. In 1941 at the other end of Europe, an official Catholic newspaper of the Croatian state, preaching extermination and hatred, bore the name "Our Lady of Lourdes" in Croatian: *Nasa Gospa Lurdska.* The first of these facts is more meaningful than the second. Werfel was not alone among European intellectuals, Jews and agnostics, who were attracted by the flickering light of the Catholic faith in the darkness cast by the Third Reich.

[69] The French used it first, in its later accepted sense.

ment, eroding many a weakening dam or muddy island of traditional belief, save for a few around which the large tide swirled, and more and
more as the tide was beginning to recede. This is what the very word
"resistance" suggests: and rightly so.

Since the end of the war a large literature of the various national
resistance movements has come into existence, furnishing many valuable
details for historians. This literature has two shortcomings, generally
speaking. It tends to exaggerate the extent as well as the popularity of the
resistance; plainly, most of this literature is not sufficiently critical. It is,
moreover, insufficiently comparative. If the principal task of historians is,
as this writer thinks it is, to deal with the history of certain problems
rather than with that of certain periods, such a comparative approach is
indeed necessary. As Professor Mastny, the historian of the Czech people under German occupation, wrote: "Nazi occupation policies during
World War II have been usually regarded as not only brutal but also
incompetent. Their success in the Protectorate suggests that they were
indeed brutal but by no means stupid. By contrast, the inadequacy of
Hitler's opponents appears evident. Circumstances peculiar to Bohemia
and Moravia assured this distressing outcome. But only further study of
the conditions in other occupied countries can ascertain to what extent
the Czech case was unique in Europe. . . . We may discover that the
people of the advanced industrial countries of Europe . . . were surprisingly susceptible to the ruthlessness of the enemy."[70]

The Czechs were the first non-German people subjugated by the
Third Reich. It was natural that the first demonstrations of popular opposition should occur among them. On 30 September 1939, the first anniversary of the Munich settlement, there was a boycott of public transportation in Prague, even though, as Mastny writes, "the initial behavior
of the population fell short of the expectations of the . . . organizers."
On 28 October, the day of Czechoslovak independence, handbills and
leaflets circulated among the people, and there were visible demonstrations on some of the streets. The Germans reacted swiftly, and ordered the closing of the Czech-language university. In early 1940 a Czech
committee of internal resistance (UVOD) came into existence. It maintained relations with the Czech politicans in exile as well as a few cautious clandestine contacts with certain members of the satellite government under German tutelage. There was hardly any sabotage in
Czechoslovakia during 1940. On 28 September 1940 the Nazi Heydrich
replaced the Swabian conservative Neurath as *Reichsprotektor* of the
Czechs. The Czech Prime Minister, Elias, was found to have had certain

---

[70] Mastny, 404.

clandestine contacts with the exiled authorities. Before a German People's Court he was convicted and condemned to death.[71] Heydrich was a diabolically clever and efficient ruler: Not only did he fully comprehend the uses of terror, but he also succeeded in keeping the Czech working class in a state of relative contentment. In 1941 the few secret contacts between the Hácha "government" and the Benes group abroad ceased to exist. Indeed, Benes was sufficiently worried about the relative pacification of his people and about the lack of visible opposition to the Germans that he ordered the plans for the assassination of Heydrich, mostly in order to demonstrate the existence of a Czech resistance to the world. The plot was carried out in May 1942, with tragic results for the Czech people, since the German reprisals were not only exceptionally brutal but also efficient. Before Heydrich's death Goebbels spoke of his work admiringly. After his death the subjection of the Czechs was completed. Less than 2,000 German officials of all classes controlled the people, with 350,000 Czech administrators doing their routine work under them.

The situation and, even more, the national temperament of the Poles were different from those of the Czechs. If the Germans' policy for the Czechs was suppression, their policy for the Poles was subjugation. Not that there were no Polish collaborators[72]; but they were few, and the Germans did not want to share any kind of power and authority with Poles. In any event, the Poles were the first people in Europe to embark on sporadic attempts of armed resistance against the Germans. The first Polish guerrilla groups were operating as early as November 1939, even before the first working contacts with the exile government had been established. A vignette of Warsaw in the first winter of the war survives, from the excellent memoirs of Stefan Korbonski:

> Military men walked with a stoop, as if they had spent all their lives behind desks, while the civilians carried themselves as straight as if they had swallowed a stick. This degenerated at times into circumlocution and impenetrable secretiveness. Some characters flitted about in the manner of actors on the stage of a provincial theatre. They moved about silent, sombre, and hesitant if they had to speak, but their gait and their whole appearance seemed to be proclaiming to all and sundry. "Look, I am a conspirator." Such silly behaviour, however, did not prevent them risking death in their daily work, and when necessary dying like heroes. While on the subject of conspiratorial practice it may be said that during the winter 1939–40 Warsaw became the centre of some peculiar fashions.

---

[71] Hitler ordered the postponement of his execution: Elias was shot in June 1942, after the assassination of Heydrich.

[72] Certain actors, artists, black-marketeers, including the conductor of the Warsaw Philharmonic, Dolzycki.

Young men of landowning families were sweeping the streets in fox-fur caps and bearskin fur-coats reaching down to their ankles. Dressed in this way they visited cafes and bars in which society ladies were working as waitresses. These were mostly the wives, sisters, or fiancées of military officers who worked there because it was fashionable to do so, and this fashion spread even behind the walls of the ghetto, where ladies of the leading Jewish families were working in a similar capacity.

Many women in Warsaw sported men's jackets with padded shoulders of all shades and colours and strutted about with masculine energy. Men had a special predilection for strong top-boots, but unfortunately the Germans soon suspected who had adopted this fashion and many a young man or boy risked arrest because of it. Nevertheless, the youngsters of the Underground Army paraded in such boots all day long, disdaining the risks involved. One of my friends, who is now pining away in a prison in Poland, happened to be arrested by a German police agent in mufti while waiting at a bus stop. When he was taken to the police station in Basket Street, which now houses the Ministry of Public Security, he only got out of bribing the agent, who seemed to be a *Volksdeutsche*. When asked by my friend why he had arrested him, the agent replied: "Why the hell do you walk about in top-boots? Don't you know what sort of people wear such boots nowadays?"[73]

By early 1941 the Polish Home Army spread its network over much of German-occupied Poland. Shortly before their invasion of Russia, the Germans relented a little in their policies of subjugation; this had few effects, however. The Poles' dislike of the Russians did not lead to an abatement of their resistance against the Germans; rather the contrary. In August 1941 the first pro-Russian and pro-Communist groups appeared in eastern Poland. Their efficacy in the field was minimal, even as their appearance, for political reasons, was ominous.

In Northern and Western Europe the early history of armed resistance groups was closely involved with the clandestine warfare directed by the British, whose secret services had left agents in these countries after the latter had been conquered by the Germans. In Norway these agents were few; the Norwegian patriotic resistance began slowly, in Denmark very slowly. In Norway its chances were enhanced by the mountainous geography of the country and by the relatively few German occupation units. Milorg, the Norwegian resistance organization, had its own conflicts with the British Special Operations Executive groups throughout most of 1941.[74] This was, to some extent, similar to problems

---

[73] Korbonski, 12.
[74] The Germans knew this, and they tried to profit from these divergences. In May 1941 Hitler decided to commute the death sentences of ten Norwegians of the underground, after Sven Hedin had intervened in their behalf.

in Holland, where inadequate liaison led to a catastrophe of the principal underground[75] SOE-Dutch group in the winter of 1941–42. In Holland the first spontaneous resistance actions began immediately after the German conquest.[76] In 1940 and in 1941, except for individual acts of sabotage, they were political rather than military, expressed by various royalist and patriotic demonstrations and through the surprisingly easy clandestine printing and circulation of underground newspapers.[77] The first large working-class strike in occupied Europe took place in Holland on 25–26 February 1941. The Belgian people who, as we have seen, were confused and dejected by the circumstances of their capitulation, began sporadic instances of demonstrative resistance against the Germans in August 1940.[78] By May 1941 there were all kinds of militant groups moving within Belgium. They would attack Rexists and other armed allies of the Germans; in May 1941 the first instances of armed attack against the latter began; hand grenades were thrown at the gates of a certain German command post. The first German punitive measures were relatively restrained; but in August the Germans began to execute patriots, including an old peasant couple in Limburg province who had hidden a British pilot. On 25 October 1941 in Belgium, as in France, the Germans announced a new policy of taking hostages: They declared that every at-

---

Still, the number of people in the Norwegian resistance who died in the Second World War was smaller than the number of Norwegian pro-Nazis who died as members of their Free Corps on the Russian front.

[75] The Dutch were among the first to bring the term "underground" into political circulation (*Onderduiken* in Dutch—to dive down).

[76] In Holland on 15 May 1940. Kwiet, 43.

[77] Principal examples: *Vrij Nederland, Het Parool, De Waarheit.* The number of clandestine newspapers was even larger in Belgium, though their circulation was more limited (15,000 to 20,000 copies, with the exception of *La Libre Belgique,* which printed 70,000 copies on one occasion in September 1941). Some of these Belgian papers were *L'Espoir, La Voix des Belges, Le Peuple, La Meuse, De Werker,* and *De Vriejheid.*

[78] In Luxembourg the first anti-German demonstration occurred as early as October 1940. Goebbels noted it. Boelcke, 561a. The main Belgian demonstrations were staged on Armistice Day, 11 November 1940; on 17 February 1941, the anniversary of the death of King Albert I, the population of Brussels boycotted the official press; on the anniversary of the German invasion, 10 May 1941, demonstrators deposited masses of flowers at the grave of the Unknown Soldier and at monuments to the war dead; on 21 July 1941, Belgium's independence day, the Germans forbade all demonstrations and the flying of flags. Still, a "Te Deum" was sung, and women wore scarves and men wore neckties with the national colors.

tack on a German would be followed by multiple arrests and by the execution of at least five Belgian hostages.

"Resistance" was the headline over an editorial in the Rightist newspaper *Petit Journal* published in Bordeaux on 16 June 1940—that is, the day before Pétain was to assume power. "The government cannot capitulate without denying itself. . . . Every citizen must be ready for total resistance till the end. . . ."[79] The next day this newspaper, too, offered its full allegiance to Pétain. This was not an act of mere opportunism. In 1940 most Frenchmen regarded Pétain as a resistant, the leader of a people who must now close their ranks and remain true to themselves, resisting all kinds of foreign temptations. This attitude, so confusing and complex in retrospect and yet so clear and unequivocal at the time, remained characteristic at least throught 1940.[80] Not until early 1941 did "resistance" mean resistance to Vichy as well as to the Germans.[81] De Gaulle and his companions found few adherents in 1940 and even in 1941.[82]

We need not again recapitulate the change in the tides of French popular sentiment in this subchapter, where the record of actions has a decided priority over that of words. The first resistance networks were organized in France during the last months of 1940 ("Interallié," "F2"). They were mostly engaged in collecting all sorts of information and transmitting it to London. With few exceptions, active sabotage and armed actions against Germans did not begin until the second half of 1941. The Germans reacted immediately, by announcing and practicing their policy of hostages: By October 1941 they had shot more than one

---

[79] One of the first examples of the new usage of the word "collaboration" may be found in a letter by the General Secretaries of the Belgian civil service, directed to the German military governor, General Reeder, on 6 June 1940: "We are glad to learn that collaboration will be possible, since you will not ask from us anything that should be incompatible with our duty of loyalty toward our country." Delandsheere, Ooms, 84. In Vichy France "collaboration" became current in July; Pétain employed it in a speech on 11 October.

[80] Many of the participants of the great student manifestation on 11 November 1940 in Paris and in Rouen (in Paris a crowd marched on the Arc de Triomphe and deposited masses of flowers there, also at the foot of Clemenceau's statue) were adherents of Pétain; their leaders included members of the *Action Française*.

[81] By that time the notion of "collaboration" had become execrable. "Collaboration" with the Germans meant, as one wit said: Give me your watch and I'll tell you the time.

[82] Of the 43,000 French troops who fought against the Anglo-Gaullist forces in Syria in July 1941, less than 6,000 chose to join the Free French; the vast majority opted for repatriation. Yet Céline in *Les Beaux Draps* around that time: "All the French are Gaullists, except for a few roustabouts."

hundred of these. The Vichy regime was particularly severe against Communists. Until June 1941 this policy had a stronge tinge of conservative hypocrisy (after all, the Communists, like the Pétainists, had opposed France's war against Germany in the beginning). With few exceptions—usually out of strong local and individual initiatives—the Communists continued to assert their opposition to the war.[83] After 22 June 1941, however, they flung themselves into the struggle against the Germans with enthusiasm.

June 1941 was a milestone in the history of the French resistance; but, then, so was December 1941. After the entry of the United States in the war, the prospects of Hitler's ultimate defeat had become visible and real. A Flemish collaborationist newspaper, *National-Socialist*, wrote these bitter words on 6 December 1941 (the date is significant): "Useless to close our eyes before reality. It is a fact that in this hour the great majority of our compatriots is hostile, or at least indifferent . . . to the great National Socialist revolution that is remaking Europe. . . ."[84]

The Last European War was now over. The European civil war had begun. In France, as also elsewhere, the armed phase of the resistance was beginning to unfold. Yet it is not enough to establish these distinctions between the developing phases of the resistance. Perhaps we ought to think of the developing phases in the life of an ordinary man. The terrible event of defeat had stunned his mind temporarily, but it did not change it. He opposes the new order, convinced as he is of its senselessness and of its ultimate defeat, and he says so privately to his family and to a few close friends. Later he finds it necessary to express such beliefs publicly, on certain propitious occasions. He now finds that he is by no means alone, that there are many people, in unexpected places and in all walks of life, who share his convictions. He is willing to do something together with them. Fraternity and conspiracy enter his everyday

---

[83] There was no substantial change in the official party line until May 1941. On 15 May 1940, when the German armies were slashing across northern France, the clandestine edition of *L'Humanité* wrote of "two gangsters struggling with each other." As late as 1 May 1941 another clandestine issue berated "the rival imperialisms . . . when the English propagandists present the Gaullist movement as if it were a democratic movement, they shamelessly lie. That noble general does not desire our freedom, he desires the triumph of the imperialist interests to whom he tied his fate." Lecoeur, 65, 67. There is an interesting correspondence (from 1955) between the then retired De Gaulle and the writer Vercors on the matter of the Communists in 1940–41 in Noguères, Degliame-Fouché, Vigier, 489–90; see also the refutation of this somewhat pretentious work in Lecoeur, 25–26.

[84] Cited in Struye, 75.

life, which goes on as usual, while a portion of it is becoming devoted to something else. He collects and transmits notes, letters, all kind of information. He meets with all kinds of people, hides some of them in his house for a few nights. The day arrives when he gets a weapon, a pistol or a rifle. There is a chance that he may have to give up his more or less normal business and that he may have to leave his house and family for days, perhaps weeks. He is now risking not only a part of his life but his entire life. Within two years he moved from the danger of imprisonment to the danger of execution, perhaps of torture. This was a gradual evolution, the successive phases of which were overlapping. It happened to thousands of people in Europe between 1940 and 1943.

After 1941 in France, as also elsewhere in Western Europe, the differences between the diverse patriotic resistance groups and the Communists had become relatively unimportant, for all kinds of reasons: De Gaulle's inspiring leadership, purposefully strong against both Germans and Vichyites, purposefully vague about the politics of postwar France; the patriotic enthusiasm with which most Communists wanted (and on occasion succeeded) to expiate their earlier ambiguous record. In Eastern Europe, however, the situation was different: both more and less propitious at the same time. It was more propitious because, as we have seen earlier, the Germans had few troops in the occupied countries of the Balkans, where the traditions of patriotic banditry had survived. It was less propitious because of the no less traditional rivalries among these bands. In addition to national and tribal rivalries the rivalry between Communists and non-Communists was developing rapidly by the end of 1941. Like elsewhere in Europe, the patriotic resistance preceded the Communist one. In the Serbian provinces of Yugoslavia, General Mihailovic became active in May 1941. Within six weeks his Cetniks were engaged in various instances of armed sabotage. The Communist Broz, alias "Tito," called for a national uprising on 4 and 12 July.[85] On 21 September and on 2–3 November Tito and Mihailovic met. They could not overcome their mutual suspicions. By December 1941 they saw each other as hardened enemies, a situation from which the Germans and Italians would often profit.[86] In Greece, too, it was in December 1941

---

[85] The Communists had the advantage of claiming to be a truly Yugoslav, instead of being a Serbian or Croatian or Macedonian, movement, something that later in the war proved to be to their advantage. In 1941, however, this claim was exaggerated. Like Mihailovic's Cetniks, more than nine out of ten of Tito's early Partisans were Serbs.

[86] Mihailovic had established contact with the exiled Royalist government; Tito had few contacts with the Soviet Union at that time. In September 1941 another force appeared, a Serbian national volunteer force led by Nedic and

that the two principal arms of the guerrillas crystallized, the nationalist EDES (National Greek Democratic Union) and EAM (National Liberation Front), dominated by Communists. Like elsewhere in Europe, the armed actions of the guerrillas in the Balkans became effective only in the second half of 1942. Unlike in Western Europe, a kind of civil war developed between anti-Communists and Communists in Greece, Yugoslavia, and to some extent in Poland, toward the end of the Second World War.

There was no full-scale national uprising against the Germans anywhere in Europe before 1944, and even then only in occasional instances (Warsaw and Paris). Thus we come back to our initial qualification. For almost all practical purposes, resistance in Europe was ineffective in 1939–41.[87] Yet there was a meaning inherent in the attitudes of the resistance, including even a relatively safe demonstration at a national monument or a mimeographed sheet. Resistance against the Third Reich in this war was something new. We have seen that it was prepared by neutrals such as the Swiss[88]; it involved publications and occasional attempts at sabotage among Germany's allies; and it included the opposition to Hitler within Germany itself.[89] It involved millions of people who

---

Lyotic. Officially pro-Fascist and pro-German, it would nevertheless collaborate with Mihailovic on occasion.

[87] Hitler recognized this. On 17 September 1940 Serrano Suñer mentioned the existence of Spanish Communists in the event of an English landing in northern Spain as a response to a German attack on Gibraltar. Hitler answered that in Norway most of the people had been pro-English, and yet the English landing there had been unsuccessful.

[88] The inner Gotthard Line was conceived by General Guisan as the line of "Swiss resistance." Besides the secret military groups such as Haussamann's ( see above, pp. 265, 374), conservative patriotic groups were formed secretly in July 1940 (example: the *Eidgenoessische Gemeinschaft*, led by the conservative newspaperman Peter Duerrenmatt, significantly welcoming Leftists as well as Rightists among its ranks). The Swiss preparations for resistance included a secret radio network, instructions on how to make radios out of cigar boxes, and the dissemination of dynamite sticks.

[89] To sum up the principal phases of German resistance conspiracies: The first crystallized in July–September 1938, composed mostly of officers in the supreme command of the Army; the second, in the autumn and winter of 1939–40, was composed mainly of people from Canaris' *Abwehr;* the third, in the winter of 1942 and the early spring of 1943, was made up by officers of Army Group Center; the July 1944 conspiracy was more general, centering around the general staff of the Home Army. It was typical of the complicated loyalties during the Second World War that the *Abwehr* personnel of German military counterintelligence played an efficient role in destroying pro-Allied resistance groups in Holland and in France.

were thinking for themselves and proved therefore immune to German and Nazi propaganda. Many of these people, especially in Western Europe, had also moved beyond their traditional nationalism.[90] In France, Italy, Belgium, and Holland, the idea of a truly international resistance began to be expressed by the men and women of certain small resistance groups in 1941, early signs of the movement toward a democratic united Europe, to which we shall now turn.

## "UNITED EUROPE"?

¶ The history of a united Europe belongs to intellectual, not political history, to the history of ideas, to the realm of grandiose plans wholly devoid of reality, easily conceivable on paper, inconceivable in practice. There were instances, short moments in the history of the Continent when some kind of a political union was in the making because of the conquest of a large portion of the Continent by a single power, as for a few years under Napoleon; but this kind of unification by force was not what the occasional idealists of a united Europe had in mind. This pattern reappeared in 1940 and after. Hitler was bringing about a more or less united Europe, where a kind of conformity would be enforced by the domination of the Third Reich. This enforced union was opposed by

---

[90] It behooves us, at this point, to make at least a cursory reference to those resistance and guerrilla movements that in 1939–41 were directed not against the occupying Germans but against the occupying Russians. In Lithuania, for example, as many as 50,000 men had risen against the retreating Russians in June 1941, with the ultimate hope that the Germans would recognize their leadership (under the nationalist Ambrazevicius) as the government of Lithuania, a hope that failed. (The Lithuanian Christian Democrats were reluctant to join this national movement because of its compromising associations with the Germans.) There were sporadic Ukrainian uprisings against the crumbling Polish state in September 1939, including the 6,000 Ukrainian nationalists who had been sequestered in Polish detention camps (Bereza Kartuska) in that year. On a larger scale, such Ukrainian risings occurred again in June 1941 as the Germans were advancing across eastern Poland. The Soviet massacres and deportations of Lithuanians, Latvians, Estonians, and Ukrainians were brutal preventive measures against such occurrences. So were their senseless deportations (including 440,000 civilians and 200,000 prisoners of war), of which the most infamous was their mass murder of 15,000 Polish officers in the camps of Starobelsk, Koziel, Ostashkov, and Katyn (at the latter place alone, 4,143 officers were killed, and the victims from the other camps were thrown into mass graves there, found by the Germans in 1943).

people who sought a union of resistance against Germany, going beyond the confines of individual nations. Some of these people were attracted by the prospect of democratic national federations after Hitler's defeat.

The reappearance of a pattern does not, however, mean that history is merely repeating itself. During the Second World War there was an element in the history of Europe that was different from the past. It was an element of consciousness, dynamic rather than static: It both preceded Hitler and the Second World War and survived it, stronger than before. This element was the consciousness of being European. In diverse (and, sometimes, in perverted and hypocritical) forms, it appeared in the thoughts and in the words of both warring camps. The desire for a united Europe, having grown beyond the realm of abstract speculations, attracted people who were willing to go along with Hitler, and others who were bitterly opposed to him.

Again we cannot, within the confines of this book, survey this development in detail. The development of a European consciousness was largely, though not exclusively, a twentieth-century phenomenon, more recent than what most people believe. It developed around 1900 in the minds of certain thinking men as a reaction to their sudden recognition that Europe was, after all, a small peninsula of Asia, that the American and Russian and Japanese empires were on the rise, against which the nations and even the traditional empires of Europe counted less and less. This recognition, not unnaturally, occurred to men whose nations had in their lifetime suffered severe defeats: the French Valéry; Spaniards such as Ortega and Madariaga; the German Spengler, whose monumental *Decline of the West* (the accurate translation of the German title is, rather, *The Sinking of the West*) was completed during the year of the German empire's lost war, in 1918. In any event, after the First World War the idea of Europe became sufficiently widespread among a certain cultural and political elite. Though it had been mostly Wilsonian in inspiration, the League of Nations was more European than the future United Nations was to be; in 1930 it even included the proposal for some kind of European political federation on its agenda, by way of a characteristically vague memorandum by Briand. More important was Count Coudenhove-Kalergi's "Pan-Europe" movement. This intelligent and cosmopolitan aristocrat in Vienna (another defeated capital on the ruins of an empire) in 1923 wrote a book with that title, proposing a confederation of all of Europe, excluding the Soviet Union. During the 1920s the Pan-Europe movement became very respectable; a series of conferences and meetings attracted the support of many eminent writers, thinkers, and politicians across the Continent. With Hitler in power, this movement, like the League of Nations, faded quickly. The rise of the Third Reich demonstrated the radical strength of nationalism, together with the inherent weakness of internationalism. In 1939 Richard Coudenhove-Kalergi found himself in Paris, in the company of thousands of Central European exiles.

As the war began, however, the reputation of the idea of a European federation, and of European federations, began to rise. There were at least two principal reasons for this. Hitler had conquered one small country after another, taking advantage of their jealousies and of their unwillingness to stand together. Strength lay in union, not in divisions[91]: The neighboring states of Europe must join together. The other reason was the attractiveness of the prospect beyond the war. To defeat the Third Reich was not enough; the Allies ought to present a grander vision of Europe as one of their aims in this war. Consequently the French government lent its official sympathy to this kind of thing during the winter of the reluctant war. They liked, for example, the proposal of the Polish Foreign Minister, Zaleski, that Poland should gain East Prussia and join in a kind of federation with Slovakia, Hungary, and Austria. They supported the historically minded federationist plans and groups of Otto von Habsburg[92] and of Coudenhove-Kalergi, both in France at the time. The idea of a Danubian federation especially appealed to the French.[93] The British government, with somewhat less enthusiasm, went along. As early as 20 December 1939, the War Cabinet recorded that it was advisable "to encourage closer co-operation between the Balkan States and closer co-operation between the various refugee groups of Poles, Czechs, Slovaks, and Austrians."[94]

---

[91] In the summer of 1939 the book by the American publicist Clarence Streit, *Union Now*, created a certain stir. His proposal for a union of the Atlantic democracies belongs, however, to the history of American, rather than of European, internationalism.

[92] The Nazis were sometimes worried by Otto's influence. This appeared in the reports of the RSHA *Meldungen*, concerning monarchist sentiments within Austria in 1939–40 (examples: MA 138, 441/4 0125; 0066, etc.). On 11 March 1940 Ribbentrop complained to Mussolini about "the machinations of Otto von Habsburg." *GD*, D, VIII, 898–99.

[93] Unlike the English, they were amenable to certain ideas of German separatism: They were interested not only in Otto von Habsburg but also in Prince Rupprecht of Bavaria. The English, on the other hand, were willing to engage in secret talks with non-Nazi Germans in the winter of 1939–40, without mentioning the restoration of Austrian independence as a condition of peace.

[94] Woodward, I, 285. From the same memorandum: "One of the weaknesses of the post-war settlement was the establishment of a number of small national States which were 'viable' neither in the military nor economic sense."

The most important and significant of these attempts toward a closer union of states was the one involving France and Great Britain, even though it failed at the dramatic moment of its presentation. It is generally assumed that this drastic proposition of a large-scale union of the two Western democracies was Churchill's[95] sudden and impetuous and desperate move before the prospect of a complete French collapse. This was not the case. The idea of joint Anglo-French institutions, including joint departments of government, was current throughout the winter of 1939–40—indeed, it was becoming an *idée reçue* in Paris, where the government as well as high political circles favored it. (Its principal proponents in England included Professor Toynbee and his circle of the Royal Institute of International Affairs in Chatham House.[96]) A significant reference to a closer association of France and Britain, extending beyond the war, was included in the last paragraph of the 28 March 1940 treaty wherein the two states bound themselves not to conclude a separate peace.[97] Churchill's surprising announcement of an Anglo-French union on 16 June 1940 did not, therefore, spring out from a void. Stimulated by the concept of a Europe that had become a kind of mental patrimony of certain aristocrats, patrician bourgeois, intellectuals, and cultivated men and women, it had been a concept especially congenial to the Francophile Churchill and to the Anglophile Reynaud, both pro-Europeans.[98]

---

[95] See above, pp. 84–85.

[96] See M. Beloff, "The Anglo-French Union Project of June 1940," *The Intellectual in Politics* (New York, 1971), 172–99. Reporting to the Foreign Office on his visit to Paris (9–12 March) "on 13 March Professor Toynbee said that he had been very struck by the general welcome for such ideas even among Frenchmen to whom the abstract ideas of federalism made no appeal. . . . The reasons for this favourable current of opinion were, he believed, that an announcement of such plans would act as a stimulus to French morale, and discourage the Nazis, and that such a union would provide a gravitational pull for the smaller neutrals, while discouraging the more powerful neutral states from pressing for an inconclusive peace." Ibid., 177. It is interesting to note that during these months the proponents of an Anglo-French union spoke frequently of adopting some of the features of the old Austro-Hungarian monarchy, whose reputation at that time was significantly high.

[97] On 29 March 1940 the *Times* of London wrote that "Anglo-French unity has already reached a more advanced point than at any other period during the last war . . . this point is but the first step toward a closer and more lasting association." The next day in *Le Figaro* Wladimir d'Ormesson saw in the declaration a historic step: "England . . . is now in Europe." Cited by Beloff, 174.

[98] Unlike Chamberlain and Pétain. Before 1940 Churchill often referred to "Europe" in his public speeches; Chamberlain seldom.

Still, the Anglo-French union plan was buried in the ruins of the collapsing house of France in June 1940. A massive shift had taken place, not only in the balance of power of the world but also in the connotation of "Europe." "Europe" was no longer some kind of a patrician association. It now meant the Continent over which the Third Reich was dominant. While the term "Europe" had been mainly employed by Franco-British propaganda in 1939–40, henceforth it was to be used by the propaganda of the Third Reich for political purposes, for the duration of the war.

Hitler had no particular interest in the idea of Europe. True, he was not much interested in colonies[99]; but he was interested in the reorganization of Europe simply to assure Germany's domination.[100] Goebbels understood this very well. His confidential propaganda instructions throughout the summer of 1940 repeated the cynical theme: Talk of a New Europe, but keep the ultimate purpose of German hegemony in mind. "If someone asks now how we visualize the new Europe, we must say that we don't know. . . . Once we shall have power . . . we shall see. . . . Everyone can imagine what he wants. But at the proper time we shall know what we want." The record of the Germans' cynicism,[101] of their eventual mismanagement of the European idea, has been surveyed by certain historians. It was also evident to certain contemporary neutral observers.[102] Within Germany the persecuted philologist Viktor Klem-

---

[99] He said to Mussolini on 4 October 1940, talking about a future peace treaty with France: Germany had gained considerable territories "in the East and in the North of Europe, and he did not intend to present large demands for colonies simply because a colonial empire would look good on the map. . . ."

[100] For this purpose he would allow a limited autonomy to the conquered lands. Already in 1939 he said that "the Czechs should be treated in a conciliatory manner, though with the greatest strictness and relentless consistency. . . ."

[101] Examples: The German political delegate Hemmen to General Huntziger of the Franco-German Armistice Commission on 22 July 1940: France will have to adjust her living standards to those of Germany. Germany wishes to reconstruct Europe; she has no interest in seeing France perish by famine or undergo the dangers of a revolution. She wants to reconstruct Europe with French participation, and suppress forever the dangers of a future war, etc. *CDA*, I, 77. This was meant for French consumption. Privately, Ribbentrop told Mussolini on 19 September 1940 that "according to the Fuehrer's intentions, France must never again play an important role in the life of Europe." Ribbentrop to Ciano: "France was to be treated absolutely as an enemy, and the instructions which the Fuehrer had issued to the German press . . . was purely tactical." *GD*, D, X, 149.

[102] George Kennan, traveling from Germany to Holland in June 1940, noted the conversation of German Nazis and of a Dutch Nazi sympathizer ("the latter, incidentally, an intelligent person" on the train. "As the train pulled into

perer noted that the idea of a New Europe had not appeared in Nazi language before 1939, but even then it was implicitly contradicted by the constant references to the Greater Germanic Reich and to its historical antecedents.[103] Whatever evidence we possess shows that German popular sentiment sensed the reality: The reports of popular opinion show no attention to the idea of Europe at all. The German people were not interested. With the beginning of the war against Russia, and especially after the first troubles in Russia, this began to change: The notion that Germany was Europe's bulwark against Asian Bolshevism appealed to the Germans.[104] But a full orchestration of this theme by Goebbels came only after 1941, later in the war, as the danger of a Russian invasion of Germany was to appear.

Still, no matter how disingenuous the Germans may have been, on the part of many Europeans there was a genuine reaction to the tremendous earthquake of 1940, a reaction that crystallized the idea of a united Europe in their minds. As early as 25 May 1940 Leopold III told the Belgian Cabinet: They must understand that the entire war may be over and something big may be beginning. The former Dutch Prime Minister,

---

The Hague, I could not help remarking to him that he would indeed have a hard time creating a Dutch National Socialist movement: for either it would be truly Dutch, in which case it would be only an unsuccessful competition for the German movement, or it would be pan-Germanic, in which case all the values of Dutch nationalism would be sacrificed and the adherents, instead of being superior Dutchmen, would only become inferior Germans. . . . By the time my inquiries into German occupational policies were completed, I was persuaded that there was, from the German viewpoint, no hopeful answer to the problem." Kennan, *M*, 128–29.

[103] Klemperer, 198–99.

[104] This argument, taken up by Hitler toward the end of the war, and employed by the Germans assiduously for the sake of impressing some of their enemies, including Americans, was, again, disingenuous. Hitler preferred the Japanese and the Chinese to some of the nations of Europe. This appears frequently from his wartime conversations and especially from his last talks, recorded by Bormann; but we have an early evidence of this from the confidential instructions issued by the party Chancellery in 1941. These warn against the recent tendency to give biological emphasis to the political and economic unity of Europe. Expressions such as the "European" or "white race" are not desirable. "So far as racial politics go, during the coming decades the German people will not seek conflicts with the populations of other continents; instead, it will have to assert its own characteristics (*seinen eigenen Anlagenbestand*) against numerous European peoples, including those closely collaborating with us. The obscuring of actual racial differences within Europe leads to the danger of inter-migration and . . . of the influence of foreign workers. . . ." P-K *Ver/Inf*, 29–52 (9 Aug. 1941).

Colijn, one of the most respected political figures in Holland, wrote in a pamphlet in June 1940: "One fact dominates everything: Germany will now lead Europe." On 10 August Colijn said in a speech: "Whatever the outcome of this war, it is not to be doubted that Germany will assume a position on the continent of Europe which may be best compared with the conductor of a great orchestra."[105] Leemans, the Secretary General in charge of economic affairs in Belgium, spoke of "a positive willingness to contribute to the making of a new order in Europe." The French people, said their Foreign Minister, Baudouin, in a speech on 22 August 1940, "prepare themselves for a new order" in Europe. On 27 August the French Finance Minister, Bouthillier, offered "full collaboration for the purpose of economic organization of the new Europe" to Hemmen of the German Armistice Commission.[106] On 30 August Laval repeated these sentiments; on 30 October Pétain, in a radio address, spoke of the honor and the unity of France "within the framework of the constructive activity of a New European order." "This war," said Laval in November 1940, "is not like the other wars, it is a revolution. . . . France, together with the other great nations of Europe, must fulfill two tasks: build the peace, and construct a [European] socialism." German propaganda in France, presided over by Abetz in Paris, worked relentlessly for this idea. In the Grand Palais an exhibition *La France européenne* ran for months in the winter of 1940–41.[107] This kind of talk was not only typical of those who had committed themselves to Hitler's cause. In June the German minister reported from Finland: "Recognition of the German leadership . . . finds spontaneous expression everywhere. Mixed in are voices which speak of a new and better Europe and perceive in a German hegemony a guarantee against the danger from the East."[108] On 12 September 1940 the Swiss President said to his people in a radio address: "The solidarity of the continent . . . is developing in an increasing manner. To deny this would be silly; and to fail to perceive it [would be] dangerous."[109]

The tidal movement of these sentiments was not synchronized with the Germans' attitudes. The latter, as we have seen, in 1940 cared little for "Europe," except for their own propagandistic purposes in the war

---

[105] Cited in Kwiet, 117.

[106] *CDA*, I, 185.

[107] In September 1940 the association of Parisian booksellers abjectly decided to withdraw the works of certain anti-German authors from their shelves because of "the wish to establish the necessary conditions for a more healthy and objective appreciation of European Problems." The list ("Otto") of the proscribed authors and books followed.

[108] Blücher (25 June 1940), cited by Krosby, 25.

[109] Wolf, 348.

against England[110]; and when after June 1941 their own interest in the idea of Europe arose, the waves of a pro-German European sentiment had already subsided, except for the few hardened collaborationists and National Socialists across the Continent.[111]

Among the latter there remained a few idealists whose commitment to the idea of Europe had preceded the rise of the Third Reich.[112] The clearest expressions of their thinking during the war may be found in the writings of Drieu la Rochelle, who, like Valéry, had seen years before that France and Europe were diminishing.[113] His commitment to Europe and to Fascism was now united.[114] "I am a Fascist because I measured the progress of decadence in Europe. I have seen in Fascism the only means to contain and to reduce this decadence; and, besides, having no more confidence in the political resources of England than in those of France, rejecting the intrusion of foreign empires such as the United States and Russia into our continent, I have seen no other recourse than that in the genius of Hitler and of Hitlerism."[115] Alfred Fabre-Luce was more

---

[110] Much of this trans-European literature in 1940–41 has not yet been studied sufficiently by historians. An Italian view in a book entitled *Toward the Balance of the New Europe*, published in 1941, for example: "In the Europe of today and tomorrow the new order requires that the small nations conform to the great ones: the strong must be strong. . . ." De Mattei, 160.

[111] Degrelle, for example, the Belgian Fascist leader who in August 1941 announced that he had volunteered with the German Army for the Russian front. He declared: "My political actions in Belgium must now remain in the background. Now when the fate of Europe is decided in the East, it is my duty to go with my followers. I do not know whether I shall return from this expedition, but I think that it is better to die nobly than to live ignobly."

[112] There were others, whose inclination toward Germany and toward a national kind of socialism preceded their interest in Europe: Knut Hamsun, for example, who wrote to his daughter in May 1941: "Next year the war will be over and light will dominate everywhere. This will be a joy! England will be crushed, and then my soul will rejoice. Europe will be properly organized—my God, how welcome this will be!"

[113] In *Mesure de la France* (1922).

[114] "(1) Ever since my first poems in 1917 I wanted to marry the love for France with the love for Europe. (2) I saw the merits and necessities in dying capitalism as well as in the birth of socialism. (3) I have sought the rebirth of aristocratic and autocratic values beyond their mere prestige from the past." Drieu, *CRP*, 9.

[115] In *La Revolution Nationale* (23 Jan. 1943). It must be said that, unlike other French pro-Nazis—Benoist-Méchin, for example, who in *Le Moisson de Quarante* (Paris, 1940) waxed rhapsodic about the German military allowing the harvesting of French peasants in the golden Beauce, and wrote that the New Europe will be like the Beauce, Germans and French working side by side—Drieu saw the prospect of German defeat early in the war. In March

careful. "Ideological variations come and go," he wrote in 1941, "but the function of Europe remains the theme of the twentieth century."[116]

We have seen that the idea of European federations had a considerable following among the exiles in Paris during the first winter of the war. After the cataclysmic summer of 1940, the attraction of such ideas revived again. Among the smaller peoples of Europe, the Belgians and the Dutch overcame their mutual distrust during their catastrophe; by early 1941 the idea of a postwar federation of the Lowlands was a common subject of talk among people in these occupied countries as well as among their exiled governments, which were beginning to draw up the first plans for their eventual customs union and federation after the war. The Finnish and Swedish governments were proposing a partial federation of their states in the fall of 1940, a plan opposed at that time by Germany as well as by the Soviet Union. The Polish and the Czechoslovak exile governments declared their plans for a postwar federation on 11 November 1940, reaffirming this in January 1942.[117] The Yugoslav and Greek exile governments declared in favor of a democratic federation of Balkan states.

At least as significant as these political projects were the inclinations of various resistance movements during the second half of 1941. They included spontaneous expressions of the idea of a supernational struggle against the Third Reich, transcending the national frontiers of matter as well as of spirit. Italian anti-Fascists, for example, played a considerable role in the first resistance organizations in the South of France in 1940–41. The first manifestos of some of these resistance groups called for a united or federated Europe after the war. Catholic resistance groups, especially the Christian Democrats in Western Europe, were especially receptive to such ideas, the further development of which would carry us beyond the confines of this book. We must, however, note their significance. During the Second World War the political, intellectual, and perhaps even spiritual ideas of the resistance, of Christian democracy, of a revivified international Socialism, and of a united

---

1942 he wrote: "The Russians in Berlin: It will be the instantaneous, irresistible victory of Communism in the entire West." Drieu, *CRP*, 340. Like Goebbels or Céline (the latter in *Rigodon:* "Europe died at Stalingrad"), Drieu was wrong.

[116] Fabre-Luce, I, 268.

[117] The history of their relations is significant, principally because of the Soviet Union. Benes, the leader of the Czechs, was inclined to subordinate his good relations with other allied nations, including the Poles, to his relations with the Soviet Union; he followed such a policy even before June 1941. In August 1941 the Russians convoked a Pan-Slav Congress in Moscow. The Polish and Yugoslav exile governments declined to participate; the Czechs did not.

Europe, were developing together; and they were popular enough to carry the peoples and the politicians of Western Europe toward the first steps of federations and common institutions after the war.

After the war, in 1946, the French writer Maurice Druon said at a meeting in Geneva, dedicated to "the European mind":

> I have known two Europes, two Europes that existed. One, the Europe of the night, which began in 1940 for us and for other peoples even earlier, was a Europe in which for a moment the same sun rising in the Caucasus set in the Atlantic. . . . I have known another Europe, a weak Europe being born, having its seat in London, a Europe made up by a few exiles, by certain volunteers, all Europeans, because they did not merely belong to the nation of their birth but because they truly belonged to a common struggle, and it is this Europe which, in the end, had won.[118]

## AMERICANIZATION

¶ In 1941 many of the peoples of Europe would have accepted the leadership of Britain on the Continent. British leadership, instead of German domination: For the subjugated peoples[119] it sounded like a dream or, rather, the promise at the end of a nightmare, a marvelous relief, just and good. And the dream had a substance in reality. The British incarnated the cause of the war against the Third Reich from the beginning. The exile governments in London, the resistance groups across the Continent, indeed, no one who opposed Hitler, doubted that Britain would be a great power after the defeat of Germany, that she would play a great role in the affairs of Europe in reconstructing her political order, that the destinies of Britain and of Europe would be closely bound together.

In 1941 even Stalin believed this, beyond the bloody edge of the blazing front in the East. Yet it was not to be. And this was to be a tragedy for Europe as well as for Britain, and probably for remnant Western civilization at large, this abdication of the British after the war, when they could have had the leadership of a united Western Europe for a song. After 1945 the Labor government was narrow, parochial, parsimonious, ultimately at the cost of what remained of British greatness. Yet already during the war Churchill himself was at least in part responsible

---

[118] Druon, 208.

[119] With the partial exception of the French, because of their feelings of shame in face of the British.

for this abdication of British leadership.[120] There were at least three main elements in this wanting British response to Europe. One was their lack of imagination—a national characteristic of sorts, which at times (as in 1940) could stand them in good stead. Another element, no less a national characteristic at the time, was pride, the insular pride of the British who stood up to the Germans when all of their European neighbors had fallen down. But the third, and the most important element, was the American factor.[121]

We have to enlarge our compass, for a moment, in order to comprehend this. In 1898, at the end of their imperial century, more than forty years before the Second World War, more than fifteen years before the First World War, there occurred a great turning point in British policy. From that moment on the British government and press never "departed from the attitude, now definitely adopted, of deliberately courting the friendship of the American Government and people."[122] This was the underlying element in the choices of British statesmanship already before and during the First World War.[123] It was, as we have

---

[120] Here is another example of the problem that often compromises what are truly inter-national relationships: the time lag in different national mentalities. We have seen that the Germans' interest in a united Europe developed too late (because of their own selfish reasons), so that they provided really no response for what had been a genuine willingness of many European nations to go along with them in 1940. In a different way the British convinced themselves to ally their fortunes to Europe in the 1960s, twenty years too late, twenty years after the peoples of Europe had been not only willing but desirous to welcome not only their presence but also their leadership.

[121] Churchill, of all people, was not wanting in imagination; rather the contrary. His English pride, too, was great and generous, and he knew enough of Europe to understand what her survival meant to Britain herself. But this man, who chafed at every retreat during his long career, abdicated to the Americans in almost every important instance. Paradoxically enough, his very imagination and his generosity, the willingness not the narrowness of his heart made him go along with the Americans even when he should have opposed them. For the irony of history is but the result of the mysterious alchemy of the human heart.

[122] Halévy, V, 44, note 2.

[123] This is why the British decided to relinquish their alliance with Japan in 1921, an event with incalculable consequences. But consider, too, what the relatively Anglophile and internationalist Franklin Roosevelt wrote to Norman Davis on 9 November 1934: "Simon and a few other Tories must be constantly impressed with the simple fact that if Great Britain is even suspected of preferring to play with Japan to playing with us, I shall be compelled, in the interest of American security, to approach public sentiment in Canada, Australia, New

seen, the dominant, though often unspoken, factor in the decision of the British government to stand up to Hitler in 1939. Had America remained truly neutral, in 1939, the British would not, because they felt they could not, stand up to Hitler.[124] This American factor influenced every decision of British strategy during the war.[125]

In this there was no difference between Chamberlain and Churchill. The latter, however, was not content with *de facto* American support. A greater, sentimental idea governed his entire political life. He believed in the necessity—indeed, in the desirability—of an ever closer union of the English-speaking peoples of the world. He wrote about it and preached it throughout his life.[126] He referred to it, in ringing tones, throughout 1940. During the Second World War he saw a chance of putting it into practice. He believed—and not without reason—that a close union of America and Britain would have prevented the First World War; it would have prevented the Second World War; even after the Second World War it could have been the greatest force for good in the world. But it did not happen. Beyond their alliances in the two world wars, the Anglo-American partnership did not develop into a closer union. During

---

Zealand and South Africa in a definite effort to make these Dominions understand clearly that their future security is linked with us in the United States." Nixon, Edgar B., *Franklin D. Roosevelt and Foreign Affairs, 1933–1937*, II, 263 cited by Pelz, 141.

[124] As early as 1 July 1939 Roosevelt told the British ambassador to Washington that, while the United States was to be neutral in the case of war, "it would be his desire that the United States government should establish a patrol over the waters of the Western Atlantic with a view of denying them to warlike operations of belligerents." This momentous declaration was made in all secrecy, with high officials of the American government, including the secretaries of State, of the Navy, and the Chief of Naval Operations present. The British ambassador's report is cited in Pelz, 195, note 42.

[125] See above, pp. 100–2. Further examples: On 31 October 1939 the British chiefs of staff, contemplating the possibility of a Russian attack on Finland, minuted that "from a military point of view we should avoid war with the U.S.S.R. The situation would be different if the United States entered the war." Woodward, I, 38. In early April 1940 Chamberlain and Churchill were pushing the French for the mine-laying in the Rhine (Royal Marine). Chamberlain told Daladier that this operation "would deflect American opinion from criticism of the [Allied] action in Norwegian territorial waters." Ibid., I, 115. The British decision to engage in Greece was also made with American opinion in mind.

[126] His political career began at the same moment, 1898, when this turning point of British imperial policy had been reached. Also, as in Hitler's case, Churchill's strong love for his mother (American by birth) was an important factor in his personality, even as these two sons sublimated their filial affections in very different ways.

the first half of the twentieth century, during a time span which corresponds almost exactly to Churchill's active political life, from about 1900
to 1955, this *Pax Anglo-Americana* was a possibility. It may have assured
the survival of Western civilization for another century to come.
Churchill was not alone in trying to further it, but he did not have his
way. Perhaps he failed to comprehend the declining influence of the
Anglo-Saxon element among the American people, a discussion of which
does not belong in this book. It was, in any event, the great failure of his
life.

The idea of an eventual Atlantic federation of the English-speaking
peoples was one thing, the idea of an eventual European union was
another. They contradicted one another; but a discussion of this, too,
does not properly belong here. More important was the fact that already
in 1939 the British government was willing to accept a subordinate role in
relation to the United States. In the summer of 1939, more than a year
before the exchange of American destroyers for British bases in the
Western Hemisphere, the British first proposed that the American Navy
occupy bases on the islands of Trinidad and St. Lucia and in the Ber-
mudas. More than two years before the arrival of American troops in
Britain, the British ambassador to Washington proposed to his government that the Americans be offered bases in the British Isles—a first in the
long history of Britain. Lothian's proposal was shelved at the time; still, it
was typical of the Anglo-American relationship that was fast developing.
The United States was not yet in the war; yet the fighting British, including Churchill, assumed more and more the role of a suppliant.[127] In the

---

[127] Churchill's relationship with Roosevelt was a complex one, as yet
insufficiently studied by historians, even as it provides the key to much of what
happened later. Churchill's attitude to Roosevelt was open and insouciant; it
had a kind of engaging simplicity of its own. Roosevelt's attitude to Churchill
was more complicated, as indeed was the American people's attitude to the
British. In spite of their actual superiority, traces of American suspicion and
feelings of inferiority toward the British still prevailed in 1940 and 1941,
though much of this would dissipate by the end of the war. (In 1941 Halifax,
then British ambassador to the United States, spoke in various American cities.
His speech in Milwaukee was a success, as the mayor of Milwaukee said afterward that "up to now there have always been some of us here who would have
expected when we meet the British ambassador that we should find him too
smart for us. After meeting Lord Halifax we don't think so any longer."
Birkenhead, *Halifax*, 489.)
   Churchill was also handicapped by bad luck. His meetings with Roosevelt
coincided with some of the worst of British defeats. At the first summit, in
August 1941, as a young American historian put it: "For physical, political,
and symbolic reasons it was necessary that Churchill undertake the larger part
of the journey, that the Old World come, as it were, cap-in-hand to the New.

long run the result of this was to be an almost total British dependence on the United States, an event with incalculable consequences for the future of Europe. In the short run, however, what matters is not what happens but what people think happens. Few people in Europe, in 1941, thought much about what the American domination over Great Britain would mean. Few cared. Whether the British would defeat Hitler alone or whether they would liberate Europe together with the Americans mattered not at all. Most people, the Germans' allies as well as their enemies, kept speaking of the "Anglo-Saxons," as if the English, the Americans, the Canadians, etc., were cousins, brothers, the same. Those who saw—or who pretended to see—further were a handful: De Gaulle in London, Hitler in Berlin,[128] probably Stalin (who always preferred the Americans to the British), and here and there a thoughtful pro-German collaborator, such as Drieu la Rochelle, who wrote on 22 May 1941: "England is now absorbed by America. America, through Wilson, revealed her dangerous incompetence in organizing peace in Europe. Clemenceau's errors at Versailles had been conditioned by those of Lloyd George and those of the latter by those of Wilson. . . . The problem of 1941 is no longer the problem of 1940. We no longer have to choose between England and Germany, but between America and Europe. . . ."[129] The vast majority of his compatriots refused this choice—for the time being, rightly so.

The prestige of the United States during the Second World War was enormous throughout Europe, as it had been at the end of the First World War. During the First World War the decisive importance of American intervention had dawned gradually on the peoples of the Continent. During the Second World War the decisive importance of American intervention was taken for granted from the beginning; indeed, in many ways it was discounted in advance. We have touched upon some of this in Part I, where we had to mention certain instances, beginning in 1939, when the government of the United States, surreptitiously or openly, intervened in European politics and in the European war. The British were not the only ones who tied their fate to the United States. Had the United States entered the war in June 1940 the French would

---

F.D.R. could not go to England." Wilson, 19. The second summit, in December 1941, came in the wake of the British naval and military disasters in the Far East. During the third summit, in June 1942, Tobruk fell to Rommel, the lowest point of Churchill's political fortunes in the war.

[128] Hitler to Serrano Suner on 25 September 1940: "England has become an American colony." Hitler did not understand that this would only strengthen the Spanish inclination not to become an enemy of the United States.

[129] Drieu, *CRP*, 309.

have probably fought on, at least in Africa.[130] Had the United States remained truly neutral in 1941 the Russians would have probably not fought
on, not even in Siberia. "The world influence of the President and government of the United States was enormous," Stalin told Harry Hopkins
on 31 July 1941.[131] Britain and Russia could not defeat Germany by themselves. The "one thing" that could defeat Hitler, "perhaps without ever
firing a shot, would be the announcement that the United States was going
to war with Germany."[132]

It was not quite as simple as that. *De facto* the United States was
waging war against Germany in 1941, many months before the Japanese
and Axis declarations of war, an undeclared naval war in the Atlantic for
which there were precedents in the history of the United States, together
with instances of a more or less clandestine political warfare in places in
Europe and in North Africa for which there were no precedents in the
history of the Republic, and some of which still deserve their serious
historian.[133] *De jure*, however, the United States was still a neutral or,
rather, officially a nonbelligerent power, until December 1941. This con-

---

[130] Reynaud knew this, even as he did not fully comprehend the constitutional
and political impossibility of such an intervention at that time. Still, he
influenced Roosevelt's mind at least in one way that is worth a footnote. It is
generally accepted that Roosevelt's speech in Charlottesville, Virginia, on 10
June 1940, condemning Mussolini's attack on France, marked a turning point
in American attitudes. The President spoke of Mussolini's "stab in the back."
This forceful, though not particularly original, metaphor must have been suggested to him by Reynaud's telegram that morning: "At the hour in which I
am addressing you, another dictator has just struck France in the back. . . ."
Reynaud, 478.
[131] Here was another example of the discrepancy between image and reality.
Actually in the summer of 1941 Roosevelt was lethargic and depressed because
of the continued strength of isolationist sentiment. People within his circle,
such as Ickes, remarked "growing discontent with the President's lack of leadership."
[132] This was when Stalin first said that he would welcome American forces
"on any part of the Russian front under the complete command of the American Army." *FRUS*, 1941, I, 805–14.
[133] Examples of this rapid development of American diplomatic practices: In
November 1940 the British asked Washington to warn Bulgaria against align-
ing herself with the Axis. The State Department refused, but not for long. By
the end of the year (coinciding with Roosevelt's decision to proceed with
Lend-lease), Washington put pressure on the Bulgarian minister, and in
January 1941 Roosevelt sent Colonel Donovan to Lisbon, Madrid, Athens,
Belgrade, and Sofia to stir up resistance against Germany. (In Lisbon Salazar
was very skeptical and concerned about American interest in the Azores.) By
1941 the activities of American consuls and agents in French Morocco had
become extensive, and the Germans protested against their presence to Vichy.

dition had certain consequences on the Continent. They are significant in retrospect, especially in view of the later policy of the United States confronting Russia after the war. Between 1939 and 1941 (and in some places and ways even afterward), the United States was the hope of certain conservatives, even more than of democrats or radicals. The British were committed to a war against Germany and Nazism to the bitter end; the Americans were not. Uncommitted by self-interest, the United States could be the great mediating world power, ultimately bringing about peace with justice. This was the hope of the Vichy French, of those conservative elements in Europe who looked with distaste at the British alliance with the Soviet Union, of the neutrals, of the Vatican, and even in certain ways of the Germans. It was a hope encouraged by the utterances of certain Americans[134]; it was to fade later during the war, reviving in 1945 and after: America the hope of Christian Europe (whatever that was) against atheistic Communism (whatever that was), with the silent assumption that the total defeat of Germany (and of Japan) had not been in the interests of the United States, after all.

The United States continued to recognize the Vichy government after the collapse of the Third Republic, for a number of reasons, including the "keeping an open window" in the middle of Hitler's Western European courtyard.[135] The purpose of this American window was not merely that of continued observation but also that of possible influence. On 23 November 1940 Roosevelt appointed one of his close advisers, Admiral Leahy, to the post of ambassador in France. Leahy arrived in Vichy on 7 January 1941. His influence was more than considerable[136] in Vichy,

---

[134] These included not only the isolationist spokesmen but also certain American diplomats such as Kennedy in London and Cudahy in Brussels. (The latter to the German minister in January 1940: "He was not entirely in agreement with the President's current policies. He would have found it more desirable for America to take a completely objective and neutral attitude. . . ." *GD*, D, VII, 693.) There was a definite political tendency in ex-President Hoover's plan to supply food, etc., to some of the German-occupied countries, especially Belgium and France. Hoover (whom Hitler liked) in a speech in August 1940 attributed equal blame to Britain and to Germany for the sufferings of small nations, and he criticized the Belgian exile government later for not supporting his campaign. The British saw the political inclinations beneath Hoover's humanitarian proposals: They were "suspect, since [they] came from elements in the United States known to be working for a compromise peace." Woodward, II, 62.

[135] For this purpose the government of Canada, too, maintained its representation by a consul-general in Vichy.

[136] "Admiral Leahy was one of those men who, although unable to converse with any Frenchman in intelligible French, believed himself the supreme exponent of French mentality." Macmillan, 160.

where all of the different and divergent politicians were unanimous in putting great hopes on the United States. They cultivated American friendship assiduously, on occasion to the point of servility.[137] The American card was the ace in the world deck. At a future day it could be played against Germany. Meanwhile, they tried to play it against the British and, of course, against De Gaulle,[138] for whom the State Department and Roosevelt cultivated a dislike that was narrow, categorical, and rigid. Unlike De Gaulle, the Vichy people would have accepted a nearly absolute dependence of France on the United States after the war—a political attitude on the part of certain French conservatives that survived the war by at least two decades. This American policy served American and Allied interests in the short run, especially in North Africa, where it led to the clandestine collaboration of certain French civil and military officials with the United States, people who would work with the Americans but not with the British. The Germans were aware of these contacts. They could do little about them. On occasion, however, they tried to profit from the American-British divergences in regard to Vichy, allowing, for example, American ships to bring grain, etc., to Vichy France in the first months of 1941.

Already in July 1940 the old Caillaux (Clemenceau's bitter enemy and a proponent of Franco-German amity before the First World War) told the new Foreign Minister, Baudouin (who had been his secretary in the twenties): "Above everything, cultivate the United States. The future is there."[139] "Above everything," wrote the French General Doyen in a confidential memorandum to the government in Vichy in July 1941,

---

[137] After Pétain's meeting with Hitler in Montoire, the former received letters from Roosevelt and from King George VI. Roosevelt's letter was the more severe of the two. Yet Pétain's answer to the American President was much more conciliatory than his answer to the King of England. Later in the winter of 1940–41 Pétain promised Roosevelt not to move French battleships without informing Washington first "to do nothing without American consent." Butler, II, 436. On Laval (whose family had a particular relationship with Hoover), see above, p. 407, n. 66. Maurras, who knew as much (indeed, probably less) about America as about the moon, wrote enthusiastic encomiums about Roosevelt and the United States in 1941, as for example at a banquet that Admiral Leahy attended (Roosevelt's "heart beats for France," he is "presiding over the fate of the world", etc.) Action Française (19 Mar. 1941). Darlan told Leahy in June 1941: "If the United States will land at Marseilles 500,000 men, 300 tanks, 3,000 planes, I, Darlan, will be ready to march with you."
[138] Laval on De Gaulle, 10 December 1940, to the Germans: "He is nothing but a vulgar agent of England . . . held in contempt by the United States." CDA, V, 456.
[139] Baudouin, 166.

"we must not lose sight of the fact that the United States remains the great arbiter of this day and of tomorrow, and it is in our vital interest not to alienate its sympathies." His clear and thoughtful memorandum went on to say that, as in 1918, the United States was the key to victory: "Whatever happens, during the coming decades the world must submit to the wishes of the United States."[140] These sentiments were shared by many of the people who had chosen to submit to the Germans. Leopold III of Belgium found it necessary to explain his decision of surrendering to Germany in a letter to Roosevelt on 28 May 1940 (drafted for him by the collaborationist Henri De Man). The Romanian Antonescu, Hitler's favorite ally, suggested to the American minister in November 1941 that Romania would not carry military operations beyond a certain line in Russia and that he hoped to maintain good relations with the United States.[141] The Finnish government followed a similar policy in regard to its participation in the war against Russia; it tried to placate the United States (with which it succeeded in maintaining diplomatic relations throughout the war, except for a short period in 1944). The Hungarian Prime Minister, Bárdossy, a *faute de mieux* Germanophile, after Pearl Harbor suggested that Hungary content herself with breaking relations with the United States and expressing her solidarity with Germany; the Germans rejected this idea, and Bárdossy was constrained to declare war on the United States.[142] The Swedes, the Swiss, the Turks, and the Spanish shared this general view about the coming American preponderance in the world and about the necessary cultivation of American goodwill.[143] So had Stalin, a neutral in the fall of 1940, when he insisted that the announcement as well as the event of Molotov's visit to Berlin be

---

[140] *CDA*, IV, 644. Doyen was a member of the Franco-German Armistice Commission.

[141] Already on 22 November 1940 Antonescu told Ribbentrop that "in view of America's probable entry into the war he believed that the war would still last a long time." He told Hitler on 14 January 1941 that he believed that the Americans would like to see the end of the war, and that they distrusted the Russians.

[142] The United States Senate did not recognize the existence of a state of war with some of the minor satellites of Germany until June 1942.

[143] Two neutrals with whom the United States had some trouble in 1940 and in 1941 were Ireland and Spain. In the case of the former, the rigid and unimaginative attitudes of the American minister to Dublin (Gray) were, to some extent, to blame; in the case of the latter, certain Spanish personages played a role, including the light-headed Spanish ambassador to Berlin, Espinosa de los Monteros, who told Hitler on 12 August 1940 that the United States was full of Jews, Freemasons, and Bolsheviks, and that God would punish America.

postponed until after the American presidential election—the first instance in history when political events in Europe were subordinated to
the American electoral calendar.

Very significant were America's relations with the Vatican. They
had domestic as well as international implications. Roosevelt was aware of
the overwhelming isolationism of American Catholics; he had had trouble
with some of the Irish-Americans within the Democratic party. On 24 October 1939 he invited Cardinal Spellman for lunch. This was the beginning of his campaign to enlist the support of the Vatican. The day before
Christmas, Roosevelt announced that he was sending Myron Taylor as his
personal representative at the Vatican. The Pope was highly pleased that
the powerful United States was paying such attention to the Vatican; he
also hoped to see in the United States a restraining and mediating power
in the war; he referred to the President's decision as a "noble and generous" act.[144] The Pope was soon to learn that Roosevelt's envoy had
both more and less than such noble matters in mind.[145] For domestic political purposes Roosevelt hoped to use the influence of the Pope to restrain the hostility of American Catholics—particularly of German-
Americans[146] and of certain Irish-Americans[147]—against his policy. His
problem became aggravated after June 1941 because of the dogmatic
anti-Communism of most American Catholics.[148] For international politi-

---

[144] The conservative and anti-German Hungarian envoy to the Holy See
(Apor) reported on 23 May 1940 that Taylor "is being treated by the Vatican
authorities with exaggerated, almost subservient, courtesy." *A Vatikáni MK*,
173.

[145] Roosevelt was worried about the continuing influence of Father Coughlin
as well as about anti-Semitism among American Catholics. He gave a memorandum about this to Taylor. Hurley notes, *VD*, I, 381.

[146] German Americans even more than the Irish (who were, to some extent,
divided) were the principal isolationists among Catholics, embittered against
Roosevelt. Example: Archbishop Beckman of Dubuque on 27 July 1941 in a
speech: How can we, in this "Christian democracy . . . account for the
coddling of Communists in every responsible branch of our Government? . . .
We have been pushed far enough in this abominable game of aid to Britain and
Bolshevism"—an early example of what would blossom into the phenomenon
of McCarthyism after the war.

[147] Examples: In an article in *America*, the Jesuit weekly, Thomas E. Davitt in
April 1939: "If the United States were allied with Russia, Catholics would be
justified in conscience in resisting conscription for military service." Bishop
Duffy of Buffalo, in such event, "would advise every Catholic boy in the
United States to refuse to serve." Monsignor Sheen in a sermon preached in St.
Patrick's: "The enemy of the world in the near future is going to be Russia."
Cited by Dawson, 86–87.

[148] The British were clever enough to recognize this. Eden memorandum, 9
July 1941: "In view of Catholic opinion in the United States, it was necessary

cal purposes Roosevelt hoped to induce the Pope to take a stand against Nazi Germany. Here, too, anti-Communism was the principal obstacle. On 3 September 1941 he addressed the Pope directly on this matter.[149] The gist of his letter may be found in these sentences: "In so far as I am informed, churches in Russia are open. . . . I believe . . . that this Russian dictatorship is less dangerous to the safety of other nations than is the German form of dictatorship. . . . I believe that the survival of Russia is less dangerous to religion, to the church as such, and to humanity in general than would be the survival of the German form of dictatorship."[150] Few, if any, communications to the Holy See were ever analyzed with such care as this one. Tardini, in charge of drafting the answer, dissected Roosevelt's letter with great care. His memorandum insisted that Roosevelt's hopes about religious freedom in Russia were unfounded. He also detected that the President's letter "reveals clearly what Roosevelt wants from American Catholics and the authority of the Holy See—he wants to obtain a large advantage in American internal politics."[151] The Pope's answer, in the end, was careful and noncommittal, couched in generalities. Roosevelt was unable to change the mind of the Holy See, which considered Communism as great a danger as Nazism—indeed, a greater danger—hoping in the long run that eventually the United States would awake to that danger.[152]

This belief—that the United States would eventually recognize the

---

to carry the United States Government with us in any step such as a political agreement with Russia." Woodward, II, 13.

[149] Taylor had traveled back to Rome, across the warring nations, including Italy. Two other confidential American emissaries were on the way (eventually their visit was adjourned). Tardini minute, 5 September 1941: "Why this flood of Americans? What will the Italian Government say, preoccupied as it is already with the coming of Taylor? Can't matters be handled with less publicity?" *VD*, 5, 185.

[150] *Wartime Correspondence*, 61–62.

[151] Tardini notes, *VD*, 5, 205; also Taylor's conversation with Cardinal Maglione: "Mr. Taylor tells me that . . . besides the Irish . . . there is a Catholic minority in the United States" causing trouble because of their inability to distinguish between Russia and Communism; "in order to avoid a deep schism among American Catholics a clarification from the Holy See would be necessary." *VD*, 5, 193. See also ibid., 202–10, 218–19, 220–23, 226–27, 229.

[152] On 22 September 1942 Tardini, after a conversation with Taylor, summed up his own opinion that the United States would be the greatest power after the war, dominating Europe according to its wishes. "After everything is said, we may conclude that, while National Socialism had prepared the war, [now] the United States are gravely afflicted by nationalism, a condition fraught with every kind of evil (*che fa presagire ogni male*). . . . *VD*, 5, 706.

dangers of Russian preponderance in Europe—was to be the principal underlying hope of German foreign policy toward the end of the war.
They tried to cultivate a certain amount of American goodwill, hoping
to profit from an American policy of a balance of power that would see
in Germany a bulwark against Communism. While this policy did not
fully crystallize until 1944–45, elements of it are detectable even in
1939–41, before the United States officially became a participant in the
war.[153] In 1939 and in 1940 Hitler and Mussolini[154] hoped to profit from
the Monroe Doctrine (just as Hitler in 1938 had profited from the Wilsonian doctrine of national self-determination)—eventually in vain. After
the fall of France, Roosevelt was coming down on the side of England.[155]
Hitler, as we have seen, tried almost everything to avoid armed conflict

---

[153] 1939–41 represent, therefore, an important phase—but only one phase—of
the general development of modern American-German relations, the starting
point of which, as in American-British relations, goes back to 1898, when there
began, on the part of the German government, an often "undignified race
with the English for American friendship." Leusser, 50, also 13–15; Waldersee,
III, 196.

[154] In answer to Roosevelt's letter warning him against intervention in May
1940, Mussolini said that an American profession of interest in the Mediterranean was "the same as Italy's interests in the Caribbean." Hitler's first reference to the Monroe Doctrine was in his speech of 28 April 1939: He had no
interest in inquiring about America's plans in South America, Roosevelt should
not interfere with German plans in Central Europe. In his June 1940 interview
with von Wiegand (see above, p. 91), Hitler returned to the idea of "America
for the Americans, Europe for the Europeans." In early July 1940 there was a
small flurry about this. Roosevelt's press secretary on 6 July spoke "on the
Monroe Doctrine discussions which have been proceeding between this
country and Germany. . . . There is an absence of any intention on the part
of this government to interfere in any territorial problem in Europe or Asia.
This government would like to see and think that there should be applied a
Monroe Doctrine for each of these continents." The Germans jumped at this
eagerly, but Roosevelt disavowed it the next day. Gruchmann, 19–20.

[155] Again, there were forewarnings of this in the longer history of German-
American relations. In 1911 Theodore Roosevelt told the German ambassador,
Eckardstein, that if, during the recent Moroccan crisis, Germany "had overrun
France, the United States would not have kept quiet." Waldersee, III, 174. The
German answered that this seemed contrary to the Monroe Doctrine.
Roosevelt: "As long as England succeeds in keeping up the 'balance of power'
in Europe, not only in principle, but in reality, well and good; should she however for some reason or other fail in doing so, the United States would be
obliged to step in at least temporarily, in order to re-establish the balance of
power in Europe, never mind against which country. . . . In fact we ourselves
are becoming, owing to our strength and geographical position, more and
more the balance of power on the whole globe." Leusser, 104.

with the United States, and playing thereby into Roosevelt's hands.[156] Hitler knew more about American politics than historians have hitherto admitted.[157] He was surely aware of American power,[158] overruling his naval chiefs on each and every occasion when these had asked that German war vessels protect themselves against American provocation. The German press, too, was forbidden to print "direct" (*unmittelbare*) attacks against Roosevelt and the American government.[159]

In sum, Hitler did not want to challenge America.[160] Nor did the German people. They, too, knew that among their opponents the American people were the least anti-German. (In 1940 the American, unlike the British and French governments, indicated that they were not in favor of the eventual partition of Germany; Roosevelt even suggested in April 1940 that the Allies make a declaration to that effect.) The sentiments of the German people went, however, beyond and beneath politics. From 1939 to 1941 the secret opinion reports reflected some of this[161]; but these inclinations reached back farther and deeper. The Ger-

---

[156] The evidence makes nonsense of Hitler's biographer Bullock's statement: "Hitler certainly never supposed—any more than Hindenburg and Ludendorff in 1917—that he would have to reckon with a major American intervention in the European war." Bullock, 662.

[157] Like Stalin, he was aware of the importance of American elections. On 20 November 1940 he told Mussolini that the Italian war against Greece should have been postponed at least "until after the American presidential election." *GD*, D, XI, 639.

[158] Re his prohibition of all incidents with American naval forces see above, also KTB III, 8 July 1941 ("avoid clashes under all circumstances"), repeated four times, Hillgruber, *HS* 448–49, also Friedlaender, 64–65, 78, 175–76, 256–57, 290, 292, 294. The first serious incident occurred on 4 September 1941 between the U.S.S. *Greer* and a German submarine. There is little doubt that the *Greer* signaled the position of the submarine to British ships nearby; it also seems that the *Greer* fired shells. (Friedlaender, 290: "The actual details of this engagement are unimportant"—a somewhat cavalier statement.)

[159] Boelcke, 307 (1 Apr. 1940). Other examples: No insults against the United States: ibid., 704 (25 Apr. 1941). Lindbergh's speeches against Roosevelt should not be emphasized: Excellent as they are, the impression that Germany stands behind Lindbergh must be avoided. Ibid., 701, 759. The official confidential newspaper service (*Zeitungsdienst*), ZD (15 Nov. 1940): "The wise restraining of the German press in regard to the presidential election . . ." No. 3546. 4268 (23 May 1941): No personal attacks on Roosevelt. No. 4641 (30 May 1941): Bernard Baruch not to be attacked(!)

[160] To Molotov on 12 November 1940: The United States will present a great danger "not in 1945" but at the earliest in 1970–80. To Ciano on 25 October 1941: "A later generation will have to face the problem Europe-America."

[161] *Meldungen*, MA 441/2, 2,057 (25 July 1940), 4,551 (July–Aug. 1941): "An inexhaustible subject of conversations are speculations about the future policy

mans liked many things about American technology, about the American way of life. Before 1933 Berlin was the most Americanized capital city in Europe. Goebbels admired American films. Many Germans liked American jazz. The German ace Major Adolf Galland named his famous ME 109 fighter plane "Mickey Mouse." "In the language of the Third Reich there are many Americanisms," the philologist Klemperer noted already in 1939.[162] We have seen earlier that Goebbels imitated not only American films but also American photo magazines. In 1940 and in 1941 nearly every issue of the *Berliner Illustrierte* had a page with pictures from America. As late as 20 November 1941 it printed a photograph of the new helmet of the U. S. Army. "After lengthy experiments they selected not the British helmet but one that resembles the German one extraordinarily." A decade later Western Germany became the closest political ally of the United States; it was, also, the most Americanized country in Europe. This was not merely the result of opportunism, nor did it develop overnight; elements of it existed during the Second World War or even before.[163]

---

of the U.S.A." 5,462–63 (15 Dec. 1941): "partial concern that the previous world-enemy Churchill has now been replaced by Roosevelt."

[162] Klemperer, 39. Goebbels (27 Feb. 1933): "The great propaganda action on the Day of the Awakening Nation is now fixed in all of its details. It will be a splendid show (*Schau*) in all of Germany." Klemperer, 179. Klemperer: "German romanticism and publicity business, Novalis and Barnum, Germany and America . . . there is a confluence of German and something that is American. . . . Americanisms of the worst kind." Ibid., 262.

[163] In Germany police authorities in 1940 and 1941 were shocked to discover the existence of juvenile gangs with American names and American preferences. In Munich the "Charlie Gang" wore "pullovers embroidered with the letters CHARLIE." "The names, monograms and badges smacked of American films with their sheriff's stars and campus conventions. Juvenile gangs of this type existed throughout the Reich." "In 1940, Frankfurt's *OK-Gang* and *Haarlem-Klub* were cleaned up . . . Their main interests were hit tunes, dancing, and lounging . . . They dressed ostentatiously and seemed uninterested in politics. Inquiries disclosed a picture of active and indiscriminate promiscuity . . . Frankfurt later spawned the *Ohio-Klub* and the *Cotton-Klub* where the *Swing-Jugend* used to congregate. While stating that the 'Swing Youngsters' were Anglophile, the police ascribed their conduct primarily a sexual license stimulated by dancing . . . In August 1941 the Minister of Propaganda received an alarming SD report from Hamburg. This claimed that 'hot and swing demonstrations' by youthful Anglophiles had recently assumed 'unpatriotic and reactionary demoralizing forms.' Records of banned swing music were in wide circulation. Young people were dancing to Anglo-American music and using English conventions and nicknames. Amateur swing bands were springing up like mushrooms . . ." Bleuel, 242 and 243, cites the police files.

The Germans were not, of course, the only people affected by this kind of Americanization. Before 1914 the image of America issued mostly from the printed and the written word: books, newspapers, the letters of emigrants. By 1939 the image was predominantly pictorial. It was, also, extraordinarily widespread.[164] In respect to America, the social and cultural distinctions that separated the upper-middle from the lower-middle class, or potential Anglophiles from potential Germanophiles, mattered little. Among the French collaborationists Rebatet, Bardèche, Brasillach, even Céline, and Drieu, had been Americanophiles, enthusiastic about American films; they saw in America and in American forms of expression of something new and fresh.[165] Across the Channel "the cultural traffic was now predominantly one-way . . . mid-Atlantic accents had become almost obligatory for popular singers, encroaching more and more on the raucous Cockney and fruity Lancashire of the old music hall . . . British bandleaders had developed their own imitation of the music of Glenn Miller and Benny Goodman. And above all, there had been the cinema."[166] Trucks of the British Army in France in 1940 had "Doc," "Grumpy," and "Sneezy" painted on them.[167] (Above them Galland piloted his "Mickimaus.") Only after 1941 did there begin among the British (and not among their lower classes) a certain kind of irritation with American omnipresence and American brashness. The British could still cite, with pride, the lines from *Richard II*:

---

[164] Here was a reverse effect of image and of reality. The main reality of American life in the thirties was the Depression, which was alleviated or, rather, cellophaned over by the glittering image of a world made in Hollywood. Few Europeans had real notions about the American Depression (even though Goebbels tried to make some propaganda from *The Grapes of Wrath*). It was the Hollywood image of American life that, for them, was the principal reality: of a rich, powerful, happy way of life of a people shining with youth and vitality. And, in 1945, so it was.

[165] Brasillach's principal books in 1937 were a eulogy of Franco's national revolution and a book on American films. Rebatet, 602: "The films of the Americans, their songs, their books, their boys and girls, I know only too well that I loved what their exuberant youth brings to the world too much not to suffer from being cut off from them." But Americans let themselves become degenerated because of Jewish influences. Later, about Vichy, ibid., 512: "The young generation hoped for salvation from America through Hollywood, 'swing,' the Marx Brothers and Duke Ellington. They thought that they were little heroes when shouting: 'Bye-bye.'"

[166] Calder, 310–11.

[167] This writer in 1938, age 15, on a visit to Paris with his mother, saw *Snow White and the Seven Dwarfs*, his first movie in color; it was there that he tasted his first Coca-Cola.

This fortress built by Nature for herself
Against infection and the hand of war;
This happy breed of men . . .

Immune from invasion, they were no longer immune from another kind of infection, this time from the far side of the sea.

In 1938 the aging Paul Valéry wrote: "Europe is now ripe to be governed by an American commission." This was to become true at the end of the war. Europe would be freed from the Germans, at the cost of an American-Russian division of the Continent, hardly avoidable at the end of the war, yet the conditions of which were aggravated by the illusions about Russia that all respectable American commissions cultivated during the war. Monuments of American respectability such as William Allen White of Kansas, who in 1940–41 took his place in the forefront of those who wanted to bring the United States into the war on the side of Britain, had written to Harold Ickes as early as 1933: "Russia is the most interesting place on the planet"—a prototypical example. The illusions lived on, and grew powerful during the war years, when an American-Soviet world of united nations seemed to be opening, full of promise. (A prototypical scene: Another monument of respectability, Mrs. Eleanor Roosevelt, reading Prokofiev's *Peter and the Wolf* in the buzzing summer night of the Berkshire music festival. . . .)

The universalist ideology represented by the Roosevelts, this particularly American form of internationalism, would not satisfy Europe; but few people saw this as early as in 1941. Among these certain Frenchmen stand out, Bernanos and De Gaulle, whose vision of France and, indirectly, of Europe was not merely opposed to German and to Russian but also to a future American hegemony. There were political reasons for this. De Gaulle suspected that Roosevelt wanted to reduce France to a client state, depriving her of her colonies in the process.[168] More sig-

---

[168] De Gaulle saw more clearly than the Vichy people, who suspected Britain first and foremost. In any event, the French experienced early the results of their reduced prestige and power, in Indochina, where in 1940 they had to agree to a partial Japanese occupation. Siam (renamed Thailand in 1938) also presented territorial demands on French Indochina, in Laos and Cambodia. The French fought them off, winning a small naval victory at Koh Chang in January 1941. Still, because of Japanese pressure, they had to cede large tracts of Indochinese lands to the Siamese (the treaty was signed aboard a Japanese cruiser). In 1941 the overlordship of the Japanese over Indochina was further extended—one of the issues over which Japan and the United States came to a break before Pearl Harbor, one of the early events that eventually led not only to the Second World War in the Pacific but also to the Vietnam War decades later.

nificant was the spiritual resistance exemplified by Bernanos in his Brazilian exile. In 1941 Bernanos saw the coming danger for France and for Europe, a kind of superficial Americanization, a France and Europe ruled by technology, in the service of a universalist ideology, the kind easily acceptable to "the conformists of the world." Like the French-Swiss Denis de Rougemont, one of the prophets of a united Europe, Bernanos saw the prospects of a spiritual desert, of despair.[169] Like the Spanish Ortega, prophet of the mass age, he knew that Europe had become too small and that the Last European War also meant the end of an age. "We can no longer pretend that European Man is Man," Bernanos was to write after the war. "But we believe that European civilization is inseparable from a certain conception of man." The same Valéry who had been among the first to recognize the decline of Europe, who in 1938 had written that Europe was ripe to be governed by an American commission, recalled Protagoras: "Man is the measure of things." And was this still true?

## End of the Bourgeois Age?

¶ "I am greatly worried about the future (in which I fancy I see a Middle Ages in disguise)" wrote Nietzsche to a friend in 1870.[170] Seventy years later this new Middle Ages seemed to become reality. In June 1940, a few days before the fall of Paris, Reynaud broadcast to the French people: If Hitler wins this war, he said, "it would be the Middle Ages again, but not illuminated by the mercy of Christ."

The collapse of France seemed to mean not only the collapse of the bourgeoisie, it also seemed to signify the end of the entire era of bourgeois civilization—of liberalism, of parliamentarism, of constitutionalism, of capitalism, of the preponderance of Western Europe, of the Age of Reason. In June 1940 it seemed that the German triumph in the West meant a return, politically speaking, to the days of the Holy German-Roman Empire, a Europe dominated by Germans, North Italians, and

---

[169] Rougemont on Times Square, New York City (23 Dec. 1940): *"Despair in Times Square.* . . . Above everything, I felt despair everywhere, in this walk of several hours, I understand it now. One asks oneself at times: What is sin, after all? It is this thing that I sensed, acutely in Times Square: the state of a world where the soul is absent. . . . In this super-humanised atmosphere of the great city I learned the mortal weight of this phrase: 'If the salt will lose its savor' . . ." Rougemont, 460.

[170] To Erwin Rohde (23 or 27 Nov. 1870). *Nietzsche SL,* 70.

Spaniards,[171] with England excluded from Europe, France divided or reduced to her shape of the late Middle Ages, and the Netherlands, Artois, Flanders, and perhaps even a reconstituted Burgundy incorporated into the Reich.[172] And there was more to this than political geography. In 1940 certain aspects of the Middle Ages had an appeal to millions of people, and not only to the triumphant Germans. Du Moulin de Labarthète, a sensitive observer of the early Vichy period, recorded in his memoirs "this kind of return to the Middle Ages, this 'instinctive medievalization,' something that Berdyaev has not foreseen."[173] A Europe pullulating with *Landsknechten*, with mercenary soldiery in the service of an imperial ideology, this German-Spanish Europe with Jews restricted, Freemasonry disappearing, capitalism replaced by a new social order,[174] corporations[175] and guilds and the tribe exalted anew—it was reminiscent of a Europe around 1500, before the Modern Age began.

This reappearance of the Middle Ages did not last. It did not survive the high noon of their triumphs. For one thing, the medieval inspiration was alien to some of Hitler's allies, including Mussolini, who wished to re-create the *condottieri*, neo-Renaissance attitudes, not medieval ones. More significantly, the medieval side was but one facet of the Third Reich and of Hitler's mind, albeit an important one. Widespread in the attitudes of the Nazi hierarchy there was something else, supermodern

---

[171] A symbolic episode: The capitulation of Brussels (which centuries before had belonged to the Spanish Empire) to the Germans on 17 May 1940 was negotiated with the help of two Spanish diplomatists. A month later Spain mediated between the Germans and Pétain, who was ready to surrender. The very name of the Spanish chargé d'affaires in Brussels, Ximenez Sandoval, in a moment of deathlike silence, somehow rang with the leaden echo of something long past but not quite dead.

[172] Goebbels would often speculate about the borders before 1500, Burgundy forming part of the Reich.

[173] Du Moulin, 300. Berdyaev, whose neo-Christian writings enjoyed a certain reputation in the 1930s, contrasted the shining virtues of the Middle Ages with the gloomy decadence of the bourgeois spirit.

[174] Henri De Man's manifesto to the working class of Belgium on 5 July 1940: "Don't think that you must resist the occupying power; accept the fact of its victory and try, rather, to reap the lessons therefrom for the building of a new social order. The war led to the collapse of the parliamentary regime and of capitalist plutocracy of the so-called deomocracies. For the working classes this collapse of a decrepit order, far from being a disaster, is a liberation. . . ."

[175] Manifestations of this neomedievalism are yet to be surveyed by historians. They were especially widespread in Vichy France. Example: The youth movement of the Pétain regime, *Compagnons de la France*, was divided into *cités, baillages, commanderies, pays, provences,* etc.

and pagan-primitive at the same time. On 18 June 1940, that crucial day in the history of the Second World War and of the twentieth century, Churchill's phraseology was both more inspiring and more precise than Reynaud's. Churchill evoked the specter, not of a return to the Middle Ages, but of a lurch into the Dark Ages. If Hitler wins and we fail, he said, "then the whole world, including the United States, including all that we have known and cared for, will sink into the abyss of a new Dark Age, made more sinister, and perhaps more protracted, by the lights of perverted science."

For there was something in the air that was different from the conservative prospect of a neomedieval age, of a helmeted and black German-Roman imperial triumph over Europe. In 1940 the summer solstice came on 24 June. The neopagan Montherlant walked out to the sea at Marseille. From the silent sea, he said, he heard the ancient words: "The great Pan is dead." No, he said, now it is translated: "You are conquered, Galilean."[176] "Now, if only now France and Germany, united under the emblem of the wheeling sun, were ready, for a certain time, to bury in their subconcious life the time of Constantine . . . To put Christianity to sleep." Across the larger ocean, at that very time, Anne Morrow Lindbergh, the wife of America's neomedieval and supermodern folk hero, wrote in *The Wave of the Future:* "I cannot see this war, then, simply and purely, as a struggle between the 'Forces of Good' and the 'Forces of Evil.' If I could simplify it into a phrase at all, it would seem truer to say that the 'Forces of the Past' are fighting against the 'Forces of the Future.' "[177] The end of an age: This is what the evolutionist Teilhard de

---

[176] Montherlant, 293.

[177] "The tragedy is, to the honest spectator, that there is so much that is good in the 'Forces of the Past,' and so much that is evil in the 'Forces of the Future.' . . ." A populist echo of this argument may be found in the debate in the pages of *The Nation* magazine, in December 1941, between the very young Arthur Schlesinger, Jr. and Senator Robert A. Taft (wrongly regarded as a true conservative). The former was trotting out the argument that the Republican party, like the Whigs in 1852, was bound to perish, because its conservative elements failed to oppose Hitler, just as the Whigs had failed to oppose slavery. Taft answered that Schlesinger was not "correct in attributing the position of the majority of Republicans to their conservatism. The most conservative members of the party—the Wall Street bankers, the society groups, nine tenths of the plutocratic (*sic*) newspapers, and most of the party's financial contributors—are the ones who favor intervention in Europe. Mr. Schlesinger's statement that the business community in general had tended to favor appeasing Hitler is simply untrue. I have received thousands of letters on both sides of the question, and I should say without question that it is the average man and woman—the farmer, the workman—who are opposed to the war. The war party is made up of the business community of the cities, the

Chardin felt in the summer of 1940. "Personally, I stick to my idea that we are watching the birth, more than the death, of a World. The scandal, for you, is that England and France should have come to this tragedy because they have sincerely tried the road of peace. But did they not precisely make a mistake on the true meaning of 'peace'? Peace cannot mean anything but a HIGHER PROCESS OF CONQUEST. . . . The world is bound to belong to its most active elements. . . . Just now, the Germans deserve to win because, however bad or mixed is their spirit, they have more spirit than the rest of the world. It is easy to criticize and despise the fifth column. But no spiritual aim or energy will ever succeed, or even deserve to succeed, unless it proves able to spread and to keep spreading a fifth column. . . ."[178] "How," asked Drieu la Rochelle in January 1941," can you believe that the winner of this war would be an empire of which every part is an anachronism from the past? Someone who today believes in the victory of England is like someone who in 1900 had prophesied the victory of China, with its mandarins with pigtails and jade buttons, over the European empires with their motors and cannons."[179] And in June: "In face of Hitler, Mussolini, Stalin, don't you see that Churchill and Roosevelt are grotesquely antiquated? To expect the re-establishment of the rule of the City and of Wall Street over Europe is as outdated as the expectations of those old bourgeois Russians in some suburb of some Western capital who are still dreaming about the return of the Tsars and of capitalism in Moscow."

This was published on 19 June 1941. Three days later Hitler attacked Stalin; Stalin became the ally of Churchill and Roosevelt; and the Russian, the British, and the American empires together defeated the German empire and won the war. They won because they were more powerful. But the spiritual power of the Germans was declining too. The latter had not gathered the youth of Europe around themselves. Their National Socialism was restricted to the German cause. After June 1941 even Communism was more patriotic, more appealing than that. And we have seen that the bourgeois classes survived; the old bourgeois virtues themselves proved to be stronger and more appealing than the Germans had thought.

A good illustration of this is reflected in an article in Goebbels' *Das Reich* magazine, entitled "Autumn in Switzerland," by an Otto Philipp Haefner:

---

newspaper and magazine writers, the radio and movie commentators, the Communists, and the university intelligentsia." *The Nation*, 6 and 13 December 1941.
[178] Letter (2 Aug. 1940) in Teilhard, *Letters*, 145.
[179] Drieu, *CRP*, 295–96.

. . . in a Swiss bourgeois house. I sit in a deep chair, far from the rumor and industry of the world, and while the lady of the house pours coffee, the clock ticks in the afternoon twilight. What time is it? 1840? 1940? No one cay say. The past breathes from the old pieces of furniture, a dream of comfort and happiness in a close family circle, the security of possessions, of solid industriousness, of honorable family life. . . . Ah, if it were only possible to halt the movement of time, the wheel of history that is sweeping the world, at least to deflect it away from one's house. What is power, what is the gleam of honor, what are flags, glorious eagles, triumphant fanfares against the peaceful afternoons in the home, the purling etude on the piano, the silent walk by the lake, the twinkling lights along the promenade, the quiet evenings at the fireplace? It is difficult to make myself understood here. The same words mean different things. Even about the facts, whether they belong to the present or to the future, we cannot agree. How can we reach a common conclusion? The enthusiasm of our youth, our determination for a brave life, the blood that we are spending for a better Europe evokes no sympathy in this bourgeois atmosphere. Whatever is old, even if it is imperfect, is better here than whatever is new and unknown. The hot breath of our times is like the kind of spring Alpine wind which gives people headaches and before which they close the windows. . . .[180]

One can detect in this article, critical of the Swiss, the seeds of a kind of exasperated respect for them. And, as the war proceeded and the prospect of disaster rose, the contempt for the bourgeois virtues incarnated by the Swiss that the champions of the new and heroic Europe had been professing would often change into a kind of envy and even admiration.[181]

During the Second World War the old civilization of Europe was still strong enough to survive the tremendous physical and mental earthquake. The attraction of its past could be inspiring; it proved stronger than most visions of the future. This included the cult of the family; as we have seen earlier, the war brought families together. We must also recognize that the European cult of the family has been more

---

[180] *Das Reich* (17 Nov. 1940).
[181] The antibourgeois Drieu in *Notes sur la Suisse,* 1943: "Switzerland is the plane of Europe, the plane where all of the physical and metaphysical crossings meet, the crucial plane—it is not in vain that her emblem is a cross—it is a sacred place." Bonneville, 106. Earlier in the war Drieu had foreseen a New Dark Ages, leather-jacketed with American-style equipment, night-fighters, and nomadic gangs with initiation rites, the *feralis exercitus* described by Tacitus, the dark Harii—it is perhaps significant that the Harii were a Germanic tribe camping two thousand years ago in what would be Switzerland later, and that the Swiss Nazis would call their league the league of the Harus.

recent than we are accustomed to think, it had been the product of the bourgeois, rather than of the medieval, age of European civilization.[182] Another example: During this barbaric war the respect for the cultural monuments of the past was both deeper and more widespread than during the earlier wars of Europe. In September 1939 the French emptied their museums, they took their most valuable treasures to the halls and vaults of châteaux, including that awfully cold half-ruin of Chambord. Along the Loire the Leonardos and the Titians preceded the sorry hegira of the politicians of the Republic and remained there after the reflux of the latter. The British carefully registered the information of their whereabouts from France (including such intelligence coming from Vichy) in order to avoid the dropping of bombs on places where the treasures of Europe lay propped against the walls and in the cellars. The British were now the cultural guardians of the European patrimony.[183] A department of the German Army worked for *Kunstschutz*, the protection of art; its chief, Count Metternich, with the aid of General Streccius, commander in occupied France, command our respect especially when they, countermanding other directives of the Nazi bureaucracy, could halt the removal of some of the French art to the Third Reich, at least in 1940. And there was Goering himself, the Vice Chief of the Reich, this admirer of Vermeer, of the quintessential painter of the Bourgeois Age of Europe, Goering who visited the Jeu de Paume a dozen times in 1940 and in 1941, on one occasion (3 November 1940) spending most of the day in its halls, lost in admiration before the marvels of French impressionist painting. . . .

In the high realms of the human spirit the Third Reich produced little that was enduring. The few enduring examples of its art—their repute remains obscured by contemporary criticism—were precisely those where the newly found energy of the German spirit had built on inspiration from the past, as in some of the paintings of Pfuhle and Dannowsky, in a few of the many sculptures by Breker, in some of the buildings of Troost and, in a few instances, of Speer. Whether, by the end of the twentieth century, the traditional civilities of Europe will still exist, I do not know. Whether the nostalgia and the respect for bourgeois values that helped them survive the Second World War will be strong enough to remain sufficiently inspiring, I don't know. It is at least possible

---

[182] A discussion of this in Lukacs, "The Bourgeois Interior," *PMA*, 191–207.
[183] This writer remembers the *frisson* that some of the French code messages of the BBC would evoke:

> *La Joconde a le sourire*
> *Van Dyck remercie Fragonard*

that the civilization of the West might succumb, not to a new Middle Ages but to a new Dark Age. In that event we will face the possibility that a new generation might respond to the half truth that Knut Hamsun wrote about the death of Hitler, a heroic figure whose "historical fate was that he flourished in a time of unexampled coarseness, which felled him at last."[184] We must face the possibility that a day might come when young people all over the world will admire both the best and the worst of Nazi art, unable to see the falseness in the worst of it, simply because of its contrast with the cancerous degeneration of art that has followed the war, continuing ever since. Even now look at the face of an American college girl as she laughs, nervously, at a photo of the reproduction of Nazi architecture, of a Nazi painting. . . . *She does not know what to think.*

"In the days when the history of the twentieth century can be written as a whole," Gerald Reitlinger said,

> it may be found that one single event dominated it, namely Hitler's invasion of Russia. This prodigious plan and its failure transformed the Russian State from the condition of a timid Asiatic country, still licking the twenty-year-old wounds of civil war, to the military power that dominated Europe from the Elbe to the Adriatic. Indirectly it brought down in impotence and shame the old balances of power in the Near and Far East. Perhaps too it will be found that the military failure of a man who rejected civilization, caused the destruction of civilization itself.[185]

Of civilization as we have known it to be. For we must not forget that the very notion of civilization, together with historical consciousness, has been the particular creation and patrimony of the Bourgeois Age in Europe, both more recent and more vulnerable than what we have been accustomed to think. How wrong was Gibbon, writing two hundred years ago, close to the noontime of the Bourgeois Age, shortly before the French Revolution, when he assured his contemporaries: What happened to ancient Rome could not happen to modern Europe. There were hardly any barbarians left, he wrote: Even in Russia "the reign of independent Barbarism is now contracted to a narrow span; and the remnant of Calmucks and Uzbecks, whose forces may be almost numbered, cannot seriously excite the apprehensions of the great republic of Europe. . . . Cannon and fortifications now form an impregnable bar-

---

[184] Cited in Hamsun, *OOP*, viii. About the essential untruth of half truths, see above, p. 325.
[185] Reitlinger, *House*, 9.

rier against the Tartar horse; and Europe is secure from any future irrup-tion of Barbarians; since, before they can conquer, they must cease to be barbarous." No: Rather the contrary is true. It was already true during the Last European War.

History is never of one piece. During the Second World War the bourgeois institutions and bourgeois spirit survived and the new Middle Ages had not come to last; but the shadow of the new Dark Ages, too, reappeared in the hearts and in the acts of people in the middle of Europe, as they reappeared on the extremes of the European world. It reappeared in the East, where in 1941, long before the Russo-Asian in-vasion of Eastern Europe in 1944–45, the unfortunate brave Poles found that among their captors the Mongols and Tartars and Uzbekhs and Kal-muks in Soviet uniform behaved even worse than their Russian and Ukrainian enemies, with a cruel and cold hatred for this defeated white people. It reappeared in the middle of Europe, in Germany, where even before Hitler rose to power, already in 1931, hidden in the dark Teutonic forests, stubbly little rockets were set toward the sky. And in the New World of the West in 1941, ten years later, the refugee scientists of Cen-tral Europe were at work on the atomic bomb, unaware that, as Georges Bernanos was to say, the splitting of the atom was the decisive triumph of technique over reason, and that this meant not the triumph but the end of the modern, or of the Bourgeois Age.

## MIND AND MATTER

¶ We are beginning this section, and ending this book, with a constatation with which we began it, that the Last European War was but a part—the last and the most dramatic part—of a larger phase in the history of Eu-rope, that began around 1870 and ended in 1945, during which Germany was the dominant power. In 1941 her military and police domination reached its apogee. The Third Reich ruled more of Europe than had any other empire in the past. By the end of that year, however, the Germans could no longer win. They held out against the overwhelming power of their enemies until 1945, a tragic milestone in the history of the German people and of the states of Europe at large.

We made another statement in the beginning of this book. Contrary to the accepted ideas of our times, in the age of materialism mind counted ever more than matter. The industry and the discipline of the German people made them powerful, at times frighteningly so; and this was due less to material factors than to their mental habits and to their governing ideas. These ideas served them well for a long time. In the end, however, German idealism degenerated into a kind of unrestrained and fanatical spiritualism, represented by Hitler. He thought that the power of that spirit was sufficient unto itself to defy most of the world, including the material power of his enemies. In 1871 Renan said to the French that the victory of the Germans had been the victory of the German schoolmaster. In 1945 the defeat of the Germans was largely the defeat of the German spirit, though perhaps not of the German mind.

We have also said, in the beginning as well as throughout this book, that German forms of thinking had a strong influence on many nations of Europe, and that 1870–1945 represented not only the political and military and economic but also the cultural predominance of Germany in most of Europe: And this is the substance with which we are here concerned. After 1870 in Europe there developed a philosophical and ideological reaction against the materialist and positivistic thought of the nineteenth century. The span of this neo-idealist reaction, 1874–1941, curiously corresponds nearly exactly with the time-span of the first, the romantic, reaction, 1770–1840, also mostly out of Germany, against the rationalist mentality of the eighteenth century. The crystallization of this reaction may be perhaps marked by Nietzsche's essay "The Use and Abuse of History" in 1874 and by Dilthey's *Ueber das Studium der Geschichte* in 1875. The decrystallization of this phase may be marked, at any rate, by 1941, meaning the coming military defeat and political bankruptcy of Germany. This event was not only a turning point in the evolution of European ideas; for the very condition that Germany, with its dominant philosophy of ideological nationalism, represented some of the most extreme and primitive applications of the reaction against materialism either alienated or disillusioned or drove underground some of the actual and potential intellectual advocates of this reaction.

Thus this antimaterialistic reaction of the European spirit from 1875 to 1941—or, more accurately, this first postmaterialist, and first postmodern, movement in its history—cannot be properly assayed without considering the history of nations at the same time. It is true that, as Péguy said, the massive intrusion of politics and of its rhetoric leads to the degeneration of truth and of thought. But it is precisely because of this massive pervasiveness of politics that the history of ideas cannot be treated in an isolated category. Not only were there correspondences between the intellectual reactions against positivism and the political reactions against parliamentarism, or between the reactions against materialism and those against capitalism, or later between philosophical neo-idealism and political Fascism. There exist, too, relationships between world political developments and the applications of new ideas, relationships not only in philosophy but also in physics. And here we arrive not only to the splitting of minds but also to the splitting of the atom, to the history of the atomic bomb, particularly to the crucial phase leading from its potential conception to its actual construction in 1939–41, corresponding to the compass of this book.

At the opening of the twentieth century, in 1900, a time that in the history of the world and of Europe was a kind of watershed, a revolution began in physics in the fundamental science of matter itself. The German physicist Planck discovered that the smallest particles of matter do not necessarily obey the classical and complete laws of mechanics. Planck's quantum principle[186] was the first leak in the Newtonian universe. In 1905 the German-Jewish Einstein discovered the principle of relativity in physics. After the First World War, Germany continued to be the focus and the center of the new physics; it was in the intellectually febrile and fertile atmosphere of Weimar Germany that the most important work and the profoundest discussions by physicists about the very nature of matter went on. Around 1925 the young German Heisenberg discovered the principle of indeterminacy in physics (which Einstein refused to accept). Thereby the foundations of a new philosophy of physics and, indirectly, of a new philosophy of human knowledge of matter had been laid.

We cannot discuss here the fundamental philosophical consequences of these discoveries except for a passing reference to them at the very end of the book, even though they are still far from being properly and sufficiently recognized. What is important, for our purposes, are the practical applications of these discoveries. Years before the outbreak of the war—indeed, even before Hitler came to power—the notion that the splitting of the atom would release enormous physical energies that might be captured and compressed into an atomic bomb had become intellectually current.[187] Shortly before the outbreak of the Second World War these speculations acquired real substance. During the the winter of 1938–39 German physicists succeeded in splitting the uranium nucleus by neutrons for the first time. This meant that the construction of an atomic bomb was now a practical, and not merely a theoretical, possibility. During the spring of 1939 this ominous news was confirmed by French and

---

[186] Planck's choice of the word "quantum" may have had something to do with the intellectual currency of the word in Germany at that time; Nietzsche, who died at the same moment (August 1900) when Planck made his discovery, had written earlier, in *The Will to Power*, about "quanta of power that determine and distinguish rank . . ."

[187] In Harold Nicolson's *Public Faces* (London, 1932), a novel of political fantasy, the British overcome the looming danger of a Second World War by their sudden possession of an atomic bomb.

British physicists.[188] On 24 April 1939 two German physicists, Harteck and Grote, wrote a letter to the German War Ministry: "We take the liberty of calling your attention to the newest developments in nuclear physics which, in our opinion, will probably make it possible to produce an explosive many orders of magnitude more powerful than the conventional ones."[189]

By that time many of the German-trained physicists, having emigrated from Germany, were in Britain and in the United States. The outstanding figure among them was Albert Einstein.[190] This famous pacifist, like most of his colleagues,[191] was now obsessed with the fear, which was not devoid of substance, that the Germans might construct an atomic bomb, with incalculable advantages to Hitler. On 2 August 1939 Einstein wrote a letter to President Roosevelt about this. Soon thereafter the President ordered that funds and assistance be given to accelerated research for the purpose of the eventual construction of an American atomic bomb.[192]

Until 1939, the brain drain of many physicists notwithstanding, Germany was still in the lead of nuclear research in the world. From 1939 to 1941 the United States was becoming even with Germany, because of the increasing facilities available to the concentration of physicists. After 1941 American research and technology pulled decisively ahead, with the result that in December 1942 the first nuclear reactor in Chicago began to function. It would seem, therefore, that from 1939 to 1941 there was something of a dramatic race for the atomic bomb between Germany and the United States. The highest authorities of the latter acted upon this assumption. Yet in some ways (though not in all), this assumption was both inaccurate and exaggerated. For a number of reasons, including personal

---

[188] Hahn and Strassmann, working with Meitner, split the uranium nucleus on 6 December 1938. In Paris, Joliot, Halban, and Kowarski succeeded with a similar experiment in March 1939.

[189] Cited in Irving, 36–37. A detailed article about this matter appeared in a German scholarly journal publicly available, *Zeitschrift fuer Naturwissenschaft*, a few months later.

[190] He had been living in Princeton since 1932. His enormous reputation obscured the condition that he was no longer able to make any significant contribution to theoretical physics, mostly because of his unwillingness to accept the indeterminacy principle.

[191] Szilard, Wigner, Teller, Weisskopf, and Fermi were Jews of Hungarian, German, and Italian birth.

[192] The French and the British governments, too, were aware of this matter. The excellent French Minister of Armaments in the Reynaud Cabinet, Raoul Dautry, rescued heavy-water supplies from Norway before the debacle, eventually getting them to the United States. Serious work on nuclear matters began in Britain in September 1940.

complexities and bureaucratic complications, something but not much was done in Germany in the matter of an atomic bomb. The very bureaucracy of the Third Reich obstructed a clear-cut and concentrated German policy on the matter, even as German physicists were at work on various atomic reactors. Sometime in September 1941 Heisenberg, a German patriot, though far from being a convinced Nazi, became certain that the construction of an atomic bomb was now a definite possibility. In October 1941, on a visit to Copenhagen, he sought out his old colleague and acquaintance, the half-Jewish Niels Bohr. During an evening walk there occurred a confused and unhappy conversation between the two men. Heisenberg tried to convince Bohr that, now when an atomic bomb had become feasible, physicists on both sides of the war should commit themselves to silence in this regard and not impress their respective governments with the feasibility of such construction. Bohr seems to have believed that Heisenberg acted with certain political purposes in mind, hoping that such an agreement would halt developments by the Allies.[193] We are back from the splitting of atoms to the splitting of minds. Suffused with suspicion, the world of the physicists and the minds of some of them were split, just as was the atomic nucleus.

We must, for the sake of reality, insist on the human element in these events. The history of science is the history of scientists, just as the history of the universe is the history of man. It is history, not science, that explains both how and why the atomic bomb was made. The "causes" of the atomic bomb are historical and, ultimately, personal; they are scientific and technical only on a secondary level of "causes." The principal causes of the making of the bomb include Hitler, the Second World War, and the persecution of Jews by the Germans. The bomb was made when it was made, where it was made, in the way it was made, and for the purposes it was made, not merely because at a certain phase in the development of science a certain stage of technological know-how was reached, but principally because at a certain time in history in the minds of certain eminent scientists, the fear had arisen that German scientists might be building an atomic bomb for Hitler. Technically speaking, the important stages in the history of the atomic bomb were the splitting of the uranium nucleus by neutrons in December 1938, the functioning

---

[193] Shortly thereafter Bohr, spirited out of Denmark, made his way through Sweden to the United States. At a conference on 3 June 1942 Heisenberg and the German physicists explained the feasibility of an atomic bomb to some of the highest authorities of the Third Reich, but the issue was not pressed and little was done about it in practice, even as important work on atomic reactors in Germany went on, sometimes with considerable prospects of success, until the end of the war.

of the first nuclear reactor in Chicago in December 1942, the exploding of the first bomb in New Mexico in July 1945, and the two bombs finally cast on Japan in August 1945; but the technological character of these stages must not obscure the principal factors in its creations which, as in every historical event, were the results of personal choices, through historical thinking, and conditioned by the political, national, religious, intellectual, and ideological inclinations of responsible men.

At this point we must once more draw attention to the correspondences between world developments and the history of the new physics. In 1900 Planck's discovery of the hole in the mechanical-physical universe occurred at the very time when the cracks appeared in the old European order. The end of the indisputability of the Newtonian universe came together with the end of the confidence of the Bourgeois Age. In the 1920s the indeterminacy revolution in physics coincided with the defeat of the "Left" in Europe[194]; and the American phase of the Second World War, after 1941, certainly corresponded with the construction of the first atomic bombs, by refugee scientists, in the United States. It also marked the coming defeat of the neo-idealist world view that Germany, the fatherland of both neo-idealism and of the new physics, had produced. Yet, as I wrote a few pages before, the defeat of Germany 1945, while the defeat of the German spirit, was perhaps not altogether the defeat of the German mind. Almost without exception, the makers of the atomic bomb had been educated in Germany. They had brought what was largely a German type of cultural baggage to their new abode in the United States. The influence of certain Germanic categories of thought, and of German-type thinkers such as Marx and Freud—both of whom had made their way to London, where they lie buried—continued in England and in the United States after the war, in many ways spreading wider than before.

---

[194] In 1930, at the Brussels-Solvay Congress of International Physics, Einstein, refusing to admit the Heisenberg uncertainty principle, suffered a humiliating defeat, which was then administered by Bohr. I am not saying that this was a political event. I am saying that this event, and the time of its occurrence, has a significance in the general cultural history of Europe, including politics to some extent. For there is a certain correspondence between Einstein's defeat in 1930 and the failure of German Marxism, with its interpretation of Economic Man, at that very historical moment. They were, both, failures of the deterministic thinking of the nineteenth century; and, in view of more universal historical developments of that time, it is at least significant that this happened in 1930. (On the more vulgar level of mass political beliefs, it is true what Klaus Mehnert wrote in 1951: "The German people's journey from Liebknecht to Hitler, and the Russian people's journey from Lenin to Stalin, were parallel performances of the same process. In both cases . . . the journey was one from dialectic to magic. . . .") Lukacs, *HC*, 298 and passim.

Still, it remains true what Georges Bernanos wrote after 1945, that the splitting of the atom was the decisive triumph of technique over reason; for this great writer also proved to be a prophet, in more ways than one. Long after his discovery of indeterminacy, and after the war, Heisenberg, as well as Weizsaecker, came to the recognition that the new discoveries of physics had even more important philosophical than technical consquences: They called for a new concept of human knowledge, and perhaps even of human nature, within the universe. By the time this book is being written Heisenberg came close to a conclusion, strangely corresponding to Bernanos, that the further smashing and splitting of atoms was not only becoming dangerous but nonsensical; for this has now become possible in an endless way. By splitting more particles the nuclear technicians were simply creating more particles. Like trying to find the very smallest or the very largest number when by merely thinking about it any child may add more, to find the very smallest building stones of the universe has become an absurd quest: It is mind creating matter, rather than the other way around.

These are, then, the consequences of the collapse of the deterministic philosophy of materialism, of a corroding world view from which neither the Western world nor the Soviet world could as yet liberate itself (as the great German-Jewish thinkers Marx, Freud, and Einstein could not). They are, as yet, far from recognized by people who ought to know better, including amateur as well as professional historians. In the introduction to his *History of the Second World War*, Liddell Hart wrote in 1970, for example:

> If you allow anyone to stoke up a boiler until the steam-pressure rises beyond danger-point, the real responsibility for any resultant explosion will lie with you. That truth of physical science applies equally to political science—especially to the conduct of international affairs.[195]

But this is quite untrue. There is a fundamental difference between the reactions of men and the reactions of other organisms; for it is precisely because of the intrusion of the human mind that the reactions of men are not merely reactions. Revolutions break out not when the pressure is greatest but when the pressure had already begun to lessen. Men cease to resist when they think that the pressure on them is irresistible; for "irresistible" is what they no longer want to resist, and "intolerable" what they no longer want to tolerate. The fundamentally primi-

---

[195] Liddell Hart, 7.

tive law of mechanical casuality—superseded now even in the world of matter by the discoveries of quantum physics—does not automatically apply to human beings. The lid of the boiler will fly off at the highest degree of pressure, something that is both predictable and measurable in advance. Human explosions will not necessarily occur at the highest point of pressure; nor are they exactly predictable or measurable. And this happens not because of some kind of surviving irrationality at the core of the evolving human species. The contrary is true. In the human world the lid is not merely a passive element—because the lid is thinking about itself.

The recognition of this principle is something from which most historians still avert their eyes.[196] They ought not do so. During this century the texture of history changed; and with it changed what I like to call the structure of events. The influence of mind over matter, the intrusion of mind into the structure of events are there for anyone who wishes to see. We have many evidences of it during 1939–41, the Last European War. We have touched on many examples of it in this book, involving subjects that still await their serious historical study.[197] The history of those years abounds with examples suggesting the very contrary of what Marx had been preaching and of what is still the accepted basis of what goes under the name of modern social science: that what people were thinking and believing was not merely the rationalization of their economic situation,

---

[196] One exception: the treatment, by Arnold Toynbee, in the workmanlike and pragmatic, nonphilosophical and factual, survey of the Royal Institute of International Affairs, *The Initial Truimph of the Axis,* of a chapter in the history of 1940, to which he gave the following title, proper and just: "The Revolution in British Feeling from 9 April to 25 June 1940."

[197] "The mental earthquake," as I wrote at the start of Part II of this book, "was bigger than the physical one." In this book I could do little else but to point some of its evidences, beginning with such physical consequences as changes in the rhythm of births, deaths, and marriages, including the changing pattern of physical illnesses. (About the latter, for example: "One curious medical phenomenon of the Second World War, both in Britain and throughout most of the Continent, was the high incidence of peptic ulcers both in the armed forces and among civilians. The contrast with the First World War was striking: In 1914–15 ulcers caused only 709 discharges from the British armed forces, while in 1939–41 the figure was over 23,000. A similar increase occurred among workers in the war industries." Wright, 93.) *Why* this was so, we cannot know with any certainty; but the understanding of *how* the thinking of people affected their lives is the principal purpose of this book, within the structure of which I attempted to deal with the intrusion of thinking in their physical lives, their economics, their soldiering, their politics, their images of other peoples, their resistance, in successive stages, along which the importance of the events of the mind became more and more evident and the causal connections clearer.

the superstructure of the material "realities." To the contrary: What people think and believe is the real substance of their lives and of their histories—and the material institutions of society are the superstructure of *that*.

For one thing, Hitler's enormous successes during these years were the results, less of the organization of German material power than of his conviction of German superiority, a conviction that he succeeded to impart to the minds of millions.[198] Conviction, too, made Churchill and De Gaulle his principal opponents. Lamenting the state of the civilization of the West between the wars, Yeats wrote his later famous lines that "the best lack all conviction/and the worst are full of passionate intensity." When Yeats died in that bleakest of Januaries, in 1939, it seemed so. And yet it wasn't so. In 1940 the best did not lack all conviction, even when the worst may have been full of passionate intensity. And this is the lesson —perhaps the only inspiring lesson—of the Last European War.

---

[198] With all of his emphasis on spirit (and we must recognize that "spirit" and "mind" in German are often the same word, *Geist*), Hitler's comprehension of the intrusion of mind into matter, while intense, was essentially shallow. Instead of mechanical determinism, he developed a kind of spiritual-biological determinism dear to his heart. For example, as we have seen above, he regarded the Jews as essentially spiritual enemies; their spirituality, however, was determined and ineluctable. Goebbels, whose thinking was closest to Hitler's, and who otherwise had a masterful understanding about how to impart convictions and ideas to the masses, was similarly affected by this kind of an essentially shallow ideological determinism, as when in June 1941 he said to his circle that Germany's victory over Russia would be very swift because of the obvious superiority of National Socialism over Communism.

Churchill, their principal opponent, had no such philosophy of history. Indeed, in a categorical sense he had no philosophy of history at all, something that British intellectuals such as Professors Rowse and Carr regretted (the former writing that Churchill's historianship was inferior to Trotsky's, since Churchill, unlike Trotsky, had "no philosophy of history." Rowse, *The End of an Epoch* (1933, 1947), 262–83; Carr, *What Is History?*, 20–21). This was all to the good. Churchill had a profound understanding of history, more profound and also more humble than Trotsky's or Hitler's. Churchill also had a good sense of humor. This writer is touched by a scene, recorded by Spears, with which he finds it proper to conclude the last footnote in the narrative text of this book. Peering into catastrophe, surrounded by the imminence of defeat, collapse, and confusion, on 31 May 1940 Churchill descended from his plane in France on the airfield of Villecoublay. He grinned at Spears and poked him in the stomach.

# Bibliographical remarks

As I conclude my work on this book (late in 1973), I estimate that the number of printed items—that is, books and articles relating to its topic—approaches 60,000.[1] Add to this the immense mass of listed papers in the archives, the files and remnants of the contemporary press, collections of photographs, picture magazines, contemporary films, radio and other recordings, etc. The usual practice of appending a large and seemingly scholarly bibliography at the end of a book such as this would, therefore, be worse than hypocrisy, since it would be devoid of practical usefulness.

An attempt at a more or less complete bibliography of its subject, the history of Europe from September 1939 to December 1941, would amount to several volumes. Most of it would, of course, duplicate items listed in several existing bibliographies of the Second World War (about which see below). However, there is another, graver, problem. Even if such a bibliography were to be made with assiduous care the result would be far from being even reasonably complete. We have reached a stage in the decay of the so-called Modern Age that is manifest by the cancerous growth of publications and of many other forms of public communications. Five hundred years ago the Modern Age began with the sudden increase of all kinds of communications, including printing. This age is now ending with a breakdown of communications, because of their inflation. There are public idiots who proclaim this flood of communications as the "knowledge explosion," instead of seeing what it is: the cancer of a civilization nearing its end.

History is both the recorded and the remembered past. The aim of

---

[1] In early 1961 the German bibliographer Gunzenhaeuser estimated the number of items relating to the Second World War as about 50,000. (Gunzenhaeuser, 529.) There is reason to believe that the volume of these items doubled during the next twelve years. In Europe the literature relating to the first two years of the war is probably as large as that dealing with the last four years of it.

professional historians has been to complete the record, from time to time. Until relatively recently this professional aim of near-complete documentation was close to being realizable, on occasion. On more and more topics during the twentieth century this has become an impossible illusion. In the past historians were plagued by the scarcity of records. During the twentieth century they are plagued by the immense flood of records. Oddly— or perhaps not so oddly—few historians have been thinking what this plague really means. Plainly, the inflation of materials, including a great variety of documents, means what every kind of inflation means: When there is more and more of something, it is worth less and less. But this happens not merely because of the decline in their subjective value. It is involved with the decline of their very authenticity. And this calls for new approaches to some of the very canons of historical research.

This is not the place to speculate about new methods. However, it is because of the above-mentioned conditions that this bibliographical appendix to this book consists of two parts: of certain remarks concerning the immense and ungovernable mass of materials relating to its topic, and of an alphabetical list giving the full titles of the books, journals, documents, and other materials that are cited, in abbreviated form, through the text.

More than thirty years have passed since the events I have tried to describe in this book. Their documentary residue in the archives and in the libraries of Europe (and also of the United States) is available for the researcher in many countries. This includes most of the governmental records of Great Britain, Holland, Belgium, Italy, and of the Scandinavian states, with the partial exception of Finland. Partial access to or publication of certain official papers of the 1939–41 period has been granted by the governments of Spain, Portugal, Greece, Switzerland, and the Holy See; in Eastern Europe by those of Yugoslavia, Poland, and Hungary. The Romanian government is said to be considering a partial opening of its state archives relating to the Second World War. The governmental records of France in Western Europe, and of the rest of the states of Eastern Europe, are still largely closed, as of course are those of the Soviet Union. The most impressive mass of papers are those of the government of the Third Reich. The orderly habits of German bureaucracy carried over into the Hitler regime, even though the latter was no longer a *Beamtenstaat*.[2] The major portions of the papers of the government of the Third Reich have been found after the war. Since during the years 1939–41 most of Europe was dominated by the Third Reich, the existence

---

[2] See a discussion of this above, p. 324.

of these papers has remained the principal asset for historians dealing with that period.

The classic problem with government archives is, of course, that they do not contain everything. A relatively small portion of the archives of Europe's states was destroyed or lost during the Second World War (the French burned some of their important diplomatic files during the panic day of 16 May 1940; portions of the Polish, Yugoslav, and Hungarian Foreign Ministry archives went up in flames during the bombardments of their capital cities; most of the government papers of the independent Baltic republics were taken to the Soviet Union; and certain German records disappeared during the chaos at the end of the war). Perhaps as much as 90 per cent of the paperwork of the various state bureaucracies of Europe during the Second World War remains extant. The experienced historian as well as the sophisticated civil servant will, however, agree: No matter how extensive the records of the bureaucracy, many of the most important decisions or events are not committed to paper—a condition especially prevalent in the twentieth century. The telephone, the teletype, the radioed instructions are mostly unrecorded for posterity. Records of certain discussions, and of certain decisions, disappear even from those archives that escaped other destructions and are reputed to be reasonably "complete."[3] In the Soviet Union not only the official compilations of histories but also some of the selected documents published from the archives of the Narkomindel are often falsified.[4] Those historians who are eagerly awaiting the day when the Soviet archives will be open for researchers are, I fear, bound to be disappointed. But, then, some of this holds for the researcher in the archives of the Western democracies. Often the honest historian must admit that they contain little of what has not been known beforehand. In the Introduction to his *1939: The Making of The Second World War*, Sidney Aster celebrates the event that "The critical [British] documents for the eve of war in 1939 . . . were declassified and made public on January 1, 1970. Here, among thousands of bound volumes and files of loose papers

---

[3] Example: Many of the files in the archives of the Italian Foreign Ministry relating to Greece in 1940 are missing. (Toscano on p. x of *DDI*, Series IX, V.) Another example: Hitler to Molotov, 13 November 1940, wrangling about the previous Soviet insistence on a corner of southeastern Bukovina: "According to an oral agreement the former Austrian territories should have fallen entirely within the German sphere of interest." *GD*, D, XI, 462. No record of this "oral agreement" exists.

[4] In May 1945 a special team of Soviet intelligence recruits attempted to track down and destroy the phonograph records of the Hitler-Ribbentrop talks with Molotov of November 1940 in Berlin, with partial success. See also Hillgruber, *HS*, 103, note 1.

of all Government departments, is contained *the vital evidence which finally reveals the making of the Second World War.*" (My italics.) Contrast this breathless statement with the more cynical one from the second volume of the autobiography of Malcolm Muggeridge, an intelligence officer during the war, who later looked up some records relating to his former activities in different German and British archives: "Diplomats and Intelligence agents, in my experience, are even bigger liars than journalists, and the historians who try to reconstruct the past out of their records are, for the most part, dealing in fantasy."[5] Both statements are exaggerations: but somehow the second rings truer than the first.

Hitler, at the summit of events, was a secretive man. He knew rather well which of his monologues he wanted to have recorded. Other, far more important, decisions he reached in secret. He read not too many documents, and he made marginal notations on few of them.[6] There is not a single paper, not even the record of a verbal instruction, that connects him with the decision for the physical extermination of the Jews. Sometimes the very texts of some of the most important records of his utterances are subjects of posthumous debates, as is the case of the famous Hossbach memorandum or of his 22 August 1939 speech to his generals.[7] Yet the partial inaccuracy, or the second-hand character, of a certain record is insufficient reason to dismiss it altogether or to reduce its significance until it fits the preconceived thesis of a historian—the error of A. J. P. Taylor and some of his followers.

On the other hand, the skeptical historian (such as Taylor at his best) is often right: The existence of a document is plainly no guarantee of its authenticity. Certain people are careful enough to cover their tracks. This has been especially true during the Second World War.[8]

---

[5] Aster, 13; Muggeridge, II, 149.

[6] One significant exception is mentioned above, p. 34.

[7] See, for example, a discussion of these documents in the article by H. W. Koch in *THJ* (1968), 125–47; also several articles in *VFZ* (April 1968, October 1968, July 1971).

[8] One exception of this covers personal diaries, the authenticity of which has not noticeably deteriorated during the Second World War. The private diaries of a writer such as George Orwell, the diaries of certain officials such as Jan Szembek (of which the French version is incomplete), of certain diplomats such as André François-Poncet, of a captive king such as Christian X of Denmark are at least as authentic as the diaries of their predecessors centuries ago. In September 1940 the Germans got hold of a letter by the King of Denmark in which he said that he had written two hundred pages in his diary in the last two months "but I am forcing myself to keep it and it is especially interesting on account of the German conversations." *GD*, D, XI, 68–72. The skepticism with which Ciano's diaries, published the year after the war, were

There is, moreover, the effect of the large governmental bureaucracies—especially in totalitarian states—when the very language of an instruction or report or dispatch is impersonal. The once sacrosanct Rankean distinction between primary and secondary sources has become blurred. On many occasions the language of the responsible official may conceal more than it reveals.[9] His language may conform to the authoritarian rhetoric of the regime he serves; his truer intention may be different.[10] A novel kind of hermeneutical intelligence is needed to comprehend the purpose, the essence, and the details of many modern documents, perhaps especially during the Second World War—a kind of knowledge that in many ways cannot be taught and that comes from experience. It was summed up by the great Burckhardt more than a century ago: *Bisogna saper leggere* (one must know how to read)—reading between the lines, which is, after all, the literal meaning of the original Latin noun of "intelligence."[11]

There is more trouble to come. History is more than past politics, especially in the twentieth century. In this book I have attempted to describe—in many instances not much more than sketch—certain matters about the lives of peoples, what many of them ate, drank, saw, read, on occasion thought. The materials for this kind of reconstruction are often scanty, unreliable, misleading. This includes the statistics on which the economic and social historian has to rely. It is not only that historically significant statistics, even in this bureaucractic age, are scattered, often in the oddest places; it is also that the historian has no way to check their accuracy or even their reliability.[12] Economic historians are especially prone to forget that what they are reading are reports of production,

---

received at the time has not been borne out by successive documents: He has been largely truthful, though of course the purposes of some of his entries are open to question—as indeed are those of any diarist or writer.

[9] Example: Goebbels' confidential instructions and remarks to his closest confidants in Boelcke. Yet often Goebbels' deeper thoughts are not reflected in his remarks, in spite of their feigned openness. Like Goering's *bonhomie*, Goebbels' "confidential" frankness was often false.

[10] See, for example, Jacobsen on the Halder diaries: Jacobsen, *HT*, passim.

[11] That experience in intelligence work does not necessarily result in superior historianship is evident in Whaley, whose *Barbarossa* is but a collection of "intelligence" evidences—mostly rumors—to the effect that in 1941 Hitler *would* attack Russia, after all.

[12] There is an additional problem. By displaying his statistics, a historian may give the false impression that he had really done his homework. Example: Professor Denis Mack Smith in *Italy: A Modern History*, in a subchapter heavily laden with statistics ("The Theory and Practice of Fascism," 389–427, reprinted in Greene), says that Mussolini's populationist policies in the 1930s were a failure. One look at Italian population figures (see above, pp. 175–76) of the years 1935–39 would have shown him that the opposite was true.

compiled by bureaucrats several steps removed from production itself; that these figures may be as tendentious (and as cloaked in respectability) as the report of a careful ecclesiastical bureaucrat in the Vatican. In plain English, we must be as skeptical of figures as we are of documents. Figures telling us that the average daily consumption of a French worker in 1941 included 1,100 calories, or that the total volume of consumer goods produced in Germany in 1941 amounted to 14.3 billion Reichsmarks, are important. But—a very simple *caveat*—they are neither more nor less accurate than the statement that in August 1940 the English were brave. Economic historians such as Petzina are pioneers in a forest where enormous tasks of clearing are ahead in order to let in the light. Perhaps their experience will allow them to come to the conclusion that their methods must be constantly rethought—indeed, that a new science of economics is sorely needed for a new world.

The same thing is true of the historian of political science, interested as he may be in the phenomena of public opinion. He must be skeptical of public-opinion polls (of which, as we have seen, a few were made during and before the war years)[13]; he should not take the confidential reports of popular sentiments compiled by assiduous government officials as complete evidence[14]; he must be wary of trying to reconstruct public opinion from the press, without knowing much about the *internal* history of certain newspapers[15]; he must be *extremely* skeptical of films and newsreels which, despite their impression of authenticity, are often falsified not only by their editing but also by their very nature, with numberless and faceless technicians cooking up the broth.[16] *Bisogna saper*

---

[13] MO ("Mass Observation") began in England in 1939 (its chief organizer, Charles Madge, moved on from poet to pollster to *Daily Mirror* reporter and eventually to professor of sociology and filmwriter). Its archives now repose in the University of Sussex. For a skeptical approach to public-opinion polls (including their insufficient distinctions between choosing and thinking, between articulate and inarticulate sentiments, between opinions and sentiments, between public and private opinions, see Lukacs, *HC*, 75–83). An interesting comparison between contemporary and later reconstructions of public opinions and sentiments among the Belgian people could be made by studying Struye; Delandsheere, Ooms; and Gerard-Libois, Gotovitch, *opera citata*, side by side.
[14] One exception is the 1938–40 reports of Bocchini, then head of OVRA, Italy's secret police, "brutally frank," in Bocchini's own words, reports of opinion given to Mussolini alone. It could be compared with the far more limited RSHA surveys, or of the *Regierungspraesidentenberichten* as compiled and edited by Witetschek, *KB*.
[15] The few such internal histories include those of the London *Times, Corriere della Sera*, and *Das Reich;* with the exception of the latter, only a short chapter or two in the above relates to the war years.
[16] See the falsification described above, p. 86, n. 23, about an episode that has entered the pages of numberless history books.

*leggere:* In the end the historian must rely on his own judgment and experience, like the good critic, about whom Samuel Butler said that he must know how to judge from insufficient evidence.

He must understand that documents do not make history. It is, rather, the other way around: It is history that made the documents. Living persons, all kinds of persons with all kinds of complexities and confused and ephemeral purposes, left us those residues in the form of records that are inevitably necessary for our reconstruction of the past. But it is experience and imagination that vitalize these residues. On the one hand, there may be more than one golden needle in the dustiest of bureaucratic haystacks. On the other hand, the historian must be honest enough to admit to himself that, in most cases, he knows what he is looking for; he re-searches the past rather than searches it; he knows what he wants to find.

There is still much that is worth looking for. There remain important matters in the history of Europe during the Last European War about which more research is needed. Most of these matters involve not so much the relations of states or the march of the armies than the relations of peoples to each other, involving the internal structure of events. The images of nations as reflected in a variety of publications and public expressions, the differences between Hitler's public and private rhetoric, discrepancies between economic statistics and realities of consumption, memories of everyday life and their relation to official records,[17] the movements of cultural and artistic life, the opportunism of certain intellectuals, the peculiar conditions and circumscriptions of the language of

---

[17] In spite (or, perhaps, because?) of the magnitude of events, few superb descriptive prose passages, comparable of Conrad's description of the sea approach to England in 1889 in *The Nigger of the "Narcissus,"* of Dangerfield's description of England in 1913–14 in *The Strange Death of Liberal England*, of Waugh's London of 1922 in *Brideshead Revisited*, of Weidlé's frozen Petrograd in 1920 in *Russia: Past and Present*, exist of the Second World War. On the other hand, Peter Fleming's footnote (139) in his excellent history of 1940 remains supremely true. Fleming cites an asinine bureaucratic statement at the time, and in the footnote he adds: "For a satirical pastiche—from which the above sentence might well be taken—purporting to describe the religious activities of the Ministry of Information in 1940 see *Put Out More Flags* by Evelyn Waugh (London, 1942). This novel is an excellent guide to the atmosphere of the period." Or the Introduction by Audiat, 5–6, about Paris during the war: ". . . psychic events (*faits psychologiques*) . . . the atmosphere of Paris during the occupation is one of these. It changed from one year to another, from one month to another, in times of crisis from one hour to the next. No one, no matter what was his situation, no matter what his erudition, can evoke this atmosphere, this air, if he had not himself breathed it . . . [And yet] this book is not a diary or a memoir; the reader will never find the word 'I' in its pages."

totalitarian diplomacy, the American influences, the movements of peoples,[18] the history of certain small communities,[19] a comparative history of military training during the first phase of the war[20]—there is a long list of topics that still await their serious historian. Many of these matters involve matters of rhetoric, the examination of which cannot be left to content analysts or to experts in structural linguistics, who so often literally do not know what they are talking about. And it is in such matters that every so often the original document *is* invaluable—not even an accurate translation will do.[21] *Bisogna saper leggere;* to which we should add: *Bisogna saper ascoltare.*[22] We must know how to read, and we must know how to listen. It is not only from a scratchy and doctored record of a Hitler speech that we can hear, literally hear, the voices and sometimes feel the very breath of the past. It was an English historian, G. M. Young, I think, who once told his students "to go on reading till you hear the people speaking."[23] And they will tell you the most extraordinary things.

At the time of this writing the greatest help to researchers would be a central guide to the various archives in Europe (and also in the United States). Unfortunately such a central and useful guide does not exist.[24]

---

[18] To Vidalenc's work about the exodus of 1940 in France one may add an entire list of the French "underground" railroad: Ippecourt, Jouan, Nouveau, Rémy, dealing with *passeurs clandestins*, etc.

[19] Many of these exist in France (e.g. Baudot on the evolution of public opinion in the *département* of the Eure); a model in Belgium is Wynants on Verviers.

[20] Careful comparisons of military unit records and histories of certain limited engagements from both sides of the hill (which will necessarily include a comparison of the very language of these records) still await their serious, and intuitive, military historians.

[21] A masterful example of how to utilize documents is De Felice, *EF*, because of many things; his perusal of a vast variety of documents not necessarily relating to his main topic; his knowledge of the manners and morals and, most important, rhetoric of Italian society of the period; and his comprehension of the very language (it must be said, less totalitarian, less circumscribed than those of the Germans) of the Italian bureaucracy of the period.

[22] And at times: *Bisogna saper vedere* (we must know how to see). Not films. Certain photographs literally remind us through a kind of instant imagination that visualizes the past which, in some way or another, is latent in our minds.

[23] This is one of the reasons why Churchill's war memoirs are worth reading again and again, in spite of (or, rather, because) of their personal character.

[24] Thomas, Case is now badly outdated, *PRO* 15 is a good guide to the Public Record Office papers in England. Jacobsen, Röseler is useful; Hillgruber, *HS*, 611–14, provides a good overview of the German archival materials. (The

A reasonably complete (though perhaps not sufficiently critical) survey of bibliographies relating to the Second World War that had been published before December 1965 was compiled by Janet Ziegler.[25] Under the heading "Generalités," Miss Ziegler lists seventeen of the principal general bibliographies (Gunzenhaeuser, Jacobsen, Röseler, and Herre-Auerbach are the most important ones).[26] A supplement, 1966–69, to this, again compiled by Miss Ziegler, was published in *RH2M* (January 1971). Her "Survey of existing bibliographical coverage of the war" in Ziegler, *WW II*,[27] xiii–xvii, is valuable because of its critical and often judicious comments. She is correct in saying that "In general, the national bibliographic coverage of publications on the war in the individual countries is spotty and inadequate."[28] Periodicals with extensive bibliographical portions include *VFZ*, *RH2M*, *IA*, and *JCH* (in descending order of completeness).[29] There is no adequate bibliography of iconography of films, photos, and audiovisual materials in any language.[30]

---

question of accessibility is another problem. James W. O'Neill, "The Accessibility of Sources for the History of the Second World War: The Archivist's Viewpoint," *Prologue* [Spring 1972] is but a sketch from the American viewpoint; but for most European countries' holdings even such a sketch is missing.)

[25] "Repertoire international des bibliographies publiées de 1945 à 1965 sur la seconde guerre mondiale," *RH2M* (July 1966), a useful and exceptionally honest piece of work in which the bibliographer marks with an asterisk those items that she had not personally seen.

[26] To these one must add the catalogues (11 and 20 volumes) of the Bibliothek für Zeitgeschichte—Weltkriegsbucherei (Stuttgart), reprinted in Boston (C. K. Hall), 1969). Its *Jahresbibliographie* "lists the annual acquisitions of the Library, supplementary to the published catalogs, and includes many short special bibliographies." Ziegler, *WW II*, xiii.

[27] Ziegler, *WW II* is a compendium of books in English 1945–65 about World War II (it is marred by various omissions).

[28] Ziegler, *WW II*, xiv.

[29] The bibliography of *VFZ* is also published separately. There are also the various *Newsletters of the American Committee on the History of the Second World War* and special news bulletins and bibliographies (not complete) published by this committee.

[30] The National Archives in Washington has useful lists of microfilm publications, of films, and of sound recordings available on tape. A summary of the latter, "Audiovisual Records in the National Archives Relating to World War II," written by Mayfield S. Bray and William T. Murphy, exists in mimeographed form. Fred E. Peteler's tape collection, *Tondokumente des III. Reiches* (Munich), available in certain American libraries, is valuable. About the extent and the limitations of radio recordings, see E. Viefhaus, "Zeitgeschichte in Tondokumenten," *Neue politische Literatur* (Oct. 1960).

To sum up: The mass of materials has become ungovernable. A complete bibliography of our topic, the history of an entire continent during two war years, is impossible. The first step toward a better order, of immeasurable help for future researchers, would be a central guide to the various archives. The second, no less useful, would be a carefully researched, counterchecked, and perhaps annotated bibliography of bibliographies, 1945–74, bringing the original Ziegler "Repertoire . . ." 1945–65 and its 1966–69 supplement up to date. The third step, after this, ought to be a critical checking of bibliographies, national section by national section, by historians and bibliographers conversant with the materials within their own countries. There are still many general works, with overlapping competences, that are too easily overlooked; and, in spite of the ocean of materials, there remain many gaps in the lists to be filled.

The following list of books and of periodicals includes *only* the titles of those items that were cited or referred to in the text, in abbreviated form. It is emphatically not a selective bibliography of the history of Europe, 1939–41. Nor is it, even remotely, an exhaustive list of the materials and the books consulted by the author.[1]

## ABBREVIATIONS OF CITED REFERENCES

*Action This Day*     *Action This day: Working with Churchill: Memoirs by Lord Normanbrook, John Colville, Sir John Martin, Sir Ian Jacob, Lord Bridges, Sir Leslie Rowen,* ed. Sir John Wheeler-Bennett (London, 1969).

Ádám, *MMV*     Ádám, M. ed. *Magyarország a második világháboruban* (Budapest, 1967).

Amery     Amery, C. *Die Kapitulation* (Hamburg, 1963).

*Annals*     *Annals of the American Academy of Political and Social Sciences,* Philadelphia.

Ansel     Ansel, W. *Hitler Confronts England* (Durham, N.C., 1960).

Aster     Aster, S. *1939–The Making of the Second World War* (London, 1973).

Audiat     Audiat, P. *Paris pendant la guerre* (Paris, 1946).

*A Vatikáni MK*     *A vatikáni magyar követ jelenti* (Budapest, 1969).

Barker     Barker, C. *Eritrea 1941* (London, 1961).

Baudhuin     Baudhuin, F. *L'economie belge sous l'occupation, 1940–1944* (Brussels, 1945).

---

[1] Articles cited appear in the footnotes of the text. The only articles listed below are those mentioned in the foregoing Bibliographical remarks.

Baudot     Baudot, M. *L'opinion publique sous l'occupation. L'exemple d'un département français (1939–1945)* (Paris, 1960).

Baudouin     *The Private Diaries of Paul Baudouin* (London, 1951).

Bayern KL     *Die kirchliche Lage in Bayern nach den Regierungspraesidentenberichten, 1933–1943*, Vol. I, Oberbayern, Vol. II, Ober- und Mittelfranken, ed. H. Witetschek (Mayence, 1966, 1967).

BD     *Documents on British Foreign Policy*, Series III (London, 1949–).

Beaufre     Beaufre, A. *1940: The Fall of France* (New York, 1960).

Behrend-Rosenfeld     Behrend-Rosenfeld, E. R. *Ich stand nicht allein* (Hamburg, 1945).

Benouville     Guillain de Benouville, P. *Le sacrifice du matin* (Paris, 1947).

Bennett     Bennett, J. *British Broadcasting and the Danish Resistance Movement* (London, 1966).

Berg     *Warsaw Ghetto: A Diary of Mary Berg*, ed. S. L. Shreiderman (New York, 1945).

Bernanos, *EC*, I     Bernanos, G. *Essais et écrits de combat*, I (Paris, 1971).

Bernanos, *GRC*     Bernanos, G. *Les grands cimetières sous la lune.* (Paris, 1938).

Bialer     Bialer, S. (ed.). *Stalin and His Generals: Soviet Military Memoirs of World War II* (New York, 1969).

Birkenhead, *Halifax*     Birkenhead, *Life of Lord Halifax* (London, 1965).

Blackstock     Blackstock, P. W. *The Secret Road to World War II: Soviet vs. Western Intelligence 1921–1939* (Chicago, 1964).

Bleuel     Bleuel, H. P. *Sex and Society in Nazi Germany* (New York, 1973).

Bloch     Bloch, M. *The Strange Defeat* (New York, 1948).

Boberach     *Meldungen aus dem Reich. Auswahl aus den geheimen Lageberichten des Sicherheitsdienstes der SS 1939–1944*, ed. H. Boberach (Munich, 1968).

Boberach, *KK*     *Berichte des SD und der Gestapo ueber Kirchen und Kirchenvolk in Deutschland, 1934–1944*, ed. H. Boberach (Mayence, 1967).

Boehme     Boehme, H. *Entstehung und Grundlagen des Waffenstillstandes von 1940* (Stuttgart, 1966).

Boelcke     Boelcke, W. A. *Kriegspropaganda, 1939–1941: Geheime Ministerkonferenzen im Reichspropagandaministerium* (Stuttgart, 1966).

Bonnefous     Bonnefous, E. *Histoire politique de la III<sup>e</sup> République*, Vol. VII (Paris, 1967).

Bonneville     Bonneville, G. *Prophètes et témoins de l'Europe* (Essai sur l'idée d'Europe dans la littérature française de 1914 a nos jours) (Leyden, 1961).

Bourget    Bourget, P. *Der Marschall: Pétain zwischen Kollaboration und Resistance* (Frankfurt, 1968).

Brenner    Brenner, H. *Die Kunstpolitik des Nationalsozialismus* (Hamburg, 1963).

Broszat    Broszat, M. *Nationalsozialistische Polenpolitik 1939–1945* (Stuttgart, 1961).

Bryant    Bryant, A. *The Turn of the Tide* (the Alanbrooke diaries) (London, 1957).

Budurowycz    Budurowycz, B. *Polish-Soviet Relations, 1933–1939* (New York, 1963).

Bullock    Bullock, A. *Hitler, a Study in Tyranny* (New York, 1966).

Burckhardt    Burckhardt, C. J. *Meine Danziger Mission, 1937–1939* (Munich, 1960).

Butler    Butler, Sir J. R. M. *Lord Lothian* (London, 1965).

Butler, GS    Butler, Sir J. R. M. (ed.). *Grand Strategy*, Vol. II. (London, 1957).

*Cadogan*    *The Diaries of Sir Alexander Cadogan, 1938–1945*, ed. D. Dilks (London, 1971).

Calder    Calder, A. *The People's War: Britain, 1939–45* (London, 1969).

Carell    Carell, P. *Unternehmen Barbarossa* (Berlin, 1968).

CDA    Commission d'armistice franco-allemande, *La délégation française auprès de la commission allemande d'armistice*, I–V (Paris, 1947–59).

Céline, *Bagatelles*    Céline, L. F. (Destouches), *Bagatelles pour un massacre* (Paris, 1937).

Cerruti    Cerruti, E. *Visti da vicino* (Milan, 1951).

Charles-Roux    Charles-Roux, F. *Cinq mois tragiques aux affairs étrangères* (Paris, 1949).

CHSGM    *Cahiers d'histoire de la deuxième guerre mondiale* (Brussels, 1971–).

Churchill, GS    Churchill, Sir W. *The Second World War*, Vol. I, *The Gathering Storm* (Boston, 1948).

Churchill, FH    Ibid., Vol. II, *Their Finest Hour* (Boston, 1949).

Churchill, GA    Ibid., Vol. III, *The Grand Alliance* (Boston, 1950).

Ciano    *The Ciano Diaries* (New York, 1946).

Ciano, EVC    Ciano, G. *L'Europa verso la catastrofe* (Milan, 1948).

Colvin, NB    Colvin, I. *None So Blind* (London, 1965).

Compton    Compton, J. V. *The Swastika and the Eagle* (London, 1968).

Conquest    Conquest, R. *The Great Terror* (London, 1969).

Conway    Conway, J. *The Nazi Persecution of the Churches* (New York, 1968).

Cross    Cross, C. *The Fascists in Britain* (New York, 1963).

Dawson    Dawson, R. *The Decision to Aid Russia, 1941* (Chapel Hill, 1959).

*DDF*    *Documents diplomatiques français 1932–1939*, Serie II (Paris, 1961–).

*DDI*    *Documenti diplomatici italiani*, Serie VIII, IX (Rome, 1952–).

De Felice, *EF*    De Felice, R. *Storia degli ebrei italiani sotto il fascismo* (Turin, 1961).

De Felice, *MR*    De Felice, R. *Mussolini rivoluzionario* (Turin, 1965).

De Gaulle    *The War Memoirs of Charles de Gaulle*, Vol. I. (New York, 1960).

De Jong, *D5K*    De Jong, L. *Die deutsche Fünfte Kolonne im Zweiten Weltkrieg* (Stuttgart, 1959).

De Jong, *Holland*    De Jong, L. *Holland Fights the Nazis* (London, 1941).

De Jong, *TW*    De Jong, L. *Total War and the Human Mind: Mass Reactions to German Occupation* (New York, 1946).

Delandsheere, Ooms    Delandsheere P.; Ooms, A. *La Belgique sous les nazis*, I–IV (Brussels, n.d. [1945 or 1946]).

*Delp PM*    *The Prison Meditations of Father Alfred Delp* (New York, 1963).

De Man, *CS*    De Man, H. *Cavalier seul* (Geneva, 1948).

De Mattei    De Mattei, G. *Verso l'equilibrio della nuova Europa* (Florence, 1941).

Derry    Derry, T. K. *The Campaign in Norway* (London, 1952).

Destrem    Destrem, M. *L'été 39* (Paris, 1969).

Deuerlein    Deuerlein, E. *Hitler—eine politische Biographie* (Munich, 1970).

Deutsch    Deutsch, H. C. *The Conspiracy Against Hitler in the Twilight War* (Minneapolis, 1968).

Djilas    Djilas, V. *Conversation with Stalin* (New York, 1967).

Dossinague    Dossinague, J. *España tenia razón* (1939–45) (Madrid, 1949).

*DPSR*    *Documents of Polish-Soviet Relations, 1939–1945* (London, 1961–).

Drieu, *CRP*    Drieu la Rochelle, P. *Chronique politique* (Paris, 1941).

Druon    Druon, M. *L'esprit européen* (Rencontres internationales de Geneve) (Geneva, 1946).

Du Moulin    Du Moulin de Labarthète, H. *Les temps des illusions* (Geneva, 1946).

Duquesne    Duquesne, J. *Les catholiques français sous l'occupation* (Paris, 1966).

Eby    Eby, C. *Alcazar* (New York, 1965).

Eden    Eden, A. *The Reckoning: The Eden Memoirs* (London, 1965).

Einstein    Einstein, L. *A Diplomat Looks Back* (New Haven, 1968).

Einzig    Einzig, P. *In the Center of Things* (London, 1960).

Ellis    Ellis, L. F. *France and Flanders 1939–1940* (London, 1953).

Erickson    Erickson, J. *The Soviet High Command* (London, 1962).

Fabre-Luce    Fabre-Luce, A. *Journal de la France*, Vol. I. (Paris, 1941; Vol. II, Geneva, 1946).

Falconi    Falconi, C. *The Silence of Pius XII* (London, 1970).

Feiling    Feiling, K. *The Life of Neville Chamberlain* (London, 1970).

Fireside    Fireside, T. *Icon and Swastika: The Russian Orthodox Church Under Nazi and Soviet Control* (Cambridge, 1971).

Fischer    Fischer, G. *The Soviet Opposition to Stalin* (London, 1970).

Fitzgibbon    Fitzgibbon, C. *The Winter of the Bombs* (London, 1958).

Fleming    Fleming, P. *Invasion 1940* (New York, 1957) (American edition of *Operation Sea Lion* [London, 1957]).

*Forrestal*    *The Forrestal Diaries*, ed. W. Millis (New York, 1954).

François-Poncet    François-Poncet, A. *Au Palais Farnèse: Souvenirs d'une ambassade à Rome, 1938–1940* (Paris, 1961).

Friedlaender    Friedlaender, S. *Pius XII et le IIIᵉ Reich: Documents* (Paris, 1964).

Friedlaender, *HUS*    Friedlaender, S. *Prelude to Downfall: Hitler and the United States, 1939–1941* (New York, 1967).

*FRUS*    *Foreign Relations of the United States* (series) (Washington, D.C.).

Fuller    Fuller, J. F. C. *The Second World War, 1939–1945: A Strategical and Tactical History* (London, 1948).

Fuller, *CW*    Fuller, J. F. C. *The Conduct of War, 1789–1961* (London, 1961).

Galland    Galland, A. *The First and the Last: The Rise and Fall of the German Fighter Forces, 1938–1945* (London, 1955).

Galtier    Galtier-Boissière, J. *Mon journal pendant l'occupation* (Paris, 1945).

*GD*    *Documents on German Foreign Policy, 1918–1945*, Series D (Washington, D.C., 1948–).

Gerard-Libois, Gotovitch    Gerard-Libois, J., Gotovitch, J. *L'an 40: La Belgique occupée* (Brussels, 1972).

Gide    *The Journals of André Gide*, Vol. II, ed. J. O'Brien (New York, 1947).

Goure, Dinerstein    Goure, L.; Dinerstein, H. *Moscow in Crisis* (Glencoe, Ill., 1955).

Greene     *Fascism: An Anthology*, ed. N. Greene (New York, 1968).

Gross     Gross B. *Willi Münzenberg—eine politische Biographie* (Stuttgart, 1967).

Gruchmann     Gruchmann, L. *Nationalsozialistische Grossraumordnung* (Stuttgart, 1962).

Guéhenno     Guéhenno, J. *Journal des années noires* (1940–44) (Paris, 1947).

Günther-Hornis     Günther-Hornis, E. *Kunstschutz in der von Deutschland besetzten Gebieten, 1939–45* (Tübingen, 1958).

Gunzenhaeuser     Gunzenhaeuser, M. "Die Bibliographien zur Geschichte des Zweiten Weltkrieges," *Jahresbibliographie 1961 der Bibliothek für Zeitgeschichte Stuttgart* (Frankfurt, 1963).

GWB     *German White Book(s)*. *Auswartiges Amt: Polnische Dokumente über die Ursachen des Krieges*, No. 1 (Berlin, 1940). *Die Geheimakten des französischen Generalstabes*, No. 6 (Berlin, 1941). *Dokumente zum Konflikt mit Jugoslawien und Griechenland*, No. 7 (Berlin, 1941).\*

Gwyer, Butler     Gwyer, J. M. A.; Butler, J. R. M. *Grand Strategy*, Vol. III (London, 1964).

Halder, *KTB*     Halder, F. *Kriegstagebuch: Tägliche Aufzeichnungen des Chefs des Generalstabes des Heeres, 1939–1942*, Vols. I–III, ed. H.-A. Jacobsen (Stuttgart, 1962–64).

Halévy     Halévy, E. *A History of the English People in the Nineteenth Century*, Vol. V (London, 1961).

Hamsun, *OOP*     Hamsun, K. *On Overgrown Paths* (New York, 1967).

Hanfstaengl     Hanfstaengl, E. *Hitler: The Missing Years* (London, 1957).

Harington     Harington, Sir C. *Tim Harington Looks Back* (London, 1937).

Hartlaub     Hartlaub, F. *Von unten gesehen* (Stuttgart, 1950).

Hartmann     Hartmann, F. H. *The Swiss Press and Foreign Affairs in World War II* (Gainesville, Fla., 1960).

---

\* Seven of these *German White Books* were published in 1940 and in 1941. A selective collection of German and captured documents, they obviously served propagandistic purposes. Three of the *White Books* were translated into English, and published in New York in 1940. In spite of the propagandistic purposes of their publication, the captured documents are authentic and often of considerable interest. It is therefore more than regrettable that they are not included in the bibliographies of most works dealing with their specific subjects. Often they are excluded from extensive bibliographies of the war. In spite of the large number of volumes printed in the United States by the German Information Center in 1940, most of these have disappeared from American libraries.

Hassell   Hassell, U. V. *Vom anderen Deutschland* (Zurich, 1946).

Hedin   *Sven Hedin's German Diary* (Dublin, 1951).

Heer, *Glaube*   Heer, F. *Der Glaube des Adolf Hitler: Anatomie einter politischen Religiositaet* (Munich, 1968).

Heine, *SW*   *Heinrich Heine's Sämtiche Werke*, ed. Elster (Leipzig and Vienna, 1893).

Heinz, Peterson   Heinz, G.; Peterson, A. F. *NSDAP Hauptarchiv*, Guide to the Hoover Institution microfilm collection (Stanford, Calif., 1964).

Henderson   Henderson, Sir N. *Failure of a Mission* (London, 1940).

Henrey   Henrey, R. *The Siege of London* (London, 1946).

Herre, Auerbach   Herre, F.; Auerbach, H. *Bibliographie zur Zeitgeschichte und zum zweiten Weltkrieg für die Jahre 1945–1950* (Munich, 1955).

Hesse   Hesse, F. *Das Spiel um Deutschland* (Munich, 1953).

Heyen   Heyen, F. J. *Nationalsozialismus im Alltag: Quellen zur Geschichte des Nationalsozialismus, vornehmlich im Raum Mainz-Koblenz-Trier* (Boppard am Rhein, 1967).

Hillgruber   Hillgruber, A. (ed.). *Von El Alamein bis Stalingrad: Aus dem Kriegstagebuch des Oberkommandos der Wehrmacht* (Munich, 1964).

Hillgruber, *HS*   Hillgruber, A. *Hitlers Strategie: Politik und Kriegsführung 1940–1941* (Dusseldorf, 1965).

Hillgruber, *SDH*   Hillgruber, A. (ed.). *Staatsmanner und Diplomaten bei Hitler: Vertrauliche Aufzeichnungen über die Unterredungen mit Vertretern des Auslandes 1939–1941* (München, 1969).

Hitler, *MK*   Hitler, A. *Mein Kampf* (New York, 1939).

Hitler *TG*   *Hitlers Tischgesprache im Führerhauptquartier*, ed. H. Picker -A. Hillgruber (Munich, 1968).

Hitler *ZB*   *Hitlers Zweites Buch* (Stuttgart, 1961).

Hitler-Bormann   *The Testament of Adolf Hitler: The Hitler-Bormann Documents, February–April 1945* (London, 1959).

Hochhuth   Hochhuth, R. *The Representative* (London, 1963).

Homze   Homze, E. *Foreign Labor in Nazi Germany* (Princeton, N.J., 1967).

Hoover, *France*   *France During the German Occupation, 1940–1944: A Collection of 292 Statements on the Government of Maréchal Pétain and Pierre Laval*, Vols. 1–3 (Stanford, Calif., 1959).

Horthy *TI*   *Horthy Miklós titkos iratai*, ed. Szinai-Szücs (Budapest, 1965).

Hytier   Hytier, A. *Two Years of French Foreign Policy, Vichy: 1940–1942* (Geneva, 1958).

*IA*   *International Affairs* (London).

*IH*     *Irish Historical Studies* (Dublin).

*IMT*     International Military Tribunal, *Nazi conspiracy and Aggression* (two series; 15 and 42 vols.) (Washington, D.C., 1947–53).

Ippecourt     Ippecourt, A. *Chemins d'Espagne: Mémoires et documents sur la guerre secrète à travers les Pyrenées* (Paris, 1948).

Irving     Irving, D. *The German Atomic Bomb* (London, 1967).

Jaeckel     Jaeckel, E. *Hitlers Weltanschauung* (Tubingen, 1969).

Jacobsen, *HT*     Jacobsen, H.-A. "Das Halder-Tagebuch als historische Quelle," *Festschrift Percy Ernst Schramm zu seinem 70. Geburtstag von Schülern und Freunden zugeeignet* (Wiesbaden, 1964).

Jacobsen, Röseler     Jacobsen, H.-A. *Zur Konzeption einer Geschichte des Zweiten Weltkrieges.* Schriften der Bibliothek für Zeitgeschichte/Weltkriegsbücherei (Stuttgart, 1964).

*JCH*     *The Journal of Contemporary History* (London).

Jouan     Jouan, C. *Comète, histoire d'une ligne d'évasion* (Brussels, 1948).

Juenger     Juenger, E. *Garten und Strassen* (Berlin, 1942).

Keep     *Contemporary History in the Soviet Mirror*, ed. J. Keep (New York, 1964).

Kennan, *M*     Kennan, G. *Memoirs 1925–1950* (Boston, 1967).

King     King, C. *A War Diary* (London, 1971).

Klein     Klein, B. H. *Germany's Economic Preparations for War* (Cambridge, 1959).

Klemperer     Klemperer, V. *LTI: Notizbuch eines Philologen* (Leipzig, 1960).

Knef     Knef, H. *The Gift Horse* (New York, 1971).

Korbonski     Korbonski, S. *Fighting Warsaw* (London, 1956).

Kot     Kot, S. *Conversations in the Kremlin and Dispatches from Russia* (London, 1961).

Krausnick     Krausnick, H. *Anatomy of the SS State* (New York, 1970).

Krosby     Krosby, H. P. *Finland, Germany, and the Soviet Union, 1940–1941: The Petsamo Dispute* (London, 1968).

Kwiet     Kwiet, K. *Reichskommissariat Niederlande* (Stuttgart, 1968).

Lampe     Lampe, D. *The Last Ditch* (London, 1968).

Lancaster     Lancaster, O. *Signs of the Times, 1939–1961* (London, 1961).

Laurière     Laurière, H. *Assassins au nom de Dieu* (Paris, 1951).

Lawrence     Lawrence, D. H. *Movements in European History* (London, 1921).

Lecoeur     Lecoeur, A. *Le parti communiste français et la résistance: Aôut 1939–Juin 1941* (Paris, 1968).

Leusser     Leusser, A. *Ein Jahrzehnt deutsch-amerikanischer Politik* (Munich, 1928).

Lewy    Lewy, G. *The Catholic Church and Nazi Germany* (New York, 1964).

Liddell Hart    Liddell Hart, B. M., *History of the Second World War* (London, 1970).

LJ    Ministere des Affaires Etrangères, Documents diplomatiques, *Livre Jaune* (French Yellow Book) (Paris, 1939).

Lloyd George, F.    Lloyd George, Frances. *The Years That Are Past* (London, 1970).

Lukacs, *HC*    Lukacs, J. *Historical Consciousness* (New York, 1968).

Lukacs, *PMA*    Lukacs, J. *The Passing of the Modern Age* (New York, 1970).

Macmillan    Macmillan, H. *The Blast of War* (New York, 1967).

Marie Thérèse    Marie Thérèse (pseud.), *Histoire d'une prostituée*, ed. M. Duras (Geneva, 1964).

Maser    Maser, W. *Adolf Hitler—Legende—Mythos—Wirklichkeit* (Munich, 1971).

Maser, *MK*    Maser, W. *Hitlers Mein Kampf* (Munich, 1966).

Mastny    Mastny, V. *The Czechs Under Nazi Rule: The Failure of National Resistance, 1939–1942* (New York, 1971).

Maurois, *Proust*    Maurois, A. *Proust: Portrait of a Genius* (New York, 1950).

*Meldungen*    *Meldungen aus dem Reich.* The numbers cited are those in the microfilm collection of the RSHA file in the library of the Institut fuer Zeitgeschichte in Munich. There is also a good printed selection: H. Boberach (ed.), *Meldungen aus dem Reich* (Munich, 1968).

Mencken, *AL*    Mencken, H. L., *Supplement One, The American Language* (New York, 1945).

Milward    Milward, A. *Die deutsche Kriegswirtschaft, 1939–1945* (Stuttgart, 1966).

Miry    Miry, R. *Belgium Under Occupation* (New York, 1946).

*Moffat*    *The Moffat Papers*, ed. Nancy Hooker Harrison (Cambridge, 1956).

Montherlant    Montherlant, H. de. *Solstice de juin* (Paris, 1940).

Moran    *Churchill. Taken from the Diaries of Lord Moran* (Boston, 1966).

Mordal, *Dunkerque*    Mordal, J. (Cras). *La bataille de Dunkerque* (Paris, 1957).

Mordal, *Norvège*    Mordal, J. *La campagne de Norvège* (Paris, 1959).

Mosley    Mosley, L. *On Borrowed Time* (New York, 1969).

Mosley, *Back*    Mosley, L. *Back to the Wall* (London, 1971).

Muggeridge    Muggeridge, M. *Chronicles of Wasted Time*, Vol. I (London, 1972; Vol. II, London, 1973).

Muggeridge, *WM*    Muggeridge, M. *Winter in Moscow* (London, 1935).

*MWB*    *Militärwochenblatt* (Berlin).

Neave    Neave, A. *The Flames of Calais* (London, 1972).

Nicolson    Nicolson, H. *Diaries and Letters*, Vol. II (1939–45), (London, 1967).

*Nietzsche SL*    *Selected letters of Friedrich Nietzsche*, ed. C. Middleton (Chicago, 1969).

Nobécourt    Nobécourt, J. *Le vicaire* (Paris, 1964).

Noguères, Degliame-Fouché, Vigier    Noguères, H., with Degliame-Fouché, M., and Vigier, J.-L. *Histoire de la résistance en France*, Vol. I., *Juin 1940–Juin 1941* (Paris, 1967).

Nouveau    Nouveau, C. H. *Des capitaines par milliers* (Paris, 1958).

*NSR*    Department of State, *Nazi-Soviet Relations* (Washington, D.C., 1948).

*OFW*    *The Origins of the First World War: Great Power Rivalry and German War Aims*, ed. H. W. Koch (London, 1972).

*OKW/KTB*    *Kriegstagebuch des Oberkommandos der Wehrmacht* (Wehrmachtsführungsstab), Vols. I–IV, ed. P. Schramm, with A. Hillgruber, W. Hubatsch, and H.-A. Jacobsen, (Frankfurt, 1961–65).

*Orwell*    *The Collected Essays, Journalism, and Letters of George Orwell*, Vols. I–IV (London, 1968).

Orwell, *Wigan Pier*    Orwell, G. (Blair). *The Road to Wigan Pier* (London, 1937).

Paikert    Paikert, G. C. *The Danube Swabians* (The Hague, 1967).

Pawle    Pawle, G. *The War and Colonel Warden* (New York, 1963).

Paxton    Paxton, R. *Parades and Politics in Vichy* (New York, 1962).

*PD*    See *GWB*, No. 1.

Pearson    Pearson, H. *Labby: The Life and Character of Henry Labouchère* (London, 1936).

Pelz    Pelz, S. E. *Race to Pearl Harbor* (Cambridge, Mass., 1974).

Perrault    Perrault, G. *L'orchestre rouge* (Paris, 1967).

Peterson    Peterson, W. *The Limits of Hitler's Power* (Chicago, 1968).

Petrov, *Lane*    Petrov, V. *A Study in Diplomacy: The Story of Arthur Bliss Lane* (Chicago, 1971).

Petzina    Petzina, D. *Autarkiepolitik im Dritten Reich: Der nationalsozialistische Vierjahresplan* (Stuttgart, 1968).

P-K, *Ver/Inf*    Partei-Kanzlei, *Vertrauliche Informationen* (in the library of the Institut für Zeitgeschichte, Munich).

*PRO 15*    *Public Record Office Handbook No. 15, The Second World War: A Guide to Documents in the Public Record Office* (London, 1972).

*PSR*    See *DPSR*.

Pulzer    Pulzer, P. *The Rise of Political Anti-Semitism in Germany and Austria* (New York, 1964).

Raczynski    Raczynski, C. *In Allied London* (London, 1962).

Rebatet    Rebatet, L. *Les décombres* (Paris, 1942).

Reck-Malleczewen    Reck-Malleczewen, R. P. *Tagebuch eines Verzweifelten* (Frankfurt, 1971).

Reitlinger, *FS*    Reitlinger, G. *The Final Solution* (New York, 1953).

Reitlinger, *House*    Reitlinger, G. *The House Built on Sand* (New York, 1960).

Rémy    Rémy, C. (pseud.). *Passeurs clandestins* (Paris, 1954).

Reynaud    Reynaud, P. *La France a sauvé l'Europe* (Paris, 1950).

*RH*    *Revue historique* (Paris).

*RH2M*    *Revue historique de la deuxième guerre mondiale* (Paris).

*Ribbentrop*    *The Ribbentrop Memoirs*, ed. Annelies v. Ribbentrop (London, 1954).

Rich    Rich, N. *Hitler's War Aims*. Vol. II (New York, 1974).

RIIA Survey    Royal Institute of International Affairs, *The Initial Triumph of the Axis* (London, 1960).

Robertson    Robertson, E. M. *Hitler's Prewar Policy and Military Plans, 1937–1939* (London, 1963).

Robien    Robien, L. de. *The Diary of a Diplomatist in Russia, 1917–1918* (London, 1969).

*Rommel*    *The Rommel Papers* (London, 1953).

*Rosenberg TB*    *Das politische Tagebuch A. Rosenbergs aus den Jahren 1934/35 und 1939/40*, ed. H.-G. Seraphim (Berlin, 1956).

Rougemont    Rougemont, D. de. *Journal d'une époque* (Paris, 1968).

Schechtman    Schechtman, J. *European Population Transfers, 1939–45* (New York, 1946).

Schmitz    Schmitz, H. *Die Bewirtschaftung der Nahrungsmittel und Verbrauchsgüter 1939–1950, dargestellt am Beispiel der Stadt Essen* (Essen, 1956).

Schramm    Schramm, P. E. *Hitler: The Man and the Military Leader* (Chicago, 1971).

Schramm-Thadden    Schramm-v. Thadden, E. *Griechenland und die Grossmaechte im II. Weltkrieg* (Wiesbaden, 1955).

Smith, *English Language*    Smith, L. P. *The English Language* (London, 1912).

Sorel    Sorel, A. *Europe and the French Revolution: The Political Conditions of the Old Regime* (London, 1968).

Spears    Spears, Sir E. L. *Assignment to Catastrophe*, I–II (London, 1954).

Speer    Speer, A. *Erinnerungen* (Frankfurt-Berlin, 1969).

Spinks    *Religion in Britain Since 1900*, ed. G. S. Spinks (London, 1952).

Stalin-Churchill    *Correspondence Between the Chairman of the Council of Ministers of the USSR and the Presidents of the U.S.A. and the Prime Ministers of Great Britain During the Great Patriotic War of 1941–1942*, Vol. I, *Correspondence with Churchill and Attlee: July 1941–November 1945* (Moscow, 1957).

Stehlin    Stehlin, P. *Témoignage pour l'histoire* (Paris, 1962).

Stewart, *Crete*    Stewart, I. McD. G. *The Struggle for Crete* (London, 1966).

Struye    Struye, P. *L'evolution du sentiment public en Belgique sous l'occupation allemande* (Brussels, 1945).

Sulzberger    Sulzberger, C. *A Long Row of Candles* (New York, 1969).

Szembek    Szembek, J. *Journal 1933–1939* (Paris, 1952).

Tanner    Tanner, V. *The Winter War* (Stanford, Calif., 1957).

Taylor    Taylor, A. J. P. *The Origins of the Second World War* (New York, 1968).

Taylor, *Beaverbrook*    Taylor, A. J. P. *Beaverbrook* (New York, 1972).

Taylor, *EH*    Taylor, A. J. P. *English History, 1914–1945* (New York, 1965).

Teilhard, *Letters*    Teilhard de Chardin, P. *Letters to Two Friends, 1926–1952* (London, 1963).

Tharaud    Tharaud, J. *L'envoyé de l'archange* (Paris, 1939).

*THJ*    *The Historical Journal* (London).

Thomas, Case    Thomas, R. P.; Case, L. M. (eds.). *Guide to the Diplomatic Archives of Western Europe* (Philadelphia, 1959).

Thompson, *1940*    Thompson, L. *1940* (New York, 1967).

Thorne    Thorne, C. *The Approach of War, 1938–39* (London, 1967).

Toscano    Toscano, M. *Una mancata intesa italo-sovietica nel 1940 e 1941* (Florence, 1953).

Turney    Turney, A. *Disaster at Moscow: Von Bock's Campaigns, 1941–1942* (London, 1972).

*TW&HM*    *Total War and the Human Mind: A Symposium* (London, 1959).

Valland    Valland, R. *Le front de l'art, 1939–45* (Paris, 1961).

*VFZ*    *Vierteljahrshefte für Zeitgeschichte* (Munich).

*VD*    *Actes et documents du Saint-Siège relatifs à la second guerre mondiale* (Vatican City, 1965–).

Vidalenc    Vidalenc, J. *L'exode de mai–juin 1940* (Paris, 1957).

Wagenführ    Wagenführ, R. *Die deutsche Industrie im Kriege 1939–1945* (Berlin, 1954).

Wahlen    Wahlen, F. *Unser Boden heute und morgen* (Zurich, 1943).

Waldeck    Waldeck, C. *Athénée-Palace* (New York, 1942).

Waldersee    Waldersee, A. *Denkwürdigkeiten*, III, ed. H. Meisner (Berlin, 1923).

*Wartime Correspondence    Wartime Correspondence Between President Roosevelt and Pope Pius XII* (New York, 1947).

Weidlé    Weidlé, W. *Les abeilles d'Aristée* (Paris, 1954).

Weininger    Weininger, O. *Geschlecht und Charakter* (Vienna, 1922).

Weizsaecker    Weizsaecker, E. V. *Memoirs* (London, 1951).

Whaley    Whaley, B. *Barbarossa* (Cambridge, 1973).

Wilson    Wilson, T. *The First Summit* (Boston, 1969).

Wiskemann    Wiskemann, E. *The Europe I Saw* (London, 1966).

Wolf    Wolf, W. *Faschismus in der Schweiz* (Zurich, 1969).

Wood-Dempster    Wood, D.-Dempster, D. *The Narrow Margin* (London, 1961).

Woodward    Woodward, Sir L. *British Foreign Policy in the Second World War*, Vols. I–III (London, 1970–).

Woodward, *BP*    Ibid., one-vol. ed. (London, 1962).

Wright    Wright, Gordon. *The Ordeal of Total War* (New York, 1968).

*WWR    Wehrwissentschaftliche Rundschau* (Frankfurt).

Wynants    Wynants, J., Jr. "Verviers, L'autorité communale en 1940–1941," *CHSGM* (Oct. 1972).

Zahn    Zahn, G. *German Catholics and Hitler's Wars* (New York, 1962).

ZD    *Zeitschriften-Dienst*, Together with "Die Innere Front/NSK-Pressedienst" in the library of the Institut für Zeitgeschichte, Munich.

Ziegler, *WW II    World War II: Books in English, 1945–65*, complied and introduced by Janet Ziegler (Stanford, Calif., 1971).

Zoller    Zoller, A. *Hitler privat* (Dusseldorf, 1949).

## Ackwonledgments

Brief portions of Part II, Chapter 1 ("The transmission of life," "*Rêveuse bourgeoisie*") were published in *Comparative Studies in Society and History* (October 1970) and *Societas: A review of Social History* (Autumn 1972), respectively.

I wish to acknowledge my indebtedness to the staffs of the Institut fuer Zeitgeschichte in Munich, especially Herr Thilo Vogelsang; of the Wiener Library in London; of La Salle College Library in Philadelphia, especially Mrs. Georgette Most; of the National Archives in Washington; of the Widener Library of Harvard University. And to the President and Trustees of Chestnut Hill College for my sabbatical semester in 1972–73; to the Social Science Research Council for a small but very useful grant in 1970. And to the following friends and students and assistants who helped me in tracking down obscure books, lost volumes, distant documents, and odd statistics: Mrs. Karen Rinehart Avenack, Messrs. Lutz Ziegenbalg, John McLaughlin, Ian Hamill, David Hines, Philip Michelini.

"Old Pickering School House"
Williams' Corner, near Phoenixville,
Pennsylvania

1967–73

# INDEX

Abetz, Otto, 354, 493
Abyssinia, 11, 132n, 175–76, 444n
*Action Française,* 68, 293
Afghanistan, 69, 132, 334n, 394n
Albania, 46, 122, 123n, 125, 172, 251, 343
  marriage, 177
  national image, 413, 423
  population, 174
Alfonso XIII, King, 221n
Algeria, 84, 113, 414
Allen, H. C., 283
Alsace-Lorraine, 346, 348, 351, 354, 431n, 438n
*Altmark* (ship), 61, 72, 250
American Red Cross, 113n, 364
Amery, Leopold, 60n, 296, 409n
Andorra, 361, 374
Antonescu, Ion 116, 123, 137, 317, 337, 345n, 353n, 504
Aosta, Duke of, 133n, 280, 411n
*Apollo,* 214
Arnold, H. H., 260
*Arriba,* 317n, 385
*Art of Guerrilla Warfare, The* (Gubbins), 264n
Ascher, G., 281n
Aster, Sidney, 530–31
*Athenia* (ship), 56n
Atomic bomb, 522–24
Attlee, Clement, 32–33
Attolico, Ambassador, 331, 333
*Au Bon Beurre* (Dutourd), 196, 283n
Auchinleck, Claude, 272, 277
Auriol, Vincent, 307
Australia, 497n–98n
Austria, 176, 184–85, 252, 386n, 440n, 489
  daily life, 193, 207
  Hitler's rise and, 9–14, 21, 30
  Jews, 428, 431, 434, 439, 452–53
  national image, 416, 428
  politics, 290, 298, 304, 310, 315
  religion, 457n, 464, 465
  as a state, 341, 348, 350
*Auto-Sport,* 376n
"Autumn in Switzerland" (Haefner), 515–16
Azaña, Manuel, 419n
Azores, 501n

Badoglio, Pietro, 280
Balbo, Marshal Italo, 310n
Baldwin, Stanley, 33n, 228
Ball, Sir Joseph, 371
Bárdossy, Prime Minister, 332n, 504
Barfield, Owen, 417
Baruch, Bernard, 508n
*Basler Nachrichten,* 291–92
Baudhuin, F., 181n
Baudouin, Paul, 83n, 212, 213n, 274, 275n, 331, 406, 493, 503n
Baudrillart, Henri, 459n, 472n
Bauer, Walther, 299n
Bavaria, 446n, 457n, 464, 466n, 469
Bavarian *Kirchenzeitung,* 467n
Beaufre, A., 43n, 272, 273
*Beaux Draps, Les* (Céline), 483n
Beaverbrook, William, 149n, 152n, 251, 299, 413n
Bebel, August, 437n
Beck, Józef, 26–27, 31, 37, 49, 330
Beckman, Archbishop, 50n
Belgium, 107n, 242, 253n, 255n, 260, 263n, 470n, 495, 502n, 504
  archives of, 529, 535n
  birthrate, 174, 177n, 179, 181n

black market, 225–26
  daily life, 197, 198, 200, 204n, 208, 209, 211, 214–16, 222–23
  early days of the war, 59, 77–79, 89
  industrial power, 234–35
  invasion of, 59
  Jews, 443
  migrations, 190–91
  morale, 275, 279–80
  national image, 393–96, 404, 413n–14n, 424
  politics, 289, 291n, 294, 301–4, 310, 311n, 315, 316, 321
  religion, 461
  resistance movement, 482–83, 487
  as a state, 335, 336, 346–52, 357–58
  stock market, 237
Bell, George, 474
Bendiscioli, Mario, 310n
Benes, Eduard, 495n
Benouville, Guilleaume de, 274
Berg, Mary, 207
Bergéry, Gaston, 319n
Bergson, Henri, 422, 439–40, 444
Beria, Lavrenti, 333
Berl, Emmanuel, 288n, 422
*Berlin Diary* (Shirer), 86n
*Berliner Illustrierte,* 402n, 509
Bernanos, Georges, 62, 325, 414, 443, 456, 511, 512, 519, 525
Bernanos, Yves, 318
Bertram, Adolph Cardinal, 465
Bessarabia, 45n, 68n, 88, 103, 118n, 185, 189
Bethlen, Count Stephen, 296
Bethmann-Hollweg, Theobald von, 51n
Bismarck, Prince Otto von, 3, 4, 6, 10, 15, 21, 117, 337, 339, 346, 349
*Bismarck* (ship), 135, 250
Black market, 224–27, 235–36
*Blackout in Gretley* (Priestley), 411n
Blaskowitz, General, 279
Bloch, Marc, 81n, 248, 279, 420
Blomberg, Werner von, 12
Blum, Léon, 228, 292n, 304–7, 319n, 460
Bock, Fedor von, 121, 144, 150, 151, 156, 157, 159
Bochme, II., 84
Bohemia, 32, 35, 193, 252, 303, 309n, 346, 428, 431, 434, 469, 479
Bohemia-Moravia, 351, 461
Bohr, Niels, 523, 524n
Bologna *Resto del Carlino,* 457n
Bonnard, Pierre, 214
Bonnet, Henri, 33, 64, 269
Bonnet, Georges, 214
Bormann, Martin, 145, 345n, 492n
Bornewasser, Monsignor, 466n
Bourgeois, the, 201–24, 512–19
Boveri, Margret, 376n
Bracken, Brendan, 98n
Braque, Georges, 214
Brauchitsch, General, 32, 105, 156, 159, 160, 164
Breker, Arno, 92
Brenner, Hildegarde, 323n
Briand, Aristide, 488
Bridges, Robert, 418
Brinon, Fernand de, 444
British Broadcasting Corporation, 39n, 135–36, 376n, 379, 380, 381n, 517
Brizgys, Bishop, 459
Bukovina, 103, 118n, 185–89, 346, 530n
Bulgaria, 5, 69, 107n, 116, 119–27, 130, 156, 166, 179, 253n, 333n, 501n
  migrations, 184, 187
  national image, 394

# Index

Jews, 203, 207–8, 240–41, 312, 362, 386, 391, 398
  brutalities, 23, 155, 165–66, 182, 186–87, 247, 317, 427–53
  emigration of, 428–31, 434, 448–49
Jodl, General Alfred, 158, 159, 165n, 253
John XXIII, Pope, 164, 368–69, 471n, 475n
*Journal* (Gide), 395–96
Jouvenel, Bertrand de, 18n, 213n, 223
Joyce, William, 379n
József, Attila, 171n
Juenger, Ernst, 280
Jung, Guido, 440n

Kallio, Kyösti, 69n
Kardoff, Ursula von, 376n
Keitel, Wilhelm, 46, 69n, 280
Kelly, Sir David, 98–99, 331
Kennan, George, 206, 491n–92n
Kennedy, John F., 339n
Kennedy, Joseph, 26, 27n, 94, 112, 371n, 502n
Kerillis, Henri de, 296
Kierkegaard, Sören, 26n
King, Cecil, 101
King, William Lyon, 102n
Klemperer, Viktor, 221–22, 252, 491–92, 509
*Klerusblatt*, 467n
Knef, Hildegarde, 395n
Koestler, Arthur, 372
Kollontay, Aleksandra, 333
Korbonski, Stefan, 199, 480–81
Korizis, Alexandros, 131n
Kot, Ambassador, 300, 330n, 389n, 442

Laidoner, Johan, 65n, 66n, 403
Lammers, Hans Heinrich, 450n
Lampe, David, 218, 263
Lancaster, Osbert, 411–12
Laski, Harold, 18
Latvia, 63, 103, 174, 181n, 185, 189, 203, 290, 351, 396, 435, 475
Laval, Pierre, 213n, 289n, 295, 304–7, 317, 319, 320n, 331, 407, 444, 456, 503n
Lawrence, D. H., 52–53
League of Nations, 66, 176, 184, 213n, 488
Leahy, William, 502, 503n
Lebrun, Albert, 287n
Leese, Arnold, 448n
Léger, Alexis, 213, 331
Lenin, Nikolai, 28, 29, 57, 63–64, 149, 151, 297, 323, 327, 362, 452, 524n
Leonhardt, Walter, 396
Leopold III, King, 221n, 294, 305, 358, 393, 492, 504
*Letters* (Bonhoeffer), 468
Lewis, C. S., 417
*Liberté*, 302n
Libya, 122, 125, 277n
Liddell Hart, B. M., 254, 525
Liebknecht, Wilhelm, 524n
Lindbergh, Anne Morrow, 315, 514
Lindbergh, Charles, 260n, 295n, 315, 508n
Lipski, Ambassador, 31, 49
List, Siegmund, 129
Lithuania, 6, 37, 44, 63, 103, 179, 203, 290
  Jews, 430, 435, 439
  national image, 396, 413, 424, 426n
  population, 174
  religion, 457n, 459
  resistance movement, 487
  as a state, 351, 368n, 380n
Litvinov, Maxim, 42, 333
Lloyd George, David, 22, 62, 97, 98, 134n, 304, 500
London *Times*, 167, 490n, 533n

Lothian, Lord, 10, 93n, 99n
Ludwig, Emil, 434n
Luxembourg, 234, 253n, 291n, 404
  birthrate, 179
  black market, 226
  population, 174, 177n, 179, 181
  religion, 461
  resistance movement, 482n
  as a state, 336, 346, 348, 351, 352

McCormack, John W., 293n
MacDonald, James Ramsay, 304
Madagascar, 429, 431n, 432
Madariaga, Salvador de, 488
Madge, Charles, 533n
Maeztu, Ramiro de, 406n
Maglione, Luigi Cardinal, 368, 471n, 476n, 506n
Magritte, René, 214
Maisky, Ivan, 333
Malta, 113n, 368
Mandel, Georges, 289, 441n, 442
Mann, Thomas, 171n, 313
Mannerheim, Carl Gustaf von, 292
Marty, André, 301
Marx, Karl, 145, 285, 297, 298n, 300, 414, 459n, 524–26
Mastny, V., 445, 479
*Matin, Le*, 376n
Matisse, Henri, 214
Matsuoka, Ambassador, 129, 143, 335n
Maulnier, Thierry, 293
Maurois, André, 422
Maurras, Charles, 287, 293, 319n, 421n, 503n
Max, Adolphe, 215
Mécs, László, 458n
Medlicott, W. N., 232
Mehnert, Klaus, 524n
Meijers, E. M., 216
*Mein Kampf* (Hitler), 8, 18–19, 29–30, 41n, 76n, 138, 143, 252, 315n, 387n, 447
*Memoirs* (Kennan), 206
Mencken, H. L., 56n
Metaxas, Joannes, 47, 117, 125n, 175, 288n
Metternich, Count, 517
Mihailovic, Draža, 485, 486n
Miry, Raoul, 226
Mistral, Frédéric, 421n
Moffat, Jay Pierrepont, 448n
Mola, Emilio, 372
Moldavia, 187
Molotov, Vyacheslav, 43, 115n, 119–20, 128, 139–40, 152, 233, 333n, 370n, 504, 508n, 530n
  early days of the war, 56–59, 63, 65, 104
  as protector of the state, 328, 330, 336, 342, 343, 365
Monckton, Sir Walter, 99n
Mongolia, 253, 270n
Montherlant, Henry de, 455–56, 514
Monzie, Anatole de, 288, 320n
Moran, Paul, 407n
Moravia, 32, 35, 303, 346, 428, 431, 434, 469, 479
Morocco, 113, 501n
Moscicki, Ignacy, 360n
Mosley, Sir Oswald, 108n, 304n, 311n
Mowinckel, Johan Ludwig, 365
*Muenchner Katholische Kirchenzeitung*, 467n
Muggeridge, Malcolm, 313, 531
Münzenberg, Willi, 289n, 300
Mussert, Anton, 316
Mussolini, Benito, 111, 122, 125, 138, 140, 145, 228, 261, 328, 336, 339, 341, 344,